Medications and Mothers' Milk

A Manual of Lactational Pharmacology

Medications and Mothers' Milk

Tenth Edition

Thomas W. Hale, R.Ph., Ph.D.
Associate Professor of Pediatrics
Associate Professor of Pharmacology
Division of Clinical Pharmacology
Texas Tech University School of Medicine
Amarillo, Texas 79106

Medications and Mothers' Milk

Tenth Edition

© Copyright 1992-2002

Pharmasoft Publishing

21 Tascocita Circle
Amarillo, Tx 79124

(806)-376-9900
(800)-378-1317

DISCLAIMER

The information contained in this publication is intended to supplement the knowledge of health care professionals regarding drug use during lactation. This information is advisory only and is not intended to replace sound clinical judgement or individualized patient care. The author disclaims all warranties, whether expressed or implied, including any warranty as to the quality, accuracy, safety, or suitability of this information for any particular purpose.

ISBN 0-9636219-6-3
RJ216 .H25 1995
96-143153

Ordering Information

Pharmasoft Publishing
21 Tascocita Circle
Amarillo, Texas, USA 79124-7301
8:00 AM to 5:00 PM CST

Call....	806-376-9900
Sales....	800-378-1317
FAX....	806-376-9901

Online Web Orders...

http://www.iBreastfeeding.com

Single Copies   **$ 24.95 US**
  Plus Shipping

(Texas Residents add 8.25% sales tax)

Common Abbreviations

T½=	Adult elimination half-life
M/P	Milk/Plasma Ratio
PK=	Time to peak plasma level
Vd	Volume of Distribution
PB=	Percent of protein binding in maternal circulation
PHL=	Pediatric elimination half-life
Oral=	Oral bioavailability (adult)
µg/L	Microgram per liter
ng/L	Nanogram per liter
mg/L	Milligram per liter
mL	Milliliter. One cc
NSAIDs	Non-steroidal anti-inflammatory
ACEi	Angiotensin converting enzyme inhibitor
MAOI	Monoamine oxidase inhibitors
Vd	Volume of Distribution
MW	Molecular Weight
µCi	Microcurie of Radioactivity
mmol	Millimole of weight
µmol	Micromole of weight
Cmax	Plasma or milk concentration at peak
AUC	Area under the Curve
BID	Twice daily
TID	Three times daily
QID	Four times daily
PRN	As needed
QD	Daily

Preface

It is now clear that exclusive breastfeeding significantly reduces the incidence of major newborn illnesses. Documented reductions in the incidence of otitis media, SIDS, viral diarrhea, necrotizing enterocolitis, lymphoma, and a reduced morbidity with respiratory syncytial virus (RSV) infections are now indisputable evidence that breastfeeding should be the preferred method for feeding an infant. Breastfeeding also protects the infant against the development of food allergies, cardiovascular disease, inflammatory diseases such as ulcerative colitis and Crohn's disease. Benefits to breastfeeding women include less postpartum blood loss, prompt uterine involution, more desirable inter-pregnancy intervals, and a lower lifetime risk of breast and ovarian cancer. This information seems to be permeating the medical profession as most health care practitioners have accepted the fact that breastfeeding should be strongly recommended.

The recent publication by the American Academy of Pediatrics recommending up to at least 1 year of breastfeeding was tacit approval by a major medical body that breastfeeding is immunologically and nutritionally the best way to feed infants. The Academy, provided with evidence by numerous publications that breastfed infants are not only healthier but may also gain in developmental skills as well, finally felt that the evidence was overwhelming and justified a stronger stance by this large body of pediatricians. Due to enormous support for breastfeeding in the medical community, many mothers are now resistant to discontinuing breastfeeding just to take a medication, particularly if the interruption is based solely on the recommendation of their physician. Although interrupting breastfeeding may seem safest to the physician it is not really necessary in most cases as the amount of drug transferred to milk is normally quite small. It is well known that most medications have few side effects in breastfeeding infants because the dose transferred via milk is almost always too low to be clinically relevant or it is poorly bioavailable to the infant.

We all know that most medications penetrate milk to some degree. With only a few exceptions the concentrations of most medications in human milk are exceedingly low and the dose delivered to the breastfed infant is often far subclinical. It is important for the clinician to closely review the documentation on drugs and their levels in human breastmilk prior to making decisions that have profound effects on nursing infants. There are almost always other suitable alternative drugs that can be used.

> It is important to remember that pharmaceutical manufacturers often discourage breastfeeding due to fear of litigation, not because the drug enters milk in clinically relevant amounts.

Because the PDR basically lists only the pharmaceutical's package insert, the standard recommendation is to not take the medication while breastfeeding. The PDR is the poorest source for obtaining accurate breastfeeding information.

The amount of drug excreted into milk depends on the following factors:

Determinants of Drug Transfer into Milk

- Plasma levels in the mother
- Lipid solubility of the drug and fat content of milk
- Milk pH
- Molecular Size of the drug
- Protein Binding of the drug in mother's plasma
- Maternal half-life of the drug
- Molecular weight of drug

However once medications are transferred into human milk then other factors are involved. One of the most important is the oral bioavailability of the medication to the infant. Numerous medications are either destroyed in the infant's gut, fail to be absorbed through the gut wall, or are rapidly picked up by the liver and either metabolized or stored in the liver. The above parameters don't always explain the transfer of drugs, but they do permit one to evaluate medications and come somewhat close to estimating the overall risk to the infant from various medications.

Drugs enter milk primarily by diffusion driven by equilibrium forces between the maternal plasma compartment and maternal milk compartment. They pass from the maternal plasma through capillary walls into the alveolar cell lining the milk buds. Medications must generally pass through both lipid membranes of the alveolar cell to penetrate milk; although early on they may pass between alveolar cells. During the first four days of life large gaps between alveolar cells exist. These gaps may permit enhanced access for most drugs, many immunoglobulins, and other maternal proteins to the milk. Soon after the first week the alveolar cells swell under the influence of prolactin; subsequently closing the intracellular gaps and limiting access to the milk. It is generally agreed that medications penetrate into milk more during the neonatal period than in mature milk. Although not identical, drug entry into human milk is restricted by a tight secretory epithelial system similar to the blood-brain barrier. In most instances the most important determinant of drug penetration into milk is the mother's plasma level. Almost without exception, as the level of the medication in the mother's plasma rises, the concentration in milk begins it's rise as well. Drugs enter milk, and in almost all cases, exit milk as a function of the mother's plasma level. As soon as the maternal plasma level of a medication begins to fall equilibrium forces drive the medication out of the milk compartment back into the maternal plasma for elimination. In some instances, drugs are ion

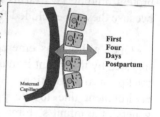

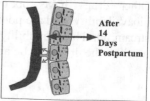

trapped in milk meaning that due to the lower pH of human milk, the physicochemical structure of the drug changes, and prevents its' exit back into the maternal circulation. This is important in weakly basic drugs such as the barbiturates. With the iodides, such as ^{131}I, the drug may concentrate in milk at high milk/plasma ratios due to the presence of a pumping system on the alveolar cell wall. Thus iodides, particularly radioactive ones, should be avoided as their milk concentrations are exceedingly high.

Two physicochemical factors are most important in evaluating drugs in breastfeeding mothers. These are the degree of protein binding, and lipid solubility. Drugs that are very lipid soluble penetrate milk in higher concentrations almost without exception. Of particular interest are the drugs that are active in the central nervous system (CNS). CNS-active drugs invariably have the unique characteristic requisite to enter milk. Therefore, if a drug is active in the central nervous system higher drug levels in milk can be expected; although they still are often subclinical. Protein binding also plays an important role. Drugs circulate in the maternal plasma either bound to albumin or freely soluble in the plasma. It is the free component (unbound) that transfers into milk while the bound fraction stays in the maternal circulation. Therefore, drugs that have high maternal protein binding (warfarin) have a reduced milk level simply because they are excluded from the milk compartment.

Once a drug has entered the mother's milk and has been ingested by the infant it must traverse through the infant's GI tract prior to absorption. Some drugs are poorly stable in this environment due to the proteolytic enzymes and acids. In general, the infant's stomach is quite acidic and can denature many drugs. This includes the aminoglycoside family, Omeprazole, and large peptide drugs such as Heparin or Insulin. Other drugs have poor oral absorption kinetics (oral bioavailability) and are poorly absorbed into the infant's blood stream. Oral bioavailability is a useful tool to estimate just how much of the drug will be absorbed by the infant. In addition, many drugs are sequestered in the liver (first pass) and may never actually reach the plasma compartment where they are active. These absorption problems tend ultimately to reduce the overall effect of many drugs. There are certainly exceptions to this rule and one must always be aware that the action of a drug in the GI tract can also be profound; producing diarrhea, constipation, and occasionally syndromes such as pseudomembranous colitis.

Although there are many exceptions, a good rule is that less than 1% of the "maternal dose" of a drug will ultimately find its way into the milk and subsequently the infant.

Considerations for use of drugs during breastfeeding*

- Avoid using medication where possible.
- When needed, evaluate the infant dose and perform individual risk assessment.
- For many drugs, a relative infant dose of < 10% is considered safe.
- Preferred drugs are those for which we have breastfeeding data.
- Avoid the peak, feed toward the end of the dose to reduce the exposure of the infant.
- Discontinuing breastfeeding for some hours/days may be required, particularly with radioactive compounds.
- Choose drugs with short half-lives, high protein binding, low oral bioavailability, or high molecular weight.
- Be more cautious with preterm or low birth weight infants.
- Many drugs are safe in breastfeeding mothers and the benefits of breastfeeding often outweigh the risks to the infant's well-being.

---

* Adapted from Hale TW, Ilett KF. Drug Therapy and Breastfeeding: From Theory to Clinical Practice, First Edition ed. London: Parthenon Publishing; 2002.

Lastly, it is terribly important to always evaluate the infant's ability to handle small amounts of medications. Some infants, such as premature or ill infants, may not be suitable candidates for certain medications. This is a critically important evaluation that should always be addressed. Always ask about the infant prior to determining the suitability of a medication.

Evaluation of the Infant

- **Infant age** - premature and newborn infants are at somewhat greater risk.
- **Infant stability** - unstable infants with poor GI stability may increase the risk of using medications.
- **Pediatric Approved Drugs** - generally are less hazardous if long-term history of safety is recognized.
- **Dose** - in a premature infant various doses may be more risky than in a 1 year old healthy infant.
- **Drugs that alter milk production** - may be much more risky during the neonatal period than much later.

General Suggestions for the Clinician

1. Determine if the drug is absorbed from the GI tract. Many drugs such as the aminoglycosides, vancomycin, cephalosporin antibiotics (third generation), morphine, magnesium salts, and large protein drugs (heparin) are so poorly absorbed that it is unlikely the infant will absorb significant quantities. At the same time observe for GI side effects from the medication trapped in the GI compartment of the infant (e.g. diarrhea).

2. Review the monograph provided herein on the drug. Review the theoretical infant dose and compare that to the pediatric dose if known. Remember, the Theoretic Infant Dose is derived from the Cmax (highest milk concentration of the drug) that is published. Unfortunately, the milk/plasma ratio is virtually worthless information unless you know the maternal plasma level. It does not provide the user with information as to the absolute amount of drug transferred to the infant via milk. Even if the drug has a high milk/plasma ratio, if the maternal plasma level of the

medication is very small (such as with propranolol), then the absolute amount (dose) of a drug entering milk will still be quite small and often subclinical.

3. Try to choose shorter half-life drugs, as they generally peak rapidly and then are eliminated from the maternal plasma thus exposing the milk compartment (and the infant) to reduced levels of medication. Urge the mother not to breastfeed while the drug is at it's peak level in the maternal plasma. Determine the time-to-peak interval as this will indicate how long the mother must wait before feeding. However, you must first determine the dosage form administered. If the tablet formulation is a prolonged release form then all prior assumptions about half-life are pointless and you must assume that the drug has a long half-life (12-24 hrs). Unfortunately, avoiding peaks early postpartum is simply not very practical and drugs with low milk levels should be chosen.

4. Be cautious of drugs (or their active metabolites) that have long pediatric half-lives as they can continually build up in the infant's plasma over time. The barbiturates, benzodiazepines, meperidine, and fluoxetine are classic examples where higher levels in the infant can and do occasionally occur.

5. If you are provided a choice, choose drugs that have higher protein binding because they are more often sequestered in the maternal circulation and do not transfer as readily to the milk or the infant. Remember, it's the free drug that transfers into the milk compartment. Without doubt, the most important parameter that determines drug penetration into milk is plasma protein binding. Choose drugs with high protein binding.

6. Although not always true, I have generally found neuroleptic drugs frequently penetrate milk in higher levels simply due to their physicochemistry. If the drug in

question produces sedation, depression, or other neuroleptic effects in the mother, it is likely to penetrate the milk and may produce similar effects in the infant. Sedative drugs (particularly phenothiazines) may contribute to an elevated risk of SIDS, although this is poorly documented.

7. Be cautious of herbal drugs as many contain chemical substances that may be dangerous to the infant. Numerous poisonings have been reported. Prior to using, advise the mother to contact a lactation consultant or herbalist who is knowledgeable about their use in breastfeeding mothers. Do not exceed standard recommended doses. Try to use pure forms, not large mixtures of unknown herbals. Do not overdose, use only minimal amounts.

8. With radioactive compounds check the NRC table in the index of this volume. The NRC recommendations are quite good. They can be copied and provided to your radiologist. They are available from the Nuclear Regulatory Commission's web page address in the appendix.

9. Use the **Theoretic Infant Dose** to estimate the maximum dose the infant would receive per kilogram per day. This data is derived from the literature and is a close estimate of the peak amount an infant would receive. Another very useful evaluation of the dose is to determine the **Relative Infant Dose.** The box below shows the calculation. In general, a Relative infant dose of < 10% is considered safe and its use is becoming increasingly popular by numerous investigators.

Relative Infant Dose

$$\textbf{RID} \quad = \quad \frac{\text{Infant Dose (mg/kg/day)}}{\text{Maternal Dose (mg/kg/day)}}$$

A Relative infant dose of < 10% is generally considered safe

Hence, it is important that the clinician evaluate all the risks of the drug in relationship to the absolute dose received by the infant and the ability of the infant to handle even that dose. It is no longer acceptable for the clinician to interrupt lactation merely because of heightened anxiety on their part. The risks of formula feeding and of the mother losing her milk supply, are significant and should not be trivialized. There are few drugs that have well documented and significant toxicity in infants as a result of breastfeeding and we know most of these. On the other hand, the clinician should always be cautious when using medications in breastfeeding mothers and in those instances where they are not necessary they should be avoided. More importantly, if they are only marginally effective (e.g. anti-influenza or herbal products), then they should probably be avoided as well.

The following review of drugs is a compilation of what we currently know, or don't know, about the use of medications during breastfeeding.

THE AUTHOR MAKES NO RECOMMENDATIONS AS TO THE SAFETY OF THESE MEDICATIONS DURING LACTATION, BUT ONLY REVIEWS WHAT IS CURRENTLY PUBLISHED IN THE SCIENTIFIC LITERATURE. INDIVIDUAL USE OF MEDICATIONS MUST BE LEFT UP TO THE JUDGEMENT OF THE PHYSICIAN, THE PATIENT AND OTHER HEALTHCARE CONSULTANTS.

The various fields of medicine have become so complicated in the last decade that few individuals are truly capable of crossing these disciplines. The purpose of this work is to assist the busy physician, lactation consultant, or mother with a tool to assess the known and unknown risks of using medications in breastfeeding mothers.

Thomas W. Hale

How to Use this Book

This section of the book is designed to aid the reader in determining risk to an infant from maternal medications and in using the pharmacokinetic parameters throughout this reference.

Drug Name and Generic Name.
Each monograph begins with the generic name of the drug. Several of the most common USA trade names are provided under the *Trade* section.

Can/Aus/UK:
Most, but not all, of the most common trade names used in Canada, Australia, and the United Kingdom are provided.

Uses:
This lists the general use of the medication, such as penicillin antibiotic, or antiemetic, or analgesic, etc. Remember, many drugs have multiple uses in many syndromes. I have only listed the most common use.

AAP:
This entry, lists the new recommendations provided by the American Academy of Pediatrics as published in their document, *The transfer of drugs and other chemicals into human milk* (Pediatrics. 2001 Sep;108(3):776-89.). *Drugs are listed in tables according to the following recommendations: Cytotoxic drugs that may interfere with cellular metabolism of the nursing infant; Drugs of abuse for which adverse effects on the infant during breastfeeding have been reported; Radioactive compounds that require temporary cessation of breastfeeding; Drugs for which the effect on nursing infants is unknown but may be of concern; Drugs that have been associated with significant effects on some nursing infants and should be given to nursing mothers with caution; Maternal medication usually compatible with breastfeeding.* In this book, the AAP recommendations have been paraphrased to reflect these recommendations. Because the AAP recommendations do not

14

cover all drugs, "Not Reviewed" simply implies that the drug has not yet been reviewed by this committee. The author recommends that each user review these recommendations for further detail.

Drug Monograph

The drug monograph lists what we currently understand about the drug, its ability to enter milk, the concentration in milk at set time intervals, and other parameters that are important to a clinical consultant. I have attempted at great length to report only what the references have documented.

Pregnancy Risk Category:

Pregnancy risk categories have been assigned to almost all medications by their manufacturers and are based on the level of risk the drug poses to the fetus during gestation. They are not useful in assigning risk via breastfeeding. The FDA has provided these five categories to indicate the risk associated with the induction of birth defects. Unfortunately they do not indicate the importance of when during gestation the medication is used, since some drugs are more dangerous during certain trimesters of pregnancy. The definitions provided below are, however, a useful tool in determining the possible risks associated with using the medication during pregnancy. Some newer medications may not yet have pregnancy classifications and are therefore not provided herein.

Category A:

Controlled studies in women fail to demonstrate a risk to the fetus in the first trimester (and there is no evidence of a risk in later trimesters) and the possibility of fetal harm appears remote.

Category B:

Either animal-reproduction studies have not demonstrated a fetal risk, but there are no controlled studies in pregnant women or animal-reproduction studies have shown an adverse effect (other than a decrease in fertility) that was not confirmed in controlled studies in women in the first trimester (and there is no evidence of a risk in later trimesters).

Category C:

Either studies in animals have revealed adverse effects on the fetus (teratogenic or embryocidal, or other) and there are no controlled studies in women, or studies in women and animals are not available. Drugs should be given only if the potential benefit justifies the potential risk to the fetus.

Category D:

There is positive evidence of human fetal risk, but the benefits from use in pregnant women may be acceptable despite the risk (e.g., if the drug is needed in a life-threatening situation or for a serious disease for which safer drugs cannot be used or are ineffective).

Category X:

Studies in animals or human beings have demonstrated fetal abnormalities, or there is evidence of fetal risk based on human experience, or both, and the risk of the use of the drug in pregnant women clearly outweighs any possible benefit. The drug is contraindicated in women who are or may become pregnant.

Lactation Risk Category:

L1 SAFEST:

Drug which has been taken by a large number of breastfeeding mothers without any observed increase in adverse effects in the infant.   Controlled studies in breastfeeding women fail to demonstrate a risk to the infant and the possibility of harm to the breastfeeding infant is remote;   or the product is not orally bioavailable in an infant.

L2 SAFER:

Drug which has been studied in a limited number of breastfeeding women without an increase in adverse effects in the infant. And/or, the evidence of a demonstrated risk which is likely to follow use of this medication in a breastfeeding woman is remote.

L3 MODERATELY SAFE:

There are no controlled studies in breastfeeding women, however the risk of untoward effects to a breastfed infant is possible; or, controlled studies show only minimal non-threatening adverse effects. Drugs should be given only if the potential benefit justifies the potential risk to the infant.

L4 POSSIBLY HAZARDOUS:

There is positive evidence of risk to a breastfed infant or to breastmilk production, but the benefits from use in breastfeeding mothers may be acceptable despite the risk to the infant (e.g. if the drug is needed in a life-threatening situation or for a serious disease for which safer drugs cannot be used or are ineffective).

L5 CONTRAINDICATED:

Studies in breastfeeding mothers have demonstrated that there is significant and documented risk to the infant based on human experience, or it is a medication that has a high risk of causing significant damage to an infant. The risk of using the drug in breastfeeding women clearly outweighs any possible benefit from breastfeeding. The drug is contraindicated in women who are breastfeeding an infant.

Theoretic Infant Dose:

This is an estimate of the maximum likely dose per kilogram per day that an infant would ingest via milk. Because the literature is highly variable, I used several methods to calculate this estimate. First, if the authors provided milk AUC information, I used this data to estimate the dose to the infant as it is much more accurate. But more commonly, the only data provided was the peak milk level, also called Cmax. In these cases I used this data to derive the theoretic infant dose. For determining dose I used the standard milk intake of 150 mL/kg/day multiplied times the concentration of medication in milk (Cmax/Liter X 0.150 mL/kg/day= TID). Please remember, this is generally the *maximum* concentration that would be transferred. Most often the actual dose to the infant would be much lower. If you know the maternal dose, calculate the **Relative Infant Dose** using the formula on page 12. It may prove very useful.

Adult Concerns:

This section lists the most prevalent undesired or bothersome side effects listed for adults. As with most medications, the occurrence of these is often quite rare, generally less than 1-10% of the time. Side effects vary from one patient to another and should not be overemphasized, since most patients do not experience untoward effects.

Pediatric Concerns:

This section lists the side effects noted in the published literature as associated with medications transferred **via human milk**. Pediatric concerns are those effects that were noted by investigators as being associated with drug transfer via milk. They are not the effects that would result from direct administration to the infant. In some sections, I have added comments that may not have been reported in the literature, but are well known attributes of this medication and are useful information to provide the mother so that she can better care for her infant ("Observe for weakness, apnea").

Drug Interactions:

Drug interactions generally indicate which medications, when taken together, may produce higher or lower plasma levels of other medications, or they may decrease or increase the effect of another medication. These effects may vary widely from minimal to dangerous. Because some medications have hundreds of interactions, and because I had limited room to provide this information, I have listed only those that may be significant. Therefore please be advised that this section may not be complete. In several references, I have suggested that due to the large number of interactions the reader consult a more complete drug interaction reference. Please remember that the drugs administered to a mother could interact with those being administered concurrently to an infant. Example: Maternal fluconazole and pediatric cisapride.

Alternatives:

Drugs listed in this section may be suitable alternate choices for the medication listed above. In many instances, if the patient cannot take the medication, or it is a poor choice due to high milk concentrations, these alternates may be suitable candidates. **WARNING**: The alternates listed are only suggestions and may not be at all proper for the syndrome in question. Only the clinician can make this judgement. For instance, nifedipine is a calcium channel blocker with good antihypertensive qualities, but poor antiarrhythmic qualities. In this case, verapamil would be a better choice.

Adult Dosage:

This is the usual adult oral dose provided in the package insert. While these are highly variable, I chose the dose for the most common use of the medication.

T½ =

This lists the most commonly recorded adult half-life of the medication. It is very important to remember that short half-life drugs are preferred. Use this parameter to determine if the mother can successfully breastfeed around the medication, by nursing the infant... then taking the medication. If the half-life is short enough (1-3 hrs), then the drug level in the maternal plasma will be declining when the infant feeds again. This is ideal. If the half-life is significantly long (12-24 hrs), and if your physician is open to suggestions, then find a similar medication with a shorter half-life (compare ibuprofen with Naproxen). I have provided "Family" tables in the back of this text, so you can compare family members for half-lives and other kinetic parameters.

PHL=

This lists the most commonly recorded pediatric half-life of the medication. Medications with extremely long half-lives in pediatric patients may accumulate to high levels in the infant's plasma if the half-life is exceeding long(>12 hrs.). Pediatric half-lives are difficult to find due to the paucity of studies.

M/P=

This lists the Milk/plasma ratio. This is the ratio of the concentration of drug in the mother's *milk* divided by the concentration in the mother's *plasma*. If high (> 1-5) it is useful as an indicator of drugs that may sequester in milk in high levels. If low (< 1) it is a good indicator that only minimal levels of the drug are transferred into milk (this is preferred). While it is best to try to choose drugs with LOW milk/plasma ratios, the amount of drug which transfers into human milk is largely determined by the level of drug in the mother's plasma compartment. Even with high M/P ratios and LOW maternal plasma levels the amount of drug that transfers is still low. Therefore, the higher M/P ratios often provide an erroneous impression that large amounts of drug are going to transfer into milk. This simply may not be true.

PK=

This lists the time interval from administration of the drug, until it reaches the highest level in the mother's plasma, which we call the *Peak*. In pharmacology literature it is most commonly abbreviated Cmax. The peak is when you do not want the mother to breastfeed her infant, rather, wait until the peak is subsiding or has at least dropped significantly. Remember, drugs enter breastmilk as a function of the maternal plasma concentration. The higher the mom's plasma level, the greater the entry of the drug into her milk. If possible, choose drugs that have short peak intervals, and don't let mom breastfeed when it peaks.

PB=

This lists the percentage of maternal protein binding. Most drugs circulate in the blood bound to plasma albumin. If a drug is highly protein bound it cannot exit the plasma compartment as well. The higher the percentage of binding the less likely the drug is to enter the maternal milk. Try to choose drugs that have high protein binding, in order to reduce the infants exposure to the medication. Good protein binding is typically greater than 90%.

Oral=

Oral bioavailability refers to the ability of a drug to reach the systemic circulation after oral administration. It is generally a good indication of the amount of medication that is absorbed into the blood stream of the patient. Drugs with low oral bioavailability are generally either poorly absorbed in the gastrointestinal tract, or they are sequestered by the liver prior to entering the plasma compartment. The oral bioavailability listed in this text is the adult value; almost none have been published for children or neonates. Recognizing this, these values are still useful in estimating if a mother or perhaps an infant will actually absorb enough drug to provide clinically significant levels in the plasma compartment of the individual. The value listed estimates the percent of an oral dose that would be found in the plasma compartment of the individual after oral administration. In many cases, the oral bioavailability of some medications is not listed by manufacturers, but instead terms such as "Complete", "Nil", or "Poor" are used. For lack of better data, I have included these terms when no data is available on the exact amount (percentage) absorbed.

Vd=

The volume of distribution is a useful kinetic term that describes how widely the medication is distributed in the body. Drugs with high volumes of distribution (Vd) are distributed in higher concentrations in remote compartments of the body, and may not stay in the blood. For instance, digoxin enters the blood compartment and then rapidly leaves to enter the heart and skeletal muscle. Most of the drug is sequestered in these remote compartments (100 fold). Therefore, drugs with high volumes of distribution (1-20 liter/kg) generally require much longer to clear from the body than drugs with smaller volumes (0.1 liter/kg). For instance, whereas it may only require a few hours to totally clear gentamycin (Vd=0.28 l/kg) it may require weeks to clear amitriptyline (Vd=10 l/kg) which has a huge volume of distribution. In addition, some drugs may have one half-life for the plasma compartment, but may have a totally different half-life for the peripheral compartment, as half-life is a function of volume of distribution. For a complete description of Vd, please consult a good pharmacology reference. In this text, the units of measure for Vd are liters/kg.

pKa=

The pKa of a drug is the pH at which the drug is equally ionic and nonionic. The more ionic a drug is, the less capable it is of transferring from the milk compartment to the maternal plasma compartment. Hence, they become trapped in milk (ion-trapping). This term is useful, because drugs that have a pKa higher than 7.2 may be sequestered to a slightly higher degree than one with a lower pKa. Drugs with higher pKa generally have higher milk/plasma ratios. Hence, choose drugs with a lower pKa.

MW=

The molecular weight of a medication is a significant determinant as to the entry of that medication into human milk. Medications with small molecular weights (< 200) can easily pass into milk by traversing small pores in the cell walls of the mammary epithelium (see ethanol). Drugs with higher molecular weights must traverse the membrane by dissolving in the lipid bilayers, which may significantly reduce milk levels. As such, the smaller the molecular weight the higher the relative transfer of that drug into milk. Protein medications (e.g. Heparin, Insulin), which have enormous molecular weights, transfer at much lower concentrations and are virtually excluded from human breastmilk. Therefore, when possible, choose drugs with higher molecular weights to reduce their entry into milk.

5-HYDROXYTRYPTOPHAN

Trade: Ditropan
Can/Aus/UK: Apo-Oxybutynin, Ditropan, Oxybutyn
Uses: Precursor of serotonin
AAP: Not reviewed

5-Hydroxytryptophan(5-HTP) is a natural aromatic amino acid which is the immediate precursor of the neurotransmitter serotonin. L-Tryptophan is another amino acid formerly used to treat depression.

L-Tryptophan:

L-tryptophan(LTP), once absorbed, is rapidly transported to the liver where some of it is incorporated into proteins, and some passes unchanged into the general circulation. It is a precursor of serotonin. One of the major problems with the use of LTP is that when used at higher doses, metabolism to kynurenine is highly induced, and the majority of LTP is subsequently metabolized rather than converted into serotonin. Even under the best of circumstances, less than 3% of the LTP is likely to be converted to serotonin in the brain.[1] L-Tryptophan crosses the blood-brain barrier only poorly. As the doses increase, the creation of the metabolite kynurenine tends to block entry of LTP into the brain. As the doses of LTP used are extraordinarily high 2000-6000 mg/d cost and adverse effects are significant.[2] Older formulations created with contaminates were responsible for the eosinophilia-myalgia syndrome.

5-HTP:

5-HTP is rapidly absorbed, and approximately 70% of the dose is bioavailable, the remaining 30% is converted to serotonin by intestinal cells which may lead to some nausea. 5-HTP readily crosses the blood-brain barrier (24% in CSF) and is one step closer to serotonin production. The dose of 5-HTP is much lower, averaging 100-300 mg/d, and some studies have found it equivalent to tricyclic antidepressants[3] and fluvoxamine (an SSRI)[4] in treating depression. Although several cases of eosinophilia-myalgia syndrome have been reported with the use of 5-HTP,[5,6] both of these patients had defective metabolic mechanisms for converting 5-HTP.

Unfortunately there are no data on the transfer of exogenously supplied LTP or 5-HTP into human milk. For instance, it is not apparently known if high maternal plasma levels would produce high milk levels. While it is true human milk contains higher levels of LTP, presumably to stimulate serotonin levels in the infant's CNS, it is not known if high maternal doses would likewise produce high milk levels. Because the infant's neurologic development is incredibly sensitive to serotonin levels, and because we do not know if supplementation with LTP or 5-HTP could produce high milk levels leading to overdose in the infant, I do not recommend the use of L-tryptophan or 5-HTP supplementation in breastfeeding mothers until we know corresponding milk levels.

Pregnancy Risk Category: B

Lactation Risk Category: L3

Theoretic Infant Dose:

Adult Concerns: Nausea, dry mouth, constipation, esophagitis, urinary hesitancy, flushing and urticaria. Palpitations, somnolence, hallucinations infrequently occur.

Pediatric Concerns: Suppression of lactation has been reported by the manufacturer.

Drug Interactions: May potentiate the anticholinergic effect of biperiden and other anticholinergics such as the tricyclic antidepressants. May counteract the effects of cisapride and metoclopramide.

Alternatives: Sertraline, paroxetine

Adult Dosage: 5 mg BID-QID

T½ = 1-2 hours	M/P =
PHL =	PB =
PK = 3-6 hours	Oral = 6%
MW = 393	pKa = 6.96
Vd =	

References:
1. Filippini GA et.al. Recent advances in tryptophan research, tryptophan and serotonin pathways. Exp Biol Med 398:1-762, 1996.
2. Murray MT, Pizzorno JE. : 5-Hydroxytryptophan, in Pizzorno JE. Churchill Livingstone(eds): Textbook of Natural Medicine, 1999.
3. van Praag HM. Management of depression with serotonin precursors. Biol Psychiatry. 16(3):291-310, 1981.
4. Poldinger W, Calanchini B, Schwarz W. A functional-dimensional approach to depression: serotonin deficiency as a target syndrome in a comparison of 5-hydroxytryptophan and fluvoxamine. Psychopathology. 24(2):53-81, 1991.
5. Sternberg EM, Van Woert MH, Young SN, Magnussen I, Baker H, Gauthier S, Osterland CK. Development of a scleroderma-like illness during therapy with L-5-hydroxytryptophan and carbidopa. N Engl J Med. 303(14):782-7, 1980.
6. Michelson D, Page SW, Casey R, Trucksess MW, Love LA, Milstien S, Wilson C, Massaquoi SG, Crofford LJ, Hallett M, et al. An eosinophilia-myalgia syndrome related disorder associated with exposure to L-5-hydroxytryptophan. J Rheumatol. 21(12):2261-5, 1994.

ACARBOSE

Trade: Precose, Prandase
Can/Aus/UK: Glucobay, Prandase
Uses: Delays carbohydrate absorption
AAP: Not reviewed

Acarbose is an oral alpha-glucosidase inhibitor used to reduce the absorption of carbohydrates in the management of Type II (NIDDM) diabetics.[1] The reduction of carbohydrate absorption reduces the rapid rise in glucose following a meal, hence glycosylated hemoglobin (Hemoglobin A1C) levels are reduced. Acarbose is less than 2% bioavailable as an intact molecule.[2] No data are available on the transfer of acarbose into human milk but with a bioavailability of less than 2%, it is very unlikely any would reach the milk compartment or be absorbed by the infant.

Pregnancy Risk Category: B

Lactation Risk Category: L3

Theoretic Infant Dose:

Adult Concerns: Adverse effects include flatulence, abdominal pain and distention, diarrhea, and borborygmi. Isolated cases of elevated liver enzymes have been reported. Elevated liver enzymes occurred in approximately 15% of acarbose-treated patients and is apparently dose related with doses > 300 mg daily.

Pediatric Concerns: None reported via milk.

Drug Interactions: May increase hypoglycemia when used with other antidiabetic medications such as the sulfonylureas.

Alternatives:

Adult Dosage: 50-100 mg TID

T½ = < 2 hours	M/P =
PHL =	PB =
PK =	Oral = 0.7- 2%
MW = 645	pKa =
Vd = 0.32	

References:
1.   Pharmaceutical manufacturers package insert, 1999.
2.   Balfour JA and McTavish D: Acarbose: an update of its pharmacology and therapeutic use in diabetes mellitus. Drugs 46:1025-1054, 1993.

ACEBUTOLOL

Trade: Sectral
Can/Aus/UK: Monitan, Sectral
Uses: Antihypertensive, beta blocker
AAP: Approved by the American Academy of Pediatrics for use in breastfeeding mothers

Acebutolol is predominately a beta-1 blocker, but can block beta-2 receptors at high doses. It is low in lipid solubility, and contains some intrinsic sympathetic activity (partial beta agonist activity). It increases cold sensitivity. Studies indicate that on a weight basis, acebutolol is approximately 10-30% as effective as propranolol. It is 35-50% bioavailable orally.[1]

After relatively high doses in animal studies, acebutolol does not appear to be overly teratogenic or harm the fetus. Acebutolol is well tolerated by pregnant hypertensive women.

In a study of seven women receiving 200-1200 mg/day acebutolol, the highest milk concentration occurred in the women receiving 1200 mg/day and was 4123 μg/L.[2] In women receiving 200, 400, or 600 mg/day of acebutolol, milk levels were 286 μg/L, 666 μg/L and 539 μg/L respectively. Acebutolol and diacetolol (its major metabolite) appear in breastmilk with a milk/plasma ratio of 1.9 to 9.2 (acebutolol) and 2.3 to 24.7 for the metabolite (diacetolol).

These levels are considered relatively high and occurred following maternal doses of 400-1200 mg/day. When the metabolite is added, the dose may approach 10% of maternal dose. Neonates appear much more sensitive to acebutolol.

Pregnancy Risk Category: B

Lactation Risk Category: L3

Theoretic Infant Dose: 615 μg/kg/day

Adult Concerns: Hypotension, bradycardia, and transient tachypnea have been reported. Drowsiness has been reported.

Pediatric Concerns: Hypotension, bradycardia, and transient tachypnea have been reported. Drowsiness has been reported.

Drug Interactions: Decreased effect when used with aluminum salts, barbiturates, calcium salts, cholestyramine, NSAIDs, ampicillin, rifampin, and salicylates. Beta blockers may reduce the effect of oral sulfonylureas (hypoglycemic agents). Increased toxicity/effect when used with other antihypertensives, contraceptives, MAO inhibitors, cimetidine, and numerous other products. See drug interaction reference for complete listing.

Alternatives: Propranolol, metoprolol

Adult Dosage: 200-400 mg BID

T½ = 3-4 hours	M/P = 7.1-12.2
PHL =	PB = 26%
PK = 1-4 hours	Oral = 35-50%
MW = 336	pKa =
Vd =	

References:
1. Drug Facts and Comparisons. 1995 ed. Facts and Comparisons, St. Louis.
2. Boutroy MJ, et.al. To nurse when receiving acebutolol: Is it dangerous for the neonate? Eur. J. Clin. Pharmacol. 30:737-9,1986.

ACETAMINOPHEN

Trade: Tempra, Tylenol, Paracetamol
Can/Aus/UK: Apo-Acetaminophen, Calpol, Dymadon, Panadol, Paracetamol, Tempra, Tylenol
Uses: Analgesic
AAP: Approved by the American Academy of Pediatrics for use in breastfeeding mothers

Only small amounts are secreted into breastmilk, and are considered too small to be hazardous. Breastmilk levels of acetaminophen are approximately 10-15 mg/Liter of milk.[1] Milk levels of 4.2 mg/L and milk/plasma ratios of 0.91 to 1.42 have been reported at 1 and 12 hours respectively and a milk half-life of 4.7 hours.[2] The authors suggest that assuming ingestion of 90 ml of milk at 3, 6, and 9 hour intervals, an estimated range of ingestion would be 0.04 to 0.23% of total maternal dose. In another study of women who ingested 1000 mg acetaminophen, milk levels averaged 6.1 mg/L and provided an average dose of 0.92 mg/kg/d according to the authors.[3]

Pregnancy Risk Category: B

Lactation Risk Category: L1

Theoretic Infant Dose: 0.9 mg/kg/day

Adult Concerns: Few when taken in normal doses. Diarrhea, gastric upset sweating in overdose. Note: numerous cases of liver toxicity have been reported following 'chronic' abuse of acetaminophen at >200 mg/kg/day.

Pediatric Concerns: None reported via milk.

Drug Interactions: Rifampin can interact to reduce the analgesic effect of acetaminophen. Increased acetaminophen hepatotoxicity when used with barbiturates, carbamazepine, hydantoins, sulfinpyrazone, and chronic alcohol abuse.

Alternatives:

Adult Dosage: 325-650 mg q 4-6 hours PRN

T½ = 2 hours	M/P = 0.91-1.42
PHL = 1-3 hours	PB = 25%
PK = 0.5-2 hours	Oral = >85%
MW = 151	pKa = 9.5
Vd = 0.8-1.0	

References:
1. Berlin CM, Jaaffee S, Ragni M. Disposition of acetaminophen in milk, saliva and plasma of lactating women. Pediatr Pharmacol 1:135-41, 1980.
2. Bitzen PO, et.al. Excretion of paracetamol in human breast milk. Eur. J. Clin. Pharmacol. 20:123-125, 1981.
3. Notarianni LJ, Oldham HG, Bennett PN. Passage of paracetamol into breast milk and its subsequent metabolism by the neonate. Br J Clin Pharmacol. 24(1):63-7, 1987.

ACETAZOLAMIDE

Trade: Dazamide, Diamox
Can/Aus/UK: Acetazolam, Apo-Acetazolamide, Diamox
Uses: Diuretic
AAP: Approved by the American Academy of Pediatrics for use in breastfeeding mothers

Acetazolamide is a carbonic anhydrase inhibitor dissimilar to other thiazide diuretics. In general, diuretics may decrease the volume of breastmilk although this is rare. In a patient receiving 500 mg of acetazolamide twice daily, acetazolamide concentrations in milk were 1.3 to 2.1 mg/L (0.06 % of maternal dose) while the maternal plasma levels ranged from 5.2-6.4 mg/L.[1] Plasma concentrations in exposed infants were 0.2 to 0.6 μg/mL two to 12 hours after breastfeeding. These amounts are unlikely to cause adverse effects in the infant.

Pregnancy Risk Category: C

Lactation Risk Category: L2

Theoretic Infant Dose: 0.3 mg/kg/day

Adult Concerns: Anorexia, diarrhea, metallic taste, polyuria, muscular weakness, potassium loss. Malaise, fatigue, depression, renal failure have been reported.

Pediatric Concerns: None reported via milk.

Drug Interactions: Increases lithium excretion, reducing plasma levels. May increase toxicity of cyclosporine. Digitalis toxicity may occur if hypokalemia results from acetazolamide therapy.

Alternatives:

Adult Dosage: 500 mg BID

T½ = 2.4-5.8 hours PHL = PK = 1-3 hours MW = 222 Vd = 0.2	M/P = 0.25 PB = 70-95% Oral = Complete pKa = 7.4

References:

1. Soderman P, Hartvig, P, Fagerlund C. Acetazolamide excretion into human breast milk. Br.J.Clin.Pharmacol.17:59-60, 1984.

ACETOHEXAMIDE

Trade: Dimelor
Can/Aus/UK: Diamox, Dimelor
Uses: Hypoglycemic agent
AAP: Not reviewed

Acetohexamide is an intermediate acting hypoglycemic sulfonylurea antidiabetic agent.[1] Its structure is similar to tolbutamide, chlorpropamide and tolazamide. No data are available on its transfer to human milk, but other sulfonylureas transfer to milk, but only in minimal levels (see tolbutamide). The use of sulfonylureas in breastfeeding mothers is somewhat controversial due to limited studies, but has not been noted in the literature to produce any problems. Observe infant closely for hypoglycemia if used.

Pregnancy Risk Category: C

Lactation Risk Category: L3

Theoretic Infant Dose:

Adult Concerns: The most common adverse effects include hypoglycemia, nausea, epigastric fullness, heartburn, and rashes.

Pediatric Concerns: None reported via milk.

Drug Interactions: Numerous drugs interact with sulfonylureas, please consult further references. Increased hypoglycemic effects occur when used with salicylates, beta blockers, MAO inhibitors, oral anticoagulants, NSAIDs, sulfonamides, insulin, etc. Reduced hypoglycemic effects may occur when used with cholestyramine, diazoxide, hydantoins, rifampin, and thiazides.

Alternatives:

Adult Dosage: 250-1000 mg daily

T½ = 1.3-6 (metabolite) hours	M/P =
PHL =	PB = 65-90%
PK = 3 hours	Oral = Good
MW = 324	pKa =
Vd = 0.2	

References:
1. Pharmaceutical Manufacturers Package Insert, 1999.

ACYCLOVIR

Trade: Zovirax
Can/Aus/UK: Aciclovir, Acyclo-V, Apo-Acyclovir, Avirax, Zovirax, Zyclir
Uses: Antiviral, for herpes simplex
AAP: Approved by the American Academy of Pediatrics for use in breastfeeding mothers

Acyclovir is converted by herpes simplex and varicella zoster virus to acyclovir triphosphate which interferes with viral HSV DNA polymerase. It is currently cleared for use in HSV infections, Varicella-Zoster, and under certain instances, cytomegalo virus and Epstein-Barr infections. There is virtually no percutaneous absorption following topical application and plasma levels are undetectable. The pharmacokinetics in children are similar to adults. In neonates, the half-life is 3.8-4.1 hours, and in children one year and older it is 1.9-3.6 hours.

Acyclovir levels in breastmilk are reported to be 0.6 to 4.1 times the maternal plasma levels.[1] Maximum ingested dose was calculated to be 1500 μg/day assuming 750 ml milk intake. This level produced no overt side effects in one infant. In a study by Meyer[2], a patient receiving 200 mg five times daily produced breastmilk concentrations averaging 1.06 mg/L. Using this data an infant would ingest less than 1 mg acyclovir daily. In another study, doses of 800 mg five times daily produced milk levels that ranged from 4.16 to 5.81 mg/L (total estimated infant ingestion per day = 0.73 mg/kg/day).[3]

Topical therapy on lesions other than nipple is probably safe. If applied to nipples, any residual acyclovir cream should be removed prior to feeding. Toxicities associated with acyclovir are few and usually minor. Acyclovir therapy in neonatal units is common and produces few toxicities. Calculated intake by infant would be less than 1 mg/day.

Pregnancy Risk Category: C

Lactation Risk Category: L2

Theoretic Infant Dose: 0.9 mg/kg/day

Adult Concerns: Nausea, vomiting, diarrhea, sore throat, edema, and skin rashes.

Pediatric Concerns: None reported via milk in several studies.

Drug Interactions: Increased CNS side effects when used with zidovudine and probenecid.

Alternatives:

Adult Dosage: 200-800 mg q 4-6 hours

T½ = 2.4 hours	M/P = 0.6-4.1
PHL = 3.2 hours (neonates)	PB = 9-33%
PK = 1.5 - 2 hours	Oral = 15-30%
MW = 225	pKa =
Vd =	

References:
1. Lau RJ, Emery MG, Galinsky RE. Unexpected accumulation of acyclovir in breast milk with estimation of infant exposure. Obstet Gynecol. 69:468-471, 1987.
2. Meyer LJ, de Miranda P, Sheth N, et.al. Acyclovir in human breast milk. Am J Obstet Gynecol. 158:586-588,1988.
3. Taddio A, Klein J, Koren G. Acyclovir excretion in human breast milk. Ann. Pharm. 28:585-7, 1994.

ADAPALENE

Trade: Differin
Can/Aus/UK: Differin
Uses: Topical acne remedy
AAP: Not reviewed

Adapalene is a retinoid-like compound (similar to Tretinoin) used topically for treatment of acne. No data are available on its transfer into human milk. However, adapalene is virtually unabsorbed when applied topically to the skin.[1] Plasma levels are almost undetectable (< 0.25 ng/mL plasma), so milk levels would be infinitesimally low and probably undetectable.[2]

Pregnancy Risk Category: C

Lactation Risk Category: L3

Theoretic Infant Dose:

Adult Concerns: Exacerbation of sunburn, irritation of skin, erythema, dryness, scaling, burning, itching.

Pediatric Concerns: None reported via milk. Very unlikely due to minimal maternal absorption.

Drug Interactions:

Alternatives: Tretinoin

Adult Dosage: apply topical QD

References:
1. Pharmaceutical Manufacturers Package Insert, 1999.
2. Drug Facts and Comparisons. 1999 ed. Facts and Comparisons, St. Louis.

ALBUTEROL

Trade: Proventil, Ventolin
Can/Aus/UK: Asmavent, Asmol, Novo-Salmol, Respax, Respolin, Salamol, Salbulin, Salbuvent, Ventolin
Uses: Bronchodilator for asthma
AAP: Not reviewed

Albuterol is a very popular beta-2 adrenergic agonist that is typically used to dilate constricted bronchi in asthmatics.[1] It is active orally, but is most commonly used via inhalation. When used orally, significant plasma levels are attained and transfer to breastmilk is possible. When used via inhalation, less than 10% is absorbed into maternal plasma. Small amounts are probably secreted into milk although no reports exist. It is very unlikely that pharmacologic doses will be transferred to the infant via milk following inhaler use. However, when used orally, breastmilk levels could be sufficient to produce tremors and agitation in infants. Commonly used via inhalation in treating pediatric asthma.

Pregnancy Risk Category: C

Lactation Risk Category: L1

Theoretic Infant Dose:

Adult Concerns: Observe infant for tremors and excitement.

Pediatric Concerns: None reported via milk

Drug Interactions: Albuterol effects are reduce when used with beta blockers. Cardiovascular effects are potentiated when used with MAO inhibitors, tricyclic antidepressants, amphetamines, and inhaled anesthetics (enflurane).

Alternatives:

Adult Dosage: 2-4 mg TID or QID

T½ = 3.8 hours	M/P =
PHL=	PB =
PK = 5-30 min.(inhaled)	Oral = 100%
MW = 239	pKa = 10.3
Vd = 2.2	

References:
1.   Pharmaceutical Manufacturers Package Insert, 1997.

ALBUTEROL and IPRATROPIUM BROMIDE

Trade: Duoneb
Can/Aus/UK:
Uses: Bronchodilators
AAP: Not reviewed

DuoNeb is a combination product containing 0.103 mg albuterol and 0.018 mg of ipratropium bromide per metered-dose inhalation. See the individual monographs on this product.

ALENDRONATE SODIUM

Trade: Fosamax
Can/Aus/UK: Fosamax
Uses: Inhibits bone resorption
AAP: Not reviewed

Alendronate is a specific inhibitor of osteoclast-mediated bone resorption, thus reducing bone loss and bone turnover.[1]   While incorporated in bone matrix, it is not pharmacologically active. Because concentrations in plasma are too low to be detected (< 5 ng/mL) it is very unlikely that it would be secreted into human milk in clinically relevant concentrations. Concentrations in human milk have not been reported.   Because this product has exceedingly poor oral bioavailability, particularly when ingested with milk, it is exceedingly unlikely that alendronate would be orally absorbed by a breastfeeding infant.

Pregnancy Risk Category: C

Lactation Risk Category: L3

Theoretic Infant Dose:

Adult Concerns: Abdominal pain, nausea, dyspepsia, constipation, muscle cramps, headache, taste perversion. There are a number of case reports of esophagitis and esophageal ulceration in patients taking Fosamax.

Pediatric Concerns: None reported via milk.

Drug Interactions: Ranitidine will double the absorption of alendronate. Calcium, milk, and other multivalent cation containing foods reduce the bioavailability of alendronate.

Alternatives:

Adult Dosage: 10 mg QD

T½ = <3 hours(plasma)	M/P =
PHL=	PB = 78%
PK =	Oral = <0.7%
MW = 325	pKa =
Vd = 0.4	

References:
1. Pharmaceutical Manufacturers Package Insert, 1997.

ALFENTANIL

Trade: Alfenta
Can/Aus/UK: Alfenta, Rapifen
Uses: Narcotic analgesic
AAP: Not reviewed

Alfentanil is secreted into breastmilk. Following a dose of 50 μg/kg I.V., the mean levels of alfentanil in colostrum at 4 hours varied from 0.21 to 1.56 μg/L of milk, levels probably too small to produce overt toxicity in breastfeeding infants.[1] In another study following 50 micrograms or more, breastmilk levels were 0.88 μg/Liter at 4 hours and 0.05 μg/Liter at 28 hours.[2] These levels are probably too low to be clinically relevant.

Pregnancy Risk Category: C

Lactation Risk Category: L2

Theoretic Infant Dose: 0.2 μg/kg/day

Adult Concerns: Observe for bradycardia, shivering, constipation and sedation. In neonates observe for severe hypotension.

Pediatric Concerns: None reported via milk.

Drug Interactions: Phenothiazines may antagonize the analgesic effects of opiates. Dextromethorphan may increase the analgesia of opiate agonists. Other CNS depressants such as benzodiazepines, barbiturates, tricyclic antidepressants, erythromycin, reserpine and beta blockers may increase the toxicity of this opiate.

Alternatives: Remifentanil

Adult Dosage: 8-40 mcg/kg total

T½ = 1-2 hours PHL= 5-6 hours (neonates) PK = immediate MW = 417 Vd = 0.3-1.0	M/P = PB = 92% Oral = pKa = 6.5

References:
1. Giesecke, AH, Rice, LJ. Lipton, JM. Alfentanil in colostrum. Anesthesiology 63:A284, 1985.
2. Spigset O. Anaesthetic agents and excretion in breast milk. Acta Anaesthesiologica Scandinavica. 38:94-103, 1994.

ALLERGY INJECTIONS
Trade:
Can/Aus/UK:
Uses: Descnsitizing injections
AAP: Not revicwed

Allergy injections consist of protein and carbohydrate substances from plants, animals, and other species. There are no reported untoward effects.

Pregnancy Risk Category:

Lactation Risk Category: L1

Theoretic Infant Dose:

Adult Concerns: Allergic pruritus, anaphylaxis, other immune reactions.

Pediatric Concerns: None.

Drug Interactions:

Alternatives:

Adult Dosage: N/A

ALLOPURINOL

Trade: Zyloprim, Lopurin
Can/Aus/UK: Alloprin, Allorin, Aluline, Apo-Allopurinol, Caplenal, Capurate, Cosuric, Hamarin, Novo-Purol, Zygout, Zyloprim, Zyloric
Uses: Reduces uric acid levels
AAP: Approved by the American Academy of Pediatrics for use in breastfeeding mothers

Allopurinol is a potent antagonist of xanthine oxidase, an enzyme involved in the production of uric acid. It is used to reduce uric acid levels in gouty individuals. In one report of allopurinol use in a nursing mother (300mg/d), the breastmilk concentration at 2 and 4 hours was 0.9 and 1.4 μg/ml respectively.[1] The concentration of the metabolite, oxypurinol, was 53.7 and 48.0 μg/ml at 2 and 4 hours respectively. The milk/plasma ratio ranged from 0.9 to 1.4 for allopurinol and 3.9 for its metabolite, oxypurinol. The average daily dose that an infant would receive from milk would be approximately 0.14-0.20 mg/kg of allopurinol and 7.2-8.0 mg/kg of oxypurinol. No adverse effects were noted in the infant after 6 weeks of therapy.

AHL= 1-3 hours (allopurinol), 18-30 hours for (oxypurinol). Pediatric dosages for ages 6 and under is generally 10 mg/kg/24 hours.

Pregnancy Risk Category: C

Lactation Risk Category: L2

Theoretic Infant Dose: 0.2 μg/kg/day

Adult Concerns: Itching skin rash. Fever, chills, nausea and vomiting, diarrhea, gastritis,

Pediatric Concerns: No adverse effects were noted in one infant after 6 weeks of therapy.

Drug Interactions: Alcohol decreases allopurinol efficacy. Inhibits metabolism of azathioprine and mercaptopurine. Increased incidence of skin rash when used with amoxicillin and ampicillin. Increased risk of kidney stones when used with high doses of vitamin C. Allopurinol prolongs half-life of oral anticoagulants, theophylline, chlorpropamide.

Alternatives:

Adult Dosage: 100-400 mg BID

T½ = 1-3 hours(allopurinol)	M/P = 0.9-1.4
PHL =	PB = 0%
PK = 2-6 hours	Oral = 90%
MW = 136	pKa =
Vd = 1.6	

References:
1. Kamilli I, and Gresser U. Allopurinol and oxypurinol in human breast milk. Clinical Investigator 71:161-164, 1993.

ALMOTRIPTAN

Trade: Axert
Can/Aus/UK: Almogran
Uses: Acute migraine treatment
AAP: Not reviewed

Almotriptan is a selective serotonin receptor antagonist similar to sumatriptan although it is slightly more bioavailable orally. No data are available on its transfer to human milk. Clinically it is not much better than oral sumatriptan[1], which has been well studied in breastfeeding women. See sumatriptan for alternative.

Pregnancy Risk Category: C

Lactation Risk Category:

Theoretic Infant Dose:

Adult Concerns: Nausea, somnolence, headache, dry mouth, tachycardia, myocardial ischemia.

Pediatric Concerns: None reported.

Drug Interactions: Higher plasma level of almotriptan could result from use with ketoconazole, amiodarone, cimetidine, clarithromycin, erythromycin, nefazodone, and other inhibitors of CYP3A4. Do not use with ergot alkaloids, MAO inhibitors, verapamil, SSRIs such as fluoxetine, sertraline, etc.

Alternatives: Sumatriptan

Adult Dosage: 6.25-12.5 mg

T½ = 3-4 hours	M/P =
PHL =	PB = 35%
PK = 2-4 hours	Oral = 80%
MW =	pKa =
Vd = 2.85	

References:
1. Spierings EL, Gomez-Mancilla B, Grosz DE, Rowland CR, Whaley FS, Jirgens KJ. Oral almotriptan vs. oral sumatriptan in the abortive treatment of migraine: a double-blind, randomized, parallel-group, optimum-dose comparison. Arch Neurol. 58(6):944-50, 2001.

ALOE VERA

Trade: Aloe Vera, Cape, Zanzibar, Socotrine
Can/Aus/UK:
Uses: Extract from A. Vera
AAP: Not reviewed

There are over 500 species of aloes. The aloe plant yields two important products, Aloe latex derived from the outer skin, and Aloe gel, a clear, gelatinous material derived from the inner tissue of the leaf. The aloe gel is the most commonly used product in cosmetic and health food products. The gel contains a polysaccharide glucomannan, similar to guar gum, which is responsible for its emollient effect. Aloe also contains tannins, polysaccharides, organic acids, enzymes, and other products. Bradykininase, a protease inhibitor, is believed to relieve pain and decrease swelling and pruritus. Other components, such as an anti-prostaglandin compound is believed to reduce inflammation.[1]

Aloe latex, a bitter yellow product derived from the outer skin, is a drastic cathartic and produces a strong purgative effect on the large intestine due to its anthraquinone barbaloin content. Do not use the latex orally in children.[1] The most common use of the aloe gel is in burn therapy for minor burns and skin irritation. Thus far, well controlled studies do not provide evidence of a clear advantage over aggressive wound care. Two FDA advisory panels failed to find sufficient evidence to show Aloe Vera is useful in treatment of minor burns, cuts, or vaginal irritation.

Recent evidence suggests that A.vera may accelerate wound healing, such as in frostbite, and in patients undergoing dermabrasion, although another study suggests a delay in healing.[2,3] Numerous studies have suggested accelerated wound healing, reduction in arthritic inflammation, and other inflammatory diseases, although these are in many cases poorly controlled.

The toxicity of A.vera gel when applied topically is minimal. Oral use of the latex derived from the outer skin of A. vera is strongly discouraged as they are drastic cathartics. Aloe emodin and other anthraquinones present in A. vera latex may cause severe gastric cramping, and should never be used in pregnant women and children.

Pregnancy Risk Category:

Lactation Risk Category: L3

Theoretic Infant Dose:

Adult Concerns: Severe gastric irritation, strong purgative effect and diarrhea when gel used orally.

Pediatric Concerns: No reports of untoward effects following maternal use or via milk ingestion.

Drug Interactions:

Alternatives:

Adult Dosage: N/A

References:
1. Review of Natural Products. Ed: Facts and Comparisons, St. Louis, Missouri, 1997.
2. Leung AY. Encyclopedia of Common Natural Ingredients used in Food, Drugs and Cosmetics. New York, NY: J Wiley and Sons, 1980.
3. Fulton JE: The stimulation of postdermabrasion would healing with stabilized aloe vera gel polyethylene oxide dressing. J. Dermatol Surg Oncol 16(5):460, 1990.
4. Schmidt JM, Greenspoon JS. Aloevera dermal wound gel is associated with a delay in wound healing. Obstet Gynecol 78(1):115, 1991.

ALOSETRON

Trade: Lotronex
Can/Aus/UK:
Uses: Treatment of Irritable Bowel Syndrome
AAP: Not reviewed

Alosetron (Lotronex) is a new 5-HT3 receptor antagonist which is used to control the symptoms of irritable bowel syndrome. No data are available on the transfer of this medication into human milk. While the manufacturer suggests it is present in animal milk, no data are provided.[1] The peak plasma levels (in young women) of this product are quite small, only averaging 9 nanogram/mL following a 1 mg dose. Although the half-life of the parent alosetron is short (1.5 hours) its metabolites have much longer half-lives but their importance is unknown. Bioavailability is lessened (-25%) when admixed with food. With this data it is unlikely milk levels will be extraordinarily high, or that the levels transferred to the infant will be clinically relevant to the infant. However its use in breastfeeding patients should be approached with caution until we have more clinical experience with this new product.

Pregnancy Risk Category: B

Lactation Risk Category: L3

Theoretic Infant Dose:

Adult Concerns: Constipation is very common, hypertension, nausea less so.

Pediatric Concerns: None reported via milk, but no studies exist.

Drug Interactions: It is unlikely alosetron will inhibit the metabolism of drugs metabolized by the major CYP 450 enzymes.

Alternatives:

Adult Dosage: 1 mg twice daily.

T½ = 1.5 hours	M/P =
PHL=	PB = 82%
PK = 1 hour	Oral = 50-60%
MW =	pKa =
Vd = 1.36	

References:
1. Manufacturers package insert, Glaxo-Wellcome, 2000.

ALPRAZOLAM

Trade: Xanax
Can/Aus/UK: Apo-Alpraz, Kalma, Novo-Alprazol, Ralozam, Xanax
Uses: Benzodiazepine antianxiety agent
AAP: Drug whose effect on nursing infants is unknown but may be of concern

Alprazolam is a prototypical benzodiazepine drug similar to Valium, but is now preferred in many instances because of its shorter half-life. In a study of 8 women who received a single oral dose of 0.5 mg, the peak alprazolam level in milk was 3.7 μg/L which occurred at 1.1 hours; the observed milk/serum ratio (using AUC method) was 0.36.[1] The neonatal dose of alprazolam in breastmilk is low. The author estimates the average between 0.3 to 5 μg/kg per day. This is approximately 3% of weight-adjusted maternal dose. While the infants in this study did not breastfeed, these doses would probably be too low to induce a clinical effect.

In a brief letter, Anderson reports that the manufacturer is aware of withdrawal symptoms in infants following exposure in utero and via breastmilk.[2] In a mother who received 0.5 mg 2-3 times daily (PO) during pregnancy, a neonatal withdrawal syndrome was evident in the breast fed infant the first week postpartum. This data suggests that the amount of alprazolam in breastmilk is insufficient to prevent a withdrawal syndrome following prenatal exposure. In another case of infant exposure solely via breastmilk, the mother took alprazolam (dosage unspecified) for nine months while breastfeeding and withdrew herself from the medication over a 3 week period. The mother reported withdrawal symptoms in the infant including irritability, crying, and sleep disturbances.

The benzodiazepine family as a rule, are not ideal for breastfeeding mothers due to relatively long half-lives and the development of dependence. However, it is apparent that the shorter-acting benzodiazepines are safest during lactation provided their use is short-term or intermittent, low dose, and after the first week of life.[3]

Pregnancy Risk Category: D

Lactation Risk Category: L3

Theoretic Infant Dose: 0.6 μg/kg/day

Adult Concerns: Drowsiness, fatigue, insomnia, confusion, dry mouth, constipation, nausea, vomiting.

Pediatric Concerns: Rarely, withdrawal syndrome reported in one breastfed infant. Observe for sedation, poor feeding, irritability, crying, insomnia on withdrawal. Use on an acute or short term basis is not contraindicated.

Drug Interactions: Decreased therapeutic effect when used with carbamazepine, disulfiram. Increased toxicity when used with oral contraceptives, CNS depressants, cimetidine and lithium.

Alternatives:

Adult Dosage: 0.5-1 mg TID

T½ = 12-15 hours	M/P = 0.36
PHL =	PB = 80%
PK = 1-2 hours	Oral = Complete
MW = 309	pKa =
Vd = 0.9-1.3	

References:
1. OO CY, Kuhn RJ, Desai N, et.al. Pharmacokinetics in lactating women: prediction of alprazolam transfer into milk. Br. J.Clin. Pharmacol. 40:231-236, 1995.
2. Anderson PO, McGuire GG. Neonatal alprazolam withdrawal: possible effects of breast feeding. DICP Annal Pharmacother. 23:614, 1989.
3. Maitra R, Menkes DB. Psychotropic drugs and lactation. N Z Med J. 28;109(1024):217-8, 1996.

ALTEPLASE

Trade: Activase
Can/Aus/UK: Actilyse
Uses: Thrombolytic agent
AAP: Not reviewed

Alteplase is a thrombolytic agent commonly known as tissue-type plasminogen activator (tPA). Alteplase is a large protein with 527 amino acids and with a large molecular weight. It binds to fibrin in a thrombus and converts the plasminogen to plasmin which subsequently leads to a breakdown of the clot. Alteplase is rapidly cleared from the plasma, with an initial half-life of 5 minutes following rapid I.V. therapy, and a somewhat longer half-life 26-46 minutes following prolonged infusion.[1,2] Its transfer into mature milk would be negligible but it could potentially pass in small amounts in colostrum. Whether it would be bioavailable in the gut of a newborn infant is questionable, but it would almost certainly not be bioavailable in an older infant. It is very unlikely it would produce adverse effects in breastfed infants.

Pregnancy Risk Category: C

Lactation Risk Category: L3

Theoretic Infant Dose:

Adult Concerns: Hemorrhage, reperfusion arrhythmias, bradycardia and possibly seizures.

Pediatric Concerns: None reported.

Drug Interactions: May potentiate hemorrhage when used with other anticoagulants such as dicoumarol, warfarin, anisindione, acenocoumarol, phenindione, heparin and etc. Nitroglycerin may increase clearance of TPA.

Alternatives:

Adult Dosage: 100 mg

T½ = 26-46 minutes	M/P =
PHL =	PB =
PK = 20-40 min.	Oral = Nil
MW = Large	pKa =
Vd = 8.1	

References:
1. Pharmaceutical manufacturers package insert, 2001.
2. Verstraete M, Su CAPF, Tanswell P et al: Pharmacokinetics and effects on fibrinolytic and coagulation parameters of two doses of recombinant tissue-type plasminogen activator in healthy volunteers. Thromb Haemost 56:1-5, 1986.

AMANTADINE

Trade: Symmetrel, Symadine
Can/Aus/UK: Endantadine, Gen-Amantadine, Mantadine, Symmetrel
Uses: Anti-viral
AAP: Not reviewed

Amantadine is a unique compound that has both antiviral activity against influenza A and is effective in treating Parkinsonian symptoms.[1]

Pediatric indications for prevention of influenza for ages 1-10 are available.

Trace amounts are believed to be secreted in milk although no reports are found. Adult plasma levels following doses of 200 mg daily are 400-900 nanograms/mL.[2] Even assuming a theoretical milk/plasma ratio of 1.0, the average daily dose to a breastfeeding infant would be far less than 0.9 mg, a dose that would be clinically irrelevant compared to the 4-8 mg/kg dose used in 1 year old infants.

However, amantadine is known to suppress prolactin production and should not be used in breastfeeding mothers, or at least used with caution while observing for milk suppression.[3,4]

Pregnancy Risk Category: C

Lactation Risk Category: L3

Theoretic Infant Dose:

Adult Concerns: Urinary retention, vomiting, skin rash in infants. Insomnia, depression, confusion, disorientation, nausea, anorexia, constipation, vomiting.

Pediatric Concerns: None reported via milk but a major reduction in prolactin levels has been reported. Avoid.

Drug Interactions: May increase anticholinergic effects when used with anticholinergic or CNS active drugs. Increased toxicity/levels when used with hydrochlorothiazide plus triamterene, or amiloride.

Alternatives:

Adult Dosage: 100 mg BID

T½ = 1-28 hours	M/P =
PHL =	PB = 67%
PK = 1-4 hours	Oral = 86-94%
MW = 151	pKa = 10.1
Vd = 4.4	

References:
1. Pharmaceutical Manufacturers Package Insert, 1997.
2. Cedarbaum JM: Clinical pharmacokinetics of anti-parkinsonian drugs. Clin Pharmacokinetics 13:141-178, 1987.
3. Correa N, Opler LA, Kay SR, Birmaher B. Amantadine in the treatment of neuroendocrine side effects of neuroleptics. J Clin Psychopharmacol. 7(2):91-5, 1987.
4. Siever LJ. The effect of amantadine on prolactin levels and galactorrhea on neuroleptic-treated patients. J Clin Psychopharmacol. 1(1):2-7, 1981.

AMIKACIN

Trade: Amikin
Can/Aus/UK: Amikin
Uses: Aminoglycoside antibiotic
AAP: Not reviewed

Amikacin is a typical aminoglycoside antibiotic used for gram negative infections. Other aminoglycoside antibiotics are poorly absorbed from GI tract in infants although they could produce changes in GI flora. Only very small amounts are secreted into breastmilk. Following 100 and 200 mg IM doses, only trace amounts have been found in breastmilk and then in only 2 of 4 patients studied.[1] In another study of 2-3 patients who received 100 mg IM, none to trace amounts were found in milk.[2]

Pregnancy Risk Category: C

Lactation Risk Category: L2

Theoretic Infant Dose:

Adult Concerns: Diarrhea, changes in GI flora.

Pediatric Concerns: None reported via milk. Commonly used in neonates.

Drug Interactions: Increased aminoglycoside toxicity when used with indomethacin, amphotericin, loop diuretics, vancomycin, enflurane, methoxyflurane, depolarizing neuromuscular blocking agents.

Alternatives:

Adult Dosage: 5-7.5 mg/kg/dose TID

T½ = 2.3 hours	M/P =
PHL = 4-5 hours	PB = 4%
PK = 0.75-2.0 hours	Oral = Poor
MW = 586	pKa =
Vd = 0.28	

References:
1. Matsuda C, et. al. A study of amikacin in the obstetrics field. Jpn J Antibiot 27:633-6,1974.
2. Matsuda S. Transfer of antibiotics into maternal milk. Biol Res Pregnancy Perinatol. 5(2):57-60, 1984.

AMINOSALICYLIC ACID (PARA)

Trade: Paser, PAS
Can/Aus/UK: Nemasol, Tubasal
Uses: Antitubercular
AAP: Drugs associated with significant side effects and should be given with caution

PARA inhibits folic acid synthesis and is selective only for tuberculosis bacteria. Following a maternal dose of 4.0 gm/day, the peak maternal plasma level was 70.1 mg/L and occurred at 2 hours. The breastmilk concentration of 5-ASA at 3 hours was 1.1 mg/L.[1] In another study, the concentration in milk ranged from 0.13 to 0.53 μmol/liter.[2] In a 29 year old mother who received 3 gm/day of 5-ASA for ulcerative colitis, the estimated intake for an infant receiving 120-200 ml of milk was 0.02 to 0.012 mg of 5-ASA.[3] The concentrations of 5-ASA and its metabolite Acetyl-5-ASA present in milk appear too low to produce overt toxicity in most infants. Only one report of slight diarrhea in one infant has been reported.

Pregnancy Risk Category: C

Lactation Risk Category: L3

Theoretic Infant Dose: 0.2 μg/kg/day

Adult Concerns: Nausea, vomiting, diarrhea.

Pediatric Concerns: Only one report of slight diarrhea in one infant has been reported.

Drug Interactions: Reduces levels of digoxin and vitamin B-12.

Alternatives:

Adult Dosage: 150 mg/kg/day BID or TID

T½ = 1 hour	M/P = 0.09-0.17
PHL =	PB = 50-73%
PK = 2 hours	Oral = >90%
MW = 153	pKa =
Vd =	

References:
1. Holdiness, MR. Antituberculosis drugs and breast-feeding. Arch. Int. Med. 144:1888, 1984.
2. Christensen, LA. Disposition of 5-aminosalicylic acid and N-acetyl-5-amintosalicylic acid in fetal and maternal body fluids during treatment with different 5-aminosalicyclic acid preparations. Acta.Obstet. Gynecol. Scand. 74:399-402, 1994.
3. Klotz U. Negligable excretion of 5-aminosalicyclic acid in breast milk. The Lancet 342:618-9, 1993.

AMIODARONE

Trade: Cordarone
Can/Aus/UK: Aratac, Cordarone
Uses: Strong antiarrhythmic agent
AAP: Drugs whose effect on nursing infants is unknown by may be of concern

Amiodarone is a potent and sometimes dangerous antiarrhythmic drug and requires close supervision by clinicians. Although poorly absorbed by the mother (<50%), maximum serum levels are attained after 3-7 hours. This drug has a very large volume of distribution, resulting in accumulation in adipose, liver, spleen and lungs and has a high rate of fetal toxicity (10-17%). It should not be given to pregnant mothers unless critically required.

Significant amounts are secreted into breastmilk at levels higher than the plasma level. Breastmilk samples obtained at birth and at 2 and 3 weeks post-partum in 2 patients, contained levels of amiodarone and desethylamiodarone varying from 1.7 to 3.0 mg/L (mean =2.3 mg/L), and 0.8 to 1.8 mg/L (mean =1.1 mg/L), respectively.[1] Despite the concentrations of amiodarone in milk, the amounts were apparently not high enough to produce plasma levels of both drugs higher than about 0.1 μg/mL, which are minimal compared to the maternal plasma levels of 1.2 μg/mL or higher.

McKenna reported amiodarone milk levels in a mother treated with 400 mg daily.[2] In this study, at 6 weeks postpartum, breastmilk levels of amiodarone and desethylamiodarone varied during the day from 2.8-16.4 mg/L and 1.1-6.5 mg/L respectively.   Reported infant plasma levels of amiodarone and desethylamiodarone were 0.4 and 0.25 respectively.   The ingested dose to the infant was approximately 1.5 μg/kg/day.   The authors suggest that the amount of amiodarone ingested was moderate and could expose the developing infant to a significant dose of the drug and should be avoided.   Because amiodarone inhibits extrathyroid deiodinases, conversion of T4 to T3 is reduced. One reported case of hypothyroidism has been reported in an infant following therapy in the mother.   Because of the long half-life and high concentrations in various organs, amiodarone could continuously build up to higher levels in the infant, although it was not reported in the above studies. This product should be used only under the most extraordinary conditions, and the infant should be closely monitored for cardiovascular and thyroid function.

Pregnancy Risk Category: C

Lactation Risk Category: L5

Theoretic Infant Dose: 1.5 mg/kg/d

Adult Concerns: Hypothyroidism, myocardial arrhythmias, pulmonary toxicity, serious liver injury, congestive heart failure.

Pediatric Concerns: Hypothyroidism has been reported. Extreme caution is urged.

Drug Interactions: Amiodarone interferes with the metabolism of a number of drugs including: oral anticoagulants, beta blockers, calcium channel blockers, digoxin, flecainide, phenytoin, procainamide, quinidine. Plasma levels of these drugs tend to be increased to hazardous levels.

Alternatives: Disopyramide, mexiletine

Adult Dosage: 200-800 mg BID

T½ = 26-107 days	M/P = 4.6-13
PHL =	PB = 99.98%
PK = 3-7 hours	Oral = 22-86%
MW = 643	pKa = 6.6
Vd = 18-148	

References:
1. Plomp TA, Vulsma T, and deVijlder JJ. Use of amiodarone during pregnancy. Eur. J. of OBstet. Gyn. and Rep. Biol. 43:201-7, 1992.
2. McKenna Wj, Harris L, et.al. Amiodarone therapy during pregnancy. Am. J. Cardiol. 51:1231-1233, 1983.

AMITRIPTYLINE

Trade: Elavil, Endep
Can/Aus/UK: Amitrol, Apo-Amitriptyline, Domical, Elavil, Endep, Lentizol, Mutabon D, Novo-Tryptin, Tryptanol
Uses: Tricyclic antidepressant
AAP: Drug whose effect on nursing infants is unknown but may be of concern

Amitriptyline and its active metabolite, nortriptyline, are secreted into breastmilk in small amounts. In one report of a mother taking 100 mg/day of amitriptyline, milk levels of amitriptyline and nortriptyline(active metabolite) averaged 143 μg/L and 55.5 μg/L respectively; maternal serum levels averaged 112 μg/L and 72.5 μg/L respectively.[1] No drug was detected in the infants serum. From this data, an infant would consume approximately 21.5 μg/kg/day, a dose that is unlikely to be clinically relevant.

In another study following a maternal dose of 25 mg/day, the amitriptyline and nortriptyline(active metabolite) levels in milk were 30 μg/L and < 30 μg/L respectively.[2] In the same study when the doseage was 75 mg/day, milk levels of amitriptyline and nortriptyline averaged 88 μg/L and 69 μg/L respectively.   Both drugs were essentially undetectable in the infant's serum.   Therefore, the authors estimated that a nursing infant would receive less than 0.1 mg/day.

Pregnancy Risk Category: D

Lactation Risk Category: L2

Theoretic Infant Dose: 21.5 μg/kg/day

Adult Concerns: Anticholinergic side effects, such as drying of secretions, dilated pupil, sedation.

Pediatric Concerns: No untoward effects have been noted in several studies.

Drug Interactions: Phenobarbital may reduce effect of amitriptyline. Amitriptyline blocks the hypotensive effect of guanethidine.   May increase toxicity of amitriptyline when used with clonidine. Dangerous when used with MAO inhibitors, other CNS depressants. May increase anticoagulant effect of coumadin, warfarin. SSRIs (Prozac, Zoloft,etc) should not be used with or soon after amitriptyline or other TCAs due to serotonergic crisis.

Alternatives: Amoxapine, imipramine

Adult Dosage: 15-150 mg BID

T½ = 31-46 hours	**M/P = 1.0**
PHL =	**PB = 94.8%**
PK = 2-4 hours	**Oral = Complete**
MW = 277	**pKa = 9.4**
Vd = 6-10	

References:
1.   Bader, T. and Newman, K. Amitriptyline in human breastmilk and the nursing infant's serum. Am. J. Psychiatry 137:855-856, 1980.
2.   Brixen-Rasmussen L, Halgrener J, Jergensen A.   Amitriptyline and nortriptyline excretion in human breast milk. Psychopharmacology 76:94-95, 1982.
3.   Matheson I, Skjaeraasen J.   Milk concentrations of flupenthixol, nortriptyline and zuclopenthixol and between-breast differences in two patients. Eur J Clin Pharmacol. 35(2):217-20, 1988.

AMLODIPINE BESYLATE

Trade: Norvasc
Can/Aus/UK: Istin, Norvasc
Uses: Antihypertensive, calcium channel blocker
AAP: Not reviewed

Amlodipine is a typical calcium channel blocker antihypertensive agent which has greater bioavailability and a longer duration of action.[1] No data are currently available on transfer of amlodipine into breastmilk. Because most calcium channel blockers (CCB) readily transfer into milk, we should assume the same for this drug. Use caution if administering to lactating women.

Pregnancy Risk Category: C

Lactation Risk Category: L3

Theoretic Infant Dose:

Adult Concerns: Hypotension, bradycardia, edema, headache, or nausea.

Pediatric Concerns: None reported but observe for bradycardia, hypotension upon prolonged use.

Drug Interactions: Cyclosporine levels may be increased when used with calcium channel blockers. Use with azole antifungals (fluconazole, itraconazole, ketoconazole, etc) may lead to enhanced amlodipine levels. Use with rifampin may significantly reduce plasma levels of calcium channel blockers.

Alternatives: Nifedipine, nimodipine

Adult Dosage: 5-10 mg QD

T½ = 30-50 hours	M/P =
PHL=	PB = 93%
PK = 6-9 hours	Oral = 64-65%
MW = 408	pKa =
Vd = 21	

References:
1. Pharmaceutical Manufacturers Package Insert, 1996.

AMOXAPINE

Trade: Asendin
Can/Aus/UK: Asendin, Asendis
Uses: Tricyclic antidepressant
AAP: Drug whose effect on nursing infants is unknown but may be of concern

Amoxapine, and its metabolite are both secreted into breastmilk at relatively low levels. Following a dose of 250 mg/day, milk levels of amoxapine were less than 20 μg/L and 113 μg/L of the active metabolite.[1] Milk levels of active metabolite varied from 113 to 168 μg/L in two other milk samples. Maternal serum levels of amoxapine and metabolite at steady state were 97 μg/L and 375 μg/L respectively.

Milk levels are generally less than 20% of the maternal plasma level.

Pregnancy Risk Category: C

Lactation Risk Category: L2

Theoretic Infant Dose: 17 μg/kg/day

Adult Concerns: Dry mouth, constipation, urine retention, drowsiness or sedation, anxiety, emotional disturbances, parkinsonism, tardive dyskinesia, seizures.

Pediatric Concerns: None reported via milk.

Drug Interactions: Decreased effect of clonidine, guanethidine. Amoxapine may increase effect of CNS depressants, adrenergic agents, anticholinergic agents. Increased toxicity with MAO inhibitors.

Alternatives:

Adult Dosage: 25 mg BID or TID

T½ = 8 hours (parent)	M/P = 0.21
PHL=	PB = 15-25%
PK = 2 hours	Oral = 18-54%
MW = 314	pKa =
Vd = 65.7	

References:
1. Gelenberg AJ. Amoxapin, a new antidepressant, appears in human milk. J. Nerv. Ment. Dis. 167:635-636, 1979.

AMOXICILLIN

Trade: Larotid, Amoxil
Can/Aus/UK: Alphamox, Amoxil, Apo-Amoxi, Betamox, Cilamox, Moxacin, Novamoxin
Uses: Penicillin antibiotic
AAP: Approved by the American Academy of Pediatrics for use in breastfeeding mothers

Amoxicillin is a popular oral penicillin used for otitis media and many other pediatric/adult infections. In one group of 6 mothers who received 1 gm oral doses, the concentration of amoxicillin in breastmilk ranged from 0.68 to 1.3 mg/L of milk (average = 0.9 mg/L).[1] Peak levels occurred at 4-5 hours. Milk/plasma ratios at 1,2, and 3 hours were 0.014, 0.013, and 0.043. Less than 0.7% of the maternal dose is secreted into milk. No harmful effects have been reported.

Pregnancy Risk Category: B

Lactation Risk Category: L1

Theoretic Infant Dose: 0.1 mg/kg/day

Adult Concerns: Diarrhea, rashes, and changes in GI flora. Pancytopenia, rarely pseudomembranous colitis.

Pediatric Concerns: None reported. Commonly used in neonates and children.

Drug Interactions: Efficacy of oral contraceptives may be reduced. Disulfiram and probenecid may increase plasma levels of amoxicillin. Allopurinol may increase the risk of amoxicillin skin rash.

Alternatives:

Adult Dosage: 500-875 mg BID

T½ = 1.7 hours	M/P = 0.014-0.043
PHL = 4 hours (neonate)	PB = 18%
PK = 1.5 hours	Oral = 89%
MW = 365	pKa =
Vd = 0.3	

References:
1. Kefetzis DA, Siafas CA, Georgakopoulous PA, et.al. Passage of cephalosporins and amoxicillin into the breast milk. Acta Paediatr Scan 70:285-286,1981.

AMOXICILLIN + CLAVULANATE

Trade: Augmentin
Can/Aus/UK: Augmentin, Clavulin
Uses: Penicillin antibiotic, extended spectrum
AAP: Not reviewed

Addition of clavulanate extends spectrum of amoxicillin by inhibiting beta lactamase enzymes. Small amounts of amoxicillin (0.9 mg/L milk) are secreted in breastmilk. No harmful effects have been reported.[1] See amoxicillin. Although clavulanic acid is well absorbed and widely distributed, no reports of secretion into human milk exist, but it should be expected (AHL= 1 hour. PB= 45%). May cause changes in GI flora, and possibly fungal (candida) overgrowth.

Pregnancy Risk Category: B

Lactation Risk Category: L1

Theoretic Infant Dose: 0.1 mg/kg/day

Adult Concerns: Diarrhea, rash, thrush, or diarrhea.

Pediatric Concerns: None reported but observe for diarrhea, rash.

Drug Interactions: Efficacy of oral contraceptives may be reduced.

Disulfiram and probenecid may increase plasma levels of amoxicillin. Allopurinol may increase the risk of amoxicillin skin rash.

Alternatives:

Adult Dosage: 875 mg BID

T½ = 1.7 hours	M/P = 0.014-0.043
PHL = 4 hours (neonate)	PB = 18%
PK = 1.5 hours	Oral = 89%
MW = 365	pKa =
Vd = 0.3	

References:
1. Kefetzis DA, Siafas CA, Georgakopoulous PA, et.al. Passage of cephalosporins and amoxicillin into the breast milk. Acta Paediatr Scan 70:285-286,1981.

AMPHETAMINES, HALLUCINOGENIC

Trade: Ecstasy, Adam, Eve, Harmony, Love
Can/Aus/UK:
Uses: Amphetamines
AAP: Contraindicated by the American Academy of Pediatrics in Breastfeeding Mothers

Hallucinogenic amphetamines are a group of illegal amphetamines synthesized specifically for inducing hallucinogenic stimulation. While their use in breastfeeding mothers is certainly contraindicated, their illicit use is increasing. There is a widely held belief among users that it is safe. In the last several years there have been a number of reports of the drug producing severe acute toxicity and death and there are concerns that it may produce long-term damage to the serotonin nerve terminals.[1] MDMA, MDEA, and MDA are three of the most prevalent of this group. Their "street names" are: MDMA=Adam, Ecstacy, MDM=XTC, Essence; MDEA= Eve; MDA=Harmony, Love, Love Drug, Speed for Lovers.   All of these agents are amphetamine derivatives, with extreme hallucinogenic and stimulant activity. As with most amphetamines, their half-lives are rather brief (less than 8 hours). Urinary excretion of these agents is generally complete within 24 hours, but this depends on dose and individual.[2] Their duration of action varies with dose and individual, but is 4-6 hours with doses of 75-150 mg.   Because their structures are similar to methamphetamine, it is likely that significant amounts can transfer into human milk. Hallucinations, extreme agitation and seizures would be likely if an infant were exposed early in the administration of these agents. It is not known when it would be safe to reinitiate breastfeeding, but 24-48 hours should be sufficient to reduce risks to the infant.   Again this depends on the dose administered.

Pregnancy Risk Category:

Lactation Risk Category: L5

Theoretic Infant Dose:

Adult Concerns: Hallucinations, agitation, seizures, acute paranoid psychosis, extreme hypertension, hyperthermia, tachyarrhythmias may occur. Effects largely depend on the dose.

Pediatric Concerns: None reported via milk but breastfeeding should be interrupted for at least 24 hours following last administration.

Drug Interactions:

Alternatives:

Adult Dosage:

T½ = < 8 hours	M/P =
PHL =	PB =
PK = 1-5 hours	Oral = Complete
MW =	pKa =
Vd =	

References:

1. Green AR, Cross AJ, Goodwin GM. Review of the pharmacology and clinical pharmacology of 3,4-methylenedioxymethamphetamine (MDMA or 'Ecstasy'). Psychopharmacology 119:247-260, 1995.
2. Verebey K, Alrazi IJ and Jaffee JH: The complications 'Ecstasy'(MDMA). J Am Vet Med Assoc 259:1649-1650, 1988.

AMPHOTERICIN B

Trade: Fungizone, Amphotec
Can/Aus/UK: Abelcet, Ambisome, Amphocel, Fungilin, Resteclin
Uses: Antifungal
AAP: Not reviewed

Amphotericin B is an intravenous antifungal effective for the treatment of Cryptococcus neoformans, Candida albicans, Histoplasma capsulatum, Coccidioides immitis, and Aspergillus infections. Amphotericin is significantly toxic and is reserved for life-threatening infections. No data are available on its transfer to human milk. However, it is virtually unabsorbed orally (< 9%) and is commonly used in pediatrics. It is quite unlikely the amount in milk would be clinically relevant to a breastfeeding infant.

Pregnancy Risk Category: B

Lactation Risk Category: L3

Theoretic Infant Dose:

Adult Concerns: Adverse effects include anemia, thrombocytopenia, congestive heart failure, thrombophlebitis, paresthesias, hypokalemia, hyperthermia, nephrotoxicity, hepatotoxicity, pulmonary toxicity, erythematous reactions, and anaphylaxis.

Pediatric Concerns: None reported. Unlikely to be absorbed orally.

Drug Interactions: Antagonism with azole antifungals. Enhanced renal toxicity with cyclosporin. Enhanced digitalis toxicity due to hypokalemia.

Alternatives:

Adult Dosage: 0.25 to 1.0 mg/kg/day I.V.

T½ = 15 days	M/P =
PHL=	PB = >90%
PK = < 1 hour	Oral = < 9%
MW = 924	pKa =
Vd = 4	

References:
1.   Pharmaceutical manufacturers package insert, 2002.

AMPICILLIN

Trade: Polycillin, Omnipen
Can/Aus/UK: Amfipen, Ampicyn, Apo-Ampi, Austrapen, Britcin, Novo-Ampicillin, NuAmpi, Penbriton, Vidopen
Uses: Penicillin antibiotic
AAP: Not reviewed

Low milk/plasma ratios of 0.2 have been reported.[1]   In a study by Matsuda of 2-3 breastfeeding patients who received 500 mg of ampicillin orally,   levels in milk peaked at 6 hours and averaged only 0.14 mg/L of milk.[2] The milk/plasma ratio was reported to be 0.03 at 2 hours.

In a group of 9 breastfeeding women sampled at various times and who received doses of 350 mg TID orally, milk concentrations ranged from 0.06 to 0.17 mg/L with peak milk levels at 3-4 hours after the dose.[3] Milk/plasma ratios varied between 0.01 and 0.58.   The highest reported milk level (1.02 mg/L) was in a patient receiving 700 mg TID. Ampicillin was not detected in the plasma of any infant.

Ampicillin is one of the most commonly used prophylactic antibiotics in pediatric neonatal nurseries. Neonatal half-life is 2.8 to 4 hours. Possible rash, sensitization, diarrhea, or candidiasis could occur, but unlikely. May alter GI flora.

Pregnancy Risk Category: B

Lactation Risk Category: L1

Theoretic Infant Dose: 0.2 mg/kg/day

Adult Concerns: Diarrhea, rash, fungal overgrowth, agranulocytosis, pseudomembranous colitis, anaphylaxis.

Pediatric Concerns: None reported but observe for diarrhea.

Drug Interactions: Efficacy of oral contraceptives may be reduced. Disulfiram and probenecid may increase plasma levels of ampicillin. Allopurinol may increase the risk of ampicillin skin rash.

Alternatives:

Adult Dosage: 250-500 mg QID

T½ = 1.3 hours	**M/P = 0.58**
PHL= 1.7 hours (neonate)	**PB = 8-20**
PK = 1-2 hours	**Oral = 50%**
MW = 349	**pKa =**
Vd = 0.38	

References:
1. Kefetzis DA, Siafas CA, Georgakopoulous PA, et.al. Passage of cephalosporins and amoxicillin into the breast milk. Acta Paediatr Scan 70:285-286,1981.
2. Matsuda S. Transfer of antibiotics into maternal milk. Biol Res Pregnancy Perinatol. 5(2):57-60, 1984.
3. Branebjerg PE, Heisterberg L. Blood and milk concentrations of ampicillin in mothers treated with pivampicillin and in their infants. J Perinat Med. 15(6):555-8, 1987.

AMPICILLIN + SULBACTAM

Trade: Unasyn
Can/Aus/UK: Dicapen
Uses: Penicillin antibiotic with extended spectrum.
AAP: Not reviewed

Small amounts of ampicillin may transfer (1 mg/L).[1] Possible rash, sensitization, diarrhea, or candidiasis could occur, but unlikely. May alter GI flora. There are no reports of sulbactam secretion into human milk, but it is probably low and largely without side effects (AHL= 1 hour. PB= 38%).

Pregnancy Risk Category: B

Lactation Risk Category: L1

Theoretic Infant Dose: 0.2 mg/kg/day

Adult Concerns: Diarrhea, rash, fungal overgrowth, agranulocytosis, pseudomembranous colitis, anaphylaxis.

Pediatric Concerns: None reported but observe for diarrhea.

Drug Interactions: Efficacy of oral contraceptives may be reduced. Disulfiram and probenecid may increase plasma levels of amoxicillin. Allopurinol may increase the risk of amoxicillin skin rash.

Alternatives:

Adult Dosage: 1.5-3 g QID

T½ = 1.3 hours	M/P = 0.01-0.5
PHL = 1.7 hrs (15-30 days old)	PB = 28%
PK = 1-2 hours	Oral = 60%
MW = 349	pKa =
Vd = 0.38	

References:
1. Kefetzis DA, Siafas CA, Georgakopoulous PA, et.al.   Passage of cephalosporins and amoxicillin into the breast milk. Acta Paediatr Scan 70:285-286,1981.

ANTHRALIN

Trade: Anthra-derm, Drithocreme, Dritho-scalp, Micanol
Can/Aus/UK: Alphodith, Anthraforte, Anthranol, Anthrascalp, Dithranol
Uses: Anti-psoriatic
AAP: Not reviewed

Anthralin is a synthetic tar derivative used topically for suppression of psoriasis.   Anthralin, when applied topically,   induces burning and inflammation of the skin, but is one of the most effective treatments for psoriasis.   Purple-brown staining of skin and permanent staining of clothing and porcelain bathroom fixtures is frequent.   Anthralin when applied topically is absorbed into the surface layers of the skin and only minimal amounts enter the systemic circulation.   That absorbed is rapidly excreted via the kidneys almost instantly, plasma levels are very low to undetectable.[1]   No data are available on its transfer into human milk.   Most anthralin is eliminated by washing off and desquamation of insolubles.[2] For this reason, when placed directly on lesions on the areola or nipple, breastfeeding should be discouraged.   Another similar anthraquinone is Senna (laxative), which even in high doses does not enter milk. While undergoing initial intense treatment, it would perhaps be advisable to interrupt breastfeeding temporarily, but this may be overly conservative. Observe the infant for diarrhea. It has been used in children < 2 years of age for psoriasis.

Pregnancy Risk Category: C

Lactation Risk Category: L3

Theoretic Infant Dose:

Adult Concerns: Pruritus, skin irritation and inflammation. Purple-brown staining of skin and permanent staining of clothing and porcelain bathroom fixtures is frequent. Anthralin may have carcinogenic properties following high doses in mice. This may have no relevance to humans at all.

Pediatric Concerns: Diarrhea, nausea, vomiting via milk, but no reports have been published.

Drug Interactions:

Alternatives:

Adult Dosage: Apply topical BID

T½ = Brief	M/P =
PHL =	PB =
PK =	Oral = Complete
MW = 226	pKa =
Vd =	

References:
1. Goodfield MJD, Hull SM and Cunliffe WJ: The systemic effect of dithranol treatment in psoriasis. Acta Dermatol Venereol (Stockh) 74:295-297, 1994.
2. Shroot B: Mode of action of dithranol, pharmacokinetics/dynamics. Acta Dermatol Venereol (Stockh) 71(suppl 172):10-12, 1992.

ANTHRAX (BACILLUS ANTHRACIS)

Trade: Anthrax Infection, Bacillus Anthracis
Can/Aus/UK:
Uses: Anthrax infection
AAP: Approved by the American Academy of Pediatrics for use in breastfeeding mothers

Anthrax is caused by the gram-positive, spore-forming bacterium bacillus anthracis. The spore may persist in nature for many years and infect grazing animals such as sheep, goats and cattle. The most common forms of the disease are inhaled, oral, and cutaneous. The Center for Disease Control has recently published guidelines for treating or prophylaxing exposed breastfeeding mothers. The web address in reference 1 below contains several treatment options.

Thus far, all of the anthrax strains released by bioterrorists have been sensitive to ciprofloxacin, doxycycline, and the penicillin family. In breastfeeding women, amoxicillin (80 mg/kg/d in 3 divided doses) is an option for antimicrobial prophylaxis when B. anthracis is known to be penicillin-susceptible and no contraindication to maternal amoxicillin use is indicated. The American Academy of Pediatrics also considers ciprofloxacin and tetracyclines (which include doxycycline) to be usually compatible with breastfeeding because the amount of either drug absorbed by infants is small, but little is known about the safety of long-term use.

Until culture sensitivity tests have been completed, the breastfeeding mother be treated with ciprofloxacin (see ofloxacin or levofloxacin as alternates) or doxycycline. Once cultures show that the anthrax strain is sensitive to penicillins, then the mother can switch to amoxicillin for long term use up to 60 days or more. Due to possible dental staining following prolonged exposure, this author would not suggest long-term use(60 days) of doxycycline in a breastfeeding mother. The CDC offers several alternative antibiotics such as rifampin, vancomycin, imipenem, clindamycin and clarithromycin in those patients will allergic conditions.[2] Check the CDC websites for the most current recommendations.[3]

References:
1. http://www.cdc.gov/mmwr/preview/mmwrhtml/mm5045a5.htm
2. CDC. Update: investigation of bioterrorism-related anthrax and interim guidelines for exposure management and antimicrobial therapy, October 2001. MMWR 2001;50:909--19.
3. Center for Disease Control Website : http://www.bt.cdc.gov/

ANTHRAX VACCINE

Trade: Anthrax Vaccine
Can/Aus/UK:
Uses: Vaccination
AAP: Not reviewed

The anthrax vaccine for humans licensed for use in the United States is a cell-free filtrate vaccine, which means it uses dead bacteria as opposed to live bacteria. The vaccine is reported to be 93% effective in protecting against cutaneous anthrax.[1] The vaccine should only be administered to healthy men and women from 18 to 65 years of age since investigations to date have been conducted exclusively in that population. Because it is not known whether the anthrax vaccine can cause fetal harm, pregnant women should not be vaccinated. There are no data or indications relative to its use in breastfeeding mothers. While it consists primarily of protein fragments of anthrax bacteria, it is very unlikely any would transfer into milk, nor even be bioavailable in the infant. Unfortunately, the CDC does not have recommendations in reference to breastfeeding mothers.

Pregnancy Risk Category: C

Lactation Risk Category: L3

Adult Concerns: Mild local reactions occur in 30% of recipients and consist of slight tenderness and redness at the injection site. A moderate local reaction can occur if the vaccine is given to anyone with a past history of anthrax infection. Severe local reactions are very infrequent and consist of extensive swelling of the forearm in addition to the local reaction. Systemic reactions occur in fewer than 0.2% of recipients and are characterized by flu-like symptoms.

Pediatric Concerns: None reported via milk.

Drug Interactions:

Alternatives:

Adult Dosage: 2-30 mg per day

References:
1. Center for Disease Control WEB Page http://www.cdc.gov/ncidod/dbmd/anthrax.htm

ANTIPYRINE

Trade: Antipyrine
Can/Aus/UK:
Uses: Analgesic, antipyretic
AAP: Not reviewed

Insignificant secretion into breastmilk. This product is no longer used in the USA due to high incidence of fatal bone marrow toxicity. Contraindicated.

Pregnancy Risk Category:

Lactation Risk Category: L5

Theoretic Infant Dose:

Adult Concerns: Severe bone marrow toxicity.

Pediatric Concerns: None reported but due to better medications, this product should never be used.

Drug Interactions:

Alternatives: Ibuprofen, acetaminophen

Adult Dosage:

T½ =	M/P = 1.0
PHL=	PB = <1%
PK = 1-2 hours	Oral =
MW = 188	pKa = 1.4
Vd = 0.56	

References:
1. Berlin, C. and Vesell, E. Antipyrine disposition in milk and saliva of lactating women. Clin Pharmacol. Ther 31:38-44, 1982.

ASCORBIC ACID

Trade: Ascorbica, Cecon, Cevi-bid, Ce-vi-sol, Vitamin C
Can/Aus/UK:
Uses: Vitamin C
AAP: Not reviewed

Ascorbic acid is an essential vitamin. Without supplementation, 75 mg/day is excreted in the urine of the average individual due to overabundance. Renal control of vitamin C is significant, and maintains plasma levels at 0.4 to 1.5 mg/dL regardless of dose. Ascorbic acid is secreted into human milk in well controlled sequence and mature milk contains 5 mg/100 ml.[1] Excessive Vitamin C intake in the mother does not alter (or increase) the controlled secretion into breastmilk. The RDA for mother is 100 mg/day. Maternal supplementation is only required in undernourished mothers.

Pregnant women should not use excessive ascorbic acid due to metabolic induction in the fetal liver, followed by a metabolic rebound scurvy early postpartum in the neonate. Ascorbic acid should not routinely be administered to breast fed infants unless to treat clinical scurvy.

Pregnancy Risk Category: A during the 1st and 2nd trimester
C during the 3rd trimester

Lactation Risk Category: L1

Theoretic Infant Dose:

Adult Concerns: Renal calculi with large doses. Faintness, flushing, dizziness, nausea, vomiting, gastritis.

Pediatric Concerns: None reported via breastmilk, but excessive use prepartum is strongly discouraged.

Drug Interactions: Ascorbic acid decreases propranolol peak concentrations. Aspirin decreases ascorbate levels and increases aspirin levels. Reduced effect of warfarin when used with ascorbic acid. Urinary acidification results in decreased retention of many basic drugs, including tricyclic antidepressants, amoxipine, amphetamines. Do not use with aluminum antacids. Ascorbic acid reduces renal elimination of aluminum leading to encephalopathy, seizures, coma.

Alternatives:

Adult Dosage: 45-60 mg QD

T½ =	M/P =
PHL=	PB =
PK = 2-3 hours	Oral = Complete
MW = 176	pKa =
Vd =	

References:
1. Sneed SM, et. al. The effects of ascorbic acid, vitamin B6, vitamin B12, and folic acid supplementation on the breast milk and maternal nutritional status of low socioeconomic lactating women. Am J Clin Nutr 34:1338-46, 1981.

ASPARTAME

Trade: Nutrasweet
Can/Aus/UK:
Uses: Artificial sweetner
AAP: Not reviewed

Aspartame consists of two linked amino acids, aspartic acid and phenylalanine. Once in the GI tract, it is rapidly metabolized to phenylalanine and aspartic acid. Maternal ingestion of 50 mg/kg aspartame will approximately double (2.3 to 4.8 μmol/dL) aspartate milk levels. Phenylalanine milk levels similarly increased from 0.5 to 2.3 μmol/dL. This dose is 3-4 times the normal dose used, and these milk levels are too low to produce significant side effects in normal infants.[1,2] Contraindicated in infants with proven phenylketonuria.

Pregnancy Risk Category: B

Lactation Risk Category: L1
L5 if used in infants with PKU

Theoretic Infant Dose:

Adult Concerns: Contraindicated in mothers/infants with PKU.

Pediatric Concerns: None reported except contraindicated in infants with documented phenylketonuria.

Drug Interactions:

Alternatives:

Adult Dosage:

T½ =	M/P =
PHL =	PB =
PK =	Oral = Complete
MW = 294	pKa =
Vd =	

References:
1. Levels of free amino acids in lactating women following ingestion of the sweetener aspartame. Nutrition Reviews. 38:183-184, 1980.
2. Stegink LD, Filer LJ, Baker GL. Plasma, erythrocyte and human milk levels of free amino acids in lactating women administered aspartame or lactose, J. Nutr. 109:2173-81, 1979.

ASPIRIN

Trade:
Can/Aus/UK: Aspro, Cartia, Coryphen, Disprin, Ecotrin, Entrophen, Novasen
Uses: Salicylate analgesic
AAP: Drugs associated with significant side effects and should be given with caution

Extremely small amounts secreted into breastmilk. Few harmful effects have been reported. Following single or multiple doses, peak levels occur at approximately 3 hours and vary from 1.12 to 1.69 mg/L.[1] In another study of a rheumatoid arthritis patient who received 4 gm/day, none was detectable in her milk (< 5mg/100cc). Extremely high doses in mother could potentially produce slight bleeding in infant. Because aspirin is implicated in Reye's Syndrome in febrile-viral illnesses, it is a poor choice of analgesic to use in breastfeeding mothers. However, in rheumatic fever patients, it is still the anti-inflammatory drug of choice and a risk-vs-benefit assessment must be done in this case. See ibuprofen or acetaminophen as a better choice.

Pregnancy Risk Category: C during 1st trimester
D during 2nd and 3rd trimester

Lactation Risk Category: L3

Theoretic Infant Dose: 0.3 mg/kg/day

Adult Concerns: GI ulceration, distress, esophagitis, nephropathy, hepatotoxicity, tinnitus, platelet dysfunction.

Pediatric Concerns: None reported via milk, but aspirin use in pediatric patients may increase risk of Reye's syndrome in viral infections.

Drug Interactions: May decrease serum levels of other NSAIDs as well as GI distress. Aspirin may antagonize effect of probenecid. Aspirin may increase methotrexate serum levels, and increase free valproic acid plasma levels and valproate toxicity. May increase anticoagulant effect of warfarin.

Alternatives: Ibuprofen, acetaminophen

Adult Dosage: 325-900 mg QID

T½ = 2.5-7 hours	**M/P = 0.03-0.08**
PHL=	**PB = 88-93%**
PK = 1-2 hours	**Oral = 80-100%**
MW = 180	**pKa =**
Vd = 0.15	

References:
1. Findlay JW, DeAngelis RI, Kearney MF, et.al. Analgesic drugs in breast milk and plasma. Clin Pharmacol. Ther. 29:625-633, 1981.
2. Erickson SH, Oppenheim GL. Aspirin in breast milk. J. Fam. Med. 8:189-190, 1979.

ATENOLOL

Trade: Tenoretic, Tenormin
Can/Aus/UK: Anselol, Antipress, Apo-Atenolol, Noten, Tenlol, Tenormin, Tensig
Uses: Antihypertensive beta blocker
AAP: Drugs associated with significant side effects and should be given with caution

Atenolol is a potent cardio-selective beta blocker. Data conflict on the secretion of atenolol into breastmilk. One author reports an incident of significant bradycardia, cyanosis, low body temp., and low blood pressure in breastfeeding infant of mother consuming 100 mg atenolol daily, while a number of others have failed to detect plasma levels in the neonate or untoward side effects.[1]

Data seem to indicate that atenolol secretion into breastmilk is highly variable but may be as high as 10 times greater than for propranolol. In one study, women taking 50-100 mg/day were found to have M:P ratios of 1.5-6.8. However, even with high M:P ratios, the calculated intake per day (at peak levels) for a breastfeeding infant would only be 0.13 mg.[2]

In a study by White, breastmilk levels in one patient were 0.7, 1.2 and 1.8 mg/L of milk at doses of 25, 50 and 100 mg daily respectively.[3] In another study, the estimated daily intake for an infant receiving 500 ml milk per day, would be 0.3 mg.[4] In these five patients who received 100 mg daily, the mean milk concentration of atenolol was 630 μg/L. In a study by Kulas, the amount of atenolol transferred into milk varied from 0.66 mg/L with a maternal dose of 25 mg, 1.2 mg/L with a maternal dose of 50 mg, and 1.7 mg/L with a maternal dose of 100 mg per day.[5] Although atenolol is approved by the AAP, some caution is recommended due to the milk/plasma ratios and the reported problem with one infant.

Pregnancy Risk Category: C

Lactation Risk Category: L3

Theoretic Infant Dose: 0.3 mg/kg/day

Adult Concerns: Persistent bardycardia, hypotension, heart failure, dizziness, fatigue, insomnia, lethargy, confusion, impotence, dyspnea, wheezing in asthmatics.

Pediatric Concerns: One report of bradycardia, cyanosis, low body temperature, and hypotension in a breastfeeding infant of mother consuming 100 mg atenolol daily, but other reports do not suggest clinical effects on breastfed infants.

Drug Interactions: Decreased effect when used with aluminum salts, barbiturates, calcium salts, cholestyramine, NSAIDs, ampicillin, rifampin, and salicylates. Beta blockers may reduce the effect of oral sulfonylureas (hypoglycemic agents). Increased toxicity/effect when used with other antihypertensives, contraceptives, MAO inhibitors, cimetidine, and numerous other products. See drug interaction reference for complete listing.

Alternatives: Propranolol, metoprolol

Adult Dosage: 50-100 mg QD

T½ = 6.1 hours	M/P = 1.5-6.8
PHL = 6.4 hours	PB = 5%
PK = 2-4 hours	Oral = 50-60%
MW = 266	pKa = 9.6
Vd = 1.3	

References:
1. Schimmel MS, Eidelman AI, Wilschanski MA, Shaw D Jr, Ogilvie RJ, Koren G, Schmimmel MS, Eidelman AJ. Toxic effects of atenolol consumed during breast feeding. J Pediatr. 114(3):476-8, 1989.
2. Liedholm H, Melander A, et.al. Accumulation of atenolol and metoprolol in human breast milk. Eur. J. Clin. Pharmcol. 20:229-31, 1981.
3. White WB, et.al. Atenolol in human plasma and breast milk. Obj. and Gyn. 63:42S-44S, 1984.
4. Thorley KJ, McAninsh J. Levels of beta-blockers atenolol and propranolol in the breast milk of women treated for hypertension in pregnancy. Biopharm Drug Dispos. 4:299-301,1983.
5. Kulas J, Lunell NO, et.al. Atenolol and metoprolol. A comparison of their excretion into human breast milk. Acta. Obstet. Gynecol. Scan. Suppl 118:65-69, 1984.

ATORVASTATIN CALCIUM

Trade: Lipitor
Can/Aus/UK: Lipitor
Uses: Cholesterol-lowering agent
AAP: Not reviewed

Atorvastatin is a typical HMG Co-A reductase inhibitor for lowering plasma cholesterol levels. It is known to transfer into animal milk, but human studies are not available.[1] Due to its poor oral absorption, and high protein binding, it is unlikely that clinically relevant amounts would transfer into human milk. Nevertheless, atherosclerosis is a chronic process and discontinuation of lipid-lowering drugs during pregnancy and lactation should have little to no impact on the outcome of long-term therapy of primary hypercholesterolemia. Cholesterol and other products of cholesterol biosynthesis are essential components for fetal and neonatal development and the use of cholesterol-lowering drugs would not be advisable under any circumstances.

Pregnancy Risk Category: X

Lactation Risk Category: L3

Theoretic Infant Dose:

Adult Concerns: Liver dysfunction, rhabdomyolysis with acute renal failure.

Pediatric Concerns: None reported, but the use of these products in lactating women is not recommended.

Drug Interactions: Increased risk of myopathy when used with cyclosporin, fibric acid derivatives, niacin, erythromycin, and azole antifungals (Diflucan, etc). Decreased plasma levels of atorvastatin when used with antacids, or colestipol.

Alternatives:

Adult Dosage: 10-80 mg daily

T½ = 14 hours	M/P =
PHL =	PB = 98%
PK = 1-2 hours	Oral = 12-30%
MW = 1209	pKa =
Vd = 8	

References:
1.   Pharmaceutical Manufacturers Package Insert, 1999.

ATOVAQUONE AND PROGUANIL

Trade: Malarone
Can/Aus/UK:
Uses: Antimalarials
AAP: Not reviewed

Malarone is a fixed combination of atovaquone (250 mg) and proguanil (100 mg) (adult dose). The pediatric chewable tablet contains atovaquone (62.5) and proguanil (25 mg). Malarone is used both to prevent and treat malaria, particularly malaria resistant to certain other drugs. Both adult and pediatric formulations are available for treating pediatric patients down to 11 kg. There are no data available for transfer of these agents into human milk although the pharmaceutical company suggests that atovaquone concentrations in rodent milk were 30% of the concurrent concentrations in the maternal plasma. It is my experience that rodent levels are much higher than found in humans. Only trace quantities of proguanil were found in human milk. Further, while the pharmacokinetics of proguanil is similar in adults and pediatric patients, the elimination half-life of atovaquone is much shorter in pediatric patients (1-2 days) than in adult patients (2-3 days). Elimination half-life ranges from 32 to 84 hours for atovaquone and 12 to 21 hours for proguanil; the half-life of cycloguanil is approximately 14 hours.

For current information contact the CDC website for information (www.cdc.gov). **According to the CDC, breastfeeding mothers with infants less than 11 kg should use mefloquine instead of Malarone.**[2]

	Atovaquone	Proguanil
T1/2	32-84 hours	12-21 hours
Oral bioavailability	23%	Complete
Protein Binding	> 99%	75%

Pedi dose: One, two or three MALARONE Pediatric Tablets (62.5 mg atovaquone and 25 mg proguanil hydrochloride) once a day depending on your child's body weight. For children over 40 kg (88 pounds) in weight, one MALARONE tablet (adult dose) once a day.

Pregnancy Risk Category: C

Lactation Risk Category: L3 for infants > 11 kg

Theoretic Infant Dose:

Adult Concerns: Headache, fever, myalgia, abdominal pain, cough, diarrhea, dyspepsia, back pain, gastritis have been reported.

Pediatric Concerns: None reported via milk.

Drug Interactions: Major reductions in plasma levels of atovaquone have been reported following the use of tetracycline (40%), metoclopramide, rifampin (50%), or rifabutin (34%).

Alternatives: Mefloquine

Adult Dosage: Atovaquone (250 mg); Proguanil (100 mg) daily.

References:
1. Pharmaceutical manufacturers package insert, 2002.
2. http://www.cdc.gov/ncidod/dpd/parasites/malaria/default.htm

ATROPINE

Trade: Belladonna, Atropine
Can/Aus/UK: Atropine Minims, Atropisol, Atropt, Eyesule, Isopto-Atropine
Uses: Anticholinergic, drying agent
AAP: Approved by the American Academy of Pediatrics for use in breastfeeding mothers

Atropine is a powerful anticholinergic that is well distributed throughout the body.[1] Only small amounts are believed secreted in milk.[2] Effects may be highly variable. Slight absorption together with enhanced neonatal sensitivity creates hazardous potential. Use caution. Avoid if possible but not definitely contraindicated.

Pregnancy Risk Category: C

Lactation Risk Category: L3

Theoretic Infant Dose:

Adult Concerns: Dry, hot skin. Decreased flow of breastmilk. Decreased bowel motility, drying of secretions, dilated pupil, and increased heart rate.

Pediatric Concerns: No reports are available, although caution is urged.

Drug Interactions: Phenothiazines, levodopa, antihistamines, may decrease anticholinergic effects of atropine. Increased toxicity when admixed with amantadine and thiazide diuretics.

Alternatives:

Adult Dosage: 0.6 mg every 6 hours

T½ = 4.3 hours	M/P =
PHL=	PB = 14-22%
PK = 1 hour	Oral = 90%
MW = 289	pKa = 9.8
Vd = 2.3-3.6	

References:
1.   Drug Facts and Comparisons. 1995 ed. Facts and Comparisons, St. Louis.
2.   Wilson, J. Drugs in Breast Milk. New York: ADIS Press, 1981.

AZATHIOPRINE

Trade: Imuran
Can/Aus/UK: Imuran, Thioprine
Uses: Immunosuppressive agent
AAP: Not reviewed

Azathioprine is a powerful immunosuppressive agent that is metabolized to 6-Mercaptopurine (6-MP). In two mothers receiving 75 mg azathioprine, the concentration of 6-Mercaptopurine in milk varied from 3.5-4.5 μg/L in one mother, and 18 μg/L in the second mother.[1] Both levels were peak milk concentrations at 2 hours following the dose.   The authors conclude that these levels would be too low to produce clinical effects in a breastfed infant. Using this data for 6-MP, an infant would absorb only 0.1 % of the weight-adjusted maternal dose which is too low to likely produce adverse effects in a breastfeeding infant.   Plasma levels in treated patients is maintained at 50 ng/mL or higher. One infant continued to breastfeed during therapy and displayed no immunosuppressive effects.

In another study of two infants who were breastfed by mothers receiving 75-100 mg/d azathioprine,   milk levels of 6-MP were not measured. But both infants had normal blood counts, no increase in infections and above-average growth rate.[2]   Caution is recommended.

Pregnancy Risk Category: D

Lactation Risk Category: L3

Theoretic Infant Dose: 2.7 μg/kg/day

Adult Concerns: Bone marrow suppression, megaloblastic anemia, infections, skin cancers, lymphoma, nausea, vomiting, hepatotoxicity, pulmonary dysfunction and pancreatitis.

Pediatric Concerns: None reported, but caution is urged.

Drug Interactions: Increased toxicity when used with allopurinol. Reduce azathioprine dose to 1/3 to 1/4 of normal.   Use with ACE inhibitors has produced severe leukopenia.

Alternatives:

Adult Dosage: 1-2.5 mg/kg/day

T½ = 0.6 hour PHL = PK = 1-2 hours MW = 277 Vd =	M/P = PB = 30% Oral = 41-44% pKa =

References:
1. Coulam, C. et.al. Breast-feeding after renal transplantation. Trans. Proc. 14:605-609, 1982.
2. Grekas DM, Vasiliou SS, Lazarides AN. Immunosuppressive therapy and breasat-feeding after renal transplantation. Nephron 37:68, 1984.

AZELAIC ACID

Trade: Azelex, Finevin
Can/Aus/UK: Skinoren
Uses: Topical treatment of acne
AAP: Not reviewed

Azelaic is a dicarboxylic acid derivative normally found in whole grains and animal products. Azelaic acid when applied as a cream, produces a significant reduction of P. acnes and an antikeratinizing effect as well. Small amounts of azelaic acid are normally present in human milk.[1] Azelaic acid is only modestly absorbed via skin (< 4%). That absorbed is rapidly metabolized.   The amount absorbed does not change the levels normally found in plasma nor milk.   Due to its poor penetration into plasma and rapid half-life (45 min) it is not likely to penetrate milk or produce untoward effects in a breastfed infant.

Pregnancy Risk Category: B

Lactation Risk Category: L3

Theoretic Infant Dose:

Adult Concerns: Pruritus, burning, stinging, erythema, dryness, peeling and skin irritation.

Pediatric Concerns: None reported via milk. Normal constituent of milk.

Drug Interactions:

Alternatives:

Adult Dosage: Apply topical BID

T½ = 45 minutes	M/P =
PHL=	PB =
PK =	Oral =
MW = 188	pKa =
Vd =	

References:

1. Pharmaceutical Manufacturers Package Insert, 1999.

AZITHROMYCIN

Trade: Zithromax
Can/Aus/UK: Zithromax
Uses: Erythromycin-like antibiotic
AAP: Not reviewed

Azithromycin belongs to erythromycin family. It has an extremely long half-life, particularly in tissues.[1] Azithromycin is concentrated for long periods in phagocytes which are known to be present in human milk. In one study of a patient who received 1 gm initially, followed by two 500mg doses at 24 hour intervals, the concentration of azithromycin in breastmilk varied from 0.64 mg/L (initially) to 2.8 mg/L on day three.[2]

The predicted dose of azithromycin received by the infant would be approximately 0.4 mg/kg/day. This would suggest that the level of azithromycin ingested by a breastfeeding infant is not clinically significant. New pediatric formulations of azithromycin have been recently introduced. Pediatric dosing is 10 mg/kg STAT, followed by 5 mg/kg per day for up to 5 days.

Pregnancy Risk Category: B

Lactation Risk Category: L2

Theoretic Infant Dose: 0.4 mg/kg/day

Adult Concerns: Diarrhea, loose stools, abdominal pain, vomiting, nausea.

Pediatric Concerns: None reported via breastmilk. Pediatric formulations are available.

Drug Interactions: Aluminum and magnesium-containing antacids may slow, but not reduce absorption of azithromycin. Increased effect/toxicity when used with tacrolimus, alfentanil, astemizole, terfenadine, loratadine, carbamazepine, cyclosporine, digoxin, disopyramide, triazolam.

Alternatives:

Adult Dosage: 250-500 mg QD

T½ = 48-68 hours	M/P =
PHL=	PB = 7-51%
PK = 3-4 hours	Oral = 37%
MW = 749	pKa =
Vd = 23-31	

References:
1. Pharmaceutical Manufacturers Package Insert, 1996.
2. Kelsey JJ, Moser LR, Jennings JC, et.al. Presence of azithromycin breast milk concentrations: A case report. Am. J. Obstct. Gynecol. 170:1375-6, 1994.

AZTREONAM

Trade: Azactam
Can/Aus/UK: Azactam
Uses: Antibiotic
AAP: Approved by the American Academy of Pediatrics for use in breastfeeding mothers

Aztreonam is a monobactam antibiotic whose structure is similar but different than the penicillins and is used for documented gram-negative scpsis. Following a single 1 g I.V. dose, breastmilk level was 0.18 mg/L at 2 hours and 0.22 mg/L at 4 hours.[1] An infant would ingest approximately 33.0 μg/kg/day or < 0.03% of the maternal dose per day. The manufacturer reports that less than 1% of a maternal dose is transferred into milk.[2] Due to poor oral absorption (<1%) no untoward effects would be expected in nursing infants, aside from changes in GI flora. Aztreonam is commonly used in pediatric units.

Pregnancy Risk Category: B

Lactation Risk Category: L2

Theoretic Infant Dose: 33 μg/kg/day

Adult Concerns: Changes in GI flora, diarrhea, rash, elevations of hepatic function tests.

Pediatric Concerns: None reported via milk.

Drug Interactions: Check hypersensitivity to penicillins and other beta-lactams. Requires dosage adjustment in renal failure.

Alternatives:

Adult Dosage: 1-2 g BID or QID

T½ = 1.7 hours	M/P = 0.005
PHL = 2.6 hours	PB = 60%
PK = 0.6-1.3 hours	Oral = <1%
MW = 435	pKa =
Vd = 0.26-0.36	

References:
1. Fleiss PM, et.al. Aztreonam in human serum and breast milk. Br. J. Clin. Pharmacol. 19(4):509-11, 1985.
2. Pharmaceutical Manufacturers Package Insert, 1996.

BACLOFEN

Trade: Lioresal, Atrofen
Can/Aus/UK: Apo-Baclofen, Clofen, Lioresal, Novo-Baclofen
Uses: Skeletal muscle relaxant
AAP: Approved by the American Academy of Pediatrics for use in breastfeeding mothers

Baclofen inhibits spinal reflexes and is used to reverse spasticity associated with multiple sclerosis or spinal cord lesions. Animal studies indicate baclofen inhibits prolactin release, and may inhibit lactation. Small amounts of baclofen are secreted into milk. In one mother given a 20 mg dose, total consumption by infant over a 26 hour period is estimated to be 22 μg, about 0.1% of the maternal dose.[1] The milk half-life was 5.6 hours. It is quite unlikely that baclofen administered intrathecally would be secreted into milk in significant quantities.

Pregnancy Risk Category: C

Lactation Risk Category: L2

Theoretic Infant Dose:

Adult Concerns: Drowsiness, excitement, dry mouth, urinary retention, tremor, rigidity, and wide pupils.

Pediatric Concerns: None reported.

Drug Interactions: Decreased effect when used with lithium. Increased effect of opiate analgesics, CNS depressants, alcohol (sedation), tricyclic antidepressants, clindamycin (neuromuscular blockade), guanabenz, MAO inhibitors.

Alternatives:

Adult Dosage: 5-25 mg TID

T½ = 3-4 hours	M/P =
PHL=	PB = 30%
PK = 2-3 hours	Oral = Complete
MW = 214	pKa =
Vd =	

References:
1. Eriksson G, Swahn CG. Concentrations of baclofen in serum and breast milk from a lactating woman. Scand. J. Clin. Lab. Invest. 41:185, 1981.

BARIUM

Trade: Barium
Can/Aus/UK: ACB, Baritop, Medebar, Medescan
Uses: Radiopaque agent
AAP: Not reviewed

Contrast agent used in radiology that is not absorbed orally. No reported harmful effects. Maternal absorption limited.

Pregnancy Risk Category:

Lactation Risk Category: L1

Theoretic Infant Dose:

Adult Concerns: Nausea, vomiting, constipation.

Pediatric Concerns: None reported, not absorbed.

Drug Interactions:

Alternatives:

Adult Dosage: N/A

BECLOMETHASONE

Trade: Vanceril, Beclovent, Beconase
Can/Aus/UK: Aldecin, Becloforte, Beclovent, Beconase, Becotide, Propadem, Propaderm, Vanceril
Uses: Intranasal, intrapulmonary steroid
AAP: Not reviewed

Beclomethasone is a potent steroid that is generally used via inhalation in asthma, or via intranasal administration for allergic rhinitis.   Due to its potency only very small doses are generally used, and therefore minimal plasma levels are attained.   Intranasal absorption is generally minimal.[1,2] Due to small doses administered, absorption into maternal plasma extremely small.   Therefore it is unlikely that these doses would produce clinical significance in a breastfeeding infant.   See corticosteroids.

Pregnancy Risk Category: C

Lactation Risk Category: L2

Theoretic Infant Dose:

Adult Concerns: When administered intranasally or via inhalation, adrenal suppression is very unlikely. Complications include headaches, hoarseness, bronchial irritation, oral candidiasis, cough. When used orally, complications may include adrenal suppression.

Pediatric Concerns: None reported via milk and inhalation or intranasal use. Oral doses could suppress the adrenal cortex, and induce premature closure of the epiphysis, but would require high doses.

Drug Interactions: Corticosteroids have few drug interactions.

Alternatives:

Adult Dosage: 504-840 mcg QD

T½ = 15 hours	M/P =
PHL=	PB = 87%
PK =	Oral = 90% (oral)
MW = 409	pKa =
Vd =	

References:
1.   Pharmaceutical Manufacturers Package Insert, 1996.
2.   McEvoy GE(ed):AFHS Drug Information, New York, NY. 1995.

BENAZEPRIL HCL

Trade: Lotensin, Lotrel
Can/Aus/UK: Lotensin
Uses: Antihypertensive, ACE inhibitor
AAP: Not reviewed

Benazepril belongs to the ACE inhibitor family. Oral absorption is rather poor(37%). The active component(benazeprilat) reaches a peak at approximately 2 hours after ingestion.[2] Generally, ACE inhibitors are seldom used during the early neonatal period due to profound neonatal hypotension. However, only minimal amounts are secreted into human milk. A newborn infant ingesting only breastmilk would receive less than 0.1% of the mg/kg maternal dose of benazepril and benazeprilat.

Pregnancy Risk Category: D

Lactation Risk Category: L3
L4 if used in neonatal period

Theoretic Infant Dose: Enalapril, captopril

Adult Concerns: Significant fetal and neonatal morbidity, hypotension.

Pediatric Concerns: Neonatal morbidity, severe hypotension after in-utero exposure.

Drug Interactions: Decreased bioavailability with antacids. Reduced hypotensive effect with NSAIDS. Phenothiazines increase hypotensive effect. Allopurinol dramatically increase hypersensitivities (Steven-Johnson Syn.). ACE inhibitors dramatically increase digoxin levels. Lithium levels may be significantly increased with ACE use. Elevated potassium levels with oral potassium supplements.

Alternatives:

Adult Dosage: 20-40 mg QD

T½ = 10-11 hours	M/P =	
PHL =	PB = 96.7%	
PK = 0.5 - 1 hour	Oral = 37%	
MW =	pKa =	
Vd =		

References:
1 Pharmaceutical Manufacturers Package Insert, 1996.

BENDROFLUMETHIAZIDE

Trade: Naturetin
Can/Aus/UK: Aprinox, Berkozide, Centyl, Naturetin, Urizid
Uses: Thiazide diuretic
AAP: Approved by the American Academy of Pediatrics for use in breastfeeding mothers

Bendroflumethiazide is a thiazide diuretic sometimes used to suppress lactation. In one study, the clinician found this thiazide to effectively inhibit lactation.[1] Use with caution. Not generally recommended in breastfeeding mothers.

Pregnancy Risk Category: D

Lactation Risk Category: L4

Theoretic Infant Dose:

Adult Concerns: Diuresis, fluid loss, leukopenia, hypotension, dizziness, headache, vertigo, reduced milk production.

Pediatric Concerns: None reported, but may inhibit lactation.

Drug Interactions: Enhanced hyponatremia and hypotension when used with ACE inhibitors.   May elevate lithium levels.

Alternatives: Hydrochlorothiazide

Adult Dosage: 2.5-10 mg QD

T½ = 3-3.9 hours	**M/P =**
PHL =	**PB = 94%**
PK = 2-4 hours	**Oral = Complete**
MW = 421	**pKa =**
Vd = 1,48	

References:
1.   Healy M. Suppressing lactation with oral diuretics. The Lancet, June 17, 1961, p 1353-4.

BENZONATATE

Trade: Tessalon Perles
Can/Aus/UK:
Uses: Antitussive
AAP: Not reviewed

Benzonatate is a non-narcotic cough suppressant similar to the local anesthetic tetracaine. It anesthetizes stretch receptors in respiratory passages, dampening their activity and reducing the cough reflex.[1] There are little pharmacokinetic data on this product, and no data on transfer into human milk. Because codeine is almost equally effective, and because we know that codeine only marginally transfers into human milk, it is probably a preferred antitussive in breastfeeding mothers.

Pregnancy Risk Category: C

Lactation Risk Category: L3

Theoretic Infant Dose:

Adult Concerns: Sedation, headache, dizziness, constipation, nausea, pruritus have been reported.

Pediatric Concerns: None reported via milk.

Drug Interactions:

Alternatives: Codeine

Adult Dosage: 100 mg TID

T½ = < 8 hours	M/P =
PHL=	PB =
PK = 20 minutes	Oral = Good
MW =	pKa =
Vd =	

References:
1.   Drug Facts and Comparisons. 1998. ed. Facts and Comparisons, St. Louis.

BEPRIDIL HCL

Trade: Vascor, Bepadin
Can/Aus/UK:
Uses: Antihypertensive, calcium channel blocker
AAP: Not reviewed

Following therapy with bepridil, milk levels were reported to approach 1/3 of serum levels.[1,2] As with other calcium channel blockers, this family has been found to produce embryotoxic effects, and should be used cautiously in pregnant women. Long half-life, enhanced oral absorption, and potency of this compound would increase the danger in nursing infant. Caution is recommended if used in nursing mother.

Pregnancy Risk Category: C

Lactation Risk Category: L4

Theoretic Infant Dose:

Adult Concerns: Bradycardia, hypotension.

Pediatric Concerns: None reported, but other calcium channel blockers may be preferred. See nifedipine.

Drug Interactions: H2 blockers may enhance oral absorption of bepridil. Beta blockers may enhance hypotensive effect.   Bepridil may increase carbamazepine, cyclosporin, digitalis, quinidine, theophylline levels when used with these products.

Alternatives: Nifedipine, nimodipine

Adult Dosage: 300 mg QD

T½ = 42 hours	M/P = 0.33
PHL=	PB = >99%
PK = 2-3 hours	Oral = 60%
MW = 367	pKa =
Vd = 8	

References:
1. Pharmaceutical Manufacturers Package Insert, 1996.
2. Drug Facts and Comparisons. 1995 ed. Facts and Comparisons, St. Louis.

BETAMETHASONE

Trade: Betameth, Celestone
Can/Aus/UK: Beben, Betadermetnesol, Betnelan, Betnovate, Celestone, Dipr, Diprolene, Diprosone
Uses: Synthetic corticosteroid
AAP: Not reviewed

Betamethasone is a potent long-acting steroid. It generally produces less sodium and fluid retention that other steroids.[1]   See prednisone.

Pregnancy Risk Category: C

Lactation Risk Category: L3

Theoretic Infant Dose:

Adult Concerns: See prednisone.

Pediatric Concerns: None reported, used in pediatric patients.

Drug Interactions:

Alternatives:

Adult Dosage: 2.4-4.8 mg BID or TID

T½ = 5.6 hours	M/P =
PHL=	PB = 64%
PK = 10-36 minutes.	Oral = Complete
MW = 392	pKa =
Vd =	

References:
1. Drug Facts and Comparisons. 1995 ed. Facts and Comparisons, St. Louis.

BETAXOLOL

Trade: Kerlone, Betoptic
Can/Aus/UK: Betoptic, Kerlone
Uses: Beta blocker antihypertensive
AAP: Not reviewed

Betaxolol is a long-acting, cardioselective beta blocker primarily used for glaucoma, but can be used orally for hypertension.   No data are available on betaxolol except one report by manufacturer of side effects which occurred in one nursing infant.[1]   Many in this family readily transfer into human milk (see atenolol, acebutolol). Manufacturer indicates that levels secreted in milk are sufficient to produce pharmacological effects in the infant.   Caution is urged.

Pregnancy Risk Category: C

Lactation Risk Category: L3

Theoretic Infant Dose:

Adult Concerns: Hypotension, bradycardia, fatigue.

Pediatric Concerns: No data are available on betaxolol except one report by manufacturer of side effects which occurred in one nursing infant.

Drug Interactions: Decreased effect when used with aluminum salts, barbiturates, calcium salts, cholestyramine, NSAIDs, ampicillin, rifampin, and salicylates. Beta blockers may reduce the effect of oral sulfonylureas (hypoglycemic agents). Increased toxicity/effect when used with other antihypertensives, contraceptives, MAO inhibitors, cimetidine, and numerous other products. See drug interaction reference for complete listing.

Alternatives: Propranolol, metoprolol

Adult Dosage: 10 mg QD

T½ = 14-22 hours	M/P = 2.5-3.0
PHL –	PB = 50%
PK = 3 hours	Oral = 89%
MW = 307	pKa =
Vd = 4.9	

References:
1.   Pharmaceutical Manufacturers Package Insert, 1995.

BETHANECHOL CHLORIDE

Trade: Urabeth, Urecholine
Can/Aus/UK: Duvoid, Myotonine, Urecholine, Urocarb
Uses: Cholinergic stimulant
AAP: Not reviewed

Bethanechol is a cholinergic stimulant useful for urinary retention. Although poorly absorbed from GI tract, no reports on entry into breastmilk are available.   However, it could conceivably cause abdominal cramps, colicky pain , nausea, salivation, bronchial constriction, or diarrhea in infants. There are several reports of discomfort in nursing infants.[1] Use cautiously.

Pregnancy Risk Category: C

Lactation Risk Category: L4

Theoretic Infant Dose:

Adult Concerns: Gastric distress such as colicky pain, cramping, nausea, salivation, breathing difficulties, diarrhea, hypotension, heart block, headache, urinary urgency.

Pediatric Concerns: Gi distress, discomfort, diarrhea.

Drug Interactions: Bethanechol when used with ganglionic blockers may lead to significant hypotension. Bethanechol effects may be antagonized by procainamide and quinidine.

Alternatives:

Adult Dosage: 10-50 mg BID-QID

T½ = 1-2 hours	M/P =
PHL =	PB =
PK = 60-90 min.(oral)	Oral = Poor
MW = 197	pKa =
Vd =	

References:
1. Shore MF. Drugs can be dangerous during pregnancy and lactation. Can Pharmaceut J 103:358, 1970.

BISACODYL

Trade: Bisacodyl, Dacodyl, Dulcolax
Can/Aus/UK: Apo-Bisacodyl, Bisacolax, Bisalax, Dulcolax, Durolax, Laxit, Paxolax
Uses: Laxative
AAP: Not reviewed

Bisacodyl is a stimulant laxative that selectively stimulates colon contractions and defecation. It has only limited secretion into breastmilk due to poor gastric absorption and subsequently minimal systemic levels.[1] Little or no known harmful effects on infants.

Pregnancy Risk Category: C

Lactation Risk Category: L2

Theoretic Infant Dose:

Adult Concerns: Diarrhea, GI cramping, rectal irritation.

Pediatric Concerns: None reported via milk.

Drug Interactions: Warfarin absorption may be reduced.

Alternatives:

Adult Dosage: 10-15 mg QD

T½ =	M/P =
PHL=	PB =
PK =	Oral = < 5%
MW = 361	pKa =
Vd =	

References:
1. Vorherr, H. Drug excretion in breast milk. Postgrad. Med. 56:97-104, 1974.

BISMUTH SUBSALICYLATE

Trade: Pepto-Bismol
Can/Aus/UK: Bismuth Liquid, Pepto-Bismol
Uses: Antisecretory, antimicrobial salt
AAP: Drug whose effect on nursing infants is unknown but may be of concern

Bismuth subsalicylate is present in many diarrhea mixtures. Although bismuth salts are poorly absorbed from the maternal GI tract, significant levels of salicylate could be absorbed from these products.[1] As such, these drugs should not be routinely used due to the association of salicylates in Reyes syndrome in children. Some forms (Parepcctolin, Infantol Pink) may contain tincture of opium (morphine).

Pregnancy Risk Category: C during 1st trimester
D during 2nd and 3rd trimester

Lactation Risk Category: L3

Theoretic Infant Dose:

Adult Concerns: Constipation, salicylate poisoning (tinnitus). May enhance risk of Reyes syndrome in children.

Pediatric Concerns: Risk of Reyes syndrome in neonates, but has not been reported with this product in a breastfed infant.

Drug Interactions: May reduce effects of tetracyclines, and uricosurics. May increase toxicity of aspirin, warfarin, hypoglycemics.

Alternatives:

Adult Dosage: 524-2096 mg QD

T½ =	M/P =
PHL =	PB =
PK =	Oral = Poor
MW = 362	pKa =
Vd =	

References:
1.   Findlay JW, DeAngelis RI, Kearney MF, et.al. Analgesic drugs in breast milk and plasma. Clin Pharmacol. Ther. 29:625-633, 1981.

BISOPROLOL

Trade: Ziac, Zebeta
Can/Aus/UK: Amizide, Dichlotride, Emcor, Monocor
Uses: Beta-adrenergic antihypertensive
AAP: Not reviewed

Bisoprolol is a typical beta blocker used to treat hypertension. The manufacturer states that small amounts (<2%) are secreted into milk of animals.[1] Others in this family are known to produce problems in lactating infants (see atenolol, acebutolol).   Ziac is a combination of bisoprolol and hydrochlorothiazide.

Pregnancy Risk Category: C

Lactation Risk Category: L3

Theoretic Infant Dose:

Adult Concerns: Bradycardia, hypotension, fatigue, excessive fluid loss.

Pediatric Concerns: None reported with this product, but other beta blockers have produced hypotension, hypoglycemia. See propranolol as alternative.

Drug Interactions: Decreased effect when used with aluminum salts, barbiturates, calcium salts, cholestyramine, NSAIDs, ampicillin, rifampin, and salicylates. Beta blockers may reduce the effect of oral sulfonylureas (hypoglycemic agents). Increased toxicity/effect when used with other antihypertensives, contraceptives, MAO inhibitors, cimetidine, and numerous other products. See drug interaction reference for complete listing.

Alternatives: Propranolol, metoprolol

Adult Dosage: 5-10 mg QD

T½ = 9-12 hours	M/P =
PHL =	PB = 30%
PK = 2 - 3 hours	Oral = 80%
MW = 325	pKa =
Vd =	

References:
1. Pharmaceutical Manufacturers Package Insert, 1995.

BLACK COHOSH

Trade: Baneberry, Black Snakeroot, Bugbane, Squawroot, Rattle Root
Can/Aus/UK:
Uses: Herbal estrogenic compound
AAP: Not reviewed

The roots and rhizomes of this herb are used medicinally. Traditional uses include the treatment of dysmenorrhea, dyspepsia, rheumatisms, and as an antitussive. It has also been used as an insect repellant. The standardized extract, called Remifemin, has been used in Germany for menopausal management.[1]   Black cohosh contains a number of alkaloids including N-methylcytosine, other tannins, and terpenoids. It is believed that the isoflavones, or formononetic components may bind to estrogenic receptors.[2]   Intraperitoneal injection of the extract selectively inhibits release of luteinizing hormone with no effect on the follicle-stimulating (FSH) hormone, or prolactin.[3]   The data seems to suggest that this product interacts strongly at certain specific estrogen receptors, and might be useful as estrogen replacement therapy in postmenopausal women, although this has not been well studied. More studies are needed to address its usefulness in postmenopausal women and osteoporotic states.[1]   Other effects of black cohosh include: hypotension, hypocholesterolemic activity, and peripheral vasodilation in vasospastic conditions (due to acteina content). Overdose may cause nausea, vomiting, dizziness, visual disturbances, bradycardia, and perspiration. Large doses may induce miscarriage...this product should not be used in pregnant women.[4]   No data are available on the transfer of Black Cohosh into human milk, but due to its estrogenic activity, it could lower milk production, although this is not known at this time. Caution is recommended in breastfeeding mothers. Use for more than 6 months is not recommended.[5]

Pregnancy Risk Category: X

Lactation Risk Category: L4

Theoretic Infant Dose:

Adult Concerns: Large doses may induce miscarriage...this product should not be used in pregnant women. Other effects of black cohosh include: hypotension, hypocholesterolemic activity, and peripheral vasodilation in vasospastic conditions. Overdose may cause nausea, vomiting, dizziness, visual disturbances, bradycardia, and perspiration.

Pediatric Concerns: None reported via milk.

Drug Interactions:

Alternatives:

Adult Dosage:

References:
1. Murray M. Am. J. Nat. Med. 4(3):3-5, 1997.
2. Jarry H. et.al. Planta Medica 4:316-319, 1885.
3. Jarry H. et.al. Planta Medica 1:46-49, 1885.
4. Newall C. et.al. Balck Cohosh Herbal Medicines. London, England:Pharmaceutical Press, 80:81, 1996.
5. The Complete German Commission E Monographs. Ed. M. Blumenthal. Amer. Botanical Council, Austin, Tx. 1998.

BLESSED THISTLE

Trade: Blessed Thistle
Can/Aus/UK:
Uses: Anorexic, antidiarrheal, febrifuge
AAP: Not reviewed

Blessed thistle contains an enormous array of chemicals, polyenes, steroids, terpenoids, and volatile oils. It is believed useful for diarrhea, hemorrhage, fevers, expectorant, bacteriostatic, and other antiseptic properties. Traditionally it has been used for loss of appetite, flatulence, cough and congestion, gangrenous ulcers, and dyspepsia. It has been documented to be antibacterial against: B. subtilis, Brucella abortis, B. bronchiseptica, E. coli, Proteus species, P. aeruginosa, Staph. aureus, and Strep. faecalis. The antibacterial and anti-inflammatory properties are due to its cnicin component.[1] While it is commonly used as a galactagogue, no data could be found suggesting this application. It is virtually nontoxic, with only occasional suggestions that high doses may induce GI symptoms.[2]

Pregnancy Risk Category:

Lactation Risk Category: L3

Theoretic Infant Dose:

Adult Concerns: Virtually nontoxic.

Pediatric Concerns: None reported via milk.

Drug Interactions:

Alternatives:

Adult Dosage:

References:
1.   Vanhaelen-Fastre R. Cnicus benedictus: Separation of antimicrobial constituents. Plant Med. Phytother 2:294-9, 1968.
2.   Newall C. et.al. Black Cohosh Herbal Medicines. London, England:Pharmaceutical Press, 80:81, 1996.

BLUE COHOSH

Trade: Blue Ginseng, Squaw Root, Papoose Root, Yellow Ginseng

Can/Aus/UK:

Uses: Uterine stimulant

AAP: Not reviewed

Blue Cohosh is also known as blue ginseng, squaw root, papoose root, yellow ginseng.   It is primarily used as a uterotonic drug, to stimulate uterine contractions.   In one recent paper, an infant born of a mother who ingested Blue Cohosh root for 3 weeks prior to delivery, suffered from severe cardiogenic shock and congestive heart failure.[1]   Blue Cohosh root contains a number of chemicals, including the alkaloid methylcytosine,   and   the   glycosides   caulospaponin   and caulophyllosaponin.   Methylcytosine is pharmacologically similar to nicotine, and may result in elevated blood pressure, gastric stimulation, and hyperglycemia. Caulosaponin and caulophyllosaponin are uterine stimulants.   They also apparently produce severe ischemia of the myocardium due to intense coronary vasoconstriction. This product should not be used in pregnant women.   No data are available as to its transfer into human milk. It is primarily used prior to delivery.

Pregnancy Risk Category: X

Lactation Risk Category: L5

Theoretic Infant Dose:

Adult Concerns: The leaves and seeds contain alkaloids and glycosides that can cause severe stomach pain when ingested. Poisoning have been reported.

Pediatric Concerns: One case of severe congestive heart failure in newborn (not breastfeeding).

Drug Interactions:

Alternatives:

Adult Dosage:

References:
1. Jones TK, Lawson BM: Profound neonatal congestive heart failure caused by maternal consumption of blue cohosh herbal medication. J. Pediatrics132(3):550-552, 1998.

BOTULISM

Trade:
Can/Aus/UK:
Uses: Botulism poisoning
AAP: Not reviewed

Botulism is a syndrome produced by the deadly toxin secreted by clostridium botulinum. This same toxin is sometimes used for the treatment of ophthalmic conditions such as strabismus and blepharospasm (Botox). Although the bacteria is wide spread, its colonization in food or the intestine of infants produces a deadly toxin. The syndrome is characterized by GI distress, weakness, malaise, lightheadedness, sore throat and nausea. Dry mouth is almost universal.

In most adult poisoning, the bacteria is absent, only the toxin is present. In most pediatric poisoning, the stomach is colonized by the bacterium, often from contaminated honey. In one published report, a woman severely poisoned by botulism toxin continued to breastfeed her infant throughout.[1] Four hours after admission, her milk was tested and was free of botulinum toxin and C. botulinum bacteria although she was still severely ill.   The infant showed no symptoms of poisoning. It is apparent from this case that neither botulinum bacteria, nor the toxin is secreted in breastmilk.

Pregnancy Risk Category:

Lactation Risk Category:

Theoretic Infant Dose:

Adult Concerns: GI distress, weakness, malaise, lightheadedness, sore throat, nausea, dry mouth.

Pediatric Concerns: None reported in one case.

Drug Interactions:

Alternatives:

Adult Dosage: 1.25-5 units IM injection

References:
1. Middaugh J. Botulism and Breast Milk. N. Engl. J. Med. 298:343, 1978

BROMIDES

Trade:
Can/Aus/UK:
Uses: Sedatives
AAP: Approved by the American Academy of Pediatrics for use in breastfeeding mothers

Small amounts are known to be secreted in milk.[1] May cause persistent rash, drowsiness, or weakness in infants. Secretion in milk has been known for many years. Bromide preparations are no longer available in the US. They are poorly effective products and have no place in modern medicine. Contraindicated in nursing mothers.

Pregnancy Risk Category: D

Lactation Risk Category: L5

Theoretic Infant Dose:

Adult Concerns: Rash, sedation.

Pediatric Concerns: Rash, drowsiness, weakness.

Drug Interactions:

Alternatives:

Adult Dosage: 3-6 g QD

References:
1. Van der Bogert F. Bromine poisoning through mother's milk. Am J Dis Child ;1921;21:167.

BROMOCRIPTINE MESYLATE

Trade: Parlodel
Can/Aus/UK: Apo-Bromocriptine, Bromolactin, Kripton, Parlodel
Uses: Inhibits prolactin secretion
AAP: Drugs associated with significant side effects and should be given with caution

Bromocriptine is an anti-parkinsonian, synthetic ergot alkaloid which inhibits prolactin secretion and hence physiologic lactation. Most of the dose of bromocriptine is absorbed first-pass by the liver, leaving less than 6% to remain in the plasma. Maternal serum prolactin levels remain suppressed for up to 14 hours after a single dose. The FDA approved indication for lactation suppression has been withdrawn, and it is no longer approved for this purpose due to numerous maternal deaths, seizures, and strokes.

Observe for transient hypotension or vomiting. It is sometimes used in hyperprolactinemic patients who have continued to breastfeed, although the incidence of maternal side-effects is significant and newer products are preferred.[1,2] In one breastfeeding patient who received 5 mg/day for a pituitary tumor, continued lactation produced no untoward effects in her infant.[3] Caution is recommended as profound postpartum hypotension has been reported. While bromocriptine is no longer recommended for suppression of lactation, a newer product cabergoline (Dostinex), is considered much safer for suppression of prolactin production.

Pregnancy Risk Category: C

Lactation Risk Category: L5

Theoretic Infant Dose:

Adult Concerns: Most frequent side effects include nausea (49%), headache (19%), and dizziness (17%), peripheral vasoconstriction. Rarely, significant hypotension, shock, myocardial infarction. Transient hypotension and hair loss. A number of deaths have been associated with this product and it is no longer cleared for postpartum use to inhibit lactation.

Pediatric Concerns: No reports of direct toxicity to infant via milk but use with caution. Inhibits lactation.

Drug Interactions: Amitriptyline, butyrophenones, imipramine, methyldopa, phenothiazines, reserpine, may decrease efficacy of bromocriptine at reducing serum prolactin. May increase toxicity of other ergot alkaloids.

Alternatives: Cabergoline

Adult Dosage: 1.25-2.5 mg BID-TID

T½ = 50 hours	M/P =
PHL=	PB = 90-96%
PK = 1-3 hours	Oral = <28%
MW = 654	pKa =
Vd = 3.4	

References:
1. Meese MG, et.al. Reassessment of bromocriptine use for lactation suppression. P and T. 17:1003-4, 1992.
2. Spalding G. Bromocriptine for suppression of lactation. Aust. and NZ J. of Obstet. and Gyn. 31:344-45, 1991.
3. Canales ES, Garcia IC, et.al. Bromocriptine as prophylactic therapy in prolactinoma during pregnancy. Fertil Steril 36:524-6, 1981.

BROMPHENIRAMINE

Trade: Dimetane, Brombay, Dimetapp, Bromfed
Can/Aus/UK: Dimetane, Dimotane
Uses: Antihistamine
AAP: Not reviewed

Brompheniramine is a popular antihistamine sold as Dimetane by itself, or in combination with phenylpropanolamine as Dimetapp, or with d-isoephedrine as Bromfed.   Although untoward effects appear limited, some reported side effects from Dimetapp preparations are known. Although only insignificant amounts appear to be secreted into breastmilk,   there are a number of reported cases of irritability, excessive crying, and sleep disturbances that have been reported in breastfeeding infants.[1]   Only modest amounts of phenylpropanolamine (PPA, Propadrine) are believed to be secreted into breastmilk.   See phenylpropanolamine.

Pregnancy Risk Category: C

Lactation Risk Category: L3

Theoretic Infant Dose:

Adult Concerns: Drowsiness, dry mucosa, excessive crying, irritability, sleep disturbances.

Pediatric Concerns: Irritability, excessive crying, and sleep disturbances have been reported.

Drug Interactions: May enhance toxicity of other CNS depressants, MAO inhibitors, alcohol and tricyclic depressants.

Alternatives: Loratadine, cetirizine

Adult Dosage: 4 mg q 4-6 hours

T½ = 24.9 hours	M/P =
PHL =	PB =
PK = 3.1 hours	Oral = Complete
MW = 319	pKa =
Vd = 11.7	

References:
1.   Paton DM, Webster DR. Clinical pharmacokinetics of H1-receptor antagonists (the antihistamines). Clin. Pharm. 10:477-497, 1985.

BUDESONIDE

Trade: Rhinocort, Pulmicort Respules
Can/Aus/UK: Entocort, Pulmicort, Rhinocort
Uses: Corticosteroid
AAP: Not reviewed

Budesonide is a new and potent corticosteroid primarily used intranasally for allergic rhinitis. As such, the systemic bioavailability is minimal with less than 20% of the intranasal dose ever reaching systemic circulation.[1] Once absorbed systemically budesonide is a weak systemic steroid and should not be used to replace other steroids. In one 5 year study of children aged 2-7 years, no changes in linear growth, weight, and bone age were noted.[2] Adrenal suppression at these doses is extremely remote. Using normal doses, it is unlikely that clinically relevant concentrations of budesonide would ever reach the milk, nor be systemically bioavailable to a breastfed infant.

Pregnancy Risk Category: C

Lactation Risk Category: L3

Theoretic Infant Dose:

Adult Concerns: Adverse effects following intranasal use include irritation, pharyngitis, cough, bleeding, candidiasis, dry mouth. No adrenal suppression has been reported.

Pediatric Concerns: None reported via milk. Pediatric use down to age 6 is permitted.

Drug Interactions:

Alternatives:

Adult Dosage: 200-400 ug BID

T½ = 2.8 hours	**M/P =**
PHL=	**PB =**
PK = 2-4 hours (oral)	**Oral = 10.7% (oral)**
MW = 430	**pKa =**
Vd = 4.3	

References:
1. Pharmaceutical Manufacturers Package Insert, 1999.
2. Volovitz B, Amir J, Malik H et al: Growth and pituitary-adrenal function in children with severe asthma treated with inhaled budesonide. N Engl J Med 329:1703-1708, 1993.

BUMETANIDE

Trade: Bumex
Can/Aus/UK: Burinex
Uses: Loop diuretic
AAP: Not reviewed

Bumetanide is a potent loop diuretic similar to Lasix.[1]   As with all diuretics, some reduction in breastmilk production may result but it is rare. It is not known if bumetanide transfers into human milk. If needed furosemide may be a better choice, as the oral bioavailability of furosemide in neonates is minimal.

Pregnancy Risk Category: D

Lactation Risk Category: L3

Theoretic Infant Dose:

Adult Concerns: Dehydration, hepatic cirrhosis, ototoxicity, potassium loss. See furosemide.

Pediatric Concerns: None reported via milk.

Drug Interactions: Numerous interactions exist, this is a partial list of the most important.   NSAIDS may block diuretic effect. Lithium excretion may be reduced.   Increased effect with other antihypertensives.   May induce hypoglycemia when added to sulfonylurea users. Clofibrate may induce an exaggerated diuresis. Increased ototoxicity with aminoglycoside antibiotics.   Increased anticoagulation with anticoagulants.

Alternatives: Furosemide

Adult Dosage: 0.5-2 mg QD-TID

T½ = 1-1.5	M/P =	
PHL = 2.5 hours (neonate)	PB = 95%	
PK = 1 hour (oral)	Oral =	
MW = 364	pKa =	
Vd =		

References:
1.   Pharmaceutical Manufacturers Package Insert, 1999.

BUPIVACAINE

Trade: Marcaine
Can/Aus/UK: Marcaine
Uses: Epidural, local anesthetic
AAP: Not reviewed

Bupivacaine is the most commonly employed regional anesthetic used in delivery because it concentrations in the fetus are the least of the local anesthetics. In one study of five patients, levels of bupivacaine in breastmilk were below the limits of detection (< 0.02 mg/L) at 2 to 48 hours postpartum.[1] These authors concluded that bupivacaine is a safe drug for perinatal use in mothers who plan to breastfeed.

In a study of 27 parturients who received an average of 183.3 mg lidocaine and 82.1 mg bupivacaine via an epidural catheter, lidocaine milk levels at 2, 6 , and 12 hours post administration were 0.86 , 0.46, and 0.22 mg/L respectively.[2] Levels of bupivacaine in milk at 2, 6, and 12 hours were 0.09, 0.06, 0.04 mg/L respectively. The milk/serum ratio bases upon area under the curve values (AUC) were 1.07 and 0.34 for lidocaine and bupivacaine respectively. Based on AUC data of lidocaine and bupivacaine milk levels, the average milk concentration of these agents over 12 hours was 0.5 and 0.07 mg/L. Most of the infants had a maximal APGAR score.

Pregnancy Risk Category: C

Lactation Risk Category: L2

Theoretic Infant Dose: 90 μg/kg/day

Adult Concerns: Sedation, bradycardia, respiratory depression.

Pediatric Concerns: None reported via milk.

Drug Interactions: Increases effect of hyaluronidase, beta blockers, MAO inhibitors, tricyclic antidepressants, phenothiazines, and vasopressors.

Alternatives:

Adult Dosage: 25-100 mg once

T½ = 2.7 hours	**M/P =**
PHL= 8.1 hours	**PB = 95%**
PK = 30-45 min.	**Oral =**
MW = 288	**pKa = 8.1**
Vd = 0.4-1.0	

References:
1. Naulty JS, Ostheimer G, et.al. Bupivacaine in breast milk following epidural anesthesia for vaginal delivery. Regional Anesthesia 8(1):44-45,

1983.

2. Ortega D, Viviand X, Lorec AM, Gamerre M, Martin C, Bruguerolle B. Excretion of lidocaine and bupivacaine in breast milk following epidural anesthesia for cesarean delivery. Acta Anaesthesiol Scand. 43(4):394-7, 1999.

BUPRENORPHINE

Trade: Buprenex
Can/Aus/UK: Subutex, Temgesic
Uses: Narcotic analgesic
AAP: Not reviewed

Buprenorphine is a potent long-acting narcotic agonist and antagonist, and may be useful as a replacement for methadone treatment in addicts. While its elimination half-life is short, it is retained on the opiate receptor site for long periods and may produce effects longer than the elimination half-life would suggest.

In one patient who received 4 mg/day to facilitate withdrawal from other opiates, the amount of buprenorphine transferred via milk was only 3.28 micrograms per day, an amount that was clinically insignificant.[1] No symptoms were noted in this breastfed infant. In another study of continuous extradural bupivacaine and buprenorphine in postcesarean women for 3 days[2], it was suggested that buprenorphine may suppress the production of milk (and infant weight gain), although this was not absolutely clear. As with most opiates, breastmilk levels are probably low, but sustained exposure should be avoided.

Pregnancy Risk Category: C

Lactation Risk Category: L3

Theoretic Infant Dose: 3.28 μg/kg/day

Adult Concerns: Typical opiate side effects include pruritus, sedation, analgesia, hallucinations, euphoria, dizziness, respiratory depression.

Pediatric Concerns: Low weight gain and reduced breastmilk levels in one study, and no effects in another study.

Drug Interactions: May enhance effects of other opiates, benzodiazepines, and barbiturates.

Alternatives:

Adult Dosage: 0.3 mg q 6 hours PRN

T½ = 1.2-7.2 hours	M/P =
PHL =	PB = 96%
PK = 15-30 minutes	Oral = 31%
MW =	pKa = 8.24, 9.92
Vd = 97	

References:
1. Marquet P, Lachatre G et.al. Buprenorphine withdrawal syndrome in a newborn. Clin. Pharmacol. Ther. 62(5):569-71, 1997.
2. Hirose M, Hosokawa T, Tanaka Y. Extradural buprenorphine suppresses breast feeding after caesarean section. Br. J. Anaesth. 79:120-1, 1997.

BUPROPION

Trade: Wellbutrin, Zyban
Can/Aus/UK: Wellbutrin, Zyban
Uses: Antidepressant, smoking deterrent
AAP: Drug whose effect on nursing infants is unknown but may be of concern

Bupropion is an older antidepressant with a structure unrelated to tricyclics. It may be teratogenic in pregnant women. One report in the literature indicates that bupropion probably accumulates in human milk, although the absolute dose transferred appears minimal.

Following one 100 mg dose in a mother the milk/plasma ratio ranged from 2.51 to 8.58, clearly suggesting a concentrating mechanism for this drug in human milk.[1] However, plasma levels of bupropion (or its metabolites) in the infant were undetectable, indicating that the dose transferred to the infant was low, and accumulation in infant plasma apparently did not occur under these conditions (infant was fed 7.5 to 9.5 hours after dosing).   The peak milk bupropion level (0.189 mg/L) occurred two hours after a 100 mg dose. This milk level would provide 0.019% of the maternal dose, a dose that is likely to be clinically insignificant to a breastfed infant.   A new formulation is currently recommended for smoking cessation therapy and is called Zyban.

Pregnancy Risk Category: B

Lactation Risk Category: L3

Theoretic Infant Dose: 28.4 μg/kg/day

Adult Concerns: Seizures, restlessness, agitation, sleep disturbances. Probably contraindicated in patients with seizure disorders.

Pediatric Concerns: None reported in one study, but this infant was only breastfed but twice daily. Observe for changes in milk production.

Drug Interactions: May increase clearance of diazepam, carbamazepine, phenytoin. May increase effects of MAO inhibitors.

Alternatives: Sertraline, paroxetine, fluvoxamine

Adult Dosage: 100 mg TID

T½ = 8-24 hours	M/P = 2.51-8.58
PHL=	PB = 75-88%
PK = 2 hours	Oral =
MW = 240	pKa = 8.0
Vd = 40	

References:
1.   Briggs GG, et.al. Excretion of bupropion in breast milk. Annals of Pharmacotherapy 27:431-433, 1993.

BUSPIRONE

Trade: Buspar
Can/Aus/UK: Apo-Buspirone, BuSpar, Buspar, Novo-Buspirone
Uses: Antianxiety medication
AAP: Not reviewed

No data exists on excretion into human milk. It is secreted into animal milk, so would expect the same in human milk.[1] Buspar is mg for mg equivalent to diazepam(Valium) in its anxiolytic properties, but does not produce significant sedation or addiction as the benzodiazepine family. Its metabolite is partially active, but has a brief half-life (4.8 hours) as well. Compared to the benzodiazepine family, this product would be a better choice for treatment of anxiety in breastfeeding women. But without accurate breastmilk levels, it is not known if the product is safe for breastfeeding women or the levels the infant would ingest daily. The rather brief half-life of this product and its metabolite would not likely lead to buildup in the infants plasma.

Pregnancy Risk Category: B

Lactation Risk Category: L3

Theoretic Infant Dose:

Adult Concerns: Dizziness, nausea, drowsiness, fatigue, excitement, euphoria.

Pediatric Concerns: None reported.

Drug Interactions: Cimetidine may increase the effect of buspirone. Increased toxicity may occur when used with MAO inhibitors, phenothiazines, CNS depressants, digoxin and haloperidol.

Alternatives:

Adult Dosage: 5 mg TID

T½ = 2-3 hours	M/P =
PHL=	PB = 95%
PK = 60-90 minutes	Oral = 90%
MW = 386	pKa =
Vd = 5.3	

References:
1.   Pharmaceutical Manufacturers Package Insert, 1996.

BUSULFAN

Trade: Myleran
Can/Aus/UK: Myleran
Uses: Antineoplastic, anticancer drug.
AAP: Not reviewed

Busulfan is a potent antineoplastic agent that can produce severe bone marrow suppression, anemia, loss of blood cells, and elevated risk of infection.[1] It is not known if busulfan is distributed to human milk. No data are available concerning breastmilk concentrations, but this agent would be extremely toxic to growing infants and continued breastfeeding would not be justified.   Use of this drug during breastfeeding is definitely not recommended.

Pregnancy Risk Category: D

Lactation Risk Category: L5

Theoretic Infant Dose:

Adult Concerns: Severe bone marrow suppression, anemia, leukopenia, pulmonary fibrosis, cholestatic jaundice.

Pediatric Concerns: Extremely cytotoxic, use is not recommended in nursing women.

Drug Interactions:

Alternatives:

Adult Dosage: 1 mg/kg/dose q 6 hours (16 doses total)

T½ = 2.6 hours.	M/P =
PHL=	PB = 14%
PK = 0.5-2 hours.	Oral = Complete
MW = 246	pKa =
Vd = 1.0	

References:
1.   McEvoy GE(ed):AHFS Drug Information, New York, NY. 1995.

BUTABARBITAL

Trade: Butisol, Butalan, Ampyrox
Can/Aus/UK:
Uses: Sedative, hypnotic
AAP: Not reviewed

Butabarbital is an intermediate acting barbiturate similar to phenobarbital. Small amounts are secreted in breastmilk.[1] No harmful effects have been reported. Watch for drowsiness and sedation.

Pregnancy Risk Category: D

Lactation Risk Category: L3

Theoretic Infant Dose:

Adult Concerns: Sedation, weakness.

Pediatric Concerns: None reported but observe for sedation.

Drug Interactions: May have a decreased effect when used with phenothiazines, haloperidol, cyclosporin, tricyclic antidepressants, doxycycline, beta-blockers. May increase effects of benzodiazepines, CNS depressants, valproic acid, methylphenidate, and chloramphenicol.

Alternatives:

Adult Dosage: 15-30 mg TID or QID

T½ = 100 hours	M/P =
PHL =	PB =
PK = 3-4 hours.	Oral = Complete
MW = 232	pKa = 7.9
Vd =	

References:
1. Tyson RM, Shrader EA, Perlman HH. Drugs transmitted through breast milk. II Barbiturates. J Pediatr. 14:86-90, 1938.

BUTALBITAL COMPOUND

Trade: Fioricet, Fiorinal, Bancap, Two-dyne
Can/Aus/UK: Fiorinal, Tecnal
Uses: Mild analgesic, sedative
AAP: Not reviewed

Mild analgesic with acetaminophen (325mg) or aspirin, caffeine (40mg), and butalbital (50mg). Butalbital is a mild, short-acting barbiturate that probably transfers into breastmilk to a limited degree, although it is unreported.[1] No data are available on the transfer of butalbital to breastmilk, but it is likely minimal.

Pregnancy Risk Category: D

Lactation Risk Category: L3

Theoretic Infant Dose:

Adult Concerns: Sedation.

Pediatric Concerns: Sedation.

Drug Interactions: Decreased effect when used with phenothiazines, haloperidol, cyclosporin, tricyclic antidepressants, and oral contraceptives.   Increased effect when used with alcohol, benzodiazepines, CNS depressants, valproic acid, methylphenidate.

Alternatives:

Adult Dosage: 50-100 mg q 4 hours

T½ = 40-140 hours	M/P =
PHL=	PB = 26%
PK = 40-60 min.	Oral = Complete
MW = 224	pKa =
Vd = 0.8	

References:
1.   McEvoy GE(ed):AHFS Drug Information, New York, NY. 1995.

BUTORPHANOL

Trade: Stadol
Can/Aus/UK: Stadol
Uses: Potent narcotic analgesic
AAP: Approved by the American Academy of Pediatrics for use in breastfeeding mothers

Butorphanol is a potent narcotic analgesic. It is available both by I.V., IM, and a nasal spray. Butorphanol passes into breastmilk in low to moderate concentrations (estimated 4 μg/L of milk following 2 mg I.M.4 times daily).[1] Levels produced in infants are considered very low to insignificant. Butorphanol undergoes first-pass extraction by the liver, hence only 17% of the oral dose reaches the plasma. Butorphanol has been frequently used in labor and delivery in women who subsequently nursed their infants although it has been noted to produce a sinusoidal fetal heart rate pattern, and dysphoric or psychotomimetic responses in postpartum women.

Pregnancy Risk Category: B during 1st and 2nd trimesters

D during 3rd trimester

Lactation Risk Category: L3

Theoretic Infant Dose: 0.6 μg/kg/day

Adult Concerns: Sedation, respiratory depression.

Pediatric Concerns: None reported via milk but sedation is possible in newborns.

Drug Interactions: May produce increased toxicity when used with CNS depressants, other opiates, phenothiazines, barbiturates, benzodiazepines, MAO inhibitors.

Alternatives:

Adult Dosage: 1-4 mg IM q 3-4 hours OR 0.5-2 mg I.V. q 3-4 hours

T½ = 3-4 hours.	M/P =
PHL =	PB = 80%
PK = 1 hour	Oral = 17 %
MW = 327	pKa = 8.6
Vd = 5	

References:

1. Pittman, K. et.al. Human perinatal distribution of butorphanol. Am. J. Obstet. Gynecol. 138:797-800, 1980.

CABERGOLINE

Trade: Dostinex
Can/Aus/UK: Dostinex
Uses: Anti-prolactin
AAP: Not reviewed

Cabergoline is a long-acting synthetic ergot alkaloid derivative which produces a dopamine agonist effect similar but much safer than bromocriptine (Parlodel). Cabergoline directly inhibits prolactin secretion by the pituitary.[1] It is primarily indicated for pathological hyperprolactinemia, but in several European studies, it has been used for inhibition of post-partum lactation. In several European countries, cabergoline is indicated for the inhibition or suppression of physiologic lactation.[2] The dose regimen used for the inhibition of physiologic lactation is cabergoline 1 mg administered as a single dose on the first day post-partum. For the suppression of established lactation, cabergoline 0.25 mg is taken every 12 hours for 2 days for a total of 1 mg. Single doses of 1 mg have been found to completely inhibit postpartum lactation. Transfer into human milk is not reported.

Pregnancy Risk Category: B

Lactation Risk Category: L4

Theoretic Infant Dose:

Adult Concerns: Headache, dizziness, fatigue, orthostatic hypotension, nose bleed, inhibition of lactation.

Pediatric Concerns: Transfer via milk is unknown. Will completely and irreversibly suppress lactation and should not be used in mothers who are breastfeeding.

Drug Interactions: Do not use with other dopamine antagonists such as the phenothiazines (Thorazine, etc), butyrophenones (Haldol), thioxanthenes, and metoclopramide (Reglan).

Alternatives:

Adult Dosage: 0.25-1 mg twice a week

T½ = 80 hours	M/P =
PHL =	PB =
PK = 2-3 hours	Oral = Complete
MW = 451	pKa =
Vd =	

References:
1. Caballero-Gordo A, et.al. Oral cabergoline: Single-dose inhibition of puerperal lactation. J. Reprod. Med. 36(10):717-721, 1991.
2. European Multicentre Study Group for Cabergoline in Lactation Inhibition. Single dose cabergoline versus bromocriptine in inhibition of puerperal lactation. Randomised, double blind, multicentre study. BMJ 302(6789):1367-71, 1991.

CAFFEINE

Trade: Vivarin, NoDoz, Coffee
Can/Aus/UK:
Uses: CNS stimulant
AAP: Approved by the American Academy of Pediatrics for use in breastfeeding mothers

Caffeine is a naturally-occurring CNS stimulant present in many foods and drinks. While the half-life in adults is 4.9 hours, the half-life in neonates is as high as 97.5 hours. The half-life decreases with age to 14 hours at 3-5 months, and 2.6 hours at 6 months and older. The average cup of coffee contains 100-150 mg of caffeine depending on preparation and country of origin. Peak levels of caffeine are found in breastmilk 60-120 minutes after ingestion.

In a study of 5 patients following an ingestion of 150 mg caffeine, peak concentrations of caffeine in serum ranged from 2.39 to 4.05 μg/mL and peak concentrations in milk ranged from 1.4 to 2.41 mg/L with a milk/serum ratio of 0.52.[1] The average milk concentration at 30, 60, and 120 minute post dose was 1.58, 1.49, and 0.926 mg/L respectively.

In another study of 7 breastfeeding mothers who consumed 750 mg caffeine/day for 5 days, and were 11-22 days postpartum, the average milk concentration was 4.3 mg/L.[2] Values ranged significantly from nondetectible to 15.7 mg/L. The mean concentration of caffeine in sera of the infants on day 5 was 1.4 μg/mL(range nondeductible to 2.8 μg/mL). In two patients whose milk levels were 13.4 and 28 mg/L the respective infant serum levels were 0.25 and 3.2 μg/mL.

In a study of 6 breastfeeding mothers who received one dose of 100 mg PO, peak levels (Cmax) in maternal serum ranged from 0.5 to 1 hour, and 0.75 to 2 hours in milk.[3] The maternal plasma Cmax ranged from 3.6 to 6.15 μg/mL, while the Cmax for their milk ranged from 1.98 to 4.3 mg/L. The average concentration of caffeine in milk was 2.45 mg/L at 1 hour. The average milk/plasma ratio (AUC) was 0.812 for both breasts. This elegant study shows that caffeine rapidly enters milk and that the decay of caffeine in milk is similar to that of plasma. In infants from 4 to 7 kg, body weight, the estimated dose to the infant would be 1.77 to 3.10 mg/d following a 100 mg maternal dose.

In a group of mothers who ingested from 35 to 336 mg of caffeine daily, the level of caffeine in milk ranged from 2.09 to 7.17 mg/L.[4] The author estimates the dose to infant at 0.01 to 1.64 mg/d or 0.06% to 1.5% of the maternal dose.

An interesting review of the nutritional effects of caffeine ingestion on infants is provided by Nehlig.[5] There is some evidence that chronic coffee drinking may reduce the iron content of milk. Irritability and insomnia may occur and have been reported. Occasional use of caffeine is not contraindicated, but persistent, chronic use may lead to high plasma levels in the infant particularly during the neonatal period.

Pregnancy Risk Category: B

Lactation Risk Category: L2

Theoretic Infant Dose: 0.4 mg/kg/day

Adult Concerns: Agitation, irritability, poor sleeping patterns.

Pediatric Concerns: Rarely, irritability and insomnia.

Drug Interactions: Reduces vasodilation of adenosine.   Reduces bioavailability of alendronate by 60%.   Cimetidine reduces caffeine clearance by 50%. Fluoroquinolone antibiotics increases half-life of caffeine by 5 to 8 hours.

Alternatives:

Adult Dosage:

T½ = 4.9 hours	M/P = 0.52 - 0.76
PHL = 80-97.5 hours	PB = 36%
PK = 60 min.	Oral = 100%
MW = 194	pKa = 0.8
Vd = 0.4-0.6	

References:

1. Tyrala EE, Dodson WE. Caffeine secretion into breast milk. Arch Dis Child. 1979 Oct;54(10):787-800.
2. Ryu JE. Caffeine in human milk and in serum of breast-fed infants. Dev Pharmacol Ther. 8(6):329-37, 1985.
3. Stavchansky S, Combs A, Sagraves R, Delgado M, Joshi A. Pharmacokinetics of caffeine in breast milk and plasma after single oral administration of caffeine to lactating mothers. Biopharm Drug Dispos. 9(3):285-99, 1988.
4. Berlin CM Jr, Denson HM, Daniel CH, Ward RM. Disposition of dietary caffeine in milk, saliva, and plasma of lactating women. Pediatrics. 73(1):59-63, 1984.
5. Nehlig A, Debry G. Consequences on the newborn of chronic maternal consumption of coffee during gestation and lactation: A review. J. Am. Coll. Nutrit. 13:6-21, 1994.

CALCITONIN

Trade: Calcimar, Salmonine, Osteocalcin, Miacalcin
Can/Aus/UK: Calcimar, Calcitare, Calsynar, Caltine, Miacalcic
Uses: Calcium metabolism
AAP: Not reviewed

Calcitonin is a large polypeptide hormone (32 amino acids) secreted by the parafollicular cells of the thyroid that inhibits osteoclastic bone resorption thus maintaining calcium homeostasis in mammals.[1] It is used for control of postmenopausal osteoporosis and other calcium metabolic diseases. Calcitonins are destroyed by gastric acids, requiring parenteral (SC, IM) or intranasal dosing. Calcitonin is unlikely to penetrate human milk due to its large molecular weight. Further, its oral bioavailability is nil, due to destruction in the GI tract. It has been reported to inhibit lactation in animals, although this has not been reported in humans.[2]

Pregnancy Risk Category: C

Lactation Risk Category: L3

Theoretic Infant Dose:

Adult Concerns: Nausea, facial flushing, shivering, edema, metallic taste, and increased urinary frequency.

Pediatric Concerns: None reported via milk. Unlikely to enter milk.

Calcitonins have been reported to inhibit lactation in animals.

Drug Interactions: It is reported that ketoprofen inhibits the calciuric and uricosuric effect of porcine calcitonin. May have additive effect with plicamycin.

Alternatives:

Adult Dosage: 50-100 units (salmon) three times weekly

T½ = 1 hour	M/P =
PHL =	PB =
PK = 2 hours	Oral = None
MW =	pKa =
Vd =	

References:
1. Pharmaceutical manufacturers package insert, Armour. 1997.
2. Fiore CE, Petralito A, Mazzarino MC et al: Effects of ketoprofen on the calciuric and uricosuric activities of calcitonin in man. J Endocrinol Invest 4:81-83, 1981.

CALENDULA

Trade: Calendula, Marigold, Garden Marigold, Holligold, Gold Bloom, Marybud
Can/Aus/UK:
Uses: Herbal wound healing
AAP: Not reviewed

Calendula, grown worldwide, has been used topically to promote wound healing, and to alleviate conjunctivitis and other ocular inflammations. It consists of a number of flavonol glycosides and saponins, but the active ingredients are unknown.[1] Despite these claims, there are almost no studies regarding its efficacy in any of these disorders. Further, there are no suggestions of overt toxicity, with exception of allergies. Although it may have some uses externally, its internal use as an antiphlogistic and spasmolytic is largely obsolete.

Pregnancy Risk Category:

Lactation Risk Category: L3

Theoretic Infant Dose:

Adult Concerns: Allergies, anaphylactoid shock.

Pediatric Concerns: None reported via milk.

Drug Interactions:

Alternatives:

Adult Dosage:

References:
1.   Bissett NG. In: Herbal Drugs and Phytopharmaceuticals. Medpharm Scientific Publishers, CRC Press, Boca Raton, 1994.

CANDESARTAN

Trade: Atacand
Can/Aus/UK:
Uses: Antihypertensive agent
AAP: Not reviewed

Candesartan is a specific blocker of the receptor site (AT1) for angiotensin II. It is typically used as an antihypertensive similar to the ACE inhibitor family.[1]   Both the ACE inhibitor family, and the specific AT1 inhibitors such as candesartan are contraindicated in the 2nd and 3rd trimesters of pregnancy due to severe hypotension, neonatal skull hypoplasia, irreversible renal failure, and death in the newborn infant. However, some ACE inhibitors can be used in breastfeeding mothers 2-3 weeks postpartum without major risk in some cases with due caution. However, no data are available on candesartan in human milk, although the manufacturer states that it is present in rodent milk. Extreme caution is recommended in the neonatal period.

Pregnancy Risk Category: C during 1st trimester
                                          D during 2nd and 3rd trimester

Lactation Risk Category: L4

Theoretic Infant Dose:

Adult Concerns: Headache, back pain, pharyngitis, and dizziness have been reported. The use of ACE inhibitors and angiotensin receptor blockers during pregnancy or the neonatal period is extremely dangerous and has resulted in hypotension, neonatal skull hypoplasia, anuria, renal failure and death.

Pediatric Concerns: None reported via milk. Caution is recommended in the early postpartum period.

Drug Interactions: None have been reported.

Alternatives: Captopril, enalapril

Adult Dosage: 4-32 mg QD

T½ = 9 hours	M/P =
PHL=	PB = >99%
PK = 3-4 hours	Oral = 15%
MW = 611	pKa =
Vd = 0.13	

References:
1. Pharmaceutical Manufacturers Package Insert, 1999.

CANNABIS

Trade: Marijuana
Can/Aus/UK:
Uses: Sedative, hallucinogen
AAP: Contraindicated by the American Academy of Pediatrics in Breastfeeding Mothers

Commonly called marijuana, the active component is delta-9-THC is rapidly distributed to the brain and adipose tissue. It is stored in fat tissues for long periods (weeks to months). Small to moderate secretion into breastmilk has been documented.[1] Analysis of breastmilk in chronic heavy users revealed an eightfold accumulation in breastmilk compared to plasma although the dose received is insufficient to produce significant side effects in the infant. Studies have shown significant absorption and metabolism in infants, although long term sequelae have not been shown. Marijuana could produce sedation and growth delay, but it is highly dose dependent. In one study of 27 women who smoked marijuana during breastfeeding, no differences were noted in outcomes on growth, mental, and motor development.[2] Studies in animals suggests that marijuana inhibits prolactin production and could inhibit lactation. Contraindicated in nursing mothers. Infants exposed to marijuana via breastmilk will test positive in urine screens for long periods (2-3 weeks).

Pregnancy Risk Category: C

Lactation Risk Category: L5

Theoretic Infant Dose:

Adult Concerns: Sedation, weakness, poor feeding patterns. Possible decreased milk production.

Pediatric Concerns: Sedation.

Drug Interactions:

Alternatives:

Adult Dosage:

T½ = 25-57 hours	**M/P** = 8
PHL =	**PB** = 99.9%.
PK =	**Oral** = Complete
MW =	**pKa** =
Vd = High	

References:
1.   Perez-Reyes M, Wall ME. Presence of tetrahydrocannabinol in human milk. N Engl J Med. 307:819-820, 1982.
2.   Tennes K, et.al. Marijuana: prenatal and postnatal exposure in the human. Natl. Inst. Drug Abuse Res. Monogr. Ser. 59:48-60, 1985.

CAPSAICIN

Trade: Zostrix, Axsain, Capsin, Capzasin-p, No-pain, Absorbine Jr. Arthritis, Arthricare
Can/Aus/UK: Axsain, Capsig, Natraflex, Zostrix
Uses: Analgesic, topical.
AAP: Not reviewed

Capsaicin is an alkaloid derived from peppers from the Solanaceae family.   After topical absorption it increases,   depletes, and then suppresses substance P release from sensory neurons, thus preventing pain sensation.   Substance P is the principal chemomediator of pain from the periphery to the CNS.[1,2]   After repeated application (days to weeks), it depletes substance P and prevents reaccumulation in the neuron.   Very little or nothing is known about the kinetics of this product. It is approved for use in children > 2 years of age.   No data are available on transfer into human milk.

Pregnancy Risk Category: C

Lactation Risk Category: L3

Theoretic Infant Dose:

Adult Concerns: Local irritation, burning, stinging, erythema. Cough and infrequently neurotoxicity. Avoid use near eyes.

Pediatric Concerns: None reported.   Avoid transfer to eye and other sensitive surfaces via hand contact.

Drug Interactions: May increase risk of cough with ACE inhibitors.

Alternatives:

Adult Dosage:

T½ = **Several hours**	**M/P** =
PHL =	**PB** =
PK =	**Oral** =
MW = **305**	**pKa** =
Vd =	

References:
1.   Bernstein JE: Capsaicin in dermatologic disease. Semin Dermatol 7:304-309, 1988.

2. Watson CPN, et.al. : The post-mastectomy pain syndrome and the effect of topical capsaicin. Pain 38:177-186, 1989.

CAPTOPRIL

Trade: Capoten
Can/Aus/UK: Acenorm, Acepril, Apo-Capto, Capoten, Enzace, Novo-Captopril
Uses: Antihypertensive drug (ACE inhibitor)
AAP: Approved by the American Academy of Pediatrics for use in breastfeeding mothers

Captopril is a typical angiotensin converting enzyme inhibitor (ACE) used to reduce hypertension. Small amounts are secreted (4.7 μg/L milk). In one report of 12 women treated with 100 mg three times daily, maternal serum levels averaged 713 μg/L, while breastmilk levels averaged 4.7 μg/L at 3.8 hours after administration.[1] Data from this study suggest that an infant would ingest approximately 0.002% of the free captopril consumed by its mother (300mg) on a daily basis. No adverse effects have been reported in this study. Use only if determined to be important to mother's health.

Pregnancy Risk Category: D

Lactation Risk Category: L3 if used after 30 days
L4 if used early postpartum

Theoretic Infant Dose: 0.7 μg/kg/day

Adult Concerns: Hypotension, bradycardia, decreased urine output and possible seizures. A decrease in taste acuity or metallic taste.

Pediatric Concerns: None reported but observe for hypotension.

Drug Interactions: Probenecid increases plasma levels of captopril. Captopril and diuretics have additive hypotensive effects. Antacids reduce bioavailability of ACE inhibitors. NSAIDs reduce hypotension of ACE inhibitors. Phenothiazines increase effects of ACEi. Allopurinol may increase risk of Steven-Johnson's syndrome with admixed with captopril. ACEi increase digoxin and lithium plasma levels. May elevate potassium levels when potassium supplementation is added.

Alternatives: Enalapril

Adult Dosage: 50 mg TID

T½ = 2.2 hours	M/P = 0.012
PHL =	PB = 30%
PK = 1 hour	Oral = 60-75%
MW = 217	pKa = 3.7, 9.8
Vd = 0.7	

References:
1.   Devlin RG, Fleiss PM. Selective resistance to the passage of captopril into
      human milk. Clin Pharmacol Ther 27:250, 1980.

CARBAMAZEPINE

Trade: Tegretol, Epitol, Carbatrol
Can/Aus/UK: Apo-Carbamazepine, Mazepine, Tegretol, Teril
Uses: Anticonvulsant
AAP: Approved by the American Academy of Pediatrics for
use in breastfeeding mothers

Carbamazepine(CBZ) is a unique anticonvulsant commonly used for
grand mal, clonic-tonic, simple and complex seizures. It is also used
in manic depression and a number of other neurologic syndromes. It is
one of the most commonly used anticonvulsants in pediatric patients.
In a brief study by Kaneko, with maternal plasma levels averaging 4.3
μg/mL, milk levels were 1.9 mg/L. [1]   In a study of 3 patients who
received from 5.8 to 7.3 mg/kg/day carbamazepine, milk levels were
reported to vary from 1.3 to 1.8 mg/L while the epoxide metabolite
varied from 0.5 to 1.1 mg/L.[2]   No adverse effects were noted in any of
the infants.   In another study by Niebyl, breastmilk levels were 1.4
mg/L in the lipid fraction, and 2.3 mg/L in the skim fraction in a mother
receiving 1000 mg daily of carbamazepine.[3] This author estimated that
the daily intake of 2 mg carbamazepine daily (0.5 mg/kg) in an infant
ingesting 1 Liter of milk per day.

In a study of CBZ and its epoxide metabolite (ECBZ) in milk, 16
patients received an average dose of 13.8 mg/kg/d.[4] The average
maternal serum levels of CBZ and ECBZ were 7.1 and 2.6 μg/mL
respectively. The average milk levels of CBZ and ECBZ were 2.5 and
1.5 mg/L respectively. The relative percent of CBZ and ECBZ in milk
were 36.4% and 53% of the maternal serum levels. A total of 50 milk
samples in 19 patients were analyzed. Of these, the lowest CBZ
concentration in milk was 1.0 mg/L; the highest was 4.8 mg/L. The
CBZ level was determined in 7 infants 4-7 days postpartum. All infants
have CBZ levels below 1.5 μg/mL.

In a study of 7 women receiving 250-800 mg/d carbamazepine, the
CBZ level ranged from 2.8-4.5 mg/L in milk to 3.2-15.0 mg/L in
plasma.[5]   The levels of ECBZ ranged from 0.5-1.7 mg/L in milk to
0.8-4.8 mg/L in plasma.

The amount of CBZ transferred to the infant is apparently quite low.
Although the half-life of CBZ in infants appears shorter than in adults,
infants should still be monitored for sedative effects.

Pregnancy Risk Category: C

Lactation Risk Category: L2

Theoretic Infant Dose: 0.5 mg/kg/day

Adult Concerns: Sedation, nausea, respiratory depression, tachycardia, vomiting, diarrhea, blood dyscrasias.

Pediatric Concerns: None reported via milk.

Drug Interactions: Carbamazepine may induce the metabolism of warfarin, cyclosporin, doxycycline, oral contraceptives, phenytoin, theophylline, benzodiazepines, ethosuximide, valproic acid, corticosteroids, and thyroid hormones. Macrolide antibiotics, isoniazid, verapamil, danazol, diltiazem may inhibit metabolism of carbamazepine and increase plasma levels.

Alternatives:

Adult Dosage: 800-1200 mg QD divided TID or QID

T½ = 18-54 hours.	M/P = 0.69
PHL = 8-28 hours.	PB = 74%
PK = 4-5 hours.	Oral = 100%
MW = 236	pKa = 7.0
Vd = 0.8-1.8	

References:
1. Kaneko S, Sato T, Suzuki K. The levels of anticonvulsants in breast milk. Br J Clin Pharmacol. 7(6):624-7, 1979.
2. Pynnonen S, Kanto J, Sillanpaa M, Erkkola R. Carbamazepine: Placental transport, tissue concentrations in foetus and newborn, and level in milk. Acta Phamacol et toxicol 41:244-253, 1977.
3. Niebyl JR, Blake DA, Freeman JM, et.al. Carbamazepine levels in pregnancy and lactation. Obstet Gynecol. 53:139-140,1979.
4. Froescher W, Eichelbaum M, Niesen M, Dietrich K, Rausch P. Carbamazepine levels in breast milk. Ther Drug Monit. 6(3):266-71, 1984.
5. Shimoyama R, Ohkubo T, Sugawara K. Monitoring of carbamazepine and carbamazepine 10,11-epoxide in breast milk and plasma by high-performance liquid chromatography. Ann Clin Biochem. 37:210-215.

CARBAMIDE PEROXIDE

Trade: Gly-oxide, Debrox, Auro Otic
Can/Aus/UK: Exterol
Uses: Antibacterial, whitening agent
AAP: Not reviewed

Carbamide peroxide is stable while immersed in glycerin, but upon contact with moisture, releases hydrogen peroxide and nascent oxygen, both strong oxidizing agents. It is used to disinfect infected lesions and for whitening of teeth and dental appliances. Hydrogen peroxide is rapidly metabolized by hydroperoxidases, peroxidases and catalase present in all tissues, plasma, and saliva. Its transfer to the plasma is minimal if at all. It would be all but impossible for any to reach breastmilk unless under extreme overdose.

Pregnancy Risk Category: C

Lactation Risk Category: L1

Theoretic Infant Dose:

Adult Concerns: Dermal irritation, mucous membrane irritation, inflammation. Overgrowth of candida and other opportunistic infections.

Pediatric Concerns: Toxic in major overdose. Exposure to small amounts may lead to inflamed membranes.

Drug Interactions:

Alternatives:

Adult Dosage:

CARBENICILLIN

Trade: Geopen, Geocillin, Carindacillin
Can/Aus/UK: Carbapen, Geopen
Uses: Extended spectrum penicillin antibiotic
AAP: Not reviewed

Carbenicillin is an extended spectrum penicillin antibiotic. Only limited levels are secreted into breastmilk (0.26 mg/liter or about 0.001% of adult dose).[1] In a study of 2-3 women who received 1000 mg IM, the maximum milk level occurred at 4 hours and averaged 0.24 mg/L.[2] The average milk/plasma ratio reported was 0.045 at 4 hours. Due to its poor oral absorption (< 10%) the amount absorbed by a nursing infant would be minimal.

Pregnancy Risk Category: B

Lactation Risk Category: L1

Theoretic Infant Dose: 39 μg/kg/day

Adult Concerns: Rash, thrush, or diarrhea.   Headache, rash, hyperthermia.

Pediatric Concerns: None reported via milk.

Drug Interactions: Co-administration of aminoglycosides (within 1 hour) may inactivate both drugs. Increased half-life with probenecid.

Alternatives:

Adult Dosage: 382-764 mg q 6 hours

T½ = 1 hour	M/P = 0.02
PHL = 0.8-1.8 hours	PB = 26-60%
PK = 1-3 hours	Oral = <10-30%
MW = 378	pKa =
Vd =	

References:
1. Pharmaceutical Manufacturers Package Insert, 1996.
2. Matsuda S. Transfer of antibiotics into maternal milk.   Biol Res Pregnancy Perinatol. 5(2):57-60, 1984.

CARBIDOPA

Trade: Lodosyn
Can/Aus/UK: Kinson, Sinacarb, Sinemet
Uses: Inhibits levodopa metabolism
AAP: Not reviewed

Carbidopa inhibits the metabolism of levodopa in parkinsonian patients therefore extending the half-life of levodopa.   Its effect on lactation is largely unknown, but skeletal malformations have occurred in pregnant rabbits.[1,2] Use discretion in administering to pregnant or lactating women.

Pregnancy Risk Category: C

Lactation Risk Category: L3

Theoretic Infant Dose:

Adult Concerns: GI distress, nausea, vomiting, diarrhea.

Pediatric Concerns:

Drug Interactions: May interact with tricyclic antidepressants leading to hypertensive reactions.

Alternatives:

Adult Dosage: 70-100 mg QD

T½ = 1-2 hours.	M/P =
PHL =	PB = 36%
PK =	Oral = 40-70%
MW = 244	pKa =
Vd =	

References:
1. Pharmaceutical Manufacturers Package Insert, 1996.
2. McEvoy GE(ed):AHFS Drug Information, New York, NY. 1995.

CARBIMAZOLE

Trade:
Can/Aus/UK: Neo-Mercazole
Uses: Thyroid inhibitor
AAP: Approved by the American Academy of Pediatrics for use in breastfeeding mothers

Carbimazole is a prodrug of methimazole and is rapidly and completely converted to the active methimazole in the plasma. Only methimazole is detected in plasma, urine and thyroid tissue. See breastfeeding specifics for methimazole. Data from Rylance suggests that subclinical levels of methimazole enter milk subsequent to administration of 30 mg/day carbimazole.[1] Free methimazole measured in milk on 10 occasions averaged 43 nanogram/mL. Plasma methimazole in twins was 45 to 52 nanograms/mL. Thyroid suppression is believed to occur only when plasma levels exceed 50-100 ng/mL. No thyroid suppression was noted in these two twins. Peak transfer into milk occurred at 2-4 hours, and the lowest at 6 hours after the dose. The authors suggest that breastfeeding is permissible if the maternal dose is less than 30 mg/day. See propylthiouracil as alternative.

Pregnancy Risk Category: D

Lactation Risk Category: L3

Theoretic Infant Dose: 6.5 ng/kg/day

Adult Concerns: Hypothyroidism, hepatic dysfunction, bleeding, drowsiness, skin rash, nausea, vomiting, fever.

Pediatric Concerns: None reported via milk, but propylthiouracil is generally preferred in breastfeeding women.

Drug Interactions: Use with iodinated glycerol, lithium, and potassium iodide may increase toxicity.

Alternatives: Propylthiouracil

Adult Dosage: < 30 mg daily

T½ = 6-13 hours	M/P = 0.3-0.7
PHL =	PB = 0%
PK = 4 hour	Oral = Complete
MW = 186	pKa =
Vd =	

References:
1. Rylance GW, Woods CG, Donnelly MC et al: Carbimazole and breastfeeding (letter). Lancet 1987; 1:928

CARISOPRODOL

Trade: Soma Compound, Solol
Can/Aus/UK: Carisoma, Soma
Uses: Muscle relaxant, CNS depressant
AAP: Not reviewed

Carisoprodol is a commonly used skeletal muscle relaxant that is a CNS depressant. It is metabolized to an active metabolite called meprobamate. As Soma Compound it also contains 325 mg of aspirin. In a study of one breastfeeding mother receiving 2100 mg/d, the average milk concentration of carisoprodol and meprobamate was 0.9 mg/L and 11.6 mg/L, respectively.[1] Based on these combined values, the relative infant dose for carisoprodol and meprobamate would be 4.1% of the weight-adjusted maternal dose. No adverse effects on the infant were noted.

Pregnancy Risk Category: C

Lactation Risk Category: L3

Theoretic Infant Dose:

Adult Concerns: Nausea, vomiting, hiccups, sedation, weakness, mild withdrawal symptoms after chronic use.

Pediatric Concerns: None reported, but observe for sedation.

Drug Interactions: Increased toxicity when added to alcohol, CNS depressants, MAO inhibitors.

Alternatives:

Adult Dosage: 350 mg TID-QID

T½ = 8 hours	M/P = 2-4
PHL =	PB =
PK =	Oral = Complete
MW = 260	pKa =
Vd =	

References:
1. Nordeng H, Zahlsen K, Spigset O. Transfer of carisoprodol to breast milk. Ther Drug Monit. 23(3):298-300, 2001.

CARTEOLOL

Trade: Cartrol
Can/Aus/UK: Teoptic
Uses: Beta-adrenergic antihypertensive
AAP: Not reviewed

Carteolol is a typical beta blocker used for hypertension. Carteolol is reported to be excreted in breastmilk of lactating animals.[1] No data available on human milk.

Pregnancy Risk Category: C

Lactation Risk Category: L3

Theoretic Infant Dose:

Adult Concerns: Hypotension, bradycardia, lethargy, and sedation.

Pediatric Concerns: None reported but observe for hypoglycemia, hypotension, bradycardia, lethargy.

Drug Interactions: Decreased effect when used with aluminum salts, barbiturates, calcium salts, cholestyramine, NSAIDs, ampicillin, rifampin, and salicylates. Beta blockers may reduce the effect of oral sulfonylureas (hypoglycemic agents). Increased toxicity/effect when used with other antihypertensives, contraceptives, MAO inhibitors, cimetidine, and numerous other products. See drug interaction reference for complete listing.

Alternatives: Propranolol, metoprolol

Adult Dosage: 2.5-5 mg QD

T½ = 6 hours	**M/P =**
PHL=	**PB = 23-30%**
PK =	**Oral = 80%**
MW = 292	**pKa =**
Vd =	

References:
1.   Pharmaceutical Manufacturers Package Insert, 1996.

CARVEDILOL

Trade: Coreg
Can/Aus/UK: Coreg, Dilatrend, Eucardic, Proreg
Uses: Antihypertensive
AAP: Not reviewed

Carvedilol is a nonselective beta-adrenergic blocking agent (and partial alpha-1 blocking activity) with high lipid solubility and no intrinsic sympathomimetic activity.[1] There are no data available on the transfer of this drug into human milk. However, due to its high volume of distribution and high lipid solubility, some may transfer. Caution is recommended.

Pregnancy Risk Category: C

Lactation Risk Category: L3

Theoretic Infant Dose:

Adult Concerns: Postural hypotension, fatigue, dizziness, lightheadedness, bradycardia, bronchospasm. Use with caution in asthmatics.

Pediatric Concerns: None reported via milk. Observe for hypotension, bradycardia, hypoglycemia.

Drug Interactions: Severe bradycardia may result when used with amiodarone. Digoxin may prolong AV conduction time. Severe hypotension when added with calcium channel blockers. Severe hypertension, bradycardia when used with epinephrine.

Alternatives: Propranolol, metoprolol

Adult Dosage: 6.25-12.5 mg BID

T½ = 6-10 hours		M/P =	
PHL =		PB =	
PK = 1-1.5 hours		Oral = 25-35%	
MW =		pKa =	
Vd = 1.88			

References:
1. Pharmaceutical Manufacturers Package Insert, 1998.

CASCARA SAGRADA

Trade: Cascara Sagrada
Can/Aus/UK: Cascara Sagrada
Uses: Laxative
AAP: Approved by the American Academy of Pediatrics for use in breastfeeding mothers

Trace amounts appear to be secreted into breastmilk.[1,2] No exact estimates have been published. May cause loose stools and diarrhea in neonates.

Pregnancy Risk Category: C

Lactation Risk Category: L3

Theoretic Infant Dose:

Adult Concerns: Diarrhea, GI cramping.

Pediatric Concerns: May loosen stools in infants.

Drug Interactions: Decreased effect of oral anticoagulants.

Alternatives:

Adult Dosage: 5 mL QD

References:
1. O'Brien, T. Excretion of drugs in human milk. Am.J. Hosp. Pharm. 31:844-854, 1974.
2. Vorherr, H. Drug excretion in breast milk. Postgrad. Med. 56:97-104, 1974.

CASPOFUNGIN ACETATE

Trade: Cancidas
Can/Aus/UK:
Uses: Antifungal
AAP: Not reviewed

Caspofungin is a unique semisynthetic lipopeptide that is active against Aspergillus fumigatus. It has a large polycyclic structure with a molecular weight of 1213 daltons. The half-life of this product is unique with a polyphasic elimination curve with 3 distinct phases. The half-life varies from 11 hours in one phase to 40-50 hours in the last phase. This is a new product and limited data are available on its use, particularly in pediatrics. The pharmaceutical manufacture states that it was found in rodent milk, no data are available for human milk. Regardless, the oral bioavailability is reported as poor and it is unlikely an infant would absorb enough to be clinically relevant but this is only speculative.

Pregnancy Risk Category: C

Lactation Risk Category: L3

Theoretic Infant Dose:

Adult Concerns: Fever, nausea, vomiting, flushing, phlebitis, anemia, headache, etc.

Pediatric Concerns: None reported via milk. Not cleared for pediatric patients.

Drug Interactions: Cyclosporin increases AUC of Cancidas. Do not use with cyclosporin unless potential benefits outweighs risk. Cancidas reduces plasma levels of tacrolimus.

Alternatives:

Adult Dosage: 70 mg STAT, 50 mg/d

T½ = > 11 hours		M/P =
PHL =		PB = 97%
PK =		Oral = Poor
MW = 1213		pKa = 5.1, 10.7
Vd =		

References:
1.   Pharmaceutical manufacturers package insert, 2001.

CASTOR OIL

Trade: Alphamul, Neoloid, Emulsoil
Can/Aus/UK: Castrol Oil, Exzem Oil, Seda-rash
Uses: Laxative
AAP: Not reviewed

Castor oil is converted to ricinoleic acid in the gut. Its transfer into milk is unknown. Caution should be used. Excess amounts could produce diarrhea, insomnia and tremors in exposed infants.

Pregnancy Risk Category: X

Lactation Risk Category: L3

Theoretic Infant Dose:

Adult Concerns: Insomnia, tremors, diarrhea.

Pediatric Concerns: Observe for diarrhea, insomnia, tremors in infants.

Drug Interactions:

Alternatives:

Adult Dosage: N/A

T½ =		M/P =
PHL =		PB =
PK = 2-3 hours.		Oral = Unknown
MW = 932		pKa =
Vd =		

CEFACLOR

Trade: Ceclor
Can/Aus/UK: Apo-Cefaclor, Ceclor, Distaclor, Keflor
Uses: Cephalosporin antibiotic
AAP: Not reviewed

Cefaclor is a commonly used pediatric cephalosporin antibiotic. Small amounts are known to be secreted into human milk. Following a 500 mg oral dose, milk levels averaged 0.16 to 0.21 mg/L.[1]   See cephalosporins.

Pregnancy Risk Category: B

Lactation Risk Category: L2

Theoretic Infant Dose: 3.15 μg/kg/day

Adult Concerns: Diarrhea, GI irritation, rash, penicillin allergy, delayed serum sickness at 14 days.

Pediatric Concerns: None reported via milk.

Drug Interactions: Probenecid may increase levels of cephalosporins by reducing renal clearance.

Alternatives:

Adult Dosage: 250-500 mg q 8 hours

T½ = 0.5-1 hour	M/P =
PHL =	PB = 25%
PK = 0.5-1 hour	Oral = 100%
MW = 386	pKa =
Vd =	

References:
1. Takase Z. Clinical and laboratory studies of cefaclor in the field of obstetrics and gynecology. Chemotherapy 27:(Suppl)668, 1979.

CEFADROXIL

Trade: Ultracef, Duricef
Can/Aus/UK: Baxan, Duricef
Uses: Cephalosporin antibiotic
AAP: Approved by the American Academy of Pediatrics for use in breastfeeding mothers

Cefadroxil is a typical first-generation cephalosporin antibiotic. Small amounts are known to be secreted into milk. Milk concentrations following a 1000 mg oral dose were 0.10 mg/L at 1 hour and 1.24 mg/L at 5 hours.[1] Milk/serum ratios were 0.009 at 1 hour and 0.019 at 3 hours.

In a study of 2-3 patients who received an oral dose of 500 mg cefadroxil, milk levels peaked at 4 hours at an average of 0.4 mg/L.[2] The milk/plasma ratio was 0.085.

Pregnancy Risk Category: B

Lactation Risk Category: L1

Theoretic Infant Dose: 0.2 mg/kg/day

Adult Concerns: Diarrhea, allergic rash.

Pediatric Concerns: None reported via milk. Observe for GI symptoms such as diarrhea.

Drug Interactions: Probenecid may decrease clearance. Furosemide, aminoglycosides may enhance renal toxicity.

Alternatives:

Adult Dosage: 0.5-1 g BID

T½ = 1.5 hours	M/P = 0.009-0.019
PHL=	PB = 20%
PK = 1-2 hours	Oral = 100%
MW = 381	pKa =
Vd =	

References:
1. Kafetzi D, Siafas C, et.al. Passage of cephalosporins and amoxicillin into the breast milk. Acta. Paediatr. Scand. 70:285-8, 1981.
2. Matsuda S. Transfer of antibiotics into maternal milk. Biol Res Pregnancy Perinatol. 5(2):57-60, 1984.

CEFAZOLIN

Trade: Ancef, Kefzol
Can/Aus/UK: Ancef, Cefamezin, Kefzol
Uses: Cephalosporin antibiotic
AAP: Approved by the American Academy of Pediatrics for use in breastfeeding mothers

Cefazolin is a typical first-generation cephalosporin antibiotic that has adult and pediatric indications. It is only used IM or I.V., never orally. In 20 patients who received a 2 gm STAT dose over 10 minutes, the average concentration of cefazolin in milk in 2, 3, and 4 hours after the dose was 1.25, 1.51, and 1.16 mg/L, respectively.[1] A very small milk/plasma ratio (0.023) indicates insignificant transfer into milk.

Cefazolin is poorly absorbed orally, therefore the infant would absorb a minimal amount. Plasma levels in infants are reported to be too small to be detected.

Pregnancy Risk Category: B

Lactation Risk Category: L1

Theoretic Infant Dose: 0.2 mg/kg/day

Adult Concerns: Allergic rash, thrush, diarrhea.

Pediatric Concerns: None reported via milk. Observe for GI symptoms such as diarrhea.

Drug Interactions: Probenecid may decrease clearance. Furosemide, aminoglycosides may enhance renal toxicity.

Alternatives:

Adult Dosage: 250-2000 mg TID

T½ = 1.2-2.2 hours	M/P = 0.023
PHL=	PB = 89%
PK = 1-2 hours	Oral = Poor
MW = 455	pKa =
Vd =	

References:
1. Yoshioka H, Cho K, Takimoto M et.al. Transfer of cefazolin into human milk. J. Pediatr. 94:151-2, 1979.

CEFDINIR

Trade: Omnicef
Can/Aus/UK:
Uses: Antibiotic
AAP: Not reviewed

Cefdinir is a broad spectrum cephalosporin antibiotic. Following administration of a 600 mg oral dose, no cefdinir was detected in human milk.

Pregnancy Risk Category: B

Lactation Risk Category: L2

Theoretic Infant Dose:

Adult Concerns: Similar for other cephalosporins, and include diarrhea, vaginal moniliasis, nausea, and rash. Allergic reactions are possible.

Pediatric Concerns: None reported via milk. Milk levels virtually undetectable.

Drug Interactions: Reduced oral absorption following use of antacids. Probenecid will decrease renal excretion and a 54% increase in peak levels, and a 50% prolongation of clearance.

Alternatives:

Adult Dosage: 14 mg/kg/day

T½ = 1.7 hours	**M/P =**
PHL=	**PB = 70%**
PK = 3 hours	**Oral = 21%**
MW = 395	**pKa =**
Vd = 0.35	

References:
1. Pharmaceutical Manufacturer package insert, 2000.

CEFDITOREN

Trade: Spectracef
Can/Aus/UK:
Uses: Cephalosporin antibiotic
AAP: Not reviewed

Cefditoren is a new third generation cephalosporin antibiotic that is indicated in the treatment of acute bacterial exacerbations of chronic bronchitis, pharyngitis, tonsillitis, and uncomplicated skin infections. It is moderately active against resistant penicillin-resistant pneumococcus. It is cleared for use in children < 12 years of age. No data on breastmilk levels are available.

Pregnancy Risk Category: B

Lactation Risk Category: L3

Theoretic Infant Dose:

Adult Concerns: Diarrhea, nausea, headache, vaginal moniliasis.

Pediatric Concerns: None reported.

Drug Interactions:

Alternatives: Cephalexin

Adult Dosage:

T½ = 1.3-2 hours	M/P =
PHL=	PB = 88%
PK = 1-3 hours	Oral = 14%
MW = 620	pKa =
Vd = 9.3	

References:
1. Pharmaceutical manufacturers package insert, 2001.

CEFEPIME

Trade: Maxipime
Can/Aus/UK: Maxipime
Uses: Cephalosporin antibiotic
AAP: Not reviewed

Cefepime is a new 'fourth-generation' parenteral cephalosporin. Cefepime is secreted in human milk in small amounts averaging 0.5 μg/mL.[1,2] In a mother consuming 2 gm/d, an infant would ingest approximately 75 μg/kg/d or only approximately 0.3 % of the maternal dose. This amount is too small to produce any clinical symptoms other than possible changes in gut flora.

Pregnancy Risk Category: B

Lactation Risk Category: L2

Theoretic Infant Dose: 75 μg/kg/day

Adult Concerns: Headache, blurred vision, dyspepsia, diarrhea, transient elevation of liver enzymes.

Pediatric Concerns: None reported via milk.

Drug Interactions: May produce additive nephrotoxic effects when used with aminoglycosides.

Alternatives:

Adult Dosage: 1-2 g BID

T½ = 2 hours	M/P = 0.8
PHL=	PB = 16-19%
PK = 0.5-1.5 hours	Oral = Poor
MW = 571	pKa =
Vd = 0.3	

References:
1. Pharmaceutical Manufacturers Package Insert, 1997.
2. Sanders CC: Cefepime: the next generation? Clin Infect Dis 17:369-379, 1993.

CEFIXIME

Trade: Suprax
Can/Aus/UK: Suprax
Uses: Cephalosporin antibiotic
AAP: Not reviewed

Cefixime is an oral third-generation cephalosporin used in treating infections. It is poorly absorbed (30-50%) by the oral route. It is secreted to a limited degree in the milk, although in one study of a mother receiving 100 mg, it was undetected in the milk from 1-6 hours after the dose.[1]

Pregnancy Risk Category: B

Lactation Risk Category: L2

Theoretic Infant Dose:

Adult Concerns: Allergic rash, diarrhea, thrush.

Pediatric Concerns: None reported. Observe for GI symptoms such as diarrhea.

Drug Interactions: Probenecid may decrease clearance. Furosemide, aminoglycosides may enhance renal toxicity.

Alternatives:

Adult Dosage: 200 mg BID

T½ = 7 hours	M/P =
PHL =	PB = 70%
PK = 2-6 hours	Oral = 30-50%
MW = 453	pKa =
Vd =	

References:
1. Pharmaceutical Manufacturers Package Insert, 1996.

CEFOPERAZONE SODIUM

Trade: Cefobid
Can/Aus/UK: Cefobid, Dicapen
Uses: Cephalosporin antibiotic
AAP: Not reviewed

Cefoperazone is a broad spectrum third-generation cephalosporin antibiotic. It is poorly absorbed from the GI tract and is only available via I.V. and IM injection. Cefoperazone is extremely labile in acid environments which would account both for its destruction and its lack of absorption via the GI tract. Following an I.V. dose of 1000 mg, milk levels ranged from 0.4 to 0.9 mg/L.[1] In a study of 2-3 women who received 1000 mg I.V., the maximum milk concentration was 0.4 mg/L at 6 hours.[2] The average milk/plasma ratio was 0.12 at 4 hours. Cefoperazone is extremely acid labile and would be destroyed in the GI tract of an infant. It is unlikely that significant absorption would occur.

Pregnancy Risk Category: B

Lactation Risk Category: L2

Theoretic Infant Dose: 0.1 mg/kg/day

Adult Concerns: Diarrhea, allergic rash, thrush.

Pediatric Concerns: None reported. Observe for GI symptoms such as diarrhea.

Drug Interactions: Probenecid may decrease clearance. Furosemide, aminoglycosides may enhance renal toxicity.

Alternatives:

Adult Dosage: 1-2 g BID

T½ = **2 hours**	M/P = **0.12**
PHL= **6-10 hours(neonatal)**	PB = **82-93%**
PK = **73-153 min.(IV)**	Oral = **Poor**
MW = **645**	pKa =
Vd =	

References:
1. Personal Communication. Pfizer/Roerig Laboratories . 1996.
2. Matsuda S. Transfer of antibiotics into maternal milk. Biol Res Pregnancy Perinatol. 5(2):57-60, 1984.

CEFOTAXIME

Trade: Claforan
Can/Aus/UK: Claforan
Uses: Cephalosporin antibiotic
AAP: Approved by the American Academy of Pediatrics for use in breastfeeding mothers

Cefotaxime is poorly absorbed orally and is only used via I.V. or IM administration. Milk levels following a 1000 mg I.V. maternal dose were 0.26 mg/L at 1 hour, 0.32 mg/L at 2 hours, and 0.30 mg/L at 3 hours.[1] No effect on infant or lactation were noted. Milk/serum ratio at 3 hours was 0.160.

In a group of 2-3 patients receiving 1000 mg I.V., none to trace amounts were found in milk after 6 hours.[2]

Pregnancy Risk Category: B

Lactation Risk Category: L2

Theoretic Infant Dose: 48 μg/kg/day

Adult Concerns: Diarrhea, allergic rash, thrush.

Pediatric Concerns: None reported. Observe for GI symptoms such as diarrhea.

Drug Interactions: Probenecid may decrease clearance. Furosemide, aminoglycosides may enhance renal toxicity.

Alternatives:

Adult Dosage: 1-2 g q BID

T½ = < 0.68 hour	**M/P = 0.027 - 0.17**
PHL= 2-3.5 hours	**PB = 40%**
PK = 30 min.	**Oral = Poor**
MW = 455	**pKa =**
Vd –	

References:
1.   Kafetzis DA, et.al. Transfer of cefotaxime in human milk and from mother to foetus. J. Antimicrob. Chemother. 6:135-41(Suppl), 1980.
2.   Matsuda S. Transfer of antibiotics into maternal milk.   Biol Res Pregnancy Perinatol. 5(2):57-60, 1984.

CEFOTETAN

Trade: Cefotan
Can/Aus/UK: Apatef, Cefotan
Uses: Cephalosporin antibiotic
AAP: Not reviewed

Cefotetan is a third generation cephalosporin that is poorly absorbed orally and is only available via IM and I.V. injection. The drug is distributed into human milk in low concentrations. Following a maternal dose of 1000mg IM every 12 hours in 5 patients, breastmilk concentrations ranged from 0.29 to 0.59 mg/L.[1] Plasma concentrations were almost 100 times higher.

In a group of 2-3 women who received 1000 mg I.V., the maximum average milk level reported was 0.2 mg/L at 4 hours with a milk/plasma ratio of 0.02.[2]

Pregnancy Risk Category: B

Lactation Risk Category: L2

Theoretic Infant Dose: 0.1 mg/kg/day

Adult Concerns: Diarrhea, allergic rash, thrush.

Pediatric Concerns: None reported. Observe for GI symptoms such as diarrhea.

Drug Interactions: Probenecid may decrease clearance. Furosemide, aminoglycosides may enhance renal toxicity.

Alternatives:

Adult Dosage: 1-2 g BID

T½ = 3-4.6 hours	M/P =
PHL=	PB = 76-91%
PK = 1.5-3 hours.	Oral = Poor
MW = 576	pKa =
Vd =	

References:
1. Novelli A. et.al. The penetration of intramuscular cefotetan disodium into human esta-vascular fluid and maternal milk secretion. Chemoterapia II(5): 337-342,1983.
2. Matsuda S. Transfer of antibiotics into maternal milk.   Biol Res Pregnancy Perinatol. 5(2):57-60, 1984.

CEFOXITIN

Trade: Mefoxin
Can/Aus/UK: Mefoxin
Uses: Cephalosporin antibiotic
AAP: Approved by the American Academy of Pediatrics for use in breastfeeding mothers

Cefoxitin is a cephalosporin antibiotic with a spectrum similar to the second generation family. It is transferred into human milk in very low levels. In a study of 18 women receiving 2000-4000 mg doses, only one breastmilk sample contained cefoxitin (0.9 mg/L), all the rest were too low to be detected.[1]

In a study of 2-3 women who received 1000 mg I.V., only trace amounts were reported in milk over 6 hours.[2]

In a group of 5 women who received an IM injection of 2000 mg, milk levels the highest milk levels were reported at 4 hours after dose.[3] The maternal plasma levels varied from 22.5 at 2 hours to 77.6 $\mu g/mL$ at 4 hours. Maternal milk levels ranged from < 0.25 to 0.65 mg/L.

Pregnancy Risk Category: B

Lactation Risk Category: L1

Theoretic Infant Dose: 0.1 mg/kg/day

Adult Concerns: Diarrhea, allergic rash, thrush.

Pediatric Concerns: None reported. Observe for GI symptoms such as diarrhea.

Drug Interactions: Probenecid may decrease clearance. Furosemide, aminoglycosides may enhance renal toxicity.

Alternatives:

Adult Dosage: 1-2 g TID

T½ = 0.7-1.1 hour	**M/P =**
PHL =	**PB = 85-99%**
PK = 20-30 min.(IM)	**Oral = Poor**
MW = 427	**pKa =**
Vd =	

References:
1.   Roex AJM, van Loenen AC, et.al. Secretion of cefoxitin in breast milk following short-term prophylactic administration in caesarean section. Eur. J. Obstet. Gynecol. Reprod. Biol. 25:299-301, 1987.
2.   Matsuda S. Transfer of antibiotics into maternal milk.   Biol Res Pregnancy Perinatol. 5(2):57-60, 1984.
3.   Dresse A, Lambotte R, Dubois M, Delapierre D, Kramp R. Transmammary passage of cefoxitin: additional results. J Clin Pharmacol. 23(10):438-40, 1983.

CEFPODOXIME PROXETIL

Trade: Vantin
Can/Aus/UK: Orelox
Uses: Cephalosporin antibiotic
AAP: Not reviewed

Cefpodoxime is a cephalosporin antibiotic that is subsequently metabolized to an active metabolite. Only 50% is orally absorbed. In a study of 3 lactating women, levels of cefpodoxime in human milk were 0%, 2%, and 6% of maternal serum levels at 4 hours following a 200 mg oral dose.[1] At 6 hours post-dosing, levels were 0%, 9%, and 16% of concomitant maternal serum levels. Pediatric indications down to 6 months of age are available.

Pregnancy Risk Category: B

Lactation Risk Category: L2

Theoretic Infant Dose:

Adult Concerns: Diarrhea, allergic rash, thrush.

Pediatric Concerns: None reported. Observe for GI symptoms such as diarrhea.

Drug Interactions: Probenecid may decrease clearance. Furosemide, aminoglycosides may enhance renal toxicity. Antacids and H2 blockers reduce GI absorption of cefpodoxime.

Alternatives:

Adult Dosage: 100-400 mg BID

T½ = 2.09-2.84 hours	M/P = 0-0.16
PHL=	PB = 22-33%
PK = 2-3 hours	Oral = 50%
MW = 558	pKa =
Vd =	

References:
1. Pharmaceutical Manufacturers Package Insert, 1996.

CEFPROZIL

Trade: Cefzil
Can/Aus/UK:
Uses: Oral cephalosporin antibiotic
AAP: Approved by the American Academy of Pediatrics for use in breastfeeding mothers

Cefprozil is a typical second-generation cephalosporin antibiotic. Following an oral dose of 1000 mg, the breastmilk concentrations were 0.7, 2.5, and 3.4 mg/L at 2, 4, and 6 hours post-dose respectively. The peak milk concentration occurred at 6 hours, and was lower thereafter.[1] Milk/plasma ratios varied from 0.05 at 2 hours to 5.67 at 12 hours. However, the milk concentration at 12 hours was small (1.3 μg/ml). Using the highest concentration found in breastmilk (3.5 mg/L) an infant consuming 800 ml of milk daily would ingest about 2.8 mg of cefprozil daily or less than 0.3% of the maternal dose. Because the dose used in this study is approximately twice that normally used, it is reasonable to assume that an infant would ingest less than 1.7 mg per day, an amount clinically insignificant. Pediatric indications for infants 6 months and older are available.

Pregnancy Risk Category: C

Lactation Risk Category: L1

Theoretic Infant Dose: 0.5 mg/kg/day

Adult Concerns: Diarrhea, allergic rash, and thrush.

Pediatric Concerns: None reported. Observe for GI symptoms such as diarrhea.

Drug Interactions: Probenecid may decrease clearance. Furosemide, aminoglycosides may enhance renal toxicity.

Alternatives:

Adult Dosage: 250 mg BID

T½ = 78 minutes		M/P = 0.05 - 5.67	
PHL =		PB = 36 %	
PK = 1.5 hours		Oral = Complete	
MW =		pKa =	
Vd =			

References:
1. Shyu WC, et.al. Excretion of cefprozil into human breast milk. Antimic. Agents & Chemo. 36(5):938-41,1992

CEFTAZIDIME

Trade: Ceftazidime, Fortaz, Tazidime, Ceptaz
Can/Aus/UK: Ceptaz, Fortaz, Fortum
Uses: Cephalosporin antibiotic
AAP: Approved by the American Academy of Pediatrics for use in breastfeeding mothers

Ceftazidime is a broad spectrum third-generation cephalosporin antibiotic. Is has poor oral absorption (<10%). In lactating women who received 2000 mg (IV) every 8 hours for 5 days, concentrations of ceftazidime in milk averaged 3.8 mg/L before the dose and 5.2 mg/L at 1 hour after the dose, and 4.5 mg/L 3 hours after the dose.[1] There is, however, no progressive accumulation of ceftazidime in breastmilk, as evidenced by the similar levels prior to, and after seven doses. The therapeutic dose for neonates is 30-50 mg/kg every 12 hours

Pregnancy Risk Category: B

Lactation Risk Category: L1

Theoretic Infant Dose: 0.8 mg/kg/day

Adult Concerns: Diarrhea, allergic rash, thrush.

Pediatric Concerns: None reported. Observe for GI symptoms such as diarrhea.

Drug Interactions: Probenecid may decrease clearance. Furosemide, aminoglycosides may enhance renal toxicity.

Alternatives:

Adult Dosage: 500-2000 mg BID

T½ = 1.4-2 hours	M/P =
PHL = 2.2-4.7 hours(neonates)	PB = 5-24%
PK = 69-90 min.	Oral = < 10%
MW = 547	pKa =
Vd =	

References:
1. Blanco JD et.al. Ceftazidime levels in human breast milk. Antimicro. Agents and Chemotherapy 23:479-480, 1983.

CEFTIBUTEN

Trade: Cedax
Can/Aus/UK: Cedax
Uses: Cephalosporin antibiotic
AAP: Not reviewed

Ceftibuten is a broad spectrum third generation oral cephalosporin antibiotic. No data yet available on penetration into human breastmilk.[1] Small to moderate amounts may penetrate into milk, but ceftibuten is cleared for pediatric use.[2] Its strength is in activity against gram negative species. Its weakness is in coverage for staphylococci, and strep. pneumonia infections (which cause many inner ear infections).

Pregnancy Risk Category: B

Lactation Risk Category: L2

Theoretic Infant Dose:

Adult Concerns: Diarrhea, vomiting, loose stools, abdominal pain.

Pediatric Concerns: None reported. Observe for GI symptoms such as diarrhea.

Drug Interactions: Probenecid may decrease clearance. Furosemide, aminoglycosides may enhance renal toxicity.

Alternatives:

Adult Dosage: 400 mg QD

T½ = 2.4 hours.	M/P =
PHL= 2-3 hours.	PB = 65%
PK = 2.6 hours.	Oral = High
MW = 410	pKa =
Vd =	

References:
1. Pharmaceutical manufactures package insert, 1996.
2. Barr WH, et.al. Pharmacokinetids of ceftibuten in children. Pediatr. Infect. Dis. J. 14:S93-101, 1995.

CEFTRIAXONE

Trade: Rocephin
Can/Aus/UK: Rocephin
Uses: Cephalosporin antibiotic
AAP: Approved by the American Academy of Pediatrics for use in breastfeeding mothers

Ceftriaxone is a very popular third-generation broad spectrum cephalosporin antibiotic. Small amounts are transferred into milk (3-4% of maternal serum level). Following a 1 gm IM dose, breastmilk levels were approximately 0.5-0.7 mg/L at between 4-8 hours.[1,2] The estimated mean milk levels at steady state were 3-4 mg/L. Another source indicates that following a 2 g/d dose and at steady state, approximately 4.4 % of dose penetrates into milk.[3] In this study, the maximum breastmilk concentration was 7.89 mg/L after prolonged therapy (7days). Using this data, the weight-adjusted relative infant dose would only be 0.35% of the maternal dose. Poor oral absorption of ceftriaxone would further limit systemic absorption by the infant. The half-life of ceftriaxone in human milk varies from 12.8 to 17.3 hours (longer than maternal serum). Even at this high dose, no adverse effects were noted in the infant.

Ceftriaxone levels in breastmilk are probably too low to be clinically relevant, except for changes in GI flora. Ceftriaxone is commonly used in neonates.

Pregnancy Risk Category: B

Lactation Risk Category: L2

Theoretic Infant Dose: 1.2 mg/kg/day

Adult Concerns: Diarrhea, allergic rash, pseudomembranous colitis, thrush.

Pediatric Concerns: None reported. Observe for GI symptoms such as diarrhea.

Drug Interactions: Probenecid may decrease clearance. Furosemide, aminoglycosides may enhance renal toxicity.

Alternatives:

Adult Dosage: 1-2 g QD-BID

T½ = 7.3 hours	M/P = 0.03
PHL=	PB = 95%
PK = 1 hour	Oral = Poor
MW = 555	pKa =
Vd =	

References:
1. Kefetzis DA, Siafas CA, Georgakopoulous PA, et.al. Passage of cephalosporins and amoxicillin into the breast milk. Acta Paediatr Scan 70:285-286,1981.
2. Kafetzis DA, Brater DC, Fanourgakis JE, et.al. Ceftriaxone distribution between maternal blood and fetal blood and tissues at parturition and between blood and milk postpartum. Antimicrob Agents Chemother. 23:870-873,1983.
3. Bourget P, et.al. Ceftriaxone distribution and protein binding between maternal blood and milk postpartum. Annals of Pharmaco. 27:294-7, 1993.

CEFUROXIME

Trade: Ceftin, Zinacef, Kefurox
Can/Aus/UK: Ceftin, Zinacef, Zinnat
Uses: Cephalosporin antibiotic
AAP: Not reviewed

Cefuroxime is a broad spectrum second generation cephalosporin antibiotic that is available orally and I.V.   The manufacturer states that it is secreted into human milk in small amounts, but the levels are not available.[1]   Thus far, no untoward effects in infants have been reported.   Cefuroxime has a very bitter taste.   The I.V. salt form, cefuroxime sodium is very poorly absorbed orally.   Only the axetil salt form is orally bioavailable.

Pregnancy Risk Category: B

Lactation Risk Category: L2

Theoretic Infant Dose:

Adult Concerns: Nausea, vomiting, diarrhea, GI distress, skin rash, allergies.

Pediatric Concerns: None reported. Observe for GI symptoms such as diarrhea.

Drug Interactions: Probenecid may decrease clearance. Furosemide, aminoglycosides may enhance renal toxicity.

Alternatives:

Adult Dosage: 250-500 mg BID

T½ = 1.4 hours	M/P =
PHL=	PB = 33-50%
PK =	Oral = 30-50%
MW = 424	pKa =
Vd =	

References:
1.   Pharmaceutical Manufacturers Package Insert, 1995.

CELECOXIB

Trade: Celebrex
Can/Aus/UK:
Uses: NSAID anti-inflammatory
AAP: Not reviewed

Celecoxib is a new anti-inflammatory NSAID that specifically blocks the cyclooxygenase-2 (COX-2) enzyme.   It is primarily used for arthritic or inflammatory pain.[1]   Due to its new introduction, we do not have data available on its transfer to human milk. Studies in rodents suggest that milk levels are similar to plasma levels (or a M/P ratio of about 1).   The peak plasma concentration is 705 μg/L. Assuming an infant ingests 150 ml/kg/day at an M/P ratio of 1.0, then the estimated dose would be about 105 μg/kg body weight per day. This would be about 3.6% of the weight adjusted maternal dose.   It is not likely this would be detrimental to an infant, but we do not know this for sure.

Pregnancy Risk Category: C

Lactation Risk Category: L3

Theoretic Infant Dose:

Adult Concerns: GI distress, diarrhea, dyspepsia, headache, aggravated hypertension and asthma.

Pediatric Concerns: None reported via milk.

Drug Interactions: Celecoxib may significantly diminish antihypertensive effects of ACE inhibitors, and the naturetic effect of furosemide. Fluconazole may increase plasma levels of celecoxib two-fold. Celecoxib may increase lithium levels by 17%.

Alternatives: Ibuprofen

Adult Dosage: 100-400 mg daily

T½ = 11.2 hours	M/P = 1.0 (rodent)
PHL=	PB = 97%
PK = 2.8 hours	Oral =
MW = 381	pKa =
Vd = 5.71	

References:
1.   Pharmaceutical Manufacturers Package Insert, 1999.

CEPHALEXIN

Trade: Keflex
Can/Aus/UK: Apo-Cephalex, Ceporex, Ibilex, Keflex, Novo-Lexin
Uses: Cephalosporin antibiotic
AAP: Not reviewed

Cephalexin is a typical first-generation cephalosporin antibiotic. Only minimal concentrations are secreted into human milk. Following a 1000 mg maternal oral dose, milk levels at 1, 2, 3, 4, and 5 hours ranged from 0.20, 0.28, 0.39, 0.50, and 0.47 mg/L respectively.[1] Milk/serum ratios varied from 0.008 at 1 hour, to 0.140 at 3 hours. These levels are probably too low to be clinically relevant.

In a group of 2-3 patients who received 500 mg orally, milk levels averaged 0.7 mg/L at 4 hours although the average milk level was 0.36 mg/L over 6 hours.[2] The milk/plasma ratio was 0.25.

Pregnancy Risk Category: B

Lactation Risk Category: L1

Theoretic Infant Dose: 0.075 mg/kg/day

Adult Concerns: Diarrhea, allergic rash, thrush.

Pediatric Concerns: None reported. Observe for diarrhea.

Drug Interactions: Probenecid may decrease clearance. Furosemide, aminoglycosides may enhance renal toxicity.

Alternatives:

Adult Dosage: 250-1000 mg q 6 hours

T½ = 50-80 minutes	M/P = 0.008-0.14
PHL=	PB = 10%
PK = 1 hour	Oral = Complete
MW = 347	pKa =
Vd =	

References:
1. Kefetzis DA, Siafas CΛ, Georgakopoulous PA, et.al. Passage of cephalosporins and amoxicillin into the breast milk. Acta Paediatr Scan 70:285-286,1981.
2. Matsuda S. Transfer of antibiotics into maternal milk. Biol Res Pregnancy Perinatol. 5(2):57-60, 1984.

CEPHALOTHIN

Trade: Keflin
Can/Aus/UK: Ceporacin, Keflin
Uses: Cephalosporin antibiotic
AAP: Not reviewed

Cephalothin is a first-generation cephalosporin antibiotic for use by IM or I.V. administration. Following a 1000 mg I.V. maternal dose, milk levels varied from 0.27, 0.41, 0.47, 0.36, and 0.28 mg/L at 0.5, 1, 2, 3, and 4 hours respectively.[1] Milk/serum ratios varied from 0.06 at 1 hour to 0.51 at 3 hours.

Pregnancy Risk Category: B

Lactation Risk Category: L2

Theoretic Infant Dose: 70.5 μg/kg/day

Adult Concerns: Diarrhea, allergic rash, thrush.

Pediatric Concerns: None reported. Observe for diarrhea.

Drug Interactions: Probenecid may decrease clearance. Furosemide, aminoglycosides may enhance renal toxicity.

Alternatives:

Adult Dosage: 500-2000 mg q 4-6 hours

T½ = 30-50 minutes	M/P = 0.06-0.5 1
PHL =	PB = 70%
PK = 1-2 hours	Oral = Poor
MW = 396	pKa =
Vd =	

References:
1. Kefetzis DA, Siafas CA, Georgakopoulous PA, et.al. Passage of cephalosporins and amoxicillin into the breast milk. Acta Paediatr Scan 70:285-286,1981.

CEPHAPIRIN

Trade: Cefadyl
Can/Aus/UK: Cefadyl
Uses: Cephalosporin antibiotic
AAP: Not reviewed

Cephapirin is a typical first-generation cephalosporin antibiotic for IM or I.V. administration. Following a 1000 mg I.V. maternal dose, milk levels varied from 0.26, 0.41, 0.43, 0.33, and 0.27 mg/L at 0.5, 1, 2, 3, and 4 hours respectively.[1] These are too low to be clinically relevant. Milk/serum ratios varied from 0.068 at 1 hour to 0.48 at 3 hours.

Pregnancy Risk Category: B

Lactation Risk Category: L1

Theoretic Infant Dose: 64.5 μg/kg/day

Adult Concerns: Diarrhea, allergic rash, thrush.

Pediatric Concerns: None reported. Observe for GI symptoms such as diarrhea.

Drug Interactions: Probenecid may decrease clearance. Furosemide, aminoglycosides may enhance renal toxicity.

Alternatives:

Adult Dosage: 500-1000 mg q 6 hours

T½ = 24-36 minutes	M/P = 0.068-0.48
PHL =	PB = 54%
PK = 1-2 hours	Oral = Poor
MW = 445	pKa =
Vd =	

References:
1. Kefetzis DA, Siafas CA, Georgakopoulous PA, et.al. Passage of cephalosporins and amoxicillin into the breast milk. Acta Paediatr Scan 70:285-286,1981.

CEPHRADINE

Trade: Velosef, Anspor
Can/Aus/UK: Nicef, Velosef
Uses: Cephalosporin antibiotic
AAP: Not reviewed

Cephradine is typical first-generation cephalosporin antibiotic. In a group of 6 lactating women receiving 500 mg orally every 6 hours for

2 days, milk levels averaged about 0.6 mg/L.[1]   In another study group by this same author, the average milk level was 1.0 mg/L.[2] These levels are too low to be clinically relevant.

Pregnancy Risk Category: B

Lactation Risk Category: L1

Theoretic Infant Dose: 0.2 mg/kg/day

Adult Concerns: Diarrhea, allergic rash, thrush, liver dysfunction.

Pediatric Concerns: None reported. Observe for GI symptoms such as diarrhea.

Drug Interactions: Probenecid may decrease clearance. Furosemide, aminoglycosides may enhance renal toxicity.

Alternatives:

Adult Dosage: 250-500 mg q 6-12 hours

T½ = 0.7-2 hours.	M/P = 0.2
PHL=	PB = 8-17%
PK = 1 hour	Oral = Complete
MW = 349	pKa =
Vd =	

References:
1. Mischler TW, et.al. Cephradine and epicillin in body fluids of lactating and pregnant women. J. Reprod. Med. 21:130-6, 1978.
2. Mischler TW, Corson SL, et.al. Presence of cephradine in body fluids of lactating and pregnant women. Clin. Pharmacol. Ther. 15:214, 1974.

CERIVASTATIN

Trade: Baycol
Can/Aus/UK: Kazak, Lipobay
Uses: Anti-cholesterol drug.
AAP: Not reviewed

Cerivastatin is a typical HMG Co-A reductase inhibitor for lowering plasma cholesterol levels. Based on preclinical data , cerivastatin is present in breastmilk at levels slightly higher than maternal plasma levels.[1]   Milk/plasma ratio was 1.3.   Atherosclerosis is a chronic process and discontinuation of lipid-lowering drugs during pregnancy and lactation should have little to no impact on the outcome of long-term therapy of primary hypercholesterolemia. Cholesterol and other products of cholesterol biosynthesis are essential components for fetal and neonatal development and the use of cholesterol-lowering drugs would not be advisable under any circumstances.

Pregnancy Risk Category: X

Lactation Risk Category: L3

Theoretic Infant Dose:

Adult Concerns: Transient increases in liver enzymes have been reported. Liver function tests are required prior to use. Rare cases of rhabdomyolysis with acute renal failure secondary to myoglobinuria have been reported with other HMG-CoA reductase inhibitors.

Pediatric Concerns: None reported via milk, but use is not recommended.

Drug Interactions:

Alternatives:

Adult Dosage: 0.3 mg daily

T½ = 2-3 hours	M/P = 1.3
PHL=	PB = 99%
PK = 2.5 hours	Oral = 60%
MW = 481	pKa =
Vd = 0.3	

References:
1. Pharmaceutical Manufacturers Package Insert, 1999.

CETIRIZINE

Trade: Zyrtec
Can/Aus/UK: Reactine, Zirtek, Zyrtec
Uses: Antihistamine
AAP: Not reviewed

Cetirizine is a popular new antihistamine useful for seasonal allergic rhinitis. It is a metabolite of hydroxyzine, and is one of the most potent of the antihistamines. It is rapidly and extensively absorbed orally, and due to a rather long half-life is used only once daily. It penetrates the CNS poorly and therefore produces minimal sedation. Compared to other new antihistamines, cetirizine is not very toxic in overdose, and produces few cardiovascular changes at higher doses.[1] Further, as with many other antihistamines, cetirizine has very few drug interactions, alcohol being the main one. Studies in dogs suggests that only 3% of the dose is transferred into milk.[2]

Pregnancy Risk Category: B

Lactation Risk Category: L2

Theoretic Infant Dose:

Adult Concerns: Sedation, fatigue, dry mouth.

Pediatric Concerns: None reported but observe for sedation.

Drug Interactions: Increased sedation with other CNS sedatives, alcohol.

Alternatives:

Adult Dosage: 5-10 mg QD

T½ = 8.3 hours		
PHL = 6.2 hours	M/P =	
PK = 1.7 hour	PB = 93%	
MW = 389	Oral = 70%	
Vd =	pKa =	

References:
1. Pharmaceutical Manufacturers Package Insert, 1996.
2. Pharmaceutical Manufacturer. Personal Communication, 1996.

CHAMOMILE, GERMAN

Trade: Hungarian Chamomile, Sweet False, Wild Chamomile
Can/Aus/UK:
Uses: Anti-inflammatory, carminative
AAP: Not reviewed

Chamomile has been used since Roman times, and is primarily used for its anti-inflammatory, carminative, antispasmodic, mild sedative, and antiseptic properties. It has been used for flatulent dyspepsia, travel sickness, diarrhea, GI irritation.[1] It has been used topically for hemorrhoids and mastitis. Chamomile contains coumarins, flavonoids such as quercetin, rutin, and others. Anti-allergic and anti-inflammatory have been well documented and are due to the azulene components of the volatile oil which inhibit histamine release.[2] Matricin is reported to be a significant anti-inflammatory agent. In humans, German chamomile has been reported to exhibit anti-inflammatory, antipeptic, and anti-spasmodic effects on the stomach.[2] Reports of allergic reactions to chamomile are common, including two cases of anaphylaxis.[3-5] Asthmatics should avoid this product. German chamomile is reported to be uterotonic and teratogenic in rats, rabbits, and dogs, although the dose in these studies was high.[6] This product should be avoided in pregnant and lactating patients.[7]

Pregnancy Risk Category:

Lactation Risk Category: L3

Theoretic Infant Dose:

Adult Concerns: Reports of allergic reactions to chamomile are common, including two cases of anaphylaxis. Asthmatics should avoid this product. German chamomile is reported to be uterotonic and teratogenic in rats, rabbits, and dogs. This product should be avoided in pregnant and lactating patients.

Pediatric Concerns: None reported via milk, but hypersensitization is possible.

Drug Interactions:

Alternatives:

Adult Dosage:

References:
1. Berry M. The chamomiles. Pharm J 254:191-3, 1995.
2. Mann C, Staba EJ. The chemistry, pharmacology, and commercial formulations of chamomile. In: Herbs, spices, and medicinal plants: Recent advances in botany, horticulture, and pharmacology. Vol. 1. Craker LE editor, Arizona:Oryx Press, 1986:235-80.
3. Hausen BM et.al. The sensitizing capacity of Compositae plants. Planta Med 50:229-34, 1984.
4. Casterline CL. Allergy to chamomile tea. JAMA 4:330-1, 1980.
5. Benner MH, Lee HJ. Anaphylactic reaction to chamomile tea. J. Allergy clin. Immunol 52:307-8,1973.
6. Habersang S et.al. Pharmacologic studies with compounds of chamomile. I.V. Studies of toxicity of 9-0-alpha-bisabolol. Planta Med 37:115-23, 1979.
7. Newall C, Anderson LA, Phillipson JD. Chamomile, German. In. Herbal Medicine. A guide for the health-care professionals. The Pharmaceutical Press, London, 1996.

CHLORAL HYDRATE

Trade: Aquachloral, Noctec
Can/Aus/UK: Dormel, Elix-Nocte, Noctec, Nortec, Novo-Chlorhydrate
Uses: Sedative, hypnotic
AAP: Approved by the American Academy of Pediatrics for use in breastfeeding mothers

Chloral Hydrate is a sedative hypnotic. Small to moderate amounts are known to be secreted into milk. Mild drowsiness was reported in one infant following administration of dichloralphenazone (1300 mg/d), which is metabolized to the same active metabolite as chloral hydrate. Infant growth and development were reported to be normal. In a study of 50 postpartum women using a 1.3 gm rectal suppository, the average milk concentration of chloral hydrate at 1 hour was 3.2 mg/L.[1] The maximum level found in this study was 15 mg/L in one patient. The oral pediatric sedative dose of chloral hydrate is generally 5-15 mg/kg/dose every 8 hours.[2]

Pregnancy Risk Category: C

Lactation Risk Category: L3

Theoretic Infant Dose: 0.5 mg/kg/day

Adult Concerns: Irritating to mucous membrane, laryngospasm, GI irritation, paradoxical excitement, delirium, hypotension, respiratory depression and sedation.

Pediatric Concerns: None reported via milk, but observe for sedation.

Drug Interactions: May potentiate effects of warfarin, CNS depressants such as alcohol, etc. Use with furosemide (IV) may induce flushing, hypotension.

Alternatives: Alprazolam, midazolam

Adult Dosage: 250 mg TID

T½ = 7-10 hours.	M/P =
PHL=	PB = 35-41%
PK = 30-60 min.	Oral = Complete
MW = 165	pKa = 10.0
Vd = 0.6	

References:
1. Bernstine JB, et. al. Maternal blood and breast milk estimation following the administration of chloral hydrate during the puerperium. J Obstet Gynecol Br Emp 63:228-31, 1956.
2. Johnson KB, ed. The Harriet Lane Handbook, Thirthteenth Edition, Mosby, 1993, p. 407.

CHLORAMBUCIL

Trade: Leukeran
Can/Aus/UK: Leukeran
Uses: Antineoplastic compound
AAP: Not reviewed

Chlorambucil is an antineoplastic, anticancer agent.[1] No data are available on concentrations secreted into human milk. This product would be extremely dangerous to growing infants and is probably contraindicated in nursing mothers.

Pregnancy Risk Category: D

Lactation Risk Category: L5

Theoretic Infant Dose:

Adult Concerns: Hepatotoxicity with jaundice. Pulmonary fibrosis, seizures, pneumonia.

Pediatric Concerns: None reported via milk, but due to overt toxicity, breastfeeding is discouraged.

Drug Interactions:

Alternatives:

Adult Dosage: 0.1-0.2 mg/kg QD

T½ = 1.3 hours	M/P =
PHL =	PB = 99%
PK = 1 hour.	Oral = 80%
MW = 304	pKa =
Vd = 0.14-0.24	

References:
1. Drug Facts and Comparisons. 1995 ed. Facts and Comparisons, St. Louis.

CHLORAMPHENICOL

Trade: Chloromycetin
Can/Aus/UK: Ak-Chlor, Biocetin, Chloromycetin, Chloroptic, Chlorsig, Sopamycetin
Uses: Antibiotic
AAP: Drug whose effect on nursing infants is unknown but may be of concern

Chloramphenicol is a broad spectrum antibiotic. In one study of 5 women receiving 250 mg PO four times daily, the concentration of chloramphenicol in milk ranged from 0.54 to 2.84 mg/L.[1] In the same study but in another group receiving 500 mg four times daily, the concentration of chloramphenicol in milk ranged from 1.75 to 6.10 mg/L. In a group of patients being treated for typhus, milk levels were lower than maternal plasma levels.[2] With maternal plasma levels of 49 and 26 mg/L in two patients, the milk levels were 26 and 16 mg/L respectively.

In a study of 2-3 patients who received a single 500 mg oral dose, the average milk concentration at 4 hours was 4.1 mg/L.[3] The milk/plasma ratio at 4 hours was 0.84. Safety in infants is highly controversial. Milk levels are too low to produce overt toxicity in infants, but could produce allergic sensitization to subsequent exposures. Generally chloramphenicol is considered contraindicated in nursing mothers, although it is occasionally used in infants. This antibiotic can be extremely toxic, particularly in newborns, and should not be used for trivial infections. Blood levels should be constantly monitored and kept below 20 μg/ml.

Pregnancy Risk Category: C

Lactation Risk Category: L4

Theoretic Infant Dose: 0.9 mg/kg/day

Adult Concerns: Numerous blood dyscrasias, aplastic anemia, fever, skin rashes.

Pediatric Concerns: None reported via milk

Drug Interactions: Phenobarbital and rifampin may reduce plasma levels of chloramphenicol.   Chloramphenicol inhibits metabolism of chlorpropamide, phenytoin, and oral anticoagulants.

Alternatives:

Adult Dosage: 50-100 mg/kg QD divided q 6 hours

T½ = 4 hours	M/P = 0.5-0.6
PHL = 22 hours(neonates)	PB = 53%
PK = 1 hour.	Oral = Complete
MW = 323	pKa = 5.5
Vd = 0.57	

References:
1.   Havelka J, Hejzlar M, et.al. Excretion of chloramphenicol in human milk. Chemotherapy 13:204-211, 1968.
2.   Smadel JE, Woodward TE, et.al. Chloramphenicol in the treatment of tsutsugamushi disease. J. Clin. Invest. 28:1196-1215, 1949.
3.   Matsuda S. Transfer of antibiotics into maternal milk.   Biol Res Pregnancy Perinatol. 5(2):57-60, 1984.

CHLORDIAZEPOXIDE

Trade: Librium, Libritabs, Solium
Can/Aus/UK: Amitrol, Apo-Chlordiazepoxide, Librium, Medilium
Uses: Antianxiety, benzodiazepine sedative
AAP: Not reviewed

Chlordiazepoxide is an older benzodiazepine that belongs to the Valium family. It is secreted in breastmilk in moderate but unreported levels.[1] See Diazepam.

Pregnancy Risk Category: D

Lactation Risk Category: L3

Theoretic Infant Dose:

Adult Concerns: Sedation.

Pediatric Concerns: Observe for sedation.

Drug Interactions: Increased CNS sedation when used with other sedative-hypnotics. May increase risk when used with anticoagulants, alcohol, tricyclic antidepressants, MAO inhibitors.

Alternatives: Alprazolam

Adult Dosage: 15-100 mg q 6-8 hours

T½ = 5-30 hours	M/P =
PHL =	PB = 90-98%
PK = 1-4 hours	Oral = Complete
MW = 300	pKa = 4.8
Vd = 0.3-0.5	

References:
1. Pharmaceutical Manufacturers Package Insert, 1996.

CHLORHEXIDINE

Trade: Peridex, Bactoshield, Betasept, Dyna-hex, Hibiclens
Can/Aus/UK: Bactigras, Hexol, Hibitane, Peridex, Savlon
Uses: Lozenge antimicrobial
AAP: Not reviewed

Chlorhexidine is a topical antimicrobial used in oral lozenges. It is poorly absorbed in humans and is not likely to cause untoward effects in nursing infant due to poor oral absorption by mother and infant as well.[1]

Pregnancy Risk Category: B

Lactation Risk Category: L2

Theoretic Infant Dose:

Adult Concerns: Staining of teeth and dentures. Keep out of eyes. Changes in taste, increased plaque, staining of tongue.

Pediatric Concerns: None reported via milk.

Drug Interactions:

Alternatives:

Adult Dosage: N/A

T½ = < 4 hours	M/P =
PHL =	PB =
PK =	Oral = Poor
MW = 505	pKa =
Vd =	

References:
1. Lacy C. et.al. Drug information handbook. Lexi-Comp Inc. Cleveland OH 1996.

CHLOROQUINE

Trade: Aralen, Novo-chloroquine
Can/Aus/UK: Aralen, Avloclor, Chlorquin
Uses: Antimalarial
AAP: Approved by the American Academy of Pediatrics for use in breastfeeding mothers

Chloroquine is an antimalarial drug. Following 5mg/kg IM injection in lactating mothers 17 days postpartum, milk levels averaged 0.227 mg/L.[1] In this study the milk level of chloroquine in 6 patients ranged from 0.192 to 0.319 mg/L. Based on these levels, the infant would consume approximately 34 μg/kg/day, an amount considered safe. Other studies have shown absorption to vary from 2.2 to 4.2% of maternal dose.[2] The breastmilk concentration of chloroquine in this study averaged 0.58 mg/L following a single dose of 600 mg. Current recommended pediatric dose for patients exposed to malaria is 8.3 mg/kg per week. Pediatric patients are exceedingly sensitive to chloroquine. If used children should be closely monitored.

Pregnancy Risk Category: C

Lactation Risk Category: L3

Theoretic Infant Dose: 34.1 μg/kg/day

Adult Concerns: Ocular disturbances including blindness, skin lesions, headache, fatigue, nervousness, hypotension, neutropenia, aplastic anemia.

Pediatric Concerns: None reported but close observation is required. Observe for diarrhea, GI distress, hypotension.

Drug Interactions: Decreased oral absorption if used with kaolin and magnesium trisilicate. Increased toxicity if used with cimetidine.

Alternatives:

Adult Dosage: 300-600 mg q day

T½ = 72-120 hours	M/P = 0.358
PHL =	PB = 61%
PK = 1-2 hours.	Oral = Complete
MW = 320	pKa = 8.4, 10.8
Vd = 116-285	

References:
1. Akintonwa A, et.al. Placental and milk transfer of chloraquine in humans.

Ther. Drug. Mon. 10:147-149, 1988.

2. Edstein MD, Veenendaal JR, Newman K. et.al. Excretion of chloroquine, dapsone and pyrimethamine in human milk. Br. J. Clin. Pharmacol. 22:733-735, 1986.

CHLOROTHIAZIDE

Trade: Hydro-Diuril
Can/Aus/UK: Chlotride, Saluric
Uses: Diuretic
AAP: Approved by the American Academy of Pediatrics for use in breastfeeding mothers

Chlorothiazide is a typical thiazide diuretic. In one study of 11 lactating women, each receiving 500 mg of chlorothiazide, the concentrations in milk samples taken one, two, and three hours after the dose were all less than 1 mg/L with a milk/plasma ratio of 0.05.[1] Although thiazide diuretics are reported to produce thrombocytopenia in nursing infants, it is remote and unsubstantiated. Most thiazide diuretics are considered compatible with breastfeeding if doses are kept low and milk production is unaffected.

Pregnancy Risk Category: D

Lactation Risk Category: L3

Theoretic Infant Dose: 0.2 mg/kg/day

Adult Concerns: Fluid loss, dehydration, lethargy.

Pediatric Concerns: None reported but observe for reduced milk production.

Drug Interactions: NSAIDs may reduce hypotensive effect of chlorothiazide. Cholestyramine resins may reduce absorption of chlorothiazide. Diuretics reduce efficacy of oral hypoglycemics. May reduce lithium clearance leading to high levels. May elevate digoxin levels.

Alternatives:

Adult Dosage: 500-2000 mg q 12-24 hours

T½ = 1.5 hours	M/P = 0.05
PHL=	PB = 95%.
PK = 1 hour.	Oral = 20%
MW = 296	pKa = 6.7, 9.5
Vd =	

References:
1.   Werthman MW, Krees SV. Excretion of chlorothiazide in human breast milk. J. Pediatr. 81:781-3,1972.

CHLORPHENIRAMINE

Trade: Aller Chlor, Chlor-Tripolon, Chlor-Trimeton
Can/Aus/UK: Alunex, Chlor-Tripolon, Demazin, Piridon
Uses: Antihistamine
AAP: Not reviewed

Chlorpheniramine is a commonly used antihistamine. Although no data are available on secretion into breastmilk, it has not been reported to produce side effects. Sedation is the only likely side effect.[1]

Pregnancy Risk Category: B

Lactation Risk Category: L3

Theoretic Infant Dose:

Adult Concerns: Sedation, dry mouth.

Pediatric Concerns: None reported but observe for sedation.

Drug Interactions: May increase sedation when used with other CNS depressants such as opiates, tricyclic antidepressants, MAO inhibitors.

Alternatives: Cetirizine, Loratadine

Adult Dosage: 4 mg q 4-6 hours

T½ = 12-43 hours	M/P =
PHL= 9.5-13 hours	PB = 70%
PK = 2-6 hours	Oral = 25-45%
MW = 275	pKa = 9.2
Vd = 5.9	

References:
1.   Paton DM, Webster DR. Clinical pharmacokinetics of H1-receptor antagonists (the antihistamines). Clin. Pharm. 10:477-497, 1985.

CHLORPROMAZINE

Trade: Thorazine, Ormazine
Can/Aus/UK: Chloractil, Chlorpromanyl, Largactil, Novo-Chlorpromazine
Uses: Tranquilizer
AAP: Drug whose effect on nursing infants is unknown but may be of concern

Chlorpromazine is a powerful CNS tranquilizer.   Small amounts are known to be secreted into milk. Following a 1200 mg oral dose, samples were taken at 60, 120, and 180 minutes.[1] Breastmilk concentrations were highest at 120 minutes and were 0.29 mg/L at that time.   The milk/plasma ratio was less than 0.5. Ayd[2] suggests that in one group of 16 women who took chlorpromazine during and after pregnancy while breastfeeding, the side effects were minimal and infant development was normal. In a group of 4 breastfeeding mothers receiving unspecified amounts of chlorpromazine, milk levels varied from 7 to 98 μg/L.[3] Maternal serum levels ranged from 16 to 52 μg/L Only the infant who ingested milk with a chlorpromazine level of 92 μg/L showed drowsiness and lethargy.

Chlorpromazine has a long half-life and is particularly sedating. Long term use of this product in a lactating mother may be risky to the breastfed infant.   Observer for sedation and lethargy.

Pregnancy Risk Category: C

Lactation Risk Category: L3

Theoretic Infant Dose: 43.5 μg/kg/day

Adult Concerns: Sedation, lethargy, extrapyramidal jerking motion.

Pediatric Concerns: One report of lethargy and sedation.

Drug Interactions: Additive effects when used with other CNS depressants. May increase valproic acid plasma levels.

Alternatives:

Adult Dosage: 200 mg QD

T½ = 30 hours	M/P = <0.5
PHL =	PB = 95%
PK = 1-2 hours.	Oral = Complete
MW = 319	pKa = 9.3
Vd = 10-35	

References:
1.   Blacker KH, Weinstein BJ, et.al. Mothers milk and chlorpromazine. Am. J. Psychol. 114:178-9, 1962.

2. Ayd FJ. Excretion of psychotropic drugs in breast milk. In : International Drug Therapy Newsletter. Ayd Medical Communications. November-December 1973. Vol. 8.
3. Wiles DH, Orr MW, Kolakowska T. Chlorpromazine levels in plasma and milk of nursing mothers. Br. J. Clin. Pharmacol. 5:272-3, 1978.

CHLORPROPAMIDE

Trade: Diabinese
Can/Aus/UK: Apo-Chlorpropamide, Diabinese, Diabinese, Melitase, Novopropamide
Uses: Oral hypoglycemic
AAP: Drug whose effect on nursing infants is unknown but may be of concern

Chlorpropamide stimulates the secretion of insulin in some patients. Following one 500 mg dose, the concentration of chlorpropamide in milk after 5 hours was approximately 5 mg/L of milk.[1] May cause hypoglycemia in infant although effects are largely unknown and unreported.

Pregnancy Risk Category: D

Lactation Risk Category: L3

Theoretic Infant Dose: 0.8 mg/kg/day

Adult Concerns: Hypoglycemia, diarrhea, edema.

Pediatric Concerns: None actually reported, but observe for hypoglycemia although unlikely.

Drug Interactions: Thiazides and hydantoins reduce hypoglycemic effect of chlorpropamide. Chlorpropamide may increase disulfiram effects when used with alcohol. Increases anticoagulant effect when used with warfarin. Sulfonamides may decrease chlorpropamide clearance.

Alternatives:

Adult Dosage: 250-500 mg QD

T½ = 33 hours	M/P =
PHL=	PB = 96%
PK = 3-6 hours	Oral = Complete
MW = 277	pKa = 4.8
Vd = 0.1-0.3	

References:
1. Pharmaceutical Manufacturers Package Insert, 1986.

CHLORPROTHIXENE

Trade: Taractan
Can/Aus/UK: Taractan, Tarasan
Uses: Sedative, tranquilizer.
AAP: Drug whose effect on nursing infants is unknown but may be of concern

Sedative commonly used in psychotic or disturbed patients. Chlorprothixene is poorly absorbed orally (<40%) and has been found to increase serum prolactin levels in mothers. Although the milk/plasma ratios are relatively high, only modest levels of chlorprothixene are actually secreted into human milk. In one patient taking 200 mg/day, maximum milk concentrations of the parent and metabolite were 19 μg/L and 28.5 μg/L respectively.[1] This is approximately 0.1% of the maternal dose.

Pregnancy Risk Category: C

Lactation Risk Category: L3

Theoretic Infant Dose: 4.3 μg/kg/day

Adult Concerns: Sedation, hypotension, pseudoparkinsonian jerking, constipation.

Pediatric Concerns: None reported, but observe for sedation.

Drug Interactions: May reduce effect of guanethidine. May increase effects of alcohol and other CNS sedatives.

Alternatives:

Adult Dosage:

T½ = 8-12 hours	M/P = 1.2-2.6
PHL =	PB =
PK = 4.25 hours	Oral = < 40%
MW = 316	pKa = 8.8
Vd = 11-23	

References:
1. Matheson I, Evang A, Fredricson OK, et.al. Presence of chlorprothixene and its metabolites in breast milk. Eur. J. Clin. Pharm. 27:611, 1984.

CHLORTHALIDONE

Trade: Hygroton
Can/Aus/UK: Apo-Chlorthalidone, Hygroton, Novo-Thalidone
Uses: Diuretic
AAP: Approved by the American Academy of Pediatrics for use in breastfeeding mothers

See hydrochlorothiazide. Avoid if possible. May reduce milk production.

Pregnancy Risk Category: D

Lactation Risk Category: L3

Theoretic Infant Dose:

Adult Concerns: Thrombocytopenia, hypotension, reduction of milk supply.

Pediatric Concerns: None reported via milk, but may reduce milk supply.

Drug Interactions: Reduces hypoglycemic effect of oral sulfonylureas used in diabetics. Increases digoxin related arrhythmias. May increase lithium levels.

Alternatives:

Adult Dosage: 50-100 mg QD

T½ = 54 hours	M/P =
PHL =	PB = 75%
PK =	Oral = Complete
MW = 339	pKa =
Vd =	

References:
1. McEvoy GE(ed):AHFS Drug Information, New York, NY. 1995.

CHOLERA VACCINE

Trade: Cholera Vaccine
Can/Aus/UK:
Uses: Cholera vaccination
AAP: Not reviewed

Cholera vaccine is a sterile solution containing equal parts of phenol inactivated Ogawa and Inaba serotypes of Vibrio cholerae bacteria. Maternal immunization with cholera vaccine significantly increases levels of anti-cholera antibodies (IgA, IgG) in their milk.[1]   It is not contraindicated in nursing mothers. Breastfed infants are generally protected from cholera transmission. Immunization is approved from the age of 6 months and older.

Pregnancy Risk Category: C

Lactation Risk Category: L3

Theoretic Infant Dose:

Adult Concerns: Malaise, fever, headache, pain at injection site.

Pediatric Concerns: None reported.

Drug Interactions: Decreased effect when used with yellow fever vaccine. Wait at least 3 weeks between.

Alternatives:

Adult Dosage: 2 0.5 mL injections (IM or SC) 1 week-month apart

References:
1. Merson MH, et. al. Maternal cholera immunization and secretory IgA in breast milk. Lancet 1:931-2, 1980.

CHOLESTYRAMINE

Trade: Questran, Cholybar
Can/Aus/UK: Novo-Cholamine, Questran
Uses: Cholesterol binding resin
AAP: Not reviewed

Cholestyramine is a bile salt chelating resin. Used orally in adults, it binds bile salts and prevents reabsorption of bile salts in the gut, thus reducing cholesterol plasma levels.[1] This resin is not absorbed from the maternal GI tract, therefore it is not secreted into breastmilk.

Pregnancy Risk Category: C

Lactation Risk Category: L1

Theoretic Infant Dose:

Adult Concerns: Constipation, skin rash, nausea, vomiting, malabsorption, intestinal obstruction.

Pediatric Concerns: None reported via milk.

Drug Interactions: Decreases oral absorption of digoxin, warfarin, thyroid hormones, thiazide diuretics, propranolol, phenobarbital, amiodarone, methotrexate, NSAIDs, and many other drugs.

Alternatives:

Adult Dosage: 16-32 grams/day

References:
1.   Pharmaceutical Manufacturers Package Insert, 1995.

CHONDROITIN SULFATE

Trade: Viscoat
Can/Aus/UK:
Uses: Biologic polymer used for arthritis
AAP: Not reviewed

Chondroitin is a biological polymer that acts as a flexible connecting matrix between the protein filaments in cartilage.   It is derived largely from natural sources such as shark or bovine cartilage and chemically is   composed   of   a   high-viscosity   mucopolysaccharide (glycosaminoglycan) polymer found in most mammalian cartilaginous tissues.[1]   Thus far, chondroitin has been found to be nontoxic.   It's molecular weight averages 50,000 daltons which is far too large to permit its entry into human milk.   Combined with a poor oral bioavailability and large molecular weight, it is unlikely to pose a problem for a breastfed infant.

Pregnancy Risk Category:

Lactation Risk Category: L3

Theoretic Infant Dose:

Adult Concerns: Virtually nontoxic and poorly absorbed orally.

Pediatric Concerns: None reported via milk.

Drug Interactions:

Alternatives:

Adult Dosage:

T½ =	M/P =	
PHL=	PB =	
PK =	Oral = 0-13%	
MW = 50,000	pKa =	
Vd =		

References:
1.   Review of Natural Products. Facts and Comparisons, St. Louis, Mo. 1996.

CHORIONIC GONADOTROPIN

Trade: A.P.L., Chorex-5, Profasi, Gonic, Pregnyl
Can/Aus/UK: APL, Humegon Pregnyl, Pregnyl, Profasi, Profasi HP, Profasik
Uses: Placental hormone
AAP: Not reviewed

Human chorionic gonadotropin (HCG) is a large polypeptide hormone produced by the human placenta with functions similar to luteinizing hormone (LH). Its function is to stimulate the corpus luteum of the ovary to produce progesterone, thus sustaining pregnancy.[1,2] During pregnancy, HCG secreted by the placenta, maintains the corpus luteum, supporting estrogen and progesterone secretion and preventing menstruation.   It is used for multiple purposes including pediatric cryptorchidism, male hypogonadism, and ovulatory failure. HCG has no known effect on fat mobilization, appetite, sense of hunger or body fat distribution. HCG has NOT been found to be effective in treatment of obesity.

Due to the large molecular weight (47,000) of HCG, it would be extremely unlikely penetrate into human milk. Further, it would not be orally bioavailable, due to destruction in the GI tract.

Pregnancy Risk Category: X

Lactation Risk Category: L3

Theoretic Infant Dose:

Adult Concerns: Headache, irritability, restlessness, depression, fatigue, edema, gynecomastia, pain at injection site.

Pediatric Concerns: None reported via milk. Absorption unlikely due to gastric digestion and poor penetration into milk.

Drug Interactions:

Alternatives:

Adult Dosage: 5000-10000 units X 1

T½ = 5.6 hours	M/P =
PHL =	PB =
PK = 6 hours	Oral = 0%
MW = 47,000	pKa =
Vd =	

References:
1.   Drug Facts and Comparisons. 1996. ed. Facts and Comparisons, St. Louis.
2.   Pharmaceutical Manufacturers Package Insert, 1997.

CHROMIUM

Trade: Chromium Picrolinate
Can/Aus/UK:
Uses: Metal supplement
AAP: Not reviewed

Trace metal, required in glucose metabolism. Less than 1% is absorbed following oral administration.   Chromium levels are depleted in multiparous women. Chromium levels in neonate are approximately 2.5 times that of mother, due to concentrating mechanism during gestation. Because chromium is difficult to measure, levels reported vary widely.

One article reports that breastmilk levels are less than 2% of the estimated safe and adequate daily intake of 10 ug (which is probably excessive and needs review).[1] Most importantly, breastmilk levels are independent of dietary intake in mother, and do not apparently increase with increased maternal intake. Chromium is apparently secreted into breastmilk by a well controlled pumping mechanism. Hence, breastmilk levels of chromium are independent of maternal plasma levels. Increased maternal plasma levels may not alter milk chromium levels.

Pregnancy Risk Category: C

Lactation Risk Category: L3

Theoretic Infant Dose:

Adult Concerns: Chromium poisoning if used in excess.

Pediatric Concerns: None reported.

Drug Interactions:

Alternatives:

Adult Dosage: 200 μg/day

T½ =	M/P =
PHL=	PB =
PK =	Oral = < 1%
MW = 52	pKa =
Vd =	

References:
1. Anderson RA, et.al. Breast milk chromium and its association with chromium intake, chromium excretion, and serum chromium. Am. J. Clin. Nutr. 57:519-23,1993.

CICLOPIROXOLAMINE

Trade: Loprox
Can/Aus/UK: Loprox
Uses: Antifungal
AAP: Not reviewed

Ciclopirox is a broad spectrum antifungal and is active again numerous species including tinea, candida albicans, and trichophyton rubrum. An average of 1.3% ciclopirox is absorbed when applied topically.[1] Topical application produces minimal systemic absorption; it is unlikely that topical use would expose the nursing infant to significant risks. The risk to a breastfeeding infant associated with application directly on the nipple is not known; only small amounts should be used. Ciclopirox and miconazole are comparable in treatment of vaginal candida.

Pregnancy Risk Category: B

Lactation Risk Category: L3

Theoretic Infant Dose:

Adult Concerns: Pruritus and burning following topical therapy.

Pediatric Concerns: None via milk.

Drug Interactions:

Alternatives: Fluconazole, Miconazole

Adult Dosage: apply topical BID

T½ = 1.7 hours	M/P =
PHL =	PB = 98%
PK = 6 hours	Oral =
MW =	pKa =
Vd =	

References:
1.   Pharmaceutical manufacturers package insert, 1998.

CIMETIDINE

Trade: Tagamet
Can/Aus/UK: Apo-Cimetidine, Magicul, Novo-Cimetine, Peptimax, Peptol, Sigmetadine, Tagamet, Zita
Uses: Reduces gastric acid production
AAP: Approved by the American Academy of Pediatrics for use in breastfeeding mothers

Cimetidine is an antisecretory, histamine-2 antagonist that reduces stomach acid secretion. Cimetidine is secreted into breastmilk in low levels. A relatively high milk/plasma ratio varies depending on dose from 4.6 to 11.76.[1] Such levels could potentially reduce infant gastric acidity, and drug metabolizing ability although these effects have not been reported and seem unlikely due to the minimal dose transferred to the infant.

The potential dose from lactation would be approximately 6 mg/L of milk, which is quite small. The pediatric dose administered I.V. for therapeutic treatment of pediatric gastroesophageal reflux averages 8-20 mg/kg/24 hours. Other choices for breastfeeding mothers should preclude the use of this drug. See famotidine, nizatidine. Short term use (days) would not be incompatible with breastfeeding.

Pregnancy Risk Category: B

Lactation Risk Category: L2

Theoretic Infant Dose: 0.9 mg/kg/day

Adult Concerns: Headache, dizziness, somnolence.

Pediatric Concerns: None reported via milk. Frequently used in pediatric patients.

Drug Interactions: Cimetidine inhibits the metabolism of many drugs and may potentially increase their plasma levels. Such drugs include: lidocaine, theophylline, phenytoin, metronidazole, triamterene, procainamide, quinidine, propranolol, warfarin, tricyclic antidepressants, diazepam, cyclosporin.

Alternatives: Famotidine, Nizatidine
Adult Dosage: 400-800 mg QID

T½ = 2 hours	M/P = 4.6-11.76
PHL= 3.6 hours(neonate)	PB = 19%
PK = 0.75-1.5 hours	Oral = 60-70%
MW = 252	pKa =
Vd =	

References:
1.   Somogyi A, Gugler R. Cimetidine excretion into breast milk. Br J Clin Pharmacol. 7:627-9,1979.

CIPROFLOXACIN

Trade: Cipro, Ciloxan
Can/Aus/UK: Ciloxan, Cipro, Ciproxin
Uses: Fluoroquinolone antibiotic
AAP: Approved by the American Academy of Pediatrics for use in breastfeeding mothers

Ciprofloxacin is a fluoroquinolone antibiotic primarily used for gram negative coverage and is presently the drug of choice for anthrax treatment and prophylaxis. Because it has been implicated in arthropathy in newborn animals, it is not normally used in pediatric patients, although it was recently approved by the AAP for use in breastfeeding mothers.   Levels secreted into breastmilk (2.26 to 3.79 mg/L) are somewhat conflicting, and vary from the low to moderate range to levels that are higher than maternal serum up to 12 hours after a dose. In one study of 10 women who received 750 mg every 12 hours, milk levels of ciprofloxacin ranged from 3.79 mg/L at 2 hours post-dose to 0.02 mg/L at 24 hours.[1]

In another study of a single patient receiving one 500 mg tablet daily at bedtime, the concentrations in maternal serum, and breastmilk were 0.21 μg/mL, and 0.98 μg/mL, respectively.[2]   Plasma levels were undetectable (< 0. 03 μg/mL) in the infant.   The dose to the 4 month old infant was estimated to be 0.92 mg/day or 0.15 mg/kg/day. No adverse effects were noted in this infant.

There has been one reported case of severe pseudomembranous colitis in an infant of a mother who self-medicated with ciprofloxacin for 6 days.[3]   In a patient 17 days postpartum who received 500 mg orally, ciprofloxacin levels in milk were 3.02, 3.02, 3.02 and 1.98 mg/L 4, 8, 12 and 16 hours postdose, respectively.[4]

If used in lactating mothers, observe the infant closely for GI symptoms.   Current studies seem to suggest that the amount of ciprofloxacin present in milk is quite low. The use of this family of antibiotics in breastfeeding mothers requires a risk-vs-benefit assessment.   The use of fluoroquinolone antibiotics in adolescent children has been associated with arthropathy, or swollen joints, although these would be at higher doses than via milk, and only occurred following several weeks of normal oral doses, not breastmilk. Ciprofloxacin was recently approved by the American Academy of Pediatrics for use in breastfeeding women.   Ciprofloxacin is available in several ophthalmic preparations (Ciloxan). As the absolute dose presented to the nursing mother is minimal, they would not be contraindicated in breastfeeding mothers.

Pregnancy Risk Category: C

Lactation Risk Category: L4

Theoretic Infant Dose: 0.6 mg/kg/day

Adult Concerns: Nausea, vomiting, diarrhea, abdominal cramps, GI bleeding. Several cases of tendon rupture have been noted.

Pediatric Concerns: Pseudomembranous colitis in one infant. Observe for diarrhea. Tooth discoloration in several infants reported.

Drug Interactions: Decreased absorption with antacids. Quinolones cause increased levels of caffeine, warfarin, cyclosporine, theophylline. Cimetidine, probenecid, azlocillin increase ciprofloxacin levels. Increased risk of seizures when used with foscarnet.

Alternatives: Norfloxacin, Ofloxacin

Adult Dosage: 250 mg BID

T½ = 4.1 hours	M/P = > 1
PHL= 2.5 hours	PB = 40%
PK = 0.5-2.3 hours	Oral = 50-85%
MW = 331	pKa = 7.1
Vd = 1.4	

References:
1. Giamarellou H, Kolokythas E, Petrikkos G, et.al. Pharmacokinetics of three newer quinolones in pregnant and lactating women. Amer. Jour. of Med. 87:5A-49S-51S, 1989.
2. Gardner DK, Gabbe SG, Harter C. Simultaneous concentrations of ciprofloxacin in breast milk and in serum in mother and breast-fed infant. Clin. Pharmacy 11(4):352-354, 1992.
3. Harmon T, Burkhart G, and Applebaum H. Perforated pseudomembranous colitis in the breast-fed infant. J. Ped. Surg. 27:744-6,1992.
4. Cover DL, Mueller BA. Ciprofloxacin penetration into human breast milk: a case report. DICP 24:703-704,1990.

CISAPRIDE

Trade: Propulsid
Can/Aus/UK: Prepulsid, Propulsid
Uses: Gastrointestinal tract stimulant
AAP: Approved by the American Academy of Pediatrics for use in breastfeeding mothers

Cisapride is a gastrointestinal stimulant used to increase lower esophageal sphincter pressure, and increase the rate of gastric emptying. It is frequently used in gastroesophageal reflux.[1] It is often preferred over metoclopramide (Reglan) due to the lack of CNS side effects. CNS concentrations are generally 2-3 fold less than the serum levels. It is frequently used in pediatric patients and neonates.

Breastmilk levels following a maternal dose of 60 mg/day for 4 days averaged 6.2 μg/L while maternal plasma levels averaged 137 μg/L.[2] The dose of cisapride absorbed in breastfeeding infants would be expected to be 600-800 times lower than the usual therapeutic dose. Manufacturers internal data suggest that breastmilk levels are less than 5% of maternal plasma levels (approximately 2.2 to 3.0 μg/L).[3]

Pregnancy Risk Category: C

Lactation Risk Category: L2

Theoretic Infant Dose: 0.9 μg/kg/day

Adult Concerns: Diarrhea, abdominal pain, cramping. Note many drug-drug interactions.

Pediatric Concerns: None reported via milk.

Drug Interactions: Increased effect of atropine and digoxin. Increased toxicity when used with warfarin, diazepam levels may be increased, cimetidine, ranitidine, CNS depressants. Cisapride levels may rise when used with azole antifungals such as ketoconazole, fluconazole, erythromycins.

Alternatives:

Adult Dosage: 10 mg QID (q AC & q HS)

T½ = 7-10 hours	M/P = 0.045
PHL=	PB = 98%
PK = 1-2 hours	Oral = 35-40%
MW = 466	pKa =
Vd =	

References:
1. McCallum RW, Prakash C, et.al. Cisapride: a preliminary review of its pharmacodynamic and pharmacokinetic properties, and therapeutic use as a prokinetic agent in gastrointestinal motility disorders. Drugs, 36(6):652-81, 1988.
2. Hofmeyr GJ, Sonnendecker WW. Secretion of the gastrokinetic agent cisapride in human milk. Eur. J. Clin. Pharmacol. 30:735-6,1986.
3. Janssen Pharmaceuticals, personal communication, 1996.

CISPLATIN

Trade: Platinol
Can/Aus/UK: Abiplatin, Cisplatin, Platinol, Platinol-AQ, Platosin
Uses: Anticancer drug
AAP: Approved by the American Academy of Pediatrics for use in breastfeeding mothers

Cisplatin is a potent and very toxic anticancer medication. Plasma and breastmilk samples were collected from a 24 year old woman treated for three prior days with cisplatin (30mg/meter).[1] On the third day, 30 minutes prior to chemotherapy, platinum levels in milk were 0.9 mg/L and plasma levels were 0.8 mg/L. In another study, no cisplatin was found in breastmilk following a dose of 100 mg/meter.[2] Other studies suggest that milk levels are 10 fold lower than serum levels in an older lactating woman. Cisplatin has multiple half-lives with the terminal half-life equal to greater than 24 to 73 hours. These studies generally support the recommendation that mothers should not breastfeed while undergoing cisplatin therapy.

Pregnancy Risk Category: D

Lactation Risk Category: L4

Theoretic Infant Dose: 0.1 mg/kg/day

Adult Concerns: Nausea, vomiting, tinnitus, ototoxicity, renal toxicity, leukopenia, peripheral neuropathy, etc.

Pediatric Concerns: None reported via milk, but due to enormous toxicity, do not use in breastfeeding women.

Drug Interactions: Increased toxicity when used with ethacrynic acid (ototoxicity). Delayed bleomycin metabolism. Sodium thiosulfate inactivates cisplatin.

Alternatives:

Adult Dosage: 20 mg/m(2) I.V. QD

T½ = 24-73 hours	M/P = > 1
PHL =	PB = 90%
PK = < 1 hour.	Oral =
MW = 300	pKa =
Vd =	

References:
1. deVries EGE, et.al. Excretion of platinum into breast milk[letter]. Lancet 1(8636):497,1989.
2. Egan PC, et. al. Doxorubicin and cisplatin excretion into human milk. Cancer Treat Rep 69:1387-9, 1985.

CITALOPRAM

Trade: Celexa
Can/Aus/UK: Cipramil
Uses: Antidepressant
AAP: Not reviewed

Citalopram is a new SSRI antidepressant similar in effect to Prozac and Zoloft. In one study of a 21 year old patient receiving 20 mg citalopram per day, citalopram levels in milk peaked at 3-9 hours following administration.[1] Peak milk levels varied during the day, but the mean daily concentration was 298 nM (range 270-311). The milk/serum ratio was approximately three. The metabolite, desmethylcitalopram, was present in milk in low levels (23-28 nM). The concentration of metabolite in milk varied little during the day. Assuming a milk intake of 150 ml/kg baby, approximately 272 nM (88 ug or 16 ng/kg) of citalopram was passed to the baby each day. This amounts to only 0.4% of the dose administered to the mother. At three weeks, maternal serum levels of citalopram were 185 nM, compared to the infants plasma level of just 7 nM. No untoward effects were noted in this breastfed infant. In another study[2], a milk/serum ratio of 1.16 to 1.88 was reported. This study suggests the infant would ingest 4.3 μg/kg/day and a relative dose of 0.7 to 5.9% of the weight-adjusted maternal dose.

In another study of 7 women receiving an average of 0.41 mg/kg/d citalopram,[3] the average peak level (Cmax) of citalopram was 154 μg/L, and 50 μg/L for demethylcitalopram (metabolite is 8 times less potent than citalopram). However, average milk concentrations (AUC) were lower and averaged 97 μg/L for citalopram and 36 μg/L for demethylcitalopram during the dosing interval. The mean peak milk/plasma AUC ratio was 1.8 for citalopram. Low concentrations of citalopram (around 2-2.3 μg/L) were detected in only three of the seven infant plasmas. No adverse effects were found in any of the infants. The authors estimate the daily intake to be approximately 3.7% of the maternal dose.

In a study of a single patient receiving 40 mg/day of citalopram, the concentration in milk and serum were 205 μg/L and 98.9 ng/mL, respectively.[4] Infant serum levels were 12.7 ng/mL. This infant was noted to have 'uneasy' sleep patterns, which were reduced upon lowering the maternal dose.

Pregnancy Risk Category: C

Lactation Risk Category: L3

Theoretic Infant Dose: 14.6 μg/kg/day

Adult Concerns: Diarrhea, headache, anxiety, dizziness, insomnia, constipation, nausea, vomiting, and tremor. Tachycardia, hypotension have been reported. Increased salivation, and flatulence. Amenorrhea, coughing, rash, pruritus, polyuria have been reported.

Pediatric Concerns: There have been two cases of excessive somnolence, decreased feeding, and weight loss in breastfed infants.

Drug Interactions: Increased citalopram levels when used with macrolide antibiotics (erythromycin), and azole antifungals such as fluconazole, itraconazole, ketoconazole, etc. Carbamazepine may reduce plasma levels of citalopram. Serious reactions may occur if citalopram is administered too soon after MAO use. Beta blocker (metoprolol) levels may increase by two fold when admixed with citalopram.

Alternatives: Sertraline, Paroxetine, Paxil

Adult Dosage: 20-40 mg daily

T½ = 36 hours	M/P = 1.16 - 3
PHL =	PB = 80%
PK = 2-4 hours	Oral = 80%
MW = 405	pKa =
Vd = 12	

References:

1. Jensen PN, Olesen OV, Bertelsen A, and Linnet K. Citalopram and desmethylcitalopram concentrations in breast milk and in serum of mother and infant. Ther. Drug. Mon. 19:236-239, 1997.
2. Spigset O, Carleborg L, Ohman R et al: Excretion of citalopram in breast milk. Br J Clin Pharmacol 44:295-298, 1997.
3. Rampono J, Kristensen JH, Hackett LP, Paech M, Kohan R, Ilett KF. Citalopram and demethylcitalopram in human milk; distribution, excretion and effects in breastfed infants. Br J Clin Pharmacol. 50(3):263-8, 2000.
4. Schmidt K, Olesen OV, Jensen PN. Citalopram and breast-feeding: Serum concentration and side effects in the infant. Biol. Psychiatary 47:164-165, 2000.

CLARITHROMYCIN

Trade: Biaxin
Can/Aus/UK: Biaxin, Klacid, Klaricid
Uses: Antibiotic
AAP: Not reviewed

Antibiotic that belongs to erythromycin family. Clarithromycin is known to transfer into animal milk, although no studies have been done on humans. This drug is a weak base and could concentrate in human milk by ion trapping.[1,2] However, it is a commonly used pediatric antibiotic and pediatric indications down to 6 months of age are available. See azithromycin as alternative.

Pregnancy Risk Category: C

Lactation Risk Category: L2

Theoretic Infant Dose:

Adult Concerns: Diarrhea, nausea, dyspepsia, abdominal pain, metallic taste.

Pediatric Concerns: None reported via milk. Pediatric indications are available.

Drug Interactions: Clarithromycin increases serum theophylline by as much as 20%. Increases plasma levels of carbamazepine, cyclosporin, digoxin, ergot alkaloids, tacrolimus, triazolam, zidovudine, terfenadine, astemizole, cisapride (serious arrhythmias). Fluconazole increases clarithromycin serum levels by 25%. Numerous other drug-drug interactions are unreported, but probably occur.

Alternatives:

Adult Dosage: 250 mg BID

T½ = 5-7 hours	M/P = >1
PHL =	PB = 40-70%
PK = 1.7 hours	Oral = 50%
MW = 748	pKa =
Vd =	

References:
1. Drug Facts and Comparisons. 1995 ed. Facts and Comparisons, St. Louis.
2. Pharmaceutical Manufacturers Package Insert, 1996.

CLEMASTINE

Trade: Tavist
Can/Aus/UK: Tavegyl, Tavist
Uses: Antihistamine
AAP: Drugs associated with significant side effects and should be given with caution

Clemastine is a long-acting antihistamine. Following a maternal dose of 1 mg twice daily a 10 week old breastfeeding infant developed drowsiness, irritability, refusal to feed, and neck stiffness.[1] Levels in milk and plasma (20 hours post dose) were 5-10 μg/L(milk) and 20 μg/L (plasma) respectively.

Pregnancy Risk Category: C

Lactation Risk Category: L4

Theoretic Infant Dose: 1.5 μg/kg/day

Adult Concerns: Drowsiness, headache, fatigue, nervousness, appetite increase, depression.

Pediatric Concerns: Drowsiness, irritability, refusal to feed, and neck stiffness in one infant. Increased risk of seizures.

Drug Interactions: Increased toxicity when mixed with CNS depressants, anticholinergics, MAO inhibitors, tricyclic antidepressants, phenothiazines.

Alternatives: Cetirizine, Loratadine

Adult Dosage: 1.34 to 2.68 mg BID or TID

T½ = 10-12 hours.	M/P = 0.25-0.5
PHL=	PB =
PK = 2-5 hours.	Oral = 100%
MW = 344	pKa =
Vd =	

References:
1. Kok THHG, Taitz LS, Bennett MJ, et.al. Drowsiness due to clemastine transmitted in breast milk. Lancet 1:914-915,1982.

CLINDAMYCIN

Trade: Cleocin
Can/Aus/UK: Cleocin, Clindatech, Dalacin
Uses: Antibiotic
AAP: Approved by the American Academy of Pediatrics for use in breastfeeding mothers

Clindamycin is a broad spectrum antibiotic frequently used for anaerobic infections. In one study of two nursing mothers and following doses of 600 mg I.V. every 6 hours, the concentration of clindamycin in breastmilk was 3.1 to 3.8 mg/L at 0.2 to 0.5 hours after dosing.[1] Following oral doses of 300 mg every 6 hours, the breastmilk levels averaged 1.0 to 1.7 mg/L at 1.5 to 7 hours after dosing. In another study of 2-3 women who received a single oral dose of 150 mg, milk levels averaged 0.9 mg/L at 4 hours with a milk/plasma ratio of 0.47.[2]

An alteration of GI flora is possible, even though the dose is low. One case of bloody stools (pseudomembranous colitis) has been associated with clindamycin and gentamycin therapy on day 5 postpartum, but this is considered rare.[3] In this case, the mother of a newborn infant was given 600 mg I.V. every 6 hours. In rare cases, pseudomembranous colitis can appear several weeks later.

In a study by Steen in 5 breastfeeding patients who received 150 mg three times daily for 7 days, milk concentration ranged from <0.5 to 3.1

mg/L with the majority of levels < 0.5 mg/L.[4]   There are a number of pediatric clinical uses of clindamycin (anaerobic infections, bacterial endocarditis, pelvic inflammatory disease, and bacterial vaginosis). The current pediatric dosage recommendation is 10-40 mg/kg/day divided every 6-8 hours.[5]

Pregnancy Risk Category: B

Lactation Risk Category: L3

Theoretic Infant Dose: 0.6 mg/kg/day

Adult Concerns: Diarrhea, rash, pseudomembranous colitis, nausea, vomiting, GI cramps.

Pediatric Concerns: One case of pseudomembranous colitis has been reported. But this is rare. It is unlikely the levels in breastmilk would be clinically relevant. Commonly used in pediatric infections. Observe for diarrhea.

Drug Interactions: Increased duration of muscle blockade when administered with neuromuscular blockers such as tubocurarine and pancuronium.

Alternatives:

Adult Dosage: 150-450 mg q 6 hours

T½ = 2.9 hours.	M/P = 0.47
PHL = 3.6 hours (term).	PB = 94%
PK = 45-60 minutes.	Oral = 90%
MW = 425	pKa = 7.45
Vd =	

References:
1. Smith JA, Morgan JR, et.al. Clindamycin in human breast milk. Can. Med. Assn. J. 112:806, 1975.
2. Matsuda S. Transfer of antibiotics into maternal milk.   Biol Res Pregnancy Perinatol. 5(2):57-60, 1984.
3. Mann CF. Clindamycin and breast-feeding. Pediatrics 66:1030-1031, 1980.
4. Steen B, Rane A. Clindamycin passage into human milk. Br J Clin Pharmacol. 13(5):661-4, 1982.
5. Johnson KB. The Harriet Lane Handbook. Thirteenth Edition. Mosby Publishing.

CLINDAMYCIN VAGINAL

Trade: Cleocin Vaginal
Can/Aus/UK: Dalacin T, Dalacin Vaginal Cream
Uses: Antibiotic
AAP: Approved by the American Academy of Pediatrics for use in breastfeeding mothers

Clindamycin when administered by I.V. has been found in breastmilk (see clindamycin). One case of bloody stools (pseudomembranous colitis) has been associated with oral clindamycin.

However, only about 5% of Clindamycin Vaginal (100 mg/dose) is absorbed into the maternal circulation, which would be approximately 5 mg clindamycin/day.[1] It is unlikely that clindamycin when administered via a vaginal gel would produce any significant danger to a breastfeeding infant.

Pregnancy Risk Category: B

Lactation Risk Category: L2

Theoretic Infant Dose:

Adult Concerns: Diarrhea, rash, GI cramps, colitis, rarely bloody diarrhea.

Pediatric Concerns:

Drug Interactions:

Alternatives:

Adult Dosage: 100 mg intravaginally q HS

T½ = 2.9 hours	M/P =
PHL =	PB = 94%
PK =	Oral = 90%
MW = 425	pKa =
Vd =	

References:
1. Pharmaceutical Manufacturers Package Insert, 1996.

CLOBAZAM

Trade: Frisium
Can/Aus/UK: Frisium, Frisum
Uses: Benzodiazepine anxiolytic
AAP: Not reviewed

Clobazam (Frisium) is a typical benzodiazepine very similar to Valium.[1] It is primarily an anxiolytic, but it is sometimes used to treat refractory seizures. The median half-life for tolerance is only 3.5 months, so it would not be suitable for long term therapy of seizures. It has a rather long half-life averaging 17-31 hours for the parent drug in young adults and 11-77 hours for the active metabolite desmethylclobazam. As with Valium, it would probably reach relatively high levels in a breastfeeding infant. No data are available on breastmilk concentrations.   See diazepam.

Pregnancy Risk Category: C

Lactation Risk Category: L3

Theoretic Infant Dose:

Adult Concerns: Sedation, drowsiness, hangover, weakness, insomnia.

Pediatric Concerns: Typical benzodiazepine, use caution. See Diazepam.

Drug Interactions: May increase effects of opiates, CNS depressants. Macrolide (erythromycin) antibiotics may increase levels of clobazam. Clobazam may increase levels of carbamazepine.

Alternatives: Alprazolam

Adult Dosage: 20-30 mg/day

T½ = 17-31 hours	M/P =
PHL=	PB = 90%
PK = 1-2 hours.	Oral = 87%
MW = 301	pKa =
Vd = 0.87-1.8	

References:
1.   Pharmaceutical Manufacturers Package Insert, 1995.

CLOFAZIMINE

Trade: Lamprene
Can/Aus/UK: Lamprene
Uses: Antimicrobial for leprosy
AAP: Drug whose effect on nursing infants is unknown but may be of concern

Clofazimine exerts a slow bacteriocidal effect on M. Leprae. In a study of 8 female leprosy patients on clofazimine (50 mg/day or 100 mg on alternate days) for 1-18 months, blood samples were take at 4-6 hours after the dose.[1]   Average plasma and milk levels were 0.9 μg/mL and 1.33 μg/mL (1.33 mg/Liter) respectively. The milk/plasma ratio varied from 1.0 to 1.7 with a mean of 1.48.   A red tint and pigmentation has been reported in breastfed infants.[2,3]

Pregnancy Risk Category: C

Lactation Risk Category: L3

Theoretic Infant Dose: 0.2 mg/kg/day

Adult Concerns: Reversible red-brown discoloration of skin and eyes. Gastrointestinal effects include nausea, abdominal cramps and pain, nausea and vomiting. Splenic infarction, crystalline deposits of clofazimine in multiple organs and tissues.

Pediatric Concerns: Reddish discoloration of milk and infant.

Drug Interactions:

Alternatives:

Adult Dosage: 100-200 mg QD

T½ = 70 days	M/P = 1,7
PHL=	PB =
PK =	Oral = 45-70%
MW = 473	pKa =
Vd =	

References:

1. Venkatesan L, Girdhar BL. et.al. Excretion of clofazimine in human milk in leprosy patients. Lepr Rev 68(3):242-6, 1997.
2. Farb H et al: Clofazimine in pregnancy complicated by leprosy. Obstet Gynecol 59:122-123, 1982.
6. Freerksen E and Seydel JK: Critical comments on the treatment of leprosy and other mycobacterial infections with clofazimine. Arzneim-Forsch Drug Res 42:1243-1245,1992.

CLOMIPHENE

Trade: Clomid, Serophene, Milophene
Can/Aus/UK: Clomid, Serophene
Uses: Ovulation stimulator for ovulatory failure
AAP: Not reviewed

Clomiphene appears to stimulate the release of the pituitary gonadotropins, follicle-stimulating hormone (FSH) and luteinizing hormone (LH), which result in development and maturation of the ovarian follicle, ovulation, and subsequent development and function of the corpus luteum. It has both estrogenic and anti-estrogenic effects. LH and FSH peak at 5-9 days after completing clomiphene therapy.

In a study of 60 postpartum women (1-4 days postpartum), clomiphene was effective in totally inhibiting unestablished lactation, and in suppressing established lactation (day 4).[1] Only 7 of 40 women receiving clomiphene to inhibit lactation had signs of congestion or discomfort. In the 20 women who received clomiphene to suppress established lactation(on day 4), a rapid amelioration of breast engorgement and discomfort was produced. After 5 days of treatment no signs of lactation were present. In another study of 177 postpartum women, clomiphene was very effective at inhibiting lactation.[2]

Clomiphene appears to be very effective in suppressing lactation when used up to 4 days postpartum. However, its efficacy in reducing milk production in women months after lactation has been established is unknown, but believed to be minimal.[3]

Pregnancy Risk Category: X

Lactation Risk Category: L4

Theoretic Infant Dose:

Adult Concerns: Dizziness, insomnia, lightheadedness, hot flashes, ovarian enlargement, depression, headache, alopecia. May inhibit lactation early postpartum.

Pediatric Concerns: Transfer and effect on infant is unreported, but may suppress early lactation.

Drug Interactions:

Alternatives:

Adult Dosage: 50 mg QD

T½ = 5-7 days	**M/P** =
PHL =	**PB** =
PK =	**Oral** = Complete
MW = 406	**pKa** =
Vd =	

References:
1. Masala, A. Clomiphene and puerperal lactation. Panminerva. Med. 20: 161-163, 1978.
2. Zuckerman, H. and Carmel, S. The inhibition of lactation by clomiphene. J. Obstet. and Gynecology of Brit. Common. 80:822-23, 1973.
3. JN. Personal communication. 2001

CLOMIPRAMINE

Trade: Anafranil
Can/Aus/UK: Anafranil, Apo-Clomipramine, Placil
Uses: Anti-obsessional, antidepressant drug
AAP: Drug whose effect on nursing infants is unknown but may be of concern

Clomipramine is a tricyclic antidepressant frequently used for obsessive-compulsive disorder.[1] In one patient taking 125 mg/day, on the 4th and 6th day postpartum, milk levels were 342.7 and 215.8 μg/L respectively.[2] Maternal plasma levels were 211 and 208.4 μg/L at day 4 and 6 respectively. Milk/plasma ratio varies from 1.62 to 1.04 on day 4 to 6 respectively. Neonatal plasma levels continued to drop from a high of 266.6 ng/mL at birth to 127.6 ng/mL at day 4, to 94.8 ng/mL at day 6, to 9.8 ng/mL at 35 days. In a study of four breastfeeding women who received doses of 75 to 125 mg/day, plasma levels of clomipramine in the breastfed infants were below the limit of detection, suggesting minimal transfer to the infant via milk.[3] No untoward effects were noted in any of the infants.

Pregnancy Risk Category: C

Lactation Risk Category: L2

Theoretic Infant Dose: 51.4 μg/kg/day

Adult Concerns: Drowsiness, fatigue, dry mouth, seizures, constipation, sweating, reduced appetite.

Pediatric Concerns: None reported in several studies.

Drug Interactions: Decreased effect when used with barbiturates, carbamazepine and phenytoin. Increased sedation when used with alcohol, CNS depressants(hypnotics). Increased dangers when used with MAO inhibitors. Additive anticholinergic effects when used with other anticholinergics.

Alternatives:

Adult Dosage: 50 mg BID

T½ = 19-37 hours	M/P = 0.84- 1.62
PHL = 92.8 hours	PB = 96%
PK =	Oral – Complete
MW = 315	pKa = 9.5
Vd = 17	

References:
1. Pharmaceutical Manufacturers Package Insert, 1996.
2. Schimmell MS, et.al. Toxic neonatal effects following maternal clomipramine therapy. J. Toxicol. Clin. Toxicol. 29:479-84, 1991.
3. Wisner KL, Perel JM, Foglia JP. Serum clomipramine and metabolite levels in four nursing mother-infant pairs.

CLONAZEPAM

Trade: Klonopin
Can/Aus/UK: Apo-Clonazepam, PMS-Clonazepam, Paxam, Rivotril
Uses: Benzodiazepine anticonvulsant
AAP: Not reviewed

Clonazepam is a typical benzo diazepam sedative, anticonvulsant. In one case report, milk levels varied between 11 and 13 μg/L (the maternal dose was omitted).[1] Milk/ serum ratio was approximately

0.33. In this report, the infant's serum level of clonazepam dropped from 4.4 μg/L at birth to 1.0 μg/L at 14 days while continuing to breastfeed.

Pregnancy Risk Category: C

Lactation Risk Category: L3

Theoretic Infant Dose: 2.0 μg/kg/day

Adult Concerns: Apnea, sedation, ataxia, hypotonia. Behavioral disturbances(in children) include aggressiveness, irritability, agitation.

Pediatric Concerns: None reported via milk. Observe for sedation.

Drug Interactions: Phenytoin and barbiturates may increase clearance of clonazepam. CNS depressants may increase sedation.

Alternatives:

Adult Dosage: 0.5-1 mg TID

T½ = 18-50 hours	**M/P** = 0.33
PHL =	**PB** = 50-86%
PK = 1-4 hours	**Oral** = Complete
MW = 316	**pKa** = 1.5, 10.5
Vd = 1.5-4.4	

References:
1.   Fisher JB, Edgren BE, et.al. Neonatal apnea associated with maternal clonazepam therapy: a case report. Obstet. Gynecol. 66:34S(Suppl), 1985.

CLONIDINE

Trade: Catapres
Can/Aus/UK: Apo-Clonidine, Catapres, Dixarit, Novo-Clonidine
Uses: Antihypertensive
AAP: Not reviewed

Clonidine is an antihypertensive that reduces sympathetic nerve activity from the brain. Clonidine is excreted in human milk. In a study of 9 nursing women receiving between 241.7 and 391.7 μg/day of clonidine, milk levels varied from approximately 1.8 μg/L to as high as 2.8 μg/L on postpartum day 10-14.[1]   In another report following a maternal dose of 37.5 ug twice daily, maternal plasma was determined to be 0.33 ng/mL and milk level was 0.60 μg/L.[2] The dose an infant would receive is estimated to be approximately 6.8 % of maternal dose (90 ng/kg/d vs 1320 ng/kg/d in adults). Clinical symptoms of neonatal toxicity are unreported and are unlikely in normal full term infants. Clonidine may reduce prolactin secretion, and could conceivably reduce milk production early postpartum.   Transdermal patches produce maternal plasma levels of 0.39, 0.84, and 1.12 ng/mL using the 3.5, 7, and 10.5 cm square patches respectively. The 3.7 square cm patch would produce maternal plasma levels equivalent to the 37.5 ug oral dose and would likely produce milk levels equivalent to the above study.

Pregnancy Risk Category: C

Lactation Risk Category: L3

Theoretic Infant Dose: 0.4 μg/kg/day

Adult Concerns: Drowsiness, dry mouth, hypotension, constipation, dizziness.

Pediatric Concerns: None reported, but may induce hypotension in infant. May reduce milk production by reducing prolactin secretion.

Drug Interactions: Tricyclic antidepressants inhibit hypotensive effect of clonidine. Beta blockers may potentiate slow heart rate when administered with clonidine. Discontinue beta blockers several days to week prior to using clonidine.

Alternatives:

Adult Dosage: 0.1-0.3 mg BID

T½ = 20-24 hours	M/P = 2
PHL =	PB = 20-40 %
PK = 3-5 hours.	Oral = 75-100%
MW = 230	pKa = 8.3
Vd = 3.2-5.6	

References:
1. Hartikainen-Sorri AL, Heikkinen JE, Koivisto M. Pharmacokinetics of clonidine during pregnancy and nursing. Obstet Gynecol. 69:598-600,1987.
2. Bunjes R, Schaefer C, and Holzinger D. Clonidine and breast-feeding. Clinical Pharmacy 12:178, 1993.

CLOPIDOGREL

Trade: Plavix
Can/Aus/UK: Plavix
Uses: Platelet aggregation inhibitor
AAP: Not reviewed

Clopidogrel selectively inhibits platelet adenosine diphosphate-induced platelet aggregation. It is used to prevent ischemic events in patients at risk (e.g. cardiovascular disease, strokes, myocardial infarct). Aspirin is generally preferred, as it is less expensive, quite tolerable, and very effective. Clopidogrel is only used in those patients who are aspirin-intolerant. It is not known if it transfers into human milk, but it does enter rodent milk.[1]   Although the plasma half-life is rather brief (8 hours), it covalently bonds to platelet receptors with a half-life of 11 days.   Because it produces an irreversible inhibition of platelet aggregation, any present in milk could inhibit an infant's platelet function for a prolonged period.   Because aspirin affects platelet aggregation similarly, and its milk levels are quite low, it would appear to be an ideal alternative.   However, aspirin also inhibits platelet aggregation for long periods as well, and may increase the risk of Reyes syndrome in infants.   The choice between using clopidogrel and aspirin must be made on clinical grounds until we know more about the levels secreted into human milk.

Pregnancy Risk Category: B

Lactation Risk Category: L4

Theoretic Infant Dose:

Adult Concerns: Contraindicated in individuals with bleeding phenomenon.

Pediatric Concerns: None reported via milk.

Drug Interactions: At high concentrations, clopidogrel inhibits Cytochrome P450 2C9, and may inhibit metabolism of phenytoin, tamoxifen, tolbutamide, warfarin, torsemide, fluvastatin, and many NSAIDs.

Alternatives:

Adult Dosage: 75 mg daily

T½ = 8 hours	**M/P =**
PHL =	**PB = 94%**
PK = 1 hour	**Oral = 50%**
MW = 420	**pKa =**
Vd =	

References:
1.   Pharmaceutical Manufacturers Package Insert, 1999.

CLOTRIMAZOLE

Trade: Gyne-Lotrimin, Mycelex, Lotrimin, Fem Care, Trivaqizole
Can/Aus/UK: Canesten, Clonea, Clotrimaderm, Hiderm, Myclo
Uses: Antifungal
AAP: Not reviewed

Clotrimazole is a broad spectrum antifungal agent. It is generally used for candidiasis, and various tinea species (athletes foot, ring worm).

Clotrimazole is available in oral lozenges, topical creams, intravaginal tablets and creams. No data are available on penetration into breastmilk. However, after intravaginal administration only 3-10% of the drug is absorbed (peak serum level= 0.01 to 0.03 μg/mL), and even less by oral lozenge.[1] Hence, from vaginal administration it seems very unlikely that levels absorbed by a breastfeeding infant would be high enough to produce untoward effects. Safety of clotrimazole lozenges in children younger than 3 years of age has not been established. The risk of contact dermatitis with this agent may be higher.[1]

Pregnancy Risk Category: B during 1st and 2nd trimesters
C during 3rd trimester

Lactation Risk Category: L1

Theoretic Infant Dose:

Adult Concerns: Nausea, vomiting from oral administration. Itching, burning , and stinging following topical application. Elevated liver enzymes in > 10% of treated.

Pediatric Concerns: None reported via milk. Limited oral absorption probably limits clinical relevance in breastfed infants.

Drug Interactions: May inhibit amphotericin activity. Clotrimazole is reported to increase cyclosporin plasma levels. May enhance hypoglycemic effect of oral hypoglycemic agents. Clotrimazole inhibits cytochrome P450 IIIA and may inhibit metabolism of any number of other medications.

Alternatives: Fluconazole, Miconazole

Adult Dosage: 500 mg intravaginally q HS

T½ = 3.5-5 hours	M/P =
PHL =	PB =
PK = 3 hours (oral)	Oral = Poor
MW = 345	pKa =
Vd =	

References:

1. McEvoy GE(ed):AFHS Drug Information, New York, NY. 1995, pp 417-26.
2. Newman, Jack. Personal communication(1999).

CLOXACILLIN

Trade: Tegopen, Cloxapen
Can/Aus/UK: Alclox, Apo-Cloxi, Kloxerate-DC, Novo-Cloxin, Orbenin
Uses: Penicillin antibiotic
AAP: Not reviewed

Cloxacillin is an oral penicillinase-resistant penicillin frequently used for peripheral (non CNS) Staphylococcus aureus and S. epidermidis infections, particularly mastitis. Following a single 500 mg oral dose of cloxacillin in lactating women, milk concentrations of the drug were zero to 0.2 mg/L one and two hours after the dose respectively, and 0.2 to 0.4 mg/L after 6 hours.[1] Usual dose for adults is 250-500 mg four times daily for at least 10-14 days.[2] As with most penicillins, it is unlikely these levels would be clinically relevant.

Pregnancy Risk Category: B

Lactation Risk Category: L2

Theoretic Infant Dose: 60.0 μg/kg/day

Adult Concerns: Rash, diarrhea, nephrotoxicity, fever, shaking, chills.

Pediatric Concerns: None reported but observe for GI symptoms such as diarrhea.

Drug Interactions: Efficacy of oral contraceptives may be reduced. Disulfiram, probenecid may increase cloxacillin levels. Increased effect of oral anticoagulants.

Alternatives:

Adult Dosage: 250-500 mg q 6 hours

T½ = 0.7-3 hours	M/P =
PHL = 0.8-1.5 hours	PB = 90-96%
PK = 0.5-2 hours	Oral = 37-60%
MW = 436	pKa =
Vd = 6.6-10.8	

References:
1. Matsuda S. Transfer of antibiotics into maternal milk. Biol Res Pregnancy Perinatol 5:57-60, 1984.
2. McEvoy GE(ed):AHFS Drug Information, New York, NY. 1995.

CLOZAPINE

Trade: Clozaril
Can/Aus/UK: Clozaril
Uses: Antipsychotic, sedative
AAP: Drug whose effect on nursing infants is unknown but may be of concern

Clozapine is an atypical antipsychotic, sedative drug somewhat similar to the phenothiazine family. In a study of one patient receiving 50 mg/d clozapine at delivery, the maternal and fetal plasma were reported to be 14.1 ng/mL and 27 ng/mL respectively. After 24 hours postpartum, the maternal plasma level was 14.7 ng/mL and maternal milk levels were 63.5 ng/mL. On day 7 postpartum and receiving a dose of 100 mg/d clozapine, the maternal plasma and milk levels were 41.1 ng/mL and 115.6 ng/mL respectively. From this data it is apparent that clozapine concentrates in milk with a milk/plasma ratio of 4.3 at a dose of 50 mg/d and 2.8 at a dose of 100 mg/d. The change from day one to seven suggests that clozapine entry into mature milk is less. From this data, the weight-adjusted relative infant dose would be 1.2% of the maternal dose.

Pregnancy Risk Category: C

Lactation Risk Category: L3

Theoretic Infant Dose: 17.3 μg/kg/day

Adult Concerns: Drowsiness, salivation, constipation, dizziness, tachycardia, nausea, GI distress, agranulocytosis.

Pediatric Concerns: None reported.

Drug Interactions: Decreased effect of epinephrine, phenytoin. Increased sedation with CNS depressants. Increased effect with guanabenz, anticholinergics. Increased toxicity with cimetidine, MAO inhibitors, tricyclic antidepressants.

Alternatives:

Adult Dosage: 300-600 mg QD

T½ = 8-12 hours	M/P = 2.8-4.3
PHL=	PB = 95%
PK = 2.5 hours	Oral = 90%
MW = 327	pKa =
Vd = 5	

References:
1. Barnas C, Bergant A, Hummer M, Saria A, Fleischhacker WW. Clozapine concentrations in maternal and fetal plasma, amniotic fluid, and breast milk. Am J Psychiatry. 151(6):945, 1994.

CO-TRIMOXAZOLE

Trade: TMP-SMZ, Bactrim, Cotrim, Septra
Can/Aus/UK: Bactrim, Novo-Trimel, Respax, Septrin, Trimogal
Uses: Sulfonamide antibiotic
AAP: Approved by the American Academy of Pediatrics for use in breastfeeding mothers

Co-trimoxazole is the mixture of trimethoprim and sulfamethoxazole. See individual monographs for each of these products.

Pregnancy Risk Category:

Lactation Risk Category: L3

Theoretic Infant Dose:

Adult Concerns:

Pediatric Concerns:

Drug Interactions:

Alternatives:

Adult Dosage: 160 mg BID

COCAINE

Trade: Crack
Can/Aus/UK:
Uses: Powerful CNS stimulant, local anesthetic
AAP: Contraindicated by the American Academy of Pediatrics
in Breastfeeding Mothers

Cocaine is a local anesthetic and a powerful central nervous system stimulant. It is well absorbed from all locations including the stomach, nasal passages, intrapulmonary tissues via inhalation, and even via ophthalmic instillation. Adverse effects include agitation, nervousness, restlessness, euphoria, hallucinations, tremors, tonic-clonic seizures, and myocardial arrhythmias. Although the pharmacologic effects of cocaine are relatively brief (20-30 min.) due to redistribution out of the brain, cocaine is slowly metabolized and excreted over a prolonged period. Urine samples can be positive for cocaine metabolites for up to 7 days or longer in adults. Breastfeeding infants will likewise become urine positive for cocaine for even longer periods. Even after the clinical effects of cocaine have subsided, the breastmilk will still probably contain significant quantities of benzoecgonine, the inactive metabolite of cocaine. The infant could still test positive for urine cocaine metabolites for long periods (days). The ingestion of small amounts of cocaine by infants via inhalation of smoke (environmental) is likely.

Studies of exact estimates of cocaine transmission to breastmilk have not been reported. Significant secretion into breastmilk is suspected with a probable high milk/plasma ratio. A number of case reports in the literature clearly indicate the transmission of maternal cocaine to the infant via milk with significant agitation in the breastfeeding infant resulting.[1,2] In one case study, a woman who applied topical cocaine to her nipples and breastfed her infant, produced extreme toxicity in the infant. Topical application to nipples is EXTREMELY dangerous and is definitely contraindicated. Oral, intranasal, and smoking of crack cocaine is dangerous and definitely contraindicated. In those individuals who have ingested cocaine, a minimum pump and dump period of 24 hours is recommended for clearance.

Pregnancy Risk Category: C during 1st and 2nd trimesters
X during 3rd trimester

Lactation Risk Category: L5

Theoretic Infant Dose:

Adult Concerns: Nausea, vomiting, CNS excitement, hypertension, tachycardia, arrhythmias.

Pediatric Concerns: Choking, vomiting, diarrhea, tremulousness, hyperactive startle reflex, gasping, agitation, irritability, hypertension, tachycardia. Extreme danger.

Drug Interactions: Increased toxicity when used with MAO inhibitors.

Alternatives:

Adult Dosage: N/A

T½ = 0.8 hour	M/P =
PHL =	PB = 91%
PK = 15 min.	Oral = Complete
MW = 303	pKa = 8.6
Vd = 1.6-2-7	

References:
1. Chaney NE, Franke J, and Wadington WB. Cocaine convulsions in a breast-feeding baby. J. Pediatr. 112:134-135, 1988.
2. Chasnoff IJ, Lewis DE, Squires L. Cocaine intoxication in a breast-fed infant. Pediatrics 80:836-838, 1987.

CODEINE

Trade: Empirin #3, # 4, Tylenol # 3, # 4
Can/Aus/UK: Actacode, Codalgin, Codral, Kaodene, Panadeine, Paveral, Penntuss, Teropin, Veganin
Uses: Analgesic
AAP: Approved by the American Academy of Pediatrics for use in breastfeeding mothers

Codeine is considered a mild opiate analgesic whose action is probably due to its metabolism to small amounts of morphine. The amount of codeine secreted into milk is low and dose dependent. Infant response is higher during neonatal period (first or second week). Four cases of neonatal apnea have been reported following administration of 60 mg codeine every 4-6 hours to breastfeeding mothers although codeine was not detected in serum of the infants tested.[1] Apnea resolved after discontinuation of maternal codeine. Number # 3 tablets contain 30 mg and #4 tablets contain 60 mg of codeine.

In another study, following a dose of 60 mg, milk concentrations averaged 140 μg/L of milk with a peak of 455 μg/L at 1 hour. Following 12 doses in 48 hours, the estimated dose of codeine in milk (2000 ml milk) was 0.7 mg which is approximately 0.1% of the maternal dose. There are few reported side effects following codeine doses of 30 mg, and it is believed to produce only minimal side effects in newborns.

Pregnancy Risk Category: C

Lactation Risk Category: L3

Theoretic Infant Dose: 68.3 μg/kg/day

Adult Concerns: Sedation, respiratory depression, constipation.

Pediatric Concerns: Several rare cases of neonatal apnea have been reported, but at higher doses. Codeine analgesics are so commonly used postpartum, that side effects are extremely rare and seldom reported. Observe for sedation, apnea in premature or weakened infants.

Drug Interactions: Cigarette smoking increases effect of codeine. Increased toxicity/sedation when used with CNS depressants, phenothiazines, tricyclic antidepressants, other opiates, guanabenz, MAO inhibitors, neuromuscular blockers.

Alternatives:

Adult Dosage: 15-60 mg q 4-6 hours

T½ = 2.9 hours	M/P = 1.3-2.5
PHL=	PB = 7%
PK = 0.5-1 hour	Oral = Complete
MW = 299	pKa = 8.2
Vd = 3.5	

References:
1. Davis JM and Bhutani VK. Neonatal apnea and maternal codeine use. Ped.Res. 19(4):170A abstract.
2. Davis JM and Bhutani VK. Neonatal apnea and maternal codeine use. Ped.Res. 19(4):170A abstract.
3. Findlay JW, DeAngelis RI, Kearney MF, et.al. Analgesic drugs in breast milk and plasma. Clin Pharmacol. Ther. 29:625-633, 1981.

COENZYME Q10

Trade:
Can/Aus/UK:
Uses: Cofactor in electron transport chain
AAP: Not reviewed

Coenzyme Q10, also known as ubiquinone and ubidecarenone, is a cofactor in the mitochondrial electron-transport chain in the synthesis of ATP within the cell. It may also possess antioxidant and membrane-stabilizing properties. Although it is a naturally occurring cofactor, it is generally synthesized within the cell. Those cells that have the highest metabolic activity are most sensitive to deficiencies.

The clinical uses of ubiquinone are quite interesting and include congestive heart disease, hypertension, periodontal disease, obesity, immune deficiencies, and angina.[1]

Ubiquinone is slowly absorbed requiring 5-10 hours to reach a peak. Following oral doses of 100 mg, peak blood levels of 1 μg/mL have been reported.[2] With doses of 300 mg/d, mean plasma levels were 5.4 μg/mL after 4 days. No data are available on ubiquinone levels in milk. However, ubiquinone is very lipid soluble and has a long plasma half-life; transfer to milk is likely. If one were to assume a milk/plasma ratio of 1.0 and a significant maternal dose of 300 mg/d, then the average daily intake via milk in an infant would be approximately 16% of the weight-adjusted maternal dose. Were these numbers correct, it is not likely that this dose would be overtly toxic to an infant. Although ubiquinone is relatively non-toxic in adults,   there are no data on the relative toxicity of this substance in infants. Most references suggest that pregnant and lactating women should avoid supplementation with this cofactor.

Pregnancy Risk Category:

Lactation Risk Category: L3

Theoretic Infant Dose:

Adult Concerns: Caution when using in patient with biliary obstruction. Caution when using with hypolipidemic agents, oral hypoglycemic agents, insulin, in patients with hepatic and renal insufficiency. Most common adverse effects include nausea, epigastric pain, diarrhea, heartburn, appetite suppression.

Pediatric Concerns: None reported but caution recommended.

Drug Interactions: Do not use with oral hypoglycemics, hypolipidemic agents. May decrease INR in patients taking warfarin.

Alternatives:

Adult Dosage:

T½ = 34 hours	M/P =
PHL =	PB =
PK = 5-10 hours	Oral = Complete
MW =	pKa =
Vd =	

References:

1.   Gaby AR.: Coenzyme Q10, in Pizzorno JE. Churchill Livingstone(eds): Textbook of Natural Medicine, 1999.
2.   Greenberg S, Frishman WH.   Co-enzyme Q10: a new drug for cardiovascular disease. J Clin Pharmacol. 30(7):596-608, 1990.

COLCHICINE

Trade: Colchicine
Can/Aus/UK: Colchicine, Colgout
Uses: Analgesic in gouty arthritis
AAP: Approved by the American Academy of Pediatrics for use in breastfeeding mothers

Colchicine is an old product primarily used to reduce pain associated with inflammatory gout. Although it reduces the pain, it is not a true analgesic, but simply reduces the inflammation associated with uric acid crystals by inhibiting leukocyte and other cellular migration into the region. However, it is quite toxic, and routine CBC should be done while under treatment.   Blood dyscrasias, hepatomegaly, and bone marrow depression are all possible, particularly in infants.   Although the plasma half-life is only 20 minutes, it deposits in blood leukocytes and many other tissues, thereby extending the elimination half-life to over 60 hours.

Little or no consistent data on breastmilk levels are available.   In the one study published, even the authors questioned the percent recovery in the breastmilk,   so the data must be considered questionable. Nevertheless, the milk concentration varied from 1.2 to 2.5 μg/L (16-19 days postpartum) in one patient receiving 0.6 mg of colchicine twice daily.[1]

Pregnancy Risk Category: D

Lactation Risk Category: L4

Theoretic Infant Dose: 0.4 μg/kg/day

Adult Concerns: Nausea, vomiting, diarrhea, myopathy, leukopenia, bone marrow suppression.

Pediatric Concerns: None reported in one case reviewed.

Drug Interactions: Colchicine reduces vitamin B-12 absorption. Avoid alcohol.

Alternatives:

Adult Dosage: 0.5-0.6 mg 1-4 times a week

T½ = 12-30 minutes	M/P =
PHL =	PB = 10-31%
PK = 1-2 hours.	Oral = Complete
MW = 399	pKa = 1.7, 12.4
Vd = 10-12	

References:
1. Milunsky JM, and Milunsky A. Breast-feeding during colchicine therapy for familial Mediterranean fever. J. Pediatr. 119: 164, 1991.

COMFREY

Trade: Russian Comfrey, Knitbone, Bruisewort, Blackwort, Slippery Root
Can/Aus/UK:
Uses: Herbal poultice
AAP: Not reviewed

Comfrey has been claimed to heal gastric ulcers, hemorrhoids and suppress bronchial congestion and inflammation.[1] The product contains allantoin, tannin, and a group of dangerous pyrrolizidine alkaloids. Ointments containing comfrey have been found to be anti-inflammatory, probably due to the allantoin content. However, when administered orally to animals, most members of this family (Boraginaceae) have been noted to induce severe liver toxicity including elevated liver enzymes and liver tumors (hepatocellular adenomas).[2,3] Bladder tumors were noted at low concentrations. Russian comfrey has been found to induce liver damage and pancreatic islet cell tumors.[4] A number of significant human toxicities have been reported including several deaths, all associated with the ingestion of comfrey teas, or yerba mate tea.[5] Even when applied to the skin, pyrrolizidine alkaloids were noted in the urine of rodents. Lactating rats excreted pyrrolizidine alkaloids into breastmilk.

Comfrey and members of this family are exceedingly dangerous and should not be used topically, ingested orally, or used in any form in breastfeeding mothers.

Pregnancy Risk Category: X

Lactation Risk Category: L5

Theoretic Infant Dose:

Adult Concerns: Liver toxicity, hepatic carcinoma, hepatocellular adenomas, hepatonecrosis.

Pediatric Concerns: Passes into animal milk. Too dangerous for breastfeeding mothers and infants.

Drug Interactions:

Alternatives:

Adult Dosage:

References:
1. Review of Natural Products. Facts and Comparisons, St. Louis, Mo. 1996.
2. Hirono et.al. Carcinogenic activity of symphytale officinale. J. Nat. Cancer Inst 61:865, 1978.
3. Yeong ML. Hepatocyte membrane injury and bleb formation following low dose comfrey toxicity in rats. Inter J of Exp Pathol 74:211, 1993.
4. Yeong ML. The effects of comfrey derived pyrrolizidine alkaloid on rat liver. Path 23:35, 1991.
5. McGee J. et.al. A case of veno-occlusive disease of the liver in Britain associated with herbal tea consumption. J. Clin. Pathol. 29:788, 1976.

COPPER-64

Trade: Copper-64
Can/Aus/UK:
Uses: Radioisotope
AAP: Radioactive compound that requires temporary cessation of breastfeeding.

Copper-64 is a radioactive compound. Radioactivity is present in milk after 50 hours. Pump and discard until radioactivity has decayed(approximately 5 half-lives = 64 hours). Radioactive half-life is 12.7 hours.

Pregnancy Risk Category:

Lactation Risk Category: L4

Theoretic Infant Dose:

Adult Concerns:

Pediatric Concerns:

Drug Interactions:

Alternatives:

Adult Dosage:

T½ = 12.7 hours.	M/P =
PHL=	PB =
PK =	Oral =
MW = 64	pKa =
Vd = 2.0	

References:

CORTICOSTEROIDS

Trade: ACTH
Can/Aus/UK:
Uses: Steroid, corticosteroid
AAP: Not reviewed

Small amounts of most corticosteroids are secreted into breastmilk. Following a 10 mg oral dose of prednisone, 2 hour milk levels of prednisolone and   prednisone were 1.6 μg/L and 26.7 μg/L respectively.[1] Doses of 80 mg/day in mothers produce insignificant absorption in infant (< 0.1% of dose). In small doses, most steroids are not contraindicated in nursing mothers. Whenever possible use low-dose alternatives such as aerosols or inhalers. Following administration, wait at least 4 hours if possible prior to feeding infant to reduce exposure. With high doses, particularly for longer periods, steroids may inhibit epiphyseal bone growth, weaken bones, and may induce gastric ulcerations in children. Brief applications of high dose steroids are probably not contraindicated, but this will require a risk-benefit assessment.

Pregnancy Risk Category: C

Lactation Risk Category: L3

Theoretic Infant Dose: 4.0 μg/kg/day

Adult Concerns: Gastric distress, gastric ulceration, glaucoma, thinning skin.

Pediatric Concerns: None reported via milk.   Limit degree and duration of exposure if possible. Use inhaled or intranasal steroids to reduce exposure.

Drug Interactions: Decreased effect when used with barbiturates, phenytoin, rifampin.

Alternatives:

Adult Dosage: N/A

T½ = 24+ hours PHL = PK = 1 hour(milk) MW = 346 Vd =	M/P = 0.25 PB = 75% Oral = Complete pKa =

References:
1. Berlin CM, Kaiser DG, Demmers L. Excretion of prednisone and prednisolone in human milk. Pharmacologist 21:264, 1979.
2. Ost L, Wettrell G. Bjorkhem I, et.al. Prednisolone excretion in human milk. J Pediatr. 106:1008-1011,1985.
3. Wilson, J. Drugs in Breast Milk. New York: ADIS Press, 1981.
4. Katz FH, Duncan BR. Entry of prednisone into human milk. N Engl J Med 293:1154, 1975.
5. Ost L, et. al. Prednisolone excretion in human milk. J Pediatr 106:1008-11, 1985.
6. Greenberger PA, et.al. Pharmacokinetics of prednisolone transfer to breast milk. Clinical Pharmacology and Therapeutics 53:324-328, 1993.

CORTICOTROPIN

Trade: ACT, Acthar, ACTH
Can/Aus/UK: Acthar
Uses: Stimulates cortisol release
AAP: Not reviewed

ACTH is secreted by the anterior pituitary in the brain and stimulates the adrenal cortex to produce and secrete adrenocortical hormones (cortisol, hydrocortisone). As a peptide product, ACTH is easily destroyed in the infants' GI tract. None would be absorbed by the infant. ACTH stimulates the endogenous production of cortisol which theoretically can transfer to the breastfed infant. However, the use of ACTH in breastfeeding mothers largely depends on the dose and duration of exposure, and the risks to the infant. Brief exposures are probably not contraindicated.

Pregnancy Risk Category: C

Lactation Risk Category: L3

Theoretic Infant Dose:

Adult Concerns: Hypersensitivity reactions, increased risk of infection, embryocidal effects, other symptoms of hypercorticalism.

Pediatric Concerns: None reported via milk.

Drug Interactions:

Alternatives:

Adult Dosage: 80 U injection (IM or SC)

T½ = 15 minutes.	M/P =
PHL =	PB =
PK =	Oral = 0%
MW =	pKa =
Vd =	

References:

CROMOLYN SODIUM

Trade: Nasalcrom, Gastrocrom, Intal
Can/Aus/UK: Cromese, Intal, Intral, Nalcrom, Opticrom, Rynacrom, Vistacrom
Uses: Antiasthmatic, antiallergic
AAP: Not reviewed

Cromolyn is an extremely safe drug that is used clinically as an antiasthmatic, antiallergic, and to suppress mast cell degranulation and allergic symptoms.   No data on penetration into human breastmilk is available, but it has an extremely low pKa, and minimal levels would be expected.[1] Less than 0.001% of a dose is distributed into milk of the monkey.   No harmful effects have been reported on breastfeeding infants. Less than 1% of this drug is absorbed from the maternal (and probably the infant's) GI tract, so it is unlikely to produce untoward effects in nursing infants. This product is frequently used in pediatric patients.

Pregnancy Risk Category: B

Lactation Risk Category: L1

Theoretic Infant Dose:

Adult Concerns: Headache, itching, nausea, diarrhea, allergic reactions, hoarseness, coughing.

Pediatric Concerns: None reported via milk.

Drug Interactions:

Alternatives:

Adult Dosage: 20 mg QID via inhalation

T½ = 80-90 minutes	M/P =
PHL =	PB =
PK = < 15 minutes	Oral = < 1%
MW = 468	pKa = Low
Vd =	

References:
1.   McEvoy GE(ed):AHFS Drug Information, New York, NY. 1995.

CYCLIZINE

Trade: Marezine
Can/Aus/UK: Diconal, Marzine, Migral, Valoid
Uses: Antihistamine, antiemetic
AAP: Not reviewed

Cyclizine is an antihistamine frequently used as an antiemetic, and for motion sickness.   In past years, this drug was frequently used for nausea and vomiting of pregnancy, although it is no longer used for this purpose.   No reports concerning its secretion into human milk are available.

Pregnancy Risk Category: B

Lactation Risk Category: L3

Theoretic Infant Dose:

Adult Concerns: Sedation, dry mouth.

Pediatric Concerns: None reported via milk.

Drug Interactions: Increased sedation with CNS depressants such as alcohol, barbiturates.

Alternatives:

Adult Dosage: 50 mg q 4-6 hours

T½ =	M/P =
PHL =	PB =
PK =	Oral =
MW = 266	pKa = 7.7
Vd =	

References:

CYCLOBENZAPRINE

Trade: Flexeril, Cycoflex
Can/Aus/UK: Flexeril, Novo-Cycloprine
Uses: Muscle relaxant, CNS depressant
AAP: Not reviewed

Cyclobenzaprine is a centrally acting skeletal muscle relaxant that is structurally and pharmacologically similar to the tricyclic antidepressants. Cyclobenzaprine is used as an adjunct to rest and physical therapy for the relief of acute, painful musculoskeletal conditions.[1] Studies have not conclusively shown whether the skeletal muscle relaxation properties are due to the sedation or placebo effects. At least one study has found it no more effective than placebo. It is not known if cyclobenzaprine is secreted in milk, but one must assume that its secretion would be similar to the tricyclics (see amitriptyline, desipramine). There are no pediatric indications for this product.

Pregnancy Risk Category: B

Lactation Risk Category: L3

Theoretic Infant Dose:

Adult Concerns: Drowsiness, dry mouth, dizziness, nausea, vomiting, unpleasant taste sensation. Tachycardia, hypotension, arrhythmias.

Pediatric Concerns: None reported, but caution is urged.

Drug Interactions: Do not use with 14 days of MAO inhibitor. Additive effect with tricyclic antidepressants. Enhances effect of alcohol, barbiturates, and other CNS depressants.

Alternatives:

Adult Dosage: 20-60 mg QD

T½ = 24-72 hours.		M/P =	
PHL =		PB = 93%	
PK = 3-8 hours		Oral = Complete	
MW = 275		pKa =	
Vd = High			

References:
1. McEvoy GE(ed):AHFS Drug Information, New York, NY. 1995.

CYCLOPHOSPHAMIDE

Trade: Neosar, Cytoxan
Can/Aus/UK: Cycloblastin, Cytoxan, Endoxan, Endoxana, Procytox
Uses: Antineoplastic
AAP: Contraindicated by the American Academy of Pediatrics in Breastfeeding Mothers

Cyclophosphamide is a powerful and toxic antineoplastic drug. A number of reports in the literature indicate that cyclophosphamide can transfer into human milk as evidenced by the production of leukopenia and bone marrow suppression in at least 3 breastfed infants. In one case of a mother who received 800 mg/week of cyclophosphamide, the infant was significancy neutropenic following 6 weeks of exposure via breastmilk.[1] Major leukopenia was also reported in a second breastfed infant following only a brief exposure.[2] Thus far, no reports have provided quantitative estimates of cyclophosphamide in milk. This agent should not be used in breastfeeding mothers.

Pregnancy Risk Category: D

Lactation Risk Category: L5

Theoretic Infant Dose:

Adult Concerns: Leukopenia, infections, anemia, GI distress, nausea, vomiting, diarrhea, hemorrhagic colitis.

Pediatric Concerns: Leukopenia and bone marrow suppression in at least 3 breastfed infants.

Drug Interactions: Cyclophosphamide may reduce digoxin serum levels. Increased bone marrow suppression when used with allopurinol, and cardiotoxicity when used with doxorubicin. May prolong effect of neuromuscular blocking agents. Chloramphenicol increases half-life of cyclophosphamide. Numerous others, see complete review.

Alternatives:

Adult Dosage: 1-5 mg/kg QD

$T\frac{1}{2}$ = 7.5 hours		M/P =	
PHL=		PB = 13%	
PK = 2-3 hours.		Oral = 75%	
MW = 261		pKa =	
Vd =			

References:
1. Amato D, Niblett JS. Neutropenia from cyclophosphamide in breast milk. Med. J. Australia 1:383-4, 1977.
2. Durodola JL. Administration of cyclophosphamide during late pregnancy and early lactation: a case report. J.Natl.Med.Assoc. 71:165-6,1979.

CYCLOSERINE

Trade: Seromycin
Can/Aus/UK: Closina, Cycloserine
Uses: Anti-tuberculosis drug
AAP: Approved by the American Academy of Pediatrics for use in breastfeeding mothers

Cycloserine is an antibiotic primarily used for treating tuberculosis. It is also effective against various staphylococcal infections. It is a small molecule with a structure similar to an amino acid, D-alanine. Following 250 mg oral dose given four times daily to mothers, milk levels ranged from 6 to 19 mg/L, an average of 72% of maternal serum levels.[1] Vorherr estimates the percent of maternal daily dose excreted in milk to be 0.6%.[2]

Pregnancy Risk Category: C

Lactation Risk Category: L3

Theoretic Infant Dose: 2.9 mg/kg/day

Adult Concerns: Drowsiness, CNS confusion, dizziness, headache, lethargy, depression, seizures. Precautions urged in epilepsy, depression, severe anxiety.

Pediatric Concerns: None reported.

Drug Interactions: Increased toxicity with alcohol, isoniazid. Phenytoin levels may be elevated due to inhibition of metabolism.

Alternatives:

Adult Dosage: 250 mg BID

T½ = 12+ hours	M/P = 0.72
PHL =	PB =
PK = 3-4 hours	Oral = 70-90%
MW = 102	pKa =
Vd =	

References:
1. Morton RF, et.al. Studies on the absorption, diffusion, and excretion of cycloserine. Antibiot. Ann. 3:169-72, 1955.
2. Vorherr, H. Drug excretion in breast milk. Postgrad. Med. 56:97-104, 1974.

CYCLOSPORINE

Trade: Sandimmune, Neoral
Can/Aus/UK: Neoral, Sandimmune
Uses: Immunosuppressant
AAP: Cytotoxic drug that may interfere with cellular metabolism of the nursing infant.

Cyclosporine is an immunosuppressant used to reduce organ rejection following transplant and in autoimmune syndromes such as arthritis, etc. In a recent report of 7 breastfeeding mothers treated with cyclosporine, the levels of cyclosporine in breastmilk ranged from 50 to 227 μg/L. Corresponding plasma levels in the breastfed infants were undetectable (<30 ng/mL) in all infants. In this study, the infants received less than 300 ug per day via breastmilk.[1] In another, following a dose of 320 mg/d, the milk level at 22 hours post dose was 16 μg/L and the milk/plasma ratio was 0.28.[2] In another report of a mother receiving 250 mg twice daily, the maternal plasma level of cyclosporine was measured at 187 μg/L, the breastmilk level was 167 μg/L.[3] None was detected in the plasma of the infant.

In a study of a breastfeeding transplant patient who received 300 mg twice daily, maternal serum levels were 193, 273, and 123 ng/mL at 23 days, 6.5 and 9.7 weeks postpartum.[4] Corresponding milk cyclosporine levels were 160, 286, and 79 μg/L respectively. Using the higher milk level, an infant would receive less than 0.4% of the weight-adjusted maternal dose. All these studies suggest that the clinical dose transferred to the infant via milk is minuscule. Cyclosporine use during lactation is subject to some risk and close observation of a breastfeeding infant is suggested.

Pregnancy Risk Category: C

Lactation Risk Category: L3

Theoretic Infant Dose: 34.1 μg/kg/day

Adult Concerns: Kidney toxicity, edema, tremor, seizures, elevated liver enzymes, hypertension, hirsutism. Use during pregnancy does not pose a major risk. Infections and possible lymphomas may result.

Pediatric Concerns: None reported, but caution is urged.

Drug Interactions: Rifampin, phenytoin, phenobarbital decrease plasma concentrations of cyclosporine. Ketoconazole, fluconazole, and itraconazole increase plasma concentrations of cyclosporine.

Alternatives:

Adult Dosage: 10-15 mg/kg QD

T½ = 5.6 hours	M/P = 0.28-0.4
PHL =	PB = 93%
PK = 3.5 hours.	Oral = 28% pediatric
MW =	pKa =
Vd = 3.1-4.3	

References:
1. Nyberg G, Haljamae U, et.al. Breast-feeding during treatment with cyclosporine. Transplantation 65(2):253-255, 1998.
2. Flechner SM, Katz AR, Rogers AJ, et.al. The presence of cyclosporine in body tissue and fluids during pregnancy. Am J Kidney Dis. 5:60-63,1985.
3. KDT. (personal communication), 1997.
4. Munoz-Flores-Thiagarajan KD, Easterling T, Davis C, Bond EF. Breast-feeding by a cyclosporine-treated mother. Obstet Gynecol. 97(5 Pt 2):816-8, 2001.

CYPROHEPTADINE

Trade: Periactin
Can/Aus/UK: PMS-Cyproheptadine, Periactin
Uses: Antihistamine
AAP: Not reviewed

Cyproheptadine is a serotonin and histamine antagonist with anticholinergic and sedative effects.   It has been used as an appetite stimulant in children, and for rashes and pruritus (itching).   No data are available on its transfer to human milk.

Pregnancy Risk Category: B

Lactation Risk Category: L3

Theoretic Infant Dose:

Adult Concerns: Sedation, nausea, vomiting, diarrhea.

Pediatric Concerns: None reported. Observe for sedation.

Drug Interactions: Additive sedation when used with other antihistamines and CNS depressants. Increased toxicity (hallucinations) when used with MAO inhibitors.

Alternatives: Hydroxyzine

Adult Dosage: 4 mg TID-QID

T½ = 16 hours		M/P =	
PHL=		PB =	
PK =		Oral =	
MW = 287		pKa = 9.3	
Vd =			

References:

CYTARABINE

Trade: Cytosar
Can/Aus/UK: Alexan, Cytosar
Uses: Antineoplastic
AAP: Not reviewed

Cytarabine is converted intra-cellularly to a nucleotide that interrupts DNA synthesis. No data has been reported on transfer into breastmilk.[1] The compound is poorly absorbed orally and is therefore used IM or I.V. only. This drug would be extremely toxic to an infant and is generally contraindicated in breastfeeding mothers.

Pregnancy Risk Category: D

Lactation Risk Category: L5

Theoretic Infant Dose:

Adult Concerns: Anemia, bone marrow suppression, nausea, vomiting, diarrhea, GI hemorrhage, elevated liver enzymes.

Pediatric Concerns: None reported via milk. But due to toxicity, this product should never be used in a breastfeeding mother.

Drug Interactions: Decreases effect of gentamycin flucytosine, digoxin. Increases toxicity of alkylating agents, radiation, purine analogs, methotrexate.

Alternatives:

Adult Dosage: 100 mg/m^2 I.V. QD

T½ = 1-3 hours.	M/P =
PHL =	PB = 13%.
PK =	Oral = <20%
MW = 243	pKa =
Vd =	

References:
1. Drug Facts and Comparisons. 1995 ed. Facts and Comparisons, St. Louis.

CYTOMEGALOVIRUS

Trade: Human Cytomegalovirus, CMV
Can/Aus/UK:
Uses: Viral infection
AAP:

Cytomegalovirus is one of the family of herpes viruses. CMV is rather ubiquitous, many infants having been exposed in utero, and later in day care centers.[1] Maternal cervical infection is very common. CMV is found in breastmilk of virtually all CMV positive women using the newer PCR techniques.[2] The timing of maternal infection is important. If the mother seroconverts early in gestation, the infant is likely to be affected. Symptoms include: small for gestational age, jaundice, microcephaly, petechia, hepatosplenomegaly, hearing loss. If the mother seroconverts late in gestation, the infant is less likely to be severely affected.   In most infants from seropositive mothers, the CMV found in breastmilk is not overtly dangerous, and these mothers can breastfeed successfully.[3] However, infants who are not provided with maternal antibodies to CMV may be exceedingly susceptible to CMV in breastmilk. Breastmilk from CMV positive mothers should never be fed to unprotected infants.

Pregnancy Risk Category:

Lactation Risk Category:

Theoretic Infant Dose:

Adult Concerns: Asymptomatic to Hepatosplenomegaly. Fever, mild hepatitis.

Pediatric Concerns: CMV transfer into breastmilk is known but of low risk to infants born of CMV positive mothers. Breastmilk from CMV positive mothers should never be fed to unprotected non-immune infants.

Drug Interactions:

Alternatives:

Adult Dosage: 50-150 mg/kg I.V. QD

References:
1. Dworsky M et.al. Cytomegalovirus infection of breast milk and transmission in infancy. Pediatrics 72:295, 1983.
2. Hotsubo T, Nagata N, et.al. Detection of human cytomegalovirus DNA in breast milk by means of polymerase chain reaction. Microbiol. Immunol. 38(10):809-811,1994.
3. Lawrence RA. Breastfeeding, A guide for the medical profession. Mosby, St. Louis, 1994.

DACTINOMYCIN

Trade: Cosmegen
Can/Aus/UK: Cosmegen
Uses: Antibiotic used in cancer chemotherapy
AAP: Not reviewed

Dactinomycin is an antineoplastic antibiotic that inhibits DNA and RNA synthesis. It is extremely dangerous and very toxic. Transfer into breastmilk is unreported.[1] Although its oral absorption is very poor, it is extremely irritating to tissues and must be administered I.V. only. Definitely contraindicated in nursing mothers.

Pregnancy Risk Category: C

Lactation Risk Category: L5

Theoretic Infant Dose:

Adult Concerns: Anemia, bone marrow suppression, skin lesions and rashes, alopecia, malaise, fatigue, fever, liver toxicity.

Pediatric Concerns: None reported, but could be extremely toxic. Caution urged.

Drug Interactions: Dactinomycin potentiates the toxicity of radiation therapy.

Alternatives:

Adult Dosage: 0.5 mg I.V. QD

T½ = 36 hours	**M/P =**
PHL =	**PB =**
PK =	**Oral = Poor**
MW = 1255	**pKa =**
Vd =	

References:
1.   Drug Facts and Comparisons. 1995 ed. Facts and Comparisons, St. Louis.

DALTEPARIN SODIUM

Trade: Fragmin, Low Molecular Weight Heparin
Can/Aus/UK: Fragmin
Uses: Anticoagulant
AAP: Not reviewed

Dalteparin is a low molecular weight polysaccharide fragment of heparin used clinically as an anticoagulant.

In a study of two patients who received 5000-10,000 IU of dalteparin, none was found in human milk.[1]

In another study of 15 post-caesarian patients early postpartum(mean = 5.7 days),   blood and milk levels of dalteparin were determined 3-4 hours post-treatment.[2]   Following subcutaneous doses of 2500 IU, maternal plasma levels averaged 0.074 to 0.308 IU/mL.   Breastmilk levels of dalteparin ranged from < 0.005 to 0.037 IU/mL of milk. The milk/plasma ratio ranged from 0.025 to 0.224.   Using this data, an infant ingesting 150 mL/kg/day would ingest approximately 5.5 IU/kg/day. Due to the polysaccharide nature of this production, oral absorption is unlikely.   Further, because this study was done early postpartum, it is possible that the levels in 'mature' milk would be lower.   The authors suggest that "it appears highly unlikely that puerperal thromboprophylaxis with LMWH has any clinically relevant effect on the nursing infant".

Pregnancy Risk Category: B

Lactation Risk Category: L2

Theoretic Infant Dose: 5.5 IU/kg/day

Adult Concerns: Anticoagulant effects in adults when administered subcutaneously.

Pediatric Concerns: None reported via milk. Molecular weight is too large to produce clinically relevant milk levels.

Drug Interactions:

Alternatives: Enoxaparin

Adult Dosage: 2500 units daily

T½ = 2.3 hours	M/P = 0.025-0.224
PHL =	PB =
PK = 2-4 hours (SC)	Oral = None
MW = 4000	pKa =
Vd = 0.06	

References:
1. Harenberg J, Leber G, Zimmermann R, Schmidt W. Prevention of thromboembolism with low-molecular weight heparin in pregnancy. Geburtshilfe Frauenheilkd 47(1):15-8, 1987.
2. Richter C, Sitzmann J, et.al. Excretion of low molecular weight heparin in human milk. Br. J. Clin. Pharmacol. 52:708-710, 2001.

DANAZOL

Trade: Danocrine
Can/Aus/UK: Azol, Cyclomen, Danocrine, Danol
Uses: Synthetic androgen, antigonadotropic agent
AAP: Not reviewed

Danazol suppresses the pituitary-ovarian axis by inhibiting output of pituitary and hypothalamic hormones. It also appears to inhibit the synthesis of sex steroids and provides antiestrogenic effects. It is primarily used for treating endometriosis. Due to its effect on pituitary hormones and its androgenic effects, it is likely to reduce the rate of breastmilk production, although this has not been documented. No data on its transfer into human milk are available.

Pregnancy Risk Category: X

Lactation Risk Category: L5

Theoretic Infant Dose:

Adult Concerns: Breast size reduction. Androgenic effects, hirsutism, acne, weight gain, edema, testicular atrophy, thrombocytopenia, thrombocytosis, hot flashes.

Pediatric Concerns: None reported, but caution is urged.

Drug Interactions: Decreased insulin requirements. May increase anticoagulation with warfarin therapy.

Alternatives:

Adult Dosage: 50-200 mg BID

T½ = 4.5 hours	M/P =
PHL =	PB =
PK = 2 hours	Oral = Complete
MW = 337	pKa =
Vd =	

References:
1. White, G. and White, M. Breastfeeding and drugs in human milk. Vet. and Human Tox. 26:supplement 1, 1984.

DANTROLENE

Trade: Dantrium
Can/Aus/UK: Dantrium
Uses: Skeletal muscle relaxant
AAP: Not reviewed

Dantrolene produces a direct skeletal muscle relaxation and is indicated for spasticity resulting from upper motor neuron disorders such as multiple sclerosis, cerebral palsy, etc.[1] It is not indicated for rheumatic disorders, or musculoskeletal trauma. No data are available on transfer into human milk.

Pregnancy Risk Category: C

Lactation Risk Category: L4

Theoretic Infant Dose:

Adult Concerns: Adverse effects are quite common and include weakness, dizziness, diarrhea, slurred speech, drooling, and nausea. Significant risk for hepatotoxicity. Visual and auditory hallucinations.

Pediatric Concerns: None reported, but caution is urged.

Drug Interactions: Increased toxicity with estrogens, CNS sedatives, MAO inhibitors, phenothiazines, calcium channel blockers, warfarin, and tolbutamide.

Alternatives:

Adult Dosage: 1-2 mg/kg TID-QID

T½ = 8.7 hours	**M/P** =
PHL = 7.3 hours	**PB** =
PK = 5 hours	**Oral** = 35%
MW = 314	**pKa** =
Vd =	

References:
1. Pharmaceutical Manufacturers Package Insert, 1997.

DAPSONE

Trade: Dapsone
Can/Aus/UK: Avlosulfon, Maloprim
Uses: Sulfone antibiotic
AAP: Approved by the American Academy of Pediatrics for use in breastfeeding mothers

Dapsone is a sulfone antibiotic useful for treating leprosy, tuberculoid leprosy, dermatitis herpetiformis, and pneumocystis carinii pneumonia. In one case report of a mother consuming 50 mg daily while breastfeeding, both the mother and infant had symptoms of hemolytic anemia.[1] Plasma levels of dapsone in mother and infant were 1622 ng/mL and 439 ng/ml respectively. Breastmilk levels were reported to be 1092 μg/L. In another study of 3 patients receiving 100 mg/day, milk levels averaged 580 μg/L, but these were not at steady state levels.[2] The authors estimated the dose via milk was 4.6 to 14.3% of the maternal dose.

Dapsone is one of those drugs which apparently has all the proper kinetic parameters to enter milk, high lipophilicity, low molecular weight, high volume of distribution, high pKb, etc. While it is approved by the AAP, this is one exception that should be used very cautiously if at all. The dose this mother was consuming was 50 mg/day which is half the normal dose.

Pregnancy Risk Category: C

Lactation Risk Category: L4

Theoretic Infant Dose: 163.8 μg/kg/day

Adult Concerns: Adverse effects reported include hemolytic anemia (particularly in G6PD deficient persons), methemoglobinemia, aplastic anemia, psychotic episodes, peripheral neuropathy, acute renal failure, nephrotic syndrome, hepatotoxicity, exfoliative dermatitis, erythema multiforme, toxic epidermal necrolysis, and hypersensitivity reactions

Pediatric Concerns: Hemolytic anemia in one breastfeeding patient.

Drug Interactions: Increased dapsone levels when taken with Amprenavir, trimethoprim, delavirdine, and probenecid. Dapsone may increase chloramphenicol plasma levels. Rifampin may decrease plasma levels of dapsone. Concomitant administration of zidovudine with drugs like dapsone which are cytotoxic or suppress bone marrow function may increase the risk of hematologic toxicity

Alternatives:

Adult Dosage: 100 mg daily

T½ = 28 hours	M/P =
PHL=	PB = 70-90%
PK = 4-8 hours	Oral = 86-100%
MW = 248	pKa =
Vd = 1-2	

References:
1. Sanders SW, Zone JJ, Foltz RL, et.al. Hemolytic Anemia induced by dapsone transmitted through breastmilk. Annals of Internal Medicine, 96(4):465-466, 1982.
2. Edstein MD, Veenendaal JR, Newman K et al: Excretion of chloroquine, dapson and pyrimethamine in human milk. Br J Clin Pharmacol 22:733-735,1986.

DESIPRAMINE

Trade: Pertofrane, Norpramin
Can/Aus/UK: Norpramin, Novo-Desipramine, Pertofran, Pertofrane
Uses: Tricyclic antidepressant
AAP: Drug whose effect on nursing infants is unknown but may be of concern

Desipramine is a prototypical tricyclic antidepressant. In one case report, a mother taking 200 mg of desipramine at bedtime had milk/plasma ratios of 0.4 to 0.9 with milk levels ranging between 17-35 μg/L.[1] Desipramine was not found in the infant's blood, although these levels are probably too low to measure. In another study of a mother consuming 300 mg of desipramine daily, the milk levels were 30% higher than the maternal serum.[2] The milk concentrations of desipramine were reported to be 316 to 328 μg/L, with peak concentrations occurring at 4 hours post-dose. Assuming an average milk concentration of 280 μg/L, an infant would receive approximately 42 μg/kg/day. This dose is approximately 1/100th the maternal dose. No untoward effects have been reported.

Pregnancy Risk Category: C

Lactation Risk Category: L2

Theoretic Infant Dose: 42.0 μg/kg/day

Adult Concerns: Anticholinergic side effects, such as drying of secretions, dilated pupil, sedation, constipation, fatigue, peculiar taste.

Pediatric Concerns: None reported in many studies.

Drug Interactions: Do not use with MAO inhibitors or within two weeks of therapy. Increased effects occur following use with stimulants, and benzodiazepines. Decreased effects occur with barbiturates, carbamazepine, and phenytoin use.

Alternatives: Amoxapine, Imipramine

Adult Dosage: 100-200 mg QD

T½ = 7-60 hours	M/P = 0.4-0.9
PHL =	PB = 82%
PK = 4-6 hours	Oral = 90%
MW = 266	pKa = 9.5
Vd = 22-59	

References:
1. Sovner R, Orsulak PJ. Excretion of imipramine and desipramine in human breast milk. Am J Psychiatry 136:451-2, 1979.
2. Stancer HC, Reed KL. Desipramine and 2-Hydroxydesipramine in human breast milk and the nursing infant's serum. Am. J. Psy. 143:1597-1600, 1986.

DESMOPRESSIN ACETATE

Trade: DDAVP, Stimate
Can/Aus/UK: DDAVP, Desmospray, Minirin, Rhinyle
Uses: Synthetic antidiuretic hormone.
AAP: Not reviewed

Desmopressin (DDAVP) is a small synthetic octapeptide antidiuretic hormone.[1] Desmopressin increases reabsorption of water by the collecting ducts in the kidneys resulting in decreased urinary flow (ADH effect). Generally used in patients who lack pituitary vasopressin, it is primarily used intranasally or intravenously. Unlike natural vasopressin, desmopressin has no effect on growth hormone, prolactin, or luteinizing hormone.

Following intranasal administration, less than 10-20% is absorbed through the nasal mucosa. This peptide has been used in lactating women without effect on nursing infants.[2,3] In a study of one breastfeeding mother receiving 10 ug twice daily of DDAVP(desmopressin), maternal plasma levels peaked at 40 minutes after the dose at approximately 7 ng/L, while milk levels were virtually unchanged at 1-1.5 ng/L.[4] Because DDAVP is easily destroyed in the gastrointestinal tract by trypsin, the oral absorption of these levels in milk would be nil.

Pregnancy Risk Category: B

Lactation Risk Category: L2

Theoretic Infant Dose:

Adult Concerns: Reduced urine production, edema, fluid retention.

Pediatric Concerns: None reported.

Drug Interactions: Lithium, demeclocycline may decrease ADH effect. Chlorpropamide, fludrocortisone may increase ADH effect.

Alternatives:

Adult Dosage: 10-40 mcg intranasally QD

T½ = 75.5 minutes.	M/P = 0.2
PHL =	PB =
PK = 40 min.	Oral = 0.16%
MW = 1069	pKa =
Vd =	

References:
1. McEvoy GE(ed):AFHS Drug Information, New York, NY. 1992, pp 417-26.
2. Hime MC, Richardson JA. Diabetes insipidus and pregnancy. Obstet. Gynecol. Surv. 33:375-379, 1978
3. Hadi HA et.al. Diabetes insipidus during pregnancy complicated by preeclampsia. A Case Report. J. Reprod. Med. 30:206, 1985.
4. Burrow GN, Wassenaar W, Robertson GL, Sehl H. DDAVP treatment of diabetes insipidus during pregnancy and the post-partum period. Acta Endocrinol (Copenh). 97(1):23-5, 1981.

DESOGESTREL and ETHINYL ESTRADIOL

Trade: Mircette
Can/Aus/UK:
Uses: Low dose oral contraceptive
AAP: Not reviewed

This is a somewhat atypical lower dose estrogen/progestin oral contraceptive. It contains a potent progestin desogestrel in combination with 10 or 20 micrograms/day of ethinyl estradiol(EE). While most oral contraceptives contain 40 micrograms of EE or more, the reduced level estrogen in this product may be less inhibitory of milk production as is occasionally seen with the higher dose products. Still, the mother should observe for reduced milk production.

Pregnancy Risk Category: X

Lactation Risk Category: L3

Theoretic Infant Dose:

Adult Concerns: Observe for reduced milk production. Breakthrough bleeding is more common with this product.   Fluid retention has been reported.   See typical oral contraceptive contraindications.

Pediatric Concerns: Reduced milk supply is possible.   Do not use early postpartum.

Drug Interactions: Reduced efficacy when used with rifampin, barbiturates, phenytoin, carbamazepine, griseofulvin, ampicillin, and tetracyclines.

Alternatives: Norethindrone

Adult Dosage:

References:
1.   Pharmaceutical Manufacturer package insert, 2000.

DEXAMETHASONE

Trade: Decadron, Ak-dex, Maxidex
Can/Aus/UK: AK-Dex
Uses: Corticosteroid anti-inflammatory
AAP: Not reviewed

Dexamethasone is a long-acting corticosteroid, similar in effect to prednisone, although more potent.   Dexamethasone 0.75 mg is equivalent to a 5 mg dose of prednisone.[1]   While the elimination half-life is brief, only 3-6 hours in adults, its metabolic effects last for up to 72 hours. No data are available on the transfer of dexamethasone into human milk. It is likely similar to that of prednisone which is extremely low.   Doses of prednisone as high as 120 mg fail to produce clinically relevant milk levels.   This product is commonly used in pediatrics for treating immune syndromes such as arthritis, and particularly acute onset asthma or other broncho constrictive diseases. It is not likely that the amount in milk would produce clinical effects unless used in high doses over prolonged periods.

Pregnancy Risk Category: C

Lactation Risk Category: L3

Theoretic Infant Dose:

Adult Concerns: In pediatrics: shortened stature, GI bleeding, GI ulceration, edema, osteoporosis, glaucoma, and other symptoms of hyperadrenalism.

Pediatric Concerns: None reported via milk.

Drug Interactions: Barbiturates, phenytoin, rifampin may reduce the corticosteroid effect of dexamethasone. Dexamethasone may decrease effects of vaccines, salicylates, and toxoids.

Alternatives: Prednisone

Adult Dosage: 0.5-9 mg daily

T½ = 3.3 hours	M/P =
PHL=	PB =
PK = 1-2 hours	Oral = 78%
MW = 392	pKa =
Vd = 2	

References:
1.   Pharmaceutical Manufacturers Package Insert, 1999.

DEXFENFLURAMINE

Trade: Redux
Can/Aus/UK: Adifax
Uses: Anorexigenic, diet pill
AAP: Not reviewed

Dexfenfluramine is the dextro stereoisomer of fenfluramine (Pondimin) and is used for its anorexiant effect in weight reduction. It is both a serotonin reuptake inhibitor and releasing agent. It is metabolized to d-norfenfluramine (active) which has a half-life of 32 hours. Its transfer to human milk has not been reported although it is secreted in animal milk.[1,2] Due to the low molecular weight, and high CNS penetration, it is likely that this product may attain moderate levels in breastmilk. Further, its long half-life and active metabolite could possibly induce higher steady state plasma levels in the neonate with corresponding anorexia and weight loss after prolonged therapy. Risk assessment with this product may not justify exposure of a breastfeeding infant.

Pregnancy Risk Category: C

Lactation Risk Category: L4

Theoretic Infant Dose:

Adult Concerns: Adverse effects include diarrhea, drowsiness, dizziness, mood disorders, sleep disorders, tiredness, dry mouth, nausea, constipation, polyuria, suicide ideations, impaired concentration and memory(18%), pulmonary hypertension (1 per 22-44,000).

Pediatric Concerns: None reported, but caution urged.

Drug Interactions: Increased risk of serotonin syndrome when used with sumatriptan, dihydroergotamine, and tricyclic antidepressants. Increased toxicity when used with MAO inhibitors. Allow at least 14 days after MAOI use. May cause false positive results on urine drug screens.

Alternatives:

Adult Dosage: 15 mg BID

T½ = 17-20 hours	M/P =
PHL =	PB = 36%
PK = 2 hours	Oral = 68%
MW = 231	pKa =
Vd = 10	

References:
1. Drug Facts and Comparisons. 1996. ed. Facts and Comparisons, St. Louis.
2. Pharmaceutical Manufacturers Package Insert, 1997.

DEXTROAMPHETAMINE

Trade: Dexedrine, Amphetamine, Oxydess, Adderall
Can/Aus/UK: Dexamphetamine, Dexedrine, Dexten
Uses: Powerful CNS stimulant
AAP: Drugs of abuse for which adverse effects have been reported.

The only data available is on racemic amphetamines. Following a 20 mg daily dose of racemic amphetamine administered at 1000, 1200, 1400 and 1600 hours each day to a breastfeeding mother, amphetamine concentrations were determined in milk at 10 days and 42 days postpartum. Samples were taken at 20 min prior to the 1000 dose, and immediately prior to the 1400 dose. Milk levels were 55 and 118 μg/L, respectively.[1] Corresponding maternal plasma levels were 20 and 40 ng/mL at the same times. Milk/plasma ratios at these times were 2.8 and 3.0 respectively. At 42 days, breastmilk levels of amphetamine were 68 and 138 μg/L while maternal plasma levels were 9 and 21 ng/mL, respectively. Milk/plasma ratios in the 42 day samples were 7.5 and 6.6 respectively. Although the milk/plasma ratios appear high, using a daily milk intake of 150 mL/kg/d, the weight-adjusted relative infant dose would be only 6.7% of the maternal dose, which probably accounts for the fact that the infant in this study was unaffected.

Pregnancy Risk Category: C

Lactation Risk Category: L4

Theoretic Infant Dose: 20.7 μg/kg/day

Adult Concerns: Nervousness, insomnia, anorexia, hyperexcitability.

Pediatric Concerns: Possible insomnia, irritability, anorexia, or poor sleeping patterns in infants.

Drug Interactions: May precipitate hypertensive crisis in patients on MAO inhibitors and arrhythmias in patients receiving general anesthetics. Increased effect/toxicity with tricyclic antidepressants, phenytoin, phenobarbital, norepinephrine, meperidine.

Alternatives:

Adult Dosage: 5-60 mg QD

T½ = 6-8 hours	M/P = 2.8-7.5
PHL =	PB = 16-20%
PK = 1-2 hours	Oral = Complete
MW = 368	pKa = 9.9
Vd = 3.2-5.6	

References:
1. Steiner E, Hallberg V. Amphetamine secretion in breastmilk. Eur J Clin Pharmacol. 27:123-124, 1959.

DEXTROMETHORPHAN

Trade: DM, Benylin, Delsym, Pertussin, Robitussin DM
Can/Aus/UK: Balminil-DM, Benylin DM, Cosylan, Delsym
Uses: Antitussive, Cough preparation
AAP: Not reviewed

Dextromethorphan is a weak antitussive commonly used in infants and adults. It is a congener of codeine and appears to elevate the cough threshold in the brain. It does not have addictive, analgesic, or sedative actions, and it does not produce respiratory depression at normal doses.[1] It is the safest of the antitussives and is routinely used in children and infants.   No data on its transfer to human milk are available. It is very unlikely that enough would transfer via milk to provide clinically significant levels in a breastfed infant.

Pregnancy Risk Category: C

Lactation Risk Category: L1

Theoretic Infant Dose:

Adult Concerns: Drowsiness, fatigue, dizziness, hyperpyrexia.

Pediatric Concerns: None reported.

Drug Interactions: May interact with MAO inhibitors producing hypotension, hyperpyrexia, nausea, coma.

Alternatives: Codeine

Adult Dosage: 10-20 mg q 4 hours

T½ = <4 hours	**M/P** =
PHL =	**PB** =
PK = 1-2 hours	**Oral** = Complete
MW = 271	**pKa** = 8.3
Vd =	

References:
1. Pender ES, Parks BR: Toxicity with dextromethorphan-containing preparations: a literature review and report of two additional cases. Pediatr Emerg Care 7:163-165, 1991.

DIAZEPAM

Trade: Valium
Can/Aus/UK: Antenex, Apo-Diazepam, Ducene, Meval, Novo-Dipam, Sedapam, Valium, Vivol
Uses: Sedative, anxiolytic drug
AAP: Drug whose effect on nursing infants is unknown but may be of concern

Diazepam is a powerful CNS depressant and anticonvulsant. Published data on milk and plasma levels are highly variable and many are poor studies. In 3 mothers receiving 10 mg three times daily for up to 6 days, the maternal plasma levels of diazepam averaged 491 ng/ml (day 4) and 601 ng/ml (day 6).[1] Corresponding milk levels were 51 ng/ml (day 4) and 78 ng/ml (day6). The milk/plasma ratio was approximately 0.1. In a case report of a patient taking 6-10 mg of diazepam daily, her milk levels varied from 7.5 to 87 μg/L.[2] In a study of 9 mothers receiving diazepam postpartum, milk levels of diazepam varied from approximately 0.01 to 0.08 mg/L.[3] Other reports suggest slightly higher values. Taken together, most results suggest that the dose of diazepam and its metabolite, desmethyldiazepam, to a suckling infant will be on average 5% and at a maximum 12% of the weight-adjusted maternal dose of diazepam.[4] The active metabolite, desmethyldiazepam, in general has a much longer half-life in adults and pediatric patients and may tend to accumulate on longer therapy. Some reports of lethargy, sedation, poor suckling have been found. The acute use, such as in surgical procedures, is not likely to lead to significant accumulation. Long-term, sustained therapy may prove troublesome. The benzodiazepine family as a rule, are not ideal for breastfeeding mothers due to relatively long half-lives and the development of dependence. However, it is apparent that the shorter-acting benzodiazepines(lorazepam, alprazolam) are safest during lactation provided their use is short-term or intermittent, low dose, and after the first week of life.[5]

Pregnancy Risk Category: D

Lactation Risk Category: L3
L4 if used chronically

Theoretic Infant Dose: 13.1 μg/kg/day

Adult Concerns: Poor suckling, sedation, lethargy, constipation.

Pediatric Concerns: Some reports of lethargy, sedation, poor suckling have been found.

Drug Interactions: May increase sedation when used with CNS depressants such as alcohol, barbiturates, opioids. Cimetidine may decrease metabolism and clearance of diazepam. Cisapride can dramatically increase plasma levels of diazepam. Valproic may displace diazepam from binding sites, thus increasing sedative effects. SSRIs (fluoxetine, sertraline, paroxetine) can dramatically increase diazepam levels by altering clearance, thus leading to sedation.

Alternatives: Lorazepam, Midazolam

Adult Dosage: 2-10 mg BID to QID

T½ = 43 hours	M/P = 0.2-2.7
PHL = 20-50 hours(full-term)	PB = 99%
PK = 1-2 hours	Oral = Complete
MW = 285	pKa = 3.4
Vd = 0.7-2.6	

References:
1. Erkkola R. Kanto J. Diazepam and breastfeeding. The Lancet, 1:1235-1236, 1972.
2. Wesson DR, Camber S, Harkey M et.al. Diazepam and desmethyldiazepam in breast milk. J Psychoactive Drugs 17:55-56, 1985.
3. Cole AP and Haley DM. Diazepam and active metabolite in breast milk and their transfer to the neonate. Arch Dis Child 50(9):741-2, 1975
4. Spigset O. Anaesthetic agents and excretion in breast milk. Acta Anaesthesiologica Scandinavica. 38:94-103, 1994.
5. Maitra R, Menkes DB. Psychotropic drugs and lactation. N Z Med J. 28;109(1024):217-8, 1996.

DIBUCAINE

Trade: Nupercainal
Can/Aus/UK: Cinchocaine, Dermacaine, Nupercainal, Nupercaine, Ultraproct
Uses: Local anesthetic
AAP: Not reviewed

Dibucaine is a long-acting local anesthetic generally used topically. It is primarily used topically in creams and ointments, and due to toxicity, has been banned in the USA for I.V. or IM injections.[1] No data are available on transfer to breastmilk. Dibucaine is effective for sunburn, topical burns, rash, rectal hemorrhoids, and other skin irritations. Long-term use and use over large areas of the body are discouraged. Although somewhat minimal, some dibucaine can be absorbed from irritated skin.

Pregnancy Risk Category: C

Lactation Risk Category: L3

Theoretic Infant Dose:

Adult Concerns: Rash or allergic symptoms.

Pediatric Concerns: None reported via milk.

Drug Interactions:

Alternatives:

Adult Dosage: 10-30 g QD

References:
1. Pharmaceutical Manufacturers Package Insert, 1995.

DICLOFENAC

Trade: Cataflam, Voltaren
Can/Aus/UK: Apo-Diclo, Fenac, Novo-Difenac, Voltaren, Voltarol
Uses: NSAID analgesic for arthritis
AAP: Not reviewed

Diclofenac is a typical nonsteroidal analgesic (NSAID). Voltaren is a sustained release product whereas Cataflam is an immediate release product. Time to peak for Voltaren is 2.0 hours In one study of six postpartum mothers receiving 100 mg of Voltaren daily, the levels of diclofenac in breastmilk were undetectable (limit of detection < 19 ng/mL).[1] The amount an infant would consume would therefore be less than 2.5 μg/kg, an amount that is not clinically relevant.

Pregnancy Risk Category: B

Lactation Risk Category: L2

Theoretic Infant Dose: 2.5 μg/kg/day

Adult Concerns: GI distress, diarrhea, nausea, vomiting.

Pediatric Concerns: None reported via milk.

Drug Interactions: May prolong prothrombin time when used with warfarin. Antihypertensive effects of ACEi family may be blunted or completely abolished by NSAIDs. Some NSAIDs may block antihypertensive effect of beta blockers, diuretics. Used with cyclosporin, may dramatically increase renal toxicity. May increase digoxin, phenytoin, lithium levels. May increase toxicity of methotrexate. May increase bioavailability of penicillamine. Probenecid may increase NSAID levels.

Alternatives: Ibuprofen

Adult Dosage: 75 mg BID

T½ = 1.1 hours	M/P =
PHL=	PB = 99.7%
PK = 1 hour (Cataflam)	Oral = Complete
MW = 318	pKa = 4.0
Vd = 0.55	

References:
1. Sioufi A, Stierlin H. et.al. Recent findings concerning clinically relevant pharmacokinetics of diclofenac sodium. In: Kass(ed), Voltaren-new findings. pp19-30, Hans Huber Publishers, Bern 1982.

DICLOXACILLIN

Trade: Pathocil, Dycill, Dynapen
Can/Aus/UK: Diclocil, Dicloxsig, Dynapen
Uses: Penicillin antibiotic
AAP: Not reviewed

Dicloxacillin is an oral penicillinase-resistant penicillin frequently used for peripheral (non CNS) infections caused by Staph. aureus and Staph. epidermidis infections, particularly mastitis. Following oral administration of a 250 mg dose, milk concentrations of the drug were 0.1, and 0.3 mg/L at 2 and 4 hours after the dose, respectively.[1] Levels were undetectable after 6 hours. Usual dose for adults is 250-500 mg four times daily for at least 10-14 days.

Pregnancy Risk Category: B

Lactation Risk Category: L1

Theoretic Infant Dose:

Adult Concerns: Elimination is delayed in neonates. Rash, diarrhea.

Pediatric Concerns: None reported via milk.

Drug Interactions: May increase effect of oral anticoagulants. Disulfiram, probenecid may increase levels of penicillin. May reduce efficacy of oral contraceptives.

Alternatives:

Adult Dosage: 125-250 mg q 6 hours

T½ = 0.6-0.8 hour	M/P =
PHL= 1.9 hours	PB = 96%
PK = 0.5-2 hours	Oral = 35-76%
MW = 470	pKa =
Vd =	

References:
1.   McEvoy GE(ed):AHFS Drug Information, New York, NY. 1995.

DICYCLOMINE

Trade: Bentyl, Antispas, Spasmoject
Can/Aus/UK: Bentylol, Formulex, Lomine, Merbentyl
Uses: Anticholinergic, drying agent.
AAP: Not reviewed.

Dicyclomine is a tertiary amine antispasmodic. It belongs to the family of anticholinergics such as atropine and the belladonna alkaloids. It was previously used for infant colic, but due to overdoses and reported apnea, it is seldom recommended for this use. Infants are exceedingly sensitive to anticholinergics, particularly in the neonatal period.

Following a dose of 20 mg in a lactating woman, a 12 day old infant reported severe apnea. The manufacturer reports milk levels of 131 μg/L with corresponding maternal serum levels of 59 μg/L.[1] The reported milk/plasma level was 2.22.

Pregnancy Risk Category: B

Lactation Risk Category: L4

Theoretic Infant Dose: 19.7 μg/kg/day

Adult Concerns: Apnea, dry secretions, urinary hesitancy, dilated pupils.

Pediatric Concerns: Severe apnea in one 12 day old infant. Observe for anticholinergic symptoms, drying, constipation, rapid heart rate.

Drug Interactions: Decreased effect with antacids, phenothiazines, haloperidol. Increased toxicity when used with other anticholinergics, amantadine, opiates, antiarrhythmics, antihistamines, tricyclic antidepressants.

Alternatives:

Adult Dosage: 20-40 mg QID

T½ = 9-10 hours.	M/P =
PHL=	PB =
PK = 1-1.5 hours.	Oral = 67%
MW = 345	pKa =
Vd =	

References:
1.   Pharmaceutical Manufacturers Package Insert, 1999.

DIETHYL ETHER

Trade: Diethyl Ether, Ether
Can/Aus/UK:
Uses: Anesthetic
AAP: Not reviewed

Ether is seldom used today. Although some would be transferred into human milk, it would rapidly redistribute back to the blood and be eliminated, particularly if the mother were to withhold breastmilk for at least 12 or more hours after administration.

Pregnancy Risk Category:

Lactation Risk Category: L4

Theoretic Infant Dose:

Adult Concerns: GI distress, unique ether odor.

Pediatric Concerns:

Drug Interactions:

Alternatives:

Adult Dosage:

T½ =	M/P =
PHL=	PB =
PK = 10-20 min.	Oral =
MW =	pKa =
Vd =	

References:

DIETHYLPROPION

Trade: Tepanil, Tenuate
Can/Aus/UK: Dospan, Tenuate
Uses: Anorexiant
AAP: Not reviewed

Diethylpropion belongs to the amphetamine family and is typically used to reduce food intake. No data available other than manufacturer states this medication is secreted into breastmilk.[1] Diethylpropion's structure is similar to amphetamines. Upon withdrawal, significant withdrawal symptoms have been reported in adults. Such symptoms could be observed in breastfeeding infants of mothers using this product. The use of this medication during lactation is simply unrealistic and not justified.

Pregnancy Risk Category: B

Lactation Risk Category: L5

Theoretic Infant Dose:

Adult Concerns: Overstimulation, insomnia, anorexia, jitteriness, rapid heart rate, elevated blood pressure.

Pediatric Concerns: None reported, but observe for anorexia, agitation, insomnia.

Drug Interactions: Increased toxicity with MAO inhibitors, CNS depressants, general anesthetics (arrhythmias), other adrenergics.

Alternatives:

Adult Dosage: 25 mg TID

T½ = 8 hours.	M/P =
PHL =	PB =
PK = 2 hours.	Oral = 70%
MW = 205	pKa =
Vd =	

References:
1. Pharmaceutical Manufacturers Package Insert, 1995.

DIETHYLSTILBESTROL

Trade:
Can/Aus/UK: Apstil, Fosfestrol, Honvan, Honvol
Uses: Synthetic estrogen
AAP: Not reviewed

Diethylstilbestrol is a synthetic estrogen that is seldom used today. It is known to produce a high risk of cervical cancer in female infants exposed during pregnancy.[1,2] It has been shown to cause anatomical abnormalities in males and females, neoplasia, reduced fertility and immunologic changes. Its effect in the breastfeeding infant is unknown but should be absolutely avoided. DES would probably inhibit milk production. Strongly suggest using other estrogens during breastfeeding if absolutely mandatory. Contraindicated.

Pregnancy Risk Category: X

Lactation Risk Category: L5

Theoretic Infant Dose:

Adult Concerns: Decreased breastmilk production.

Pediatric Concerns: None reported via milk, but this product is too dangerous for use in breastfeeding mothers.

Drug Interactions:

Alternatives:

Adult Dosage: 15 mg QD

T½ =	M/P =
PHL =	PB =
PK =	Oral = Complete
MW = 268	pKa =
Vd =	

References:
1. O'Brien, T. Excretion of drugs in human milk. Am.J. Hosp. Pharm. 31:844-854, 1974.
2. Shapiro S, Sloan D. The effects of exogenous female sex hormones on the fetus. Epidemiol Rev I:110, 1979.

DIFLUNISAL

Trade: Dolobid
Can/Aus/UK: Apo-Diflunisal, Dolobid, Novo-Diflunisal
Uses: Nonsteroidal anti-inflammatory analgesic
AAP: Not reviewed

Diflunisal is a derivative of salicylic acid. Diflunisal is excreted into human milk in concentrations 2-7% of the maternal plasma levels.[1] No reports of side-effects have been located. This product is potentially a higher risk NSAID and other less toxic compounds should be used.

Pregnancy Risk Category: C during 1st trimester
D during 3rd trimester

Lactation Risk Category: L3

Theoretic Infant Dose:

Adult Concerns: Prolonged bleeding time, headache, GI distress, diarrhea, GI cramping, fluid retention. Ulcer complications. Worsening hypertension.

Pediatric Concerns: None reported but alternatives advised.

Drug Interactions: Antacids reduce effect. Increased toxicity of digoxin, methotrexate, anticoagulants, phenytoin, sulfonylureas, lithium, acetaminophen.

Alternatives: Ibuprofen

Adult Dosage: 500 mg BID or TID

T½ = 8-12 hours	M/P =
PHL =	PB = 99%
PK = 2-3 hours	Oral = Complete
MW = 250	pKa =
Vd = 0.1-0.2	

References:
1.   Pharmaceutical Manufacturers Package Insert, 1995.

DIGITOXIN

Trade: Crystodigin
Can/Aus/UK: Digitaline
Uses: Cardiac stimulant
AAP: Not reviewed

No data available on digitoxin and its transfer to human milk.[1]

Occasionally given to infants. High lipid solubility and good oral bioavailability would suggest some transfer into breastmilk. See digoxin.

Pregnancy Risk Category: C

Lactation Risk Category: L3

Theoretic Infant Dose:

Adult Concerns: Nausea, vomiting, anorexia, cardiac arrhythmias.

Pediatric Concerns: None reported thus far.

Drug Interactions: Reduced plasma levels when used with antacids, penicillamine, bran fiber, sucralfate, cholestyramine, rifampin, etc. Increased toxicity when used with diltiazem, ibuprofen, cimetidine, omeprazole, etc.

Alternatives:

Adult Dosage: 0.15 mg QD

$T\frac{1}{2}$ = 6.7 days	M/P =
PHL =	PB = 97%
PK = 4 hours	Oral = 90-100%
MW = 765	pKa =
Vd = 7 (variable)	

References:
1. Levy, M. et.al. Excretion of drugs in human milk, New Engl. J. Med. 297:789, 1977.

DIGOXIN

Trade: Lanoxin, Lanoxicaps
Can/Aus/UK: Lanoxin, Novo-Digoxin
Uses: Cardiac stimulant
AAP: Approved by the American Academy of Pediatrics for use in breastfeeding mothers

Digoxin is a cardiac stimulant used primarily to strengthen the contractile process. In one mother receiving 0.25 mg digoxin daily, the amount found in breastmilk ranged from 0.96 to 0.61 μg/L at 4 and 6 hours post-dose respectively.[1] Mean peak breastmilk levels varied from 0.78 μg/L in one patient to 0.41 μg/L in another. Plasma levels in the infants were undetectable. In another study of 5 women receiving digoxin therapy, the average breastmilk concentration was 0.64 μg/L.[2] From these studies, it is apparent that a breastfeeding infant would receive less than 1 μg/day of digoxin, too low to be clinically relevant. The small amounts secreted into breastmilk have not produced problems in nursing infants. Poor and erratic GI absorption could theoretically reduce absorption in nursing infant.

Pregnancy Risk Category: C

Lactation Risk Category: L2

Theoretic Infant Dose: 96.0 ng/kg/day

Adult Concerns: Nausea, vomiting, bradycardia, arrhythmias.

Pediatric Concerns: None reported in several studies.

Drug Interactions: Too numerous to list all. Decreased digoxin effect when used with antacids, bran fiber, sucralfate, sulfasalazine, diuretics, phenytoin, cholestyramine, aminoglutethimide. Increase digoxin effects may result when used with diltiazem, ibuprofen, cimetidine, omeprazole, bepridil, reserpine, amphotericin B, erythromycin, quinine, tetracycline, cyclosporine, etc.

Alternatives:

Adult Dosage: 0.125-0.5 mg QD

T½ = 39 hours PHL = 20-180 hours PK = 1.5-3 hours MW = 781 Vd = 5.1-7.4	M/P = <0.9 PB = 25% Oral = 65-85% pKa =

References:

1. Loughnan PM. Digoxin excretion in human breast milk. J. Pediatr. 92:1019-1020,1978.
2. Levy, M. et.al. Excretion of drugs in human milk, New Engl. J. Med. 297:789, 1977.

DILTIAZEM HCL

Trade: Cardizem SR, Dilacor-XR, Diltiazem Hcl, Cardizem CD
Can/Aus/UK: Adizem, Apo-Diltiaz, Apo-Diltiazem, Britiazim, Cardcal, Cardizem, Coras, Dilzem, Tildiem
Uses: Antihypertensive, calcium channel blocker
AAP: Approved by the American Academy of Pediatrics for use in breastfeeding mothers

Diltiazem is a typical calcium channel blocker antihypertensive.[1] One report indicates levels in milk parallel those of serum (Milk/plasma ratio is approximately 1.0).[2] Peak level in milk (and plasma) was slightly higher than 200 μg/L and occurred at 8 hours. Remember, many formulations are extended release preparations (12-24 hours..SR,XR,CD) and it would be difficult to breastfeed between the peak levels. Best choice of CCB may be nifedipine (< 5% of dose transferred). Authors recommend against using diltiazem in breastfeeding mothers.

Pregnancy Risk Category: C

Lactation Risk Category: L3

Theoretic Infant Dose: 30.0 μg/kg/day

Adult Concerns: Hypotension, bradycardia.

Pediatric Concerns: Hypotension, bradycardia is possible. See nifedipine.

Drug Interactions: H-2 blockers may increase bioavailability of diltiazem. Beta blockers may increase cardio depressant effect. May increase cyclosporine, and carbamazepine levels. Fentanyl may increase hypotension.

Alternatives: Nifedipine, Nimodipine, Verapamil

Adult Dosage: 30-90 mg QID

T½ = 3.5-6 hours	M/P = 1.0
PHL =	PB = 78%
PK = 2-3 hours	Oral = 40-60%
MW = 433	pKa =
Vd = 1.7	

References:
1. Pharmaceutical Manufacturers Package Insert, 1995.
2. Okada M, Inoue H, Nakamura Y, et.al. Excretion of diltiazem in human milk. N. Eng. J. Med. 312:992,1985.

DIMENHYDRINATE

Trade: Marmine, Dramamine
Can/Aus/UK: Andrumin, Dramamine, Gravol, Travacalm, Traveltabs
Uses: Antihistamine for vertigo and motion sickness
AAP: Not reviewed

Consists of 55% diphenhydramine and 45% of 8-chlorotheophylline. Diphenhydramine (Benadryl) is considered to be the active ingredient. See Benadryl.

Pregnancy Risk Category: B

Lactation Risk Category: L2

Theoretic Infant Dose:

Adult Concerns: Sedation, dry secretions.

Pediatric Concerns:

Drug Interactions: May enhance CNS depressants, anticholinergics, tricyclic antidepressants, and MAO exhibitors. Increased toxicity of antibiotics, especially aminoglycosides "ototoxicity".

Alternatives: Hydroxyzine

Adult Dosage: 50-100 mg q 4-6 hours

T½ = 8.5 hours	M/P =
PHL=	PB = 78%
PK = 1-2 hours	Oral =
MW = 470	pKa =
Vd =	

References:
1.   Pharmaceutical Manufacturers Package Insert, 1995.

DINOPROSTONE

Trade: Prostin E2, Prepidil, Cervidil
Can/Aus/UK: Cervidil, Propress
Uses: Prostaglandin E-2
AAP: Not reviewed

Dinoprostone is a naturally occurring prostaglandin E2 that is primarily used for induction of labor, for cervical ripening, as an abortifacient, for postpartum bleeding, and for uterine atony.[1] Available as a vaginal gel or insert, it is slowly absorbed into the plasma where it is rapidly cleared and metabolized by most tissues and the lung. Its half-life is brief 2.5 to 5 minutes although absorption from the vaginal mucosa is slow. Neonatal effects from maternal dinoprostone include fetal heart rate abnormalities, and neonatal jaundice. The amount of dinoprostone entering milk is not known, but a brief wash out period would preclude any possible side effects.

However, dinoprostone has been used to suppress lactation. When used orally (Prostin E2, 2 mg orally/d on day 3and 4; then 6 mg/d thereafter) it has been found to significantly suppress milk production.[2,3] However, the use of prostaglandin E2 products for cervical ripening (during delivery) is generally brief and probably does not clinically impact the production of breastmilk many hours or days later.

Pregnancy Risk Category: C during 1st and 2nd trimester
                                  X during 3rd trimester

Lactation Risk Category: L3

Theoretic Infant Dose:

Adult Concerns: Side effects of vaginal dinoprostone are numerous and include, abortion, labor induction, blood loss, hypotension, syncope, tachycardia, dizziness, hyperthermia, nausea, vomiting, diarrhea, and taste disorders.

Pediatric Concerns: None reported via milk, but a washout period is suggested.

Drug Interactions:

Alternatives:

Adult Dosage: 10-20 mg X 1-2

T½ = 2.5-5 minutes	M/P =
PHL=	PB = High
PK = 0.5-1 hour	Oral =
MW =	pKa =
Vd =	

References:
1. Pharmaceutical Manufacturers Package Insert, 1999.
2. Caminiti F, De Murtas M, Parodo G, Lecca U, Nasi A. Decrease in human plasma prolactin levels by oral prostaglandin E2 in early puerperium. J Endocrinol. 87(3):333-7, 1980.
3. Nasi A, De Murtas M, Parodo G, Caminiti F. Inhibition of lactation by prostaglandin E2. Obstet Gynecol Surv. 35(10):619-20, 1980.

DIPHENHYDRAMINE

Trade: Benadryl, Cheracol
Can/Aus/UK: Allerdryl, Benadryl, Delixir, Insomnal, Nytol, Paedamin
Uses: Antihistamine, antitussive
AAP: Not reviewed

Small but unreported levels are thought to be secreted into breastmilk.[1,2] In rodents, milk/plasma ratio has been reported to be 3.85-9.54, although the total transfer was minimal.   Only probable side effect would be slight drowsiness in infant.

Pregnancy Risk Category: C

Lactation Risk Category: L2

Theoretic Infant Dose:

Adult Concerns: Sedation, drowsiness.

Pediatric Concerns: None reported, but observe for sedation.

Drug Interactions: Increased sedation when used with other CNS depressants. MAO inhibitors may increase anticholinergic side effects.

Alternatives: Cetirizine, Hydroxyzine, Loratadine

Adult Dosage: 25-50 mg TID or QID

T½ = 4.3 hours	**M/P =**
PHL=	**PB = 78%**
PK = 2-3 hours	**Oral = 43-61%**
MW = 255	**pKa = 8.3**
Vd = 3-4	

References:
1. O'Brien, T. Excretion of drugs in human milk. Am.J. Hosp. Pharm. 31:844-854, 1974.
2. Paton DM, Webster DR. Clinical pharmacokinetics of H1-receptor antagonists (the antihistamines). Clin. Pharm. 10:477-497, 1985.

DIPHENOXYLATE

Trade: Lomotil, Lofene
Can/Aus/UK: Lofenoxal, Lomotil, Tropergen
Uses: Antidiarrheal
AAP: Not reviewed

Lomotil is a combination product of diphenoxylate and atropine.[1] Diphenoxylate belongs to the opiate family(meperidine) and acts on the intestinal tract inhibiting GI motility and excessive GI propulsion. The drug has no analgesic activity.   Although no reports are available, it is probably secreted in breastmilk but in very small quantities.[2] Some authors consider diphenoxylate to be contraindicated but this is questionable.

Pregnancy Risk Category: C

Lactation Risk Category: L3

Theoretic Infant Dose:

Adult Concerns: Anticholinergic effects, such as drying, constipation, and sedation.

Pediatric Concerns: None reported, but observe for dryness, constipation, sedation.

Drug Interactions: Increased toxicity when used with MAO inhibitors, CNS depressants, anticholinergics.

Alternatives:

Adult Dosage: 5 mg QID

T½ = 2.5 hours	M/P =
PHL=	PB =
PK = 2 hours	Oral = 90%
MW = 453	pKa = 7.1
Vd = 3.8	

References:
1. Drug Facts and Comparisons. 1994 ed. Facts and Comparisons, St. Louis.
2. Stewart JJ. Gastrointestinal drugs. In Wilson JT, ed. Drugs in Breast Milk. Balgowlah, Australia;ADIS Press, 71, 1981.

DIPHTHERIA and TETANUS TOXOID

Trade: DT, TD
Can/Aus/UK: ADT, CDT, Triple Antigen
Uses: Vaccine
AAP: Not reviewed

Diphtheria and tetanus toxoid contains large molecular weight protein toxoids.   It is extremely unlikely proteins of this size would be secreted in breastmilk. No reported harmful effects.

Pregnancy Risk Category: C

Lactation Risk Category:

Theoretic Infant Dose:

Adult Concerns: Swelling, fretfulness, drowsiness, anorexia, vomiting.

Pediatric Concerns: None reported via breastmilk exposure.

Drug Interactions:

Alternatives:

Adult Dosage: 0.5 ml injection (IM)

References:

DIPHTHERIA-TETANUS-PERTUSSIS

Trade: DTAP, Acel-Imune, Tripedia, Tetramune, DPT
Can/Aus/UK:
Uses: Vaccine
AAP: Not reviewed

DTP injections come in two forms, one including acellular pertussis (Acel-Imune, Tripedia), and one including whole-cell pertussis, and Haemophilus Influenzae Type B Conjugate (Tetramune). Both are inactivated bacterial vaccines or toxoids.

The use of pertussis vaccinations in individuals over 7 years of age is generally contraindicated. Hence there is no indication for administering this vaccine to adult mothers. Because these are inactivated bacterial products, there is no specific contraindication in breastfeeding following injection with these vaccines. The CDC states that all vaccines are safe for breastfeeding mothers.

Pregnancy Risk Category: B

Lactation Risk Category:

Theoretic Infant Dose:

Adult Concerns: Pain, fever, swelling

Pediatric Concerns: None reported via breastmilk.

Drug Interactions: Immunosuppressive agents, high dose corticosteroids, may reduce immunogenicity.

Alternatives:

Adult Dosage: N/A

References:
1. Pharmaceutical Manufacturers Package Insert, 1996.

DIPIVEFRIN

Trade: Ak-pro, Propine
Can/Aus/UK: PSM-Dipivefrin, Propine
Uses: Adrenergic for glaucoma
AAP: Not reviewed

Dipivefrin is a synthetic amine prodrug that is metabolized to epinephrine. Because of its structure, it is more lipophilic and better absorbed into the eye, hence it is more potent.[1,2] Following absorption into the eye, it reduces intraocular pressure. It is not known if dipivefrin enters milk, but small amounts may be present. It is unlikely that any dipivefrin or epinephrine present in milk would be orally bioavailable to the infant.

Pregnancy Risk Category: B

Lactation Risk Category: L2

Theoretic Infant Dose:

Adult Concerns: Infrequently, tachycardia, arrhythmias, hypertension have occurred with intraocular epinephrine. Burning, itching, tearing, hyperemia of eyes, redness of the eyes, burning and stinging have been reported.

Pediatric Concerns: None via milk.

Drug Interactions: When admixed with a pilocarpine Ocusert system, a transient increase in myopia was reported.

Alternatives:

Adult Dosage: 1 drop affected eye q 12 hours

T½ =	M/P =
PHL =	PB =
PK = 1 hour	Oral = Minimal
MW =	pKa =
Vd =	

References:
1. Pharmaceutical Manufacturers Package Insert, 1999.
2. McEvoy GE(ed):AFHS Drug Information, New York, NY. 1999.

DIPYRIDAMOLE

Trade: Persantine
Can/Aus/UK: Apo-Dipyridamole, Novo-Dipiradol, Persantin
Uses: Vasodilator, antiplatelet agent
AAP: Not reviewed

Dipyridamole is most commonly used in addition to coumarin anticoagulants to prevent thromboembolic complications of cardiac valve replacement. According to the manufacturer, only small amounts are believed to be secreted in human milk. No reported untoward effects have been reported.

Pregnancy Risk Category: C

Lactation Risk Category: L3

Theoretic Infant Dose:

Adult Concerns: Headache, dizziness, GI distress, nausea, vomiting, diarrhea, flushing.

Pediatric Concerns: No untoward effects have been reported.

Drug Interactions: When used with Heparin, may increase anticoagulation. Theophylline may reduce the hypotensive effect of dipyridamole.

Alternatives:

Adult Dosage: 75-100 mg QID

T½ = 10-12 hours	M/P =
PHL=	PB = 91-99%
PK = 45-150 min.	Oral = Poor
MW = 505	pKa =
Vd = 2-3	

References:
1. Pharmaceutical Manufacturers Package Insert, 1995.
2. Briggs GG, Freeman R, Yaffe S. Drugs in Pregnancy and Lactation, 4th ed. Baltimore, Williams and Wilkins 1994.

DIRITHROMYCIN

Trade: Dynabac
Can/Aus/UK:
Uses: Macrolide antibiotic
AAP: Not reviewed

Dirithromycin is a macrolide antibiotic similar to the erythromycins, but is characterized by low serum levels and high tissue levels.[1] Dirithromycin is metabolized to erythromycyclamine which is the active component. No data on the transfer of erythromycyclamine into human milk is available, but it is known to transfer into animal milk. Due to the kinetics of dirithromycin and its distribution largely to tissues, it is unlikely that major levels in milk will result. Suitable alternatives include erythromycin and azithromycin.

Pregnancy Risk Category: C

Lactation Risk Category: L3

Theoretic Infant Dose:

Adult Concerns: GI distress, abdominal pain, diarrhea, nausea, vomiting, skin rash, headache and dizziness. Changes in liver function have been reported.

Pediatric Concerns: None reported via milk. Suitable alternatives are erythromycin and azithromycin.

Drug Interactions: Increased anticoagulant effect when used with warfarin, dicoumarol, phenindione, and anisindione. Dirithromycin may increase the level of astemizole significantly. May increase digoxin levels. Acute and dangerous toxicity have resulted following use of dirithromycin with ergot alkaloids. Increased serum levels of pimozide and triazolam may result.

Alternatives: Dirithromycin

Adult Dosage: 500 mg QD

T½ = 20-50 hours	**M/P =**
PHL=	**PB = 15-30%**
PK = 3.9 hours	**Oral = 6-14%**
MW =	**pKa =**
Vd = 11	

References:
1.   Pharmaceutical Manufacturers Package Insert, 1998.

DISOPYRAMIDE

Trade: Norpace, Napamide
Can/Aus/UK: Isomide, Norpace, Rhythmodan, Rythmodan
Uses: Antiarrhythmic
AAP: Approved by the American Academy of Pediatrics for use in breastfeeding mothers

Disopyramide is used for treating cardiac arrhythmias similar to quinidine and procainamide. Small levels are secreted into milk. Following a maternal dose of 450 mg every 8 hours for two weeks, the milk/plasma ratio was approximately 1.06 for disopyramide, and 6.24 for its active metabolite.[1] Although no disopyramide was measurable in the infant's plasma, the milk levels were 2.6-4.4 mg/L (disopyramide), and 9.6-12.3 mg/L (metabolite). Infant urine collected over an 8 hour period contained 3.3 mg/L of disopyramide. Such levels are probably too small to affect infant. No reported side effects.

In another study, in a woman receiving 100 mg five times daily, the maternal serum level was 10.3 μmol/L and the breastmilk level was 4.0 μmol/L, giving a milk/serum ratio of 0.4.[2]   From these levels, an infant ingesting 1 liter of milk would receive only 1.5 mg per day. Lowest milk levels are at 6-8 hours post-dose.

Pregnancy Risk Category: C

Lactation Risk Category: L2

Theoretic Infant Dose: 0.7 mg/kg/day

Adult Concerns: Dry mouth, constipation, edema, hypotension, nausea, vomiting, diarrhea.

Pediatric Concerns: None reported.

Drug Interactions: Increased side effects with drugs such as phenytoin, phenobarbital, rifampin. Increased effects/toxicity with rifamycin. Increased plasma levels of digoxin.

Alternatives:

Adult Dosage: 150 mg q 6 hours

T½ = 8.3-11.65 hours	M/P = 0.4-1.06
PHL =	PB = 50%
PK = 2.3 hours	Oral = 60-83%
MW = 339	pKa = 8.4
Vd = 0.6-1.3	

References:

1. MacKintosh D, Buchanan N. Excretion of disopyramide in human breast milk. Br J Clin Pharmacol 19:856-7, 1985.
2. Ellsworth AJ, et.al. Disopyramide and N-monodesalkyl disopyramide in serum and breast milk. DICP 23(1):56-7,1989.

DISULFIRAM

Trade: Antabuse
Can/Aus/UK: Antabuse
Uses: Inhibitor of alcohol metabolism.
AAP: Not reviewed

Disulfiram is an old product that is occasionally used to prevent alcohol consumption in chronic alcoholics.[1,2] Disulfiram inhibits the enzyme, aldehyde dehydrogenase (ADH) which is one of two enzymes responsible for the metabolism of alcohol. Patients receiving disulfiram, and who ingest alcohol, become extremely nauseated due to elevated plasma levels of acetaldehyde. This also results in flushing, thirst, palpitations, chest pain, vertigo and hypotension. All sources of alcohol should be avoided, including mouthwash, cough syrups, and after shave. There are no data on the transfer of disulfiram into human milk, but due to its small molecular weight, it likely penetrates milk to some degree. Because it produces an irreversible inhibition of aldehyde dehydrogenase, any absorbed via milk could potentially produce long-lasting inhibition of the infants' ADH. With the ingestion of any alcohol containing product, the infant could become seriously ill. Further, because the enzyme is permanently inhibited, the individual will be susceptible to alcohol toxicity for up to 2 weeks following discontinuing of the medication. Because so many products contain small amounts of alcohol (cough syrups, etc), the use of this product in breastfeeding mothers is extremely risky and probably does not justify continued breastfeeding unless the mother is warned and compliant.

Pregnancy Risk Category: C

Lactation Risk Category: L5

Theoretic Infant Dose:

Adult Concerns: Symptoms primarily occur following ingestion of alcohol, and include: ectopic heartbeats, tachycardia, chest pain, angina, palpitations, hypertension, headache, severe nausea and vomiting, leg and muscle cramps, dyspnea and shortness of breath.

Pediatric Concerns: None reported via milk, but with ingestion of alcohol could produce profound symptoms in infant.

Drug Interactions: Severe reactions may occur with any product containing alcohol. Concomitant therapy with amitriptyline or metronidazole has resulted in a confusional and psychotic mental state. When used with anisindione or dicumarol, an increased hypoprothrombinemic effect has been documented. Use with bacampicillin has resulted in an disulfiram-type reaction. Significantly increased plasma levels of chlordiazepoxide and diazepam, phenytoin and fosphenytoin when co-administered with disulfiram. An increased half-life and plasma level of desipramine.

Alternatives:

Adult Dosage: 250 mg daily

T½ =		**M/P** =	
PHL =		**PB** = 96%	
PK = 1-2 hours		**Oral** = 80-90%	
MW = 296		**pKa** =	
Vd =			

References:
1. Pharmaceutical Manufacturers Package Insert, 1999.
2. McEvoy GE(ed):AFHS Drug Information, New York, NY. 1999.

DOCUSATE

Trade: Colace, Docusate, Softgels, Dialose, Surfak
Can/Aus/UK: Albert Docusate, Audinorm, Colace, Colax-C, Coloxyl, Diocytl-medo, Rectalad, Surfak, Waxsol
Uses: Laxative, stool softener
AAP: Not reviewed

Docusate is a detergent commonly used as a stool softener. The degree of oral absorption is poor, but some is known to be absorbed and resecreted in the bile. Although some drug is absorbed by mother via her GI tract transfer into breastmilk is unknown but probably minimal. Watch for loose stools in infant. It is not likely this would be overly detrimental to a breastfed infant.

Pregnancy Risk Category: C

Lactation Risk Category: L2

Theoretic Infant Dose:

Adult Concerns: Nausea, diarrhea.

Pediatric Concerns: None reported.

Drug Interactions: Decreased effect of Coumadin with high doses of docusate. Increased toxicity with mineral oil, phenolphthalein.

Alternatives:

Adult Dosage: 50-200 mg QD

T½ =	M/P =
PHL=	PB =
PK =	Oral = Poor
MW = 444	pKa =
Vd =	

References:

DOLASETRON MESYLATE

Trade: Anzemet
Can/Aus/UK:
Uses: Antinauseant and antiemetic
AAP: Not reviewed

Dolasetron and its active metabolite, hydrodolasetron, are selective serotonin 5-HT3 receptor antagonists, primarily in the chemoreceptor trigger zone responsible for control of nausea and vomiting. It is believed that chemotherapeutic agents release serotonin in the gastrointestinal tract that then activates the 5-HT3 receptors on the vagus nerve that initiates the vomiting reflex. This product is used prior to treatment with cancer chemotherapeutic agents, or prior to surgery and general anesthesia.[1]

No data are available on its transfer to milk. The maximum concentration in maternal plasma would be 556 ng/mL, which is quite low. At this plasma level, an infant would likely receive far less than a milligram daily. It has been safely used in children 2 years of age at doses of 1.2 mg/kg.

Pregnancy Risk Category: B

Lactation Risk Category: L3

Theoretic Infant Dose:

Adult Concerns: Changes in ECG intervals (PR, QT, JT prolongation, and QRS widening) have been reported but are dose related. Use cautiously in patients with hypokalemia or hypomagnesemia, patients on diuretics, or patients on other antiarrhythmics. Side effects include: headache, fatigue, diarrhea, bradycardia.

Pediatric Concerns: None reported via milk.

Drug Interactions: Drug-drug interactions are few, but include rifampin, and cimetidine.

Alternatives:

Adult Dosage: 100 mg orally.

T½ = 8.1 hours	M/P =
PHL=	PB = 77%
PK = 1 hour	Oral = 75%
MW = 438	pKa =
Vd = 5.8	

References:
1.   Pharmaceutical Manufacturer package insert, 2000.

DOMPERIDONE

Trade: Motilium
Can/Aus/UK: Motilidone, Motilium
Uses: Nausea and vomiting, stimulates lactation
AAP: Approved by the American Academy of Pediatrics for use in breastfeeding mothers

Domperidone (Motilium) is a peripheral dopamine antagonist (similar to Reglan) generally used for controlling nausea and vomiting, dyspepsia, and gastric reflux. It blocks peripheral dopamine receptors in the GI wall and in the CTZ (nausea center) in the brain stem and is currently used in Canada as an antiemetic.[1] Unlike Reglan, it does not enter the brain compartment and it has few CNS effects such as depression.

It is also known to produce significant increases in prolactin levels and has proven useful as a galactagogue.[1] Serum prolactin levels have been found to increase from 8.1 ng/mL to 124.1 ng/mL in non-lactating women after one 20 mg dose.[2]   Concentrations of domperidone reported in milk vary according to dose but following a dose of 10 mg three times daily, the average concentration in milk was only 2.6 μg/L.[3] In a study by da Silva, 16 mothers with premature infants and low milk production (mean= 112.8 mL/d in domperidone group; 48.2 mL/d in placebo group) were randomly chosen to receive placebo (n=9) or domperidone (10mg TID) (n = 7) for 7 days.[4] Milk volume increased from 112.8 to 162.2 mL/d in the domperidone group and 48.2 to 56.1 mL/d in the placebo group. Prolactin levels increased from 12.9 to 119.3 μg/L in the domperidone group, and 15.6 to 18.1 μg/L in the placebo group. On day 5, the mean domperidone concentration was 6.6 ng/mL in plasma and 1.2 ng/mL in breastmilk of the treated group (n=6). No adverse effects were reported in infants or mothers.

The usual oral dose for controlling GI distress is 10-20 mg three to four times daily although for nausea and vomiting the dose can be higher(up to 40 mg). The galactagogue dose is suggested to be 10-20 mg orally 3-4 times daily. At present, this product is unavailable in the USA.

Pregnancy Risk Category:

Lactation Risk Category: L2

Theoretic Infant Dose: 0.4 μg/kg/day

Adult Concerns: Dry mouth, skin rash, itching, headache, thirst, abdominal cramps, diarrhea, drowsiness.   Seizures have occurred rarely.

Pediatric Concerns: None reported.

Drug Interactions: Cimetidine, famotidine, nizatidine, ranitidine (H-2 blockers) reduce absorption of domperidone. Prior use of bicarbonate reduces absorption of domperidone.

Alternatives: Metoclopramide, Cisapride

Adult Dosage: 10-20 mg 3-4 times daily

T½ = 7-14 hours(oral)	M/P = 0.25
PHL=	PB = 93%
PK = 30 min.	Oral = 13-17%
MW = 426	pKa =
Vd =	

References:
1.   Hofmeyr GJ and van Iddekinge B. Domperidone and lactation. Lancet i, 647, 1983.
2.   Brouwers JR, Assies J, Wiersinga WM, Huizing G, Tytgat GN. Plasma prolactin levels after acute and subchronic oral administration of domperidone and of metoclopramide: a cross-over study in healthy volunteers. Clin Endocrinol (Oxf) 12(5):435-40, 1980.
3.   Hofmeyr GJ, et.al. Domperidone: secretion in breast milk and effect on

puerperal prolactin levels. Brit. J. Obs. and Gyn. 92:141-144, 1985.
4.   da Silva OP, Knoppert DC, Angelini MM, Forret PA.   Effect of
      domperidone on milk production in mothers of premature newborns: a
      randomized, double-blind, placebo-controlled trial. CMAJ. 164(1):17-21,
      2001.

DOPAMINE-DOBUTAMINE

Trade: Intropin
Can/Aus/UK: Inotropin, Intropin, Revimine–Dobutrex
Uses: Adrenergic stimulants
AAP: Not reviewed

Dopamine and dobutamine are catecholamine pressor agents used in shock and severe hypotension.[1] They are rapidly destroyed in the GI tract and are only used I.V. It is not known if they transfer into human milk, but the half-life is so short they would not last long. Dopamine, while in the plasma, significantly (> 60%) inhibits prolactin secretion and would likely inhibit lactation while being used.

Pregnancy Risk Category: C

Lactation Risk Category: L2

Theoretic Infant Dose:

Adult Concerns: Stimulation, agitation, tachycardia.

Pediatric Concerns: None reported. No GI absorption.

Drug Interactions: Increased effect when used with monoamine oxidase inhibitors MAO, alpha and beta adrenergic blockers, general anesthetics, and phenytoin.

Alternatives:

Adult Dosage: 5-50 mcg/kg/min I.V.

T½ = 2 minutes	M/P =
PHL= 7 minutes	PB =
PK = 5 minutes.	Oral = Poor
MW = 153	pKa =
Vd =	

References:
1.   McEvoy GE(ed):AHFS Drug Information, New York, NY. 1995.

DORNASE

Trade: Pulmozyme
Can/Aus/UK: Pulmozyme
Uses: Mucolytic enzyme
AAP: Not reviewed

Dornase is a mucolytic enzyme used in the treatment of cystic fibrosis. It is a large molecular weight peptide (260 amino acids, 37,000 daltons) that selectively digests DNA.[1] It is poorly absorbed by the pulmonary tissues. Serum levels are undetectable. Even if it were to reach the milk, it would not be orally bioavailable in the infant.

Pregnancy Risk Category: B

Lactation Risk Category: L2

Theoretic Infant Dose:

Adult Concerns: In adults: hoarseness, sore throat, facial edema.

Pediatric Concerns: None reported.

Drug Interactions:

Alternatives:

Adult Dosage: 2.5 mg via inhalation

T½ =		M/P =
PHL =		PB =
PK =		Oral = None
MW =		pKa =
Vd =		

References:
1. Pharmaceutical Manufacturers Package Insert, 1995.

DORZOLAMIDE

Trade: Trusopt
Can/Aus/UK: Trusopt
Uses: Glaucoma treatment
AAP: Not reviewed

Dorzolamide is a carbonic anhydrase-II inhibitor used for the treatment of increased intraocular pressure in glaucoma patients. It reduces intraocular pressure by reducing the production of aqueous humor.[1] Some systemic absorption of dorzolamide is known and is primarily associated with red blood cell carbonic anhydrase. It produces sustained inhibition of erythrocyte carbonic anhydrase (T1/2 = 147 days). No data are available on levels in milk. This is an incredibly potent and long-lasting inhibitor of carbonic anhydrase. Transfer of small amounts into breastmilk over a sustained period could prove detrimental to breastfed infants. Exercise caution when using with breastfeeding mothers.

Pregnancy Risk Category: C

Lactation Risk Category: L4

Theoretic Infant Dose:

Adult Concerns: Headache, vertigo, taste disorders, renal stones, burning, stinging, conjunctivitis.

Pediatric Concerns: None reported via milk. Exercise caution.

Drug Interactions:

Alternatives:

Adult Dosage: 1 drop in affected eye TID

References:
1. Pharmaceutical manufacturers package insert, 1997.

DOTHIEPIN

Trade: Prothiaden
Can/Aus/UK: Dothep, Prothiaden
Uses: Tricyclic antidepressant
AAP: Drug whose effect on nursing infants is unknown but may be of concern

New analog of the older tricyclic antidepressant amitriptyline. Dothiepin appears in breastmilk in a concentration of 11 μg/L following a dose of 75 mg/day, while the maternal plasma level was 33 μg/L.[1] If the infant ingests 150 ml/kg/day of milk, the total daily dose of dothiepin ingested by the infant in this case would be approximately 1.7 μg/kg/day, approximately 1/650th of the adult dose. In an outcome study of 15 mother/infant pairs 3-5 years postpartum, no overall cognitive differences were noted in dothiepin treated mothers/infants, suggesting that this medication did not alter cognitive abilities in breastfed infants.[2]

In a study by Ilett[3], dothiepin concentrations in the milk of 8 mothers was determined (dose ranged from 25-225 mg/day). The mean post-feeding milk/plasma ratio was 1.59 and the mean post-feeding dothiepin concentration in milk ranged from 20-475 μg/L(median=52 μg/L). Mean daily infant doses on a weight basis (in dothiepin equivalents) was 4.4% for dothiepin and its metabolites. Blood levels in all 5 infants were low (> 10 μg/L). No untoward effects were noted in any of the 8 infants following chronic maternal use.

Pregnancy Risk Category: D

Lactation Risk Category: L2

Theoretic Infant Dose: 7.8 μg/kg/day

Adult Concerns: Anticholinergic side effects, such as drying of secretions, dilated pupil, sedation, dizziness, drowsiness, urinary retention.

Pediatric Concerns: None reported in numerous studies.

Drug Interactions: Phenobarbital may reduce effect of dothiepin. Dothiepin blocks the hypotensive effect of guanethidine. May increase toxicity of dothiepin when used with clonidine. Dangerous when used with MAO inhibitors, other CNS depressants. May increase anticoagulant effect of coumadin, warfarin. SSRIs (Prozac, Zoloft, etc) should not be used with or soon after dothiepin or other TCAs due to serotonergic crisis.

Alternatives:

Adult Dosage: 75-300 mg/day

T½ = 14.4-23.9 hours.	M/P = 0.3
PHL =	PB =
PK = 3 hours.	Oral = 30%
MW = 295	pKa =
Vd = 20-92	

References:
1. Rees JA, Glass RC, Sporne GA. Serum and breast milk concentrations of dothiepin. Practitioner 217:686, 1976.
2. Buist A, Janson H. Effect of exposure to dothiepin and northiaden in breast milk on child development. Brit. J. Psy. 167:370-373, 1995.
3. Ilett KF, Lebedevs TH, Wojnar-Horton RE, et.al. the excretion of dothiepin and its primary metabolites in breast milk. Br. J.Clin. Pharmacol. 33:635-9, 1993.

DOXAZOSIN MESYLATE

Trade: Cardura
Can/Aus/UK: Cardura, Carduran
Uses: Antiadrenergic antihypertensive
AAP: Not reviewed

Studies in lactating animals indicate milk levels that are 20 times that of maternal plasma levels, suggesting a concentrating mechanism in breastmilk.[1] It is not known if this occurs in human milk. Extreme caution recommended.

Pregnancy Risk Category: B

Lactation Risk Category: L4

Theoretic Infant Dose:

Adult Concerns: Low blood pressure, malaise, and edema.

Pediatric Concerns: None reported, but extreme caution is recommended.

Drug Interactions: Decreased antihypertensive effect with NSAIDs. Increased effect with other diuretics, antihypertensive medications particularly beta blockers.

Alternatives: Propranolol, Metoprolol

Adult Dosage: 2-4 mg QD

T½ = 9-22 hours	M/P = 20
PHL =	PB = 98%
PK = 2 hours	Oral = 62-69%
MW = 451	pKa =
Vd =	

References:
1. Pharmaceutical Manufacturers Package Insert, 1995.

DOXEPIN

Trade: Adapin, Sinequan
Can/Aus/UK: Deptran, Novo-Doxepin, Sinequan, Triadapin
Uses: Antidepressant
AAP: Drug whose effect on nursing infants is unknown but may be of concern

---

Small but significant amounts are secreted in milk. Two published reports indicate absorption by infant varying from significant to modest. One report of dangerous sedation and respiratory arrest in one infant.[1] Doxepin has an active metabolite with long half-life (37 hours). In one study, peak milk doxepin levels were 27 and 29 μg/L four-five hours after a dose of 25 mg, and the level of metabolite was 9 μg/L.[2] In this infant, the metabolite was believed responsible for the severe depression. Although the milk concentrations were low, the infant's plasma level of metabolite was similar to the maternal plasma level. It is apparent, that the active metabolite of doxepin can concentrate in nursing infants and may be hazardous.

In another case report of a mother ingesting 35 mg/d, the infant was readmitted to the neonatal intensive care unit at day 9 postpartum because of poor sucking and swallowing, muscle hypotonia, vomiting, drowsiness and jaundice.[3] Doxepin levels in the infant were found in small amounts. Breastmilk levels were reported at 60-100 μg/L with a milk/plasma ratio of 1.0-1.7. Upon discontinuing of breastfeeding the infant rapidly became lively and active.

Pregnancy Risk Category: C

Lactation Risk Category: L5

Theoretic Infant Dose: 4.4 μg/kg/day

Adult Concerns: Respiratory arrest, sedation, dry mouth.

Pediatric Concerns: One report of dangerous sedation and respiratory arrest in an infant. Poor sucking and swallowing, muscle hypotonia, vomiting, drowsiness and jaundice reported in a second infant.

Drug Interactions: Decreased effect of Doxepin when used with bretylium, guanethidine, clonidine, levodopa, ascorbic acid and cholestyramine. Increased toxicity when used with carbamazepine, amphetamines, thyroid preparations. Increased toxicity with fluoxetine, thyroid preparations, MAO inhibitors, albuterol, CNS depressants such as benzodiazepines and opiate analgesics, anticholinergics, cimetidine.

Alternatives: Sertraline, Paroxetine

Adult Dosage: 75-300 mg QD

T½ = 8-24 hours	M/P = 1.08-1.66
PHL =	PB = 80-85%
PK = 2 hours	Oral = Complete
MW = 279	pKa = 8.0
Vd = 9-33	

References:
1.   Matheson I, et. al. Respiratory depression caused by N-desmethyldoxepin in breast milk. Lancet 2:1124, 1985.
2.   Kemp J, et. al. Excretion of doxepin and N-desmethyldoxepin in human milk. Br J Clin Pharmacol 20:497-9, 1985.
3.   Frey OR, Scheidt P, von Brenndorff AI. Adverse effects in an newborn infant breast-fed by a mother treated with doxepin. The Annals of Pharmacotherapy. 33:690-693, 1999.

DOXEPIN CREAM

Trade: Zonalon Cream
Can/Aus/UK: Zonalon
Uses: Antipruritic cream
AAP: Drug whose effect on nursing infants is unknown but may be of concern

Doxepin cream is an antihistamine-like cream used to treat severe itching. In one study of 19 women, plasma levels ranged from zero to 47 μg/L following transcutaneous absorption.[1] Target therapeutic ranges in doxepin antidepressant therapy is 30-150 ng/ml. Small but significant amounts are secreted in milk. Two published reports indicate absorption by infant varying from significant to modest, but only in mother consuming oral doses.[2,3] See doxepin.

Pregnancy Risk Category: B

Lactation Risk Category: L4

Theoretic Infant Dose: 7.1 μg/kg/day

Adult Concerns: Respiratory arrest, sedation, dry mouth.

Pediatric Concerns: Sedation, respiratory arrest have been reported following oral administration.

Drug Interactions: Decreased effect of Doxepin when use with bretylium, guanethidine, clonidine, levodopa, ascorbic acid and cholestyramine. Increased toxicity when used with carbamazepine, amphetamines, thyroid preparations. Increased toxicity with fluoxetine, thyroid preparations, MAO inhibitors, albuterol, CNS depressants such as benzodiazepines and opiate analgesics, anticholinergics, cimetidine.

Alternatives:

Adult Dosage: 150-300 mg QD

T½ = 28-52 hours	M/P = 1.08, 1.66
PHL=	PB = 80-85%
PK = 2 hours	Oral = Complete
MW = 279	pKa =
Vd =	

References:
1. Drug Facts and Comparisons. 1994 ed. Facts and Comparisons, St. Louis.
2. Kemp J, et. al. Excretion of doxepin and N-desmethyldoxepin in human milk. Br J Clin Pharmacol 20:497-9, 1985.
3. Matheson I, et. al. Respiratory depression caused by N-desmethyldoxepin in breast milk. Lancet 2:1124, 1985.

DOXORUBICIN

Trade: Adriamycin
Can/Aus/UK: Adriamycin
Uses: Anticancer drug
AAP: Contraindicated by the American Academy of Pediatrics in Breastfeeding Mothers

Doxorubicin and its metabolite are secreted in significant amounts in breastmilk. Following a dose of 70 mg/meter sq., peak milk levels of doxorubicin and metabolite occurred at 24 hours and were 128 and 111 μg/L respectively.[1] The highest milk/plasma ratio was 4.43 at 24 hours Due to the extraordinary toxicity of this compound, breastfeeding is not recommended.

Pregnancy Risk Category: D

Lactation Risk Category: L5

Theoretic Infant Dose: 19.2 μg/kg/day

Adult Concerns: Bone marrow suppression, cardiac toxicity, arrhythmias, nausea, vomiting, stomatitis, liver toxicity.

Pediatric Concerns: This product could be extremely toxic to a breastfeeding infant and is not recommended.

Drug Interactions: Doxorubicin may decrease digoxin plasma levels and renal excretion. Allopurinol, and verapamil may increase cytotoxicity of doxorubicin.

Alternatives:

Adult Dosage: 20-75 mg/sq. meter I.V.

T½ = 17-30 hours	M/P = 4.43
PHL =	PB = 85%
PK = 24 hours	Oral = Poor
MW = 544	pKa =
Vd = 25	

References:
1. Egan PC, et. al. Doxorubicin and cisplatin excretion into human milk. Cancer Treat Rep 69:1387-9, 1985.

DOXYCYCLINE

Trade: Doxychel, Vibramycin, Peristat
Can/Aus/UK: Apo-Doxy, Doryx, Doxycin, Doxylar, Doxylin, Vibra-Tabs, Vibramycin
Uses: Tetracycline antibiotic
AAP: Not reviewed

Doxycycline is a long half-life tetracycline antibiotic. In a study of 15 subjects, the average doxycycline level in milk was 0.77 mg/L following a 200 mg oral dose.[1] One oral dose of 100 mg was administered 24 hours later, and the breastmilk levels were 0.380 mg/L. Tetracyclines administered orally to infants are known to bind in teeth producing discoloration and inhibit bone growth, although doxycycline and oxytetracycline stain teeth the least severe. Although most tetracyclines secreted into milk are generally bound to calcium, thus inhibiting their absorption, doxycycline is the least bound (20%), and may be better absorbed in a breastfeeding infant than the older tetracyclines. While the absolute absorption of older tetracyclines may be dramatically reduced by calcium salts, the newer doxycycline and minocycline analogs bind less and their overall absorption while slowed, may be significantly higher than earlier versions. Prolonged use could potentially alter GI flora, stain teeth, and reduce bone growth. Short term use (several weeks) is not contraindicated. No harmful effects have yet been reported in breastfeeding infants but prolonged use is not advised.

Pregnancy Risk Category: D

Lactation Risk Category: L3
                              L4 if used chronically

Theoretic Infant Dose: 0.1 mg/kg/day

Adult Concerns: Nausea, vomiting, diarrhea, photosensitivity. Doxycycline decreased prothrombin activity.

Pediatric Concerns: None reported, but prolonged exposure may lead to dental staining, and decreased bone growth.

Drug Interactions: Reduced absorption with aluminum, calcium, or magnesium salts, iron or bismuth subsalicylate. Reduced doxycycline half-life when used with barbiturates, phenytoin, and carbamazepine. Concurrent use with methoxyflurane has resulted in fatal renal toxicity. May render oral contraceptives less effective.

Alternatives:

Adult Dosage: 100 mg daily

T½ = 15-25 hours	M/P = 0.3-0.4
PHL =	PB = 90%
PK = 1.5-4 hours	Oral = 90-100%
MW = 462	pKa =
Vd =	

References:
1.   Morganti G, et. al. Comparative concentrations of a tetracycline antibiotic in serum and maternal milk. Antibiotica 6:216-23, 1968.

DOXYLAMINE

Trade: Unisom Nighttime
Can/Aus/UK: Dozile, Mersyndol, Panalgesic, Syndol
Uses: Antihistamine, sedative.
AAP: Not reviewed

Doxylamine is an antihistamine similar in structure to Benadryl. Because it has significant sedative properties, it is primarily used in over-the-counter sleep aids. Like other antihistamines, it should not be used in infants, and particularly in premature or full-term neonates due to paradoxical effects such as CNS stimulation, or even sedation.[1,2] Levels in breastmilk are not known.

Pregnancy Risk Category: B

Lactation Risk Category: L4

Theoretic Infant Dose:

Adult Concerns: Sedation, paradoxical CNS stimulation, agitation.

Pediatric Concerns: None reported via milk, but observe for sedation and paradoxical CNS stimulation. Do not use in infants with apnea.

Drug Interactions: Increased CNS sedation when added to other antihistamines and CNS sedative-hypnotics.

Alternatives:

Adult Dosage:

T½ = 10.1 hours.	M/P =
PHL =	PB =
PK = 2.4 hours.	Oral = Complete
MW = 270	pKa = 9.2
Vd = 2.7	

References:

1. Friedman H, Greenblatt DJ, Scavone JM et al: Clearance of the antihistamine doxylamine reduced in elderly men but not in elderly women. Clin Pharmacokinet 16:312-316, 1989.
2. Friedman H & Greenblatt DJ: The Pharmacokinetics of doxylamine: use of automated gas chromatography with nitrogen-phosphorus detection. J Clin Pharmacol 25:448-451, 1985..

DROPERIDOL

Trade: Inapsine
Can/Aus/UK: Droleptan, Inapsine
Uses: Tranquilizer, antiemetic
AAP: Not reviewed

Droperidol is a powerful tranquilizer. It is sometimes used as preanesthetic medication in labor and delivery because of fewer respiratory effects in neonates. In pediatric patients 2-12 years of age, it is sometimes used as an antiemetic (20-75 micrograms/kg IM, I.V.).[1,2] It apparently crosses the placenta only very slowly. There are no data available on secretion into breastmilk. Due to the potent sedative properties of this medication, caution is urged.

Pregnancy Risk Category: C

Lactation Risk Category: L3

Theoretic Infant Dose:

Adult Concerns: Sedation, hypotension, dizziness, chills, shivering, unusual ocular movements.

Pediatric Concerns: None reported via milk, but observe for sedation, hypotension.

Drug Interactions: Can cause peripheral vasodilation and hypotension when used with certain anesthesia medications. Can potentiate effects of other CNS depressants and antidepressants such as barbiturates.

Alternatives: Haloperidol

Adult Dosage: 2.5-10 mg injection (IM)

T½ = 2.2 hours	M/P =
PHL=	PB = High
PK = 10-30 min.(IM)	Oral =
MW = 379	pKa =
Vd = 2.0	

References:
1. McEvoy GE(ed):AFHS Drug Information, New York, NY. 1992, pp 417-26.
2. Pharmaceutical manufacturers package insert, 1995.

DYPHYLLINE

Trade: Dilor, Lufyllin, Dyphylline
Can/Aus/UK: Broncho-Grippol, Noradran, Silbephylline
Uses: Anti-asthmatic drug
AAP: Approved by the American Academy of Pediatrics for use in breastfeeding mothers

Dyphylline is a methylzanthine bronchodilator similar to theophylline. It is apparently secreted into milk in small quantities. Following a 5 mg/kg dose IM, the milk/plasma ratio was 2.08. and the estimated maximum milk concentration was 72 μg/mL.[1] No reported untoward effects. Observe infant for irritability, insomnia, elevated heart rate.

Pregnancy Risk Category: C

Lactation Risk Category: L3

Theoretic Infant Dose: 10.8 mg/kg/day

Adult Concerns: Irritability, insomnia, tachycardia, arrhythmias, GI distress, headache, seizures, hyperglycemia.

Pediatric Concerns: None reported via milk, but observe for irritability, insomnia, tachycardia.

Drug Interactions: Probenecid significantly increases half-life of dyphylline and increases plasma levels.

Alternatives: Theophylline

Adult Dosage:

T½ = 3-12.8 hours	M/P = 2.08
PHL =	PB = 56%
PK = 1-2 hours(oral)	Oral = Complete
MW = 254	pKa =
Vd = 0.6-1.1	

References:
1. Jarboe CH, et. al. Dyphylline elimination kinetics in lactating women: blood to milk transfer. J Clin Pharmacol 21:405-10, 1981.

ECHINACEA

Trade: Echinacea Angustifolia, Echinacea Purpurea, American Cone Flower, Black Susans, Snakeroot
Can/Aus/UK: Antifect
Uses: Herbal immunostimulant
AAP: Not reviewed

Echinacea is a popular herbal remedy in the central U.S. and has been traditionally used topically to stimulate wound healing, and internally to stimulate the immune system. The plant contains a complex mixture of compounds and thus far, no single component appears responsible for its immunostimulant properties. A number of in vitro and animal studies have documented the activation of immunologic properties although most of these are via intraperitoneal injections, not orally. The activity of orally administered extracts is unknown. Echinacea extracts appear to stimulate phagocytosis of macrophages, increase cellular respiration, and increase the mobility of phagocytic leukocytes.[1] Extracts of E. Purpurea are highly effective in activating macrophages to engulf tumor cells, to produce tumor necrosis factor, interleukin-1, and interferon beta-2. One study suggests a radioprotective effect (antioxidant) of Echinacea. Another study in humans suggests that while single doses may stimulate the immune system, repeated daily doses may actually suppress the immune response.[2] Thus far, little is known about the toxicity of this plant although its use has been widespread for many years. Apparently, purified Echinacea extract is relatively non-toxic even at high doses.[3,4] No data are available on its transfer into human milk, or its effect on lactation. It should not be used for more than 8 weeks.[5]

Pregnancy Risk Category:

Lactation Risk Category: L3

Theoretic Infant Dose:

Adult Concerns: None reported.

Pediatric Concerns: None reported via milk.

Drug Interactions:

Alternatives:

Adult Dosage:

References:
1. Steinmuller C. et.al. Polysaccharides isolated from plant cell cultures of Echinacea purpurea enhance the resistance of immunosuppressed mice against systemic infections with Candida albicans and Listeria monocytogenes. Int J. Immunopharmacol 15(5):605, 1993.
2. Coeugniet EG, Elek E. Immunomodulation with Viscum album and Echinacea purpurea extracts. Onkologie 10(supp 3):27, 1987.
3. Review of Natural Products. Facts and Comparisons, St. Louis, Mo. 1996.
3. Bissett NG. In: Herbal Drugs and Phytopharmaceuticals. Medpharm Scientific Publishers, CRC Press, Boca Raton, 1994.
4. The Complete German Commission E Monographs. Ed. M. Blumenthal. Amer. Botanical Council, Austin, Tx. 1998.

ENALAPRIL MALEATE

Trade: Vasotec
Can/Aus/UK: Amprace, Innovace, Renitec, Vasotec
Uses: Antihypertensive, ACE inhibitor
AAP: Approved by the American Academy of Pediatrics for use in breastfeeding mothers

Enalapril maleate is an ACE inhibitor used as an antihypertensive. Upon absorption, it is rapidly metabolized by the adult liver to enalaprilat, the biologically active metabolite.

In one study of 5 lactating mothers who received a single 20 mg dose, the mean maximum milk concentration of enalapril and enalaprilat was only 1.74 μg/L and 1.72 μg/L respectively. [1] The author suggests that an infant consuming 850 mL of milk daily would ingest less than 2 ug of enalaprilat daily. The milk/plasma ratios for enalapril and enalaprilat averaged 0.013 and 0.025 respectively. However, this was only a single dose study, and the levels transferred into milk at steady state may be slightly higher.

In a study by Rush[2] of a patient receiving 10 mg/day, the total amount of enalapril and enalaprilat measured in milk during the 24 hour period was 81.9 ng and 36.1 ng, respectively, or 1.44 μg/L and 0.63 μg/L of milk, respectively.

Exercise caution when administering to lactating women particularly early postnatal, although the data thus far indicates the levels secreted into milk are clinically insignificant.

Pregnancy Risk Category: C if used 1st trimester
D if used 2nd and 3rd trimesters

Lactation Risk Category: L2
L4 if used early postpartum

Theoretic Infant Dose: 885.0 ng/kg/day

Adult Concerns: Hypotension, bradycardia, headache, fatigue, diarrhea, rash, cough.

Pediatric Concerns: None reported via milk, but observe for hypotension.

Drug Interactions: Bioavailability of ACEIs may be decreased when used with antacids. Capsaicin may exacerbate coughing associated with ACE inhibitor treatment. Pharmacologic effects of ACE inhibitors may be increased. Increased plasma levels of digoxin may result. Increased serum lithium levels may result when used with ACE inhibitors.

Alternatives: Captopril, Benazepril

Adult Dosage: 10-40 mg QD

T½ = 35 hours(metabolite)	M/P =
PHL =	PB = 60%
PK = 0.5-1.5 hours	Oral = 60%
MW = 492	pKa =
Vd =	

References:
1. Redman CG, Kelly JG, Cooper WD. The excretion of enalapril and enalaprilat in human breast milk. Eur. J. Clin. Pharmacol 38:99, 1990.
2. Rush JE, Snyder BA, Barrish A, et.al. Comment. Clin. Nephrol. 35:234, 1991

ENCAINIDE

Trade: Enkaid
Can/Aus/UK:
Uses: Antiarrhythmic agent.
AAP: Not reviewed

Encainide is a local anesthetic-type antiarrhythmic agent.   It was voluntarily removed from the market in 1991, but is available on a limited basis for certain patients with life-threatening arrhythmias. The plasma kinetics are highly variable depending on the metabolic capabilities of the maternal liver. The oral bioavailability is extremely variable, and varies from 25-65% in extensive metabolizers to 80-90% in poor metabolizers. Half-lives are variable as well according to the metabolic capacity of the individual's liver.[1]

However, encainide and its 3 active metabolites are excreted into human milk.   Milk concentrations of encainide and o-demethyl encainide are 200-400 μg/L and 100-200 μg/L respectively.[2] These concentrations are similar to the maternal serum levels.

Pregnancy Risk Category: B

Lactation Risk Category: L3

Theoretic Infant Dose: 60.0 μg/kg/day

Adult Concerns: Arrhythmias, chest pain, congestive heart failure, abdominal pain.

Pediatric Concerns: None reported, but extreme caution is recommended.

Drug Interactions: Use caution when encainide is used with any other drug that effects cardiac conduction.   Cimetidine increases plasma concentrations of encainide.

Alternatives:

Adult Dosage:

T½ = 2-36 hours.	M/P = 1
PHL =	PB = 70.5-78%
PK = 1.7 hours.	Oral = Variable
MW = 352	pKa =
Vd = 2.7-4.3	

References:
1. Pharmaceutical Manufactures Product Information, 1992.
2. Briggs GS, et.al. Drugs in Pregnancy and Lactation. Williams and Wilkins, 1998.

ENOXACIN

Trade: Penetrex
Can/Aus/UK: Comprecin, Enoxin
Uses: Antibiotic
AAP: Not reviewed

Enoxacin is a typical fluoroquinolone antibiotic similar to ciprofloxacin, norfloxacin, and others. At present the flouroquinolones are not cleared for use in pediatric patients due to arthropathy in young animals. No data on the transfer of enoxacin into human milk are available. See ofloxacin and norfloxacin as alternatives.

Pregnancy Risk Category: C

Lactation Risk Category: L4

Theoretic Infant Dose:

Adult Concerns: Nausea, vomiting, diarrhea, abdominal cramps, GI bleeding, increased intracranial pressure, tremor, restlessness, other CNS reactions. Photosensitivity.

Pediatric Concerns: None reported via milk, but caution urged. See norfloxacin.

Drug Interactions: Decreased absorption with antacids. Quinolones cause increased levels of caffeine, warfarin, cyclosporine, theophylline. Cimetidine, probenecid, azlocillin increase ciprofloxacin levels. Increased risk of seizures when used with foscarnet.

Alternatives: Ofloxacine, Norfloxacine, Trovafloxacin

Adult Dosage: 200-400 mg BID

T½ = 3-6 hours	M/P =
PHL =	PB = 40%
PK =	Oral = 90%
MW =	pKa =
Vd = 2.5	

ENOXAPARIN

Trade: Lovenox, Low Molecular Weight Heparin
Can/Aus/UK: Clexane, Lovenox
Uses: Anticoagulant
AAP: Not reviewed

Enoxaparin is a low molecular weight fraction of heparin used clinically as an anticoagulant.   In a study of 12 women receiving 20-40 mg of enoxaparin daily for up to 5 days postpartum for venous pathology (n=4) or caesarian section (n=8), no change in anti-Xa activity was noted in the breastfed infants.[1]   Because it is a peptide fragment of heparin, its molecular weight is large (2000-8000 daltons). The size alone would largely preclude its entry into human milk at levels clinically relevant. Due to minimal oral bioavailability, any present in milk would not be orally absorbed by the infant. A similar compound, dalteparin, has been studied and milk levels are extremely low as well. See dalteparin.

Pregnancy Risk Category: B

Lactation Risk Category: L3

Theoretic Infant Dose:

Adult Concerns: Anticoagulant effects in adults when administered subcutaneously.

Pediatric Concerns: None reported via milk. Molecular weight is too large to produce clinically relevant milk levels.

Drug Interactions: Anticoagulants and platelet inhibitors. NSAIDS may increase risk of bleeding.

Alternatives: Dalteparin

Adult Dosage: 30 mg BID

T½ = 4.5 hours	M/P =
PHL =	PB =
PK = 3-5 hours	Oral = None
MW = 8000	pKa =
Vd = 0.1	

References:
1.   L'allaitement est possible en cas de traitement maternel par l'enoxaparine. Guillonneau M; de Crepy A; Aufrant C; Hurtaud-Roux MF; Jacqz-Aigrain E. ,Arch Pediatr 3(5):513-4, 1996.

EPHEDRINE

Trade: Vatronol Nose Drops
Can/Aus/UK: Adalixin, Amsec, Anestan, Anodesyn, Bethal, Cam
Uses: Adrenergic stimulant, anti-asthmatic.
AAP: Not reviewed

Ephedrine is a mild stimulant that belongs to the adrenergic family and functions similar to the amphetamines. Small amounts of d-isoephedrine, a close congener of ephedrine, is believed to be secreted into milk, although no data are available on ephedrine itself.[1] This product is commonly used to support blood pressure of parturients during delivery. On an acute basis, it is not likely to harm a breastfeeding infant.

Pregnancy Risk Category: C

Lactation Risk Category: L4

Theoretic Infant Dose:

Adult Concerns: Anorexia, tachycardia, arrhythmias, agitation, insomnia, hyperstimulation.

Pediatric Concerns: None reported, but observe for anorexia, irritability, crying, disturbed sleeping patterns, excitement.

Drug Interactions: May increase toxicity and cardiac stimulation when used with theophylline. MAO inhibitors or atropine may increase blood pressure.

Alternatives:

Adult Dosage: 25-50 mg injection

T½ = 3-5 hours	M/P =
PHL=	PB =
PK = 15-60 min.	Oral = 85%
MW = 165	pKa = 9.6
Vd =	

References:
1.   Mortimer EA J. Drug toxicity from breast milk? Pediatrics 60:780-1, 1977.

EPINEPHRINE

Trade: Adrenalin, Sus-Phrine, Medihaler, Primatene
Can/Aus/UK: Adrenalin, Adrenaline, Adrenutol, Bronkaid, Epi-Pen, Eppy, Simplene
Uses: Stimulant
AAP: Not reviewed

Epinephrine is a powerful adrenergic stimulant. Although likely to be secreted in milk, it is rapidly destroyed in the GI tract.[1] It is unlikely that any would be absorbed by the infant unless in the early neonatal period or premature.

Pregnancy Risk Category: C

Lactation Risk Category: L1

Theoretic Infant Dose:

Adult Concerns: Nervousness, tremors, agitation, tachycardia.

Pediatric Concerns: None reported, but observe for brief stimulation.

Drug Interactions: Increase cardiac irritability when used with halogenated inhaled anesthetics, alpha blocking agents. Do not use with MAO inhibitors.

Alternatives:

Adult Dosage: 0.1-0.25 mg injection (IV)

T½ = 1 hour(inhalation)	M/P =
PHL =	PB =
PK = <1-10 min.	Oral = Poor
MW = 183	pKa =
Vd =	

References:
1. Wilson, J. Drugs in Breast Milk. New York: ADIS Press, 1981.

EPOETIN ALFA

Trade: Epogen
Can/Aus/UK:
Uses: Stimulates red blood cell production
AAP: Not reviewed

Epoetin alfa is a glycoprotein which stimulates red blood cell production. Structurally similar to the natural erythropoietin, it consists of 165 amino acids manufactured by recombinant DNA technology. It has a molecular weight of 30,400 daltons. Large molecular weight proteins in general are poorly transferred into human milk. Further, due to its protein nature, it would not likely be absorbed orally to any degree by the infant.

Pregnancy Risk Category: C

Lactation Risk Category: L3

Theoretic Infant Dose:

Adult Concerns: Headache, hypertension, arthralgias, nausea, edema, vomiting and chest pain have been reported in adults.

Pediatric Concerns: None reported via milk.

Drug Interactions: None.

Alternatives:

Adult Dosage: 50-100 Units three times weekly

T½ = 4-13 hours	M/P =
PHL = 4-13 hours	PB =
PK = 5-24 hours	Oral = Nil
MW = 30,400	pKa =
Vd =	

References:
1. Pharmaceutical manufacturers package insert, 2001.

EPOPROSTENOL

Trade: Flolan
Can/Aus/UK:
Uses: Vasodilator, platelet function inhibitor
AAP: Not reviewed

Epoprostenol (Prostacyclin; PGX; PGI-2) is a naturally occurring prostaglandin that is a potent inhibitor of platelet aggregation and a vasodilator. It is commonly used to treat primary pulmonary hypertension. It is rapidly metabolized in plasma to 6-keto-prostaglandin F1-alpha, which is biologically inactive, and has a half-life of only 3-5 minutes.[1] Prostaglandins are known to be transferred into human milk, but they are believed derived from mammary tissue including synthesis by the cellular components of breastmilk.[2] With the extraordinarily short half-life of this product, it is unlikely any would penetrate into milk, be retained for very long, or be stable in the infant's gut. Oral absorption by the infant is unlikely.

Pregnancy Risk Category: B

Lactation Risk Category: L3

Theoretic Infant Dose:

Adult Concerns: Flushing, headache, nausea, vomiting, hypotension, anxiety, chest pain, dizziness, bradycardia, abdominal pain.

Pediatric Concerns: None reported, unlikely to be absorbed.

Drug Interactions: May decrease clearance of digoxin. Decreased oral clearance of furosemide.

Alternatives:

Adult Dosage: 2 ng/kg per minute

T½ = 6 minutes	M/P =
PHL =	PB =
PK =	Oral = Nil
MW = 374	pKa =
Vd = 357 mL	

References:
1. Pharmaceutical manufacturers package insert, 2002.
2. Friedman Z. Prostaglandins in breast milk. Endocrinol Exp. 20(2-3):285-91, 1986.

EPSTEIN-BARR VIRUS

Trade: Mononucleosis, EBV
Can/Aus/UK:
Uses: Herpesvirus infection (EBV)
AAP: Not reviewed

The Epstein-Barr virus (EBV) is one of the causes of infectious mononucleosis. EBV belongs to the herpesvirus family. Symptoms include fever, exudative pharyngitis, lymphadenopathy, hepatosplenomegaly, and atypical lymphocytosis. Close personal contact is generally required for transmission and it is not known if EBV is secreted into human milk, although it is likely. Studies by Kusuhara[1] indicate that the seroprevalence of EBV at 12-23 months was the same in bottle-fed, and in breastfed infants. This data suggests that breastmilk is not a significant source of early EBV infections.

Pregnancy Risk Category:

Lactation Risk Category:

Theoretic Infant Dose:

Adult Concerns:

Pediatric Concerns:

Drug Interactions:

Alternatives:

Adult Dosage:

References:
1. Kushhara K, Takabayashi A, et.al. Breast milk is not a significant source for early Epstein-Barr virus or human herpesvirus 6 infection in infants: a Seroepidemiologic study in 2 endemic areas of human T-Cell lymphotropic virus Type 1 in Japan. Microbiol. Immunol. 41(4):309-312, 1997.

ERGONOVINE MALEATE

Trade: Ergotrate, Ergometrine
Can/Aus/UK: Ergometrine, Ergotrate, Syntometrine
Uses: Postpartum uterine bleeding
AAP: Not reviewed

Ergonovine and its close congener, methylergonovine maleate, directly stimulate uterine and vascular smooth muscle contractions. They are primarily used to prevent/treat postpartum hemorrhage. Although pharmacologically similar, many clinicians prefer methylergonovine because it produces less hypertension than ergonovine. In a study of 8 postpartum women receiving 0.125 mg three times daily until day 5 when a 0.25 mg tablet was introduced, measurable ergonovine was only found in 4 of 8 patients, and averaged 0.8 μg/L.[1] These authors suggested that use of the drug during breastfeeding would not affect the infant.

In addition, the effect of ergonovine on prolactin levels is controversial. In one study methylergonovine did not alter postpartum maternal prolactin levels[2], while another study[3] indicated a significant inhibition of prolactin production by ergonovine. Ergonovine use in lactating women would presumably suppress lactation, whereas methylergonovine may not.

When used at doses of 0.2mg up to 3-4 times daily, only small quantities of ergonovine are found in milk. Short-term (1 week) low-dose regimens of these agents do not apparently pose problems in nursing mothers or their infants. Methylergonovine is preferred because it does not inhibit lactation and levels in milk are minimal. The prolonged use of ergot alkaloids should be avoided and can lead to severe gangrenous manifestations.

Pregnancy Risk Category: X

Lactation Risk Category: L3

Theoretic Infant Dose: 120.0 ng/kg/day

Adult Concerns: Hypertension, seizures, vomiting, diarrhea, cold extremities.

Pediatric Concerns: None reported, but long term exposure is not recommended. Methyl-ergonovine is commonly recommended early postpartum for breastfeeding mothers to reduce uterine bleeding.

Drug Interactions:

Alternatives: Methylergonovine

Adult Dosage: 0.2 mg injection (IM) q 2-4 hours

T½ = 0.5-2 hours	M/P =
PHL=	PB =
PK = 30- 180 min.	Oral = >60%
MW = 441	pKa =
Vd =	

References:
1. Erkkola R, et.al. Excretion of methylergometrine (methylergonovine) into the human breast milk. Int. J. Clin. Pharmacol. 16:579-80,1978.
2. Del Pozo E, Brun del Rey R, Hinselmann M. Lack of effect of methyl-ergonovine on postpartum lactation. Am. J. Obstet. Gynecol. 123:845-6,1975.
3. Canales ES, Facog JT et.al. Effect of ergonovine on prolactin secretion and milk Let-Down. Obstet. Gynecol. 48:2228-9, 1976.

ERGOTAMINE TARTRATE

Trade: Wigraine, Cafergot, Ergostat, Ergomar, DHE45
Can/Aus/UK: Cafergot, Ergodryl, Ergomar, Gynergen, Lingraine, Migral
Uses: Anti-migraine, inhibits prolactin
AAP: Drugs associated with significant side effects and should be given with caution

Ergotamine is a potent vasoconstrictor, generally used in acute phases of migraine headache. It is never used chronically for prophylaxis of migraine. Although early reports suggest ergotamine compounds are secreted in breastmilk[1] and cause symptoms of ergotism (vomiting, and diarrhea) in infants, other authors [2] suggest that the short term use of ergotamine (0.2 mg postpartum) generally presents no problem to a nursing infant. This is likely, due to the fact that less than 5% of ergotamine is orally absorbed in adults. However, excessive dosing and prolonged administration may inhibit prolactin secretion and hence lactation. Although the initial plasma half-life is only 2 hours, ergotamine is stored for long periods in various tissues producing long-lasting effects (terminal half-life = 21 hours). Use during lactation should be strongly discouraged.

Pregnancy Risk Category: X

Lactation Risk Category: L4

Theoretic Infant Dose:

Adult Concerns: Ergotism, peripheral artery insufficiency, nausea, vomiting, paresthesia, cold skin temperatures, headache.

Pediatric Concerns: One case of ergotism reported and included symptoms such as vomiting and diarrhea. Long term exposure is contraindicated.

Drug Interactions: Rifamycin and other macrolide antibiotics may enhance ergot toxicity.

Alternatives: Propranolol, Sumatriptan

Adult Dosage: 2 mg q 30 minutes

T½ = 21 hours(terminal)	M/P =
PHL =	PB =
PK = 0.5-3 hours	Oral = < 5%
MW = 581	pKa =
Vd =	

References:
1. Fomina PI. Untersuchungen uber den Ubergang des aktiven agens des Muttrkorns in die milch stillender Mutter. Arch Gynecol 157:275, 1934.
2. White GJ & White MK: Breast feeding and drugs in human milk. Vet Hum Toxicol 1980; 22(Suppl 1):18.

ERYTHROMYCIN

Trade: E-mycin, Ery-tab, Eryc, Ilosone
Can/Aus/UK: Ceplac, E-Mycin, E-mycin, EES, EMU-V, Eryc, Erycen, Erythrocin, Erythromid, Ilosone, Ilotyc, Novo-Rythro, PCE
Uses: Macrolide antibiotic
AAP: Approved by the American Academy of Pediatrics for use in breastfeeding mothers

Erythromycin is an older narrow spectrum antibiotic. In one study of patients receiving 400 mg three times daily, milk levels varied from 0.4 to 1.6 mg/L.[1] Doses as high as 2 gm per day produced milk levels of 1.6 to 3.2 mg/L. One case of hypertrophic pyloric stenosis apparently linked to erythromycin administration has been reported.[2] In a study of 2-3 patients who received a single 500 oral dose, milk levels at 4 hours ranged from 0.9 to 1.4 mg/L with a milk/plasma ratio of 0.92.[3] Newer macrolide-like antibiotics(azithromycin) may preclude the use of erythromycin.

Pregnancy Risk Category: B

Lactation Risk Category: L1

Theoretic Infant Dose: 0.5 mg/kg/day

Adult Concerns: Abdominal cramping, nausea, vomiting, hepatitis, ototoxicity, and hypersensitivity.

Pediatric Concerns: One case of pyloric stenosis reported, but this is extremely rare. Erythromycin is commonly used in children.

Drug Interactions: Erythromycin may decrease clearance of carbamazepine, cyclosporin, triazolam. Erythromycin may decrease theophylline clearance by as much as 60%. May increase terfenadine plasma levels and increase Q/T intervals. May potentiate anticoagulant effect of warfarin.

Alternatives: Azithromycin, Clarithromycin

Adult Dosage: 500-800 mg QID

T½ = 1.5-2 hours	M/P = 0.92
PHL =	PB = 84%
PK = 2-4 hours	Oral = Variable
MW = 734	pKa =
Vd =	

References:
1. Knowles JA. Drugs in milk. Pediatr Currents 1:28-32, 1972.
2. Stang H: Pyloric stenosis associated with erythromycin ingested through breast milk. Minn Med 69:669-682, 1986
3. Matsuda S. Transfer of antibiotics into maternal milk.   Biol Res Pregnancy Perinatol. 5(2):57-60, 1984.

ESMOLOL

Trade: Brevibloc
Can/Aus/UK: Brevibloc
Uses: Beta blocker antiarrhythmic
AAP: Not reviewed

Esmolol is an ultra short-acting beta blocker agent with low lipid solubility.   It is of the same family as propranolol.   It is primarily used for treatment of supraventricular tachycardia. It is only used I.V. and has an extremely   short half-life.   It is almost completely hydrolyzed in 30 minutes.[1,2] No data on breastmilk levels are available.

Pregnancy Risk Category: C

Lactation Risk Category: L3

Theoretic Infant Dose:

Adult Concerns: Hypotension, bradycardia, dizziness, somnolence.

Pediatric Concerns: None reported.

Drug Interactions: Beta blockers may decrease the effect of sulfonylureas. Increased effect with calcium channel blockers, contraceptives, ciprofloxacin, MAO inhibitors, thyroid hormones, haloperidol, and numerous other medications.

Alternatives: Propranolol, Metoprolol

Adult Dosage: 100 μg/kg/minute

T½ = 9 minutes	M/P =
PHL = 4.5 min.	PB = 55%
PK = 15 min.	Oral = Poor
MW = 295	pKa =
Vd =	

References:
1. McEvoy GF(ed):AHFS Drug Information, New York, NY. 1995.
2. Lacy C. et.al. Drug information handbook. Lexi-Comp, Hudson(Cleveland), Oh. 1996.

ESOMEPRAZOLE

Trade: Nexium
Can/Aus/UK: Nexium
Uses: Reduces gastric acid secretion
AAP: Not reviewed

Esomeprazole is just the L isomer of omeprazole(Prilosec) and is essentially identical to Prilosec. See omeprazole for breastfeeding recommendations.

Pregnancy Risk Category: C

ESTAZOLAM

Trade: Prosom
Can/Aus/UK:
Uses: Benzodiazepine sedative.
AAP: Not reviewed

Estazolam is a benzodiazepine sedative hypnotic that belongs to the Valium family. Estazolam, like other benzodiazepines, is secreted into rodent milk, although the levels are unpublished.[1,2] No data are available on human milk levels. It is likely that some is secreted into human milk as well.

Pregnancy Risk Category: X

Lactation Risk Category: L3

Theoretic Infant Dose:

Adult Concerns: Sedation.

Pediatric Concerns: None reported via milk, but observe for sedation, apnea.

Drug Interactions: Certain enzyme inducers such as barbiturates may increase the metabolism of estazolam. CNS depressants may increase adverse effects of estazolam. Cimetidine may decrease metabolism of estazolam.

Alternatives: Lorazepam, Midazolam, Alprazolam

Adult Dosage: 1-2 mg daily

T½ = 10-24 hours	M/P =
PHL=	PB = 93%
PK = 0.5-3 hours	Oral = Complete
MW = 295	pKa =
Vd =	

References:
1. Pharmaceutical Manufacturers Package Insert, 1995.
2. Drug Facts and Comparisons. 1995 ed. Facts and Comparisons, St. Louis.

ESTROGEN-ESTRADIOL

Trade: Estratab, Premarin, Menest
Can/Aus/UK: Delestrogen, Estinyl, Estrace, Estraderm, Estring, Evorel
Uses: Estrogen hormone
AAP: Approved by the American Academy of Pediatrics for use in breastfeeding mothers

Although small amounts may pass into breastmilk, the effects of estrogens on the infant appear minimal. Early post-partum use of estrogens may reduce volume of milk produced and the protein content, but it is variable and depends on dose and the individual.[1-4]

Breastfeeding mothers should attempt to wait until lactation is firmly established (6-8 weeks) prior to use of estrogen-containing oral contraceptives.   In one study of six lactating women who received 50 or 100 mg vaginal suppositories of estradiol, the plasma levels peaked at 3 hours.[5] These doses are extremely large and are not used clinically. In this study of 11 women, the mean concentration of estradiol in breastmilk was found to be 113 picograms/ml[6], which is very close to that seen when the woman begins ovulating during lactation.   If oral contraceptives are used during lactation, the transfer of estradiol to human milk will be low and will not exceed the transfer during physiologic conditions when the mother has resumed ovulation. See oral contraceptives.

Pregnancy Risk Category: X

Lactation Risk Category: L3

Theoretic Infant Dose:

Adult Concerns: Estrogen use has been associated with breast tenderness, increased risk of thromboembolic disorders, headache, nausea, vomiting, etc.

Pediatric Concerns: None reported. Infantile feminization is unlikely at normal dosages.

Drug Interactions: Rifampin reduces the serum levels of estrogen. Exogenous estrogens increase toxicity of hydrocortisone, and thromboembolic events with anticoagulants such as warfarin.

Alternatives: Norethindrone

Adult Dosage: 10 mg TID

T½ = 60 minutes	**M/P = 0.08**
PHL=	**PB = 98%**
PK = Rapid	**Oral = Complete**
MW = 272	**pKa =**
Vd =	

References:
1.   Booker DE, Pahyl IR. Control of postpartum breast engorgement with oral contraceptives. Am J Obstet Gynecol 98:1099-1101, 1967.
2.   Kamal I, Hefnawi F, Ghoneim M, Talaat M, Younis N, Tagui A, Abdalla M. Clinical, biochemical, and experimental studies on lactation. II. Clinical effects of gestagens on lactation. Am J Obstet Gynecol. 105(3):324-34, 1969.
3.   Kora SJ. Effect of oral contraceptives on lactation. Fertil Steril. 20(3):419-23, 1969.
4.   Koetsawang S, Bhiraleus P, Chiemprajert T. Effects of oral contraceptives on lactation. Fertil Steril. 23(1):24-8, 1972.
5.   Laukaran VH. The effects of contraceptive use on the initiation and duration of lactation. Int J Gynecol Obstet. 25(suppl)129-142, 1987
6.   Nilsson S, et.al. Transfer of estradiol to human milk. Am. J. Obstet. Gynecol. 132:653-7, 1978.

ETANERCEPT

Trade: Enbrel
Can/Aus/UK: Enbrel
Uses: Anti-arthritic
AAP: Not reviewed

Etanercept is a dimeric fusion protein consisting of the extracellular ligand-binding portion of tumor necrosis factor bound to human IgG1. Etanercept binds specifically to tumor necrosis factor (TNF) blocks its inflammatory and immune activity in rheumatoid arthritis patients.[1,2] Elevated levels of TNF are found in the synovial fluid of arthritis patients. No data are available on the transfer of etanercept to human milk. However, due to its enormous molecular weight (150,000 daltons), it is extremely unlikely clinically relevant amounts would transfer into milk. In addition, due to its protein structure, it would not be orally bioavailable in an infant. Infliximab is somewhat similar and is apparently not secreted into human milk (see infliximab).

Pregnancy Risk Category: B

Lactation Risk Category: L3

Theoretic Infant Dose:

Adult Concerns: Etanercept may suppress the immune system and increase the risk of infections significantly. Incidence of infections is 38%. Headache, dizziness, cough, and rhinitis have been reported.

Pediatric Concerns: None reported via milk.

Drug Interactions: Do not administer live vaccines concurrent with etanercept.

Alternatives: Infliximab

Adult Dosage: 25 mg twice weekly

T½ = 115 hours	M/P =
PHL =	PB =
PK = 72 hours	Oral = Nil
MW = 150000	pKa =
Vd = 0.24	

References:
1.   Pharmaceutical Manufacturers Package Insert, 1999.
2.   Drug Facts and Comparisons. 1999 ed. Facts and Comparisons, St. Louis.

ETHACRYNIC ACID

Trade: Edecrin
Can/Aus/UK: Edecril, Edecrin
Uses: Powerful loop diuretic
AAP: Not reviewed

Ethacrynic acid is a potent short acting loop diuretic similar to Lasix. It is listed by the manufacturer as contraindicated in nursing women. A significant decrease in maternal blood pressure, or blood volume may reduce milk production. No data on transfer into human milk are available.[1,2]

Pregnancy Risk Category: B

Lactation Risk Category: L3

Theoretic Infant Dose:

Adult Concerns: Diuresis, hypotension, diarrhea.

Pediatric Concerns: None reported.

Drug Interactions: Increased toxicity when used with antihypertensives, other diuretics, aminoglycosides. Increased risk of arrhythmias when used with digoxin. Probenecid reduces diuresis of this product.

Alternatives: Furosemide

Adult Dosage: 50-200 mg QD

T½ = 2-4 hours.	M/P =
PHL =	PB = 90%
PK = 2 hours(oral)	Oral = 100%
MW = 303	pKa =
Vd =	

References:
1. Pharmaceutical Manufacturers Package Insert, 1996.
2. Lacy C. et.al. Drug information handbook. Lexi-Comp, Hudson(Cleveland), Oh. 1996.

ETHAMBUTOL

Trade: Ethambutol, Myambutol
Can/Aus/UK: Etibi, Myambutol
Uses: Antitubercular drug
AAP: Approved by the American Academy of Pediatrics for use in breastfeeding mothers

Ethambutol is an antimicrobial used for tuberculosis. Small amounts are secreted in milk, although no studies are available which clearly document levels. In one unpublished study, the mother had an ethambutol plasma level of 1.5 mg/L three hours after a dose of 15 mg/kg. Following a similar dose, the concentration in milk was 1.4 mg/L.[1] In another patient, the plasma level was 4.62 mg/L and the corresponding milk concentration was 4.6 mg/L (no dose available).

Pregnancy Risk Category: B

Lactation Risk Category: L2

Theoretic Infant Dose: 0.7 mg/kg/day

Adult Concerns: Optic neuritis, dizziness, confusion, nausea, vomiting, anorexia.

Pediatric Concerns: None reported, but caution is recommended.

Drug Interactions: Aluminum salts may decrease oral absorption.

Alternatives:

Adult Dosage: 15-25 mg/kg QD

T½ = 3.1 hours	**M/P = 1.0**
PHL =	**PB = 8-22%**
PK = 2-4 hours	**Oral = 80%**
MW = 204	**pKa =**
Vd =	

References:
1. Snider DE, Powell KE. Should women taking antituberculosis drugs breast-feed? Arch Inter Med. 144:589-590, 1984.

ETHANOL

Trade: Alcohol
Can/Aus/UK:
Uses: Depressant
AAP: Approved by the American Academy of Pediatrics for use in breastfeeding mothers

Significant amounts of alcohol are secreted into breastmilk, although it is not considered harmful to the infant if the amount and duration are limited. The absolute amount of alcohol transferred into milk is generally low. Beer, but not ethanol, has been reported in a number of studies to stimulate prolactin levels and breastmilk production.[1-3] Thus it is presumed that the polysaccharide from barley may be the prolactin-stimulating component of beer.[4] Non-alcoholic beer is equally effective.

In a study of twelve breastfeeding mothers who ingested 0.3 g/kg of ethanol in orange juice(equivalent to 1 can of beer for the average sized woman), the mean maximum concentration of ethanol in milk was 320 mg/L.[5] This report suggests a 23% reduction (156 to 120 mL) in breastmilk production following ingestion of beer, and an increase in milk odor as a function of ethanol content.

Excess levels may lead to drowsiness, deep sleep, weakness, and decreased linear growth in infant. Maternal blood alcohol levels must attain 300 mg/dl before significant side effects are reported in the infant. Reduction of letdown is apparently dose-dependent and requires alcohol consumption of 1.5 to 1.9 gm/kg body weight.[6] Other studies have suggested psychomotor delay in infants of moderate drinkers (2+ drinks daily). Avoid breastfeeding during and for 2-3 hours after drinking alcohol.

In an interesting study of the effect of alcohol on milk ingestion by infants, the rate of milk consumption by infants during the 4 hours immediately after exposure to alcohol (0.3 g/kg) in 12 mothers was significantly less.[7] Compensatory increases in intake were then observed during the 8-16 hours after exposure when mothers refrained from drinking.

Adult metabolism of alcohol is approximately 1 oz in 3 hours, so that mothers who ingest alcohol in moderate amounts can generally return to breastfeeding as soon as they feel neurologically normal. Chronic or heavy consumers of alcohol should not breastfeed.

Pregnancy Risk Category: D

Lactation Risk Category: L3

Theoretic Infant Dose:

Adult Concerns: Sedation, decreased milk supply, altered milk taste.

Pediatric Concerns: Sedation, irritability, weak sucking, decreased milk supply, increased milk odor.

Drug Interactions: Increased CNS depression when used with barbiturates, benzodiazepines, chloral hydrate, and other CNS depressants. A disulfiram-like reaction (flushing, weakness, sweating, tachycardia, etc) may occur when used with cephalosporins, chlorpropamide, disulfiram, furazolidone, metronidazole, procarbazine. Increased hypoglycemia when used with sulfonylureas and other hypoglycemic agents. Intolerance of bromocriptine.

Alternatives:

Adult Dosage:

T½ = 0.24 hours	M/P = 1.0
PHL =	PB = 0%
PK = 30-90 min.(oral)	Oral = 100%
MW = 46	pKa =
Vd = 0.53	

References:

1. Marks V, Wright JW. Endocrinological and metabolic effects of alcohol. Proc R Soc Med. 70(5):337-44, 1977.
2. De Rosa G, Corsello SM, Ruffilli MP, Della Casa S, Pasargiklian E. Prolactin secretion after beer. Lancet. 2(8252):934, 1981.
3. Carlson HE, Wasser HL, Reidelberger RD. Beer-induced prolactin secretion: a clinical and laboratory study of the role of salsolinol. J Clin Endocrinol Metab. 60(4):673-7, 1985.
4. Koletzko B, Lehner F. Beer and breastfeeding. Adv Exp Med Biol. 478:23-8, 2000.
5. Mennella JA and Beauchamp, GK. The transfer of alcohol to human milk. Effects on flavor and the infant's behavior. NEJM 325:981-985, 1991.
6. Cobo E. Effect of different doses of ethanol on the milk ejecting reflex in lactating women. Am J obstet Gynecol. 115:817-821, 1973.
7. Mennella JA. Regulation of milk intake after exposure to alcohol in mothers' milk. Alcohol Clin Exp Res. 25(4):590-3, 2001.

ETHOSUXIMIDE

Trade: Zarontin
Can/Aus/UK: Zarontin
Uses: Anticonvulsant used in epilepsy
AAP: Approved by the American Academy of Pediatrics for use in breastfeeding mothers

Ethosuximide is an anticonvulsant used in epilepsy.   Rane's data suggest that although significant levels of ethosuximide are transferred into human milk, the plasma level in the infant is quite low.[1] A peak milk concentration of approximately 55 mg/L was reported at 1 month postpartum.   Milk/plasma ratios were reported to be 1.03 on day 3 postpartum, and 0.8 during the first three months of therapy.   The infant's plasma reached a peak (2.9 mg/dl) at approximately 1.5 months postpartum and then declined significantly over the next 3 months suggesting increased clearance by the infant. Although these levels are considered sub-therapeutic, it is suggested that the infant's plasma levels be occasionally tested.

In another study of a women receiving 500 mg twice daily, her milk levels as estimated from a graph averaged 60-70 mg/L.[2] A total daily exposure to ethosuximide of 3.6-11 mg/kg as a result of nursing was predicted.

In a study by Kuhnz of 10 epileptic breastfeeding mothers (and 13 infants) receiving 3.5 to 23.6 mg/kg/day,   the breastmilk concentrations were similar to those of the maternal plasma (milk/serum: 0.86) and the breastfed infants maintained serum levels between 15 and 40 μg/mL.[3] Maximum milk concentration reported was 77 mg/L although the average was 49.54 mg/L.   Neonatal behavior complications such as poor suckling, sedation, and hyperexcitability occurred in 7 of the 12 infants.   Interestingly, one infant who was not breastfed, exhibited severe withdrawal symptoms such as tremors, kloni, restlessness, insomnia, crying and vomiting which lasted for 8 weeks causing a slow weight gain.   Thus the question remains, is it safer to breastfeed and avoid these severe withdrawal reactions?

These studies clearly indicate that the amount of ethosuximide transferred to the infant is significant. With milk/plasma ratios of approximately 0.86-1.0 and relatively high maternal plasma levels, the maternal plasma levels are a good indication of the dose transferred to the infant. Milk levels are generally high. Caution is recommended.

Pregnancy Risk Category: C

Lactation Risk Category: L4

Theoretic Infant Dose: 8.3 mg/kg/day

Adult Concerns: Drowsiness, ataxia, nausea, vomiting, anorexia, rash.

Pediatric Concerns; Neonatal behavior complications such as poor suckling, sedation, and hyperexcitability occurred in 7 of 12 infants in one study. Milk levels are significant. Caution is recommended.

Drug Interactions: Decreased efficacy of ethosuximide when used with phenytoin, carbamazepine, primidone, phenobarbital (may reduce plasma levels). Elevated levels of ethosuximide may result when used with isoniazid.

Alternatives:

Adult Dosage: 250-750 mg BID

T½ = 30-60 hours	M/P = 0.94
PHL = 32-38 hours	PB = 0%
PK = 4 hours	Oral = Complete
MW = 141	pKa = 9.3
Vd = 0.72	

References:
1.   Rane, A and Tunnell, R. Ethosuximide in human milk and in plasma of a mother and her nursed infant. Br. J. Clin. Pharmacol. 12:855-58, 1981.
2.   Koup JR, Rose JQ, Cohen ME. Ethosuximide pharmacokinetics in a pregnant patient and her newborn. Epilepsia 19(6):535-9, 1978.
3.   Kuhnz W, Koch S, Jakob S, Hartmann A, Helge H, Nau H. Ethosuximide in epileptic women during pregnancy and lactation period. Placental transfer, serum concentrations in nursed infants and clinical status. Br J Clin Pharmacol 18(5):671-7, 1984

ETHOTOIN

Trade: Peganone
Can/Aus/UK:
Uses: Anticonvulsant
AAP: Not reviewed

Ethotoin is a typical phenytoin-like anticonvulsant. Although no data are available on concentrations in breastmilk, it's similarity to phenytoin would suggest that some is secreted via breastmilk.[1] No data are available in the literature. See phenytoin.

Pregnancy Risk Category: D

Lactation Risk Category: L3

Theoretic Infant Dose:

Adult Concerns: Drowsiness, dizziness, insomnia, headache, blood dyscrasias.

Pediatric Concerns: None reported, but see phenytoin.

Drug Interactions: See phenytoin.

Alternatives:

Adult Dosage:

T½ = 3-9 hours	M/P =
PHL =	PB = Low-41%
PK = 1-2 hours	Oral = Complete
MW = 204	pKa =
Vd =	

References:
1. McEvoy GE(ed):AHFS Drug Information, New York, NY. 1995.

ETIDRONATE

Trade: Didronel
Can/Aus/UK: Didronel
Uses: Slows bone turnover
AAP: Not reviewed

Etidronate is a bisphosphonate that slows the dissolution of hydroxyapatite crystals in the bone, thus reducing bone calcium loss in certain syndromes such as Paget's syndrome.[1] Etidronate also reduces the remineralization of bone and can result in osteomalacia over time.

It is not known how the administration of this product during active lactation would effect the maternal bone porosity. It is possible that milk calcium levels could be reduced, although this has not been reported. Etidronate is poorly absorbed orally (1%) and must be administered in between meals on an empty stomach. Its penetration into milk is possible due to its small molecular weight, but it has not yet been reported. However, due to the presence of fat and calcium in milk, its oral bioavailability in infants would be exceedingly low. Whereas the plasma half-life is approximately 6 hours, the terminal elimination half-life (from bone) is > 90 days.

Pregnancy Risk Category: B

Lactation Risk Category: L3

Theoretic Infant Dose:

Adult Concerns: Untoward effects include loss of taste, nephrotoxicity, risk of fractures, and focal osteomalacia after prolonged use. Fever, convulsions, bone pain.

Pediatric Concerns: None reported via milk.   Although unreported, it could result in reduced milk calcium levels. Oral absorption in infant would be minimal.

Drug Interactions: I.V. Ranitidine doubles the oral absorption of alendronate (similar to etidronate). Oral products containing calcium or magnesium will significantly reduce oral bioavailability. Take on empty stomach.

Alternatives:

Adult Dosage: 5-10 mg/kg daily

T½ = 6 hours(plasma)	M/P =
PHL =	PB =
PK = 2 hours	Oral = 1-2.5%
MW = 206	pKa =
Vd = 1.37	

References:
1.   Drug Facts and Comparisons. 1996. ed. Facts and Comparisons, St. Louis.

ETODOLAC

Trade: Etodolac, Lodine
Can/Aus/UK: Lodine, Ultradol
Uses: Non-steroidal analgesic, antipyretic
AAP: Not reviewed

Etodolac is a prototypical   nonsteroidal anti-inflammatory agent (NSAID) with analgesic, antipyretic, and anti-inflammatory properties.[1]

Thus far no data are available regarding its secretion into human breast milk. Shorter half-life varieties are preferred.

Pregnancy Risk Category: C

Lactation Risk Category: L3

Theoretic Infant Dose:

Adult Concerns: Dyspepsia, nausea, diarrhea, indigestion, heartburn, abdominal pain, and gastrointestinal bleeding.

Pediatric Concerns: None reported via milk, but observe for nausea, diarrhea, indigestion. Ibuprofen probably preferred at this time.

Drug Interactions: May prolong prothrombin time when used with warfarin. Antihypertensive effects of ACEi family may be blunted or completely abolished by NSAIDs. Some NSAIDs may block antihypertensive effect of beta blockers, diuretics. Used with cyclosporin, may dramatically increase renal toxicity. May increase digoxin, phenytoin, lithium levels. May increase toxicity of methotrexate. May increase bioavailability of penicillamine. Probenecid may increase NSAID levels.

Alternatives: Ibuprofen, Voltaren

Adult Dosage: 200-400 mg q 6-8 hours

T½ = 7.3 hours	M/P =
PHL =	PB = 95-99%
PK = 1-2 hours	Oral = 80-100%
MW = 287	pKa = 4.7
Vd = 0.4	

References:
1. Pharmaceutical Manufacturers Package Insert, 1995.

ETRETINATE

Trade: Tegison
Can/Aus/UK: Tigason
Uses: Antipsoriatic
AAP: Not reviewed

Etretinate is an oral Vitamin A derivative primarily used for psoriasis and sometimes acne. It is teratogenic and should not be administered to pregnant women or women about to become pregnant. Etretinate is known to transfer into animal milk although no data are available on human milk.[1,2] Etretinate is still detectable in human serum up to 2.9 years after administration has ceased due to storage at high concentrations in adipose tissue. Mothers who wish to breastfeed following therapy with this compound should be informed of its long half-life in the human. The manufacturer considers this drug to be contraindicated in breastfeeding mothers due to the potential for serious adverse effects.

Pregnancy Risk Category: X

Lactation Risk Category: L5

Theoretic Infant Dose:

Adult Concerns: Dry nose, chapped lips, nose bleeds, hair loss, peeling of skin on soles, palms, sunburns, and headaches. Elevated liver enzymes, lipids. Fatigue, headache, fever.

Pediatric Concerns: None reported but great caution is urged. Premature epiphyseal closure has been reported in children treated with this product.

Drug Interactions: Milk increases absorption of oral etretinate. Exogenous vitamin A increases toxicity.

Alternatives:

Adult Dosage: 0.5-0.75 mg/kg BID

T½ = 120 days (terminal)	**M/P =**
PHL =	**PB = >99%**
PK = 2-6 hours	**Oral = Complete**
MW = 354	**pKa =**
Vd = High	

References:
1. Pharmaceutical Manufacturers Package Insert, 1995.
2. Lacy C. et.al. Drug information handbook. Lexi-Comp, Hudson(Cleveland), Oh. 1996.

EVENING PRIMROSE OIL

Trade: EPO
Can/Aus/UK: Efamol
Uses: Nutritional supplement
AAP: Not reviewed

Evening primrose oil is a rich source of essential polyunsaturated fatty acids (EFA) particularly gamma linoleic acid (GLA). Human milk is generally rich in 6-desaturated essential fatty acids including arachidonic, GLA, and dihomoj-GLA (DGLA), which may play an important role in development of the infants brain. The brain contains about 20% of 6-desaturated EFAs. Supplementation in pregnant women has been found to significantly increase EFA content in human breastmilk.[1] Although there is some evidence that GLA may be beneficial in syndromes such as cardiovascular disease, rheumatoid arthritis, multiple sclerosis, atopic dermatitis, many of these studies were sponsored by the manufacturer and need independent confirmation.[2,3] Overt toxicity of this product appears quite low. A number of studies in adults using GLA at rather high doses have not been found to produce significant toxicity.

Pregnancy Risk Category:

Lactation Risk Category: L3

Theoretic Infant Dose:

Adult Concerns: Major untoward effects are largely unreported, although some patients have quit various studies for unspecified reasons.

Pediatric Concerns: None reported.

Drug Interactions:

Alternatives:

Adult Dosage:

References:
1. Cant A, Shay J, Horrobin DF. The effect of maternal supplementation with linoleic and gamma-linolenic acids on the fat composition and content of human milk: a placebo-controlled trial. J.Nutr. Sci Vitaminol 37(6):573-9, 1991.
2. Horrobin DF Manku MS. How do polyunsaturated fatty acids lower plasma cholesterol levels? Lipids 18:558-62, 1983.
3. Review of Natural Products. Facts and Comparisons, St. Louis, Mo. 1996.

FAMCICLOVIR

Trade: Famvir
Can/Aus/UK: Famvir
Uses: Antiviral for Herpes Zoster
AAP: Not reviewed

Famciclovir is an antiviral use in the treatment of uncomplicated herpes zoster infection (shingles) and genital herpes. It is rapidly metabolized to the active metabolite, penciclovir. Although similar to Acyclovir, no data are available on levels in human milk. Oral bioavailability of famciclovir (77%) is much better than acyclovir (15-30%). Studies with rodents suggest that the milk/plasma ratio is greater than 1.0.[1,2] Because famciclovir provides few advantages over acyclovir, at this point acyclovir would probably be preferred in a nursing mother although the side-effect profile is still minimal with this product.

Pregnancy Risk Category: B

Lactation Risk Category: L2

Theoretic Infant Dose:

Adult Concerns: Headache, dizziness, nausea, diarrhea, fever, anorexia.

Pediatric Concerns: None reported via milk.

Drug Interactions: Cimetidine increases plasma levels of the active metabolite penciclovir. Famciclovir increases digoxin plasma levels by 19%. Probenecid significantly increased penciclovir plasma levels.

Alternatives: Acyclovir

Adult Dosage: 125 mg BID

T½ = 2-3 hours	M/P = >1
PHL=	PB = <20%
PK = 0.9 hours	Oral = 77%
MW =	pKa =
Vd = 1,13	

References:
1.   Drug Facts and Comparisons. 1994 ed. Facts and Comparisons, St. Louis.
2.   Pharmaceutical Manufacturers Package Insert, 1995.

FAMOTIDINE

Trade: Pepcid, Axid-AR, Pepcid-AC
Can/Aus/UK: Amfamox, Apo-Famotidine, Novo-Famotidine, Pepcid, Pepcidine
Uses: Reduces gastric acid secretion
AAP: Not reviewed

Famotidine is a typical Histamine-2 antagonist that reduces stomach acid secretion. In one study of 8 lactating women receiving a 40 mg/day dose, the peak concentration in breastmilk was 72 μg/L and occurred at 6 hours post-dose.[1] The milk/plasma ratios were 0.41, 1.78, and 1.33 at 2, 6, and 24 hours respectively.   These levels are apparently much lower than other histamine H-2 antagonists (ranitidine, cimetidine) and make it a preferred choice.

Pregnancy Risk Category: B

Lactation Risk Category: L2

Theoretic Infant Dose: 10.8 μg/kg/day

Adult Concerns: Headache, constipation, increased liver enzymes.

Pediatric Concerns: None reported. Pediatric indications are available.

Drug Interactions: Famotidine reduces bioavailability of ketoconazole, itraconazole due to reduced oral absorption of these two products.

Alternatives: Nizatidine

Adult Dosage: 20-40 mg BID

T½ = 2.5-3.5 hours	M/P = 0.41-1.78
PHL =	PB = 17%
PK = 1-3.5 hours	Oral = 50%
MW = 337	pKa =
Vd =	

References:
1. Courtney TP, Shaw RW, et.al. Excretion of famotidine in breast milk. Br.J.Clin.Pharmacol. 26:639, 1988.

FELBAMATE

Trade: Felbatol
Can/Aus/UK:
Uses: Anticonvulsant
AAP: Not reviewed

Felbamate is an oral antiepileptic agent for partial seizures and Lennox-Gastaut syndrome. Due to serious side effects, the FDA recommends that felbamate be given only to patients with serious seizures refractory to all other medications. Felbamate has been reported to be secreted in rodent milk, and was detrimental to their offspring.[1] No data are available on human milk. Due to the incidence of severe side effects, extreme caution is recommended with this medication in breastfeeding mothers.

Pregnancy Risk Category: C

Lactation Risk Category: L4

Theoretic Infant Dose:

Adult Concerns: Aplastic anemia, weight gain, flu-like symptoms, tachycardia, nausea, vomiting, headache, insomnia.

Pediatric Concerns: None reported, but caution is urged.

Drug Interactions: Felbamate causes an increase in phenytoin plasma levels. Phenytoin produces a 45% decrease in felbamate levels. Carbamazepine levels may be decreased, whereas felbamate levels may drop by 40%. Valproic acid plasma levels may be increased.

Alternatives:

Adult Dosage:

T½ = 20-23 hours	M/P =
PHL=	PB = 25%
PK = 1-4 hours	Oral = 90%
MW =	pKa =
Vd = 0.7-1.0	

References:
1. Pharmaceutical Manufacturers Package Insert, 1995.

FELODIPINE

Trade: Plendil
Can/Aus/UK: Agon SR, Plendil, Plendil ER, Renedil
Uses: Calcium channel blocker, antihypertensive
AAP: Not reviewed

Felodipine is a calcium channel antagonist structurally related to nifedipine.[1] Because we have numerous studies on others in this family, it is advisable to use nifedipine or others that have breastfeeding studies available.

Pregnancy Risk Category: C

Lactation Risk Category: L3

Theoretic Infant Dose:

Adult Concerns: Headache, dizziness, edema, flushing, hypotension, constipation, cardiac arrhythmias.

Pediatric Concerns: None reported via milk, but caution is recommended.

Drug Interactions: Barbiturates may reduce bioavailability of calcium channel blockers (CCB). Calcium salts may reduce hypotensive effect. Dantrolene may increase risk of hyperkalemia and myocardial depression. H2 blockers may increase bioavailability of certain CCBs. Hydantoins may reduce plasma levels. Quinidine increases risk of hypotension, bradycardia, tachycardia. Rifampin may reduce effects of CCBs. Vitamin D may reduce efficacy of CCBs. CCBs may increase carbamazepine, cyclosporin, encainide, prazosin levels.

Alternatives: Nifedipine, Nimodipine, Verapamil

Adult Dosage: 2.5-10 mg QD

T½ = 11-16 hours	M/P =
PHL=	PB = >99%
PK = 2.5-5 hours	Oral = 20%
MW = 384	pKa =
Vd =	

References:
1. Pharmaceutical Manufacturers Package Insert, 1996.

FENNEL

Trade: Sweet Fennel, Bitter Fennel, Carosella, Florence Fennel, Finocchio, Garden Fennel, Wild Fennel
Can/Aus/UK:
Uses: Estrogenic
AAP: Not reviewed

Fennel is an herb native to southern Europe and Asia Minor. The oils of sweet and bitter fennel contain up to 90% trans-anethole, and up to 20% fenchone, and numerous other lesser oils. An acetone extract of fennel has been shown to have estrogenic effects on the genital organs of male and female rats.[1] As an herbal medicine it is reputed to increase milk secretion, promote menstruation, facilitate birth, and increased libido. The estrogenic component is believed to be a polymer of the anethole, such as dianethole or photoanethole.[2] Ingestion of the volatile oil may induce nausea, vomiting, seizures and pulmonary edema, and hallucinations.[3,4] An older survey of fennel samples in Italy found viable aerobic bacteria, including coliforms, fecal streptococci, and salmonella species, suggesting the plant may serve as a vector for infectious gastrointestinal diseases.[5] Fennel is a popular herb that has been used since ancient times. It is primarily believed to be estrogenic. Since estrogens are known to suppress breastmilk production, its use in lactating women is questionable.

Pregnancy Risk Category:

Lactation Risk Category: L4

Theoretic Infant Dose:

Adult Concerns: Allergic reactions, photodermatitis, contact dermatitis, and bacterial contamination.

Pediatric Concerns: None reported via milk. May potentially suppress milk production.

Drug Interactions:

Alternatives:

Adult Dosage:

References:
1. Malini T. et.al. The effects of foeniculum vulgare. Mill seed extract on the genital organs of male and female rats. Indian J. Physiol. Pharmacol. 29:21, 1985.
2. Albert-Puleo M. Fennel and anise as estrogenic agents. J. Ethnopharmacol. 2:337, 1980.
3. Marcus C. Lichtenstein EP. J. Agric Food Chem 27:1217, 1979.
4. Duke JA. Handbook of Medicinal Herbs. Boca Raton, Fl.: CRC Press, 1985.
5. Ercolani GL. Bacteriological quality assessment of fresh marketed lettuce and fennel. Appl. Environ. Microbiol. 31:847, 1976.

FENOPROFEN

Trade: Nalfon
Can/Aus/UK: Fenopron, Nalfon, Progesic
Uses: NSAID, nonsteroidal analgesic
AAP: Not reviewed

Fenoprofen is a typical nonsteroidal anti-inflammatory and analgesic. Following 600 mg four times daily for 4 days postpartum, the milk/plasma ratio was approximately 0.017 and fenoprofen levels in milk were too low to be accurately detected and was estimated to be approximately 1/60 th of the maternal plasma level.[1] Fenoprofen was undetectable in cord blood, amniotic fluid, saliva or washed red blood cells after multiple doses.

Pregnancy Risk Category: B during 1st and 2nd trimesters
D during 3rd trimester

Lactation Risk Category: L2

Theoretic Infant Dose:

Adult Concerns: GI distress and bleeding, dyspepsia, nausea, constipation, ulcers, hepatotoxicity, rash, tinnitus.

Pediatric Concerns: None reported.

Drug Interactions: May prolong prothrombin time when used with warfarin. Antihypertensive effects of ACEi family may be blunted or completely abolished by NSAIDs. Some NSAIDs may block antihypertensive effect of beta blockers, diuretics. Used with cyclosporin, may dramatically increase renal toxicity. May increase digoxin, phenytoin, lithium levels. May increase toxicity of methotrexate. May increase bioavailability of penicillamine. Probenecid may increase NSAID levels.

Alternatives: Ibuprofen

Adult Dosage: 300-600 mg q 4-6 hours

T½ = 2.5 hours PHL= PK = 1-2 hours MW = 242 Vd = 0.08-0.10	M/P = 0.017 PB = 99% Oral = 80% pKa = 4.5

References:
1.   Rubin A, et. al. A profile of the physiological disposition and gastrointestinal effects of fenoprofen in man. Curr Med Res Opin 2:529-44, 1974.

FENTANYL

Trade: Sublimaze
Can/Aus/UK: Duragesic, Sublimaze
Uses: Opiate analgesic
AAP: Approved by the American Academy of Pediatrics for use in breastfeeding mothers

Fentanyl is a potent narcotic analgesic used (IV, IM, transdermally) during labor and delivery. When used parenterally, its half-life is exceedingly short.[1]

The transfer of fentanyl into human milk has been documented, but is low. In a group of ten women receiving a total dose of 50 to 400 ug fentanyl I.V. during labor[2], the concentration of fentanyl in milk was exceedingly low, generally below the level of detection (<0.05 ng/mL). In a few samples, the levels were between 0.05 and 0.15 ng/mL. Using this data, an infant would ingest less than 3% of the weight-adjusted maternal dose per day.

In another study of 13 women who received 2 μg/kg I.V. after delivery and cord clamping, fentanyl concentration in colostrum was extremely low.[3]   Peak colostrum concentrations occurred at 45 minutes follow intravenous administration and averaged 0.4 μg/L.   Colostrum levels dropped rapidly and were undetectable after 10 hours.   The authors conclude that with these small concentrations and fentanyl's low oral bioavailability, intravenous fentanyl analgesia may be used safely in breastfeeding women.

The relatively low level of fentanyl found in human milk is presumably a result of the short maternal half-life, and the rather rapid redistribution out of the maternal plasma compartment. It is apparent that fentanyl transfer to milk under most clinical conditions is poor and is probably clinically unimportant.

Pregnancy Risk Category: B

Lactation Risk Category: L2

Theoretic Infant Dose: 60.0 ng/kg/day

Adult Concerns: Apnea, respiratory depression, muscle rigidity, hypotension, bradycardia.

Pediatric Concerns: No adverse effects reported via milk.

Drug Interactions: Increased toxicity when used with other CNS depressants, phenothiazines, tricyclic antidepressants.

Alternatives:

Adult Dosage: 2-20 μg/kg injection (IV)

T½ = 2-4 hours.	**M/P** =
PHL = 3-13 hours(neonates)	**PB** = 80-86%
PK = 7-8 min.(IV)	**Oral** = 25-75%
MW = 336	**pKa** = 8.4
Vd = 3-8	

References:
1. Madej TH, Strunin L. Comparison of epidural fentanyl with sufentanil. Anaesthesia 42:1156-1161, 1987.
2. Leuschen MP, Wolf LJ, Rayburn WF: Fentanyl excretion in breast milk. Clin Pharm 1990; 9:336-337.

FENUGREEK
Trade:
Can/Aus/UK:
Uses: Herbal spice
AAP: Not reviewed

Fenugreek is commonly sold as the dried ripe seed and extracts are used as an artificial flavor for maple syrup.[1] The seeds contain from 0.1 to 0.9% diosgenin.[2] Several coumarin compounds have been noted in the seed as well as a number of alkaloids such as trigonelline, gentianine, and carpaine.   The seeds also contain approximately 8% of a foul-smelling oil.

Fenugreek has been noted to reduce plasma cholesterol in animals when 50% of their diet contained fenugreek seeds.[3]   The high fiber content may have accounted for this change although it may be due to the steroid saponins.   A hypoglycemic effect has also been noted.   When added to the diet of diabetic dogs, a decrease in insulin dose and hyperglycemia was noted.[4]   It is not known if these changes are due to the fiber content of the seeds or a chemical component.   Fenugreek has been reported to increase the anticoagulant effect of warfarin.[5]   One case of GI bleeding in a premature infant (30 weeks) following introduction of fenugreek to the mother has been received.[6] The implication of fenugreek in this hemorrhage is speculative.

In a group of 10 women (non-placebo controlled) with infants born between 24 to 38 weeks gestation (mean=29 weeks) who ingested 3 fenugreek capsules 3 times daily (Nature's Way) for a week, the average milk production during the week increased significantly from a mean of 207 mL/day (range 57 - 1057 mL) to 464 mL/day (range 63-1140 mL).[8] No untoward effects were reported.

When dosed in moderation, fenugreek has limited toxicity and is listed in the US as a GRAS herbal (Generally Regarded As Safe). A maple syrup odor via urine and sweat is commonly reported. Higher doses may produce hypoglycemia. A stimulant effect on the isolated uterus (guinea pig) has been reported and its use in late pregnancy may not be advisable. Fenugreek's reputation as a galactagogue is widespread but undocumented.   The dose commonly employed is variable but is approximately 2-3 capsules taken three times daily.   The transfer of fenugreek into milk is unknown, but untoward effects have not been reported.

Pregnancy Risk Category:

Lactation Risk Category: L3

Theoretic Infant Dose:

Adult Concerns: Maple syrup odor in urine and sweat. Diarrhea, hypoglycemia, dyspnea (exaggeration of asthmatic symptoms) have been reported.   One case of suspected GI bleeding in a premature infant has been reported.[6] Two cases of fenugreek allergy have been reported.[7]

Pediatric Concerns: One case of suspected GI bleeding in a premature infant has been reported.[6]

Drug Interactions:

Alternatives: Metoclopramide, Domperidone

Adult Dosage:

References:
1.   Review of Natural Products. Facts and Comparisons, St. Louis, Mo. 1996.
2.   Sauvaire Y, Baccou JC. Extraction of diosgenine, (25R)-spirost-5-ene-3beta-ol; problems of the hydrolysis of the saponins. Lloydia 41:247, 1978.
3.   Valette G. et.al. Hypocholesterolaemic effect of fenugreek seeds in dogs. Atherosclerosis 50(1):105, 1984.
4.   Ribes G, et.al. Effects of fenugreek seeds on endocrine pancreatic secretions in dogs. Ann Nutr Metab 28(1): 37, 1984.
5.   Lambert JP, Cormier A. Potential interaction between warfarin and boldo-fenugreek. Pharmacotherapy. 21(4):509-12, 2001
6.   DH. Personnal communication, 2001.
7.   Patil SP, Niphadkar PV, Bapat MM. Allergy to fenugreek (Trigonella foenum graecum). Ann Allergy Asthma Immunol. 78(3):297-300, 1997.

8. Swafford S and Berens P. Effect of fenugreek on breast milk production. Abstract. ABM News and Views 6(3): 2000. Annual meeting abstracts Sept 11-13, 2000.

FEXOFENADINE

Trade: Allegra
Can/Aus/UK: Allegra
Uses: Antihistamine
AAP: Approved by the American Academy of Pediatrics for use in breastfeeding mothers

Fexofenadine is a non-sedating histamine-1 receptor antagonist and is the active metabolite of terfenadine (Seldane). It is indicated for symptoms of allergic rhinitis and other allergies. Unlike Seldane, no cardiotoxicity has been reported with this product.

In a study of 4 women receiving 60 mg/d terfenadine, no terfenadine was found in milk. However, the metabolite (fexofenadine) was present in small amounts. The average milk level of fexofenadine was 41 μg/L, while the maternal plasma averaged 309 ng/mL. The time to peak for milk was 4.3 hours and the half-life in milk was 14.2 hours. The AUC(0-12)(ng.hr/mL) was 320 for milk and 1590 for plasma. The authors estimate that only 0.45% of the weight-adjusted maternal dose would be ingested by the infant.

Pregnancy Risk Category: C

Lactation Risk Category: L3

Theoretic Infant Dose: 6.2 μg/kg/day

Adult Concerns: Drowsiness, fatigue, leukopenia, nausea, dyspepsia, dry mouth, headache and throat irritation have been reported. Thus far, no cardiotoxicity has been reported .

Pediatric Concerns: None reported.

Drug Interactions: Erythromycin and ketoconazole (and potentially other azole antifungals and macrolide antibiotics) may elevate the plasma level of fexofenadine(82%) significantly.

Alternatives:

Adult Dosage: 60 mg BID

T½ = 14.4 hours	M/P = 0.21
PHL =	PB = 60-70%
PK = 2.6 hours	Oral = Complete
MW = 538	pKa =
Vd =	

References:
1. Lucas BD Jr, Purdy CY, Scarim SK, Benjamin S, Abel SR, Hilleman DE. Terfenadine pharmacokinetics in breast milk in lactating women. Clin Pharmacol Ther. 57(4):398-402, 1995.

FILGRASTIM

Trade: Neupogen
Can/Aus/UK: Neupogen
Uses: Synthetic hematopoietic agent.
AAP: Not reviewed

Filgrastim is a large molecular weight biosynthetic protein used to stimulate neutrophil production. It is more commonly called granulocyte colony stimulating factor (G-CSF).[1] There are no data on its entry into human milk, but due to its large molecular weight (18,800 daltons) it is extremely remote that any would enter milk. Following use, the plasma levels in most individuals is often undetectable or in the picogram range. Further, due to its protein structure, it would not likely be orally bioavailable to the infant.

Pregnancy Risk Category: C

Lactation Risk Category: L2

Theoretic Infant Dose:

Adult Concerns: Transient rash, nausea and vomiting, erythema and swelling at injection site, and splenomegaly.

Pediatric Concerns: None reported via milk.

Drug Interactions: Use caution with drugs such as lithium that induce release of neutrophils.

Alternatives:

Adult Dosage: 5 mcg/kg daily

T½ = 3.5 hours	M/P =
PHL =	PB =
PK = 2-8 hours	Oral = None
MW = 18,800	pKa =
Vd = 150	

References:
1. Pharmaceutical manufacturers package insert, 1999.

FLAVOXATE

Trade: Urispas
Can/Aus/UK: Urispas
Uses: Urinary tract antispasmodic
AAP: Not reviewed

Flavoxate is used as an antispasmodic to provide relief of painful urination, urgency, nocturia, urinary frequency, or incontinence.[1] It exerts a direct smooth muscle relaxation on the bladder wall and has been used in children for enuresis. No data are available on its transfer into human milk.

Pregnancy Risk Category: B

Lactation Risk Category: L3

Theoretic Infant Dose:

Adult Concerns: Drowsiness, dry mouth and throat, nervousness, headache, confusion, nausea, vomiting, blurred vision. Do not use with pyloric or duodenal obstruction, GI hemorrhage, or obstructive uropathies.

Pediatric Concerns: None reported via milk.

Drug Interactions:

Alternatives:

Adult Dosage: 100-200 mg TID-QID

T½ = < 10 hours	M/P =
PHL =	PB =
PK = 2 hours	Oral = Complete
MW = 391	pKa =
Vd =	

References:
1. Pharmaceutical manufacturers package insert, 1997.

FLECAINIDE ACETATE

Trade: Tambocor
Can/Aus/UK: Tambocor
Uses: Antiarrhythmic agent
AAP: Approved by the American Academy of Pediatrics for use in breastfeeding mothers

Flecainide is a potent antiarrhythmic used to suppress dangerous ventricular arrhythmias. In a group of 11 breastfeeding mothers receiving 100 mg oral flecainide (mean =3.2 mg/kg/day) every 12 hours for 5.5 days beginning 1 day postpartum, apparent steady-state levels of flecainide in both milk and plasma were achieved in most cases by day 4 of the study.[1] Highest daily average concentration of flecainide in milk ranged from 270 to 1529 μg/L (mean= 953 μg/L) for the 11 subjects. Mean Milk/plasma ratios were 3.7, 3.2, 3.5, and 2.6 on study days 2, 3, 4, and 5, respectively. After the last dose of flecainide, peak milk levels of the drug occurred at 3 to 6 hours and then declined monoexponentially. The half-life for elimination of flecainide from milk was 14.7 hours and is very similar to the plasma elimination half-life of flecainide in healthy human subjects. Based on the pharmacokinetics of flecainide in infants, the expected average steady-state plasma concentration of flecainide in a newborn infant consuming all of the milk production of its mother (approximately 700 ml/day at the highest flecainide level of 1529 μg/L) then the average daily intake by the infant would average 1.07 mg. In a normal 4 kg infant, the average plasma concentration in a breastfed infant would not be expected to exceed about 62 ng/mL. The average plasma level in infants treated with therapeutic doses is 360 ng/mL.

In another study of one patient receiving 100 mg every 12 hours, milk levels of flecainide averaged 0.99 mg/L on day 4 and 5 postpartum.[2]

Pregnancy Risk Category: C

Lactation Risk Category: L4

Theoretic Infant Dose: 143.0 μg/kg/day

Adult Concerns: Flecainide may induce arrhythmias in certain patients and congestive heart failure in approximately 2-5% of patients due to negative inotropy. Dizziness, nausea, blurred vision, dyspnea, and vomiting are reported. Flecainide should be reserved for patients with life-threatening arrhythmias. Withdrawal from flecainide therapy should be gradual due to the possibility of fatal cardiac arrest.

Pediatric Concerns: None yet reported via milk, but observe for dizziness, faintness, dyspnea, headache, nausea, constipation.

Drug Interactions: Flecainide concentrations may be increased by digoxin and amiodarone. Arbutamine may exacerbate the arrhythmogenic effects of flecainide. Beta blockers, disopyramide, verapamil may enhance the negative inotropic effect of flecainide. Concurrent oral use of flecainide and cimetidine has been associated with a 46 to 65% increase in the elimination half-life, a 7 to 11% reduction in renal clearance, and a 15 to 32% reduction in the nonrenal clearance of flecainide.

Alternatives:

Adult Dosage: 50-100 mg BID

T½ = 7-22 hours	M/P = 2.6-3.7
PHL =	PB = 50%
PK = 4.5 hours	Oral = 90%
MW = 414	pKa =
Vd =	

References:

1. McQuinn RL, Pisani, A, Wafa, S. et.al. Flecainide excretion in human breast milk. Clin. Pharmacol. Ther. 48(3):262-267, 1990.
2. Wagner X, Jouglard J, et.al. Coadministration of flecainide acetate and sotalol during pregnancy: lack of teratogenic effects, passage across the placenta, and excretion in human breast milk. Amer. Heart J. 119:700-702, 1990.

FLOXACILLIN

Trade: Flucil
Can/Aus/UK: Flopen, Floxapen, Flu Clomix, Flu-Amp, Fluclox, Flucloxacillin, Magnapen, Staphylex
Uses: Penicillin antibiotic
AAP: Not reviewed

Floxacillin, also called flucloxacillin, is a penicillinase-resistant penicillin frequently used for resistant staphylococcal infections. Only trace amounts are secreted into human milk.[1] Its congener, cloxacillin, is commonly used to treat mastitis in breastfeeding mothers and has been used in thousands of breastfeeding patients without problem. Changes in gut flora are possible but unlikely.

Pregnancy Risk Category: B1

Lactation Risk Category: L1

Theoretic Infant Dose:

Adult Concerns: Adverse effects of FLOXACILLIN are similar to those of other penicillins, and include nausea, vomiting, diarrhea, constipation, and skin rashes; hemolytic anemia and interstitial nephritis have been reported rarely. Cases of acute hepatic cholestasis related to floxacillin therapy has been reported.

Pediatric Concerns: None reported via milk.

Drug Interactions: Concomitant penicillin and aminoglycoside therapy has been reported to result in inactivation of the aminoglycoside. Small changes in methotrexate plasma levels have been reported.

Alternatives: Cloxacillin, Dicloxacillin

Adult Dosage: 250-500 mg four times daily

T½ = 1.5 hours	M/P =
PHL=	PB = 94%
PK = 1 hour	Oral = 50%
MW = 454	pKa =
Vd = 0.11	

References:
1.   Pharmaceutical manufacturers package insert, 2000.

FLUCONAZOLE

Trade: Diflucan
Can/Aus/UK: Diflucan
Uses: Antifungal, particularly candida infections
AAP: Approved by the American Academy of Pediatrics for use in breastfeeding mothers

Fluconazole is a synthetic triazole antifungal agent and is frequently used for vaginal, oropharyngeal and esophageal candidiasis.   Many of the triazole antifungals (itraconazole, terconazole,) have similar mechanisms of action and are considered fungistatic in action.   Studies in vivo have found fluconazole to have fungistatic activity against a variety of fungal strains including   C. albicans,   C. tropicalis, T. glabrata, and C. neoformans.

The pharmacokinetics are similar following both oral and I.V. administration.   The drug is almost completely absorbed orally (>90%).   Peak plasma levels occur in 1-2 hours after oral administration.   Unlike ketoconazole and itraconazole, fluconazole absorption is unaffected by gastric pH and does not require an acid pH to be absorbed.   Steady state plasma levels are only attained after 5-10 days of therapy, but can be achieved on day two with a loading dose (twice the daily dose) on the first day.   Average plasma levels are 4.12 to 8.1 μg/ml.   Fluconazole is widely and evenly distributed in most tissues and fluids and is distributed in total body water.   Concentrations in skin and urine may be 10 fold higher than plasma levels.   CSF concentrations are 50-94% of the plasma levels.   Plasma protein binding is minimal at about 11%.   Fluconazole is primarily excreted renally.

Oral fluconazole is currently cleared for pediatric candidiasis for infants 6 months and older, and has an FDA Safety Profile for neonates 1 day and older.   Clinical cure rate for oropharyngeal candidiasis in pediatric patients is reported at 86% with fluconazole (2-3 mg/kg/day) compared to 46% of nystatin treated patients.   Fluconazole is transferred into human milk with a milk/plasma ratio of approximately 0.85.[1]   Following a single 150 mg dose, the following milk levels have been reported.

Fluconazole Milk Levels[1]

	2 hours	5 hours	24 hours	48 hours
Milk Level (mg/L)	2.93	2.66	1.76	0.98
Plasma (mg/L)	6.4	2.79	2.52	1.19
Milk/Plasma Ratio	0.46	0.85	0.85	0.83

Plasma Half-Life = 35 hours   Breastmilk Half-life = 30 hours

From these data, and assuming an average milk level of 2.3 mg/L, an infant consuming 150 cc/kg/d of milk would receive an average of 0.34 mg/kg/d of fluconazole or 16% of the weight-adjusted maternal dose, and less than 5.8% of the pediatric dose (6 mg/kg/d).

In another study of one patient receiving 200 mg daily(twice the above dose) for 18 days, the peak milk concentration was 4.1 mg/L at 2 hours following the dose.[2] However, the mean concentration of fluconazole in milk was not reported.

Side effects: Of the antifungals, fluconazole is very well tolerated. Adverse effects have only been reported in about 5-30% of patients, and in these, only 1-2.8% of patients have required discontinuation of the medication. Although adverse hepatic effects have been reported, they are very rare, and many occur coincident with the administration of other medications in AIDS patients. The most common complications include vomiting, diarrhea, abdominal pain, and skin rashes.

Pediatric Indications: While fluconazole is not cleared by the FDA for neonates, it is commonly used (90% of practitioners use it). It is however, cleared for infants 6 months and older. Due to the emergence of resistance to other antifungals, particularly nystatin, the use of fluconazole in pediatrics is increasing. Numerous reports now suggest that fluconazole is an effective and safe antifungal in low birth weight infants and neonates.[3-6,10] In one study of 40 low birth weight infants receiving fluconazole for up to 48 days, fluconazole produced few side effects.[7] Elevated liver enzymes were reported in only 2 of 40 serious ill LBW infants and due to other drugs, it is not known if this was associated with fluconazole therapy.

Dosage Recommendations:
Vaginal Candidiasis: 150 mg PO-single dose.

Oropharyngeal Candidiasis: Varies, but 200 mg STAT followed by 100 mg daily for up to 14 days is recommended.

Ductal Candidiasis: Because symptoms of ductal candidiasis are sometimes slow to resolve, many clinicians now recommend up to two to three weeks of therapy. For ductal candidiasis in breastfeeding mothers, doses can vary from 200-400 mg STAT followed by 100-200 mg daily depending on the severity of symptoms and resistance of organism. The duration of therapy is variable, but a minimum of 2-3 weeks is mandatory to clear systemic infections. For persistent or chronic infections, fluconazole has been used prophylactically in immunocompromised patients at a dose of 150 mg weekly to prevent recurrence[8,9] and this may be suitable for deep ductal candidiasis that is difficult to resolve. The recommended pediatric dosing for oral candidiasis is 6 mg/kg STAT followed by 3 mg/kg/day. For systemic candidiasis, 6-12 mg/kg/day is generally recommended.[10] These current recommendations are for infants 6 months and older. The manufacturer states that a number of infants 1 day old and older have been safely treated. One study of premature infants suggests that the dose in very low birth weight infants should be 6 mg/kg every 2 to 3 days.[11]

Fluconazole Dosage*

Indication	Day 1	Daily Therapy	Minimum Duration of Therapy
Oropharyngeal candidiasis	200 mg	100 mg	14 d
Esophageal candidiasis	200 mg	100 mg	21 d
Systemic candidiasis	400 mg	200 mg	28 d

Cryptococcal meningitis
  acute
 	
  relapse
	
	400 mg
	
	200 mg
		
		200 mg
		
		200 mg
			10-12 wk after CSF culture becomes negative

*Pharmaceutical Manufacturers Package Insert

Availability:
50, 100, 200 mg tablets. Oral suspensions = 10 mg/ml and 40 mg/ml

Pregnancy Risk Category: C

Lactation Risk Category: L2

Theoretic Infant Dose: 0.4 mg/kg/day

Adult Concerns: Side effects are minimal and usually include GI symptoms such a s vomiting, diarrhea, abdominal pain. Skin rashes, liver toxicity, elevated bilirubin in neonates may occur.

Pediatric Concerns: Pediatric complications from oral ingestion include GI symptoms such as vomiting, nausea, diarrhea, abdominal pain. Nephrotoxicity has not been reported. No complications from exposure to breastmilk have found.

Drug Interactions: Decreased hepatic clearance of fluconazole results from use with cyclosporin, zidovudine, rifabutin, theophylline, oral hypoglycemics (glipizide and tolbutamide), warfarin, phenytoin, and terfenadine. Decreased plasma levels of fluconazole have resulted following administration with rifampin, and cimetidine.

Alternatives:

Adult Dosage: 50-200 mg QD

T½ = 30 hours	**M/P = 0.46-0.85**
PHL = 88.6 hours(neonate)	**PB = 15%.**
PK = 1-2 hours	**Oral = >90%**
MW = 306	**pKa =**
Vd =	

References:
1. Force RW. Fluconazole concentrations in breast milk. Pedi. Infectious Dis. 14(3).235-236, 1995.
2. Schilling CG, Sea RE, Larson TA, et.al. Excretion of fluconazole in human breast milk(abstract # 130) Pharmacotherapy 13:287, 1993.
3. Wainer S, Cooper PA, et.al. Prospective study of fluconazole therapy in systemic neonatal fungal infection. Ped. Inf. Dis. J. 16(8):763-767.
4. Wiest DB, Fowler Sl. et.al. Fluconazole in neonatal disseminated candidiasis. Arch. Dis. Child. 66(8):1002.
5. Gurses N and Kalayci AG. Fluconazole monotherapy for candidal meningitis in a premature infant. Clin. Inf. Dis. 23:645-6, 1996.
6. Driessen M, Ellis JB, et.al. Fluconazole vs. amphotericin B for the treatment of neonatal fungal septicemia:a prospective study. Pediatr. Infect. Dis. J. 15:1107-12, 1996.
7. Huttova M, Hartmanova I, et.al. Candida fungemia in neonates treated with fluconazole: report of forty cases, includidng eight with meningitis. Pediatr. Infedt. Dis. J. 17:1012-15, 1998.
8. Leen CLS, et.al. Once-weekly fluconazole to prevent recurrence of oropharyngeal candidiasis. J. Infection 21:55-60, 1990.
9. Winston DJ, Chandrasekar PH, Lazarus HM et al: Fluconazole prophylaxis of fungal infections in patients with acute leukemia. Ann Intern Med 118:495-503, 1993.
10. Viscoli C, Castagnola E, et.al. Fluconazole therapy in an underweight infant. Eur. J. Clin. Microbiol. Infect. Dis 8:925-926, 1989.
11. Saxen H. et.al. Pharmacokinetics of fluconazole in very low birth weight infants during the first two weeks of life. Clin. Pharmax. and Ther. 54:269, 1993.

FLUDEOXYGLUCOSE F 18

Trade: Fludeoxyglucose F 18
Can/Aus/UK:
Uses: PET Scanning pharmaceutical
AAP: Not reviewed

Fludeoxyglucose F 18 is a positron-emitting radiopharmaceutical used in conjunction with positron emission tomography (PET Scanning) to detect alterations in tissue glucose metabolism, and is useful in detecting brain tumors, certain malignancies, chronic coronary artery disease, partial epilepsy and Alzheimer's disease.[1-3]

Fludeoxyglucose F 18 is rapidly distributed to all parts of the body that have significant glucose metabolism, including the breast. No levels in breastmilk have been reported, but it probably penetrates milk to some degree. The half-life of the F-18 is short, only 110 minutes. Due to concentration in some tissues, such as the bladder, radiation exposure could be a problem and emptying of the breast at routine intervals would reduce radiation exposure to breast tissue. The USPDI(1994) recommends interruption of breastfeeding for 12-24 hours. At 9 hours, 97% of the radioisotope would be decayed away.[4] It is likely that after 12 hours, almost all radioisotope would be decayed to almost background levels. Recommend pumping and dumping of breastmilk after the procedure for at least 12-24 hours.

Pregnancy Risk Category:

Lactation Risk Category: L3

Theoretic Infant Dose:

Adult Concerns: No untoward effects have been reported for this product.

Pediatric Concerns: None reported, but possible radiation exposure if breastfed prior to 12-24 hours after dose.

Drug Interactions:

Alternatives:

Adult Dosage:

T½ = 110 minutes	M/P =
PHL =	PB = Minimal
PK = 30 minutes	Oral = Complete
MW =	pKa =
Vd =	

References:
1.   Jamieson D, Alavi A, Jolles P et al: Positron emission tomography in the

investigation of central nervous system disorders. Radiol Clin North Am 26:1075-1088, 1988.

2. Jones SC, Alavi A, Christman D et al: The radiation dosimetry of 2-(F-18)fluoro-2-deoxy-d-glucose in man. Nucl Med 23:613-617, 1982

3. Som P, Atkins HL, Bandoypadhyay D, Fowler JS et al: A fluorinated glucose analog, 2-fluoro-2-deoxy-d-glucose (F-18): nontoxic tracer for rapid tumor detection. J Nucl Med 21:670-675, 1980.

4. Jones SC, Alavi A, Christman D et al: The radiation dosimetry of 2-(F-18)fluoro-2-deoxy-d-glucose in man. J Nucl Med 23:613-617, 1982.

FLUDROCORTISONE

Trade: Florinef, Myconef
Can/Aus/UK: Florinef
Uses: Mineralocorticoid.
AAP: Not reviewed

Fludrocortisone is a halogenated derivative of hydrocortisone, with very potent mineralocorticoid activity and is generally used to treat Addison's disease.[1,2] Although its glucocorticoid effect is 15 times more potent than hydrocortisone, it is primarily used for its powerful ability to retain sodium in the vascular compartment (mineralocorticoid activity). It is not known if fludrocortisone penetrates into milk, however it is very unlikely the amounts in milk will be clinically relevant until extremely high doses are used. Some caution is recommended.

Pregnancy Risk Category: C

Lactation Risk Category: L3

Theoretic Infant Dose:

Adult Concerns: Hypertension, sodium retention, cardiac hypertrophy, congestive heart failure, and headache.

Pediatric Concerns: None via milk.

Drug Interactions: Excessive potassium levels may result from use with amphotericin B. Use with loop diuretics may dramatically increase potassium loss. Phenytoin, rifampin, phenobarbital, and fosphenytoin may increase hepatic metabolism of fludrocortisone and reduce its efficacy. Lithium may reduce efficacy of fludrocortisone. Tuberculin reactions may be suppressed for periods up to 6 weeks in patients receiving fludrocortisone.

Alternatives:

Adult Dosage: 0.1-0.4 mg daily

T½ = 3.5 hours		M/P =	
PHL=		PB = 42%	
PK = 1.7 hours		Oral = Complete	
MW = 380		pKa =	
Vd =			

References:
1.   Pharmaceutical Manufacturers Package Insert, 1999.
2.   Drug Facts and Comparisons. 1999 ed. Facts and Comparisons, St. Louis.

FLUNARIZINE

Trade: Sibelium
Can/Aus/UK: Novo-Flunarizine, Sibelium
Uses: Antihypertensive
AAP: Not reviewed

Flunarizine is a calcium channel blocker primarily indicated for use in migraine headache prophylaxis and peripheral vascular disease. It has a very long half-life, and a huge volume of distribution, which contributes to the long half-life.[1] No data are available on the transfer of this product into human milk. However, due to its incredibly long half-life,   and high volume of distribution, it is possible that this product over time could build up and concentrate in a breastfed infant. Other calcium channel blockers may be preferred. Use with extreme caution.

Pregnancy Risk Category:

Lactation Risk Category: L4

Theoretic Infant Dose:

Adult Concerns: Extrapyramidal symptoms in elderly patients, depression, porphyria, thrombophlebitis, drowsiness, headache, dizziness.

Pediatric Concerns: None reported via milk, but caution is advised.

Drug Interactions: Prolonged bradycardia with adenosine. Sinus arrest when used with amiodarone. Hypotension and bradycardia when used with beta blockers. Increase of carbamazepine and cyclosporin plasma levels when used with flunarizine.

Alternatives: Nifedipine, Nimodipine

Adult Dosage: 10 mg daily

T½ = 19 days	M/P =
PHL = 23 days	PB = 99%
PK = 2-4 hours	Oral = Complete
MW =	pKa =
Vd = 43.2	

References:
1. Pharmaceutical manufacturers package insert, 1998.

FLUNISOLIDE

Trade: Nasalide, Aerobid
Can/Aus/UK: Bronalide, PMS-Flunisolide, Rhinalar, Syntaris
Uses: Inhaled and intranasal steroid.
AAP: Not reviewed

Flunisolide is a potent corticosteroid used to reduce airway hyperreactivity in asthmatics. It is also available as Nasalide for intranasal use for allergic rhinitis. Generally, only small levels of flunisolide are absorbed systemically (about 40%), thereby reducing systemic effects and presumably breastmilk levels as well.[1,2] After inhalation of 1 mg flunisolide, systemic availability was only 40% and plasma level was 0.4-1 nanogram/mL. Adrenal suppression in children has not been documented even after therapy of 2 months with 1600 μg/day. Once absorbed flunisolide is rapidly removed from the plasma compartment by first-pass uptake in the liver. Although no data on breastmilk levels are yet available, it is unlikely that the level secreted in milk is clinically relevant.

Pregnancy Risk Category: C

Lactation Risk Category: L3

Theoretic Infant Dose:

Adult Concerns: Most common side effect is irritation, due to vehicle not drug itself. Loss of taste, nasal irritation, flu-like symptoms, sore throat, headache.

Pediatric Concerns: None reported. Can be used in children down to age 6.

Drug Interactions:

Alternatives:

Adult Dosage: 1 mg QD

T½ = 1.8 hours	M/P =
PHL =	PB =
PK = 30 min.	Oral = 21% (oral)
MW = 435	pKa =
Vd = 1.8	

References:
1. Pharmaceutical Manufacturers Package Insert, 1995.
2. Drug Facts and Comparisons. 1995 ed. Facts and Comparisons, St. Louis.

FLUNITRAZEPAM

Trade: Rohypnol
Can/Aus/UK: Hypnodorm, Raohypnol, Rohypnol
Uses: Benzodiazepine sedative
AAP: Not reviewed

Flunitrazepam is a prototypical benzodiazepine. Frequently called the "Date Rape Pill", it induces rapid sedation and significant amnesia, particularly when admixed with alcohol.[1,2] Effects last about 8 hours. It is recommended for adult insomnia, and for pediatric preanesthetic sedation.

Pregnancy Risk Category: D

Lactation Risk Category: L3
L4 if used chronically

Theoretic Infant Dose:

Adult Concerns: Drowsiness, sedation, ataxia, headache, memory impairment, tremors.

Pediatric Concerns: None reported via milk, but observe for sedation.

Drug Interactions: Clarithromycin and other macrolide antibiotics may increase plasma levels for benzodiazepines by inhibiting metabolism. May have enhanced effect when added to fentanyl, ketamine, nitrous oxide. Addition of even small amounts of alcohol may produce profound sedation, psychomotor impairment, and amnesia. Theophylline may reduce the sedative effects of benzodiazepines.

Alternatives: Lorazepam, Alprazolam

Adult Dosage: 2 mg QD

T½ = 20-30 hours	M/P =
PHL =	PB = 80%
PK = 2 hours	Oral = 80-90%
MW = 313	pKa =
Vd = 3.6	

References:
1. Kanto J, Erkkola R, Kangas L et al: Placental transfer of flunitrazepam following intramuscular administration during labour. Br J Clin Pharmacol 23:491-494, 1987.
2. Kanto J, Kangas L, Leppanen T: A comparative study of the clinical effects of oral flunitrazepam, medazepam, and placebo. Int J Clin Pharmacol Ther Toxicol 20:431-433, 1982.

FLUORESCEIN

Trade:
Can/Aus/UK:
Uses: Diagnostic dye in angiography
AAP: Approved by the American Academy of Pediatrics for use in breastfeeding mothers

Sodium fluorescein is a yellow water-soluble dye. A 2% fluorescein ophthalmic solution or an impregnated fluorescein strip is used topically to detect corneal abrasions, and for fitting of hard contact lenses, and intravenously for fluorescein angiography. Fluorescein is used in two ways, one in which a small amount is added directly to the eye generally by ophthalmologists and optometrists, and secondly, when much larger quantities are administered intravenously (5 mL of 10% solution).

In a study of one patient who received an intravenous dose of fluorescein (5 mL of 10% fluorescein = 500 mg), breastmilk levels were monitored for over 76 hours.[1] Concentrations of 372 μg/L at 6 hours, and 170 μg/L at 76 hours after the dose were reported. In this patient, the half-life of fluorescein in breastmilk appeared quite long, approximating 62 hours. While the authors conclude that this is a high dose via milk, in another patient who received slightly more (910 mg I.V.), the patients' plasma levels of fluorescein monogluconoride were 37,000 μg/L.[2] Using this data, it would appear that an approximation of the milk/plasma ratio would be about 0.018, which suggests that very little of the absolute maternal dose enters milk. Nevertheless, fluorescein-induced phototoxicity remains a possibility in an infant fed breastmilk containing sodium fluorescein. One case of severe fluorescein phototoxicity has been reported in an infant receiving fluorescein intravenously.[3] If the infant is not undergoing phototherapy, it would appear that there is little risk to a breastfeeding infant.

Pregnancy Risk Category: C

Lactation Risk Category: L3

Theoretic Infant Dose: 55.8 μg/kg/day

Adult Concerns: Fluorescein-induced phototoxicity. Nausea, vomiting, dizziness, syncope, pruritus, seizures, following I.V. therapy. Severe reactions are rare. Oral fluorescein appears to elicit very few adverse reaction.

Pediatric Concerns: None reported via milk, but avoid phototherapy if used.

Drug Interactions: Interferes with numerous laboratory tests.

Alternatives:

Adult Dosage: 500 mg intravenous

T½ = 4.4 hours(metab.)	**M/P =**
PHL =	**PB = 70-85%**
PK = 1 hour	**Oral = 50%**
MW = 376	**pKa =**
Vd = 0.5	

References:

1. Maquire AM, Bennett J. Fluorescein elimination in human breast milk. Arch Ophthalmol. 106(6):718-9, 1988.
2. Kearns GL, Williams BJ & Timmons OD: Fluorescein phototoxicity in a premature infant. J Pediatr 107:796-798, 1985.
3. Kearns GL, Williams BJ, Timmons OD. Fluorescein phototoxicity in a premature infant. J Pediatr. 107(5):796-8, 1985.

FLUORIDE

Trade: Pediaflor, Flura
Can/Aus/UK: Fluor-A-Day, Fluorigard, Fluotic
Uses: Hardening enamel of teeth
AAP: Reported as having no effect on breastfeeding

Fluoride is an essential element required for bone and teeth development. It is available as salts of sodium, and stannis (tin). Excessive levels are known to stain teeth irreversibly. One study shows breastmilk levels of 0.024 - 0.172 ppm in milk (mean=0.077 ppm) of a population exposed to fluoridated water (0.7ppm).[1]

In another study of breastfeeding women from areas low and rich in fluoride, milk fluoride levels were similar.[2] The mean fluoride concentration was 0.36 μmol/L for colostrum and 0.37 μmol/L for mature milk in the region with 1 ppm fluoride enriched water. In the region with 0.2 ppm fluoride, the mean fluoride concentration of colostrum was 0.28 μmol/L. There was no statistical difference in any of these milk fluoride levels.

Fluoride probably forms calcium fluoride salts in milk which may limit the oral bioavailability of the fluoride provided by human milk. Maternal supplementation is unnecessary and not recommended in areas with high fluoride content (> 0.7 ppm) in water.[3]   Allergy to fluoride has been reported in one infant.[4] Younger children (2-6 yrs) should be instructed to use minimal quantities of toothpaste and to not swallow large amounts.   The American Academy of Pediatrics no longer recommends supplementing of breastfed infants with oral fluoride.

Fluoride Ion

Fluoride Content of Drinking Water	Daily Dose, Oral (mg) In Non-Breastfed Infants
<0.3 ppm Birth - 2 y	0.25
2-3 y	0.5
3-12 y	1
0.3-0.7 ppm Birth - 2 y	0
2-3 y	0.25
3-12 y	0.5

Pregnancy Risk Category: C

Lactation Risk Category: L2

Theoretic Infant Dose:

Adult Concerns: Stained enamel, allergic rash.

Pediatric Concerns: Allergy to fluoride has been reported in one infant. Do not use maternal doses > 0.7 ppm.

Drug Interactions: Decreased absorption when used with magnesium, aluminum, and calcium containing products.

Alternatives:

Adult Dosage: 1 mg QD

T½ = 6 hours	M/P =
PHL =	PB =
PK =	Oral = 90% (Na)
MW = 19	pKa =
Vd = 0.5-0.7	

References:
1.   Latifah R and Razak IA. Fluoride levels in mother's milk. J. Pedodontics 13:149, 1989.
2.   Spak CJ, Hardell LI, deChateau P. Fluoride in human milk. Acta Paediatr

Scand. 72:699-701, 1983.
3.   Green JC. Fluoride supplementation of the breast-fed infant. JAMA 263:2179, 1990.
4.   Shea, J. et.al. Allergy to fluoride. Ann. Allergy 25:388, 1967.

FLUOROURACIL

Trade: 5FU, Adrucil, Efudex, Fluoroplex
Can/Aus/UK: Adrucil, Efudex, Efudix, Fluoroplex
Uses: Anticancer drug, actinic keratosis
AAP: Not reviewed

Fluorouracil is a potent antineoplastic agent generally used topically for various skin cancers, and I.V. for various carcinomas.   No data are available on its transfer into breastmilk. 5FU is an extremely toxic and dangerous compound, and is probably contraindicated in breastfeeding women following I.V. therapy.[1] It is rapidly cleared by the liver and two long-half-life metabolites (FdUMP, FUTP) are formed.   The clinical effect and half-life of these metabolites is unknown.

5FU is commonly used topically as a cream for actinic or solar keratosis. The topical absorption of 5FU is minimal, reported to be less than 6%.   Although it is unlikely that significant quantities of 5FU would be transferred to a breastfed infant following topical application to small areas, caution is urged.

Pregnancy Risk Category: D if used in 1st and 2nd trimesters
                                                      X if used in 3rd trimester

Lactation Risk Category: L5

Theoretic Infant Dose:

Adult Concerns: Nausea, vomiting, anorexia, blood dyscrasias, bone marrow suppression, myocardial toxicity, dyspnea, cardiogenic shock, rashes.

Pediatric Concerns: None reported but caution is urged.

Drug Interactions: Drug interactions are numerous and include allopurinol, cimetidine, methotrexate, leukovorin and others.

Alternatives:

Adult Dosage: 6-12 mg/kg injection (IV) QD

T½ = 8-22 minutes	M/P =
PHL =	PB = 8-12%
PK = Immediate(IV)	Oral = 0-80%
MW = 130	pKa =
Vd = 0.12	

References:
1.   McEvoy GE(ed):AHFS Drug Information, New York, NY. 1995.

FLUOXETINE

Trade: Prozac
Can/Aus/UK: Apo-Fluoxetine, Lovan, Novo-Fluoxetine, Prozac, Zactin
Uses: Antidepressant
AAP: Drug whose effect on nursing infants is unknown but may be of concern

Fluoxetine is a very popular serotonin reuptake inhibitor (SSRI) currently used for depression and a host of other syndromes. Fluoxetine absorption is rapid and complete and the parent compound is rapidly metabolized to norfluoxetine, which is an active, long half-life metabolite (360 hours). Both fluoxetine and norfluoxetine appear to permeate breastmilk to levels approximately 1/5 to 1/4 of maternal plasma. In one patient at steady-state (dose=20mg/day), plasma levels of fluoxetine were 100.5 μg/L and levels of norfluoxetine were 194.5 μg/L.[1] Fluoxetine levels in milk were 28.8 μg/L and norfluoxetine levels were 41.6 μg/L. Milk/plasma ratios were 0.286 for fluoxetine, and 0.21 for norfluoxetine.

In another patient receiving 20 mg daily at bedtime, the milk concentration of fluoxetine was 67 μg/L and norfluoxetine 52 μg/L at four hours.[2] At 8 hours postdose, the concentration of fluoxetine was 17 μg/L and norfluoxetine was 13 μg/L. Using this data, the authors estimated that the total daily dose was only 15-20 μg/kg per day which represents a low exposure.

In another study of 10 breastfeeding women receiving 0.39 mg/kg/day of fluoxetine, the average breastmilk levels for fluoxetine and norfluoxetine ranged from 24.4-181.1 μg/L and 37.4-199.1 μg/L respectively.[3] Peak milk concentrations occurred within 6 hours. The milk/plasma ratios for fluoxetine and norfluoxetine were 0.88 and 0.72, respectively. Fluoxetine plasma levels in one infant were undetectable (< 1 ng/ml). Using this data, an infant consuming 150 ml/kg/day would consume approximately 9.3-57 μg/kg/day total fluoxetine (and metabolite), which represents 5-9% of the maternal dose. No adverse effects were noted in the infants in this study.

Severe colic, fussiness, and crying have been reported in one case report.[4] The mother was receiving a dose of 20 mg fluoxetine per day. Concentrations of fluoxetine and norfluoxetine in breastmilk were 69 μg/L and 90 μg/L respectively.   The plasma levels in the infant for fluoxetine and norfluoxetine were 340 ng/mL and 208 ng/mL respectively which is almost twice that of normal maternal ranges.   The author does not report the maternal plasma levels but suggests they were similar to Isenberg's adult levels (100.5 ng/mL and 194.5 ng/ml for fluoxetine and norfluoxetine). In this infant, the plasma levels would approach those of a mother receiving twice the above 20 mg dose per day (40 mg/day). The symptoms resolved upon discontinuation of fluoxetine by the mother.

In a study by Brent[5], an infant exposed in utero and postpartum via milk, had moderate plasma fluoxetine levels that increased in the three weeks postpartum due to breastmilk ingestion. The infant's plasma levels of fluoxetine went from none detectable at day 13 to 61 ng/mL at day 21. The mean adult therapeutic range is 145 ng/mL. The infant in this study exhibited slight seizure activity at 3 weeks, 4 months, and 5 months.

Ilett reports that in a group of 14 women receiving 0.51 mg/kg/day fluoxetine, the mean M/P ratio was 0.67 (range 0.35 to 0.13) and 0.56 for norfluoxetine.[6] Mean total infant dose in fluoxetine equivalents was 6.81% of the weight-adjusted maternal dose. The reported infant fluoxetine and norfluoxetine plasma levels ranged from 20-252 μg/L and 17-187 μg/L respectively.

It is not known if these reported side effects (seizures, colic, fussiness, crying) are common, although this author has received numerous other personal communications similar to this. Indeed in one case, the infant became comatose at 11 days postpartum with high plasma levels of norfluoxetine.[7] At present, fluoxetine is the only antidepressant cleared for use in pregnancy. This may pose an added problem in breastfed infants. Infants born of mothers receiving fluoxetine are born with full steady state plasma levels of the medication, and each time they are breastfed the level in the infant is likely to rise further. While perhaps controversial, I believe it is advisable to discontinue the use of fluoxetine prior to or following delivery in these infants, and if possible switch to an alternate SSRI immediately following birth. Age at institution of therapy is of importance, use in older infants (4-6 months or older) is probably not as hazardous because they can metabolize and excrete the medication more rapidly. Data published in 1999 also suggest that weight gain in infants breastfed from mothers who were taking fluoxetine demonstrated a growth curve significantly below that of infants who were breastfed by mothers who did not take the drug.[8] The average deficit in measurements taken between 2 and 6 months of age was 392 grams body weight. None of these infants were noted to have unusual behavior.

Another recent report suggests that fluoxetine may induce a state of anesthesia of the vagina and nipples.[9] The author has had another report of a paroxetine-induced reduction of milk ejection reflex. Whether or not a loss of MER is related to an anesthesia of the nipples is purely speculative.

Thus far, neurobehavioral development seems to be normal at least in one small study.[10]

Current data on Sertraline, and Paroxetine suggest these medications have difficulty entering milk, and more importantly, the infant. Therefore they may be preferred agents over fluoxetine for therapy of depression in breastfeeding mothers.

Pregnancy Risk Category: B

Lactation Risk Category: L2 in older infants
L3 if used in neonatal period

Theoretic Infant Dose: 9.3-57 μg/kg/day

Adult Concerns: Nausea, tachycardia, hypotension, headache, anxiety, nervousness, insomnia, dry mouth, anorexia and visual disturbances.

Pediatric Concerns: Severe colic, fussiness, and crying have been reported in one case study.

Drug Interactions: Cimetidine may increase plasma levels 50%. Hallucinations have occurred when used with dextromethorphan. Serious fatal reactions have occurred when used after MAO inhibitors. Phenytoin may reduce plasma levels of fluoxetine by 50%. CNS toxicity may result if used with L-tryptophan. Fluoxetine may increase plasma levels of tricyclic antidepressants. Significant increase in propranolol levels have been reported. Effects of buspirone may be decreased. Serum carbamazepine levels may be increased resulting in toxicity. Bradycardia has been reported when used with diltiazem. Use with digoxin reduces digoxin levels by 15%. Lithium levels may be increased by fluoxetine with possible neurotoxicity. Sertraline did not effect lithium levels. Methadone levels have been significantly increased with SSRIs. Clearance of theophylline may be decreased by three fold. When used with warfarin, a significant increase in bleeding time has been reported.

Alternatives: Sertraline, Paroxetine, Citalopram

Adult Dosage: 20-40 mg QD

T½ = 2-3 days(fluoxetine)	M/P = 0.286-0.67
PHL =	PB = 94.5%
PK = 1.5 - 12 hours	Oral = 100%
MW = 309	pKa =
Vd = 2.6	

References:
1. Isenberg KE. Excretion of fluoxetine in human breast milk. J Clin Psychiatry 51:169, 1990.
2. Burch KJ, and Well BG. Fluoxetine/Norfluoxetine concentrations in human milk. Pediatrics 89:676, 1992.
3. Taddio A, Ito S, Koren G. Excretion of fluoxetine and its metabolite in

human breast milk. Pediatric Res 35(4, part 2): 149a, 1994. Abstract.

4.   Lester, BM et.al. Possible association between fluoxetine hydrochloride and colic in an infant. J. Am. Acad. Child. Adolesc. Psychiatry 32(6): 1253-1255, 1993.

5.   Brent NB, Wisner KL. Fluoxetine and Carbamazepine concentrations in a nursing mother/infant pair. Clinical Pediatrics 37:41-44, 1998.

6.   Kristensen JH; Ilett KF; Hackett LP; Yapp P; Paech M; Begg EJ. Distribution and excretion of fluoxetine and norfluoxetine in human milk. Br J Clin Pharmacol 48(4):521-7,1999.

7.   Hale TW, Shum S, Grossberg M. Fluoxetine toxicity in a breastfed infant. Clin Pediatr (Phila). 40(12):681-4, 2001.

8.   Chambers CD, Anderson PO, et.al. Weight gain in infants breastfed by mothers who take fluoxetine. Pediatrics 104(5) November 1999. http://www.pediatrics.org/cgi/content/full/104/5/e61

9.   Michael A, Mayer C. Fluoxetine-induced anaesthesia of vagina and nipples. Br J Psychiatry. 176:299, 2000.

10. Yoshida K, Smith B, Craggs M, Kumar RC. Fluoxetine in breast-milk and developmental outcome of breast-fed infants. Br J Psychiatry. 172:175-8, 1998.

FLUPHENAZINE

Trade: Prolixin, Permitil
Can/Aus/UK: Anatensol, Apo-Fluphenazine, Modecate, Moditen
Uses: Psychotherapeutic agent
AAP: Not reviewed

Fluphenazine is a phenothiazine tranquilizer and presently has the highest milligram potency of this family. Fluphenazine decanoate injections (IM) provide extremely long plasma levels with half-lives approaching 14.3 days at steady state. Members of this family generally have milk/plasma ratios ranging from 0.5 to 0.7.[1] No specific reports on fluphenazine breastmilk levels have been located.

Pregnancy Risk Category: C

Lactation Risk Category: L3

Theoretic Infant Dose:

Adult Concerns: Depression, seizures, appetite stimulation, blood dyscrasias, weight gain, hepatic toxicity, sedation.

Pediatric Concerns: None reported, but observe for sedation.

Drug Interactions: Increased toxicity when administered with ethanol. CNS effects may be increased when used with lithium. May stimulate the effects of narcotics including respiratory depression.

Alternatives:

Adult Dosage: 1-5 mg QD

T½ = 10-20 hours	M/P =
PHL =	PB = 91-99%
PK = 1.5 - 2 hours	Oral = Complete
MW = 438	pKa = 3.9, 8.1
Vd = 220	

References:
1. Ayd FJ. Excretion of psychotropic drugs in breast milk. In . International Drug Therapy Newsletter. Ayd Medical Communications. November-December 1973. Vol. 8.

FLURAZEPAM

Trade: Dalmane
Can/Aus/UK: Apo-Flurazepam, Dalmane, Novo-Flupam
Uses: Sedative, hypnotic
AAP: Not reviewed

Flurazepam is a sedative, hypnotic generally used as an aid for sleep. It belongs to the benzodiazepine (Valium) family. It is rapidly and completely metabolized to several long half-life active metabolites. Because most benzodiazepines are secreted into human milk, flurazepam entry into milk should be expected.[1] However, no specific data on flurazepam breastmilk levels are available. See diazepam.

Pregnancy Risk Category: X

Lactation Risk Category: L3

Theoretic Infant Dose:

Adult Concerns: Sedation, tachycardia, jaundice, apnea.

Pediatric Concerns: None reported, but caution is recommended. Observe for sedation.

Drug Interactions: Decreased effect when used with enzyme inducers such as barbiturates. Increased toxicity when used with other CNS depressants and cimetidine.

Alternatives: Lorazepam, Alprazolam

Adult Dosage: 15-30 mg QD

T½ = 47-100 hours	M/P =
PHL =	PB = 97%
PK = 0.5-1 hours	Oral = Complete
MW = 388	pKa = 1.9, 8.2
Vd = 3.4-5.5	

References:
1.   Drug Facts and Comparisons. 1995 ed. Facts and Comparisons, St. Louis.

FLURBIPROFEN

Trade: Ansaid, Froben, Ocufen
Can/Aus/UK: Ansaid, Froben, Ocufen
Uses: Analgesic
AAP: Not reviewed

Flurbiprofen is a nonsteroidal analgesic similar in structure to ibuprofen, but used both as an ophthalmic preparation (in eyes) and orally.   In one study of 12 women and following nine oral doses (50mg/dose, 3-5 days postpartum) the concentration of flurbiprofen in two women ranged from 0.05 to 0.07 mg/L of milk,   but was < 0.05 mg/L in 10 of the 12 women.[1]   Concentrations in breastmilk and plasma of nursing mothers suggest that a nursing infant would receive less than 0.1 mg flurbiprofen per day, a level considered exceedingly low.

In another study of 10 nursing mothers following a single 100 mg dose, the average peak concentration of flurbiprofen in breastmilk was 0.09 mg/L, or about 0.05% of the maternal dose.[2]   Both of these studies suggest that the amount of flurbiprofen transferred in human milk would be clinically insignificant to the infant.

Pregnancy Risk Category: **B during 1st and 2nd trimesters**
C during 3rd trimester

Lactation Risk Category: L2

Theoretic Infant Dose: 13.5 μg/kg/day

Adult Concerns: GI distress, diarrhea, constipation, cramping, may worsen jaundice.

Pediatric Concerns: None reported.

Drug Interactions: May prolong prothrombin time when used with warfarin. Antihypertensive effects of ACEi family may be blunted or completely abolished by NSAIDs.   Some NSAIDs may block antihypertensive effect of beta blockers, diuretics.   Used with cyclosporin, may dramatically increase renal toxicity. May increase digoxin, phenytoin, lithium levels.   May increase toxicity of methotrexate.   May increase bioavailability of penicillamine. Probenecid may increase NSAID levels.

Alternatives: Ibuprofen

Adult Dosage: 200-300 mg QD

T½ = 3.8-5.7 hours	M/P = 0.008 - 0.013
PHL = 2.71 hours(children)	PB = 99%
PK = 1.5 hours	Oral = Complete
MW = 244	pKa = 4.2
Vd = 0.1	

References:
1. Smith IJ, et.al. Flurbiprofen in post-partum women: plasma and breast milk disposition. J. Clin. Pharmacol. 29(2):174-84,1989.
2. Cox SR, Forbes KK, Excretion of flurbiprofen into breast milk. Pharmacother. 7:211-215, 1987.

FLUTICASONE

Trade: Flonase, Flovent, Cutivate
Can/Aus/UK: Flixonase, Flixotide, Flonase, Flovent
Uses: Intranasal, inhaled steroid
AAP: Not reviewed

Fluticasone is a typical steroid primarily used intranasally for allergic rhinitis, and intrapulmonary for asthma. Intranasal form is called Flonase, inhaled form is Flovent. When instilled intranasally, the absolute bioavailability is less than 2%, so virtually none of the dose instilled is absorbed systemically.[1] Oral absorption following inhaled fluticasone is approximately 30%, although almost instant first-pass absorption virtually eliminates plasma levels of fluticasone.[2] Peak plasma levels following inhalation of 880 ug is only 0.1 to 1.0 nanogram/mL. Adrenocortical suppression following oral, or even systemic absorption at normal doses is extremely rare due to limited plasma levels.[3] Plasma levels are not detectible when using suggested doses. Although fluticasone is secreted into milk of rodents, the dose used was many times higher than found under normal conditions. With the above oral and systemic bioavailability, and rapid first-pass uptake by the liver, it is not likely that milk levels will be clinically relevant, even with rather high doses.

Pregnancy Risk Category: C

Lactation Risk Category: L3

Theoretic Infant Dose:

Adult Concerns: Intranasal: pruritus, headache (1-3%), burning (3-6%), epistaxis. Adverse effects associated with inhaled fluticasone include headache, nasal congestion, and oral candidiasis.

Pediatric Concerns: When used topically on large surface areas, some adrenal suppression has been noted. No effects have been reported in breastfeeding infants. In children receiving up to 5 times the normal inhaled dose (1000 μg/day), some growth suppression was noted.

Drug Interactions:

Alternatives:

Adult Dosage: 50-110 mcg inhalation QD

T½ = 7.8 hours.	M/P =
PHL =	PB =
PK = 15-60 minutes	Oral = Oral(1%), Inhaled(18%)
MW = 500	pKa =
Vd = 4.2	

References:
1. Pharmaceutical Manufacturers Package Insert, 1996.
2. Harding SM: The human pharmacology of fluticasone propionate. Respir Med 84(Suppl A):25-29, 1990.
3. Todd G, Dunlop K, McNaboe J et al: Growth and adrenal suppression in asthmatic children treated with high-dose fluticasone propionate. Lancet 348:27-29, 1996.

FLUTICASONE and SALMETEROL

Trade: Advair
Can/Aus/UK:
Uses: Anti-asthmatic
AAP: Not reviewed

Advair is a combination product containing fluticasone and salmeterol, used for the treatment of asthma. See individual monographs for fluticasone(Flovent) and Salmeterol(Serevent).

FLUVASTATIN

Trade: Lescol, Lescol Xl
Can/Aus/UK: Lescol, Vastin
Uses: Reduces blood cholesterol levels
AAP: Not reviewed

Fluvastatin is an inhibitor of cholesterol synthesis in the liver. Fluvastatin levels in human milk are reported to be 2 fold that of serum levels.[1,2] Effect on infant is unknown but could reduce cholesterol synthesis in infant. Atherosclerosis is a chronic process and discontinuation of lipid-lowering drugs during pregnancy and lactation should have little to no impact on the outcome of long-term therapy of primary hypercholesterolemia. Cholesterol and other products of cholesterol biosynthesis are essential components for fetal and neonatal development and the use of cholesterol-lowering drugs would not be advisable under any circumstances.

Pregnancy Risk Category: X

Lactation Risk Category: L3

Theoretic Infant Dose:

Adult Concerns: Headache, insomnia, dyspepsia, diarrhea, gas, elevated liver enzymes.

Pediatric Concerns: None reported, but reduced plasma cholesterol levels could occur.

Drug Interactions: Anticoagulant effect of warfarin may be increased.

Alternatives:

Adult Dosage: 20-40 mg QD

T½ = 1.2 hours	M/P = 2.0
PHL =	PB = > 98%
PK = < 1 hour	Oral = 20-30%
MW =	pKa =
Vd =	

References:
1. Drug Facts and Comparisons. 1994 ed. Facts and Comparisons, St. Louis.
2. Pharmaceutical Manufacturers Package Insert, 1995.

FLUVOXAMINE

Trade: Luvox
Can/Aus/UK: Alti-Fluvoxamine, Apo-Fluvoxamine, Faverin, Floxyfral, Luvox, Myroxim
Uses: Antidepressant
AAP: Drug whose effect on nursing infants is unknown but may be of concern

Although structurally dissimilar to the other serotonin reuptake inhibitors, fluvoxamine provides increased synaptic serotonin levels in the brain. It has several hepatic metabolites which are not active. Its primary indications are for the treatment of obsessive-compulsive disorders (OCD) although it also functions as an antidepressant. There are a number of significant drug-drug interactions with this product.

In a case report of one 23 year old mother and following a dose of 100 mg twice daily for 2 weeks, the maternal plasma level of fluvoxamine base was 0.31 mg/L and the milk concentration was 0.09 mg/L.[1] The authors reported a theoretical dose to infant of 0.0104 mg/kg/day of fluvoxamine, which is only 0.5% of the maternal dose. According to the authors, the infant suffered no unwanted effects as a result of this intake and that this dose poses little risk to a nursing infant.

In a study of one patient receiving 100 mg twice daily, the AUC milk/serum ratio averaged 1.32. The absolute daily dose of fluvoxamine ingested by the newborn was calculated to be 48 μg/kg/d and the relative dose was calculated to be 1.58% of the weight-adjusted maternal dose.[2]

In another study of two breastfeeding women, the AUC average concentration of fluvoxamine in milk was 36 and 256 μg/L respectively.[3] The absolute infant dose was estimated at 5.4 and 38.4 μg/kg/d with a relative infant dose (% of maternal dose) of 0.8% and 1.38%. A Denver assessment on one infant indicated normal development. Fluvoxamine was not detected in the plasma of either infant (limit of detection = 2 μg/L).

In a case report of a single mother receiving 25 mg three times daily, the highest milk concentration was 40 μg/L.[4] Using this data, an infant would ingest approximately 6 μg/kg/day which is 0.62% of the maternal weight-adjusted dose. Interestingly, the maternal serum concentration at 10 hours was 20 ng/mL while the infant plasma level was 9 ng/mL. Considering the clinical dose to the infant is low, this plasma level in the infant appears high. The authors suggest this may be an atypical case, or that this infant's clearance of fluvoxamine is poor. The infant showed no symptoms of adverse effects.

Yoshida reported a case of a mother receiving 100 mg/day, and an infant 15 weeks postpartum.[5] In this case the concentration of fluvoxamine in maternal serum and milk was 170 μg/L and 50 μg/L respectively and a milk/plasma ratio of 0.29. The authors estimated the dose to the infant at 7.5 μg/kg/day. Developmental assessments of the infant at 4 months and 21 months suggested normal development.

In a report of 2 breastfeeding women receiving 300 mg/d, Piontek was unable to detect any fluvoxamine in the plasma of two breastfed infants.[6]

In summary, the data from these 8 cases suggests that only minuscule amounts of fluvoxamine are transferred to infants, that plasma levels in infants are too low to be detected, and no adverse effects have been noted.

Pregnancy Risk Category: C

Lactation Risk Category: L2

Theoretic Infant Dose: 5.4-38.4 μg/kg/day

Adult Concerns: Somnolence, insomnia, nervousness, nausea.

Pediatric Concerns: None reported in one study.

Drug Interactions: Increased toxicity may result when used with terfenadine and astemizole. Sometimes serious fatal reactions have occurred close following the use of MAO inhibitors. Smokers have a 25% increase in the metabolism of fluvoxamine. Enhanced CNS toxicity when used with L-tryptophan. Plasma tricyclic antidepressant levels may be increased when used with fluvoxamine. Plasma levels of propranolol have been increased by five fold when used with fluvoxamine. Bradycardia has resulted when used with diltiazem. Lithium levels may be increased by fluvoxamine with possible neurotoxicity. Increased bleeding time may result when used with warfarin.

Alternatives: Sertraline, Paroxetine

Adult Dosage: 50-300 mg QD

T½ = 15.6 hours	**M/P = 1.34**
PHL =	**PB = 80%**
PK = 3-8 hours	**Oral = 53%**
MW = 318	**pKa =**
Vd =	

References:
1. Wright S, Dawling S et.al. Excretion of fluvoxamine in breast milk (letter). Br. J. Clin. Pharmacol. 31:209, 1991.
2. Hagg S, Granberg K, Carleborg L. Excretion of fluvoxamine into breast milk(letter). Br. J. Clin. Pharmacol. 49:286-288, 2000.
3. Kristensen JH, Hackett LP, Kohan R, Paech M, Ilett KF. The amount of fluvoxamine in milk is unlikely to be a cause of adverse effects in breastfed infants. Journal of Human Lactation (in press, 28 September, 2001).
4. Arnold LM. Suckow RF. Lichtenstein PK. Fluvoxamine concentrations in breast milk and in maternal and infant sera. Journal of Clinical Psychopharmacology. 20(4):491-3, 2000.
5. Yoshida K, Smith B, Kumar RC. Fluvoxamine in breast-milk and infant development. Br J Clin Pharmacol. 44(2):210-1, 1997.
6. Piontek CM, Wisner KL, Perel JM, Peindl KS. Serum fluvoxamine levels in breastfed infants. J Clin Psychiatry. 62(2):111-3, 2001.

FOLIC ACID

Trade: Folacin, Wellcovorin
Can/Aus/UK: Accomin, Apo-Folic, Bioglan Daily, Folvite, Megafol, Novo-Folacid
Uses: Vitamin
AAP: Approved by the American Academy of Pediatrics for use in breastfeeding mothers

Folic acid is an essential vitamin. Individuals most susceptible to folic acid deficiency are the pregnant patient, and those receiving anticonvulsants or birth control medications. Folic acid supplementation is now strongly recommended in women prior to becoming pregnancy due to a documented reduction of spinal cord malformations. Folic acid is actively secreted into breastmilk even if mother is deficient.[1] If maternal diet is adequate, folic acid is not generally required. The infant receives all required from a normal milk supply. Cooperman[1] determined milk folic acid content to be 15.2 ng/ml in colostrum, 16.3 ng/ml in transitional, and 33.4 ng/ml in mature milk.

In one study of 11 breastfeeding mothers receiving 0.8-1 mg/day of folic acid, the folic acid secreted into human milk averaged 45.6 μg/L.[3] Excessive doses (> 1 mg/day) are not generally recommended.

Pregnancy Risk Category: **A during 1st and 2nd trimesters**
C during 3rd trimester

Lactation Risk Category: L1

Theoretic Infant Dose: 6.8 μg/kg/day

Adult Concerns: Allergies, rash, nausea, anorexia, bitter taste.

Pediatric Concerns: None reported.

Drug Interactions: May increase phenytoin metabolism and reduce levels. Phenytoin, primidone, sulfasalazine, and para-aminosalicylic acid may decrease serum folate concentrations and cause deficiency. Oral contraceptives also impair folate metabolism producing depletion.

Alternatives:

Adult Dosage: 0.4-0.8 mg QD

T½ =	M/P =
PHL=	PB =
PK = 30-60 min.	Oral = 76-93%
MW = 441	pKa =
Vd =	

References:
1. Cooperman JM, et. al. The folate in human milk. Am J Clin Nutr 36:576-80, 1982.
2. Tamura T, et. al. Human milk folate and folate status in lactating mothers and their infants. Am J Clin Nutr 33:193-7, 1980.
3. Smith AM, et.al. Folate supplementation during lactation: maternal folate status, human milk folate content, and their relationship to infant folate status. J.Pediatr. Gastroenterol.Nutrit. 2:622-628, 1983.

FORMALDEHYDE

Trade: Formaldehyde, Formalin, Methyl Aldehyde
Can/Aus/UK:
Uses: Preservative
AAP: Not reviewed

Formaldehyde exposure in laboratory or embalming environments is strictly controlled by federal regulations to a permissible level of 2 ppm.

At room temperature it is a colorless gas with a pungent, irritating odor detectable at 0.5 ppm. At exposure to 1-4 ppm, formaldehyde is a strong mucous membrane irritant, producing burning and lacrimation.[1] Formaldehyde is rapidly destroyed by plasma and tissue enzymes and it is very unlikely than any would enter human milk following environmental exposures. However, acute intoxications following high oral or inhaled doses could lead to significant levels of maternal plasma formic acid which could enter milk. There is no data suggesting untoward side effects in nursing infants as a result of mild to minimal environmental exposure of the mother.

Pregnancy Risk Category: X

Lactation Risk Category: L4

Theoretic Infant Dose:

Adult Concerns: Cough, mucous membrane irritation, chest pain, dyspnea, and wheezing occur in individuals exposed to 5-30 ppm.

Pediatric Concerns: None reported via milk.

Drug Interactions:

Alternatives:

Adult Dosage:

T½ =	M/P =
PHL =	PB =
PK =	Oral =
MW = 30	pKa =
Vd =	

References:
1. Ellenhorn MJ, Barceloux DG. In: Medical Toxicology, Elsevier, New York, USA, 1988.

FORMOTEROL FUMARATE

Trade: Foradil Aerolizer
Can/Aus/UK:
Uses: Bronchodilator
AAP: Not reviewed

Formoterol is a long-acting selective beta-2 adrenoceptor agonist used for asthma and COPD. Following inhalation of a 120 ug dose, the maximum plasma concentration of 92 picograms/mL occurred within 5 minutes.[1] No data are available on its transfer into human milk, but the extremely low plasma levels would suggest that milk levels would be incredibly low, if even measurable. Studies of oral absorption in adults suggests that while absorption is good, plasma levels are still below detectable levels, and may require large oral doses prior to attaining measurable plasma levels.[2] It is not likely the amount present in human milk would be clinically relevant to a breastfed infant.

Pregnancy Risk Category: C

Lactation Risk Category: L3

Theoretic Infant Dose:

Adult Concerns: Tremor, headache, dizziness, restlessness, palpitations, nausea, dry mouth, muscle cramps, and cough. Low serum potassium and elevated blood glucose levels can occur with high doses. Blood pressure and heart rate are minimally affected.

Pediatric Concerns: None reported via milk.

Drug Interactions: Concurrent use of xanthin derivatives, steroids, or diuretics may potentiate any hypokalemic effect. Do not use with MAO inhibitors, tricyclic antidepressants, or drugs known to prolong QTc interval. Beta-adrenergic agents may inhibit effect of formoterol.

Alternatives: Salmeterol, Albuterol

Adult Dosage: 12 ug every 12 hours

T½	**= 10 hours**	**M/P**	**=**
PHL	**=**	**PB**	**= 64%**
PK	**= 5 minutes**	**Oral**	**= Good**
MW	**= 840**	**pKa**	**=**
Vd	**=**		

References:
1. Pharmaceutical manufacturers package insert, 2001.
2. Tattersfield AE. Long-acting beta 2-agonists. Clin Exp Allergy. 22(6):600-5, 1992.
3. Maesen FP, Smeets JJ, Gubbelmans HL, Zweers PG. Bronchodilator effect of inhaled formoterol vs salbutamol over 12 hours. Chest. 97(3):590-4,1990.

FOSCARNET SODIUM

Trade: Foscavir
Can/Aus/UK: Foscavir
Uses: Antiviral for herpes, CMV infections
AAP: Not reviewed

Foscarnet is an antiviral used to treat mucocutaneous herpes simplex manifestations, and cytomegalovirus retinal infections in patients with AIDS. It is not known if foscarnet is secreted into human milk, but studies in animals indicate levels in milk were three times higher than serum levels (suggesting a Milk/plasma ratio of 3.0).[1,2] Foscarnet is a potent and potentially dangerous drug including significant renal toxicity, seizures, and deposition in bone and teeth.

Pregnancy Risk Category: C

Lactation Risk Category: L4

Theoretic Infant Dose:

Adult Concerns: Fever, nausea, diarrhea, vomiting, tremor, headache, fatigue, kidney toxicity, anemia due to bone marrow suppression.

Pediatric Concerns: None reported but caution is urged.

Drug Interactions: Increased hypocalcemia with pentamidine, and increased seizures with ciprofloxacin.

Alternatives:

Adult Dosage: 34-51 mg/kg injection (IV) QD

T½ = 3 hours	M/P = 3.0
PHL=	PB = 14-17%
PK = Immediate(IV)	Oral = 12-21%
MW = 192	pKa =
Vd =	

References:
1. Pharmaceutical Manufacturers Package Insert, 1995.
2. Sjovall J, et al. Pharmacokinetics and absorption of foscarnet after intravenous and oral administration to patients with human immunodeficiency virus. Clin Pharmacol Ther 44:65-73, 1988.

FOSFOMYCIN TROMETAMOL

Trade: Monurol
Can/Aus/UK: Monuril
Uses: Urinary antibiotic
AAP: Not reviewed

Fosfomycin is a broad-spectrum antibiotic used primarily for uncomplicated urinary tract infections. It is believed safe for use in pregnancy and has been used in children less than 1 year of age. Fosfomycin absorption is largely dependent on the salt form, trometanol salts are modestly absorbed (34-58%), and calcium salts are poorly absorbed (< 12%). Fosfomycin secreted into human milk would likely be in the calcium form and is unlikely to be absorbed as secreted in human milk. Foods and the acidic milieu of the stomach both significantly reduce oral absorption.[1-3]

Levels secreted into human milk have been reported to be about 10% of the maternal plasma level.[4] Generally, a single 3 gm oral dose is effective treatment for many urinary tract infections in women. It is not likely that the levels present in breastmilk would produce untoward effects in a breastfeeding infant.

Pregnancy Risk Category: B

Lactation Risk Category: L3

Theoretic Infant Dose:

Adult Concerns: GI symptoms include nausea, vomiting, diarrhea, epigastric discomfort, anorexia. Skin rashes and pruritus have been reported.

Pediatric Concerns: None reported via milk.

Drug Interactions: Antacids, calcium salts and foods will reduce absorption. Metoclopramide reduces serum concentration, by reducing oral bioavailability.

Alternatives:

Adult Dosage: 3 g daily

T½ = 4-8 hours		M/P = 0.1	
PHL = 5-7 hours		PB = < 3%	
PK = 1.5-3 hours		Oral = 34-58%	
MW = 138		pKa =	
Vd = 0.22			

References:
1. Bergan T: Degree of absorption, pharmacokinetics of fosfomycin trometamol and duration of antibacterial activity. Infection 8(suppl 2):S65-S69, 1990.
2. Bergan T: Pharmacokinetic comparison between fosfomycin and other phosphonic acid derivatives. Chemotherapy 36(suppl 1):10-18, 1990.
3. Segre G, Bianchi E, Cataldi A et al: Pharmacokinetic profile of fosfomycin trometamol (Monuril). Eur Urol 13(suppl 1):56-63,1987.
4. Kirby WMM. Pharmacokinetics of fosfomycin. Chemotherapy 23, suppl 1: 141-151,1977.

FOSINOPRIL

Trade: Monopril
Can/Aus/UK: Monopril, Staril
Uses: Antihypertensive, ACE inhibitor
AAP: Not reviewed

Fosinopril is a prodrug that is metabolized by the gut and liver upon absorption to fosinoprilat, which is an ACE inhibitor used as an antihypertensive. The manufacturer reports that the ingestion of 20 mg daily for three days resulted in barely detectable levels in human milk, although no values are provided.[1,2] See enalapril, benazepril, captopril as alternatives.

Pregnancy Risk Category: D

Lactation Risk Category: L3
L4 if used in neonatal period

Theoretic Infant Dose:

Adult Concerns: Anemia, dry cough, headache, dizziness, diarrhea, fatigue, nausea, vomiting, hypotension.

Pediatric Concerns: None reported.

Drug Interactions: Bioavailability of ACEIs may be decreased when used with antacids. Capsaicin may exacerbate coughing associated with ACEi treatment. Pharmacologic effects of ACE inhibitors may be increased. Increased plasma levels of digoxin may result. Increased serum lithium levels may result when used with ACE inhibitors.

Alternatives: Enalapril, Benazepril, Captopril

Adult Dosage: 20-40 mg QD

T½ = 11-35 hours		M/P =	
PHL=		PB = 95 %	
PK = 3 hours		Oral = 30-36%	
MW = 564		pKa =	
Vd =			

References:
1.   Drug Facts and Comparisons. 1995 ed. Facts and Comparisons, St. Louis.
2.   Pharmaceutical Manufacturers Package Insert, 1995.

FURAZOLIDONE

Trade: Furoxone
Can/Aus/UK: Furoxone
Uses: Gastrointestinal antibiotic.
AAP: Not reviewed

Furazolidone belongs to the nitrofurantoin family of antibiotics (see nitrofurantoin).   It has a broad spectrum of activity against gram-positive and gram-negative enteric organisms including cholera, but is generally used for giardiasis.[1]

Following an oral dose, furazolidone is poorly absorbed (< 5%) and is largely inactivated in the gut. Concentrations transferred to milk are unreported, but the total amounts would be exceedingly low due to the low maternal plasma levels attained by this product.   Due to poor oral absorption, systemic absorption in a breastfeeding infant would likely be minimal.   Caution should be observed in early postpartum newborns.

Pregnancy Risk Category: C

Lactation Risk Category: L3

Theoretic Infant Dose:

Adult Concerns: Hemolytic anemia in newborns, nausea, vomiting, diarrhea, abdominal pain. Dark yellow to brown discoloration of urine.

Pediatric Concerns: Caution is urged in neonates < 1 month due to possibility of hemolytic anemia.

Drug Interactions: Increased effect when used with sympathomimetic amines, tricyclic antidepressants, MAO inhibitors, meperidine, dextromethorphan, fluoxetine, paroxetine, sertraline, trazodone.

Alternatives:

Adult Dosage:

T½ =	M/P =
PHL=	PB =
PK =	Oral = < 5%
MW = 225	pKa =
Vd =	

References:
1.   McEvoy GE(ed):AHFS Drug Information, New York, NY. 1995.

FUROSEMIDE

Trade: Lasix
Can/Aus/UK: Apo-Furosemide, Frusemide, Frusid, Lasix, Novo-Semide, Uremide
Uses: Loop diuretic
AAP: Not reviewed

Furosemide is a potent loop diuretic with a rather short duration of action. Furosemide has been found in breastmilk although the levels are unreported. Diuretics, by reducing blood volume, could potentially reduce breastmilk production, although this is largely theoretical.[1] Furosemide is frequently used in neonates in pediatric units, so pediatric use is common. The oral bioavailability of furosemide in newborns is exceedingly poor and very high oral doses are required (1-4mg/kg BID).[2] It is very unlikely the amount transferred into human milk would produce any effects in a nursing infant, although its maternal use could suppress lactation.

Pregnancy Risk Category: C

Lactation Risk Category: L3

Theoretic Infant Dose:

Adult Concerns: Hypotension, fluid loss, potassium loss.

Pediatric Concerns: None reported.

Drug Interactions: Furosemide interferes with hypoglycemic effect of antidiabetic agents. NSAIDS may reduce diuretic effect of furosemide. Effects of antihypertensive agents may be increased. Renal clearance of lithium is decreased. Increases ototoxicity of aminoglycosides.

Alternatives:

Adult Dosage: 40-80 mg BID

T½ = 92 minutes	M/P =
PHL=	PB = >98%
PK = 1-2 hours	Oral = 60-70%
MW = 331	pKa =
Vd =	

References:
1. Healy M. Suppressing lactation with oral diuretics, Lancet 1:1353-1354, 1961.
2. Pharmaceutical Manufacturers Package Insert, 1995.

GABAPENTIN

Trade: Neurontin
Can/Aus/UK: Neurontin
Uses: Anticonvulsant
AAP: Not reviewed

Gabapentin is a newer anticonvulsant used primarily for partial (focal) seizures with or without secondary generalization. Unlike many anticonvulsants, gabapentin is almost completely renally excreted without metabolism, it does not induce hepatic enzymes, and is remarkably well tolerated.[1-3] No published reports are available on its transfer into human milk. However, in preliminary results from two patients studied in our own laboratories indicate a modest infant dose via milk.[4] In one breastfeeding mother who was receiving 1800 mg/d, milk levels were 11.1, 11.1, 11.3, and 11.0 mg/L at 0, 2, 4, and 8 hours, respectively, following a dose of 600 mg. The maternal and infant plasma levels at 2 hours post dose were 16.6 mg/L and less than 0.3 mg/L respectively. In another mother receiving 2400 mg/d milk levels were 4.6, 9.8, 9.0, and 7.2 mg/L at 0, 2, 4, and 8 hours respectively, after a dose of 800 mg. The maternal plasma level at 2 hours post dose was 15.1 mg/L. Using these limited data, the calculated relative infant doses were approximately 6.0% to 3.1% respectively, of the weight-adjusted maternal dose. No adverse events were noted in either of these two infants.

Pregnancy Risk Category: C

Lactation Risk Category: L3

Theoretic Infant Dose: 1.7 mg/kg/day

Adult Concerns: Dizziness, somnolence, weight gain, vomiting, tremor, and CNS depression. Abrupt withdrawal may induce severe seizures.

Pediatric Concerns: None reported. Cleared for children > 12 yrs.

Drug Interactions: Antacids reduce gabapentin absorption by 20%. Cimetidine may decrease clearance of gabapentin. No interaction has been reported with other anticonvulsants. Antacids may reduce oral absorption by 20%.

Alternatives:

Adult Dosage: 300-600 mg TID

T½ = 5-7 hours	M/P =
PHL =	PB = < 3%
PK = 1-3 hours	Oral = 50-60%
MW =	pKa =
Vd = 0.8	

References:
1. Goa KL & Sorkin EM: Gabapentin: a review of its pharmacological properties and clinical potential in epilepsy. Drugs 46:409-427, 1993.
2. Ramsay RE: Clinical efficacy and safety of gabapentin. Neurology 44(Suppl 5):S23-S30, 1994.
3. Dichter MA & Brodie MJ: New antiepileptic drugs. J Med 334:1583-1590, 1996
4. Hale TW, Ilett KF, Hackett P. Personnal communication, 2002.

GADOPENTETATE

Trade: Magnevist, Gadolinium
Can/Aus/UK: Magnevist
Uses: Radiocontrast agent (MRI)
AAP: Approved by the American Academy of Pediatrics for use in breastfeeding mothers

Gadopentetate is a radiopaque agent used in magnetic resonance imaging of the kidney. It is nonionic, non-iodinated and has low osmolarity and contains a gadolinium ion as the radiopaque entity. Following a dose of 7 mmol (6.5 gm), the amount of gadopentetate secreted in breastmilk was 3.09, 2.8, 1.08, and 0.5 μmol/L at 2, 11, 17, and 24 hours respectively.[1] The cumulative amount excreted from both breasts in 24 hours was only 0.023% of the administered dose. Oral absorption is minimal, only 0.8% of gadopentetate is absorbed. These authors suggest that only 0.013 micromole of a gadolinium-containing compound would be absorbed by the infant in 24 hours, which is incredibly low. They further suggest that 24 hours of pumping would eliminate risks, although this seems rather extreme in view of the short (1.6 hour) half-life, poor oral bioavailability, and limited milk levels.

In another study of 19 lactating women who received 0.1 mmol/kg and one additional woman who received 0.2 mmol/kg the cumulative amount of gadolinium excreted in breastmilk during 24 hours was 0.57 μmol.[2] This resulted in an excreted dose of < 0.04% of the I.V. administered maternal dose. A similar amount was noted in the patient receiving a double dose (0.2 mmol/kg). Thus for any neonate weighing more than 1000 gm, the maximal orally ingested dose would be less than 1% of the permitted intravenous dose of 0.2 mmol/kg. According to the authors, "that the very small amount of gadopentetate dimeglumine transferred to a nursing infant does not warrant a potentially traumatic 24-hour suspension of breast feeding for lactating women."

Pregnancy Risk Category: C

Lactation Risk Category: L2

Theoretic Infant Dose: 0.4 mg/kg/day

Adult Concerns: Headache, rash, nausea, dry mouth, altered taste.

Pediatric Concerns: Virtually none enters milk. No reported side-effects via milk.

Drug Interactions:

Alternatives:

Adult Dosage:

T½ = 1.6 hours	M/P =
PHL =	PB =
PK = Immediate((V)	Oral = 0.8%
MW = 938	pKa =
Vd =	

References:
1. Rofsky NM, et.al. Quantitative analysis of gadopentetate dimeglumine secreted in breast milk. J. Magnetic Resonance Imaging. 3:131, 1993.
2. Kubik-Huch RA, Gottstein-Aalame NM, Frenzel T, Seifert B, Puchert E, Wittek S, Debatin JF. Gadopentetate dimeglumine excretion into human breast milk during lactation. Radiology. 216(2):555-8, 2000.

GADOTERIDOL

Trade: Prohance
Can/Aus/UK: Prohance
Uses: Radiocontrast agent for MRI
AAP: Not reviewed

Gadoteridol is a nonionic, non-iodinated gadolinium chelate complex used as a radiocontrast agent in MRI scans. The metabolism of gadoteridol is unknown, but a similar gadolinium salt (gadopentetate) is not metabolized at all.[1] The half-life is brief (1.6 hours) and the volume of distribution is very small, suggesting that gadoteridol does not penetrate tissues well, and is unlikely to penetrate milk in significant quantities. A similar compound, gadopentetate, is barely detectable in breastmilk. Although not reported, the oral bioavailability is probably similar to gadopentetate, which is minimal to none. No data are available on the transfer of gadoteridol into human milk, although it is probably minimal. A brief interruption of breastfeeding for 12-24 hours should remove risk, although it is may not be necessary.

Pregnancy Risk Category: C

Lactation Risk Category: L3

Theoretic Infant Dose:

Adult Concerns: Nausea, bad taste, headache, rash, urticaria, chest pain rarely.

Pediatric Concerns: None reported via milk.

Drug Interactions:

Alternatives: Gadopentetate

Adult Dosage: 0.2-0.4 mL/kg X 2

T½ = 1.6 hours	**M/P =**
PHL =	PB =
PK =	Oral = Poor
MW =	pKa =
Vd = 0.2	

References:
1. Pharmaceutical Manufacturers package insert, 1997.

GALLIUM-67 CITRATE

Trade: Gallium-67 Citrate
Can/Aus/UK:
Uses: Radioactive isotope
AAP: Radioactive compound that requires temporary cessation of breastfeeding.

Gallium-67 Citrate is a radioactive substance used for bone scanning. In one breastfeeding mother who received 3 mCi, the radioactive content in breastmilk was 0.15, 0.045, and 0.01 μCi/mL at 3, 7, and 14 days respectively.[1] If the infant ingested milk, the whole body exposure would have been very significant, 1.4-2.0 rad/mCi. This is significantly more than the mother's exposure of only 0.26 rad/mCi. Therefore, a significant radioactive hazard exists. Whole body scans showed intense radiation in the breast tissue of the mother. With a 14 day waiting period, the theoretical whole body dose to the infant would be 0.04 rads and 0.07 rads to the skeleton. Radioactive half-life of Gallium-67 is 78.3 hours, while the biological half-life of the gallium ion is 9 days. These approximations suggest that breastfeeding should be interrupted for a minimum of 1 week following a dose of 0.2 mCi, 2 weeks for 1.3 mCi, or 1 month for 4 mCi. Check the NRC guidelines in the appendix.

Pregnancy Risk Category:

Lactation Risk Category: L4

Theoretic Infant Dose:

Adult Concerns:

Pediatric Concerns: Significant radiation exposure. Remove from breast for 14 days.

Drug Interactions:

Alternatives:

Adult Dosage: 200 mg/sq. meter I.V. daily

T½ = 78.3 hours	**M/P =**
PHL =	**PB =**
PK =	**Oral =**
MW =	**pKa =**
Vd =	

References:
1. Tobin, R. and Schneider, P. Uptake of 67-Ga in the lactating breast and its persistence in milk: a case report.. J. Nucl. Med. 17: 1055-56, 1976.

GARLIC

Trade: Allium, Stinkin Rose, Rustic Treacle, Camphor Of The Poor
Can/Aus/UK:
Uses: Herbal antioxidant
AAP: Not reviewed

Garlic contains a number of sulfur-containing compounds, which when ground, are metabolized to allicin, which is responsible for the pungent odor of garlic, and the pharmacologic effects attributed to garlic.[1,2] Garlic has been reported to increase the levels of important plasma antioxidants, glutathione and catalase, probably due to the allicin content. Five sulfur containing compounds have been isolated which produce profound inhibition of lipid peroxidation in liver cells. A number of studies have found hypolipidemic effects of garlic oil, reducing plasma cholesterol, triglyceride levels and elevating HDL levels significantly. Garlic oil also inhibits platelet aggregation, thus reducing risk of thrombosis. Taken together, there is significant evidence to suggest that garlic oil may reduce the risks of cardiovascular disease, reducing plasma lipids, and reducing the risk of clot formation. Garlic is known to be modestly antimicrobial, having about 1% of the antimicrobial potency of penicillin. Interestingly, the hypolipidemic and antimicrobial properties appear to reside in the oviferous constituents, and may not be present in the "deodorized" oils.

Although garlic oil is commonly used, the safety for long term use is still unresolved. The extract has caused a reduction in liver and kidney protein in animal studies, and a potential interaction with other anticoagulants (warfarin) should be expected. Transfer of the odorous components in human milk has been documented.[3,4]

Pregnancy Risk Category:

Lactation Risk Category: L3

Theoretic Infant Dose:

Adult Concerns: Few reported, but observe for excessive bleeding.

Pediatric Concerns: None reported.

Drug Interactions: May enhance anticoagulant effects of warfarin.

Alternatives:

Adult Dosage:

References:
1. Bissett NG. In: Herbal Drugs and Phytopharmaceuticals. Medpharm Scientific Publishers, CRC Press, Boca Raton, 1994.
2. Review of Natural Products. Facts and Comparisons, St. Louis, Mo. 1996.
3. Mennella JA, Beauchamp GK. Maternal diet alters the sensory qualities

of human milk and the nursling's behavior. Pediatrics. 88(4):737-44, 1991.

4.   Mennella JA, Beauchamp GK. The effects of repeated exposure to garlic-flavored milk on the nursling's behavior. Pediatr Res. 34(6):805-8, 1993.

GATIFLOXACIN

Trade: Tequin
Can/Aus/UK:
Uses: Fluoroquinolone antibiotic
AAP: Not reviewed

Gatifloxacin is a fluoroquinolone antibiotic similar to ofloxacin, levofloxacin and ciprofloxacin. As such its use in pediatric age patients is not generally recommended. While the manufacturer reports that gatifloxacin is secreted into animal milk, no data are available on humans. Of the numerous fluoroquinolone antibiotics, ofloxacin[1] and levofloxacin are probably preferred in breastfeeding patients due to lower milk levels. The only major risk to an infant is a change in gut flora and the possibility of overgrowth of C. Difficile (pseudomembranous colitis). If used, observe for bloody diarrhea.

Pregnancy Risk Category: C

Lactation Risk Category: L3

Theoretic Infant Dose:

Adult Concerns: Diarrhea, nausea, vaginitis, headache, dizziness, allergic reaction, chills, fever, palpitations, abdominal pain and other symptoms have been reported. CNS agitation, nervousness, insomnia, and paranoia have been reported. Hypo and hyperglycemia have been reported in diabetic patients.

Pediatric Concerns: None reported via milk, but no studies yet.

Drug Interactions: Probenecid may increase plasma levels of gatifloxacin by 42%. Absorption of gatifloxacin is reduced by concomitant administration with ferrous sulfate, or antacids containing aluminum and magnesium salts. A minor increase in digoxin plasma levels has been reported.

Alternatives: Ofloxacin, Levofloxacin

Adult Dosage: 400 mg daily

T½ = **7.1 hours**	**M/P** =
PHL =	**PB** = **20%**
PK = **1-2 hours**	**Oral** = **96%**
MW = **402**	**pKa** =
Vd = **1.5**	

References:
1. Giamarellou H, Kolokythas E, Petrikkos G, et.al. Pharmacokinetics of three newer quinolones in pregnant and lactating women. Amer. Jour. of Med. 87:5A-49S-51S, 1989.

GEMFIBROZIL

Trade: Lopid, Gemcor
Can/Aus/UK: Apo-Gemfibrozil, Ausgem, Gemhexal, Lopid
Uses: Antilipemic agent
AAP: Not reviewed

Gemfibrozil is a hypolipidemic agent primarily used to lower triglyceride levels by decreasing serum very low density lipoproteins. A slight reduction in serum cholesterol may likewise occur. Following a dose of 800 mg mean peak plasma levels were 33 $\mu g/mL$. There are no data on its transfer into human milk. Reproductive studies in rodents at high doses have not revealed any evidence of harm to the fetus. But the risks of using lipid lowering drugs while pregnant, and probably while breastfeeding, may be higher than the overall risks of hyperlipidemia, and therefore are not usually justified.

Pregnancy Risk Category: C

Lactation Risk Category: L3

Theoretic Infant Dose:

Adult Concerns: Epigastric pain, dry mouth, constipation, diarrhea and flatulence. Changes in blood chemistry including hematocrit, white blood cells, hemoglobin. Elevation of liver enzymes.

Pediatric Concerns: None reported via milk, but risk vs benefit evaluation is recommended.

Drug Interactions: Stimulation of anticoagulants including Anisindione, dicoumarol, warfarin. Increased risk of myopathy when coadministered with HMG-CoA reductase inhibitors such as atorvastatin, fluvastatin, and other statins. Increased risk of hypoglycemia when used with glyburide, and perhaps other hypoglycemics.

Alternatives:

Adult Dosage: 600 mg BID

T½ = 1.5 hours	M/P =
PHL =	PB = 99%
PK = 1-2 hours	Oral = 97%
MW = 250	pKa =
Vd =	

References:
1.   McEvoy GE(ed):AFHS Drug Information, New York, NY. 1999.

GENTAMICIN

Trade: Garamycin
Can/Aus/UK: Alocomicin, Cidomycin, Garamycin, Garatec, Palacos, Septopal
Uses: Aminoglycoside antibiotic
AAP: Not reviewed

Gentamicin is a narrow spectrum antibiotic generally used for gram negative infections. The oral absorption of gentamicin (<1%) is generally nil with exception of premature neonates where small amounts may be absorbed.[1] In one study of 10 women given 80 mg three times daily IM for 5 days postpartum, milk levels were measured on day 4.[2] Gentamicin levels in milk were 0.42, 0.48, 0.49, and 0.41 mg/L at 1, 3, 5, and 7 hours respectively. The milk/plasma ratios were 0.11 at one hour and 0.44 at 7 hours. Plasma gentamicin levels in neonates were small, were found in only 5 of the 10 neonates, and averaged 0.41 μg/ml. The authors estimate that daily ingestion via breastmilk would be 307 ug for a 3.6 kg neonate (normal neonatal dose = 2.5 mg/kg every 12 hours). These amounts would be clinically irrelevant in most infants.

Pregnancy Risk Category: C

Lactation Risk Category: L2

Theoretic Infant Dose: 73.5 μg/kg/day

Adult Concerns: Changes in GI flora, diarrhea, kidney damage, etc.

Pediatric Concerns: None reported.

Drug Interactions: Increased toxicity when used with certain penicillins, cephalosporins, amphotericin B, loop diuretics, and neuromuscular blocking agents.

Alternatives:

Adult Dosage: 1.5-2.5 mg/kg q 8 hours

T½ = 2-3 hours	**M/P = 0.11-0.44**
PHL = 3-5.5 hours(neonates)	**PB = <10-30 %.**
PK = 30-90 min.(IM)	**Oral = < 1%**
MW =	**pKa = 8.2**
Vd = 0.28(adult)	

References:
1.   McCracken, G and Nelson, J. The Current status of gentamicin for the

neonate and young infant. Am. J. Dis. Child. 124:13-14, 1972.
2. Celiloglu M, Celiker S, Guven H, et.al. Gentamicin excretion and uptake from breast milk by nursing infants. Obstet. Gynecol. 84(2):263-5, 1994.

GENTIAN VIOLET

Trade: Crystal Violet, Methylrosaniline Chloride, Gentian Violet
Can/Aus/UK:
Uses: Antifungal, antimicrobial
AAP: Not reviewed

Gentian violet is an older product that when used topically and orally is an exceptionally effective antifungal and antimicrobial.[1] It is a strong purple dye that is difficult to remove. Gentian violet has been found to be equivalent to ketoconazole and far superior to nystatin in treating oral (not esophageal) candidiasis in patients with advanced AIDS.

Gentian violet (GV) solutions generally come as 1-2% Gentian violet dissolved in a 10% solution of alcohol. For use with infants, the solution should be diluted with distilled water to 0.25 to 0.5% Gentian violet. This reduces the irritant properties of GV and reduces the alcohol content as well. While the alcohol is irritating to the nipple, it is not detrimental to the infant.[2] Higher concentrations of GV are known to be very irritating, leading to oral ulceration and necrotic skin reactions in children. If used, a small swab should be soaked in the solution, and then have the baby suck on the swab, or apply it directly to the affected areas in the mouth no more than once or twice daily for no more than 3-7 days. Direct application to the nipple has been reported and is indicated for candidiasis of the nipple.

Pregnancy Risk Category: C

Lactation Risk Category: L3

Theoretic Infant Dose:

Adult Concerns: Oral ulceration, stomatitis, staining of skin and clothing, nausea, vomiting, diarrhea.

Pediatric Concerns: Irritation leading to buccal ulcerations and necrotic skin reactions if used excessively and in higher concentrations. Nausea, vomiting, diarrhea.

Drug Interactions:

Alternatives:

Adult Dosage: N/A

T½ =		M/P =	
PHL =		PB =	
PK =		Oral =	
MW = 408		pKa =	
Vd =			

References:
1.   McEvoy GE(ed): AHFS Drug information, New York, NY. 1995.
2.   Newman J. Personal communication, 1997.

GINKGO BILOBA

Trade: Ginko
Can/Aus/UK:
Uses: Herbal antioxidant
AAP: Not reviewed

Ginkgo Biloba is the world's oldest living tree. Extracts of the leaves (GBE) contain numerous chemical compounds including dimeric flavones and their glycosides, amino acids such as 6-hydroxyknurenic acid, and numerous other compounds. The seeds contain ginkgotoxin, which is particularly toxic, and should not be consumed. Numerous studies reviewing gingko have been reported, including treatments for cerebral insufficiency, asthma, dementia and circulatory disorders. Gingko appears particularly efficient at increasing cerebral blood flow, with increases varying from 20-70%.[1,2]   Older patients were more responsive. This supports the clinical use of GBE to treat cognitive impairment in the elderly. The anxiolytic properties of GBE have been reported to be due to MAO inhibition in animal studies. Ginkgolides inhibit platelet-activating factor and is believed responsible for the anti-allergic and anti-asthmatic properties of this extract.   No data are available on the transfer of GBE into human milk.   Thus far, with exception of the seeds, GBE appears relatively non-toxic.

Pregnancy Risk Category:

Lactation Risk Category: L3

Theoretic Infant Dose:

Adult Concerns: Headache, dizziness, heart palpitations, GI symptoms, dermatologic reactions.

Pediatric Concerns: None reported via human milk.

Drug Interactions:

Alternatives:

Adult Dosage:

References:

1.   Review of Natural Products. Facts and Comparisons, St. Louis, Mo. 1998.
2.   Newall CA, Anderson LA, Phillipson JD. In: Herbal Medicines, A guide for the Health-care Professionals, The Pharmaceutical Press, London, 1996.

GINSENG

Trade: Panax
Can/Aus/UK: Minomycin, Red Kooga
Uses: Herbal tonic
AAP: Not reviewed

Ginseng is perhaps the most popular and widely recognized product in the herbal remedy market. It is available in many forms, but the most common is the American root called Panax quinquefolium L. The root primarily contains steroid-like saponin glycosides (ginsenosides), of which there are at least two dozen and vary as a function of species, age, location, and season when harvested.[1]

Early claims have suggested that ginseng provided "strengthening" effects, and included increased mental capacity for work. Animal studies have suggested that ginseng can increase swimming time, prevent stress-induced ulcers, stimulate certain immune cells, etc. A number of studies, mostly small and poorly controlled, have been reported and many suggest beneficial effects of ingesting ginseng, with minimal side effects. Reported toxicities have included estrogen-like effects including diffuse mammary nodularity, vaginal bleeding, etc.[2] The most commonly reported event is nervousness, excitation, morning diarrhea, and inability to concentrate. In one case report, germanium, an ingredient in ginseng preparations, produced a significant diuretic resistance.[3] No data was found concerning transfer into human milk. It is recommended that it not be used for more than 6 weeks.[4]

Pregnancy Risk Category:

Lactation Risk Category: L3

Theoretic Infant Dose:

Adult Concerns: Excitement, nervousness, inability to concentrate, diarrhea, skin eruptions, hypertension, hypoglycemia, mammary nodularity. Ginseng products sometimes contain germanium, which can induce a state of severe loop-diuretic resistance.

Pediatric Concerns: None reported, but caution is urged.

Drug Interactions:

Alternatives:

Adult Dosage:

References:

1. Review of Natural Products. Facts and Comparisons, St. Louis, Mo. 1996.
2. Bissett NG. In: Herbal Drugs and Phytopharmaceuticals. Medpharm Scientific Publishers, CRC Press, Boca Raton, 1994.
3. Becker BN, Green J, et.al. ginseng induced diuretic resistance. JAMA Aug 28:276, 1996.
4. The Complete German Commission E Monographs. Ed. M. Blumenthal. Amer. Botanical Council, Austin, Tx. 1998.

GLATIRAMER

Trade: Copaxone
Can/Aus/UK:
Uses: Relapsing multiple sclerosis
AAP: Not reviewed

Glatiramer is a synthetic polypeptide indicated for the treatment of relapsing, remitting multiple sclerosis. It is primarily indicated for those who do not respond to interferons. Glatiramer is a mixture of random polymers of four amino acids, L-alanine, L-glutamic acid, L-lysine, and L-tyrosine. Its molecular weight ranges from 4,700 to 13,000 daltons which would reduce its ability to enter milk. It is antigenically similar to myelin basic protein , a natural component of the myelin sheath of neurons. No data are available on its transfer into human milk, but it is unlikely. If ingested orally, it would likely be depolymerized into individual amino acids, so toxicity is unlikely.

Pregnancy Risk Category: B

Lactation Risk Category: L3

Theoretic Infant Dose:

Adult Concerns: Dizziness, chest pain, palpitations, anxiety, hypertonia, sweating, nausea, weakness. Rash, hives, or severe pain where the shot is given

Pediatric Concerns: None via milk.

Drug Interactions:

Alternatives:

Adult Dosage: 20 mg subcutaneously once daily

T½ =	M/P =
PHL=	PB =
PK =	Oral = **Minimal**
MW = **4700+**	pKa =
Vd =	

References:
1. Pharmaceutical manufacturers package insert. 2000.

GLIMEPIRIDE

Trade: Amaryl
Can/Aus/UK:
Uses: Lowers plasma glucose.
AAP: Not reviewed

Glimepiride is a second-generation sulfonylurea used to lower plasma glucose in patients with non-insulin dependent diabetes mellitus. No data are available on the transfer of this product into human milk. However, rodent studies demonstrated significant transfer and elevated plasma levels in pups.[1,2] Caution is urged if used in breastfeeding humans. Observe for hypoglycemia.

Pregnancy Risk Category: B

Lactation Risk Category: L4

Theoretic Infant Dose:

Adult Concerns: Hypoglycemia, nausea, hyponatremia, dizziness, headache, elevated liver enzymes, blurred vision.

Pediatric Concerns: None reported via milk. Observe for hypoglycemia.

Drug Interactions: The hypoglycemic effect of sulfonylureas may be increased by non-steroidal analgesics, salicylates, sulfonamides, coumarins, probenecid, and other drugs with high protein binding. Numerous other interactions exist, see product information.

Alternatives:

Adult Dosage: 1-4 mg daily

T½ = 6-9 hours	M/P =
PHL =	PB = >99.5%
PK = 2-3 hours	Oral = 100%
MW = 490	pKa =
Vd = 0.113	

References:
1. Pharmaceutical manufactures package insert, 1998.
2. Bressler R & Johnson DG: Pharmacological regulation blood glucose levels in non-insulin-dependent diabetes mellitus. Arch Intern Med 157:836-848, 1997.

GLIPIZIDE

Trade: Glucotrol Xl, Glucotrol
Can/Aus/UK: Glibenese, Melizide, Minidiab, Minodiab
Uses: Prolonged release hypoglycemic agent
AAP: Not reviewed

Glipizide is a potent hypoglycemic agent that belongs to sulfonylurea family. It is formulated in regular and extended release formulations and it is used only for non insulin-dependent (Type II) diabetes. Thus the half-life and time-to-peak depends on the formulation used. It reduces glucose levels by stimulating insulin secretion from the pancreas.[1] No reports on transfer into human milk were found. Other sulfonylureas (tolbutamide, chlorpropamide) are known to pass into milk in low concentrations. Although hypoglycemia in infants is a potential problem, no reports of such have been published. AHL= 2-5 hours (Glucotrol), 24 hours (Glucotrol-XL).

Pregnancy Risk Category: C

Lactation Risk Category: L3

Theoretic Infant Dose:

Adult Concerns: Hypoglycemia, jaundice, nausea, vomiting, diarrhea, constipation.

Pediatric Concerns: None reported, but observe for hypoglycemia.

Drug Interactions: The hypoglycemic effect may be enhanced by : anticoagulants, chloramphenicol, clofibrate, fenfluramine, fluconazole, H2 antagonists, magnesium salts, methyldopa, MAO inhibitors, probenecid, salicylates, TCAs, sulfonamides. The hypoglycemic effect may be reduced by: beta blockers, cholestyramine, diazoxide, phenytoin, rifampin, thiazide diuretics.

Alternatives:

Adult Dosage: 15-40 mg QD

T½ = 1.1-3.7 hours.	M/P =
PHL=	PB = 92-99 %
PK = 6-12 hours (XL)	Oral = 80-100%
MW = 446	pKa =
Vd =	

References:
1. Pharmaceutical Manufacturers Package Insert, 1996.

GLUCOSAMINE

Trade: Glucosamine
Can/Aus/UK:
Uses: Antiarthritic
AAP: Not reviewed

Glucosamine is an endogenous aminomonosaccharide that has been reported effective in resolving symptoms of osteoarthritis. Administered in large doses, most is sequestered in the liver with only minimal amounts reaching other tissues, thus oral bioavailability is low. Most of the oral dose is hepatically metabolized and subsequently incorporated into other plasma proteins.[1] No data are available on transfer into human milk. Because glucosamine is primarily sequestered and metabolized in the liver, and because the plasma levels are almost undetectable, it is unlikely that much would enter human milk. Further, because it is poorly bioavailable, it is unlikely that an infant would ingest clinically relevant amounts.

Pregnancy Risk Category:

Lactation Risk Category: L3

Theoretic Infant Dose:

Adult Concerns: Minimal but include nausea, dyspepsia, vomiting, drowsiness, headache and skin rash. Peripheral edema and tachycardia have been reported.

Pediatric Concerns: None reported via milk.

Drug Interactions:

Alternatives:

Adult Dosage:

T½ = 0.3 hours	M/P =
PHL =	PB = 0%
PK =	Oral = < 26%
MW = 179	pKa =
Vd = 0.035	

References:
1. Setnikar I, Palumbo R, Canali S et al: Pharmacokinetics of glucosamine in man. Arzneimittelforschung 43:1109-1113, 1993.

GLYBURIDE

Trade: Micronase, Diabeta, Glynase, Glucovance
Can/Aus/UK: Daonil, Diabeta, Diaformin, Euglucon, Gen-Glybe
Uses: Hypoglycemic, antidiabetic agent
AAP: Not reviewed

Glyburide is a "second generation" sulfonylurea agent useful in the treatment of non insulin-dependent (Type II) diabetes mellitus. It belongs to the sulfonylurea family (tolbutamine, glipizide) of hypoglycemic agents of which glyburide is one of the most potent.[1,2] Glyburide apparently stimulates insulin secretion, thus reducing plasma glucose. Although no data exist on the secretion of glyburide into breastmilk, others in this family are secreted in low levels, and it is likely that this product may attain even lower levels than the first generation family. Glyburide apparently does not even cross the placenta. Although we do not have reports of breastmilk levels, it is likely (theoretical) that breastmilk levels will be very low as well. The product Glucovance contains metformin and glyburide.

Pregnancy Risk Category: B

Lactation Risk Category: L3

Theoretic Infant Dose:

Adult Concerns: Hypoglycemia, headache, anorexia, nausea, heartburn, allergic skin rashes.

Pediatric Concerns: None reported but observe for hypoglycemia, weakness.

Drug Interactions: Thiazide diuretics and beta blockers may decrease efficacy of glyburide. Increased toxicity may result from use with phenylbutazone, oral anticoagulants, hydantoins, salicylates, NSAIDS, sulfonamides. Alcohol increases disulfiram effect.

Alternatives:

Adult Dosage: 1.25-20 mg daily

T½ = 4-13.7 hours	M/P =	
PHL =	PB = 99%	
PK = 2-3 hours	Oral = Complete	
MW = 494	pKa =	
Vd = 0.73		

References:
1. Pharmaceutical Manufacturers Package Insert, 1998.
2. McEvoy GE(ed):AHFS Drug Information, New York, NY. 1995.

GLYCOPYRROLATE

Trade: Robinul
Can/Aus/UK: Robinul
Uses: Anticholinergic
AAP: Not reviewed

Glycopyrrolate is a quaternary ammonium anticholinergic used prior to surgery to dry secretions. After administration, its plasma half-life is exceedingly short (< 5 min.) with most of the product being distribution out of the plasma compartment rapidly.[1,2] No data are available on its transfer into human milk. But due to its short plasma half-life and its quaternary structure, it is very unlikely that significant quantities would penetrate milk. Further, along with the poor oral bioavailability of this product, it is very remote that glycopyrrolate would pose a significant risk to a breastfeeding infant.

Pregnancy Risk Category: B

Lactation Risk Category: L3

Theoretic Infant Dose:

Adult Concerns: Blurred vision, dry mouth, tachycardia.

Pediatric Concerns: None reported via milk.

Drug Interactions: May reduce effect of levodopa. Increased toxicity when used with amantadine and cyclopropane.

Alternatives:

Adult Dosage: 1-2 mg TID

T½ = 1.7 hours	M/P =
PHL=	PB =
PK = 5 hours(oral)	Oral = 10-25%
MW = 398	pKa =
Vd = 0.64	

References:
1. Lacy C. et.al. Drug information handbook. Lexi-Comp, Hudson(Cleveland), Oh. 1996.
2. Drug Facts and Comparisons. 1996. ed. Facts and Comparisons, St. Louis.

GOLD COMPOUNDS

Trade: Ridaura, Myochrysine, Solganal
Can/Aus/UK: Myochrysine, Myocrisin, Ridaura
Uses: Antiarthritic
AAP: Approved by the American Academy of Pediatrics for use in breastfeeding mothers

Gold salts are potent and toxic, anti-inflammatory agents used to treat rheumatoid arthritis. Two injectable forms exist, gold sodium thiomalate (Myochrysine) and sodium aurothioglucose (Solganal). One oral form exists, auranofin (Ridura). The plasma kinetics of the gold salts are highly variable and are difficult to report, but in general, their half-lives are very extended and increase as duration of treatment continues. Auranofin is the only orally available salt form and is approximately 20-25% bioavailable. They are all probably secreted into breastmilk in small quantities.

In a study by Blau [1], milk levels of gold following a cumulative dose of 135 mg ranged from 0.86-0.99 mg/100ml. These are quite high and exceed the data of others.

In one study of a patient receiving Myochrysine, 50 mg/week for 7 weeks, the concentration of gold sodium thiomalate varied from 0.022 to 0.04 mg/L at 66 hours and 7 days post-dose respectively.[2] Although the infant showed no signs or symptoms of toxicity at this time, the authors noted that 3 months after treatment the infant developed transient facial edema of unexplained origin.

Approximately 10% or more of the concentration of gold measured in maternal serum appears in breastmilk. In two patients treated with 50 mg aurothiomalate, levels in milk varied from 27-153 µg/L.[3] Gold is retained in the human body for long periods of time (months). For this reason prolonged exposure of a nursing infant may not be justified.

Pregnancy Risk Category: C

Lactation Risk Category: L5

Theoretic Infant Dose: 23.0 µg/kg/day

Adult Concerns: GI distress, diarrhea, nausea, vomiting, exfoliative dermatitis, nephrotoxicity, proteinuria, and blood dyscrasias.

Pediatric Concerns: Possible facial edema 3 months after therapy. Relationship is questionable.

Drug Interactions: Decreased gold effects with penicillamine and acetylcysteine.

Alternatives:

Adult Dosage: 25-50 mg q week

T½ = 3-26 days	M/P = 0.02-0.3
PHL=	PB = 95%
PK = 3-6 hours(IM)	Oral = 20-25%(auranofin)
MW =	pKa =
Vd = 0.1	

References:
1. Blau SP. Metabolism of gold during lactation. Arthritis Rheum 16:777-778,1973.
2. Bell RAF, and Dale IM. Gold Secretion in maternal milk. Arth. Rheum. 19:1374, `1976.
3. Ostensen M, et.al. Excretion of gold into human breast milk. Eur. J. Clin. Pharmcol. 31:251-2, 1986.

GONADORELIN ACETATE

Trade: Lutrepulse
Can/Aus/UK: Fertiral, Lutrepulse, Wyerth-Ayerst HRF
Uses: Gonadotropin-releasing hormone
AAP: Not reviewed

Gonadorelin is used for the induction of ovulation in anovulatory women with primary hypothalamic amenorrhea. Gonadorelin is a small decapeptide identical to the physiologic GnRH secreted by the hypothalamus which stimulates the pituitary release of luteinizing hormone(LH) and to a lesser degree follicle stimulating hormone (FSH). LH and FSH subsequently stimulate the ovary to produce follicles.

Gonadorelin plasma half-life is very brief (< 2-4 minutes) and it is primarily distributed to the plasma only.[1]   Gonadorelin has been detected in human breastmilk at concentrations of 0.1 to 3 nanograms/mL (adult dose = 20-100 micrograms), although its oral bioavailability in the infant would be minimal to none.[2]

Pregnancy Risk Category: B

Lactation Risk Category: L3

Theoretic Infant Dose: 0.5 μg/kg/day

Adult Concerns: Ovarian hyperstimulation, bronchospasm, tachycardia, flushing, urticaria, induration at injection site.

Pediatric Concerns: None reported via milk.

Drug Interactions:

Alternatives:

Adult Dosage: 1-20 mcg QD

T½ = 2-4 minutes	M/P =
PHL=	PB =
PK =	Oral = None
MW =	pKa =
Vd = 0.14	

References:
1. Reynolds JEF (Ed): Martindale: The Extra Pharmacopoeia (electronic version). Micromedex, Inc, Denver, CO, 1990.
2. Drug Facts and Comparisons. 1996. ed. Facts and Comparisons, St. Louis.

GRANISETRON

Trade: Kytril
Can/Aus/UK:
Uses: Antiemetic
AAP: Not reviewed

Granisetron is an antinauseant and antiemetic agent commonly used with chemotherapy. Following a 1 mg I.V. dose, the peak plasma concentration was only 3.63 ng/mL.[1] No data are available on its transfer into human milk but its levels are likely to be low. Further, this family of products (see ondansetron) are not highly toxic and are commonly used in children(2 years +). It is unlikely that this product will be overtly toxic to a breastfed infant. However, when used with chemotherapeutic agents, long waiting periods should be used for elimination of the chemotherapeutic agents anyway.

Pregnancy Risk Category: B

Lactation Risk Category: L3

Theoretic Infant Dose:

Adult Concerns: Headache, asthenia, somnolence, diarrhea, dyspepsia, abdominal pain, constipation, and fever. Rarely elevations of liver enzymes been reported.

Pediatric Concerns: None reported via milk.

Drug Interactions: Ketoconazole may inhibit the metabolism of granisetron.

Alternatives: Odansetron

Adult Dosage: 2 mg Orally

T½ = 3-14 hours	M/P =
PHL=	PB = 65%
PK = 1 hour	Oral = 60%
MW = 312	pKa =
Vd = 2-4	

References:
1. Pharmaceutical manufacturers package insert, 2002.

GREPAFLOXACIN

Trade: Raxar
Can/Aus/UK: Raxar
Uses: Fluoroquinolone antibiotic
AAP: Not reviewed

Grepafloxacin is a typical fluoroquinolone antibiotic similar to Ciprofloxacin. The manufacturer suggests that grepafloxacin is detectable in human milk after a 400 mg dose, but does not provide the exact levels.[1] Studies in rodents suggest a concentrating mechanism of about 16 times that of the plasma compartment. Because this fluoroquinolone has a rather long half-life, high volume of distribution, the ability to enter many body compartments, and is concentrated in rodent milk, it is probably advisable to use this product with extreme caution, if at all, in breastfeeding women.

Pregnancy Risk Category: C

Lactation Risk Category: L4

Theoretic Infant Dose:

Adult Concerns: Nausea, taste perversion, dizziness, headache, diarrhea, abdominal pain.

Pediatric Concerns: None reported with this product, but diarrhea and pseudomembranous colitis has been reported with ciprofloxacin. Arthropathy has been reported following pediatric use of fluoroquinolones.

Drug Interactions: Decreased absorption with antacids. Quinolones cause increased levels of caffeine, warfarin, cyclosporine, theophylline. Cimetidine, probenecid, azlocillin increase ciprofloxacin levels. Increased risk of seizures when used with foscarnet.

Alternatives: Norfloxacin, Ofloxacin, Levofloxacin, Ciprofloxacin

Adult Dosage: 400-600 mg QD

T½ = **15.7 hours**	M/P =
PHL =	PB = **50%**
PK = **2-3 hours**	Oral = **72%**
MW = **422**	pKa =
Vd = **5.07**	

References:
1. Pharmaceutical Manufacturers Package Insert, 1999.

GRISEOFULVIN

Trade: Fulvicin, Gris-peg
Can/Aus/UK: Fulcin, Fulvicin, Griseostatin, Grisovin, Grisovin-FP
Uses: Antifungal
AAP: Not reviewed

Griseofulvin is an older class antifungal. Much better safety profiles with the newer families of antifungals have reduced the use of griseofulvin. The drug is primarily effective against tinea species and not candida albicans.[1,2] There are no data available for humans. In one study in cows following a dose of 10mg/kg/day for 5 days (human dose => 5 mg/kg/day) milk concentrations were 0.16 mg/L. Although these data cannot be directly extrapolated to humans, they indicate transfer to milk in some species. Oral use in adults is associated with low risk of hepatic cancer. Griseofulvin is still commonly used in pediatric tinea capitis (ringworm) where it is a preferred medication.

Pregnancy Risk Category: C

Lactation Risk Category: L2

Theoretic Infant Dose:

Adult Concerns: Headache, depression, hepatotoxicity, skin rashes, hallucinations. Symptoms of overdose include lethargy, vertigo, blurred vision, nausea, vomiting, and diarrhea.

Pediatric Concerns: None reported from breastmilk.

Drug Interactions: Barbiturates may reduce plasma levels. May inhibit warfarin activity. May reduce effectiveness of oral contraceptives. May produce increased toxicity and tachycardia when used with alcohol.

Alternatives: Fluconazole

Adult Dosage: 500-1000 mg QD (micro) or 330-375 mg daily (ultra)

T½ = 9-24 hours	M/P =
PHL =	PB =
PK = 4-8 hours	Oral = Poor to 50%
MW = 353	pKa =
Vd =	

References:
1. McEvoy GE(ed):AHFS Drug Information, New York, NY. 1995.
2. Hiddeston WA: Antifungal activity of penicillium griseofulvin mycelium. Vet Rec 86:75-76, 1970.

GUAIFENESIN

Trade: GG, Robitussin
Can/Aus/UK: Balminil, Benylin-E, Orthoxicol, Respenyl, Resyl, Robitussin
Uses: Expectorant, loosens respiratory tract secretions
AAP: Not reviewed

Guaifenesin is an expectorant used to irritate the gastric mucosa and stimulate respiratory tract secretions in order to reduce phlegm viscosity. It does not suppress coughing and should not be used in persistent cough such as with smokers. No data are available on transfer into human breastmilk. In general, clinical studies documenting the efficacy of guaifenesin are lacking, and the usefulness of this product as an expectorant is highly questionable.[1] Poor efficacy of these drugs (expectorants in general) would suggest that they do not provide enough justification for use in lactating mothers. But untoward effects have not been reported. Pediatric dose: < 2 years = 12 mg/kg/day in 6 divided doses; 2-5 years = 50-100 mg every 4 hours; 6-11 years = 100-200 mg every 4 hours; Children > 12 years and adults = 200-400 mg every 4 hours for a maximum of 2.4 gm/day. Always dose with large volumes of fluids.

Pregnancy Risk Category: C

Lactation Risk Category: L2

Theoretic Infant Dose:

Adult Concerns: Vomiting, diarrhea, nausea, sedation, skin rash, GI dyspepsia.

Pediatric Concerns: None reported.

Drug Interactions:

Alternatives:

Adult Dosage: 200-400 mg q 4 hours

T½ = < 7 hours.	M/P =
PHL =	PB =
PK =	Oral = Complete
MW = 198	pKa =
Vd = 1.0	

References:
1. Lacy C. et.al. Drug information handbook. Lexi-Comp, Hudson(Cleveland), Oh. 1996.

GUANFACINE

Trade: Tenex
Can/Aus/UK:
Uses: Antihypertensive
AAP: Not reviewed

Guanfacine is a centrally acting antihypertensive that stimulates alpha-2 adrenergic receptors (similar to Clonidine). Studies in animals indicate that guanfacine is secreted into milk (M:P ratio = 0.75), but human studies are lacking.[1,2] Because this product has a low molecular weight (246), a high volume of distribution 6.3 L/kg), and penetrates the CNS at high levels, it is likely to penetrate milk at significant levels. Caution is urged.

Pregnancy Risk Category: B

Lactation Risk Category: L3

Theoretic Infant Dose:

Adult Concerns: Bradycardia, hypotension, dry mouth, sedation, weakness, constipation.

Pediatric Concerns: None reported but observe for hypotension, sedation, weakness.

Drug Interactions: Decreased hypotensive effect when used with tricyclic antidepressants. Increased effect when used with other antihypertensive agents.

Alternatives:

Adult Dosage: 1 mg QD

T½ = 17 hours	M/P =
PHL =	PB = 20-30%
PK = 2.6 hours	Oral = 81-100%
MW = 246	pKa =
Vd = 6.3	

References:
1. Pharmaceutical Manufacturers Package Insert, 1995.
2. Lacy C. et.al. Drug information handbook. Lexi-Comp, Hudson (Cleveland), Oh. 1996.

HAEMOPHILUS B CONJUGATE VACCINE

Trade: Hibtiter, Haemophilus B Vaccine
Can/Aus/UK: Act-HIB, HibTiter, PedvaxHIB
Uses: H. influenza Vaccine
AAP: Not reviewed

Hib Vaccine is a purified capsular polysaccharide vaccine made from haemophilus influenza bacteria. It is non-infective. It is currently recommended for initial immunizations in children at 2 months, and at 2 month intervals, for a total of 3 injections.[1] A booster is recommended at 12-15 months. Although there are no reasons for administering to adult mothers, it would not be contraindicated in breastfeeding mothers.

Pregnancy Risk Category: C

Lactation Risk Category: L3

Theoretic Infant Dose:

Adult Concerns: Itching, skin rash, injection site reaction, vomiting, fever. Few anaphylactoid-type reaction.

Pediatric Concerns: Itching, skin rash, injection site reaction, vomiting, fever. Few anaphylactoid-type reaction.

Drug Interactions: Decreased immunogenicity when used with immunosuppressive agents. Using immunoglobulins with 1 month may decrease antibody production.

Alternatives:

Adult Dosage:

References:
1. Pharmaceutical Manufacturers Package Insert, 1996.

HALAZEPAM

Trade: Paxipam
Can/Aus/UK:
Uses: Benzodiazepine antianxiety drug
AAP: Not reviewed

Halazepam is a benzodiazepine (Valium family) used to treat anxiety disorders. Halazepam is metabolized to desmethyldiazepam, which has an elimination half-life of 50-100 hours.[1] Although no information is available on halazepam levels in human milk, it should be similar to diazepam. See diazepam.

Pregnancy Risk Category: D

Lactation Risk Category: L3

Theoretic Infant Dose:

Adult Concerns: Sedation, bradycardia, euphoria, disorientation, confusion, nausea, constipation, hypotension.

Pediatric Concerns: None reported, but see diazepam.

Drug Interactions:

Alternatives: Alprazolam, Lorazepam

Adult Dosage: 20-40 mg TID-QID

T½ = 14 hours.	M/P =
PHL=	PB = High
PK = 1-3 hours	Oral = Complete
MW = 353	pKa =
Vd = 1.0	

References:

1.   Drug Facts and Comparisons. 1995 ed. Facts and Comparisons, St. Louis.

HALOPERIDOL

Trade: Haldol

Can/Aus/UK: Apo-Haloperidol, Haldol, Novo-Peridol, Peridol, Serenace

Uses: Antipsychotic

AAP: Drug whose effect on nursing infants is unknown but may be of concern

Haloperidol is a potent antipsychotic agent than is reported to increase prolactin levels in some patients.   In one study of a woman treated for puerperal hypomania and receiving 5 mg twice daily, the concentration of haloperidol in milk was 0.0, 23.5, 18.0, and 3.25 μg/L on day 1, 6, 7 and 21 respectively.[1]   The corresponding maternal plasma levels were 0, 40, 26, and 4 μg/L at day 1, 6, 7, and 21 respectively.   The milk/plasma ratios were 0.58, 0.69, and 0.81 on days 6, 7, and 21 respectively.   After 4 weeks of therapy the infant showed no symptoms of sedation and was feeding well.

In another study after a mean daily dose of 29.2 mg, the concentration of haloperidol in breastmilk was 5 μg/L at 11 hours post-dose.[2] In a study of 3 women on chronic haloperidol therapy receiving 3, 4, and 6 mg daily, milk levels were reported to be 32, 17, and 4.7 ng/mL.[3] The latter levels(4.7 ng) were taken from a patient believed to be noncompliant.

Bennett calculates the relative infant dose to be 0.2-2.1% to 9.6% of the weight-adjusted maternal daily dose.[4]

Pregnancy Risk Category: C

Lactation Risk Category: L2

Theoretic Infant Dose: 3.5 μg/kg/day

Adult Concerns: Extrapyramidal symptoms, sedation, anemia, tachycardia, hypotension.

Pediatric Concerns: None reported via milk. Observe for sedation, weakness.

Drug Interactions: Carbamazepine may increase metabolism and decrease effectiveness of haloperidol. CNS depressants may increase adverse effects. Epinephrine may cause hypotension. Concurrent use with lithium has caused acute encephalopathy syndromes.

Alternatives:

Adult Dosage: 0.5-5 mg BID-TID

T½ = 12-38 hours	M/P = 0.58-0.81
PHL =	PB = 92%
PK = 2-6 hours	Oral = 60%
MW = 376	pKa = 8.3
Vd = 18-30	

References:
1. Whalley LJ, et. al. Haloperidol secreted in breast milk. Br Med J 282:1746-7, 1981.
2. Stewart RB, et. al. Haloperidol excretion in human milk. Am J Psychiatry 137:849-50, 1980.
3. Ohkubo T, Shimoyama R, Sugawara K. Measurement of haloperidol in human breast milk by high-performance liquid chromatography. J Pharm Sci 81(9):947-9, 1992.
4. Bennett PN: Use of the monographs on drugs. In: Drugs and Human Lactation. Amsterdam, Elsevier; 1996:442-443.

HALOTHANE

Trade: Fluothane
Can/Aus/UK: Fluothane
Uses: Anesthetic gas
AAP: Approved by the American Academy of Pediatrics for use in breastfeeding mothers

Halothane is an anesthetic gas similar to enflurane, methoxyflurane, and isoflurane. Approximately 60-80% is rapidly eliminated by exhalation the first 24 hours postoperative, and only 15% is actually metabolized by the liver. Cote (1976) reviewed the secretion of halothane in breastmilk. After a 3 hour surgery, only 2 ppm was detected in milk. At another exposure in one week, only 0.83 and 1.9 ppm were found. The authors assessed the exposure to the infant as negligible.

Halothane is probably stored in the adipose tissue and eliminated for several days. There is no available information on the oral bioavailability of halothane. Pumping and dumping milk the first 24 hours postoperatively is generally recommended, but is probably unnecessary.

Pregnancy Risk Category: C

Lactation Risk Category: L2

Theoretic Infant Dose:

Adult Concerns: Nausea, vomiting, sedation, transient hepatotoxicity.

Pediatric Concerns: None reported.

Drug Interactions: When used with rifampin, or phenytoin, may have increased risk of hepatotoxicity.

Alternatives:

Adult Dosage:

T½ =	M/P =
PHL =	PB =
PK = 10-20 min.	Oral =
MW = 197	pKa =
Vd = 1	

References:
1. Cote CJ, Kenepp NB, Reed SB, Strobel GE. Trace concentrations of halothane in human breast milk. Br J Anaesth. Jun;48(6):541-3, 1976.

HCTZ +TRIAMTERENE

Trade: Dyrenium, Maxzide
Can/Aus/UK: Dyazide, Hydrene, Novo-Triamzide
Uses: Diuretic
AAP: Not reviewed

Numerous diuretic products contain varying combinations of hydrochlorothiazide (HCTZ) and triamterene. For specifics on HCTZ, see the monograph on hydrochlorothiazide. Triamterene is a potassium sparing diuretic. Following a dose of 100-200 mg, it attains plasma levels in adults of 26-30 ng/mL.[1] It is secreted in small amounts in cow's milk but no human data are available. Assuming a high milk/plasma ratio of one, an infant ingesting 125 ml/kg/day would theoretically ingest less than 4 μg/kg/day, an amount unlikely to provide clinical problems.

Pregnancy Risk Category: B

Lactation Risk Category: L3

Theoretic Infant Dose:

Adult Concerns: Diarrhea, nausea, vomiting, hepatitis, leukopenia, hyperkalemia.

Pediatric Concerns: None reported. Hyperkalemia.

Drug Interactions: Increased risk of hyperkalemia when given with amiloride, spironolactone, and ACE inhibitors. Increased risk of toxicity with amantadine.

Alternatives:

Adult Dosage: 25-50 mg HCTZ (37.5-75 mg Triamterene) QD

T½ = 1.5-2.5 hours	M/P =
PHL =	PB = 55%
PK = 1.5-3 hours	Oral = 30-70%
MW = 253	pKa = 6.2
Vd =	

References:
1. Pharmaceutical Manufacturers Package Insert, 1998.

HEPARIN

Trade: Heparin
Can/Aus/UK: Canusal, Hepalean, Heplok, Pularin
Uses: Anticoagulant
AAP: Not reviewed

Heparin is a large protein molecule.[1] It is used SC, IM and I.V. because it is not absorbed orally in mother or infant. Due to its high molecular weight (40,000 Daltons), it is unlikely any would transfer into breastmilk. Any that did enter the milk would be rapidly destroyed in the gastric contents of the infant.

Pregnancy Risk Category: C

Lactation Risk Category: L1

Theoretic Infant Dose:

Adult Concerns: Hemorrhage.

Pediatric Concerns: None reported via milk.

Drug Interactions: Increased toxicity with NSAIDS, aspirin, dipyridamole, hydroxychloroquine.

Alternatives:

Adult Dosage: 4,000-5,000 units q 4 hours

T½ = 1-2 hours	M/P =
PHL=	PB =
PK = 20 min.	Oral = None
MW = 30000	pKa =
Vd =	

References:
1.   McEvoy GE(ed):AHFS Drug Information, New York, NY. 1995.

HEPATITIS A INFECTION

Trade:
Can/Aus/UK:
Uses: Hepatitis A infection
AAP: Approved by the American Academy of Pediatrics for use in breastfeeding mothers

Hepatitis A is an acute viral infection characterized by jaundice, fever, anorexia, and malaise. In infants, the syndrome is either asymptomatic or causes only mild nonspecific symptoms.[1]   Current therapy recommended following exposure to Hepatitis A is an injection of gamma globulin. A majority of the population is immune to Hepatitis A due to prior exposure.   Fulminant hepatitis A infection is rare in children and a carrier state is unknown. It is spread through fecal-oral contact and can be spread in day care centers. Viral shedding continues from onset up to 3 weeks. Unless the mother is jaundiced and acutely ill, breastfeeding can continue without interruption.[2]   Proper hygiene should be stressed.   Protect infant with IM gamma globulin.

Pregnancy Risk Category:

Lactation Risk Category:

Theoretic Infant Dose:

Adult Concerns: Jaundice, fever, malaise.

Pediatric Concerns: None reported. Protect with gamma globulin injection.

Drug Interactions:

Alternatives:

Adult Dosage:

References:
1. American Academy of Pediatrics. Committee on Infectious Diseases. Red Book 1997.
2. Gartner L (personal communication) 1997.

HEPATITIS A VACCINE

Trade: Havrix
Can/Aus/UK: Havrix, Vaqta
Uses: Vaccine
AAP: Not reviewed

Hepatitis A vaccine is an inactivated, noninfectious viral vaccination for Hepatitis A. Although there is no specific data on the use of Hepatitis A vaccine in breastfeeding women, Hepatitis A vaccine can be used in pregnant women after 14 weeks, and in children 2 years of age.[1,2] There is little likelihood that Hepatitis A vaccinations in breastfeeding women would cause untoward effects in breastfed infants.

Pregnancy Risk Category: C

Lactation Risk Category: L3

Theoretic Infant Dose:

Adult Concerns: Lymphadenopathy. Headache, insomnia, vertigo, fatigue and malaise, fever, anorexia and nausea, photophobia, injection-site soreness.

Pediatric Concerns: None reported via milk.

Drug Interactions:

Alternatives:

Adult Dosage: 1 mL X 2 over 6-12 months

References:
1. Drug Facts and Comparisons. 1997. ed. Facts and Comparisons, St. Louis.
2. Pharmaceutical Manufacturers Package Insert, 1997.

HEPATITIS B IMMUNE GLOBULIN

Trade: H-BIG, Hep-b-Gammagee, Hyperhep
Can/Aus/UK:
Uses: Anti-Hepatitis B Immune globulins
AAP:

HBIG is a sterile solution of immunoglobulin (10-18% protein) containing a high titer of antibody to hepatitis B surface antigen.[1] It is most commonly used as prophylaxis therapy for infants born to hepatitis B surface antigen positive mothers. The carrier state can be prevented in about 75% of such infections in newborns given HBIG immediately after birth. HBIG is generally administered to infants from HBsAg positive mothers who wish to breastfeed. The prophylactic dose for newborns is 0.5 ml IM (thigh) as soon after birth as possible, preferably with 1 hour.[2] The infant should also be immunized with Hepatitis B vaccine (0.5 mL IM) within 12 hours of birth (use separate site), and again at 1 and 6 months.

Pregnancy Risk Category: C

Lactation Risk Category:

Theoretic Infant Dose:

Adult Concerns: Pain at injection site, erythema, rash. Dizziness, malaise.

Pediatric Concerns: Pain at injection site, erythema, rash.

Drug Interactions:

Alternatives:

Adult Dosage: 0.06 ml/kg post-exposure X 3 over 6 weeks

T½ =	M/P =
PHL =	PB =
PK = 1-6 days	Oral = None
MW =	pKa =
Vd =	

References:
1. Pharmaceutical Manufacturers Package Insert, 1995.
2. Lawrence RA. Breastfeeding, A guide for the medical profession. Mosby, St. Louis, 1994.

HEPATITIS B INFECTION

Trade: Hepatitis B Infection
Can/Aus/UK:
Uses: Hepatitis B exposure.
AAP: Not reviewed

Hepatitis B virus (HBV) causes a wide spectrum of infections, ranging from a mild asymptomatic form to a fulminant fatal hepatitis. Mild asymptomatic illness is most common in pediatric patients, although the chronic infectious state occurs in as many as 90% of infants who become infected by perinatal transmission. Chronically infected individuals are at increased risk for chronic liver diseases and liver cancer in later life. HBV is transmitted through blood or body fluids. Hepatitis B antigen has been detected in breastmilk.[1-3]

Infants of mothers who are HBV positive (HBsAg) should be given Hepatitis immune globulin (HBIG) (preferably within 1 hour of birth) and a Hepatitis B vaccination AT BIRTH which is believed to effectively reduce the risk of post-natal transmission, particularly via breastmilk.[4] Inject in different sites. Thus far, several older studies have indicated that breastfeeding poses no additional risk of transmission, and thus far no cases of horizontal transmission of Hepatitis B via breastmilk have been reported.

Pregnancy Risk Category:

Lactation Risk Category:

Theoretic Infant Dose:

Adult Concerns: Hepatitis, increased risk of liver cancer.

Pediatric Concerns: None reported if immunized with HBIG and HB vaccination.

Drug Interactions:

Alternatives:

Adult Dosage:

References:
1. Boxall EH, Flewett TH, Dane DS et.al. Hepatitis-B surface antigen in breast milk. Lancet 2:1007-8, 1974.
2. Beasley RP, Shiao I-S, Stevens CE et.al. Evidence against breast-feeding as a mechanism for vertical transmission of hepatitis B. Lancet 2:740-1, 1975.
3. Woo D, Cummins M, et.al. Vertical transmission of hepatitis B surface antigen in carrier mothers, in two west London hospitals. Arch Dis. Child 54:670-5, 1979.
4. American Academy of Pediatrics. Committee on Infectious Diseases. Red Book 1994.

HEPATITIS B VACCINE

Trade: Heptavax-b, Engerix-b, Recombivax Hb
Can/Aus/UK:
Uses: Hepatitis B vaccination
AAP: Not reviewed

Hepatitis B vaccine is an inactivated non-infectious hepatitis B surface antigen vaccine. It can be used in pediatric patients at birth. No data are available on its use in breastfeeding mothers, but it is unlikely to produce untoward effects on a breastfeeding infant. Hepatitis B vaccination is approximately 80-95% effective in preventing acute hepatitis B infections.[1,2] It requires at least 3 immunizations and the immunity lasts about 5-7 years. In infants born of HB surface antigen positive mothers, the American Academy of Pediatrics recommends hepatitis B vaccine (along with HBIG) should be administered to the infant within 1-12 hours of birth (0.5 mL IM) and again at 1 and 6 months. If so administered, breastfeeding poses no additional risk for acquisition of HBV by the infant.

Pregnancy Risk Category: C

Lactation Risk Category:

Theoretic Infant Dose:

Adult Concerns: Pain at injection site, swelling, erythema, fever.

Pediatric Concerns: Fever, malaise, fatigue when directly injected. None reported via breastmilk.

Drug Interactions: Immunosuppressive agents would decrease effect.

Alternatives:

Adult Dosage: 20 mcg each for three injections over 7 months

References:
1. Pharmaceutical Manufacturers Package Insert, 1996.
2. American Academy of Pediatrics. Committee on Infectious Diseases. Red Book 1997.

HEPATITIS C INFECTION

Trade: Hepatitis C Infection
Can/Aus/UK:
Uses: Hepatitis exposure
AAP: Not reviewed

Hepatitis C (HCV) is characterized by a mild or asymptomatic infection with jaundice and malaise. On average, 50% of patients develop chronic liver disease, including cirrhosis, and liver cancer in later life. HCV infection can be spread by blood-blood transmission, although most are not associated with blood transfusions and may be transmitted by other unknown methods.

Although perinatal transmission can occur, its incidence is known to be very low.[2] The average incubation period is 7-9 weeks. Mothers infected with HCV should be advised that transmission of HCV by breastfeeding is possible but has not been documented. In one study, while transmission of HCV was significantly high (21%) in HIV infected individuals, perinatal transmission was not associated with breastfeeding.[1]

It is not known with certainty if the virus is shed in breastmilk, although several studies so suggest. In one study of 17 HCV positive mothers, 11 of the 17 had HCV antibody present in milk, but zero of 17 had HCV-RNA in milk after birth, suggesting that the virus itself was not detected in milk.[3] Although it is possible that during episodes of direct exposure to blood, such as from bleeding nipples, or following initial infection and viremia, that transmission could occur, this does not appear to be certain at this time.

Currently a number of other studies have yet to document vertical transmission of HCV by breastmilk.[4,5] Available data seem to suggest an elevated risk of vertical transmission to the infant occurs in HIV infected women and women with elevated titers of HCV RNA. The risk of transmission of HCV via breastmilk is unknown at this time. HCV-infected women should be counseled that transmission of HCV by breastfeeding is theoretically possible, but has not yet been documented.[6,7] The Center for Disease Control (CDC) does not consider chronic hepatitis C infection in the mother as a contraindication to breastfeeding. The decision to breastfeed should be based largely on informed discussion between the mother and her health care provider.

References:
1. Paccagnini S, et.al. Perinatala transmission and manifestations of hepatitis C virus infection in a high risk population. Ped. Infect. Dis J. 14:195-9, 1995.
2. Nagata I, Shiraki K, et.al. Mother to infant transmission of hepatitis C virus. J. Pediatrics 120:432-4, 1992
3. Grayson ML, Braniff KM, et.al. Breastfeeding and the risk of virtical transmission of hepatitis C virus. Med. J. Australia 163:107, 1995.
4. Lin HH, et.al. Absence of infection in breastfed infants born to Hepatitis C infected mothers. J. pediatr. 126(4):589-91, 1995.
5. Zanetti, et.al. Mother to infant transmission of hepatitis C virus. Lancet 345(8945):289-91, 1995.
6. American Academy of Pediatrics. Committee on Infectious Diseases. Red Book 1997.
7. Lawrence RA. Breastfeeding, A guide for the medical profession. Mosby, St. Louis, 1994.

HERBAL TEAS

Trade: Herbal Teas
Can/Aus/UK:
Uses: Herbal teas, tablets, powders, antioxidants.
AAP: Not reviewed

Herbal teas should be used with great caution, if at all. A number of reports in the literature indicate potential toxicity in pregnant women from some herbal teas which contain pyrrolizidine alkaloids (PA).[1,2] Such alkaloids have been associated with feticide, birth defects and liver toxicity.

Other reports of severe hepatotoxicity requiring liver transplant have occurred with an herbal antioxidant called "Chaparral".[3] A Chinese herbal product called "Jin Bu Huan" has been implicated in clinically recognized hepatitis in 7 patients.[3] Other hepatotoxic remedies include germander, comfrey, mistletoe and skullcap, margosa oil, mate tea, Gordolobo yerba tea, and pennyroyal (squawmint) oil.[4,5] A recent report of seven poisonings with anticholinergic symptoms following ingestion of "Paraguay Tea" was published and was an apparent adulteration. A recent report on Blue Cohosh suggests it may be cardiotoxic when used late in pregnancy(see blue cohosh).

Because exact ingredients are seldom listed on many teas, this author strongly suggests that lactating mothers limit exposure to these substances as much as possible. Never consume herbal remedies of unknown composition. Remember, breastfeeding infants are much more susceptible to such toxicants than are adults.

Pregnancy Risk Category:

Lactation Risk Category: L4

Theoretic Infant Dose:

Adult Concerns: Severe toxicity including hepatotoxicity, anticholinergic poisoning, etc.

Pediatric Concerns: None reported via breastmilk, but caution is recommended. Agents listed above would be contraindicated.

Drug Interactions:

Alternatives:

Adult Dosage:

References:
1. Anonymous. Drug Therapy 16:64, 1993
2. Ellenhorn, MJ. and Barceloux, DG. Medical Toxicology. Elsevier Publishing Co. 1988. p. 1292-1299.
3. Gordon DW, Rosenthal G, Hart J, et.al. Chaparral Ingestion. JAMA, 273:(6),489-502, 1995.
4. Hsu CK, et.al. Anticholinergic poisoning associated with herbal tea. Arch. Intern. Med. 155:2245-48, 1995.
5. Siegel, RK. Herbal Intoxication. JAMA 236:473-477, 1976.
6. Rosti L. et.al. Toxic effects of a herbal tea mixture in two newborns. Acta. Pediatr 83:683, 1994.

HEROIN

Trade: Heroin
Can/Aus/UK:
Uses: Narcotic analgesic
AAP: Contraindicated by the American Academy of Pediatrics in Breastfeeding Mothers

Heroin is diacetyl-morphine (diamorphine), a prodrug that is rapidly converted by plasma cholinesterases to 6-acetylmorphine and more slowly to morphine. With oral use, rapid and complete first-pass metabolism occurs in the liver. The half-life of diamorphine is only 3 minutes, with the large majority of the prodrug converted to morphine. Peak levels of morphine occur in about 30 minutes following oral doses. As an analgesic, morphine is generally considered to be an ideal choice for breastfeeding mothers when used postoperatively or for other forms of pain "in normal dosage ranges". Unfortunately, addicts and recreational users may use extraordinarily large doses of heroin, and at such doses, it is likely to be very dangerous for a breastfed infant. Heavily dependent users should be advised against breastfeeding and their infants converted to formula. While it could be argued that recreational users could continue to breastfeed if they avoid doing so while under the influence of the heroin or prior to its use, this still may not be advisable as it requires some understanding of the kinetics of morphine and its elimination. Heroin, as is morphine, is known to transfer into breastmilk.[1,2] See morphine for kinetics.

Pregnancy Risk Category: B

Lactation Risk Category: L4

Theoretic Infant Dose:

Adult Concerns: Sedation, hypotension, euphoria, nausea, vomiting, dry mouth, respiratory depression, constipation.

Pediatric Concerns: Caution, observe for sedation. Tremors, restlessness, vomiting, poor feeding.

Drug Interactions:

Alternatives:

Adult Dosage:

T½ = 1.5-2 hours	M/P = 2.45
PHL =	PB = 35%
PK = 0.5-1 hours	Oral = Poor
MW = 369	pKa = 7.6
Vd = 25	

References:
1. Feilberg VL, Rosenborg D, Broen Christensen C, et.al. Excretion of morphine in human breast milk. Acta Anaesthiol Scan. 33:426-428, 1989.
2. Wittels Bk, Scott DT, Sinatra RS. Exogenous opioids in human breast milk and acute neonatal neurobehavior: a preliminary study. Anesthesiology 73:864-869, 1990.

HERPES SIMPLEX INFECTIONS

Trade:

Can/Aus/UK:

Uses: Herpes simplex type I, II

AAP: Breastfeeding is acceptable if no lesions are on the breast or are adequately covered.

HSV-1 and HSV-2 have been isolated from human milk, even in the absence of vesicular lesions or drainage.[1,2] Transmission after birth can occur and herpetic infections during the neonatal period are often severe and fatal.[3] Exposure to the virus from skin lesions of caregivers, including lesions of the breast, have been described. On average however, perinatal infection is generally believed to occur during delivery rather than through breastmilk. Breastmilk does not appear to be a common mode of transmission, although women with active lesions around the breast and nipple should refrain from breastfeeding until the lesions are adequately covered. Lesions directly on the nipple generally preclude breastfeeding.   A number of cases of herpes simplex transmission via breastmilk have been reported.[4,5] Women with active lesions should be extremely meticulous in handwashing to prevent spread of the disease from other active lesions.   Lawrence[6] provides a good review of the risks.

Pregnancy Risk Category:

Lactation Risk Category:

Theoretic Infant Dose:

Adult Concerns: Skin eruptions, CNS changes, gingivostomatitis, skin lesions, fever.

Pediatric Concerns: Transfer of virus to infants has been reported, but may be from exposure to lesions. Cover lesions on breast.

Drug Interactions:

Alternatives:

Adult Dosage: N/A

References:
1. Light IJ. Postnatal acquisition of herpes simplex virus by the newborn infant: a review of the literature. Pediatrics 63:480-2, 1979.
2. Sullivan-Bolyai JZ, Fife KH et.al. Disseminated neonatal herpes simplex virus type-1 from a maternal breast lesion. Pediatrics 71:455-7, 1983.
3. Whitley RJ, et.al. The natural history of herpes simples virus infection of mother and newborn. Pediatrics 66:489, 1980.
4. Dunkle LM, Schmidt RR, O'Connor DM. Neonatal herpes simplex infection possibly acquired via maternal breastmilk. Pediatrics 63:250, 1979.
5. Quinn PT, Lofberg JV. Maternal herpetic breast infection: another hazard of neonatal herpes simplex. Med. J. Aust. 2:411, 1978.

6.   Lawrence RA. Breastfeeding, A guide for the medical profession. Mosby, St. Louis, 1994.

HEXACHLOROPHENE

Trade: Septisol, Phisohex, Septi-soft
Can/Aus/UK: Dermalex, Sapoderm, pHisoHex
Uses: Antiseptic scrub
AAP: Not reviewed

Hexachlorophene is an antibacterial which is an effective inhibitor of gram positive organisms.[1] It is generally used topically as a surgical scrub and sometimes vaginally in mothers.   Due to its lipophilic structure, it is well absorbed through intact and denuded skin producing significant levels in plasma, brain, fat and other tissues in both adults and infants.   It has been implicated in causing brain lesions (spongioform myelinopathy), blindness and respiratory failure in both animals and humans.[2]   Although there are no studies reporting concentrations of this compound in breastmilk, it is probably transferred to some degree.   Transfer into breastmilk is known to occur in rodents. Topical use in infants is absolutely discouraged due to the high absorption of hexachlorophene through an infant's skin and proven toxicity.

Pregnancy Risk Category: C

Lactation Risk Category: L4

Theoretic Infant Dose:

Adult Concerns: Seizures, respiratory failure, hypotension, brain lesions, blindness in overdose.

Pediatric Concerns: Following direct application, CNS injury, seizures, irritability have been reported in neonates. Toxicity via breastmilk has not been reported.

Drug Interactions:

Alternatives:

Adult Dosage:

T½ =	M/P =
PHL = 6.1-44.2 hours	PB =
PK =	Oral = Complete
MW = 407	pKa =
Vd =	

References:
1. Pharmaceutical Manufacturers Package Insert, 1996.
2. Tyrala EE, Hillman RE and Dodson WE. Clinical pharmacology of hexachlorophene in newborn infants. J Pediatr 91:481-6, 1977.

HIV INFECTION

Trade: Aids
Can/Aus/UK:
Uses: Aids, HIV infections
AAP: Advise not to breastfeed.

The AIDS (HIV) virus has been isolated from human milk. In addition, recent reports from throughout the world have documented the transmission of HIV through human milk, although they are controversial.[1-3] At least 9 or more cases in the literature currently suggest that HIV-1 may be secreted and can be transmitted horizontally to the infant via breastmilk. Although these studies clearly indicate a risk, currently no studies clearly show the exact risk associated with breastfeeding in HIV infected women. However, women who develop a primary HIV infection while breastfeeding may shed especially high concentrations of HIV viruses and pose a high risk of transmission to their infants. In some studies, the risk of transmission during primary infection was 29%. In various African populations, recent reports suggest the incremental risk of transmitting HIV via breastfeeding ranges from 3-12%.[6] Because the risk is now well documented, HIV infected mothers in the USA and others countries with safe alternative sources of feeding should be advised to not breastfeed their infants.[7] Mothers at-risk for HIV should be screened and counseled prior to initiating breastfeeding.

Pregnancy Risk Category:

Lactation Risk Category:

Theoretic Infant Dose:

Adult Concerns:

Pediatric Concerns: HIV transmission has been documented. HIV infected women are advised not to breastfeed.

Drug Interactions:

Alternatives:

Adult Dosage:

References:
1. Committee on Pediatric AIDS. Human milk, breastfeeding, and transmission of human immunodeficiency virus in the United States. Pediatrics 96:977-9, 1995.
2. Oxtoby MJ. Human immunodeficiency virus and other viruses in human

milk: placing the issues in broader perspective. Pediatr. Infect. Dis. 7:825-835, 1988.
3. Goldfarb J. Breastfeeding: Aids and other infectious diseases. Clin. Perinatol 20:225-243, 1993.
4. Van de Perre P. et.al. Infective and anti-infective properties of breastmilk from HIV-1-infected women. Lancet 341:914-18, 1993.
5. Dunn DT, et.al. Risk of human immunodeficiency virus type I transmission through breastfeeding. Lancet 340:585-588, 1992.
6. St.Louis ME. et.al. The timing of HIV-1 transmission in an African setting. Presented at the First National Conference on Human Retroviruses and Related Infections. December 12-16, 1993; Washington DC.
7. Report of the Committee on Infectious Diseases. American Academy of Pediatrics, 1994.

HYDRALAZINE

Trade: Apresoline
Can/Aus/UK: Alphapress, Apo-Hydralazine, Apresoline, Novo-Hylazin
Uses: Antihypertensive
AAP: Approved by the American Academy of Pediatrics for use in breastfeeding mothers

Hydralazine is a popular antihypertensive used for severe pre-eclampsia and gestational and postpartum hypertension. In a study of one breastfeeding mother receiving 50 mg three times daily, the concentrations of hydralazine in breastmilk at 0.5 and 2 hours after administration was 762, and 792 nmol/L respectively.[1] The respective maternal serum levels were 1525, and 580 nmol/L at the aforementioned times. From these data, an infant consuming 1000 cc of milk would consume only 0.17 mg of hydralazine, an amount too small to be clinically relevant. The published pediatric dose for hydralazine is 0.75 to 1 mg/kg/day.

Pregnancy Risk Category: C

Lactation Risk Category: L2

Theoretic Infant Dose: 25.5 μg/kg/day

Adult Concerns: Hypotension, tachycardia, renal failure, liver toxicity, paresthesias.

Pediatric Concerns: None reported but observe for hypotension, sedation, weakness.

Drug Interactions: Increased effect with other antihypertensives, MAO inhibitors. Decreased effect when used with indomethacin.

Alternatives:

Adult Dosage: 10-25 mg QID

T½ = 1.5-8 hours.	M/P = 0.49-1.36
PHL =	PB = 87%
PK = 2 hours	Oral = 30-50%
MW = 160	pKa = 7.1
Vd = 1.6	

References:
1. Liedholm H, et. al. Transplacental passage and breast milk concentrations of hydralazine, Eur J Clin Pharmacol 21:417-9,1982.

HYDROCHLOROTHIAZIDE

Trade: Hydrodiuril, Esidrix, Oretic
Can/Aus/UK: Amizide, Apo-Hydro, Direma, Diuchlor H, Dyazide, Esidrex, Hydrodiuril, Modizide, Novo-Hydrazide
Uses: Thiazide diuretic
AAP: Approved by the American Academy of Pediatrics for use in breastfeeding mothers

Hydrochlorothiazide (HCTZ) is a typical thiazide diuretic. In one study of a mother receiving a 50 mg dose each morning, milk levels were almost 25% of maternal plasma levels.[1] The dose ingested (assuming milk intake of 600 ml) would be approximately 50 μg/day, a clinically insignificant amount. The concentration of HCTZ in the infant's serum was undetectable(< 20 ng/ml). Some authors suggest that HCTZ can produce thrombocytopenia in nursing infant, although this is remote and unsubstantiated. Thiazide diuretics could potentially reduce milk production by depleting maternal blood volume, although it is seldom observed. Most thiazide diuretics are considered compatible with breastfeeding if doses are kept low.

Pregnancy Risk Category: D

Lactation Risk Category: L2

Theoretic Infant Dose:

Adult Concerns: Fluid loss, hypotension. May reduce milk supply.

Pediatric Concerns: None reported via milk, but may reduce milk supply in mother.

Drug Interactions: May increase hypoglycemia with antidiabetic drugs. May increase hypotension associated with other antihypertensives. May increase digoxin associated arrhythmias. May increase lithium levels.

Alternatives:

Adult Dosage: 25-100 mg QD

T½ = 5.6-14.8 hours	M/P = 0.25
PHL =	PB = 58%
PK = 2 hours	Oral = 72%
MW = 297	pKa = 7.9, 9.2
Vd = 3	

References:

1. Miller ME, Cohn RD, and Burghart PH. Hydrochlorothiazide disposition in a mother and her breast-fed infant. J. Pediatr. 101:789-91, 1982.

HYDROCODONE

Trade: Lortab, Vicodin
Can/Aus/UK: Actron, Hycodan, Hycomine, Robidone
Uses: Analgesic for pain
AAP: Not reviewed

Hydrocodone is a narcotic analgesic and antitussive structurally related to codeine although somewhat more potent. It is commonly used in breastfeeding mothers throughout the USA. Most authors suggest that doses of 5 mg every 4 hours or more has a minimal effect on nursing infants, particularly older infants.[1-3] To reduce exposure of the infant, attempt to feed infant prior to medicating. Neonates may be more sensitive to this product, observe for sedation or constipation. Lortab and Vicodin also contain acetaminophen.

Pregnancy Risk Category: B

Lactation Risk Category: L3

Theoretic Infant Dose:

Adult Concerns: Sedation, dizziness, apnea, bradycardia, nausea, or constipation.

Pediatric Concerns: None reported via milk, but observe closely for sedation, apnea, constipation.

Drug Interactions: May reduce analgesia when used with phenothiazines. May increase toxicity associated with CNS depressants and tricyclic antidepressants.

Alternatives: Codeine

Adult Dosage: 5-10 mg q 4-6 hours

T½ = 3.8 hours.	M/P =
PHL =	PB =
PK = 1.3 hours	Oral = Complete
MW = 299	pKa = 8.9
Vd = 3.3-4.7	

References:

1. Horning MG, Identification and quantification of drugs and drug metabolites in human milk using GC-MS-COM methods. Mod Probl Paediatr 15:73-9,1975.
2. Kwit NT, Hatcher RA. Excretion of drugs in milk. Am J Dis Child 49:900-4,1935.
3. Anderson PO. Medication use while breast feeding a neonate. Neonatal Pharmacology Quarterly 2:3-12,1993.

HYDROCORTISONE TOPICAL

Trade: Westcort
Can/Aus/UK: Aquacort, Cortate, Cortef, Cortone, Dermacort, Dermaid, Egocort, Emo-Cort, Hycor
Uses: Corticosteroid
AAP: Not reviewed

Hydrocortisone is corticosteroid with glucocorticoid and mineralocorticoid activity. When applied topically it suppresses inflammation and enhances healing. Initial onset of activity when applied topically is slow and may require several days for response. Absorption topically is dependent on placement; percutaneous absorption is 1% from the forearm, 2% from rectum, 4% from the scalp, 7% from the forehead, and 36% from the scrotal area.[1] The amount transferred into human milk has not been reported, but as with most steroids, is believed minimal. Topical application to the nipple is generally approved by most authorities if amounts applied, and duration of use are minimized. Only small amounts should be applied and then only after feeding; larger quantities should be removed prior to breastfeeding. 0.5 to 1 % ointments, rather than creams, are generally preferred.

Pregnancy Risk Category: C

Lactation Risk Category: L2

Theoretic Infant Dose:

Adult Concerns: Local irritation.

Pediatric Concerns: None reported via milk.

Drug Interactions:

Alternatives:

Adult Dosage: apply topical QID

T½ = 1-2 hours	M/P =
PHL=	PB = 90%
PK =	Oral = 96%
MW = 362	pKa =
Vd = 0.48	

References:
1. Derendorf H, Mollmann H, Barth J et al: Pharmacokinetics and oral bioavailability of hydrocortisone. J Clin Pharmacol 31:473-476, 1991.

HYDROMORPHONE

Trade: Dilaudid
Can/Aus/UK: Dilaudid, Hydromorph Contin, Palladone
Uses: Opiate analgesic
AAP: Not reviewed

Hydromorphone is a potent synthetic narcotic analgesic used to alleviate moderate to severe pain. See morphine.

Pregnancy Risk Category: C

Lactation Risk Category: L3

Theoretic Infant Dose:

Adult Concerns: Dihydromorphine is highly addictive. Adverse effects include dizziness, sedation, agitation, hypotension, respiratory depression, nausea, and vomiting.

Pediatric Concerns:

Drug Interactions:

Alternatives: Codeine, Hydrocodone

Adult Dosage: 2-10 mg q 3-6 hours PRN

T½ = 2.5 hours	M/P =
PHL=	PB =
PK =	Oral =
MW =	pKa =
Vd =	

References:

HYDROXYCHLOROQUINE

Trade: Plaquenil
Can/Aus/UK: Plaquenil, Plaqueril
Uses: Antimalarial, Antirheumatic, Lupus
AAP: Approved by the American Academy of Pediatrics for use in breastfeeding mothers

Hydroxychloroquine (HCQ) is effective in the treatment of malaria, but is also used in immune syndromes such as rheumatoid arthritis and Lupus erythematosus. HCQ is known to produce significant retinal damage and blindness if used over a prolonged period, and this could occur (theoretically) in breastfed infants. Patients on this product should see an ophthalmologist routinely. In one study of a mother receiving 400 mg HCQ daily, the concentrations of HCQ in breastmilk were 1.46, 1.09, and 1.09 mg/L at 2, 9.5, and 14 hours after the dose.[1] The average milk concentration was 1.1 mg/L. The milk/plasma ratio was approximately 5.5. Assuming a daily intake of 1 Liter of milk, an infant would ingest approximately 1.1 mg. This dose is 0.35% of the daily maternal dose of 310 mg. On a body weight basis, the infant's dose would be 2% of the maternal dose. HCQ is mostly metabolized to chloroquine and has an incredibly long half-life. The pediatric dose for malaria prophylaxis is 5 mg/kg/week. See chloroquine.

Pregnancy Risk Category: C

Lactation Risk Category: L2

Theoretic Infant Dose: 0.2 mg/kg/day

Adult Concerns: Blood dyscrasias, nausea, vomiting, diarrhea, retinopathy, rash, aplastic anemia, psychosis, porphyries, psoriasis, corneal deposits.

Pediatric Concerns: None reported, but observe for retinal damage, blood dyscrasias.

Drug Interactions: Increased risk of blood dyscrasias when used with aurothioglucose. May increase serum digoxin levels.

Alternatives:

Adult Dosage: 400 mg q week X 10 weeks

T½ = >40 days	M/P = 5.5
PHL=	PB = 63%
PK = 1-2 hours	Oral = 74%
MW = 336	pKa =
Vd =	

References:
1. Nation RL, Hackett LP, Dusci LJ. Excretion of hydroxychloroquine in human milk. Br. J. Clin. Pharm. 17:368-9, 1984.

HYDROXYUREA

Trade: Hydrea
Can/Aus/UK: Hydrea
Uses: Antineoplastic agent
AAP: Not reviewed

Hydroxyurea is an antineoplastic agent used to treat melanoma, leukemias, and other neoplasms. It is well absorbed orally and rapidly metabolized to urea by the liver. In one study following a dose of 500 mg three times daily for 7 days, milk samples were collected two hours after the last dose.[1] The concentration of hydroxyurea in breastmilk averaged 6.1 mg/L (range 3.8 to 8.4 mg/L). Hydroxyurea is rapidly cleared from the plasma compartment and appears to leave no residuals or metabolites. Approximately 80% of the dose is excreted renally with 12 hours.

Pregnancy Risk Category: D

Lactation Risk Category: L2

Theoretic Infant Dose: 0.9 mg/kg/day

Adult Concerns: Bone marrow suppression, drowsiness, convulsion, hallucinations, fever, nausea, vomiting, diarrhea, constipation.

Pediatric Concerns: None reported via milk, but extreme caution is recommended due to overt toxicity of this product.

Drug Interactions: May have increased toxicity and neurotoxicity when used with fluorouracil.

Alternatives:

Adult Dosage: 80 mg/kg q 3 days

T½ = 2-3 hours	M/P =
PHL=	PB =
PK = 2 hours	Oral = Complete
MW = 76	pKa =
Vd =	

References:
1.   Sylvester RK, Lobell M, Teresi ME et al. Excretion of hydroxyurea into milk. Cancer 60:2177-2178, 1987.

HYDROXYZINE

Trade: Atarax, Vistaril
Can/Aus/UK: Apo-Hydroxyzine, Atarax, Novo-Hydroxyzin
Uses: Antihistamine, antiemetic
AAP: Not reviewed

Hydroxyzine is an antihistamine structurally similar to cyclizine and meclizine. It produces significant CNS depression, anticholinergic side effects (drying), and antiemetic side effects.[1] Hydroxyzine is largely metabolized to cetirizine (Zyrtec). No data are available on secretion into breastmilk.

Pregnancy Risk Category: C

Lactation Risk Category: L1

Theoretic Infant Dose:

Adult Concerns: Sedation, hypotension, dry mouth.

Pediatric Concerns: None reported via milk, but observe for sedation, tachycardia, dry mouth.

Drug Interactions: May reduce epinephrine vasopressor response. Increased sedation when used with CNS depressants. Increased anticholinergic side effects when admixed with other anticholinergics.

Alternatives: Cetirizine, Loratadine

Adult Dosage: 50-100 mg QID

T½ = 3-7 hours.	M/P =
PHL = 7.1 hours	PB =
PK = 2 hours	Oral = Complete
MW = 375	pKa = 2.1, 7.1
Vd = 13-31	

References:
1. Paton DM, Webster DR. Clinical pharmacokinetics of H1-receptor antagonists (the antihistamines). Clin. Pharm. 10:477-497, 1985.

HYLAN G-F 20

Trade: Synvisc
Can/Aus/UK:
Uses: Joint lubricant for arthritic pain
AAP: Not reviewed

Synvisc is a elastoviscous fluid containing hylan polymers produced from chicken combs. Hylans are a natural complex sugar of the glycosaminoglycan family.[1] Hylans are large molecular weight polymers and would not be expected to enter milk. Average molecular weight is 6 million daltons.

Pregnancy Risk Category:

Lactation Risk Category: L2

Theoretic Infant Dose:

Adult Concerns: Knee pain or swelling, rash, itching, nausea, vomiting.

Pediatric Concerns: None reported via milk.

Drug Interactions:

Alternatives:

Adult Dosage:

T½ =	M/P =
PHL=	PB =
PK =	Oral = None
MW = 6 mil	pKa =
Vd =	

References:
1. Pharmaceutical Manufacturers Package Insert, 1999.

HYOSCYAMINE

Trade: Anaspaz, Levsin, Nulev
Can/Aus/UK: Buscopan, Hyoscine, Levsin
Uses: Anticholinergic, antisecretory agent
AAP: Not reviewed

Hyoscyamine is an anticholinergic, antisecretory agent that belongs to the belladonna alkaloid family. Its typical effects are to dry secretions, produce constipation, dilate pupils, blurry vision, and may produce urinary retention.[1,2] Although no exact amounts are listed, hyoscyamine is known to be secreted into breastmilk in trace amounts.[3] Thus far, no untoward effects from breastfeeding while using hyoscyamine have been found. Levsin (hyoscyamine) drops have in the past been used directly in infants for colic, although it is no longer recommended for this use. As with atropine, infants and children are especially sensitive to anticholinergics and their use is discouraged. Atropine is composed of two isomers of hyoscyamine. See atropine. Use with caution.

Pregnancy Risk Category: C

Lactation Risk Category: L3

Theoretic Infant Dose:

Adult Concerns: Tachycardia, dry mouth, blurred vision, constipation, urinary retention.

Pediatric Concerns: Decreased heart rate, anticholinergic effects from direct use, but none reported from breastmilk ingestion. Never use directly in infants with projectile vomiting, or in infants with bilious (green) vomitus.

Drug Interactions: Decreased effect with antacids. Increased toxicity with amantadine, antimuscarinics, haloperidol, phenothiazines, tricyclic antidepressants, MAO inhibitors.

Alternatives:

Adult Dosage: 0.125-0.25 mg QID

T½ = 3.5 hours		M/P =	
PHL =		PB = 50%	
PK = 40-90 min.(oral)		Oral = 81%	
MW = 289		pKa =	
Vd =			

References:
1. Drug Facts and Comparisons. 1995 ed. Facts and Comparisons, St. Louis.
2. Pharmaceutical Manufacturers Package Insert, 1995.
3. Wilson, J. Drugs in Breast Milk. New York: ADIS Press, 1981.

I-125 I-131 I-123

Trade:
Can/Aus/UK:
Uses: Radioactive iodine
AAP: Radioactive compound that requires temporary cessation of breastfeeding.

Radioactive Iodine concentrates in the thyroid gland, as well as in breastmilk, and if ingested by an infant, may suppress its thyroid function, or increase the risk of future thyroid carcinomas. High levels may be transferred to infant producing thyroid destruction. Radioactive iodine is clinically used to ablate or destroy the thyroid (dose= 355 MBq), or in much smaller doses (7.4 MBq), to scan the thyroid for malignancies. Following ingestion, radioactive iodine concentrates in the thyroid and lactating tissues, and it is estimated 27.9% of total radioactivity is secreted via breastmilk.[1]

Two potential half-lives exist for radioactive iodine. One is the radioactive half-life which is solely dependent on radioactive decay of the molecule. And two, the biological half-life which is often briefer, and is the half-life of the iodine molecule itself in the human being. The latter half-life is influenced most by elimination via the kidneys and other routes.

Previously published data have suggested that Iodine-125 is present in milk for at least 12 days and Iodine-131 is present for 2-14 days, but these studies may be in error as they ignored the second component of the biexponential breastmilk disappearance curve.[2] The radioactive half-life of I-131 is 8.1 days. The half-life of I-125 is 60.2 days and the half-life of I-123 is 13.2 hours. The biological half-life may be shorter due to excretion in urine, feces, and milk.

A well done study by Dydek[3] reviewed the transfer of both tracer, and ablation doses of I-131 into human milk. If the tracer doses are kept minimal (0.1 μCi or 3.7 kBq) breastfeeding could resume as early as the eighth day. However, if larger tracer doses (8.6 μCi or 0.317 MBq) are used, nursing could not resume until 46 days following therapy. Doses used for ablation of the maternal thyroid (111 MBq) would require an interruption of breastfeeding for a minimum of 106 days or more. However, an acceptable dose to an infant as a result of ingestion of radioiodine is a matter for debate, although an effective dose of < 1 mSv has been suggested.

Another study of I-131 use in a mother was followed for 32 days. These authors recommend discontinuing breastfeeding for up to 50-52 days, to ensure safety of the infant thyroid. Thyroid scans use either radioactive iodine or technetium-99m pertechnetate. Technetium has a very short half-life and should be preferred in breastfeeding mothers for thyroid scanning.[3]

Another alternative is I-123, a newer isotope that is increasing in popularity. I-123 has a short half-life of only 13.2 hours and is radiologically ideal for thyroid and other scans. If radioactive iodine compounds are mandatory for various scanning procedures, I-123 should be preferred, followed by pumping and dumping for 12-24 hours depending on the dose. However, the return to breastfeeding following I-123 therapy is dependent on the purity of this product. During manufacture of I-123, I-124 and I-125 are created. If using I-123, breastfeeding should be temporarily interrupted (see table in appendices). I-123 is not normally used for ablation of the thyroid.

Due to the fact that significant concentrations of I-131 are concentrated in breastmilk, women should discontinue breastfeeding prior to treatment, as the cumulative exposure to breast tissues could be excessively high. It is generally recommended that women discontinue breastfeeding several days to weeks before undergoing therapy, or that they pump and discard milk for several weeks after exposure to iodine to reduce the overall radioactive exposure to breast tissues. The estimated dose of radioactivity to the breasts would give a "theoretical" probability of induction of breast cancer of 0.32%.[1] In addition, holding the infant close to the breast or thyroid gland for long periods may expose the infant to gamma irradiation and is not recommended. Patients should consult with the radiologist concerning exposure of the infant.

One case of significant exposure was reported in a breastfed infant.[4] The mother received a 3.02 millicurie dose of I-131 and continued to breastfeed for the next 7 days before the mother admitted breastfeeding. During this 7 day period, the infant's thyroid contained 2.7 microcuries of iodine-131 which is an effective dose equivalent of 5.5 rads. Had the mother continued to breastfeed, the dose would have been much larger and potentially dangerous.

The Nuclear Regulatory Commission has released a table of instructions to mothers concerning the use of radioisotopes (see appendix). These instructions conclude that patients should not breastfeed following the use of I-131. In a study by Hammami, radioactive I-131 was found to transfer into breasts weeks following cessation of lactation.[5] They suggest the breast is a "radioiodine reservoir".

Pregnancy Risk Category:

Lactation Risk Category: L4

Theoretic Infant Dose:

Adult Concerns: Ablation of thyroid function. Theoretical risk of breast cancer if used in lactating women.

Pediatric Concerns: None reported, but damage to thyroid is probable if the infant is breastfed while I-131 levels are high.

Drug Interactions:

Alternatives: Technetium-99 M

Adult Dosage:

References:
1. Robinson PS, Barker P, Campbell A, et.al. Iodine-131 in breast milk following therapy for thyroid carcinoma. J. Nuci. Med. 35:1797-1801, 1994.
2. Palmer, KE. Excretion of 125-I in breast milk following administration of labelled fibrinogen. Br. J. Radiol. 52:672, 1979
3. Dydek GJ, Blue PW. Human breast milk excretion of iodine-131 following diagnostic and therapeutic administration to a lactating patient with Graves' disease. J. Nuclear Med. 29(3):407-10, 1988.
4. Iodine-131 dose for whole body scan administered to a breast-feeding patient. Preliminary notification of event or unusual occurrence PNO-I-98-038. NRC. http://www.nrc.gov/OPA/pn/pn19838.htm
5. Bakheet SM, Hammami MM. Patterns of radioiodine uptake by the lactating breast. Eur J Nucl Med. 21(7):604-8, 1994.

IBUPROFEN

Trade: Advil, Nuprin, Motrin, Pediaprofen
Can/Aus/UK: ACT-3, Actiprofen, Advil, Amersol, Brufen, Motrin, Nurofen, Rafen
Uses: Analgesic, antipyretic
AAP: Approved by the American Academy of Pediatrics for use in breastfeeding mothers

Ibuprofen is a nonsteroidal anti-inflammatory analgesic. It is frequently used for fever in infants. Ibuprofen enters milk only in very low levels (less than 0.6% of maternal dose). Even large doses produce very small milk levels. In one patient receiving 400 mg twice daily, milk levels were less than 0.5 mg/L.[1]

In another study of twelve women who received 400 mg doses every 6 hours for a total of 5 doses, all breastmilk levels of ibuprofen were less than 1.0 mg/L, the lower limit of the assay.[2] Data in these studies document that no measurable concentrations of ibuprofen are detected in breastmilk following the above doses. Ibuprofen is presently popular for therapy of fever in infants. Current recommended dose is 5-10 mg/kg every 6 hours.

Pregnancy Risk Category: B during 1st and 2nd trimesters
D during 3rd trimester

Lactation Risk Category: L1

Theoretic Infant Dose: 75.0 μg/kg/day

Adult Concerns: Nausea, epigastric pain, dizziness, edema, GI bleeding.

Pediatric Concerns: None reported from breastfeeding.

Drug Interactions: Aspirin may decrease serum ibuprofen levels. May prolong prothrombin time when used with warfarin. Antihypertensive effects of ACEi family may be blunted or completely abolished by NSAIDs. Some NSAIDs may block antihypertensive effect of beta blockers, diuretics. Used with cyclosporin, may dramatically increase renal toxicity. May increase digoxin, phenytoin, lithium levels. May increase toxicity of methotrexate. May increase bioavailability of penicillamine. Probenecid may increase NSAID levels.

Alternatives: Acetaminophen

Adult Dosage: 400 mg q 4-6 hours

T½ = 1.8-2.5 hours	M/P =
PHL=	PB = >99%
PK = 1-2 hours	Oral = 80%
MW = 206	pKa = 4.4
Vd = 0.14	

References:
1. Weibert RT, Townsend RJ, Kaiser DG, et.al. Lack of ibuprofen secretion into human milk. Clin Pharm 1:457-458,1982.
2. Townsend RJ, et. al. Excretion of ibuprofen into breast milk. Am J Obstet Gynecol 149:184-6, 1984.

IMIPENEM-CILASTATIN

Trade: Primaxin
Can/Aus/UK: Primaxin
Uses: Antibiotic
AAP: Not reviewed

Imipenem is structurally similar to penicillins and acts similarly. Cilastatin is added to extend the half-life of imipenem. Both imipenem and cilastatin are poorly absorbed orally and must be administered IM or I.V.[1,2] Imipenem is destroyed by gastric acidity. Transfer into breastmilk is probably minimal. Changes in GI flora could occur but is probably remote.

Pregnancy Risk Category: C

Lactation Risk Category: L2

Theoretic Infant Dose:

Adult Concerns: Nausea, diarrhea, vomiting, abdominal pain, decreased white blood cells, decreased hemoglobin, seizures.

Pediatric Concerns:

Drug Interactions: May have increased toxicity when used with other beta lactam antibiotics. Probenecid may increase toxic potential.

Alternatives:

Adult Dosage: 500-750 mg BID

T½ = 0.85-1.3 hour	M/P =
PHL = 1.5-2.6 hours(neonate)	PB = 20-35%
PK = Immediate(IV)	Oral = Poor
MW = 317	pKa =
Vd =	

References:
1. Pharmaceutical Manufacturers Package Insert, 1995.
2. McEvoy GE(ed):AHFS Drug Information, New York, NY. 1995.

IMIPRAMINE

Trade: Tofranil, Janimine
Can/Aus/UK: Apo-Imipramine, Impril, Melipramine, Novo-Pramine, Tofanil, Tofranil
Uses: Tricyclic antidepressant
AAP: Drug whose effect on nursing infants is unknown but may be of concern

Imipramine is a classic tricyclic antidepressant. Imipramine is metabolized to desipramine, the active metabolite. Milk levels approximate those of maternal serum. In a patient receiving 200 mg daily at bedtime, the milk levels at 1, 9, 10, and 23 hours were 29, 24, 12, and 18 μg/L respectively.[1] However, in this previous study the mother was not in a therapeutic range.[2] In a mother with full therapeutic levels, it is suggested that an infant would ingest approximately 0.2 mg/Liter of milk. This represents a dose of only 30 μg/kg/day, far less than the 1.5 mg/kg dose recommended for older children. The long half-life of this medication in infants could, under certain conditions, lead to high plasma levels, although they have not been reported. Although no untoward effects have been reported, the infant should be monitored closely. Therapeutic plasma levels in children 6-12 yrs are 200-225 ng/ml. Two good reviews of psychotropic drugs in breastfeeding patients are available.[3,4]

Pregnancy Risk Category: D

Lactation Risk Category: L2

Theoretic Infant Dose: 30.0 μg/kg/day

Adult Concerns: Dry mouth, sedation, hypotension, arrhythmias, confusion, agitation, seizures.

Pediatric Concerns: None reported, but observe for sedation, dry mouth.

Drug Interactions: Barbiturates may lower serum levels of TCAs. Central and respiratory depressant effects may be additive. Cimetidine has increased serum TCA concentrations. Anticholinergic symptoms may be exacerbated. Use with clonidine may produce dangerous elevation in blood pressure and hypertensive crisis. Dicumarol anticoagulant capacity may be increased when used with TCAs. Co-use with fluoxetine may increase the toxic levels and effects of TCAs. Symptoms may persist for several weeks after discontinuation of fluoxetine. Haloperidol may increase serum concentrations of TCAs. MAO inhibitors should never be given immediately after or with tricyclic antidepressants. Oral contraceptives may inhibit the metabolism of tricyclic antidepressants and may increase their plasma levels.

Alternatives: Amoxapine, amitriptyline

Adult Dosage: 75-100 mg QD

T½ = 8-16 hours	**M/P = 0.5-1.5**
PHL =	**PB = 90%**
PK = 1-2 hours	**Oral = 90%**
MW = 280	**pKa = 9.5**
Vd = 20-40	

References:
1. Sovner R, Orsulak PJ. Excretion of imipramine and desipramine in human breast milk. Am J Psychiatry 136:451-2, 1979.
2. Erickson SH, et. al. Tricyclics and breast feeding. Am J Psychiatry 136:1483, 1979.
3. Buist A, Norman T, and Dennerstein L. Breastfeeding and the use of psychotropic medication: a review. J. Affective Disorders 19:197-206,1990.
4. Wisner KL, Perel JM, Findling RL: Antidepressant treatment during breast-feeding. Am J Psychiatry 153(9): 1132-1137, 1996.

INDAPAMIDE

Trade: Lozol
Can/Aus/UK: Apo-Indapamide, Dapa-Tabs, Gen-Indapamide, Lozide, Nadide, Napamide, Natrilix
Uses: Antihypertensive diuretic
AAP: Not reviewed

Indapamide is the first of a new class of indoline diuretics used to treat hypertension. No data exists on transfer into human milk.[1] Some diuretics may reduce the production of breastmilk. See hydrochlorothiazide as alternative.

Pregnancy Risk Category: D

Lactation Risk Category: L3

Theoretic Infant Dose:

Adult Concerns: Sodium and potassium loss, hypotension, dizziness, nausea, vomiting, constipation.

Pediatric Concerns: None reported, but observe for reduction in milk supply, and volume depletion.

Drug Interactions: May reduce effect of oral hypoglycemics. Cholestyramine may reduce absorption of indapamide. May increase the effect of furosemide and other diuretics. May increased toxicity and levels of lithium.

Alternatives:

Adult Dosage: 2.5-5 mg QD

T½ = 14 hours	M/P =
PHL =	PB = 71%
PK = 0.5-2 hours	Oral = Complete
MW = 366	pKa =
Vd =	

References:
1.   Pharmaceutical Manufacturers Package Insert, 1996.

INDIUM - 111M

Trade:
Can/Aus/UK:
Uses: Radioactive diagnostic agent
AAP: Radioactive compound that requires temporary cessation
of breastfeeding.

Indium-111 is a radioactive material used for imaging neuroendocrine tumors. While the plasma half-life is extremely short (<10 minutes), with the majority of this product leaving the plasma compartment and distributing to tissue sites, the radioactive half-life is 2.8 days.   In one patient receiving 12 MBq (0.32 mCi), the concentration in milk at 6 and 20 hours was   0.09 Bq/ml and 0.20 Bq/ml per MBq injected.[1] These data indicate that breastfeeding may be safe if this radiopharmaceutical is used. Assuming an ingestion of 500 cc daily, the infant would receive approximately 100 Bq per MBq given to the mother (approximately 0.1 μCi).   The NRC recommends a waiting period of 1 week with doses of 20 Mbq (0.5 mCi). See appendix.

Pregnancy Risk Category:

Lactation Risk Category: L4

Theoretic Infant Dose:

Adult Concerns: Nausea, dizziness, headache, flushing, hypotension.

Pediatric Concerns: None reported, but slight risk of radiation exposure.

Drug Interactions:

Alternatives:

Adult Dosage:

T½ = 2.8 days	M/P =
PHL =	PB =
PK = Immediate(IV)	Oral =
MW = 358	pKa =
Vd =	

References:
1. Pullar M. and Hartkamp, A. Excretion of radioactivity in breastmilk following administration of an 113- Indium labelled chelate complex. Br. J. Radial 50:846, 1977.

INDOMETHACIN

Trade: Indocin
Can/Aus/UK: Apo-Indomethacin, Arthrexin, Hicin, Indocid, Indoptol, Novo-Methacin
Uses: Non-steroidal anti-inflammatory
AAP: Approved by the American Academy of Pediatrics for use in breastfeeding mothers

Indomethacin is a potent nonsteroidal anti-inflammatory agent frequently used in arthritis. It is also used in newborns in neonatal units to close a patent ductus arteriosus. There is one reported case of convulsions in an infant of a breastfeeding mother early postpartum (day 7).[1] Another report of 16 women and 7 of their infants, indicates a median milk/plasma ratio of 0.37.[2] Total infant dose, assuming daily milk intake of 150 ml/kg, ranged from 0.07% to 0.98% of the weight adjusted maternal dose. Plasma samples derived from 6 of the 7 infants were below the sensitivity of the assay (< 20 μg/L) and 47 μg/L in only one infant. Dose calculations for all 16 infants showed that absolute dose rate ranged from < 0.003 to 0.017 mg/kg/day while relative dose in milk ranged from 0.11% to 0.98% (median 0.18%). In six of seven infants, indomethacin levels were below detection. In one infant the plasma level was 47 μg/L. No adverse affects were noted in this study.

Pregnancy Risk Category: B during 1st and 2nd trimesters
D during 3rd trimester

Lactation Risk Category: L3

Theoretic Infant Dose: 17.0 μg/kg/day

Adult Concerns: Renal dysfunction, GI distress, gastric bleeding, diarrhea, clotting dysfunction.

Pediatric Concerns: One case of seizures in neonate. Additional report suggests no untoward effects. Frequently used in neonatal nurseries for patent ductus.

Drug Interactions: May prolong prothrombin time when used with warfarin. Antihypertensive effects of ACEi family may be blunted or completely abolished by NSAIDs. Some NSAIDs may block antihypertensive effect of beta blockers, diuretics. Used with cyclosporin, may dramatically increase renal toxicity. May increase digoxin, phenytoin, lithium levels. May increase toxicity of methotrexate. May increase bioavailability of penicillamine.

Probenecid may increase NSAID levels.

Alternatives: Ibuprofen

Adult Dosage: 25-50 mg BID-TID

T½ = 4.5 hours	M/P = 0.37
PHL = 30 hours (prematures)	PB = >90%
PK = 1-2 :2-4(SR) hours	Oral = 90%
MW = 357	pKa = 4.5
Vd = 0.33-0.40	

References:

1. Eeg-Olofsson O, et. al. Convulsions in a breast-fed infant after maternal indomethacin. Lancet 1978;2:215.
2. Lebedevs TH, et.al. Excretion of indomethacin in breast milk. Brit. J. Clin. Pharmacol. 32(6):751-4,1991.

INFLIXIMAB

Trade: Remicade
Can/Aus/UK: Remicade
Uses: Treatment of Crohns, Rheumatoid arthritis
AAP: Not reviewed

Infliximab is a monoclonal antibody to tumor necrosis factor-alpha (TNF-alpha) used to treat Crohns disease and rheumatoid arthritis. Infliximab is a very large molecular weight antibody and is largely retained in the vascular system. In a study of one breastfeeding patient who received 5 mg/kg I.V., infliximab levels were determined in milk at 0, 2, 4, 8, 24, 48, 72 hours, and 4, 5, and 7 days.[1] None was detected in milk at any time (detection limit < 0.1 μg/mL). While these are preliminary study results that are continuing, infliximab is probably too large to enter milk in clinically measurable amounts. It would not be orally bioavailable.

Pregnancy Risk Category: C

Lactation Risk Category: L2

Theoretic Infant Dose:

Adult Concerns: Infusion-related reactions include fever, chills, pruritus, urticaria, chest pain, hypotension. A state of immunosuppression is induced thus serious infection including sepsis, disseminated tuberculosis and other infections have been reported.

Pediatric Concerns: None reported in one patient.

Drug Interactions:

Alternatives:

Adult Dosage: 5 mg/kg (Crohns)

T½ = 8-9.5 days	M/P =
PHL=	PB =
PK =	Oral = Nil
MW = 149100	pKa =
Vd = 3	

References:
1. Hale, TW. and Fasanmade, A. Unpublished data. 2002.

INFLUENZA VIRUS VACCINE

Trade: Vaccine- Influenza, Flu-Imune, Fluogen, Fluzone
Can/Aus/UK: Fluviral, Fluzone
Uses: Vaccine
AAP: Not reviewed

Influenza vaccine is prepared from inactivated, non-viable influenza viruses and infection of the neonate via milk would not be expected. There are no reported side effects, nor published contraindications for using influenza virus vaccine during lactation.[1,2]

Pregnancy Risk Category: C

Lactation Risk Category: L3

Theoretic Infant Dose:

Adult Concerns: Fever, myalgia.

Pediatric Concerns: None reported in breastfeeding mothers.

Drug Interactions: Do not administer within seven days after DTP immunizations. Decreased effect with immunosuppressants.

Alternatives:

Adult Dosage: 0.5 ml injection once

References:
1. Kilbourne ED. Questions and answers. Artificial influenza immunization of nursing mothers not harmful. JAMA 226:87, 1973.
2. Pharmaceutical manufacturer package insert, 1996.

INSECT STINGS

Trade: Insect Stings, Spider Stings, Bee Stings
Can/Aus/UK:
Uses: Insect stings, envenomations
AAP: Not reviewed

Insect stings are primarily composed of small peptides, enzymes such as hyaluronidase, and other factors such as histamine. Because the total injectant is so small, most reactions are local. In cases of systemic reactions, the secondary release of maternal reactants produces the allergic response in the injected individual. Nevertheless, the amount of injection is exceedingly small. In the case of black widow spiders, the venom is so large in molecular weight, it would not likely penetrate milk. In addition, most of the venoms and allergens would be destroyed in the acidic milieu of the infant's stomach. The sting of the Loxosceles spider (brown recluse, fiddleback) is primarily a local necrosis without systemic effects. No reports of toxicity to nursing infants has been reported from insect stings.

Pregnancy Risk Category:

Lactation Risk Category:

Theoretic Infant Dose:

Adult Concerns: Nausea, vomiting.

Pediatric Concerns: None reported via milk.

Drug Interactions:

Alternatives:

Adult Dosage: N/A

References:

INSULIN

Trade: Humulin
Can/Aus/UK: Humalog, Humulin, Iletin, Mixtard, Monotard, Novolin, Protaphane
Uses: Human insulin
AAP: Not reviewed

Insulin is a large peptide that is not secreted into milk. Even if secreted, it would be destroyed in the infant's GI tract leading to minimal or no absorption.

Pregnancy Risk Category: B

Lactation Risk Category: L1

Theoretic Infant Dose:

Adult Concerns: Hypoglycemia.

Pediatric Concerns: None reported via milk.

Drug Interactions: A decreased hypoglycemic effect may result when used with oral contraceptives, corticosteroids, diltiazem, epinephrine, thiazide diuretics, thyroid hormones and niacin. Increased hypoglycemic effects may result when used with alcohol, beta blockers, fenfluramine, MAO inhibitors, salicylates, tetracyclines.

Alternatives:

Adult Dosage:

T½ =	M/P =
PHL =	PB =
PK =	Oral = 0%
MW = >6000	pKa =
Vd = 0.37	

References:

INTERFERON ALPHA-N3

Trade: Alferon N, Interferon Alpha
Can/Aus/UK:
Uses: Immune modulator, antiviral.
AAP: Not reviewed

Interferon alpha is a pure clone of a single interferon subspecies with antiviral, antiproliferative, and immunomodulatory activity . The alpha-interferons are active against various malignancies and viral syndromes such as hairy cell leukemia, melanoma, AIDS-related Kaposi's sarcoma, condyloma acuminata, and chronic hepatitis B and C infection.[1]

Very little is known about the secretion of interferons in human milk, although some interferons are known to be secreted normally and may contribute to the antiviral properties of human milk. However, interferons are large in molecular weight (16-28,000 daltons) which would limit their transfer into human milk. Following treatment with a massive dose of 30 million units I.V. in one breastfeeding patient, the amount of interferon alpha transferred into human milk was 894, 1004, 1551, 1507, 788, 721 units at 0 (baseline), 2, 4, 8, 12, and 24 hours respectively.[2] Hence, even following a massive dose, no change in breastmilk levels were noted. One thousand international units is roughly equivalent to 500 nanograms of interferon.

The oral absorption of interferons is controversial, and is believed to be minimal. Interferons are relatively nontoxic unless extraordinarily large doses are administered parenterally. Interferons are sometimes used in infants and children to treat idiopathic thromboplastinemia (ITP) in huge doses.

Pregnancy Risk Category: C

Lactation Risk Category: L3

Theoretic Infant Dose:

Adult Concerns: Thrombocytopenia and neutropenia. Flu-like syndrome which occurs 30 minutes after administration and persists for several hours. Fatigue, hyperglycemia, nausea and vomiting.

Pediatric Concerns: None reported via milk.

Drug Interactions: Hematologic abnormalities (granulocytopenia, thrombocytopenia) may occur when used with ACE inhibitors.

Alternatives:

Adult Dosage: 0.05-0.5 mL per wart twice weekly

T½ = 5-7 hours	M/P =
PHL=	PB =
PK = Immediate	Oral = Low
MW = 28,000	pKa =
Vd = 0.44	

References:
1. Pharmaceutical Manufacturers Package Insert, 1997.
2. Kumar, A. and Hale, T. Excretion of human interferon alpha-n3 into human milk. J Hum Lact 16(3):226-8,2000.

INTERFERON BETA - 1A

Trade: Avonex, Rebif
Can/Aus/UK: Avonex, Rebif
Uses: Immune modulator
AAP: Not reviewed

Interferon Beta-1A is a glycoprotein with antiviral, antiproliferative, and immunomodulator activity presently used for reducing the severity and frequency of exacerbations of relapsing-remitting multiple sclerosis.[1] Very little is known about the secretion of interferons in human milk, although some interferons are known to be secreted normally and may contribute to the antiviral properties of human milk. However, interferons are large in molecular weight, generally containing 166 amino acids, which would limit their transfer into human milk. Their oral absorption is controversial, but is believed to be minimal. However, interferons are relatively nontoxic unless extraordinarily large doses are administered parenterally. Interferons are sometimes used in infants and children to treat idiopathic thromboplastinemia (ITP) in huge doses. See Interferon Alpha, Interferon 1B.

Pregnancy Risk Category: C

Lactation Risk Category: L3

Theoretic Infant Dose:

Adult Concerns: Headache, myalgia, nausea, diarrhea, dyspepsia, fever, chills, malaise, sweating, depression, flu-like symptoms. These effects generally follow huge doses.

Pediatric Concerns: None reported via milk.

Drug Interactions: Do not use with live viral vaccines.

Alternatives:

Adult Dosage: 30 ug weekly IM

T½ = 10 Hours	M/P =
PHL=	PB =
PK = 3-15 hours	Oral = Minimal
MW = 22,500	pKa =
Vd = 61.6 L	

References:
1. Chofflon M: Recombinant human interferon beta in relapsing-remitting multiple sclerosis: a review of the major clinical trials. Eur J Neurol 7:369-380,2000.

INTERFERON BETA-1B

Trade: Betaseron
Can/Aus/UK: Betaferon, Betaseron
Uses: Antiviral, immunomodulator
AAP: Not reviewed

Interferon Beta-1B is a glycoprotein with antiviral, antiproliferative, and immunomodulatory activity presently used for treatment of multiple sclerosis.[1,2] Very little is known about the secretion of interferons in human milk, although some interferons are known to be secreted and may contribute to the antiviral properties of human milk. However, interferons are large in molecular weight, generally containing 165 amino acids, which would limit their transfer into human milk. Their oral absorption is controversial, but is believed to be minimal. However, interferons are relatively nontoxic unless extraordinarily large doses are administered parenterally. Interferons are sometimes used in infants and children to treat idiopathic thromboplastinemia (ITP) in huge doses. See Interferon Alpha.

Pregnancy Risk Category: C

Lactation Risk Category: L3

Theoretic Infant Dose:

Adult Concerns: Headache, myalgia, nausea, diarrhea, dyspepsia, fever, chills, malaise, sweating, depression, flu-like symptoms. These effects generally follow huge doses.

Pediatric Concerns: None reported.

Drug Interactions: Hematologic abnormalities (granulocytopenia, thrombocytopenia) may occur when added to ACE inhibitors.

Alternatives:

Adult Dosage: 0.25 mg every other day

T½ = 4.3 hours	M/P =
PHL=	PB =
PK = 3-15 hours (IM)	Oral = Poor
MW =	pKa =
Vd = 2.9	

References:
1. Chiang J, Gloff CA, et.al. Pharmacokinetics of recombinant human interferon-Bser in healthy volunteers and its effect on serum neopterin. Pharm. Res. 10:567-72, 1993.
2. Wills RJ. Clinical pharmacokinetics of interferons. Clin. Pharmacokinet. 19:390-399, 1990.

IODINATED GLYCEROL

Trade: Organidin, Iophen, R-gen
Can/Aus/UK: Organidin
Uses: Expectorant
AAP: Not reviewed

This product contains 50% organically bound iodine. High levels of iodine are known to be secreted in milk.[1] Milk/plasma ratios as high as 26 have been reported. Following absorption by the infant, high levels of iodine could lead to severe thyroid depression in infants. Normal iodine levels in breastmilk are already four times higher than the RDA for an infant. Expectorants, including iodine, work very poorly. Recently, many iodine containing products have been replaced with guaifenesin, which is considered safer. High levels of iodine-containing drugs should not be used in lactating mothers.

Pregnancy Risk Category: X

Lactation Risk Category: L4

Theoretic Infant Dose:

Adult Concerns: Depressed thyroid function. Diarrhea, nausea, vomiting. Acne, dermatitis. Metallic taste.

Pediatric Concerns: Iodine concentrates in milk and should not be administered to breastfeeding mothers. Infantile thyroid suppression is likely.

Drug Interactions: Increased toxicity with disulfiram, metronidazole, procarbazine, MAO inhibitors, CNS depressants, lithium.

Alternatives:

Adult Dosage:

T½ =	M/P =
PHL =	PB =
PK =	Oral = Complete
MW = 258	pKa =
Vd =	

References:

1. Postellon DC, Aronow R. Iodine in mother's milk. JAMA 247:463, 1982.

IOHEXOL

Trade: Omnipaque
Can/Aus/UK: Omnipaque
Uses: Radiopaque agent
AAP: Approved by the American Academy of Pediatrics for use in breastfeeding mothers

Iohexol is a nonionic radiocontrast agent. Radiopaque agents (except barium) are iodinated compounds used to visualize various organs during X-ray, CAT scans, and other radiological procedures. These compounds are highly iodinated benzoic acid derivatives. Although under usual circumstances, iodine products are contraindicated in nursing mothers (due to ion trapping in milk), these products are unique in that they are extremely inert and are largely cleared without metabolism. The iodine is organically bound to the structure and is not biologically active.

In a study of 4 women who received 0.755 g/kg (350 mg iodine/mL) of iohexol I.V., the mean peak level of iohexol in milk was 35 mg/L at 3 hours post-injection.[1] The average concentration in milk was only 11.4 mg/L over 24 hours. Assuming a daily milk intake of 150 mL/kg body weight, the amount of iohexol transferred to an infant during the first

24 hours would be 1.7 mg/kg which corresponds to 0.2 % of the maternal dose.

As a group, these radiocontrast agents are virtually unabsorbed after oral administration (< 0.1%). Iohexol has a brief half-life of just 2 hours and the estimated dose ingested by the infant is only 0.2 % of the radiocontrast dose used clinically for various scanning procedures in infants.   Although most company package inserts suggest that an infant be removed from the breast for 24 hours, no untoward effects have been reported with these products in breastfed infants. Because the amount of iohexol transferred into milk is so small, the authors conclude that breastfeeding is acceptable after intravenously administered iohexol.

Pregnancy Risk Category: B

Lactation Risk Category: L2

Theoretic Infant Dose: 1.7 mg/kg/day

Adult Concerns: Hypersensitivity to iodine.   Arrhythmias, renal failure. Volume expansion.

Pediatric Concerns: None reported via milk in one study.

Drug Interactions: Lower seizure threshold when used with amitriptyline, other tricyclics, CNS stimulants, MAO inhibitors. Should not be used in patients on metformin therapy.

Alternatives:

Adult Dosage: 10-75 mL X 1

T½ = 2 hours	**M/P =**
PHL=	**PB =**
PK = 3-10 minutes	**Oral = Nil**
MW =	**pKa =**
Vd = 0.55	

References:
1.   Nielsen ST et.al. Excretion of iohexol and metrizoate in human breast milk. Acta. Radiol. 28:523-26, 1987.

IOPAMIDOL

Trade: Isovue-128
Can/Aus/UK: Ascorbef, Gastromiro
Uses: Radiocontrast agent
AAP: Not reviewed

Iopamidol is a nonionic radiocontrast agent used for numerous radiological procedures. Although it contains significant iodine content, the iodine is covalently bound to the parent molecule and the bioavailability of the iodine molecule is minuscule.[1]   As with other ionic and nonionic radiocontrast agents, it is primarily extracellular and intravascular, its does not pass the blood-brain barrier, and it would be extremely unlikely that it would penetrate into human milk. However, no data are available on its transfer into human milk.   As with most of these products, it is poorly absorbed from the GI tract and rapidly excreted from the maternal circulation due to a extremely short half-live.

Pregnancy Risk Category:

Lactation Risk Category: L3

Theoretic Infant Dose:

Adult Concerns: Infrequently seizures, deformed and dehydrated red blood cells. Hot flashes, angina, flushing.

Pediatric Concerns: None reported.

Drug Interactions:

Alternatives:

Adult Dosage: 10-60 mL X 1

T½ = < 2 hours.	M/P =
PHL =	PB = < 2 hours
PK = Immediate	Oral = None
MW = 777	pKa =
Vd = 0.35	

References:
1.   Pharmaceutical Manufacturers Package Insert, 1997.

IOPANOIC ACID

Trade: Telepaque
Can/Aus/UK: Telepaque
Uses: Radiocontrast agent
AAP: Approved by the American Academy of Pediatrics for use in breastfeeding mothers

Iopanoic acid is a radiopaque organic iodine compound similar to dozens of other radiocontrast agents. It contains 66.7% by weight of iodine. As with all of these compounds, the iodine is organically bound to the parent molecule, and only minimal amounts are free in solution, or metabolized by the body. In a group of 5 breastfeeding mothers who received an average of 2.77 gm of iodine (as Iopanoic acid), the amount of iopanoic acid excreted into human milk during the following 19-29 hours was 20.8 mg, or 0.08% of the maternal dose.[1]   No untoward effects were noted in the infants.

Pregnancy Risk Category: D

Lactation Risk Category: L2

Theoretic Infant Dose:

Adult Concerns: Nausea, vomiting, diarrhea, cramps.

Pediatric Concerns: None reported via milk. Levels are low.

Drug Interactions:

Alternatives:

Adult Dosage: 3 g X 1-2

T½ = 24 hours	M/P =
PHL=	PB = 97%
PK =	Oral = Poor
MW = 571	pKa = 4.8
Vd =	

References:
1. Holmdahl KH. Cholecystography during lactation. Acta Radiol 45:305-7, 1956.

IPRATROPIUM BROMIDE

Trade: Atrovent
Can/Aus/UK: Apo-Ipravent, Atrovent, Atrovnet
Uses: Bronchodilator in asthmatics
AAP: Not reviewed

Ipratropium is an anticholinergic drug that is used via inhalation for dilating the bronchi of asthmatics.[1] Ipratropium is a quaternary ammonium compound, and although no data exists, it probably penetrates into breastmilk in exceedingly small levels due to its structure. It is unlikely that the infant would absorb any due to the poor tissue distribution and oral absorption of this family of drugs.

Pregnancy Risk Category: B

Lactation Risk Category: L2

Theoretic Infant Dose:

Adult Concerns: Nervousness, dizziness, nausea, GI distress, drug mouth, bitter taste.

Pediatric Concerns: None reported. Commonly used in pediatric patients.

Drug Interactions: Albuterol may increase effect of ipratropium. May have increased toxicity when used with other anticholinergics.

Alternatives:

Adult Dosage: 36 mcg QID

T½ = 2 hours.	M/P =
PHL =	PB =
PK = 1-2 hours	Oral = 0-2%
MW = 412	pKa =
Vd =	

References:
1. Pharmaceutical Manufacturers Package Insert, 1996.

IRBESARTAN

Trade: Avapro
Can/Aus/UK: Accuretic, Adizem, Amizide, Avalide, Avapro
Uses: Antihypertensive
AAP: Not reviewed

Irbesartan is an angiotensin-II receptor antagonist, used as an antihypertensive. Low concentrations are known to be secreted into rodent milk, but human studies are lacking.[1] Both the ACE inhibitor family, and the specific AT1 inhibitors such as irbesartan are contraindicated in the 2nd and 3rd trimesters of pregnancy due to severe hypotension, neonatal skull hypoplasia, irreversible renal failure, and death in the newborn infant. However, some of ACE inhibitors can be used in breastfeeding mothers 2-3 months postpartum without major risk in some cases with due caution. Extreme caution is recommended.

Pregnancy Risk Category: C in 1st trimester
D in 2nd or 3rd trimester

Lactation Risk Category: L3
L4 if used in neonatal period

Theoretic Infant Dose:

Adult Concerns: Headache, back pain, pharyngitis, and dizziness have been reported. The use of ACE inhibitors and angiotensin receptor blockers during pregnancy or the neonatal period is extremely dangerous and has resulted in hypotension, neonatal skull hypoplasia, anuria, renal failure and death.

Pediatric Concerns: None reported via milk, but caution is recommended.

Drug Interactions: None reported thus far.

Alternatives: Captopril, Enalapril

Adult Dosage: 150-300 mg QD

T½ = 11-15 hours	M/P =
PHL =	PB = 90%
PK = 1.5-2 hours	Oral = 60-80%
MW = 428	pKa =
Vd = 1.3	

References:
1.   Pharmaceutical Manufacturers Package Insert, 1999.

IRON

Trade: Fer-in-sol
Can/Aus/UK: Feospan, Infufer, Jectofer, Slow-Fe
Uses: Metal supplement
AAP: Not reviewed

The secretion of iron salts into breastmilk appears to be very low although the bioavailability of that present in milk is high. One recent study suggests that supplementation is not generally required until the 4th month postpartum when some breastfed infants may become iron deficient, although these assumptions are controversial.[1] Premature infants are more susceptible to iron deficiencies, because they do not have the same hepatic stores available as full term infants.   These authors recommend iron supplementation, particularly in exclusively breastfed infants, beginning at 4th month.[1]   Supplementation in pre-term infants should probably be initiated earlier.   Again, avoid excessively high doses.

Pregnancy Risk Category:

Lactation Risk Category: L1

Theoretic Infant Dose:

Adult Concerns: Constipation, GI distress.

Pediatric Concerns: None reported via milk.

Drug Interactions: Decreased iron absorption when used with antacids, cimetidine, levodopa, penicillamine, quinolones, tetracyclines. Slightly increased absorption with ascorbic acid.

Alternatives:

Adult Dosage: 50-100 mg TID

T½ =	M/P =
PHL =	PB =
PK =	Oral = <30%
MW = 56	pKa =
Vd =	

References:

1. Calvo EB, Galindo AC, and Aspres NB. Iron status in exclusively breast-fed infants. Pediatrics 90:375-9,1992.

IRON DEXTRAN

Trade: Infed
Can/Aus/UK:
Uses: Iron supplement
AAP: Not reviewed

Iron dextran is a colloidal solution of ferric hydroxide in a complex with partially hydrolyzed low molecular weight dextran. It is used for severe iron deficiency anemia. Its molecular weight is approximately 180,000 daltons. Approximately 99% of the iron in iron dextran is present as a stable ferric-dextran complex. Following IM injection, iron dextran is absorbed from the site principally through the lymphatic system and subsequently transferred to the reticuloendothelial system in the liver for metabolism. The initial phase of absorption lasts 3 days, which accounts for 60% of an IM dose. The other 40% requires up to 1-3 weeks to several months for complete absorption. While there are no data available on the transfer of iron dextran into human milk, it is extremely unlikely due to its massive molecular weight. Further, iron is transferred into human milk by a tightly controlled pumping system that first chelates the iron to a high molecular weight protein, and then transfers it into the milk compartment. It is generally well known that dietary supplements of iron do not change milk levels of iron.[1] Please note: while the pregnancy risk category is only C, it has been shown to be teratogenic in other species. Great care should be used in pregnant women.

Pregnancy Risk Category: C

Lactation Risk Category: L2

Theoretic Infant Dose:

Adult Concerns: Local reactions at the site of injection. Abdominal pain, dyspepsia, nausea, vomiting and diarrhea. Headache, paresthesias, weakness, changes in taste perception, faintness, syncope, folic acid deficiency, and leukocytosis. Please note: while the pregnancy risk category is only C, it has been shown to be teratogenic in other species and great care should be used in pregnant women.

Pediatric Concerns: None via breastmilk.

Drug Interactions:

Alternatives:

Adult Dosage:

References:
1. Lawrence RA. Breastfeeding, A guide for the medical profession. Mosby, St. Louis, 1994.

ISOETHARINE

Trade: Bronkosol, Bronkometer
Can/Aus/UK: Numotac
Uses: Bronchodilator
AAP: Not reviewed

Isoetharine is a selective beta-2 adrenergic bronchodilator for asthmatics. There are no reports on its secretion into human milk.[1] However, plasma levels following inhalation are exceedingly low, and breastmilk levels would similarly be low. Isoetharine is rapidly metabolized in the GI tract, so oral absorption by the infant would likely be minimal.

Pregnancy Risk Category: C

Lactation Risk Category: L2

Theoretic Infant Dose:

Adult Concerns: Tremors and excitement, hypertension, anxiety, insomnia.

Pediatric Concerns: None reported.

Drug Interactions: May have decreased effect with beta blockers and increased toxicity with other adrenergic stimulants such as epinephrine.

Alternatives:

Adult Dosage:

T½ = 1-3 hours	M/P =
PHL =	PB =
PK = 5-15 min.(inhaled)	Oral =
MW = 239	pKa =
Vd =	

References:
1. Drug Facts and Comparisons. 1995. ed. Facts and Comparisons, St. Louis.

ISOMETHEPTENE MUCATE

Trade: Midrin
Can/Aus/UK: Midrin
Uses: For tension and migraine headache.
AAP: Not reviewed

Isometheptene is a mild stimulate (sympathomimetic) that apparently acts by constricting dilated cranial and cerebral arterioles, thus reducing vascular headaches. It is listed as "possibly" effective by the FDA and is probably only marginally effective.[1]   Midrin also contains acetaminophen and a mild sedative dichloralphenazone, of which little is known.

No data are available on transfer into human milk. Due to its size and molecular composition, it is likely to attain low to moderate levels in breastmilk. Because better drugs exist for migraine therapy, this product is probably not a good choice for breastfeeding mothers. See sumatriptan, amitriptyline, or propranolol as alternatives.

Pregnancy Risk Category:

Lactation Risk Category: L3

Theoretic Infant Dose:

Adult Concerns: Dizziness, skin rash, hypertension, sedation.

Pediatric Concerns: None reported. Observe for stimulation.

Drug Interactions:

Alternatives: Sumatriptan, Amitriptyline, Propanolol

Adult Dosage:

References:
1.   Drug Facts and Comparisons. 1995. ed. Facts and Comparisons, St. Louis.

ISONIAZID

Trade: INH, Laniazid
Can/Aus/UK: Isotamine, PMS Isoniazid, Pycazide, Rimifon
Uses: Antituberculosis agent
AAP: Approved by the American Academy of Pediatrics for use in breastfeeding mothers

Isoniazid (INH) is an antimicrobial agent primarily used to treat tuberculosis. It is secreted into milk in quantities ranging from 0.75 to 2.3% of the maternal dose. Following doses of 5 and 10 mg/kg, one report measured peak milk levels at 6 mg/L and 9 mg/L respectively.[1]

Isoniazid was not measurable in the infant's serum, but was detected in the urine of several infants.

In another study, following a maternal dose of 300 mg of isoniazid, the concentration of isoniazid in milk peaked at 3 hours at 16.6 mg/L while the acetyl derivative (AcINH) was 3.76 mg/L.[2] The 24 hour excretion of INH in milk was estimated at 7 mg. The authors felt this dose was potentially hazardous to a breastfed infant.

Caution and close monitoring of infant for liver toxicity and neuritis are recommended. Peripheral neuropathies, common in INH therapy, can be treated with 10-50 mg/day pyridoxine in adults. PHL= 8-20 hours (neonate), 2-5 hours (1.5-15 yrs).

Pregnancy Risk Category: C

Lactation Risk Category: L3

Theoretic Infant Dose: 2.4 mg/kg/day

Adult Concerns: Mild hepatic dysfunction, peripheral neuritis, nausea, vomiting, dizziness.

Pediatric Concerns: None reported, but the infant should be closely monitored for toxicity including hepatitis, vision changes. Observe for fatigue, weakness, malaise, anorexia, nausea, vomiting.

Drug Interactions: Decreased effect/plasma levels of isoniazide with aluminum products. Increased toxicity/levels of oral anticoagulants, carbamazepine, cycloserine, phenytoin, certain benzodiazepines. Disulfiram reactions.

Alternatives:

Adult Dosage: 5 mg/kg QD

T½ = 1.1 - 3.1 hours	M/P =
PHL= 8-20 hours(neonate)	PB = 10-15%
PK = 1-2 hours(oral)	Oral = Complete
MW = 137	pKa = 1.9, 3.5,
Vd = 0.6	

References:
1. Snider DE, Powell KE. Should women taking antituberculosis drugs breast-feed? Arch Inter Med. 144:589-590, 1984.
2. Berlin CM, Lee C. Isoniazid and acetylisoniazid disposition in human milk, saliva and plasma. Fed. Proc. 38:426, 1979.

ISOPROTERENOL

Trade: Medihaler-Iso, Isuprel
Can/Aus/UK: Isoprenaline, Isuprel, Medihaler-Iso, Saventrine
Uses: Bronchodilator
AAP: Not reviewed

Isoproterenol is an old class adrenergic bronchodilator.[1] Currently it is seldom used for this purpose. There are no data available on breastmilk levels. It is probably secreted into milk in extremely small levels. Isoproterenol is rapidly metabolized in the gut, and it is unlikely a breastfeeding infant would absorb clinically significant levels.

Pregnancy Risk Category: C

Lactation Risk Category: L2

Theoretic Infant Dose:

Adult Concerns: Insomnia, excitement, agitation, tachycardia.

Pediatric Concerns: None reported.

Drug Interactions: Increased toxicity when used with other adrenergic stimulants and elevation of blood pressure. When used with isoproterenol, general anesthetics may cause arrhythmias.

Alternatives: Albuterol

Adult Dosage: 10-30 mg QID

T½ = 1-2 hours	**M/P =**
PHL=	PB =
PK = 10 min.(Inhaled)	Oral = Poor
MW = 211	pKa = 8.6
Vd = 0.5	

References:
1. Drug Facts and Comparisons. 1995 ed. Facts and Comparisons, St. Louis.

ISOTRETINOIN

Trade: Accutane
Can/Aus/UK: Accure, Accutane, Isotrex, Roaccutane
Uses: Vitamin A derivative used for acne
AAP: Not reviewed

Isotretinoin is a synthetic derivative of the Vitamin A family called retinoids. Isotretinoin is known to be incredibly teratogenic producing profound birth defects in exposed fetuses.[1] It is primarily used for cystic acne where it is extremely effective if used by skilled physicians. While only 25% reaches the plasma, the remaining is either metabolized in the GI tract or removed first-pass by the liver. It is distributed to the liver, adrenals, ovaries, and lacrimal glands. Unlike vitamin A, isotretinoin is not stored in the liver. Secretion into milk is unknown, but is likely as with other retinoids. Isotretinoin is extremely lipid soluble, and concentrations in milk may be significant. The manufacturer strongly recommends against using isotretinoin in a breastfeeding mother.

Pregnancy Risk Category: X

Lactation Risk Category: L5

Theoretic Infant Dose:

Adult Concerns: Cheilitis(inflammation of the lips), dry nose, pruritus, elevated serum triglycerides, arthralgia, altered CBC, fatigue, headache, anorexia, nausea, vomiting, abnormal liver function tests, birth defects.

Pediatric Concerns: None reported, but this product poses too many risks to use in a lactating woman.

Drug Interactions: May increased clearance of carbamazepine. Avoid use of other vitamin A products.

Alternatives:

Adult Dosage: 0.5-2 mg/kg QD

T½ = >20 hours	M/P =
PHL=	PB = 99.9%
PK = 3.2 hours	Oral = 25%
MW = 300	pKa =
Vd =	

References:
1. Zbinden G. Investigation on the toxicity of tretinoin administered systemically to animals. Acta Derm Verereol Suppl(Stockh) 74:36-40,1975.

ISRADIPINE

Trade: Dynacirc
Can/Aus/UK: Prescal
Uses: Calcium channel blocker, antihypertensive
AAP: Not reviewed

It is not known if isradipine is secreted into milk but it should be expected.[1] Exercise caution if used during lactation. Observe for lethargy, low blood pressure, and headache. See nifedipine as alternative.

Pregnancy Risk Category: C

Lactation Risk Category: L4

Theoretic Infant Dose:

Adult Concerns: Hypotension, headache, dizziness, fatigue, bradycardia, nausea, dyspnea.

Pediatric Concerns: None reported, but observe for hypotension, fatigue, bradycardia, apnea.

Drug Interactions: H2 blockers may increase oral absorption of isradipine. Carbamazepine levels may be increased. Cyclosporine levels may be increased. May increase hypotension associated with fentanyl use. Digitalis levels may be increased. May increase quinidine levels including bradycardia, arrhythmias, and hypotension.

Alternatives: Nifedipine, Verapamil, Nimodipine

Adult Dosage: 2.5-10 mg BID

T½ = 8 hours		M/P =	
PHL =		PB = 95%	
PK = 1.5 hours		Oral = 17%	
MW = 371		pKa =	
Vd =			

References:
1. Pharmaceutical Manufacturers Package Insert, 1996.

ITRACONAZOLE

Trade: Sporanox
Can/Aus/UK: Sporanox
Uses: Antifungal
AAP: Not reviewed

Itraconazole is an antifungal agent active against a variety of fungal strains. It is extensively metabolized to hydroxyitraconazole, an active metabolite.[1,2] Itraconazole has an enormous volume of distribution, and large quantities (20 fold compared to plasma) concentrate in fatty tissues, liver, kidney and skin. In a study of two women who received two oral doses of 200 mg itraconazole 12 hours apart, the average milk concentrations at 4, 24, and 48 hours after the second dose were 70, 28, and 16 μg/L respectively.[3] After 72 hours, itraconazole levels in one mother were 20 μg/L and undetectable in the other. Reported milk/plasma ratios at 4, 24, and 48 hours were 0.51, 1.61, and 1.77 respectively. However, itraconazole oral absorption in an infant is somewhat unlikely as it requires an acidic milieu for absorption, which is unlikely in a diet high in milk.

Never use with terfenadine or astemizole. Itraconazole has also been reported to induce significant bone defects in newborn animals, and it is not cleared for pediatric use. Until further studies are done, fluconazole is probably a preferred choice in breastfeeding mothers.

Pregnancy Risk Category: C

Lactation Risk Category: L2

Theoretic Infant Dose: 10.5 μg/kg/day

Adult Concerns: Nausea, vomiting, diarrhea, epigastric pain, dizziness, rash, hypertension, abnormal liver enzymes.

Pediatric Concerns: None reported via breastmilk. Absorption via milk is unlikely.

Drug Interactions: Decreased serum levels with isoniazid, rifampin and phenytoin. Decreased absorption under alkaline conditions. Agents which increase stomach pH such as H-2 blockers (cimetidine, famotidine, nizatidine, ranitidine), omeprazole, sucralfate, and milk significantly reduce absorption. Cyclosporin levels are significantly increased by 50%. May increase phenytoin levels, inhibit warfarin metabolism, and increase digoxin levels. Significantly increases terfenadine, astemizole plasma levels.

Alternatives: Fluconazole

Adult Dosage: 200-400 mg daily

T½ = 64 hours	M/P = 0.51-1.77
PHL =	PB = 99.8%
PK = 4 hours	Oral = 55%
MW = 706	pKa =
Vd = 10	

References:
1. Drug Facts and Comparisons. 1994 ed. Facts and Comparisons, St. Louis.
2. Pharmaceutical Manufacturers Package Insert, 1996.
3. Janssen Pharmaceuticals, 1996.

IVERMECTIN

Trade: Mectizan
Can/Aus/UK: Stromectol
Uses: Antiparasitic
AAP: Approved by the American Academy of Pediatrics for use in breastfeeding mothers

Ivermectin is now widely used to treat human onchocerciasis and lymphatic filariasis, other worms and parasites such as head lice. In a study of 4 women given 150 μg/kg orally, the maximum breastmilk concentration averaged 14.13 μg/L.[1] Milk/plasma ratios ranged from 0.39 to 0.57 with a mean of 0.51. Highest breastmilk concentration was at 4-6 hours Average daily ingestion of ivermectin was calculated at 2.1 μg/kg which is 10 fold less than the adult dose. No adverse effects were reported.

Pregnancy Risk Category: C

Lactation Risk Category: L3

Theoretic Infant Dose: 2.1 μg/kg/day

Adult Concerns: Headaches, pruritus, transient hypotension.

Pediatric Concerns: None reported.

Drug Interactions:

Alternatives:

Adult Dosage: 150-200 mcg/kg once

T½ = 28 hours	M/P = 0.39-0.57
PHL=	PB –
PK = 4 hours	Oral = Variable
MW =	pKa =
Vd =	

References:
1. Ogbuokiri JE, Ozumba BC, Okonkwo PO. Ivermectin levels in human breast milk. Eur. J. Clin. Pharm. 46:89-90, 1994.

KANAMYCIN

Trade: Kantrex
Can/Aus/UK: Kannasyn
Uses: Antibiotic
AAP: Approved by the American Academy of Pediatrics for use in breastfeeding mothers

Kanamycin is an aminoglycoside antibiotic primarily used for gram negative infections. In a study of 2-3 patients who received 1000 mg I.V., milk levels at 1, 2, 4, and 6 hours were zero, 0.1 mg/L, 0.3 mg/L, and 0.5 mg/L respectively.[1] The milk/plasma ratio at 6 hours was 0.045. Poor oral absorption (only 1%) in infant would limit amount absorbed. Could potentially alter GI flora in infant.

Pregnancy Risk Category: D

Lactation Risk Category: L2

Theoretic Infant Dose: 0.1 mg/kg/day

Adult Concerns: Diarrhea, ototoxicity, nephrotoxicity.

Pediatric Concerns: None reported, but observe for diarrhea.

Drug Interactions: May have increased toxicity when used with penicillins, cephalosporins, amphotericin B, and diuretics. May increase neuromuscular blockade when used with neuromuscular blocking agents.

Alternatives:

Adult Dosage: 5-7.5 mg/kg q 8-12 hours

T½ = 2.4 hours	M/P = 0.045
PHL = 4-18 hours	PB = 0%.
PK = 1 hour	Oral = 1%
MW =	pKa = 7.2
Vd = 0.2-0.3	

References:
1. Matsuda S. Transfer of antibiotics into maternal milk. Biol Res Pregnancy Perinatol. 5(2):57-60, 1984.

KAOLIN - PECTIN

Trade: Kaolin, Kaopectate
Can/Aus/UK: Donnagel-MB, Kao-Con, Kaopectate
Uses: Antidiarrhea
AAP: Not reviewed

Kaolin and pectin (attapulgite) are used as antidiarrhea agents. Kaolin is a natural hydrated aluminum silicate. Pectin is a purified polymerized carbohydrate obtained from citrus fruits. Kaolin and pectin are not absorbed following oral use. Some preparations may contain opiate compounds and atropine-like substances. Observe bottle for ingredients. Never use in children less than 3 years of age.

Pregnancy Risk Category: C

Lactation Risk Category: L2

Theoretic Infant Dose:

Adult Concerns: Constipation, fecal impaction, reduce drug absorption.

Pediatric Concerns: None reported via milk.

Drug Interactions: Decreases oral absorption of clindamycin, tetracyclines, penicillamine, digoxin.

Alternatives:

Adult Dosage: 60-120 mL PRN

T½ =	M/P =
PHL =	PB =
PK =	Oral = 0%
MW =	pKa =
Vd =	

References:

KAVA-KAVA

Trade: Awa, Kew, Tonga
Can/Aus/UK:
Uses: Sedative and sleep enhancement
AAP: Not reviewed

Kava is the dried rhizome and roots of Piper methysticum. While more than 20 varieties are know, the black and white grades are most popular. Kava drink is prepared from the rhizome by steeping the pulverized root in hot water. It is then filtered and drunk. It is indigenous to the islands of the South Pacific where it is used similar to alcohol to induce relaxation.[1] The activity of kava appears related to several dihydropyrones that possess CNS activity, including methysticin, kawain, dihydromethysticin, and yangonin. Studies of these agents suggest that they may induce mephenesin-like muscle relaxation in animals, similar in effect to the local anesthetics. Masticated kava induces a local anesthetic effect in the mouth. It is not known with certainty how these agents work, but it is apparently not at the opiate receptors, but they do induce sleep and reduce anxiety. The CNS activity of kava is due to the lipid components, not the more polar water soluble components. In humans, kava produces mild euphoria, happiness, fluent and lively speech. High doses may lead to muscle weakness, visual and auditory changes. Heavy users are underweight, have reduced plasma protein levels, facial edema, scaly rashes, elevated HDL cholesterol, blood in the urine, and abnormal CBS (elevated RBCs, reduced platelets, and lymphocytes). Discolored, flaky skin, and reddened eyes is common. Ethanol dramatically increases the toxicity of kava, and should not be co-mixed. No data are available on its use in breastfeeding mothers, but care should be exercised. The German Commission E monographs state that it is contraindicated in pregnant and lactating women.[2]

Pregnancy Risk Category:

Lactation Risk Category: L5

Theoretic Infant Dose:

Adult Concerns: High doses may lead to muscle weakness, visual and auditory changes. Heavy users are underweight, have reduced plasma protein levels, facial edema, scaly rashes, elevated HDL cholesterol, blood in the urine, and abnormal CBS (elevated RBCs, reduced platelets, and lymphocytes). Discolored, flaky skin, and reddened eyes is common. Ethanol dramatically increases the toxicity of kava, and should not be co-mixed.

Pediatric Concerns: None reported but caution is recommended.

Drug Interactions: Admixing with alcohol dramatically increases toxicity of kava.

Alternatives:

Adult Dosage:

References:
1. Review of Natural Products. Facts and Comparisons, St. Louis, Mo. 1996.
2. The Complete German Commission E Monographs. Ed. M. Blumenthal. Amer. Botanical Council, Austin, Tx. 1998.

KETOCONAZOLE

Trade: Nizoral Shampoo, Nizoral
Can/Aus/UK: Nizoral
Uses: Antifungal, anti-dandruff
AAP: Approved by the American Academy of Pediatrics for use in breastfeeding mothers

Ketoconazole is an antifungal similar in structure to miconazole and clotrimazole. It is used orally, topically, and via shampoo.[1] Ketoconazole is not detected in plasma after chronic shampooing. Ketoconazole levels in milk following oral use as systemic antifungal have not been reported but it is probably secreted to some degree. The absorption of ketoconazole is highly variable, and could be reduced in infants due to the alkaline condition induced by milk ingestion.[2] Ketoconazole requires acidic conditions to be absorbed, and its absorption and distribution in children is not known. A number of clinical studies show fluconazole to be superior for oral and vaginal candidiasis and achieve higher tissue and salivary fluid levels. See fluconazole as alternative.

Pregnancy Risk Category: C

Lactation Risk Category: L2

Theoretic Infant Dose:

Adult Concerns: Itching, dizziness, fever, chills, hypertension, hepatotoxicity.

Pediatric Concerns: None reported.

Drug Interactions: Decreased ketoconazole levels occur with rifampin, isoniazide and phenytoin use. Theophylline levels may be reduced. Absorption requires acid pH, so anything increasing gastric pH will significantly reduce absorption. This includes cimetidine, ranitidine, famotidine, omeprazole, sucralfate, antacids, etc. Do not coadminister with cisapride or terfenadine (very dangerous). May increase cyclosporin levels by 50%, inhibits warfarin metabolism and prolongs coagulation.

Alternatives: Fluconazole

Adult Dosage: 200-400 mg QD

T½ = 2-8 hours	**M/P =**
PHL=	**PB = 99%**
PK = 1-2 hours	**Oral = Variable (75%)**
MW = 531	**pKa =**
Vd =	

References:
1. Pharmaceutical Manufacturers Package Insert, 1996.
2. Force RW, Nahata MC. Salivary concentrations of ketoconazole and fluconazole: implications for drug efficacy in oropharyngeal and esophageal candidiasis. Ann Pharmacother 29:10-15, 1995.

KETOPROFEN

Trade: Orudis, Oruvail
Can/Aus/UK: Apo-Keto, Orudis, Oruvail, Rhodis, Rhovail
Uses: NSAID analgesic
AAP: Not reviewed

Ketoprofen is a typical nonsteroidal analgesic. It is structurally similar to ibuprofen. Due to tablet formulation (Oruvail), maternal absorption is prolonged during the day, requiring 6-7 hours to peak levels.[1] Studies in animals indicate the milk concentration to be 4-5% of maternal plasma levels. There is no information available on levels produced in human breastmilk. See ibuprofen as alternative.

Pregnancy Risk Category: B

Lactation Risk Category: L3

Theoretic Infant Dose:

Adult Concerns: GI distress, diarrhea, vomiting, gastric bleeding.

Pediatric Concerns: None reported, but observe for GI symptoms including diarrhea, cramping.

Drug Interactions: May prolong prothrombin time when used with warfarin. Antihypertensive effects of ACEi family may be blunted or completely abolished by NSAIDs. Some NSAIDs may block antihypertensive effect of beta blockers, diuretics. Used with cyclosporin, may dramatically increase renal toxicity. May increase digoxin, phenytoin, lithium levels. May increase toxicity of methotrexate. May increase bioavailability of penicillamine. Probenecid may increase NSAID levels.

Alternatives: Ibuprofen

Adult Dosage: 50-75 mg TID-QID

T½ = 2-4 hours	M/P =
PHL=	PB = >99%
PK = 1.2	Oral = 90%
MW = 254	pKa = 4.0
Vd = 0.1-0.5	

References:
1. Pharmaceutical Manufacturers Package Insert, 1996.

KETOROLAC

Trade: Toradol, Acular
Can/Aus/UK: Acular, Toradol
Uses: Non-steroidal anti-inflammatory, analgesic
AAP: Approved by the American Academy of Pediatrics for use in breastfeeding mothers

Ketorolac is a popular nonsteroidal analgesic. Although previously used in labor and delivery, its use has subsequently been contraindicated because it is believed to adversely effect fetal circulation and inhibit uterine contractions, thus increasing the risk of hemorrhage.

In a study of 10 lactating women who received 10 mg orally four times daily, milk levels of ketorolac were not detectible in 4 of the subjects.[1] In the 6 remaining, the concentration of ketorolac in milk 2 hours after a dose ranged from 5.2 to 7.3 μg/L on day 1 and 5.9 to 7.9 μg/L on day two. In most patients, the breastmilk level was never above 5 μg/L. The maximum daily dose an infant could absorb (maternal dose = 40 mg/day) would range from 3.16 to 7.9 μg/day assuming a milk volume of 400 ml or 1000 ml. An infant would therefore receive less than 0.4% of the daily maternal dose (Please note, the original paper contained a misprint on the daily intake of ketorolac (mg instead of ug).

Pregnancy Risk Category: B during 1st and 2nd trimesters
D during 3rd trimester

Lactation Risk Category: L2

Theoretic Infant Dose: 1.2 μg/kg/day

Adult Concerns: GI irritability, dry mouth, nausea, vomiting, edema, or rash.

Pediatric Concerns: None reported.

Drug Interactions: May prolong prothrombin time when used with warfarin. Antihypertensive effects of ACEi family may be blunted or completely abolished by NSAIDs. Some NSAIDs may block antihypertensive effect of beta blockers, diuretics. Used with cyclosporin, may dramatically increase renal toxicity. May increase digoxin, phenytoin, lithium levels. May increase toxicity of methotrexate. May increase bioavailability of penicillamine. Probenecid may increase NSAID levels.

Alternatives: Ibuprofen

Adult Dosage: 30 mg q 6 hours

T½ = 2.4-8.6 hours	M/P = 0.015-0.037
PHL=	PB = 99%
PK = 0.5 - 1 hour	Oral = >81%
MW = 255	pKa = 3.5
Vd = 0.15-0.33	

References:
1. Wischnik A, Manth SM, Lloyd J. The excretion of ketorolac tromethamine into breast milk after multiple oral dosing. Eur. J. Clin. Pharm. 36:521-524, 1989.

KOMBUCHA TEA

Trade:
Can/Aus/UK:
Uses: Herbal tea
AAP: Not reviewed

Kombucha tea is a popular health beverage made by incubating the Kombucha mushroom in sweet black tea. During 1995, several reported cases of toxicity and one fatality were reported to the CDC.[1] Based on these reports, the Iowa Department of Health has recommended that persons refrain from drinking Kombucha tea until the role of the tea in these cases has been resolved.

Pregnancy Risk Category:

Lactation Risk Category:

Theoretic Infant Dose:

Adult Concerns: Shortness of breath, respiratory distress, fatigue, metabolic acidosis, disseminated intravascular coagulopathy.

Pediatric Concerns:

Drug Interactions:

Alternatives:

Adult Dosage: N/A

References:
1. Anonymous. Unexplained severe illness possibly associated with consumption of Kombucha Tea - Iowa, 1995. MMWR 44:892-900, December 1995.

LABETALOL

Trade: Trandate, Normodyne
Can/Aus/UK: Labrocol, Presolol, Trandate
Uses: Antihypertensive, beta blocker
AAP: Approved by the American Academy of Pediatrics for use in breastfeeding mothers

Labetalol is a selective beta blocker with moderate lipid solubility that is used as an antihypertensive and for treating angina.   In one study of 3 women receiving 600 mg, 600 mg, or 1200 mg/day, the peak concentration of labetalol in breastmilk was 129, 223, and 662 μg/L respectively.[1] In only one infant were measurable plasma levels found, 18 μg/L following a maternal dose of 600 mg.   Therefore, only small amounts are secreted into human milk (0.004% of maternal dose). Others report 0.05 to 0.07% of maternal dose. Peak levels in milk occurred between 2-3 hours.

Pregnancy Risk Category: C

Lactation Risk Category: L2

Theoretic Infant Dose: 99.3 μg/kg/day

Adult Concerns: Bradycardia, hypotension, dizziness, nausea, aggravation of asthma, lethargy.

Pediatric Concerns: None reported, but observe for hypotension, apnea.

Drug Interactions: Decreased effect when used with aluminum salts, barbiturates, calcium salts, cholestyramine, NSAIDs, ampicillin, rifampin, and salicylates. Beta blockers may reduce the effect of oral sulfonylureas (hypoglycemic agents). Increased toxicity/effect when used with other antihypertensives, contraceptives, MAO inhibitors, cimetidine, and numerous other products. See drug interaction reference for complete listing.

Alternatives: Propranolol, Metoprolol

Adult Dosage: 200-400 mg BID

T½ = 6-8 hours	M/P = 0.8-2.6
PHL=	PB = 50%
PK = 1-2 hours(oral)	Oral = 30-40%
MW = 328	pKa = A7.4, B8.7
Vd = 10	

References:
1.   Lunnell NO, Kulas J. Rane A. Transfer of labetalol into amniotic fluid and breast milk in lactating women. Eur. J. Clin. Pharmacol. 28:597-9, 1985.

LAMOTRIGINE

Trade: Lamictal
Can/Aus/UK: Lamictal
Uses: Anticonvulsant
AAP: Drug whose effect on nursing infants is unknown but may be of concern

Lamotrigine is a new anticonvulsant primarily indicated for treatment of simple and complex partial seizures.   In a study of a 24 year old female receiving 300 mg/day lamotrigine during pregnancy, maternal serum levels and cord levels of lamotrigine at birth were 3.88 μg/ml in the mother and 3.26 μg/mL in the cord blood.[1] By day 22, the maternal serum levels were 9.61 μg/mL, the milk concentration was 6.51 mg/L, and the infant's serum level was 2.25 μg/mL. Following a reduction in dose, the prior levels decreased significantly over the next weeks. The milk/plasma ratio at the highest maternal serum level, was 0.562.   The estimated dose to infant would be approximately 2-5 mg per day assuming a maternal dose of 200-300mg per day. The infant developed normally in every way.

In another study of a single mother receiving 200 mg/day lamotrigine, milk levels of lamotrigine immediately prior to the next dose (trough) at steady state were 3.48 mg/L (13.6 uM).[2]   The authors estimated the daily dose to the infant would be 0.5 mg/kg/day. The above authors suggest that infants, while developing normally, should probably be monitored periodically for plasma levels of lamotrigine.

The manufacturer reports that in a group of 5 women(no dose listed), breastmilk concentrations of lamotrigine ranged from 0.07-5.03 mg/L.[3] Breastmilk levels averaged 40-45% of maternal plasma levels. No ill effects were noted in the infants.

In a study by Ohman of 9 breastfeeding women at 3 weeks postpartum, the median milk/plasma ratio was 0.61, and the nursed infants maintained lamotrigine concentrations of approximately 30% of the mother's plasma levels.[4] The authors estimated the dose to the infant at >= 0.2-1 mg/kg/d. No adverse effects were noted in the infants.

Pregnancy Risk Category: C

Lactation Risk Category: L3

Theoretic Infant Dose: 0.5 mg/kg/day

Adult Concerns: Rash, fatigue, ataxia, dizziness, somnolence, tremor, nausea, vomiting, and headache. Breast pain has been infrequently reported.

Pediatric Concerns: Not indicated for children less than 16 years of age, but has been studied safely in patients down to 5 years of age.

Drug Interactions: Acetaminophen reduces lamotrigen half-life by 15-20% and may require increased doses. Carbamazepine, phenytoin, phenobarbital, and other anticonvulsants may reduce plasma levels of lamotrigen by increasing clearance, but this is highly variable.

Alternatives:

Adult Dosage: 150-250 mg BID

T½ = 29 hours	M/P = 0.562
PHL=	PB = 55%
PK = 1-4 hours	Oral = 98%
MW = 256	pKa = 5.7
Vd = 0.9-1.3 L/kg	

References:
1. Rambeck B, Kurlemann G, Stodieck SR, May TW, and Jurgens U. Concentrations of lamotrigine in a mother on lamotrigine treatment and her newborn child. Eur J Clin Pharmacol 51(6):481-4. 1997.
2. Tomson T, Ohman I, Vitols S. Lamotrigine in pregnancy and lactation: A Case Report. Epilepsia 38(9):1039-1041, 1997.
3. Biddlecombe RA. Analysis of breast milk samples for lamotrigine. Internal document BDCR/93/0011. GlasoWellcome.
4. Ohman I, Vitols S, Tomson T. Lamotrigine in pregnancy: pharmacokinetics during delivery, in the neonate, and during lactation. Epilepsia. 41(6):709-13, 2000.

LANSOPRAZOLE

Trade: Prevacid, Prevpac
Can/Aus/UK: Prevacid, Zoton
Uses: Reduces stomach acid secretion.
AAP: Not reviewed

Lansoprazole is a new proton pump inhibitor that suppresses the release of acid protons from the parietal cells in the stomach, effectively raising the pH of the stomach. Structurally similar to omeprazole, it is very unstable in stomach acid and to a large degree is denatured by acidity of the infant's stomach.[1]   A new study shows milk levels of omeprazole are minimal (see omeprazole) and it is likely milk levels of lansoprazole are small as well.   Although there are no studies of lansoprazole in breastfeeding mothers,   transfer to milk, and its oral absorption (via milk) is likely to be minimal in a breastfed infant.

Lansoprazole is secreted in animal milk, although no data is available on the amount secreted in human milk.   The only likely untoward effects would be a reduced stomach acidity.   This product has no current pediatric indications although it is occasionally used in severe cases of erosive gastritis.

Prevpac contains Lansoprazole, Amoxicillin, and Clarithromycin. It is primarily indicated for treatment of H.Pylori infections which cause stomach ulcers.

Pregnancy Risk Category: B

Lactation Risk Category: L3

Theoretic Infant Dose:

Adult Concerns: Reduced stomach acidity.   Diarrhea, nausea, elevated liver enzymes.

Pediatric Concerns: None reported via milk.   It is unlikely to be absorbed while dissolved in milk due to instability in acid.

Drug Interactions: Decreased absorption of ketoconazole, itraconazole, and other drugs dependent on acid for absorption. Theophylline clearance is increased slightly. Reduced lansoprazole absorption when used with sucalfate (30%).

Alternatives: Omeprazole, Famotidine

Adult Dosage: 15-30 mg TID

T½ = 1.5 hours	M/P =
PHL=	PB = 97%
PK = 1.7 hours	Oral = 80%(Enteric only)
MW = 369	pKa =
Vd =	

References:
1.   Pharmaceutical Manufacturers Package Insert, 2000.

LATANOPROST

Trade: Xalatan
Can/Aus/UK: Betim, Optimol, Xalatan
Uses: Prostaglandin for glaucoma
AAP: Not reviewed

Latanoprost is a prostaglandin F2-alpha analogue used for the treatment of ocular hypertension and glaucoma. One drop used daily is usually effective.[1] No data are available on the transfer of this product into human milk but it is unlikely. Prostaglandins are by nature, rapidly metabolized. Plasma levels are barely detectable, and then only for 1 hour after use. Combined with the short half-life, and minimal plasma levels, poor oral bioavailability, untoward effects via milk are unlikely.

Pregnancy Risk Category: C

Lactation Risk Category: L3

Theoretic Infant Dose:

Adult Concerns: Ocular irritation, headache, rash, muscle aches, joint pain.

Pediatric Concerns: None reported via milk.

Drug Interactions:

Alternatives:

Adult Dosage: 1 drop in affected eye QD

T½ = < 30 minutes	M/P =
PHL =	PB =
PK = < 1 hour	Oral = Nil
MW =	pKa =
Vd = 0.16	

References:
1.   Pharmaceutical manufacturers package insert, 1998.

LEAD

Trade:
Can/Aus/UK:
Uses: Environmental pollutant
AAP: Not reviewed

Lead is an environmental pollutant.   It serves no useful purpose in the body and tends to accumulate in the body's bony structures based on their exposure.   Due to the rapid development of the nervous system, children are particularly sensitive to elevated levels.

Lead apparently transfers into human milk at a rate proportional to maternal blood levels, but the absolute degree of transfer is controversial.   Studies of milk lead levels vary enormously and probably reflect the enormous difficulty in accurately measuring lead in milk.

One study evaluated lead transfer into human milk in population of women with an average blood lead of 45 μg/dL (considered very high).[1] The average lead level in milk was 2.47 μg/dL. Using these parameters, the average intake in an infant would be 8.1 μg/kg/d. The daily permissible level by WHO is 5.0 μg/kg/d. Using these parameters, mothers contaminated with lead should not breastfeed their infants.

However, in another study of two lactating women whose blood lead levels were 29 and 33 mcg/dl, the breastmilk levels were < 0.005 μg/ml and < 0.010 μg/ml respectively.[2] Although both infants had high lead levels (38 μg/dl and 44 μg/dl), it was probably derived from the environment or in-utero. Using this data, breastfeeding would appear to be safe.

In a larger study of Shanghai mothers (n=165) the transfer of lead to the fetus was highly correlated with maternal blood lead levels (maternal blood vs cord = 13.2 μg/dL and 6.9 μg/dL).[3] Lead levels in the cord blood and breastmilk increased with the lead level in the maternal blood, with coefficient of correlation of 0.714 and 0.353, respectively. The average concentration of lead in breastmilk for 12 occupationally exposed women (lead-exposed jobs) was 52.7 μg/L, which was almost 12 times higher than that for the occupationally non-exposed population(4.43 mg/dL). These results suggest that lead levels in milk could pose a potential health hazard to the breastfed infant, but only in those moms with high plasma lead levels.

In another rather elegant study of milk lead levels, Gulson et.al. collected samples from 21 mothers and 24 infants over a 6 month period.[4] They reported lead concentrations in milk ranging from 0.09-3.1 ug Pb/kg or ppb (mean 0.73 μg/kg) while the blood lead levels were all less than 5 μg/dL with exception of one mother. The major source of lead to the infant during this period was from maternal bone and diet.

Nashashibi reports on the transfer of lead from the mother to fetus, and into her breastmilk.[5] In a group of 47 women, the mean maternal blood lead concentration was 14.9 μg/dL, while in milk the mean lead level was 2.0 μg/dL. Mean lead level in cord blood was 13.1 μg/dL. These data suggest a close correlation between maternal blood and cord blood lead levels, and maternal blood and milk levels.

In the last decade, the permissible blood level (according to CDC) in children has dropped from 25 to less than 10 μg/dL. Lead poisoning is known to significantly alter IQ, and neuropsychologic development, particularly in infants. Therefore, infants receiving breastmilk from mothers with high lead levels should be closely monitored, and both mother and infant may require chelation and the infant transferred to formula. Depending on the choice of chelator, mothers undergoing chelation therapy to remove lead may mobilize significant quantities of lead and should not breastfeed during the treatment period unless the chelator is Succimer.

Pregnancy Risk Category:

Lactation Risk Category: L5

Theoretic Infant Dose:

Adult Concerns: Constipation, abdominal pain, anemia, anorexia, vomiting, lethargy.

Pediatric Concerns: Pediatric lead poisoning, but appears unlikely via milk. More likely environmental.

Drug Interactions:

Alternatives:

Adult Dosage:

T½ = 20-30 years(bone)	M/P =
PHL =	PB =
PK =	Oral = 5-10%
MW = 207	pKa =
Vd =	

References:
1. Namihira D. et.al. Lead in human blood and milk from nursing women living near a smelter in Mexico City. J. Toxicol. Envir. Health 38(3):225-32,1993.
2. Baum C, Shannon M. Lead-Poisoned lactating women have insignificant lead in breast milk. Abstract # 144 J. Clin. Toxicol. 33(5):540-1, 1995.
3. Li PJ, Sheng YZ, Wang QY, Gu LY, Wang YL. Transfer of lead via placenta and breast milk in human. Biomed Environ Sci. 13(2):85-9, 2000.
4. Gulson BL, Jameson CW, Mahaffey KR, Mizon KJ, Patison N, Law AJ, Korsch MJ, Salter MA. Relationships of lead in breast milk to lead in blood, urine, and diet of the infant and mother. Environ Health Perspect. 106(10):667-74, 1998.
5. Nashashibi N, Cardamakis E, Bolbos G, Tzingounis V. Investigation of kinetic of lead during pregnancy and lactation. Gynecol Obstet Invest. 48(3):158-62, 1999.

LEFLUNOMIDE

Trade: Arava
Can/Aus/UK: Arava
Uses: Antimetabolite anti-inflammatory
AAP: Not reviewed

Leflunomide is a new anti-inflammatory agent used for arthritis. It is an immunosuppressant that reduces pyrimidine synthesis.[1] Leflunomide is metabolized to the active metabolite referred to as M1, which has a long half-life and slow elimination. This product is a potent immunosuppressant with a potential elevated risk of malignancy and teratogenicity in pregnant women. It is not known if it transfers into human milk, but use of this product while breastfeeding would be highly risky.

Pregnancy Risk Category: X

Lactation Risk Category: L4

Theoretic Infant Dose:

Adult Concerns: Hypertension, diarrhea, respiratory infection, alopecia and rash are the most common adult side effects.

Pediatric Concerns: None via milk, but due to the danger of this product, breastfeeding is not recommended.

Drug Interactions: Cholestyramine produces a rapid reduction of plasma levels of the active metabolite. A significant increase in hepatotoxicity with admixed with other hepatotoxic drugs. Increased plasma drug levels (M1) when used with NSAIDs and rifampin May increase plasma free drug levels of tolbutamide.

Alternatives:

Adult Dosage: 20 mg daily

T½ = > 15-18 hours	M/P =
PHL=	PB =
PK = 6-12 hours	Oral = 80%
MW = 270	pKa =
Vd =	

References:
1. Pharmaceutical Manufacturers Package Insert, 1999.

LEUPROLIDE ACETATE

Trade: Lupron, Viadur
Can/Aus/UK: Lupron, Prostap
Uses: Gonadotropin-Releasing Hormone Analog
AAP: Not reviewed

Leuprolide is a synthetic nonapeptide analog of naturally occurring gonadotropin-releasing hormone with greater potency than the naturally occurring hormone. After initial stimulation, it inhibits gonadotropin release from the pituitary and after sustained use, suppresses ovarian and testicular hormone synthesis (2-4 weeks).[1]   Almost complete suppression of estrogen, progesterone, and testosterone result.[2] Although Lupron is contraindicated in pregnant women, no reported birth defects have been reported in humans. It is commonly used prior to fertilization, but should never be used during pregnancy.

It is not known whether Leuprolide transfers into human milk, but due to its nonapeptide structure, it is not likely that its transfer would be extensive. In addition, animal studies have found that it has zero oral bioavailability, therefore it is unlikely it would be orally bioavailable in the human infant if ingested via milk. Its effect on lactation is unknown, but it could suppress lactation particularly early postpartum.[3] Lupron would reduce estrogen and progestin levels to menopausal ranges, which may or may not suppress lactation, depending on the duration of lactation. Interestingly, several studies show no change in prolactin levels, although these were not in lactating women. One study of a hyperprolactinemic patient showed significant suppression of prolactin.

Pregnancy Risk Category: X

Lactation Risk Category: L5

Theoretic Infant Dose:

Adult Concerns: Vasomotor hot flashes, gynecomastia, edema, bone pain, thrombosis, and GI disturbances. Body odor, fever, headache.

Pediatric Concerns: May suppress lactation, particularly early in lactation.

Drug Interactions:

Alternatives:

Adult Dosage: 3.75 mg q month

T½ = 3.6 hours	M/P =
PHL =	PB = 43-49%
PK = 4-6 hours	Oral = None
MW = 1400	pKa =
Vd = 0.52	

References:
1. Sennello LT, Finley RA, et.al. Single-dose pharmacokinetics of leuprolide in humans following intravenous and subcutaneous administration. J. Pharm Sci 75(2):158-160, 1986.
2. Chantilis SJ, et.al. The effect of gonadotropin-releasing hormone agonist on thyroid-stimulating hormone and prolactin secretion in adult premenopausal women. Fertil Steril 64:698-702, 1995.
3. Frazier, SH. Personnal Communication, 1997.

LEVALBUTEROL

Trade: Xopenex
Can/Aus/UK:
Uses: Bronchodilator
AAP: Not reviewed

Levalbuterol is the active (R)-enantiomer of the drug substance racemic albuterol.   It is a popular and new bronchodilator used in asthmatics. No data are available on breastmilk levels. After inhalation, plasma levels are incredibly low, averaging 1.1 nanogram/mL.   It is very unlikely that enough would enter milk to produce clinical effects in an infant. This product is commonly used in infancy for asthma and other bronchoconstrictive illnesses.

Pregnancy Risk Category: C

Lactation Risk Category: L2

Theoretic Infant Dose:

Adult Concerns: Tachycardia, tremors, dizziness, dyspepsia.

Pediatric Concerns: None reported via milk.

Drug Interactions: Levalbuterol effects are reduce when used with beta blockers. Cardiovascular effects are potentiated when used with MAO inhibitors, tricyclic antidepressants, amphetamines, and inhaled anesthetics (enflurane).

Alternatives:

Adult Dosage: 0.63 mg every 6-8 hours by nebulization

T½ = 3.3 hours	M/P =
PHL=	PB =
PK = 0.2 (inhalation)	Oral = 100%
MW = 275	pKa =
Vd =	

References:
1.   Pharmaceutical manufacturers package insert, 2000.

LEVETIRACETAM

Trade: Keppra
Can/Aus/UK: Keppra
Uses: Anticonvulsant
AAP: Not reviewed

Levetiracetam is an new broad-spectrum antiepileptic agent. It is structurally and pharmacologically dissimilar to all the other known anticonvulsants. No data are available on its transfer into human milk. Kinetics alone would suggest that milk levels will be moderate, as it is not bound by protein, it is low in molecular weight, it is 100% orally bioavailable, it is lipophilic, and it is neuroactive. Although this product is popular for its limited side effect profile, some caution is recommended until data are available.

Pregnancy Risk Category: C

Lactation Risk Category: L4

Theoretic Infant Dose:

Adult Concerns: Somnolence, weakness, infection, headache, and dizziness.

Pediatric Concerns: None reported, but caution is recommended.

Drug Interactions: Levetiracetam may significantly increase phenytoin plasma levels by as much as 52%.

Alternatives:

Adult Dosage: 1000 - 3000 mg daily.

T½ = 6-8 hours	M/P =
PHL =	PB = <10%
PK = 1 hour	Oral = 100%
MW = 170	pKa =
Vd = 0.7	

References:
1.   Pharmaceutical manufacturers package insert, 2001.

LEVOBUNOLOL

Trade: Bunolol
Can/Aus/UK: Betagan, Ophtho-Bunolol
Uses: Beta blocker for glaucoma
AAP: Not reviewed

Levobunolol is a typical beta blocker used intraophthalmic for treatment of glaucoma.[1] Some absorption has been reported, with resultant bradycardia in patients. No data on transfer to human milk are available.

Pregnancy Risk Category: C

Lactation Risk Category: L3

Theoretic Infant Dose:

Adult Concerns: Bradycardia, hypotension, headache, dizziness, fatigue, lethargy.

Pediatric Concerns: None reported via milk, but transfer of some beta blockers is reported. Observe for lethargy, hypotension, bradycardia, apnea.

Drug Interactions: May have increased toxicity when used with other systemic beta adrenergic blocking agents. May produce bradycardia following use with quinidine and verapamil.

Alternatives:

Adult Dosage: 1-2 drops BID

T½ = 6.1 hours	M/P =
PHL=	PB =
PK = 3 hours	Oral = Complete
MW = 291	pKa =
Vd = 5.5	

References:
1.   Pharmaceutical Manufacturers Package Insert, 1997.

LEVOCABASTINE

Trade: Livostin
Can/Aus/UK: Livostin
Uses: Ophthalmic antihistamine for itching
AAP: Not reviewed

Levocabastine is an antihistamine primarily used via nasal spray and eye drops.[1] It is used for allergic rhinitis and ophthalmic allergies. After application to eye or nose, very low levels are attained in the systemic circulation (<1 ng/ml).   In one nursing mother, it was calculated that the daily dose of levocabastine in the infant was about 0.5 μg, far too low to be clinically relevant.

Pregnancy Risk Category: C

Lactation Risk Category: L2

Theoretic Infant Dose:

Adult Concerns: Sedation, dry mouth, fatigue, eye and nasal irritation.

Pediatric Concerns: None reported via milk.

Drug Interactions:

Alternatives:

Adult Dosage: 1 drop QID

T½ = 33-40 hours.	M/P =
PHL =	PB =
PK = 1-2 hours	Oral = 100%
MW =	pKa =
Vd =	

References:
1. Pharmaceutical Manufacturers Package Insert, 1996.

LEVODOPA

Trade: Dopar, Larodopa
Can/Aus/UK: Brocadopa, Eldopa, Endo Levodopa/Carbidopa, Kinson, Madopar, Prolopa, Sinemet, Weldopa
Uses: Antiparkinsonian
AAP: Not reviewed

Levodopa is a prodrug of dopamine used primarily for parkinsonian symptoms. Its use during pregnancy is extremely dangerous. In one group of 30 patients, levodopa significantly reduced prolactin plasma levels.[1] It could under certain circumstances reduce milk production as well.

Pregnancy Risk Category: C

Lactation Risk Category: L4

Theoretic Infant Dose:

Adult Concerns: Nausea, vomiting, anorexia, orthostatic hypotension. Reduces prolactin levels and may reduce milk production. Do not use in glaucoma patients with MAO inhibitors, asthmatics, peptic ulcer disease, or parkinsonian disease.

Pediatric Concerns: None reported.

Drug Interactions: MAO inhibitors may predispose to hypertensive reactions. Decreased effect when administered with phenytoin, pyridoxine, phenothiazines.

Alternatives:

Adult Dosage: 1-2 g TID

T½ = 1-3 hours.	M/P =
PHL =	PB = <36%
PK = 1-2 hours.	Oral = 41%-70%
MW = 197	pKa =
Vd =	

References:
1. Barbieri C, Ferrari C, et al. Growth hormone secretion in hypertensive patients: evidence for a derangement in central adrenergic function. Clin Sci 58:135-8, 1980.

LEVOFLOXACIN

Trade: Levaquin, Quixin
Can/Aus/UK: Levaquin
Uses: Antibiotic
AAP: Not reviewed

Levofloxacin is a pure (S) enantiomer of the racemic fluoroquinolone Ofloxacin. Its kinetics including milk levels should be identical.[1,2] See ofloxacin for specifics.

Pregnancy Risk Category: C

Lactation Risk Category: L3

Theoretic Infant Dose:

Adult Concerns: Nausea, vomiting, diarrhea, abdominal cramps, GI bleeding.

Pediatric Concerns: None reported, see ofloxacin.

Drug Interactions: Decreased absorption with antacids. Quinolones cause increased levels of caffeine, warfarin, cyclosporine, theophylline. Cimetidine, probenecid, azlocillin may increase ofloxacin levels. Increased risk of seizures when used with foscarnet.

Alternatives: Norfloxacin, Ofloxacin, Trovafloxacin

Adult Dosage: 500 mg daily

T½ = 6-8 hours	M/P =
PHL=	PB = 24-38%
PK = 1-1.8 hours	Oral = 99%
MW = 370	pKa =
Vd = 1.27	

References:
1. Pharmaceutical Manufacturers Package Insert, 1998.
2. McEvoy GE(ed):AHFS Drug Information, New York, NY. 1997.

LEVONORGESTREL

Trade: Norplant
Can/Aus/UK: Levelen, Microlut, Microval, Norgeston, Norplant, Triquilar
Uses: Implant contraceptive
AAP: Approved by the American Academy of Pediatrics for use in breastfeeding mothers

Levonorgestrel (LNG) is the active progestin in Norplant. From several studies, it appears to produce limited if any effect on milk volume or quality.[1] One report of 120 women with implants at 5-6 weeks postpartum showed no change in lactation.[2] The level of progestin in the infant is approximately 10% that of maternal circulation. In a study of 9 women who were taking LNG oral minipills (30 ug daily) and 10 women who were using the subdermal implants, Norplant(R)-2, from 4-15 weeks postpartum, no significant differences in infant follicle stimulating hormone(FSH), luteinizing hormone(LH), or testosterone levels in urine were noted when compared to controls.[3] These results suggest that the sexual development of children exposed via milk to trace levels of LNG is normal.

Pregnancy Risk Category: X

Lactation Risk Category: L1

Theoretic Infant Dose:

Adult Concerns: Interruption of the menstrual cycle and spotting, with headache, weight gain, and occasional depression.

Pediatric Concerns: None reported.

Drug Interactions: Reduced effect of carbamazepine and phenytoin.

Alternatives:

Adult Dosage: Six 36 mg capsules subcutaneously

T½ = 11-45 hours	M/P =
PHL =	PB =
PK =	Oral = Complete
MW = 312	pKa =
Vd =	

References:
1. Shaaban MM, Salem HT, Abdullah KA. Influence of levonorgestrel contraceptive implants, Norplant, initiated early postpartum upon lactation and infant growth. Contraception 32:623-635, 1985.
2. Shaaban MM. Contraception with progestogens and progesterone during lactation. J. Steroid Biochem. & Mole. Biol. 40:705-10, 1991.
3. Shikary ZK, Betrabet SS, Toddywala WS, Patel DM, Datey S, Saxena BN. Pharmacodynamic effects of levonorgestrel (LNG) administered either

orally or subdermally to early postpartum lactating mothers on the urinary levels of follicle stimulating hormone (FSH), luteinizing hormone (LH) and testosterone (T) in their breast-fed male infants. Contraception. 34(4):403-12, 1986.

LEVOTHYROXINE

Trade: Synthroid, Levothroid, Unithyroid, Eltroxin, Levoxyl, Thyroid, Levoxyl
Can/Aus/UK: Eltroxin, Oroxine, Synthroid, Thyroxine
Uses: Thyroid supplements
AAP: Approved by the American Academy of Pediatrics for use in breastfeeding mothers

Levothyroxine is also called T4. Most studies indicate that minimal levels of maternal thyroid are transferred into human milk, and further, that the amount secreted is extremely low and insufficient to protect a hypothyroid infant even while nursing.[1-3] The amount secreted after supplementing a breastfeeding mother is highly controversial and numerous reports conflict. Anderson[4] indicates that levothyroxine is not detectable in breastmilk, while others using sophisticated assay methods have shown extremely low levels (4 ng/ml). It is generally recognized that some thyroxine will transfer but the amount will be extremely low. It is important to remember that supplementation with levothyroxine is designed to bring the mother into a euthyroid state, which is equivalent to the normal breastfeeding female. Hence, the risk of using exogenous thyroxine is no different than in a normal euthyroid mother. Liothyronine (T3) appears to transfer into milk in higher concentrations than levothyroxine (T4), but liothyronine is seldom used in clinical medicine due to its short half-life (<1 day).[4]

Pregnancy Risk Category: A

Lactation Risk Category: L1

Theoretic Infant Dose: 0.6 ng/kg/day

Adult Concerns: Nervousness, tremor, agitation, weight loss.

Pediatric Concerns: None reported via milk.

Drug Interactions: Phenytoin may decrease levothyroxine levels. Cholestyramine may decreased absorption of levothyroxine. May increase oral hypoglycemic requirements and doses. May increase effects of oral
anticoagulants. Use with tricyclic antidepressants may increase toxicity.

Alternatives:

Adult Dosage: 75-125 ug daily

T½ = 6-7 days.	M/P =
PHL =	PB = 99%
PK = 2-4 hours.	Oral = 50-80%
MW = 798	pKa =
Vd =	

References:

1. Mizuta H, Amino N, Ichihara K et al: Thyroid hormones in human milk and their influence on thyroid function of breast-fed babies. Pediatr Res 17:468-471, 1983.
2. Oberkotter LV, Hahn HB. Thyroid function and human breast milk. Am J Dis Child. 137:1131, 1983
3. Sack J. et. al. Thyroxine concentration in human milk. J Clin Endocrinol Metab 45:171-3, 1977.
4. Anderson PO. Drugs and breast feeding - a review. Drug Intell Clin Pharm 11:208, 1977.
5. Varma SK, et.al. Thyroxine, triiodothyronine, and reverse triiodothyronine concentrations in human milk. J. Pediatr. 93:803-6, 1978.

LIDOCAINE

Trade: Xylocaine
Can/Aus/UK: EMLA, Lignocaine, Xylocaine, Xylocard
Uses: Local anesthetic
AAP: Approved by the American Academy of Pediatrics for use in breastfeeding mothers

Lidocaine is an antiarrhythmic and a local anesthetic. In one study of a breastfeeding mother who received I.V. lidocaine for ventricular arrhythmias, the mother received approximately 965 mg over 7 hours including the bolus starting doses.[1] At seven hours, breastmilk samples were drawn and the concentration of lidocaine was 0.8 mg/L, or 40% of the maternal plasma level (2.0 mg/L). Assuming that the mothers' plasma was maintained at 5 μg/ml (therapeutic = 1.5-5 μg/ml), an infant consuming 1 L per day of milk would ingest approximately 2 mg/day. This amount is exceeding low in view of the fact that the oral bioavailability of lidocaine is very poor (35%). The lidocaine dose recommended for pediatric arrhythmias is 1 mg/kg given as a bolus. Once absorbed by the liver, lidocaine is rapidly metabolized. These authors suggest that a mother could continue to breastfeed while on parenteral lidocaine.

Dryden and Lo have reported the transfer of lidocaine following tumescent liposuction in a 80 kg patient.[2] The areas undergoing liposuction were infiltrated with a 52 .5 mg/kg dose of lidocaine dissolved in 8400 cc of solution(total=4200 mg). Milk samples were drawn 17 hours, and plasma levels were drawn 18 hours following the procedure because other studies show lidocaine peaks in the plasma compartment at this time postoperatively. Milk levels of lidocaine were 0.55 mg/L while plasma levels were 1.2 mg/L. Breastmilk levels were 46% of the serum level. The authors conclude that it is unlikely toxic levels would be reached in a nursing infant.

In a study of 27 parturients who received an average of 82.1 mg bupivacaine and 183.3 mg lidocaine via an epidural catheter, lidocaine milk levels at 2, 6 , and 12 hours post administration were 0.86 , 0.46, and 0.22 mg/L respectively.[3]   Levels of bupivacaine in milk at 2, 6, and 12 hours were 0.09, 0.06, 0.04 mg/L respectively. The milk/serum ratio bases upon area under the curve values (AUC) were 1.07 and 0.34 for lidocaine and bupivacaine respectively.   Based on AUC data of lidocaine and bupivacaine milk levels, the average milk concentration of these agents over 12 hours was 0.5 and 0.07 mg/L. Most of the infants had a maximal APGAR score.

In a study of 7 nursing mothers who received 3.6-7.2 mL of 2% lidocaine without adrenaline, the concentration of lidocaine in milk 3 and 6 hours after injection averaged 97.5 μg/L and 52.7 μg/L respectively.[4] These authors suggest that mothers who receive local injections of lidocaine can safely breastfeed.

Recommended doses are as follows: Caudal blockade, <300 mg; Epidural blockade, < 300 mg; Dental nerve block, < 100 mg; tumescent liposuction, 4200 mg   When administered as a local anesthetic for dental and other surgical procedures, only small quantities are used, generally less than 40 mg. However, following liposuction, the amount used via instillation in the tissues is quite high. Nevertheless, maternal plasma and milk levels don't see to approach high concentrations and the oral bioavailability in the infant would be quite low (<35%).

Pregnancy Risk Category: C

Lactation Risk Category: L3

Theoretic Infant Dose: 120.0 μg/kg/day

Adult Concerns: Bradycardia, confusion, cardiac arrest, drowsiness, seizures, bronchospasm.

Pediatric Concerns: None reported via milk.

Drug Interactions: Use of local anesthetics with sulfonamides may reduce antibacterial efficacy.

Alternatives:

Adult Dosage: 50-100 mg PRN

T½ = 1.8 hours	M/P = 0.4
PHL = 3 hours(neonate)	PB = 70%
PK = Immediate(IM, I.V.)	Oral = <35%
MW = 234	pKa = 7.9
Vd = 1.3	

References:
1. Zeisler JA, Gaarder TD, De Mesquita SA. Lidocaine excretion in breast milk. Drug Intell. Clin. Pharm. 20:691-3, 1986.
2. Dryden R, Lo, MW. Breast milk lidocaine levels in tumescent liposuction. Plastic and Reconstruc. Surgery. 105(6):2267-2268, 2000.
3. Ortega D, Viviand X, Lorec AM, Gamerre M, Martin C, Bruguerolle B. Excretion of lidocaine and bupivacaine in breast milk following epidural anesthesia for cesarean delivery. Acta Anaesthesiol Scand. 43(4):394-7, 1999.
4. Giuliani M, Grossi GB, Pileri M, Lajolo C, Casparrini G. Could local anesthesia while breast-feeding be harmful to infants? J Pediatr Gastroenterol Nutr. 32(2):142-4, 2001.

LINCOMYCIN

Trade: Lincocin
Can/Aus/UK: Lincocin
Uses: Antibiotic
AAP: Not reviewed

Lincomycin is an effective antimicrobial used for gram positive and anaerobic infections. It is secreted into breastmilk in small but detectable levels. In a group of 9 mothers who received 500 mg every 6 hours for 3 days, breastmilk concentrations ranged from 0.5 to 2.4 mg/L (mean = 1.28). In this same group, the maternal plasma levels averaged 1.37 mg/L.[1] Although effects on infant are unlikely, some modification of gut flora or diarrhea is possible.

Pregnancy Risk Category: B

Lactation Risk Category: L3

Theoretic Infant Dose: 0.2 mg/kg/day

Adult Concerns: Diarrhea, changes in GI flora, colitis, blood dyscrasias, jaundice.

Pediatric Concerns: None reported via milk, but observe for GI symptoms such as diarrhea.

Drug Interactions: GI absorption of lincomycin is decreased when used with kaolin-pectin antidiarrheals. The actions of neuromuscular blockers may be enhanced when used with lincomycin.

Alternatives: Clindamycin

Adult Dosage: 500 mg q 6-8 hours

T½ = 4.4-6.4 hours	M/P = 0.9
PHL =	PB = 72%
PK = 2-4 hours	Oral = <30%
MW = 407	pKa =
Vd =	

References:
1.   Medina A, Fiske N, Hjelt-Harvey I, Brown CD, Prigot A. Absorption, diffusion, and excretion of a new antibiotic, lincomycin. Antimicrob. Agents Chemother. 3:189-96, 1963.

LINDANE

Trade: Kwell, G-well, Scabene
Can/Aus/UK: Desitan, Hexit, Kwellada, PMS-Lindane, Quellada
Uses: Pediculicide, scabicide
AAP: Not reviewed

Lindane is an older pesticide also called gamma benzene hexachloride. It is primarily indicated for treatment of pediculus capitis (head lice) and less so for scabies (crab lice).[1,2] Because of its lipophilic nature, it is significantly absorbed through the skin of neonates (up to 13%) and has produced elevated liver enzymes, seizures disorders and hypersensitivity. It is not recommended for use in neonates or young children.   Lindane is transferred into human milk although the exact amounts are unpublished.   Estimates by the manufacturer indicate a total daily dose of an infant ingesting 1 Liter of milk daily (30 ng/mL), would be approximately 30 μg/day, an amount that would probably be clinically insignificant.

If used in children, lindane should not be left on the skin for more than 6 hours before being wash off, as peak plasma levels in occur in children at about 6 hours after application.   Although there are reports of some resistance, head lice and scabies should generally be treated with permethrin products (NIX, Elimite) which are much safer in pediatric patients. See permethrin.

Pregnancy Risk Category: B

Lactation Risk Category: L3

Theoretic Infant Dose:

Adult Concerns: Dermatitis, seizures (excess dose), nervousness, irritability, anxiety, insomnia, dizziness, aplastic anemia, thrombocytopenia, neutropenia.

Pediatric Concerns: Lindane is not recommended for children. Potential CNS toxicity includes lethargy, disorientation, restlessness, and tonic-clonic seizures.

Drug Interactions: Oil based hair dressings may enhance skin absorption.

Alternatives:

Adult Dosage: Topical

T½ = 18-21 hours	M/P =
PHL = 17-22 hours	PB =
PK = 6 hours	Oral =
MW = 290	pKa =
Vd =	

References:

1. Pharmaceutical Manufacturers Package Insert, 1996.
2. Drug Facts and Comparisons. 1996. ed. Facts and Comparisons, St. Louis.

LINEZOLID

Trade: Zyvox
Can/Aus/UK:
Uses: Antibiotic
AAP: Not reviewed

Linezolid is a new oxazolidinone family of antibiotics primarily used for gram positive infections, but has some spectrum for gram negative and anaerobic bacteria. It is active against many strains, including resistant staph aureus, streptococcus pneumonia, streptococcus pyogenes, and others. It is indicated for use in patients with vancomycin resistant enterococcus faceulum infections, staph aureus pneumonias, resistant streptococcus pneumonia infections, etc. Linezolid was found in the milk of lactating rats at concentrations similar to plasma levels although the dose was not indicated (rat milk levels are always higher than humans). Using this data, with an average maternal plasma concentration of 11.5 μg/mL and a theoretical milk/plasma ratio of 1.0 then an infant would ingest approximately 1.7 mg/kg/day following a maternal dose of 1200 mg/day. This amount is likely a high estimate as doses given animals are extraordinarily high. Observe for changes in gut flora and diarrhea.

Pregnancy Risk Category: C

Lactation Risk Category: L3

Theoretic Infant Dose: 0.0 mg/kg/day

Adult Concerns: Thrombocytopenia has been reported in one patient. Observe for diarrhea, sometimes induced by overgrowth of C. Difficile (pseudomembranous colitis). Side effects include headache, nausea, tongue discoloration, taste perversion, and vomiting. Note numerous drug-drug interactions.

Pediatric Concerns: None via milk but observe for diarrhea.

Drug Interactions: Linezolid is a reversible, nonselective inhibitor of monoamine oxidase. Therefore , it has the potential for interaction with adrenergic and serotonergic agents. This includes phenylephrine, phenylpropanolamine, pseudoephedrine, dopamine, and epinephrine. Thus far coadministration with SSRIs has not posed a problem, but caution is recommended.

Alternatives:

Adult Dosage: 400-600 mg every 12 hours

T½ = 5.2 hours	**M/P =**
PHL =	**PB = 31%**
PK = 1.5-2.2 hours	**Oral = 100%**
MW = 337	**pKa =**
Vd = 0.71	

References:
1. Pharmaceutical manufacturers package insert, 2000.

LIOTHYRONINE

Trade: Cytomel
Can/Aus/UK: Cytomel, Tertroxin
Uses: Thyroid supplement
AAP: Not reviewed

Liothyronine is also called T3. It is seldom used for thyroid replacement therapy due to its short half-life. It is generally recognized that only minimal levels of thyroid hormones are secreted in human milk, although several studies have shown that hypothyroid conditions only became apparent when breastfeeding was discontinued.[1,2] Although some studies indicate that breastfeeding may briefly protect hypothyroid infants, it is apparent that the levels of T4 and T3 are too low to provide long-term protection from hypothyroid disease.[3,5,6] Levels of T3 reported in milk vary, but in general are around 238 ng/dl and considerably higher than T4 levels. The maximum amount of T3 ingested daily by an infant would be 357 ng/kg/day, or approximately 1/10 the minimum requirement. From these studies, it is apparent that only exceedingly low levels of T3 are secreted into human milk and are insufficient to protect an infant from hypothyroidism.

Pregnancy Risk Category: A

Lactation Risk Category: L2

Theoretic Infant Dose: 357.0 ng/kg/day

Adult Concerns: Tachycardia, tremor, agitation, hyperthyroidism.

Pediatric Concerns: None reported via milk.

Drug Interactions: Cholestyramine and colestipol may reduce absorption of thyroid hormones. Estrogens may decrease effectiveness of thyroid hormones. The anticoagulant effect of certain medications is increased. Serum digitalis levels are reduced in hyperthyroidism or when the hyperthyroid patient is converted to the euthyroid state. Therapeutic effects of digitalis glycosides may be reduced. A decrease in theophylline clearance can be expected.

Alternatives:

Adult Dosage: 25-75 mcg QD

T½ = 25 hours.	**M/P =**
PHL =	**PB = Low**
PK = 1-2 hours	**Oral = 95 %**
MW = 651	**pKa =**
Vd =	

References:
1. Bode HH, et.al. Mitigation of cretinism by breast-feeding. Pediatrics 62:13-6, 1978.
2. Rovet, F. Does breastfeeding protect the hypothyroid infant whose condition is diagnosed by newborn screening. AJDC 144:319-323, 1990.
3. Varma SK, et.al. Thyroxine, triiodothyronine, and reverse triiodothyronine concentrations in human milk. J. Pediatr. 93:803-6, 1978.
4. Hahn HB, et.al. Thyroid function tests in neonates fed human milk. Am. J. Dis. Child. 137:220-222, 1983.
5. Letarte J. et.al. Lack of protective effect of breastfeeding in congenital hypothyroidism: report of 12 cases. Pediatrics 65:703-5, 1980.
6. Franklin R. et.al. Neonatal thyroid function:comparison between breast-fed and bottle-fed infants. J. Pediatr. 106: 124-6, 1985.

LISINOPRIL

Trade: Prinivil, Zestril
Can/Aus/UK: Apo-Lisinopril, Carace, Prinivil, Prinvil, Zestril
Uses: Antihypertensive, ACE inhibitor
AAP: Not reviewed

Lisinopril is a typical long-acting ACE inhibitor used as an antihypertensive.[1] No breastfeeding data are available on this product. Use caution. Neonates are exceedingly sensitive to ACE inhibitors, but they can be used in older infants. See enalapril, benazepril, captopril as alternatives.

Pregnancy Risk Category: D

Lactation Risk Category: L3
L4 if used in neonatal period

Theoretic Infant Dose:

Adult Concerns: Hypotension, headache, cough, GI upset, diarrhea, nausea.

Pediatric Concerns: None reported, but observe for hypotension, weakness.

Drug Interactions: Probenecid increases plasma levels of ACEi. ACEi and diuretics have additive hypotensive effects. Antacids reduce bioavailability of ACE inhibitors. NSAIDS reduce hypotension of ACE inhibitors. Phenothiazines increase effects of ACEi.   ACEi increase digoxin and lithium plasma levels. May elevate potassium levels when potassium supplementation is added.

Alternatives: Captopril, Enalapril

Adult Dosage: 20-40 mg QD

T½ = 12 hours	M/P =
PHL =	PB = Low
PK = 7 hours	Oral = 29%
MW = 442	pKa =
Vd =	

References:
1.   McEvoy GE(ed):AHFS Drug Information, New York, NY. 1995.

LITHIUM CARBONATE

Trade: Lithobid, Eskalith
Can/Aus/UK: Camcolit, Carbolith, Duralith, Liskonum, Lithane, Lithicarb, Phasal
Uses: Antimanic drug in bipolar disorders
AAP: Approved by the American Academy of Pediatrics for use in breastfeeding mothers

Lithium is a potent antimanic drug used in bipolar disorder. Its use in the first trimester of pregnancy may be associated with a number of birth anomalies, particularly cardiovascular.[1] If used during pregnancy, the dose required is generally elevated due to the increased renal clearance during pregnancy. Soon after delivery, maternal lithium levels should be closely monitored as the mother's renal clearance drops to normal in the next several days. Several cases have been reported of lithium toxicity in newborns.

In a study of a 36 year old mother who received lithium during and after pregnancy[2], the infant's serum lithium level was similar to the mothers at birth (maternal dose =400 mg), but dropped to 0.03 mmol/L by the sixth day. While the mother's dose increased to 800 mg/day postpartum, the infant's serum level did not rise above 10% of the maternal serum levels. At 42 days postpartum, the maternal and infant serum levels were 1.1 and 0.1 mmol/L respectively.

Some toxic effects have been reported. In a mother receiving 600-1200 mg lithium daily during pregnancy[3], the concentration of lithium in breastmilk at 3 days was 0.6 mEq/L. The maternal and infant plasma levels were 1.5 mEq/L and 0.6 mEq/L respectively at 3 days. In this case the infant was floppy, unresponsive and exhibited inverted T waves which are indicative of lithium toxicity. In another study[4], 7 days postpartum, the milk and infant plasma levels were 0.3 mEq/L each, while the mother's plasma lithium levels were 0.9 mEq/L In a case report of a mother receiving 300 mg three times daily, and breastfeeding her infant at two weeks postpartum, the mother and infant's lithium levels were 0.62 and 0.31 mmol/L respectively. The infant's neurobehavioral development and thyroid function were reported normal.[5]

From these studies it is apparent that lithium can permeate milk and is absorbed by the breastfed infant. If the infant continues to breastfeed, it is strongly suggested that the infant be closely monitored for serum lithium levels. Lithium does not reach steady state levels for approximately 10 days. Clinicians may wish to wait at least this long prior to evaluating the infant's serum lithium level, or sooner if symptoms occur. In addition, lithium is known to reduce thyroxine production, and periodic thyroid evaluation should be considered. Because hydration status of the infant can alter lithium levels dramatically, the clinician should observe changes in hydration carefully. A number of studies of lithium suggest that lithium administration is not an absolute contraindication to breastfeeding, if the physician monitors the infant closely for elevated plasma lithium. Current studies, as well as unpublished experience, suggest that the infant's plasma levels rise to about 30-40% of the maternal level, most often without untoward effects in the infant. Recent evidence suggests that certain anticonvulsants such as carbamazepine, valproic acid, and others, may be equally effective as lithium in treating mania. Because these medications are probably safer to use in breastfeeding mothers, the clinician may wish to explore the use of these medications in certain manic breastfeeding mothers.[6]

Pregnancy Risk Category: D

Lactation Risk Category: L4

Theoretic Infant Dose: 0.1 mEq/kg/day

Adult Concerns: Nausea, vomiting, diarrhea, frequent urination, tremor, drowsiness.

Pediatric Concerns: In one study cyanosis, T-wave abnormalities, and decreased muscle tone were reported. Other studies report no side effects. It is advisable to evaluate both infant and maternal lithium levels.

Drug Interactions: Decreased lithium effect with theophylline and caffeine. Increased toxicity with alfentanil. Thiazide diuretics reduce clearance and increase toxicity. NSAIDS, haloperidol, phenothiazines, fluoxetine and ACE inhibitors may increase toxicity.

Alternatives: Valproic acid, Carbamazepine

Adult Dosage: 600 mg TID

T½ = 17-24 hours	**M/P = 0.24-0.66**
PHL = 17.9 hours.	**PB = 0%**
PK = 2-4 hours	**Oral = Complete**
MW = 74	**pKa =**
Vd = 0.7-1.0	

References:
1. Schou M. Lithium treatment during pregnancy, delivery, and lactation: an update. J Clin Psychiatry 51:410-413, 1990.
2. Sykes PA, Quarrie J, Alexander FW. Lithium carbonate and breast-feeding. Br Med J. 2:1299, 1976.
3. Tunnessen WW, Hertz CG. Toxic effects of lithium in newborn infants: a commentary. J. Pediatr 81:804-7, 1972.
4. Fries H. Lithium in pregnancy. Lancet 1:1233, 1970.
5. Montgomery A., Use of lithium for treatment of bipolar disorder during pregnancy and lactation. Academy of breastfeeding Medicine News and Views 3 (1): 4-5, 1997.
6. Llewellyn A, Stowe ZN, Strader JR. The use of lithium and management of women with bipolar disorder during pregnancy and lactation. J. Clin. Psychiatry 1998 59(suppl 6):57-64.

LOMEFLOXACIN

Trade: Maxaquin
Can/Aus/UK: Okacyn
Uses: Flouroquinolone antibiotic
AAP: Not reviewed

Lomefloxacin belongs the fluoroquinolone family of antimicrobials. The use of fluoroquinolone antibiotics in adolescent children has been associated with arthropathy, or swollen joints.[1] These were following several weeks of normal oral doses, not breastmilk. In addition, the FDA is reviewing several pediatric indications for this group. At least one case of bloody colitis (pseudomembranous colitis) has been reported in a breastfeeding infant whose mother ingested ciprofloxacin. It is reported that lomefloxacin is excreted in the milk of lactating animals, although levels are low.

Pregnancy Risk Category: C

Lactation Risk Category: L3

Theoretic Infant Dose:

Adult Concerns: GI distress, diarrhea, colitis, headaches, phototoxicity.

Pediatric Concerns: None reported with this drug. Colitis has been reported with another member of this family. Observe closely for bloody diarrhea.

Drug Interactions: Antacids, iron salts, sucralfate, and zinc salts may interfere with the GI absorption of the fluoroquinolones resulting in decreased serum levels. Cimetidine may interfere with the elimination of the flouroquinolones. Nitrofurantoin may interfere with the antibacterial properties of the fluoroquinoline family. Probenecid may reduce renal clearance as much as 50%. Nephrotoxic side effects of cyclosporine may be significantly increased when used with fluoroquinolones. Phenytoin serum levels may be reduced producing a decrease in therapeutic effects. Anticoagulant effects may be increased when used with flouroquinolones. Decreased clearance and increased plasma levels and toxicity of theophylline have been reported with the use of the flouroquinolones.

Alternatives: Norfloxacin, Ofloxacin.

Adult Dosage: 400 mg QD

T½ = 8 hours	M/P =
PHL=	PB = 20.6 %
PK = 0.7-2.0 hours	Oral = 92%
MW = 351	pKa =
Vd = 2	

References:
1. Pharmaceutical Manufacturers Package Insert, 1996.

LOPERAMIDE

Trade: Imodium, Pepto Diarrhea Control, Maalox Anti-diarrheal Caplets, Kaopectate Ii Caplets
Can/Aus/UK: Gastro-Stop, Imodium, Novo-Loperamide
Uses: Antidiarrheal drug
AAP: Approved by the American Academy of Pediatrics for use in breastfeeding mothers

Loperamide is an antidiarrheal drug. Because it is only minimally absorbed orally (0.3%), only extremely small amounts are secreted into breastmilk. Following a 4 mg oral dose, milk levels 6 hours after the second dose were 0.27 μg/L.[1] A breastfeeding infant consuming 165 mL/kg/day of milk would ingest 2000 times less than the recommended daily dose. Loperamide (as with any antidiarrheal) is not generally recommended in children.   One case of mild delirium has been reported in a 4 year old infant.

Pregnancy Risk Category: B

Lactation Risk Category: L2

Theoretic Infant Dose: 40.5 ng/kg/day

Adult Concerns: Fatigue, dry mouth, respiratory depression, dry mouth, and constipation.

Pediatric Concerns: One case of mild delirium has been reported in a 4 year old infant.

Drug Interactions: CNS depressants, phenothiazines, and TCA antidepressants may potentiate adverse effects.

Alternatives:

Adult Dosage: 4 mg PRN

T½ = 10.8 hours	M/P = 0.37
PHL =	PB =
PK = 4-5 hours(capsules)	Oral = 0.3%
MW = 477	pKa –
Vd =	

References:
1. Nikodem VC, and Hofmeyr GJ. Secretion of the antidiarrheal agent loperamide oxide in breast milk. Eur.J.Clin.Pharmacol. 42:695-6, 1992.

LORACARBEF

Trade: Lorabid
Can/Aus/UK:
Uses: Synthetic penicillin-like antibiotic
AAP: Not reviewed

Loracarbef is a synthetic beta-lactam antibiotic. It is structurally similar to the cephalosporin family.[1]   It is used for gram negative and gram positive infections. Pediatric indications are available for infants 6 months and children to 12 years of age. No data are available on levels in breastmilk.

Pregnancy Risk Category: B

Lactation Risk Category: L2

Theoretic Infant Dose:

Adult Concerns: Nausea, vomiting, diarrhea, allergic rashes.

Pediatric Concerns: None reported. Observe for GI changes such as diarrhea.

Drug Interactions: Probenecid may increase levels of cephalosporins by reducing renal clearance.

Alternatives:

Adult Dosage: 200-400 mg BID

T½ = 1 hour	M/P =
PHL=	PB = 25%
PK = 1.2 hours	Oral = 90%
MW =	pKa =
Vd =	

References:
1.   Pharmaceutical Manufacturers Package Insert, 1995.

LORATADINE

Trade: Claritin
Can/Aus/UK: Claratyne, Claritin, Clarityn
Uses: Long-acting antihistamine
AAP: Approved by the American Academy of Pediatrics for use in breastfeeding mothers

Loratadine is a long-acting antihistamine with minimal sedative properties. During 48 hours following administration, the amount of loratadine transferred via milk was 4.2 μg, which was 0.01% of the administered dose.[1] Through 48 hours, only 6.0 ug of descarboethoxyloratadine (metabolite) (7.5 ug loratadine equivalents) were excreted into breastmilk, or 0.029% of the administered dose of loratadine or its active metabolite were transferred via milk to the infant. A 4 kg infant would receive only 0.46% of the loratadine dose received by the mother on a mg/kg basis (2.9 μg/kg/day). It is very unlikely this dose would present a hazard to infants.   Loratadine does not transfer into the CNS of adults, so it is unlikely to induce sedation even in infants.   The half-life in neonates is not known although it is likely quite long. Pediatric formulations are available.

Pregnancy Risk Category: B

Lactation Risk Category: L2

Theoretic Infant Dose: 2.9 μg/kg/day

Adult Concerns: Sedation, dry mouth, fatigue, nausea, tachycardia, palpitations.

Pediatric Concerns: None reported, but observe for sedation, dry mouth, tachycardia.

Drug Interactions: Increased plasma levels of loratadine may result when used with ketaconazole, the macrolide antibiotics, and other products.

Alternatives: Cetirizine

Adult Dosage: 10 mg QD

T½ = 8.4-28 hours	M/P = 1.17
PHL =	PB = 97%
PK = 1.5 hours	Oral = Complete
MW = 383	pKa =
Vd =	

References:
1. Hilbert J, Radwanski E, Affrime MB et al. Excretion of loratadine in human breast milk. J Clin Pharmacol 28:234-9, 1988.

LORAZEPAM

Trade: Ativan
Can/Aus/UK: Almazine, Apo-Lorazepam, Ativan, Novo-Lorazepam
Uses: Antianxiety, sedative drug
AAP: Drug whose effect on nursing infants is unknown but may be of concern

Lorazepam is a typical benzodiazepine from the Valium family of drugs. It is frequently used prenatally and presurgically as a sedative agent. In one prenatal study, it has been found to produce a high rate of depressed respiration, hypothermia, and feeding problems in newborns.[1] Newborns were found to secrete lorazepam for up to 11 days postpartum. In McBrides's study[2], the infants were unaffected following the prenatal use of 2.5 mg I.V. prior to delivery. Plasma levels of lorazepam in infants were equivalent to those of the mothers. The rate of metabolism in mother and infant appears slow, but equal following delivery. In this study there were no untoward effects noted in any of the infants.

In one patient receiving 2.5 mg twice daily for 5 days postpartum, the breastmilk levels were 12 μg/L.[3] In another patient four hours after an oral dose of 3.5 mg, milk levels averaged 8.5 μg/L.[4] Summerfield[4] reports an average concentration in milk of 9 μg/L and an average milk/plasma ratio of 0.22. It would appear from these studies that the amount of lorazepam secreted into milk would be clinically insignificant under most conditions.

The benzodiazepine family as a rule, are not ideal for breastfeeding mothers due to relatively long half-lives and the development of dependence. However, it is apparent that the shorter-acting benzodiazepines are safest during lactation provided their use is short-term or intermittent, low dose, and after the first week of life.[5]

Pregnancy Risk Category: D

Lactation Risk Category: L3

Theoretic Infant Dose: 1.8 μg/kg/day

Adult Concerns: Sedation, agitation, respiratory depression, withdrawal syndrome.

Pediatric Concerns: None reported via milk, but observe for sedation.

Drug Interactions: Increased sedation when used with morphine, alcohol, CNS depressants, MAO inhibitors, loxapine, and tricyclic antidepressants.

Alternatives: Midazolam

Adult Dosage: 1-3 mg BID-TID

T½ = 12 hours	M/P = 0.15-0.26
PHL =	PB = 85%
PK = 2 hours	Oral = 90%
MW = 321	pKa = 1.3, 11.5
Vd = 0.9-1.3	

References:
1. Johnstone M. Effect of maternal lorazepam on the neonate. Br Med J 282:1973, 1981.
2. McBride RJ, et.al. A study of the plasma concentrations of lorazepam in mother and neonate.
3. Whitelaw AGL, Cummings AJ, McFadyen IR. Effect of maternal lorazepam on the neonate. Brit. Med. J. 282:1106-1108, 1981.
4. Summerfield RJ, Nielson MS. Excretion of lorazepam into breast milk. Br.J. Anaesth. 57:1042-43, 1985
5. Maitra R, Menkes DB. Psychotropic drugs and lactation. N Z Med J. 28;109(1024):217-8, 1996.

LOSARTAN

Trade: Cozaar, Hyzaar
Can/Aus/UK: Cozaar
Uses: ACE-like antihypertensive
AAP: Not reviewed

Losartan is a new ACE-like antihypertensive. Rather than inhibiting the enzyme that makes angiotensin such as the ACE inhibitor family, this medication selectively blocks the ACE receptor site preventing attachment of angiotensin II.[1,2] No data are available on its transfer to human milk.   Although it penetrates the CNS significantly, its rather high protein binding would probably reduce its ability to enter milk. This product is only intended for those few individuals who cannot take ACE inhibitors.   No data are available on transfer into human milk. The trade name Hyzaar contains losartan plus hydrochlorothiazide.

Pregnancy Risk Category: C in 1st trimester
                               D in 2nd and 3rd trimester

Lactation Risk Category: L3
                               L4 if used in neonatal period

Theoretic Infant Dose:

Adult Concerns: Dizziness, insomnia, hypotension, anxiety, ataxia, confusion, depression. Cough, nor angioedema, commonly associated with ACE inhibitors does not apparently occur with losartan.

Pediatric Concerns: None reported.

Drug Interactions: Decreased effect when used with phenobarbital, ketoconazole, troleandomycin, sulfaphenazole. Increased effect when used with cimetidine, moxonidine.

Alternatives: Captopril, Enalapril

Adult Dosage: 25-50 mg QD-BID

T½ = 4-9 hours(metabolite)	M/P =
PHL =	PB = 99.8%
PK = 1 hour	Oral = 25-33%
MW =	pKa =
Vd = 12	

References:
1. Lacy C. et.al. Drug information handbook.   Lexi-Comp, Hudson(Cleveland), OH. 1996.
2. Pharmaceutical Manufacturers Package Insert, 1997.

LOVASTATIN

Trade: Mevacor
Can/Aus/UK: Apo-Lovastatin, Mevacor
Uses: Hypocholesterolemic
AAP: Not reviewed

Lovastatin is an effective inhibitor of hepatic cholesterol synthesis. It is primarily used for hypercholesterolemia.   Pregnancy normally elevates maternal cholesterol and triglyceride levels. Following delivery, lipid levels gradually decline to pre-pregnancy levels within about 9 months.

Small but unpublished levels are known to be secreted into human breastmilk.[1] Less then 5% of a dose reaches the maternal circulation due to extensive first-pass removal by the liver. The effect on the infant is unknown but it could reduce hepatic cholesterol synthesis. There is little justification for using such a drug during lactation, but due to the extremely small maternal plasma levels, it is unlikely that the amount in breastmilk would be clinically active. Others in this same family of drugs include simvastatin, pravachol, atorvastatin and fluvastatin. Atherosclerosis is a chronic process and discontinuation of lipid-lowering drugs during pregnancy and lactation should have little to no impact on the outcome of long-term therapy of primary hypercholesterolemia. Cholesterol and other products of cholesterol biosynthesis are essential components for fetal and neonatal development and the use of cholesterol-lowering drugs would not be advisable under any circumstances.

Pregnancy Risk Category: X

Lactation Risk Category: L3

Theoretic Infant Dose:

Adult Concerns: Diarrhea, dyspepsia, flatulence, constipation, headache.

Pediatric Concerns: None reported but its use is not recommended.

Drug Interactions: Increased toxicity when added to gemfibrozil (myopathy, myalgia, etc), clofibrate, niacin (myopathy), erythromycin, cyclosporine, oral anticoagulants (elevated bleeding time).

Alternatives:

Adult Dosage: 20-80 mg QD

T½ = 1.1-1.7	M/P =
PHL =	PB = >95%
PK = 2-4 hours	Oral = 5-30%
MW = 405	pKa =
Vd =	

References:
1. Pharmaceutical Manufacturers Package Insert, 1999.

LOXAPINE

Trade: Loxitane
Can/Aus/UK: Loxapac, PMS-Loxapine
Uses: CNS tranquilizer
AAP: Not reviewed

Loxapine produces pharmacologic effects similar to the phenothiazines and haloperidol family.[1]   The drug does not appear to have antidepressant effects and may lower the seizure threshold. It is a powerful tranquilizer and has been found to be secreted into the milk of animals, but no human data are available.   This is a potent tranquilizer than could produce significant sequella in breastfeeding infants. Caution is urged.

Pregnancy Risk Category: C

Lactation Risk Category: L4

Theoretic Infant Dose:

Adult Concerns: Drowsiness, tremor, rigidity, extrapyramidal symptoms.

Pediatric Concerns: None reported, but extreme caution is recommended.

Drug Interactions: Increased toxicity when used with CNS depressants, metrizamide, and MAO inhibitors.

Alternatives: Haloperidol

Adult Dosage: 10-50 mg BID-QID

T½ = 19 hours	M/P =
PHL =	PB =
PK = 1-2 hours	Oral = 33%
MW = 328	pKa = 6.6
Vd =	

References:
1.   McEvoy GE(ed):AHFS Drug Information, New York, NY. 1995.

LSD

Trade:
Can/Aus/UK:
Uses: Hallucinogen
AAP: Not reviewed

LSD is a power hallucinogenic drug.[1] No data are available on transfer into breastmilk. However, due to its extreme potency and its ability to pass the blood-brain-barrier, LSD is likely to penetrate milk and produce hallucinogenic effects in the infant. This drug is definitely CONTRAINDICATED. Maternal urine may be positive for LSD for 34-120 hours post ingestion.

Pregnancy Risk Category:

Lactation Risk Category: L5

Theoretic Infant Dose:

Adult Concerns: Hallucinations, dilated pupil, salivation, nausea.

Pediatric Concerns: None reported via milk, but due to potency, hallucinations are likely. Contraindicated.

Drug Interactions:

Alternatives:

Adult Dosage:

T½ = 3 hours	M/P =
PHL=	PB =
PK = 30-60 min.(oral)	Oral = Complete
MW = 268	pKa =
Vd =	

References:
1.   Ellenhorn MJ and Barceloux DG. In: Medical Toxicology. Elsevier, New York, NY. 1988.

LYME DISEASE

Trade: Lyme Disease, Borrelia
Can/Aus/UK:
Uses: Borrelia Burgdorferi infections.
AAP: Not reviewed

Lyme disease is caused by infection with the spirochete, borrelia burgdorferi. This spirochete is transferred in-utero to the fetus, and is secreted into human milk[1] and can cause infection in breastfed infants.[2] If diagnosed postpartum or in a breastfeeding mother, the mother and infant should be treated immediately. In children (> 7 yrs) and adults, preferred therapy is doxycycline (100 mg PO twice daily for 14-21 days), or, Amoxicillin (500 mg three times daily for 21 days). In breastfeeding patients, amoxicillin therapy is probably preferred. In the infant, amoxicillin (40 mg/kg/day (max 3 gm) with probenecid (25 mg/kg/day) divided in three doses/day for a duration of 21 days.[3]

Alternative therapy for adults includes clarithromycin (500 mg PO twice daily for 21 days), or azithromycin (500 mg PO daily for 14-21 days), or cefuroxime axetil (500 mg PO twice daily for 21 days).[4] Although doxycycline therapy is not definitely contraindicated in breastfeeding mothers, alternates such as amoxicillin, cefuroxime, clarithromycin or azithromycin should be preferred.

Pregnancy Risk Category:

Lactation Risk Category:

Theoretic Infant Dose:

Adult Concerns:

Pediatric Concerns:

Drug Interactions:

Alternatives:

Adult Dosage:

References:
1. Schmidt BL, Aberer E, Stockenhuber C, Klade H, Breier F, Luger A. Detection of Borrelia burgdorferi DNA by polymerase chain reaction in the urine and breast milk of patients with Lyme borreliosis. Diagn Microbiol Infect Dis. 21(3):121-8, 1995.
2. Stiernstedt G: Lyme borreliosis during pregnancy. Scan. J. Infect. Dis. Suppl 71:99, 1990.
3. Bartlett JG. In: Pocket Book of Infectious Disease Therapy. Williams and Wilkins, Baltimore, USA. 1996.
4. Nelson JD. In: Pocket Book of Pediatric Antimicrobial Therapy. Williams and Wilkins, Baltimore, USA. 1995.

LYME DISEASE VACCINE

Trade: Lymerix
Can/Aus/UK:
Uses: Lyme Disease Vaccine
AAP: Not reviewed

LYMErix is a noninfectious recombinant vaccine containing a lipoprotein from the outer surface of Borrelia burgdorferi. The lipoprotein from this causative agent is a single polypeptide chain of

257 amino acids with lipids covalently bonded to the N terminus.[1] No substance of animal origin is used in the manufacturing process. It is primarily indicated for individuals 15-70 years of age.   It is very unlikely to enter milk.   Officials from the CDC suggest that it is not contraindicated for use in breastfeeding patients.[2]

Pregnancy Risk Category: C

Lactation Risk Category: L2

Theoretic Infant Dose:

Adult Concerns: Pain at injection site, headache, fatigue, arthralgia, myalgia.

Pediatric Concerns: None reported via milk. Unlikely to enter milk compartment.

Drug Interactions: No known interactions have been published. Avoid use in patients taking anticoagulants.

Alternatives:

Adult Dosage:

References:
1.   Pharmaceutical Manufacturers Package Insert, 2000.
2.   Hayes, N. Center for Disease Control,   Personnal Communication, 2000.

LYSINE

Trade: Lysine, L-lysine
Can/Aus/UK:
Uses: Amino acid food supplement
AAP: Not reviewed

Lysine is a naturally occurring amino acid; the average American ingests from 6-10 grams daily.   Aside from its use as a supplement in patients with poor nutrition, it is most often used for the treatment of recurrent herpes simplex infections.   The clinical efficacy of lysine in herpes infections is highly controversial with some advocates,[1,2] and many detractors.[3]   Upon absorption, most is sequestered in the liver but blood levels do rise transiently.   However, the risk of toxicity is considered quite low in both adults and infants.   Rather high doses have been studied in infants as young as 4 months, with doses from 60 to 1080 mg L-lysine per 8 ounces of milk.[4]   At the higher level, 5.18 grams of L-lysine was consumed. Plasma lysine levels varied only with normal limits, while urinary lysine levels were roughly proportional to the amount of supplementation.

Thomas et.al. has reported an elegant study of the transfer of radiolabeled L-lysine into numerous compartments, including milk.[5,6] In a group of 5 lactating women who received L-lysine (15N-lysine and 13C-lysine (5 mg/kg/each)), milk levels of labeled lysine reached a peak at approximately 150 minutes. Labeled lysine levels in milk were slightly higher with M/P ratios ranging from 1.29 to 1.43. However, the total amount of radiolabeled lysine present in milk was low. Only 0.54% of the administered dose of lysine was secreted into milk proteins. Further, the lysine present in milk was present as protein, not free amino acid.

Therefore supplementation of breastfeeding mothers with L-lysine will probably not result in excess levels of free lysine in milk.

Pregnancy Risk Category:

Lactation Risk Category:

Theoretic Infant Dose:

Adult Concerns: Gi distress. Lysine may cause cholesterol and triglyceride levels in the blood to rise.

Pediatric Concerns: None reported.

Drug Interactions:

Alternatives:

Adult Dosage:

T½ = 3.66 hours	M/P =
PHL =	PB =
PK =	Oral = 83%
MW = 146	pKa =
Vd =	

References:

1. Griffith RS, Walsh DE, Myrmel KH, Thompson RW, Behforooz A. Success of L-lysine therapy in frequently recurrent herpes simplex infection. Treatment and prophylaxis. Dermatologica. 175(4):183-90, 1987.
2. Walsh DE, Griffith RS, Behforooz A. Subjective response to lysine in the therapy of herpes simplex. J Antimicrob Chemother. 12(5):489-96, 1983.
3. DiGiovanna JJ, Blank H. Failure of lysine in frequently recurrent herpes simplex infection. Treatment and prophylaxis. Arch Dermatol. 120(1):48-51, 1984.
4. Anderson SA, Raiten DJ(eds):"Safety of Amino Acids in Dietary Supplements." Life Sciences Research Office, Bethesda, MD: FASEB Special Publications Office, pp22,59, 199.
5. Thomas MR, Irving CS, Reeds PJ, Malphus EW, Wong WW, Boutton TW, Klein PD. Lysine and protein metabolism in the young lactating woman. Eur J Clin Nutr. 45(5):227-42, 1991.
6. Irving CS, Malphus EW, Thomas MR, Marks L, Klein PD. Infused and ingested labeled lysines: appearance in human-milk proteins. Am J Clin Nutr. 47(1):49-52, 1988.

MAGNESIUM HYDROXIDE

Trade: Milk Of Magnesia
Can/Aus/UK: Citro-Mag, Gastrobrom, Mylanta, Phillips' Milk of Magnesia
Uses: Laxative, antacid
AAP: Not reviewed

Poorly absorbed from maternal GI tract. Only about 15-30 % of an orally ingested magnesium product is absorbed. Magnesium rapidly deposits in bone (> 50%) and is significantly distributed to tissue sites. See magnesium sulfate.

Pregnancy Risk Category: B

Lactation Risk Category: L1

Theoretic Infant Dose:

Adult Concerns: Hypotension, diarrhea, nausea.

Pediatric Concerns: None reported.

Drug Interactions: Decreased absorption of tetracyclines, digoxin, indomethacin, and iron salts.

Alternatives:

Adult Dosage: 5-30 mL PRN

T½ =		M/P =	
PHL =		PB = 33%	
PK =		Oral = 15-30%	
MW = 58		pKa =	
Vd =			

References:

MAGNESIUM SULFATE

Trade: Epsom Salt
Can/Aus/UK: Epsom Salts, Magnoplasm, Salvital, Zinvit
Uses: Saline laxative and anticonvulsant (IV,IM)
AAP: Approved by the American Academy of Pediatrics for use in breastfeeding mothers

Magnesium is a normal plasma electrolyte. It is used pre and postnatally as an effective anticonvulsant in preeclamptic patients. In one study of 10 preeclamptic patients who received a 4 gm I.V. loading dose followed by 1 gm per hour I.V. for more than 24 hours, the average milk magnesium levels in treated subjects was 6.4 mg/dl, only slightly higher than controls (untreated) which were 4.77 mg/dl.[1] On day 2, the average milk magnesium levels in treated groups was 3.83 mg/dl which was not significantly different from untreated controls, 3.19 mg/dl. By day 3, the treated and control groups breastmilk levels were identical (3.54 vs 3.52 mg/dl). The mean maternal serum magnesium level on day 1 in treated groups was 3.55 mg/dl, which was significantly higher than control untreated, 1.82 mg/dl. In both treated and control subjects, levels of milk magnesium were approximately twice those of maternal serum magnesium levels, with the milk-to-serum ratio being 1.9 in treated subjects, and 2.1 in control subjects.

This study clearly indicates a normal concentrating mechanism for magnesium in human milk. It is well known that oral magnesium absorption is very poor, averaging only 4-30%. Further, this study indicates that in treated groups, infants would only receive about 1.5 mg of oral magnesium more than the untreated controls. It is very unlikely that the amount of magnesium in breastmilk would be clinically relevant.

Pregnancy Risk Category: B

Lactation Risk Category: L1

Theoretic Infant Dose: 9.6 mg/kg/day

Adult Concerns: I.V.-hypotension, sedation, muscle weakness.

Pediatric Concerns: None reported via milk. Sedation, hypotonia following in-utero exposure.

Drug Interactions: May decrease the hypertensive effect of nifedepine. May increase the depression associated with other CNS depressants, neuromuscular blocking agents, and the cardiotoxicity associated with ritodrine.

Alternatives:

Adult Dosage: 1-2 g q 4-6 hours PRN

T½ = < 3 hours	M/P = 1.9
PHL =	PB = 0%
PK = Immediate(IV)	Oral = 4-30%
MW = 120	pKa =
Vd =	

References:
1. Cruikshank DP, Varner MW, Pitkin RM. Breast milk magnesium and calcium concentrations following magnesium sulfate treatment. AM J Obstet Gynecol. 143:685-688, 1982.

MAPROTILENE

Trade: Ludiomil
Can/Aus/UK: Ludiomil, Novo-Maprotilene
Uses: Antidepressant
AAP: Not reviewed

Maprotilene is a unique structured (tetracyclic) antidepressant dissimilar to others but has clinical effects similar to the tricyclic antidepressants. While it has fewer anticholinergic side effects than the tricyclics, it is more sedating and has similar toxicities in overdose. In one study following an oral dose of 50 mg three times daily, milk and maternal blood levels were greater than 200 μg/L.[1] Milk/plasma ratios varied from 1.3 to 1.5. While these levels are quite low, it is not known if they are hazardous to a breastfed infant, but caution is recommended.

Pregnancy Risk Category: B

Lactation Risk Category: L3

Theoretic Infant Dose: 30.0 μg/kg/day

Adult Concerns: Side effects include drowsiness, sedation, vertigo, blurred vision, dry mouth, and urinary retention. Skin rashes, seizures, myoclonus, mania and hallucinations have been reported.

Pediatric Concerns: None reported via milk, but caution is recommended.

Drug Interactions: Maprotilene levels may be decreased by barbiturates, phenytoin, and carbamazepine. Increased toxicity may result when used with CNS depressants, quinidine, MAO inhibitors, anticholinergics, sympathomimetics, phenothiazines (seizures), benzodiazepines. Due to hazard of increased QT intervals, do not admix with cisapride.

Alternatives: Sertraline, Venlafaxine, Paroxetine

Adult Dosage: 25-75 mg daily

T½ = 27-58 hours	M/P = 1.5
PHL=	PB = 88%
PK = 12 hours	Oral = 100%
MW = 277	pKa =
Vd = 22.6	

References:
1. Riess W: The relevance of blood level determinations during the evaluation of maprotiline in man. In: Murphy (ed): Research and Clinical Investigations in Depression. Cambridge Medical Publications, Northhampton, p 19, 1976.

MEBENDAZOLE

Trade: Vermox
Can/Aus/UK: Sqworm, Vermox
Uses: Anthelmintic
AAP: Not reviewed

Mebendazole is an anthelmintic used primarily for pin worms, although it is active against round worms, hookworms, and a number of other nematodes. Mebendazole is poorly absorbed orally. Following oral administration of multiple doses in two adults, mean peak plasma levels were only $0.08\ \mu g/ml$ after 2 hours. In children following multiple oral doses, the mean peak plasma levels were less than $0.03\ \mu g/ml$.

No data are available on its penetration into human milk. Considering the poor oral absorption and high protein binding, it is unlikely to be transmitted to the infant in clinically relevant concentrations. However, in one patient after two days therapy with mebendazole, it was reported to significantly reduce production of breastmilk to the point that milk production ceased after one week.[1] This is the only report which has noted this side effect.

Pregnancy Risk Category: C

Lactation Risk Category: L4

Theoretic Infant Dose:

Adult Concerns: Diarrhea, abdominal pain, nausea, vomiting, headache. Observe mother for reduced production of breastmilk.

Pediatric Concerns: None reported via milk. May inhibit milk production.

Drug Interactions: Carbamazepine and phenytoin may increase metabolism of mebendazole.

Alternatives: Pyrantel

Adult Dosage: 100 mg BID

T½ = 2.8-9 hours.	**M/P =**
PHL =	**PB = High**
PK = 0.5-7.0 hours.	**Oral = 2-10%**
MW = 295	**pKa =**
Vd =	

References:
1. Rao TS, Does mebendazole inhibit lactation? NZ Medical J. 96:589-590, 1983.

MECLIZINE

Trade: Antivert, Bonine
Can/Aus/UK: Ancolan, Bonamine, Sea-legs
Uses: Antiemetic, antivertigo, motion sickness
AAP: Not reviewed

Meclizine is an antihistamine frequently used for nausea, vertigo, and motion sickness, although it is inferior to scopolamine. Meclizine was previously used for nausea and vomiting of pregnancy.[1] No data are available on its secretion into breastmilk. There are no pediatric indications for this product.

Pregnancy Risk Category: B

Lactation Risk Category: L3

Theoretic Infant Dose:

Adult Concerns: Drowsiness, sedation, dry mouth, blurred vision.

Pediatric Concerns: None reported.

Drug Interactions: May have increased sedation when used with CNS depressants and other neuroleptics and anticholinergics.

Alternatives: Hydroxyzine, Cetirzine

Adult Dosage: 25-100 mg QD

T½ = 6 hours	M/P =
PHL =	PB =
PK = 1-2 hours	Oral = Complete
MW = 391	pKa =
Vd =	

References:
1. Vorherr, H. Drug excretion in breast milk. Postgrad. Med. 56:97-104, 1974.

MEDROXYPROGESTERONE

Trade: Provera, Depo-provera, Cycrin
Can/Aus/UK: Alti-MPA, Depo-Provera, Divina, Farlutal, Gen-Medroxy, Provelle, Provera, Ralovera
Uses: Injectable progestational agent
AAP: Approved by the American Academy of Pediatrics for use in breastfeeding mothers

Depo Medroxyprogesterone (DMPA) is a synthetic progestin

compound.   It is used orally for amenorrhea, dysmenorrhea, uterine bleeding, and infertility. It is used intramuscularly for contraception. Due to its poor oral bioavailability, it is seldom used orally.

Saxena has reported that the average concentration in milk is 1.03 μg/L.[1] Koetswang reported average milk levels of 0.97 μg/L.[2]   In a series of huge studies, the World Health Organization reviewed the developmental skills of children and their weight gain following exposure to progestin-only contraceptives during lactation.[3,4]   These studies documented that no adverse effects on overall development, or rate of growth, were notable. Further, they suggested there is no apparent reason to deny lactating women the use of progestin-only contraceptives, preferably after 6 weeks postpartum.

There have been consistent and controversial studies suggesting that males exposed to early postnatal progestins have higher feminine scores. However, Ehrhardt's studies have provided convincing data that males exposed to early progestins were no different than controls.[5] A number of other short and long-term studies available on development of children have found no differences with control groups.[6,7]

Interestingly, an excellent study of the transfer of DMPA into breastfed infants has been published.[8] In this study of 13 breastfeeding women who received 150 mg injections of DMPA on day 43 and again on day 127 postpartum, urine and plasma collections in infants(n=??) from day 38 to day 137 were collected.   Urinary follicle stimulating hormone(FSH), luteinizing hormone(LH), unconjugated testosterone, unconjugated cortisol, medroxyprogesterone and metabolites were measured. No differences (from untreated controls) were found in LH, FSH, or unconjugated testosterone urine levels in the infants. Urine cortisol levels were not altered from those of control infants. Medroxyprogesterone or its metabolites were at no time detected in any of the infant urine samples. This data concludes that only small trace amounts of MPA are transferred to breastfeeding infants and that these amounts are not expected to have any influence on breastfeeding infants. In support of this, using calculations based on MPA levels in the blood of DMPA users and a plasma to milk MPA ratio, Benagiano and Fraser suggest that the actual amounts of MPA in the infant's system is probably at or below trace levels.[9] Koetsawang states that the small amount of MPA present in milk is unlikely have any significant clinical adverse effects on the infant.[2]   A long-term follow-up study by Jimenez found no changes in growth, development and health status in 128 breast-fed infants at 4.5 years of age.[10] DMPA mothers lactated significantly longer than controls in this study.

The use of Depo-Provera in breastfeeding women is common but will probably always be somewhat controversial. Depo Provera has been documented to significantly elevate prolactin levels in breastfeeding mothers[11], and increase milk production.[12]

It is well known that estrogens suppress milk production.   With progestins, it has been suggested that some women may experience a decline in milk production, or arrested early production, following injection of DMPA, particularly when the progestin is used early postpartum (12-48 hours).[13] At present there is no published data to support this, nor is the relative incidence of this untoward effect known. Therefore, in some instances, it might be advisable to recommend treatment with oral progestin-only contraceptives postpartum, so that women who experience reduced milk supply could easily withdraw from the medication without significant loss of breastmilk supply. No progestin should be used before at least 3 days postpartum and perhaps longer.[13]

Pregnancy Risk Category: D

Lactation Risk Category: L1
                           L4 if used first 3 days postpartum

Theoretic Infant Dose:

Adult Concerns: Fluid retention, GI distress, menstrual disorders, breakthrough bleeding, weight gain.

Pediatric Concerns: None reported via milk, although unsubstantiated reports of depressed milk supply have been made.

Drug Interactions: Aminoglutethimide may increase the hepatic clearance of medroxyprogesterone, reducing its efficacy.

Alternatives:

Adult Dosage: 5-10 mg daily

T½ = 14.5 hours.	M/P =
PHL=	PB =
PK =	Oral = 0.6-10%
MW = 344	pKa =
Vd =	

References:
1. Saxena Nb, et.al. Level of contraceptive steroids in breast milk and plasma of lactating women. Contraception 16:605-613, 1977.
2. Koetsawang S, Nukulkarn P, Fotherby K, Shrimanker K, Mangalam M, Towobola K. Transfer of contraceptive steroids in milk of women using long-acting gestagens. Contraception. 25(4):321-31, 1982.
3. WHO Task Force for Epidemiological Research on Reproductive Health. Progestogen-only contraceptives during lactation: I. Infant Growth. Contraception 50:35-53, 1994.
4. WHO Task Force for Epidemiological Research on Reproductive Health. Progestogen-only contraceptives during lactation: II. Infant development. Contraception 50:55-68, 1994.
5. Ehrhardt AA. et.al. Prenatal exposure to medroxyprogesterone acetate (MPA) in girls. Psycho-neuroendocrinol 2:391, 1977.
6. Schwallie PC. The effect of depo-medroxyprogesterone acetate on the fetus and nursing infant: a review. Contraception 23:375-86, 1981.
7. Pardthaison T, Yenchit C, Gray R. The long-term growth and development

of children exposed to Depo-Provera during pregnancy or lactation. Contraception 45:313-24,1992.

8. Virutamasen P, Leepipatpaiboon S, Kriengsinyot R, Vichaidith P, Muia PN, Sekadde-Kigondu CB, Mati JK, Forest MG, Dikkeschei LD, Wolthers BG, d'Arcangues C. Pharmacodynamic effects of depot-medroxyprogesterone acetate (DMPA) administered to lactating women on their male infants. Contraception. 54(3):153-7, 1996.
9. Benagiano G, Fraser I. The Depo-Provera debate. Commentary on the article "Depo-Provera, a critical analysis". Contraception. 24(5):493-528, 1981. Review.
10. Jimenez J, Ochoa M, Soler MP, Portales P. Long-term follow-up of children breast-fed by mothers receiving depot-medroxyprogesterone acetate. Contraception. 30(6):523-33, 1984.
11. Ratchanon S, Taneepanichskul S. Depot medroxyprogesterone acetate and basal serum prolactin levels in lactating women. Obstet Gynecol. 96(6):926-8, 2000.
12. Fraser IS. Long acting injectable hormonal contraceptives. Clin Reprod Fertil. 1(1):67-88, 1982.
13. Kennedy KI, Short RV, Tully MR. Premature introduction of progestin-only contraceptive methods during lactation. Contraception. 55(6):347-50, 1997.

MEDROXYPROGESTERONE and ESTRADIOL CYPIONATE

Trade: Lunelle
Can/Aus/UK:
Uses: Once-a-month birth control injection.
AAP: Not reviewed

Lunelle is a new once-a-month injectable birth control product. It contains medroxyprogesterone acetate (25 mg) which is the active ingredient in Depo-Provera, and also contains 5 mg estradiol cypionate, which is a repository form of estrogen that is slowly released from the injection site over 30 days.

The amount of medroxyprogesterone for this one month injection is 25 mg. The amount of Depo-Provera providing 3 months coverage is 150 mg. Because this injection contains estrogen, it may potentially reduce the production of milk and caution is recommended.[1] Although small amounts of estrogens and progestins may pass into breastmilk, the effects of these hormones on an infant appear minimal. Use of estrogen containing products, particularly early postpartum, may dramatically reduce the volume of milk produced. Mothers should attempt to delay use of these products for as long as possible postpartum (at least 6-8 weeks), if at all. Because of the estrogen content, and the prolonged release formula, caution is recommended in breastfeeding mothers.

Pregnancy Risk Category: X

Lactation Risk Category: L3

Theoretic Infant Dose:

Adult Concerns: Side effects are typical of oral contraceptives and include thromboembolism, cerebral hemorrhage, hypertension, infarction, cerebral ischemia, gallbladder disease, pulmonary embolism, thrombophlebitis. Abdominal pain, acne, etc. See package insert for numerous others.

Pediatric Concerns: Possibility of reduce milk supply. Long term followup of infants has shown no untoward effects.

Drug Interactions: Aminogluthethamide may decrease effectiveness and serum concentration of MPA. Rifampin may increase metabolism of estrogens/progestins.   Anticonvulsants such as phenobarbital, phenytoin, and carbamazepine have been shown to increase metabolism of some estrogens and progestins and could reduce contraceptive effectiveness.   Some antibiotics (ampicillin, tetracycline and griseofulvin) may reduce contraceptive effectiveness. St. Johns wort may also reduce contraceptive effectiveness by enhancing metabolism of numerous drugs.

Alternatives: Micronor, Ovrette

Adult Dosage: 25 mg MPA, 5 mg estradiol cypionate monthly

T½ = 14.5 hours	M/P =
PHL =	PB =
PK =	Oral = <10%
MW =	pKa =
Vd =	

References:
1.   Booker DE, Pahyl IR. Control of postpartum breast engorgement with oral contraceptives. Am J Obstet Gynecol 98:1099-1101, 1967.

MEFLOQUINE

Trade: Lariam
Can/Aus/UK: Lariam
Uses: Antimalarial
AAP: Not reviewed

Mefloquine is an antimalarial and a structural analog of quinine. It is concentrated in red cells and therefore has a long half-life.[1]   Following a single 250 mg dose in two women, the milk/plasma ratio was only 0.13 to 0.16 the first 4 days of therapy.[2]   The concentration of mefloquine in milk ranged from 32 to 53 μg/L. Unfortunately, these studies were not carried out after steady state conditions, which would probably increase to some degree the amount transferred to the infant.

According to the manufacturer, mefloquine is secreted in small concentrations approximating 3% of the maternal dose. Assuming a milk level of 53 μg/L, and a daily milk intake of 150 mL/kg/day, an infant would ingest approximately 8 μg/kg/day of mefloquine which in not sufficient to protect the infant from malaria. The therapeutic dose for malaria prophylaxis is 62 mg in a 15-19 kg infant. Thus far, no untoward effects have been reported.

Pregnancy Risk Category: C

Lactation Risk Category: L2

Theoretic Infant Dose: 8.0 μg/kg/day

Adult Concerns: GI upset, dizziness, elevated liver enzymes, possible retinopathy.

Pediatric Concerns: None reported but discontinue lactation if neuropsychiatric disturbances occur.

Drug Interactions: Decreases effect of valproic acid. Increased toxicity of beta blockers, chloroquine, quinine, quinidine.

Alternatives:

Adult Dosage: 1.25 g once OR 250 mg q week

T½ = 10-21 days.	M/P = 0.13-0.27
PHL =	PB = 98%
PK = 1-2 hours.	Oral = 85%
MW = 414	pKa =
Vd = 19	

References:
1. Pharmaceutical Manufacturers Package Insert, 1995.
2. Edstein MD, Veenendaal JR & Hyslop R: Excretion of mefloquine in human breast milk. Chemothcrapy 34:165-9, 1988.

MELATONIN

Trade:
Can/Aus/UK:
Uses: Hormone
AAP: Not reviewed

Melatonin (N-acetyl-5-methoxytryptamine) is a normal hormone secreted by the pineal gland in the human brain. It is circadian in rhythm, with nighttime values considerably higher than daytime levels. It is postulated to induce a sleep-like pattern in humans. It is known to be passed into human milk, and is believed responsible for entraining the newborn brain to phase shift its circadian clock to that of the mother by communicating the time of day information to the newborn.

On the average, the amount of melatonin in human milk is about 35% of the maternal plasma level, but can range to as high as 80%.[1] Postfeeding milk levels appear to more closely reflect the maternal plasma level than prefeeding values, suggesting that melatonin may be transported into milk at night, during the feeding, rather than being stored in foremilk. In neonates, melatonin levels are low and progressively increase up to the age of 3 months when the characteristic diurnal rhythm is detectible.[2] Night-time melatonin levels reach a maximum at the age of 1-3 years and thereafter decline to adult values.[3-5] While night-time maternal serum levels average 280 pmol/L, milk levels averaged 99 pmol/L in a group of ten breastfeeding mothers.[1] The effect of orally administered melatonin on newborns is unknown, but melatonin has thus far not been associated with significant untoward effects.

Pregnancy Risk Category:

Lactation Risk Category: L3

Theoretic Infant Dose:

Adult Concerns: Headache and confusion, drowsiness, fatigue, hypothermia, and dysphoria in depressed patients.

Pediatric Concerns: None reported.

Drug Interactions:

Alternatives:

Adult Dosage:

T½ = 30-50 minutes	M/P = 0.35-0.8
PHL =	PB =
PK = 0.5-2 hours	Oral = Complete
MW = 232	pKa =
Vd =	

References:
1. Illnerova H, Buresova M, Presl J. : Melatonin rhythm in human milk. J. Clin. Endocrin. and Metab. 77(3):838-841, 1993.
2. Hartman L et.al. Plasma and urinary melatonin in male infants during the first 12 months of life. Clin. Chim. Acta. 121:37-42, 1982.
3. Aldhous M, Franey C, Wright J et al: Plasma concentrations of melatonin in man following oral absorption of different preparations. Br J Clin Pharmacol 19:517-521, 1985.
4. Attanasio A. et.al. Ontogeny of circadian rhythmicity for melatonin, serotonin and N-acetylserotonin in humans. J. Pineal Res 3:251-256, 1986.
5. Dollins AB, Lunch HJ, Wurtman RJ et al: Effect of pharmacological daytime doses of melatonin on human mood and performance. Psychopharmacology 112:490-496, 1993.

MELOXICAM

Trade: Mobic
Can/Aus/UK: Mobic
Uses: Nonsteroidal anti-inflammatory agent
AAP: Not reviewed

Meloxicam is a nonsteroidal anti-inflammatory drug that appears more selective for the COX-2 receptor. No data are available for transfer into human milk, although it does transfer into rodent milk. Due to its long half-life and good bioavailability, another NSAID would probably be preferred.

Pregnancy Risk Category: C

Lactation Risk Category: L4

Theoretic Infant Dose:

Adult Concerns: Leukopenia, elevated liver enzymes, headache, abdominal pain, constipation, diarrhea, angina, anaphylaxis in aspirin sensitive patients.

Pediatric Concerns: None reported via milk.

Drug Interactions: May reduce coagulation in patients using anticoagulants and other platelet inhibitory drugs. NSAIDs may decrease the antihypertensive effect of ACE inhibitors. May increase blood pressure in hypertensive patients using beta blockers and other antihypertensives. May increase risk of gastric hemorrhage with calcium channel blockers. Numerous other drug-drug interactions listed, consult another text.

Alternatives: Ibuprofen

Adult Dosage: 7.5 mg/d

T½ = 20.1 hours	M/P =	
PHL =	PB = 99.4	
PK = 4.9 hours	Oral = 89%	
MW = 351	pKa = 4.2	
Vd = 0.14		

References:
1. Pharmaceutical manufacturers package insert, 2002.

MENOTROPINS

Trade: Pergonal, Humegon
Can/Aus/UK: Humegon, Pergonal
Uses: Produces follicle growth
AAP: Not reviewed

Menotropins is a purified preparation of gonadotropins hormones extracted from the urine of postmenopausal women. It is a biologically standardized form containing equal activity of follicle stimulating hormone(FSH) and luteinizing hormone (LH).[1-3] It is primarily used to stimulate follicle growth in women and sperm production in men. FSH and LH are large molecular weight peptides and would not likely penetrate into human milk. Further, they are unstable in the GI tract and their oral bioavailability would be minimal to zero even in an infant.

Pregnancy Risk Category: X

Lactation Risk Category: L3

Theoretic Infant Dose:

Adult Concerns: Ovarian enlargement, cysts, hemoperitoneum, fever, chills, aches, joint pains, nausea, vomiting, abdominal pain, diarrhea, bloating, rash, dizziness.

Pediatric Concerns: None reported via milk.

Drug Interactions:

Alternatives:

Adult Dosage: 75-150 units each FSH & LH QD

T½ = 3.9 and 70.4 hours	M/P =
PHL=	PB =
PK = 6 hours	Oral = 0%
MW = 34,000	pKa =
Vd = 1.08	

References:
1. Sharma V, Riddle A, et al: Studies on folliculogenesis and in vitro fertilization outcome after the administration of follicle-stimulating hormone at different times during the menstrual cycle. Fertil Steril 51:298-303, 1989.
2. Kjeld JM, Harsoulis P, et al: Infusions of hFSH and hLH in normal men: kinetics of human follicle stimulating hormone. Acta Endocrinologica 81:225-233, 1976.
3. Yen SSC, Llerena LA, Pearson OH et al: Disappearance rates of endogenous follicle-stimulating hormone in serum following surgical hypophysectomy in man. J Clin Endocrinol 30:325-329, 1970.

MEPERIDINE

Trade: Demerol
Can/Aus/UK: Demerol, Pethidine
Uses: Narcotic analgesic
AAP: Approved by the American Academy of Pediatrics for use in breastfeeding mothers

Meperidine is a potent opiate analgesic. It is rapidly and completely metabolized by the adult and neonatal liver to an active form, normeperidine. Significant but small amounts of meperidine are secreted into breastmilk. In a study of 9 nursing mothers two hours after a 50 mg IM injection, the average concentration of meperidine in milk was 82 μg/L and a milk/plasma ratio of 1.12.[1] The highest concentration of meperidine in breastmilk at 2 hours after dose was 0.13 mg/L.

In another study the maximum concentration of meperidine in milk ranged from 134 to 244 μg/L in 5 patients at 1-2 hours after administration, and 76 to 318 μg/L at 2-4 hours after administration of 25 mg intravenously (in 3 patients).[2] According to these authors, the maximum dose to an infant would be approximately 9.5 μg/kg or 1.2% to 3.5% of the weight-adjusted maternal dose.

In a study of two nursing mothers who received varying amounts of meperidine following delivery(up to 1275 mg within 72 hours), the concentration of meperidine ranged from 36.2 to 314 μg/L with an average of 225 μg/L. Breastmilk levels of normeperidine ranged from zero to 333 μg/L with an average of 142 μg/L.[3] This study clearly shows a much longer half-life for the active metabolite, normeperidine. Normeperidine levels were detected after 56 hours post-administration in human milk (8.1 ng/ml) following a single 50 mg dose. The milk/plasma ratios varied from 0.82 to 1.59 depending on dose and timing of sampling.

Published half-lives for meperidine in neonates (13 hours) and normeperidine (63 hours) are long and with time could concentrate in the plasma of a neonate. Wittels studies clearly indicate that infants from mothers treated with meperidine (PCA post-cesarian) were neurobehaviorally depressed after three days. Infants from similar groups treated with morphine were not affected.

Pregnancy Risk Category: B

Lactation Risk Category: L2
        L3 if used early postpartum

Theoretic Infant Dose: 41.3 μg/kg/day

Adult Concerns: Sedation, respiratory depression.

Pediatric Concerns: Sedation, poor suckling reflex, neurobehavioral delay.

Drug Interactions: Phenytoin may decrease analgesic effect. Meperidine may aggravate adverse effects of isoniazid. MAO inhibitors, Fluoxetine and other SSRIs, and tricyclic antidepressants may greatly potentiate the effects of meperidine.

Alternatives: Morphine, Fentanyl, Hydrocodone

Adult Dosage: 50-100 mg q 3-4 hours PRN

T½ = 3.2 hours	M/P = 0.84-1.59
PHL = 6-32 hours(neonates)	PB = 65-80 %
PK = 30-50 min.(IM)	Oral = <50%
MW = 247	pKa = 8.6
Vd = 3.7-4.2	

References:
1. von Peiker G, et. al. Excretion of pethidine in mother's milk. Zentralbl Gynaekol 102:537-41, 1980
2. Borgatta L, Jenny RW, Gruss L, Ong C, Barad D. Clinical significance of methohexital, meperidine, and diazepam in breast milk. J Clin Pharmacol. 37(3):186-92, 1997.
3. Quinn PG, Kuhner BR, Kaine CJ, and Syracuse CD. Measurement of meperidine and normeperidine in human breast milk by selected ion monitoring. Biomed. & Environ. Mass. Spec. 13(3):133-5, 1986.
4. Wittels Bk, Scott DT, Sinatra RS. Exogenous opioids in human breast milk and acute neonatal neurobehavior: a preliminary study. Anesthesiology 73:864-869, 1990.

MEPIVACAINE

Trade: Carbocaine, Polocaine
Can/Aus/UK: Carbocaine, Polocaine
Uses: Local anesthetic
AAP: Not reviewed

Mepivacaine is a long acting local anesthetic similar to bupivacaine.[1-3] Mepivacaine is used for infiltration, peripheral nerve blocks, and central nerve blocks (epidural or caudal anesthesia). No data are available on the transfer of mepivacaine into human milk, however its structure is practically identical to bupivacaine and one would expect its entry into human milk is similar and low. Bupivacaine enters milk in exceedingly low levels (see bupivacaine). Due to higher fetal levels, and reported toxicities, mepivacaine is never used antenatally. For use in breastfeeding patients, bupivacaine is preferred.

Pregnancy Risk Category: C

Lactation Risk Category: L3

Theoretic Infant Dose:

Adult Concerns: Sedation, bradycardia, respiratory sedation, transient burning, anaphylaxis.

Pediatric Concerns: None reported via milk.   Neonatal depression and convulsive seizures occurred in 7 neonates 6 hours after delivery.

Drug Interactions: Increases effect of hyaluronidase, beta blockers, MAO inhibitors, tricyclic antidepressants, phenothiazines, and vasopressors.

Alternatives:

Adult Dosage: 50-300 mg X 1

T½ = 1.9-3.2 hours	M/P =
PHL = 8.7-9 hours	PB = 60-85%
PK = 30 minutes	Oral =
MW =	pKa = 7.6
Vd =	

References:
1.   Pharmaceutical manufacturers package insert, 1997.
2.   Hillman LS, Hillman RE & Dodson WE: Diagnosis, treatment, and follow-up of neonatal mepivacaine intoxication secondary to paracervical and pudendal blocks during labor. Pediatrics 95:472-477, 1979.
3.   Teramo K and Rajamaki A. Foetal and maternal plasma levels of mepivacaine and foetal acid-base balance and heart rate after paracervical block during labour. Br J Anesth 43:300-312, 1971.

MEPROBAMATE

Trade: Equanil, Miltown
Can/Aus/UK: Apo-Meprobamate, Equanil, Meprate, Novo-Mepro
Uses: Antianxiety drug
AAP: Not reviewed

Meprobamate is an older antianxiety drug.[1]   It is secreted into milk at levels 2-4 times that of the maternal plasma level.[2]   It could produce some sedation in a breastfeeding infant.

Pregnancy Risk Category: D

Lactation Risk Category: L3

Theoretic Infant Dose:

Adult Concerns: Blood dyscrasias, sedation, hypotension, withdrawal reactions.

Pediatric Concerns: None reported, but observe for sedation.

Drug Interactions: May have increased CNS depression when used with other neuroleptic depressants.

Alternatives: Lorazepam, Alprazolam

Adult Dosage: 300-400 mg TID-QID

T½ = 6-17 hours	M/P = 2-4
PHL=	PB = 15%
PK = 1-3 hours	Oral = Complete
MW = 218	pKa =
Vd = 0.7	

References:
1. Pharmaceutical Manufacturers Package Insert, 1993, 1994.
2. Wilson JT, et. al. Drug excretion in human breast milk: principles, pharmacokinetics and projected consequences. Clin Pharmacokinet 5:1-66, 1980.

MERCAPTOPURINE

Trade: Purinethol
Can/Aus/UK: Puri-Nethol, Purinethol
Uses: Antimetabolite
AAP: Not reviewed

Mercaptopurine is an anticancer drug that acts intracellularly as an purine antagonist, ultimately inhibiting DNA and RNA synthesis.[1] It is an extremely toxic drug producing significant bone marrow suppression. Because it has a pKa of 7.6, it would likely penetrate milk, although no data are available. Mercaptopurine is probably too dangerous and toxic to expose a breastfeeding infant.   Toxic risks probably outweigh benefits of breastfeeding.

Pregnancy Risk Category: D

Lactation Risk Category: L5

Theoretic Infant Dose:

Adult Concerns: Bone marrow suppression, liver toxicity, nausea, vomiting, diarrhea.

Pediatric Concerns: None reported, but this product is probably too dangerous to continue breastfeeding.

Drug Interactions: When used with allopurinol, reduced mercaptopurine to 1/3 to 1/4 the usual dose.   When used with trimethoprim sulfamethoxazole, may enhance bone marrow suppression.

Alternatives:

Adult Dosage: 1.5-2.5 mg/kg daily

T½ = 0.9 hour	M/P =
PHL =	PB = 19%
PK = 2 hours	Oral = 50%
MW = 152	pKa = 7.6
Vd =	

References:
1.   Pharmaceutical Manufacturers Package Insert, 1995.

MERCURY

Trade:
Can/Aus/UK:
Uses: Environmental contaminate
AAP: Not reviewed

Mercury is an environmental contaminate that is available in multiple salt forms. Elemental mercury, or the form in thermometers, is poorly absorbed orally (0.01%), but completely absorbed via inhalation (>80%).[1] Inorganic mercury causes most forms of mercury poisoning and is available in mercury disk batteries (7-15% orally bioavailable). Organic mercury (methy mercury fungicides, phenyl mercury) is readily absorbed (90% orally). Mercury poisoning produces encephalopathy, acute renal failure, severe GI necrosis, and numerous other systemic toxicities. Mercury transfers into human milk with a milk/plasma ratio that varies according to the mercury form. Pitkin reports that in the USA that 100 non-exposed women had 0.9 μg/L total mercury in their milk.[2]

Oskarsson reported mercury levels of 0.6 ng/g in Swedish women which is one-half the tolerable daily intake for adults recommended by the WHO.[3] The levels of mercury were directly correlated with the number of amalgam dental fillings and the ingestion of fish. The major transfer of mercury seems to occur during gestation, with cord blood levels approximately twice that of maternal blood levels.[4,5] The majority of mercury present in milk is in the inorganic form which is poorly absorbed orally (2-38%)[6]. Nevertheless, breastfeeding women should limit their ingestion of fish while breastfeeding in countries where fish mercury levels are higher, and should not have amalgam fillings removed. Mothers known to be contaminated with mercury should not breastfeed.

Pregnancy Risk Category:

Lactation Risk Category: L5

Theoretic Infant Dose:

Adult Concerns: Brain damage, acute renal failure, severe GI necrosis, and numerous other systemic toxicities.

Pediatric Concerns: Mercury transfer into milk is reported. Risks are too high to continue exposure of the infant if mother is contaminated.

Drug Interactions:

Alternatives:

Adult Dosage:

T½ = 70 days	M/P =
PHL=	PB =
PK =	Oral = Variable
MW = 201	pKa =
Vd =	

References:
1. Wofff MS. Occupationally derived chemicals in breast milk. Amer. J. Indust. Med. 4:359-281, 1983.
2. Pickin RM, Bahns JA, Filer LJ, Reynolds WA. Mercury in human maternal and cord blood, placenta, and milk. Proc. Soc. Exp. Med. 151:65-567, 1976.
3. Oskarsson A, Schultz A, Skerfving S, Hallen IP, Ohlin B, Lagerkvist BJ. Total and inorganic mercury in breast milk in relation to fish consumption and amalgam in lactating women. Arch Environ Health. 51(3):234-41, 1996.
4. Ramirez GB, Cruz MC, Pagulayan O, Ostrea E, Dalisay C. The Tagum study I: analysis and clinical correlates of mercury in maternal and cord blood, breast milk, meconium, and infants' hair. Pediatrics. 106(4):774-81, 2000.
5. Vahter M, Akesson A, Lind B, Bjors U, Schutz A, Berglund M. Longitudinal study of methylmercury and inorganic mercury in blood and urine of pregnant and lactating women, as well as in umbilical cord blood. Environ Res. 84(2):186-94, 2000.
6. Abadin HG, Hibbs BF, Pohl HR. Breast-feeding exposure of infants to cadmium, lead, and mercury: a public health viewpoint. Toxicol Ind Health. 13(4):495-517, 1997.

MESALAMINE

Trade: Asacol, Pentasa, Rowasa, Canasa, Colazal
Can/Aus/UK: Asacol, Mesalazine, Mesasal, Quintasa, Salofalk
Uses: Anti-inflammatory in ulcerative colitis
AAP: Should be given to nursing mothers with caution.

Mesalamine is an anti-inflammatory agent used in ulcerative colitis. Although it contains 5-aminosalicylic acid, the mechanism of action is unknown. Some 5-aminosalicylic acid (5-ASA) can be converted into salicylic acid and absorbed, but the amount is very small. Acetyl-5-aminosalicyclic (Acetyl-5-ASA) acid is the common metabolite and has been found in breastmilk. The effect of mesalamine is primarily local on the mucosa of the colon itself. Mesalamine is poorly absorbed from the GI tract. Only 5-35% of a dose is absorbed. Oral tablets are enteric coated for delayed absorption.

In one patient receiving 500 mg mesalamine orally three times daily, the concentration of 5-ASA in breastmilk was 0.11 mg/L, and the Acetyl-5-ASA metabolite was 12.4 mg/L of milk. The milk/plasma ratio for 5-ASA was 0.27, and for Acetyl-5-ASA was 5.1.[1] Using this data, the weight-adjusted relative infant dose would be 7.5%.

In another patient receiving 1000 mg PO three times daily, milk levels of 5-ASA following 7 and 11 days of treatment and 5 hours following the dose were both 0.1 mg/L and the milk/plasma ratios were 0.07 and 0.09.[2]

Mesalamine is useful in patients allergic to sulfasalazine, or salicylazosulfapyridine. At least one report of a watery diarrhea in an infant whose mother was using rectal 5-ASA has been reported.[3] Each time treatment was reinstated, diarrhea recurred. A new product, Colazal(Balsalazide) is a prodrug of mesalamine (5-aminosalicylic acid; 5-ASA).

Pregnancy Risk Category: B

Lactation Risk Category: L3

Theoretic Infant Dose: 1.9 mg/kg/day

Adult Concerns: Watery diarrhea, abdominal pain, cramps, flatulence, nausea, headache.

Pediatric Concerns: Watery diarrhea in one breastfed patient, although this appears rare.

Drug Interactions: May significantly reduce bioavailability of digoxin.

Alternatives:

Adult Dosage: 800 mg TID

T½ = 5-10 hours(metabolite)	**M/P = 0.27, 5.1**
PHL =	**PB = 55%**
PK = 4-12 hours	**Oral = 15-35%**
MW = 153	**pKa =**
Vd =	

References:
1. Jenss H, Weber P, Hartman F. 5-Aminosalicyclic acid and its metabolite in breast milk during lactation. Am. J. Gastroenterol. 85:331, 1990.
2. Klotz U, Harings-Kaim A. Negligible excretion of 5-aminosalicylic acid in breast milk. Lancet. 342(8871):618-9, 1993.
3. Nelis GF. Diarrhoea due to 5-aminosalicyclicacid in breast milk. Lancet 1:383, 1989.

MESORIDAZINE

Trade: Serentil
Can/Aus/UK: Serentil
Uses: Phenothiazine antipsychotic
AAP: Drug whose effect on nursing infants is unknown but may be of concern

Mesoridazine is a typical phenothiazine antipsychotic used for treatment of schizophrenia. No data on transfer into human milk are available.[1] However, the use of the phenothiazine family in breastfeeding mothers is risky and may increase the risk of SIDS.

Pregnancy Risk Category: C

Lactation Risk Category: L4

Theoretic Infant Dose:

Adult Concerns: Adverse effects include leukopenia, eosinophilia, thrombocytopenia, anemia, aplastic anemia, hypotension, drowsiness, agitation, dystonic reactions, seizures, galactorrhea, gynecomastia, dry mouth, nausea, vomiting, constipation, priapism, incontinence, and phototoxicity.

Pediatric Concerns: None reported via milk, but use in breastfeeding mothers is discouraged due to possible sedation in infant and elevated risk of SIDS.

Drug Interactions: Decreased effect with anticonvulsants, anticholinergics. Increased toxicity when used with CNS depressants, metrizamide(increased seizures) and propranolol.

Alternatives:

Adult Dosage: 25-50 mg TID

T½ = 24-48 hours	M/P =
PHL=	PB = 91%
PK = 4 hours	Oral = Erratic
MW =	pKa =
Vd =	

References:
1. Ayd FJ. Excretion of psychotropic drugs in breast milk. In : International Drug Therapy Newsletter. Ayd Medical Communications. November-December 1973. Vol. 8.

METAXALONE

Trade: Skelaxin
Can/Aus/UK:
Uses: Sedative, skeletal muscle relaxant
AAP: Not reviewed

Metaxalone is a centrally acting sedative used primarily as a muscle relaxant.[1] Its ability to relax skeletal muscle is weak and is probably due to its sedative properties. Hypersensitivity reactions in adults (allergic) have occurred as well as liver toxicity. No data are available on its transfer into breastmilk.

Pregnancy Risk Category:

Lactation Risk Category: L3

Theoretic Infant Dose:

Adult Concerns: Sedation, nausea, vomiting, GI upset, hemolytic anemia, abnormal liver function.

Pediatric Concerns: None reported. No data available.

Drug Interactions:

Alternatives:

Adult Dosage: 800 mg TID-QID

T½ = 2-3 hours	M/P =
PHL =	PB =
PK = 2 hours	Oral =
MW = 221	pKa =
Vd =	

References:
1. McEvoy GE(ed):AHFS Drug Information, New York, NY. 1995.

METFORMIN

Trade: Glucophage, Glucovance
Can/Aus/UK: Diabex, Diaformin, Diguanil, Gen-Metformin, Glucophage, Glucphage, Glycon
Uses: Oral hypoglycemic agent for diabetes
AAP: Not reviewed

Metformin belongs to the biguanide family and is used to reduce glucose levels in non-insulin dependent diabetics. Oral bioavailability is only 50%. In a preliminary study of 5 women who received 500 mg three times daily, milk levels were extremely low.[1] While the average milk/plasma ratio was 0.34, the average dose to the infant was 0.0405 mg/kg/d or 0.26% of the weight-adjusted maternal dose. In this study, no adverse effects were noted in any infant. The product Glucovance contains metformin and glyburide.

Pregnancy Risk Category: B

Lactation Risk Category: L3

Theoretic Infant Dose:

Adult Concerns: Diarrhea, nausea, vomiting, bloating, lactic acidosis, hypoglycemia.

Pediatric Concerns: None reported, but observe for hypoglycemia.

Drug Interactions: Alcohol potentiates the effect of metformin on lactic metabolism. Cimetidine produces a 60% increase in peak metformin plasma levels. Furosemide may increase metformin plasma levels by 22%. Use of iodinated contrast material in patients receiving metformin has produced acute renal failure and been associated with lactic acidosis. Use of nifedepine increases oral bioavailability of metformin by 20%.

Alternatives:

Adult Dosage: 500 mg BID

T½ = 6.2 hours(plasma)	M/P = 1.0
PHL =	PB = Minimal
PK = 2.75 hours	Oral = 50%
MW = 129	pKa = 11.5
Vd = 3.7	

References:
1.   Hale TW, Ilett KF, Hackett P. Unpublished data. 2002.

METHADONE

Trade: Dolophine
Can/Aus/UK: Biodone forte, Methex, Physeptone
Uses: Narcotic analgesic
AAP: Approved by the American Academy of Pediatrics for use in breastfeeding mothers

Methadone is a potent and very long-acting opiate analgesic. It is primarily used to prevent withdrawal in opiate addiction. In one study of 10 women receiving methadone 10-80 mg/day, the average milk/plasma ratio was 0.83.[1] Due to the variable doses used, the milk concentrations ranged from 0.05 mg/L in one patient receiving 10 mg/day, to 0.57 mg/L in a patient receiving 80 mg/day. One infant death has been reported in a breastfeeding mother receiving maintenance methadone therapy[2], although it is not clear that the only source of methadone to this infant was from breastmilk.

In a more recent study of 12 breastfeeding women on methadone maintenance doses ranging from 20-80 mg/day, the mean concentration of methadone in plasma and milk was 311 (207-416) μg/L and 116 (72-160) μg/L respectively yielding a mean M/P ratio of 0.44 (0.24-0.64).[3] The mean absolute oral dose to infant was 17.4 (10.8-24) μg/kg/day. This equates to a mean of 2.79% of the maternal dose per day. In this study, 64% of the infants exhibited neonatal abstinence syndrome requiring treatment.

In two women receiving 30 mg twice daily, and another who received 73 mg of methadone once daily, the average breastmilk methadone concentrations was 0.169 mg/L and 0.132 mg/L, respectively.[4] The milk/plasma ratios were 1.215 and 0.661 respectively. While the infant of the second mother died at 31/2 months of SIDS, it was apparently not due to methadone, as none was present in the infant's plasma and the infant was significancy supplemented with formula.

In an excellent study 8 mother/infant pairs ingesting from 40 to 105 mg/day methadone, the average (AUC) concentration of R-methadone and S-methadone enantiomers varied from 42-259 μg/L and 26-126 μg/L respectively.[5] The relative infant dose was estimated to be 2.8% of the maternal dose. Interestingly, there was little difference in methadone milk levels in immature and mature milk.

Most studies thus far show that only small amounts of methadone pass into breastmilk despite doses as high as 105 mg/day. In fact, neonatal abstinence syndromes are well known to occur in breastfeeding infants following delivery. In one study, 58% of infants developed neonatal abstinence syndrome while still breastfeeding.[6] However, some methadone is undoubtedly transferred via milk, and abrupt cessation of breastfeeding during high dose therapy, has resulted in neonatal abstinence in some infants.[7]

In summary, the dose of R plus S methadone transferred via milk is largely dose dependent, but generally averages less than 2.8% of the maternal dose.[5] This is significantly less than the conventional cut-off value of 10% of the maternal dose corrected for weight. However, the amount in milk is insufficient to prevent neonatal withdrawal syndrome. The Academy of Pediatrics recently place methadone in the approved category for breastfeeding women.

Pregnancy Risk Category: B

Lactation Risk Category: L3

Theoretic Infant Dose: 38.9 μg/kg/day

Adult Concerns: Nausea, vomiting, constipation, respiratory depression, sedation, withdrawal syndrome.

Pediatric Concerns: Observe for sedation, respiratory depression, addiction, withdrawal syndrome. Neonatal abstinence syndrome.

Drug Interactions: Phenytoin, pentazocine, and rifampin may increase metabolism of methadone and produce withdrawal syndrome. CNS depressants, phenothiazines, tricyclic antidepressants, and MAO inhibitors may increase adverse effects of methadone.

Alternatives:

Adult Dosage: 2.5-10 mg q 3-4 hours PRN

T½ = 13-55 hours.	M/P = 0.68(R)
PHL =	PB = 89%
PK = 0.5-1 hours.	Oral = 50%
MW = 309	pKa = 8.6
Vd = 4-5	

References:
1. Blinick G, et. al. Methadone assays in pregnant women and progeny. Am J Obstet Gynecol 121:617-21, 1975.
2. Smialek JE, et. al. Methadone deaths in children-a continuing problem. JAMA 238:2516-7, 1977.
3. Wojnar-Horton RE, Kristensen JH, Yapp P, Ilett KF, Dusci LJ, Hackett LP. Methadone distribution and excretion into breast milk of clients in a methadone maintenance programme. Br. J. Clin. Pharmacol. 44:543-547, 1997.
4. Geraghty B, Graham EA, Logan B, Weiss EL. Methadone levels in breast milk. J. Human Lact. 13:227-230, 1997.
5. Begg EJ, Malpas TJ, Hackett LP, Ilett KF. Distribution of R- and S-methadone into human milk during multiple, medium to high oral dosing. Br J Clin Pharmacol. 52(6):681-685, 2001.
6. Wojnar-Horton RE, Kristensen JH, Yapp P, Ilett KF, Dusci LJ, Hackett LP. Methadone distribution and excretion into breast milk of clients in a methadone maintenance programme. Br J Clin Pharmacol. 44(6):543-7, 1997.
7. Malpas TJ, Darlow BA. Neonatal abstinence syndrome following abrupt cessation of breastfeeding. N Z Med J. 112(1080):12-3, 1999.

METHICILLIN

Trade: Staphcillin, Celebenin
Can/Aus/UK: Celbenin, Metin
Uses: Penicillin antibiotic
AAP: Not reviewed

Methicillin is a penicillin antibiotic only available by IM and I.V. formulations.[1] It is extremely unstable at acid pH (stomach), hence it would have only limited oral absorption. No data available on transfer into breastmilk, although it would appear to be similar to other penicillins.

Pregnancy Risk Category: B

Lactation Risk Category: L3

Theoretic Infant Dose:

Adult Concerns: Allergic rash, thrush, diarrhea, drug fever, changes in GI flora, renal toxicity, pseudomembranous colitis.

Pediatric Concerns: None reported via milk.

Drug Interactions: The effect of oral contraceptives may be reduced. Disulfiram and probenecid may significantly increase penicillin levels. Methicillin may increase the effect of anticoagulants.

Alternatives:

Adult Dosage: 1 g q 6 hours

T½ = 1-2 hours	M/P =
PHL = 1.4-2.4 hours(neonates)	PB = 40%
PK = 30-60 min.	Oral = Poor
MW = 402	pKa =
Vd =	

References:
1. Drug Facts and Comparisons. 1994 ed. Facts and Comparisons, St. Louis.

METHIMAZOLE

Trade: Tapazole
Can/Aus/UK: Tapazole
Uses: Antithyroid agent
AAP: Approved by the American Academy of Pediatrics for use in breastfeeding mothers

Methimazole, carbimazole, and propylthiouracil are used to inhibit the secretion of thyroxine. Carbimazole is metabolized to the active metabolite, methimazole. Levels depend on maternal dose, but appear too low to produce clinical effect. In one study of a patient receiving 2.5 mg methimazole every 12 hours, the milk:serum ratio was 1.16, and the dose per day was calculated at 16-39 ug methimazole.[1] This was equivalent to 7-16% of the maternal dose. In a study of 35 lactating women receiving from 5 to 20 mg/day of methimazole, no changes in the infant thyroid function were noted in any infant, even those at higher doses.[2]

Further, studies by Lamberg in 11 women who were treated with the methimazole derivative carbimazole (5-15 mg daily, equal to 3.3 -10 mg methimazole), found all 11 infants had normal thyroid function following maternal treatments.[3] Thus, in small maternal doses, methimazole may also be safe for the nursing mother. In a study of a woman with twins who was receiving up to 30 mg carbimazole daily, the average methimazole concentration in milk was 43 μg/L.[4] The average plasma concentrations in the twin infants were 45 and 52 ng/mL, which is below therapeutic range. Methimazole milk concentrations peaked at 2-4 hours after a carbimazole dose. No changes in thyroid function in these infants were noted.

In a large study of over 139 thyrotoxic lactating mothers and their infants, even at methimazole doses of 20 mg/day, no changes in infant TSH, T4 or T3 were noted in over 12 months of study.[5] The authors conclude conclusively that both PTU and methimazole can safely be administered during lactation. However, during the first few months of therapy, monitoring of infant thyroid functioning is recommended.

Pregnancy Risk Category: D

Lactation Risk Category: L3

Theoretic Infant Dose: 6.5 μg/kg/day

Adult Concerns: Hypothyroidism, hepatic dysfunction, bleeding, drowsiness, skin rash, nausea, vomiting, fever.

Pediatric Concerns: None reported in several studies, but propylthiouracil may be a preferred choice in breastfeeding women.

Drug Interactions: Use with iodinated glycerol, lithium, and potassium iodide may increase toxicity.

Alternatives:

Adult Dosage: 5-30 mg QD

T½ = 6-13 hours	**M/P** = 1.0
PHL =	**PB** = 0%
PK = 1 hour	**Oral** = 80-95%
MW = 114	**pKa** =
Vd =	

References:
1. Tegler L, Lindstrom B. Antithyroid drugs in milk. Lancet 2:591,1980.
2. Azizi F. Effect of methimazole treatment of maternal thyrotoxicosis on thyroid function in breast-feeding infants. J. Pediatr. 128:855-58, 1996.
3. Lamberg BA, Ikonen E, et.al. Antithyroid treatment of maternal hyperthyroidism during lactation. Clin. Endocrinol. 21(1):81-7, 1984.
4. Rylance GW; Woods CG; Donnelly MC; Oliver JS; Alexander WD. Carbimazole and breastfeeding [letter]. Lancet 18;1(8538):928, 1987.
5. Azizi F, Khoshniat M, Bahrainian M, Hedayati M. Thyroid function and intellectual development of infants nursed by mothers taking methimazole. J Clin Endocrinol Metab. 85(9):3233-8, 2000.

METHOCARBAMOL

Trade: Robaxisal, Robaxin
Can/Aus/UK: Robaxin
Uses: Muscle relaxant
AAP: Approved by the American Academy of Pediatrics for use in breastfeeding mothers

Methocarbamol is a centrally acting sedative and skeletal muscle relaxant. Only minimal amounts have been found in milk.[1] Observe for sedation.

Pregnancy Risk Category: C

Lactation Risk Category: L3

Theoretic Infant Dose:

Adult Concerns: Drowsiness, nausea, metallic taste, vertigo, blurred vision, fever, headache.

Pediatric Concerns: None reported, but studies are limited.

Drug Interactions: May see increased toxicity when used with CNS depressants.

Alternatives:

Adult Dosage: 4-4.5 g q 4-6 hours

T½ = 0.9-1.8 hours	M/P =
PHL =	PB =
PK = 1-2 hours	Oral = Complete
MW = 241	pKa =
Vd =	

References:
1. Pharmaceutical Manufacturers Package Insert, 1995.

METHOHEXITAL

Trade: Brevital
Can/Aus/UK: Brietal
Uses: Anesthetic agent
AAP: Approved by the American Academy of Pediatrics for use in breastfeeding mothers

Methohexital is an ultra short-acting barbiturate used for induction in anesthesia. The duration of action is approximately ½ that of thiopental sodium or less than 8 minutes depending on dose. Within 30 minutes, there is complete redistribution of methohexital to tissues other than the brain, primarily the liver.[1,2] While it is not known if methohexital enters milk, it is very unlikely that milk levels will be significant, because the drug is so rapidly cleared from the plasma compartment and redistributed to other compartments. A brief interval of a few hours (2-4) following administration will significantly reduce any risk.

Pregnancy Risk Category: B

Lactation Risk Category: L3

Theoretic Infant Dose:

Adult Concerns: Hypotension, lethargy, restlessness, confusion, headache, delirium and excitation

Pediatric Concerns: None reported via milk.

Drug Interactions: CNS depressants such as barbiturates, benzodiazepines, etc, may potentiate sedation with methohexital.

Alternatives:

Adult Dosage: 20-40 mg q 4-7 minutes during surgery

T½ = **3.9 hours**		**M/P** =	
PHL =		**PB** =	
PK = **Instant**		**Oral** =	
MW = **284**		**pKa** =	
Vd =			

References:
1. Drug Facts and Comparisons. 1999 ed. Facts and Comparisons, St. Louis.
2. McEvoy GE(ed):AFHS Drug Information, New York, NY. 1999.

METHOTREXATE

Trade: Folex, Rheumatrex
Can/Aus/UK: Arthitrex, Ledertrexate, Methoblastin, Rheumatrex
Uses: Antimetabolite, anticancer, antirheumatic
AAP: Contraindicated by the American Academy of Pediatrics in Breastfeeding Mothers

Methotrexate is a potent and potentially dangerous folic acid antimetabolite used in arthritic and other immunologic syndromes. It is also used as an abortifacient in tubal pregnancies. Methotrexate is secreted into breastmilk in small levels. Following a dose of 22.5 mg to one patient two hours post-dose, the methotrexate concentration in breastmilk was 2.6 μg/L of milk with a milk/plasma ratio of 0.8.[1] The cumulative excretion of methotrexate in the first 12 hours after oral administration was only 0.32 ug in milk. These authors conclude that methotrexate therapy in breastfeeding mothers would not pose a contraindication to breastfeeding. However, methotrexate is believed to be retained in human tissues (particularly neonatal GI cells and ovarian cells) for long periods (months)[2], and one study has indicated a higher risk of fetal malformation in mothers who received methotrexate months prior to becoming pregnant.[3] Therefore, pregnancy should be delayed if either partner is receiving methotrexate for at least 3 months following therapy.

Pregnancy Risk Category: D

Lactation Risk Category: L3 for acute use
**   L5 for chronic use**

Theoretic Infant Dose: 0.4 μg/kg/day

Adult Concerns: Bone marrow suppression, anemia, vasculitis, vomiting, diarrhea, GI bleeding, stomatitis, bloody diarrhea, kidney damage, seizures, etc.

Pediatric Concerns: None reported via milk, but caution is recommended.

Drug Interactions: Aminoglycosides may significantly decrease absorption of methotrexate. Etretinate has produced hepatotoxicity in several patients receiving methotrexate. The use of folic acid or its derivatives may reduce the response to MTX. The use of NSAIDs with methotrexate is contraindicated, several deaths have occurred due to elevated MTX levels. Phenytoin serum levels may be decreased. Procarbazine may increase nephrotoxicity of MTX.

Alternatives:

Adult Dosage: 10-30 mg

T½ = 7.2 hours	**M/P = >0.08**
PHL=	**PB = 34-50 %**
PK = 1-2 hours	**Oral = 33-90%**
MW = 454	**pKa = 4.3, 5.5**
Vd = 2.6	

References:
1.   Johns DG, Rutherford L, Leighton PC, et.al. Secretion of methotrexate into human milk. Am J Obstet Gynecol. 112:978-980,1972.
2.   Fountain JR et.al. Persistence of amethopterin in normal mouse tissues. Proc.Soc. Exp. Med. 83:396-400, 1953.
3.   Walden P and Bagshawe K. Pregnancies after chemotherapy for gestational trophoblastic tumours. Lancet 2:1241, 1979.

METHYLDOPA

Trade: Aldomet
Can/Aus/UK: Aldomet, Aldopren, Apo-Methlydopa, Dopamet, Hydopa, Novo-Medopa, Nudopa
Uses: Antihypertensive
AAP: Approved by the American Academy of Pediatrics for use in breastfeeding mothers

Alpha-methyldopa is a centrally acting antihypertensive. It is frequently used to treat hypertension during pregnancy. In a study of 2 lactating women who received a dose of 500 mg, the maximum breastmilk concentration of methyldopa ranged from 0.2 to 0.66 mg/L.[1] In another patient who received 1000 mg dose, the maximum concentration in milk was 1.14 mg/L.[1] The milk/plasma ratios varied from 0.19 to 0.34. The authors indicated that if the infant were to ingest 750 ml of milk daily (with a maternal dose= 1000mg), the maximum daily ingestion would be less than 855 ug or approximately 0.02 % of the maternal dose.

In another study of 7 women who received 0.750-2.0 gm/day of methyldopa, the free methyldopa concentrations in breastmilk ranged from zero to 0.2 mg/L while the conjugated metabolite had concentrations of 0.1 to 0.9 mg/L.[2] These studies generally indicate that the levels of methyldopa transferred to a breastfeeding infant would be too low to be clinically relevant.

However, gynecomastia and galactorrhea has been reported in one fullterm two week old female neonate following seven days of maternal therapy with methyldopa, 250 mg three times daily.[3]

Pregnancy Risk Category: C

Lactation Risk Category: L2

Theoretic Infant Dose: 165.0 μg/kg/day

Adult Concerns: Hemolytic anemia, hepatitis, fever, rashes, dizziness, hypotension, sleep disturbances, dry mouth, depression, colitis.

Pediatric Concerns: None reported in several studies. Gynecomastia and galactorrhea in one personal communication.

Drug Interactions: Iron supplements can interact and cause a significant increase in blood pressure. Increased toxicity with lithium has been reported.

Alternatives:

Adult Dosage: 250-500 mg BID-QID

T½ = 105 min.	M/P = 0.19-0.34
PHL=	PB = Low
PK = 3-6 hours	Oral = 25-50%
MW = 211	pKa =
Vd = 0.3	

References:
1.   White WB, Andreoli JW, Cohn RD. Alpha-methyldopa disposition in mothers with hypertension and in their breast-fed infants. Clin. Pharmacol. Ther. 37:378-90, 1985.
2.   Jones HMR, Cummings AJ. A study of the transfer of alpha methyldopa to the human foetus and newborn infant. Br.J.Clin. Pharmacol. 6:432-4,1978.
3.   EDM. Personal communication, 9/1997.

METHYLERGONOVINE

Trade: Methergine
Can/Aus/UK: Ergometrine, Methergine, Methylerometrine
Uses: Vasoconstrictor, uterine stimulant
AAP: Not reviewed

Methylergonovine is an amine ergot alkaloid used to control postpartum uterine bleeding. The ergots are powerful vasoconstrictors. In a group of 8 postpartum women receiving 0.125 mg three times daily for 5 days, the concentration of methylergonovine ranged from < 0.5 in 4 patients to 1.3 μg/L in one patient at one hour postdose.[1]   In this study only 5 of 16 milk samples had detectable methylergonovine levels.

Using a dose of 1.3 μg/L of milk, and infant would only consume approximately 0.2 μg/kg/day which is incredibly low compared to the usual 0.375 mg daily dose.   The milk/plasma ratio averaged about 0.3. Short-term (1 week), low-dose regimens of these agents do not apparently pose problems in nursing infants/mothers.[2]   In those situations with longer therapy, a benefit to risk assessment is required, but it is not likely to be overly hazardous to the infant. Methylergonovine is preferred over ergonovine because it does not inhibit lactation to the same degree, and levels in milk are minimal.

Pregnancy Risk Category: C

Lactation Risk Category: L2
                                        L4 for chronic use

Theoretic Infant Dose: 0.2 μg/kg/day

Adult Concerns: Nausea, vomiting, diarrhea, dizziness, rapid pulse.

Pediatric Concerns: None reported, but long term exposure is not recommended. Methylergonovine is commonly recommended early postpartum for breastfeeding mothers with bleeding.

Drug Interactions: Use caution when using with other vasoconstrictors or pressor agents.

Alternatives:

Adult Dosage: 0.2-0.4 mg q 6-12 hours PRN

T½ = 20-30 minutes	M/P = 0.3
PHL =	PB = 36%
PK = 0.5-3 hours	Oral = 60%
MW = 339	pKa =
Vd =	

References:

1. Erkkola R, et.al. Excretion of methylergometrine (methylergonovine) into the human breast milk. Int. J. Clin. Pharmacol. 16:579-80,1978.
2. Del Pozo E, Brun del Rey R, Hinselmann M. Lack of effect of methyl-ergonovine on postpartum lactation. Am. J. Obstet. Gynecol. 123:845-6,1975.

METHYLPHENIDATE HCL

Trade: Ritalin, Concerta, Metadate Cd, Metadate Er, Methylin
Can/Aus/UK: PMS-Methylphenidate, Riphenidate, Ritalin
Uses: Mild CNS stimulant
AAP: Not reviewed

The pharmacologic effects of methylphenidate are similar to those of amphetamines and include CNS stimulation.[1] It is presently used for narcolepsy and attention deficit hyperactivity syndrome. At present, there are no data available on transfer of this compound into breastmilk. However, due to its small molecular weight and other kinetic data, one must assume that methylphenidate readily enters breastmilk and would be absorbed by the infant. A prolonged release tablet formulation is commonly used and would extend the half-life. Risk of toxicity must be weighed against need of the mother.

Pregnancy Risk Category: C

Lactation Risk Category: L4

Theoretic Infant Dose:

Adult Concerns: Nervousness, hyperactivity, insomnia, agitation, and lack of appetite.

Pediatric Concerns: None reported, but observe for stimulation, insomnia, anorexia.

Drug Interactions: Methylphenidate may reduce the effects of guanethidine and bretylium. May increased serum levels of tricyclic antidepressants, phenytoin, warfarin, phenobarbital, and primidone.

Use with MAOI may produce significant increased effects of methylphenidate.

Alternatives:

Adult Dosage: 10 mg BID-TID

T½ = 1-3 hours	**M/P** =
PHL =	**PB** =
PK = 1 - 3 hours	**Oral** = 95%
MW = 233	**pKa** = 8.8
Vd = 11-33	

References:
1. Pharmaceutical Manufacturers Package Insert, 1996.

METHYLPREDNISOLONE

Trade: Solu-medrol, Depo-medrol, Medrol
Can/Aus/UK: Advantan, Depo-Medrol, Medrol, Neo-Medrol, Solu-Medrol
Uses: Corticosteroid
AAP: Approved by the American Academy of Pediatrics for use in breastfeeding mothers

Methylprednisolone(MP) is the methyl derivative of prednisolone. Four milligrams of methylprednisolone is roughly equivalent to 5 mg of prednisone. Multiple dosage forms exist and include the succinate salt which is rapidly active, or the methylprednisolone base which is the tablet formulation for oral use, and the methylprednisolone acetate suspension (Depo-Medrol) which is slowly absorbed over many days to weeks. Depo-Medrol is generally used intrasynovially, IM, or epidurally, and is slowly absorbed from these sites. They would be very unlikely to affect a breastfed infant, but this depends on dose and duration of exposure. For a complete description of corticosteroid use in breastfeeding mothers see the prednisone monograph. In general, the amount of methylprednisolone and other steroids transferred into human milk is minimal as long as the dose does not exceed 80 mg per day.[1] However, relating side effects of steroids administered via breastmilk and their maternal doses is rather difficult and each situation should be evaluated individually. Extended use of high doses could predispose the infant to steroid side effects including decreased linear growth rate, but these require rather high doses. Low to moderate doses are believed to have minimal effect on breastfed infants. See prednisone.

High dose pulsed intravenous or oral administrations of methylprednisolone (MP) have become increasingly important as a treatment for acute relapses or progressively worsening of multiple sclerosis (MS).[2-6]   Even though prednisolone is approved by the American Academy of Pediatrics for use in breastfeeding women, when MP is used in such high doses in patients with MS, questions concerning when mothers can return to breastfeeding have arisen. While there are extensive kinetic data on the plasma levels, metabolism and clearance of methylprednisolone from normal and MS patients,[7,8] no data are available on the transfer of MP into human milk subsequent to using such high pulse I.V. doses in breastfeeding mothers. Simulation of MP elimination curves shows a rapid and complete elimination from the maternal plasma compartment.[9]   From this simulation, it would appear a brief pumping and discarding of milk for a period of 8-24 hours following the I.V. administration of MP (at doses up to 1 gm) would significantly reduce an infant's exposure to this corticosteroid.   This simulation estimates the infant dose at 12 hours post-administration of MP to be approximately 1.24 μg/kg/day. These are only theoretical predictions as no one yet has published milk levels following I.V. administration of 1 gram doses.

Pregnancy Risk Category: C

Lactation Risk Category: L2

Theoretic Infant Dose:

Adult Concerns: In pediatrics: shortened stature, GI bleeding, GI ulceration, edema, osteoporosis.

Pediatric Concerns: None reported via breastmilk. Limit dose and length of exposure if possible. High doses and prolonged durations may inhibit epiphyseal bone growth, induce gastric ulcerations, glaucoma, etc.

Drug Interactions: Barbiturates may significantly reduce the effects of corticosteroids.   Cholestyramine may reduce absorption of methylprednisone.   Oral contraceptives may reduce half-life and concentration of steroids.   Ephedrine may reduce the half-life and increase clearance of certain steroids.   Phenytoin may increase clearance. Corticosteroid clearance may be decreased by ketaconazole. Certain macrolide antibiotics may significantly decrease clearance of steroids. Isoniazid serum concentrations may be decreased.

Alternatives: Prednisone

Adult Dosage: 2-60 mg daily

T½ = 2.8 hours	M/P =
PHL=	PB =
PK =	Oral = Complete
MW = 374	pKa =
Vd = 1.5	

References:
1.   Anderson PO: Corticosteroid use by breast-feeding mothers. Clin Pharm 6:445, 1987.

2. Miller DM, Weinstock-Guttman B, Bethoux F, et al: A meta-analysis of methylprednisolone in recovery from multiple sclerosis exacerbations. Mult Scler 6:267-273, 2000.

3. Hommes OR, Barkhof F, Jongen PJ, Frequin ST: Methylprednisolone treatment in multiple sclerosis: effect of treatment, pharmacokinetics, future. Mult Scler 1:327-328, 1996.

4. Goas JY, Marion JL, Missoum A: High dose intravenous methyl prednisolone in acute   exacerbations of multiple sclerosis. J Neurol Neurosurg Psychiatry 46:99, 1983.

5. Sellebjerg F, Frederiksen JL, Nielsen PM, Olesen J: Double-blind, randomized,   placebo-controlled study of oral, high-dose methylprednisolone in attacks of MS. Neurology 51:529-534, 1988.

6. Barnes D, Hughes RA, Morris RW, et al: Randomised trial of oral and intravenous   methylprednisolone in acute relapses of multiple sclerosis. Lancet 349:902-906, 1997.

7. Vree TB, Lagerwerf AJ, Verwey-van Wissen CP, Jongen PJ: High-performance liquid   chromatography analysis, preliminary pharmacokinetics, metabolism and renal excretion of methylprednisolone with its C6 and C20 hydroxy metabolites in multiple sclerosis patients   receiving high-dose pulse therapy. J Chromatogr B Biomed Sci Appl 732:337-348, 1999.

8. Vree TB, Verwey-van Wissen CP, Lagerwerf AJ, et al: Isolation and identification of the   C6-hydroxy and C20-hydroxy metabolites and glucuronide conjugate of methylprednisolone by preparative high-performance liquid chromatography from urine of patients receiving high-dose pulse therapy. J Chromatogr B Biomed Sci Appl 726:157-168, 1999.

9. H a l e ,   T W   a n d   I l e t t ,   K . http://neonatal.ama.ttuhsc.edu/rbupdates/MP/mp.html

METOCLOPRAMIDE

Trade: Reglan
Can/Aus/UK: Apo-Metoclop, Emex, Gastromax, Maxeran, Maxolon, Paramid, Pramin, Reglan
Uses: GI stimulant, prolactin stimulant
AAP: Drug whose effect on nursing infants is unknown but may be of concern

Metoclopramide has multiple functions, but is primarily used for increasing the lower esophageal sphincter tone in gastroesophageal reflux in patients with reduced gastric tone. In breastfeeding, it is sometimes used in lactating women to stimulate prolactin release from the pituitary and enhance breastmilk production. Since 1981, a number of publications have documented major increases in breastmilk production following the use of metoclopramide, domperidone, or sulpiride. With metoclopramide, the increase in serum prolactin and breastmilk production appears dose-related up to a dose of 15 mg three times daily.[1] Many studies show 66 to 100 % increases in milk production depending on the degree breastmilk supply in the mother prior to therapy and maybe her initial prolactin levels. Doses of 15 mg/day were found ineffective, whereas doses of 30-45 mg/day were most effective. In most studies, major increases in prolactin were observed, such as from 125 ng/mL to 172 ng/mL in one patient.[2]

In Kauppila's study[3] of 37 women, the concentration of metoclopramide in milk was consistently higher than the maternal serum levels. The peak occurred at 2-3 hours after administration of the medication. During the late puerperium, the concentration of metoclopramide in the milk varied from 20 to 125 μg/L, which was less than the 28 to 157 μg/L noted during the early puerperium. The authors estimated the daily dose to infant to vary from 6 to 24 μg/kg/day during the early puerperium, and from 1 to 13 μg/kg/day during the late phase. These doses are minimal compared to those used for therapy of reflux in pediatric patients (0.1 to 0.5 mg/kg/day). In these studies, only 1 of 5 infants studied had detectable blood levels of metoclopramide, hence no accumulation or side effects were observed. While plasma prolactin levels in the newborns were comparable to those in the mothers prior to treatment, Kaupilla found slight increases in prolactin levels in 4 of 7 newborns following treatment with metoclopramide, although a more recent study did not find such changes.[6] However, prolactin levels are highly variable and subject to diurnal rhythm, thus timing is essential in measuring prolactin levels and could account for this inconsistency.

In another study[4] of 23 women with premature infants, milk production increased from 93 mL/day to 197 mL/day between the first and 7th day of therapy with 30 mg/day. Prolactin levels, although varied, increased from 18.1 to 121.8 ng/mL. While basal prolactin levels were elevated significantly, metoclopramide seems to blunt the rapid rise of prolactin when milk was expressed. Nevertheless, milk production was still elevated.

Gupta[5] studied 32 mothers with inadequate milk supply. Following a dose of 10 mg three times daily, a 66-100% increase in milk supply was noted. Of twelve cases of complete lactation failure, 8 responded to treatment in an average of 3-4 days after starting therapy. In this study, 87.5% of the total 32 cases responded to metoclopramide therapy with greater milk production. No untoward effects were noted in the infants.

In a study of 5 breastfeeding women who were receiving 30 mg/day, daily milk production increased significantly from 150.9 mL/day to 276.4 mL/day in this group.[6] However, the plasma prolactin levels in breastfed infants were determined as well on the 5th postnatal day and no changes were noted; thus the amount of metoclopramide transferred in milk was not enough to change the infant's prolactin levels.

In a study by Lewis in ten patients who received a single oral dose of 10 mg, the mean maternal plasma and milk levels at 2 hours was 68.5 ng/mL and 125.7 μg/L respectively.[7]

It is well recognized that metoclopramide increases a mother's milk supply, but it is exceedingly dose dependent, and yet some mothers simply do not respond. In those mothers who do not respond,

Kauppila's work suggests that these patients may already have elevated prolactin levels. In his study, 3 of the 5 mothers who did not respond with increased milk production, had the highest basal prolactin levels (300-400 ng/mL).[3] Thus it may be advisable to do plasma prolactin levels on under-producing mothers prior to instituting metoclopramide therapy to assess the response prior to treating.

Side effects such as gastric cramping and diarrhea limit the compliance of some patients but are rare. Further, it is often found that upon rapid discontinuation of the medication, the supply of milk may in some instances reduce significantly. Tapering of the dose is generally recommended and one possible regimen is to decrease the dose by 10 mg per week. Long-term use of this medication (>4 weeks) may be accompanied by increased side effects such as depression in the mother although some patients have used it successfully for months. Another dopamine antagonist, domperidone, is a preferred choice, but is unfortunately not available in the USA.

Pregnancy Risk Category: B

Lactation Risk Category: L2

Theoretic Infant Dose: 18.8 μg/kg/day

Adult Concerns: Diarrhea, sedation, gastric upset, nausea, extrapyramidal symptoms, severe depression.

Pediatric Concerns: None reported in infants via milk. Commonly used in pediatrics.

Drug Interactions: Anticholinergic drugs may reduce the effects of metoclopramide. Opiate analgesics may increased CNS depression.

Alternatives: Domperidone

Adult Dosage: 10-15 mg QID

T½ = 5-6 hours	**M/P = 0.5-4.06**
PHL =	**PB = 30%.**
PK = 1-2 hours(oral)	**Oral = 30-100%**
MW = 300	**pKa =**
Vd =	

References:
1. Kauppila A. et.al. A dose response relation between improved lactation and metoclopramide. The Lancet 1:1175-77, 1981.
2. Budd SC. et.al. Improved lactation with metoclopramide. Clinical Pediatrics 32:53-57, 1993.
3. Kauppila A, et.al. Metoclopramide and Breast Feeding: Transfer into milk and the newborn. Eur. J. Clin Pharmacol. 25:819-23, 1983.
4. Ehrenkranz RA. et.al. Metoclopramide effect on faltering milk production by mothers of premature infants. Pediatrics 78:614-620, 1986.
5. Gupta AP and Gupta PK. Metoclopramide as a lactogogue. Clinical Pediatrics 24:269-72, 1985.
6. Ertl T, Sulyok E, Ezer E, Sarkany I, Thurzo V, Csaba IF. The influence of

metoclopramide on the composition of human breast milk. Acta Paediatr Hung. 31(4):415-22, 1991.
7. Lewis PJ, Devenish C, Kahn C. Controlled trial of metoclopramide in the initiation of breast feeding. Br J Clin Pharmacol. 9(2):217-9, 1980.

METOPROLOL

Trade: Toprol-XL, Lopressor
Can/Aus/UK: Apo-Metoprolol, Betaloc, Lopresor, Lopressor, Loressor, Minax, Novo-Metoprol
Uses: Antihypertensive, beta blocker
AAP: Approved by the American Academy of Pediatrics for use in breastfeeding mothers

At low doses, metoprolol is a very cardioselective Beta-1 blocker, and it is used for hypertension, angina, and tachyarrhythmias. In a study of 3 women 4-6 months postpartum who received 100 mg twice daily for 4 days, the peak concentration of metoprolol ranged from 0.38 to 2.58 μmol/L, whereas the maternal plasma levels ranged from 0.1 to 0.97 μmol/L.[1] The mean milk/plasma ratio was 3.0. Assuming ingestion of 75 ml of milk at each feeding, and the maximum concentration of 2.58 μmol/L, an infant would ingest approximately 0.05 mg metoprolol at the first feeding, and considerably less at subsequent feedings.

In another study of 9 women receiving 50-100 mg twice daily[2], the maternal plasma and milk concentrations ranged from 4-556 nmol/L and 19-1690 nmol/L respectively. Using this data, the authors calculated an average milk concentration throughout the day as 280 μg/L of milk. This dose is 20-40 times less than a typical clinical dose. The milk/plasma ratio in these studies averaged 3.72.

Although the milk/plasma ratios for this drug are relatively high, the maternal plasma levels are quite small, so the absolute amount transferred to the infant are quite small. Although these levels are probably too low to be clinically relevant, clinicians should use metoprolol under close supervision.

Pregnancy Risk Category: B

Lactation Risk Category: L3

Theoretic Infant Dose: 42.0 μg/kg/day

Adult Concerns: Hypotension, weakness, depression, bradycardia.

Pediatric Concerns: None reported in several studies, but close observation for hypotension, weakness, bradycardia is advised.

Drug Interactions: Decreased effect when used with aluminum salts, barbiturates, calcium salts, cholestyramine, NSAIDs, ampicillin, rifampin, and salicylates. Beta blockers may reduce the effect of oral sulfonylureas (hypoglycemic agents). Increased toxicity/effect when used with other antihypertensives, contraceptives, MAO inhibitors, cimetidine, and numerous other products. See drug interaction reference for complete listing.

Alternatives: Propranolol

Adult Dosage: 100-450 mg QD

T½ = 3-7 hours	M/P = 3-3.72
PHL =	PB = 12%
PK = 2.5-3 hours	Oral = 40-50%
MW = 267	pKa = 9.7
Vd = 2.5-5.6	

References:
1. Liedholm H, et. al. Accumulation of atenolol and metoprolol in human breast milk. Eur J Clin Pharmacol 20:229-31, 1981.
2. Sandstrom B, Regardh CG. Metoprolol excretion into breast milk. Br. J.Clin.Pharmacol. 9:518-9, 1980.
3. Kulas J, et.al. Atenolol and metoprolol. A comparison of their excretion into human breast milk. Acta. Obstet. Scand. 118(Suppl):65-9, 1984.

METRIZAMIDE

Trade: Amipaque
Can/Aus/UK: Amipaque
Uses: Radiocontrast agent
AAP: Approved by the American Academy of Pediatrics for use in breastfeeding mothers

Metrizamide is a water-soluble non-ionic, radiographic contrast medium used mainly in myelography. It contains 48% bound iodine. The iodine molecule is organically bound, and is not available for uptake into breastmilk due to minimal metabolism. Following subarachnoid administration of 5.06 gm the peak plasma level of 32.9 μg/mL occurred at 6 hours. Cumulative excretion in milk increased with time, but was extremely small with only 1.1 mg or 0.02% of the dose being recovered in milk within 44.3 hours.[1] The drug's high water solubility, nonionic characteristic, and its high molecular weight (789) also support minimal excretion into breastmilk. This agent is sometimes used as an oral radiocontrast agent.[2] Only minimal oral absorption occurs (<0.4%) . The authors suggest that the very small amount of metrizamide secreted in human milk is unlikely to be hazardous to the infant.

Pregnancy Risk Category: B

Lactation Risk Category: L2

Theoretic Infant Dose:

Adult Concerns: Nausea, vomiting, headache, backache, neck stiffness, seizures.

Pediatric Concerns: None reported in one study. Milk levels are too low.

Drug Interactions: Chlorpromazine, ketamine, other phenothiazines, and any medication which lowers seizure threshold, should be discontinued 5 days prior to exposure to metrizamide. Major seizures may occur. Lactic acidosis and acute renal failure may occur when used with metformin.

Alternatives:

Adult Dosage: 5-12 mL X 1

T½ = > 24 hours	M/P =
PHL=	PB =
PK = 6 hours	Oral = < 0.4 %
MW = 789	pKa =
Vd = 1.3	

References:
1. Ilett KF, Hackett LP,Paterson JW: Excretion of metrizamide in milk. Br J Radiol 54:537-538, 1981.
2. Johansen JG. Assessment of a Non-ionic contrast medium (Amipaque) in the gastrointestinal tract. Invest. Radiol. 13:523-527, 1978.

METRIZOATE

Trade: Isopaque
Can/Aus/UK: Isopaque
Uses: Radiocontrast agent
AAP: Approved by the American Academy of Pediatrics for use in breastfeeding mothers

Metrizoate an ionic radiocontrast agent. Radiopaque agents (except barium) are iodinated compounds used to visualize various organs during X-ray, CAT scans, and other radiological procedures. These compounds are highly iodinated benzoic acid derivatives. Although under usual circumstances, iodine products are contraindicated in nursing mothers (due to ion trapping in milk), these products are unique in that they are extremely inert and are largely cleared without metabolism.

In a study of 4 women who received metrizoate 0.58 g/kg (350 mg Iodine/mL) I.V., the peak level of metrizoate in milk was 14 mg/L at 3 and 6 hours post-injection.[1] The average milk concentration during the first 24 hours was only 11.4 mg/L. During the first 24 hours following injection, it is estimated that a total of 1.7 mg/kg would be transferred to the infant which is only 0.3% of the maternal dose.

As a group, radiocontrast agents are virtually unabsorbed after oral administration (< 0.1%). Metrizoate has a brief half-life of just 2 hours and the estimated dose ingested by the infant is only 0.2 % of the radiocontrast dose used clinically for various scanning procedures in infants. Although most company package inserts suggest that an infant be removed from the breast for 24 hours, no untoward effects have been reported with these products in breastfed infants. Because the amount of metrizoate transferred into milk is so small, the authors conclude that breastfeeding is acceptable after intravenously administered metrizoate.

Pregnancy Risk Category: B

Lactation Risk Category: L2

Theoretic Infant Dose: 2.1 mg/kg/day

Adult Concerns: Hypersensitivity to iodine. Arrhythmias, renal failure. Volume expansion.

Pediatric Concerns: None reported via milk in one study.

Drug Interactions: Anaphylaxis.

Alternatives:

Adult Dosage:

T½ = < 2 hours	M/P =
PHL=	PB = < 5%
PK =	Oral = Nil
MW = 628	pKa =
Vd =	

References:
1.   Nielsen ST et.al. Excretion of iohexol and metrizoate in human breast milk. Acta. Radiol. 28:523-26, 1987.

METRONIDAZOLE

Trade: Flagyl, Metizol, Trikacide, Protostat, Noritate
Can/Aus/UK: Apo-Metronidazole, Flagyl, Metrozine, NeoMetric, Novo-Nidazol, Rozex
Uses: Antibiotic, amebicide
AAP: Drug whose effect on nursing infants is unknown but may be of concern

Metronidazole is indicated in the treatment of vaginitis due to Trichomonas Vaginalis, and various anaerobic bacterial infections including Giardiasis, H. Pylori, B. Fragilis, and Gardnerella vaginalis. Metronidazole has become the treatment of choice for pediatric giardiasis (AAP).

Metronidazole absorption is time and dose dependent and also depends on the route of administration (oral vs vaginal). Following a 2 gm oral dose milk levels were reported to peak at 50-57 mg/L at 2 hours. Milk levels after 12 hours were approximately 19 mg/L and at 24 hours were approximately 10 mg/L.[1] The average drug concentration reported in milk at 2, 8, 12, and 12-24 hours was 45.8, 27.9, 19.1, and 12.6 mg/L respectively. If breastfeeding were to continue uninterrupted, an infant would consume 21.8 mg via breastmilk. With a 12 hour discontinuation, an infant would consume only 9.8 mg.

In a group of 12 nursing mothers receiving 400 mg three times daily, the mean milk/plasma ratio was 0.91.[2] The mean milk metronidazole concentration was 15.5 mg/L. Infant plasma metronidazole levels ranged from 1.27 to 2.41 μg/mL. No adverse effects were attributable to metronidazole therapy in these infants.

In another study in patients receiving 600 and 1200 mg daily, the average milk metronidazole concentration was 5.7 and 14.4 mg/L respectively.[3] The plasma levels of metronidazole (2 hours) at the 600 mg/d dose were 5 μg/mL (mother) and 0.8 μg/mL(infant). At the 1200 mg/d dose (2 hours), plasma levels were 12.5 μg/mL (mother) and 2.4 μg/mL (infant).   The authors estimated the daily metronidazole dose received by the infant at 3.0 mg/kg with 500 ml milk intake per day, which is well below the advocated 10-20 mg/kg recommended therapeutic dose for infants.

For treating trichomoniasis, many physicians now recommend 2 gm single oral dose, with an interruption of breastfeeding for 12-24 hours, then reinstitute breastfeeding. Thus far, no reports of untoward effects in breastfed infants have been published for the 2 gm STAT dose, or the 250 mg three times daily for 10 day dosage regimen.

In a study of 6 women receiving 400 mg TID for 3 days, the average milk concentration was 13.5 mg/L with a milk/plasma ratio of 0.9.[4]

For intravaginal use see Metrogel. Metrogel vaginal jel produces only 2% of the mean peak serum level concentration of a 500 mg oral metronidazole tablet. The maternal plasma level following use of each dose of vaginal gel averaged only 237 μg/L, far less than orally administered tablet formulations. Milk levels following intravaginal use would probably be exceeding low. Milk/plasma ratios, although published for oral metronidazole, may be different for this route of administration.

It is true that the relative infant dose via milk is moderately high depending on the dose and timing. Infants whose mothers ingest 1.2 gm/d will receive approximately 12.6% or less, of the maternal dose or approximately 2.3 mg/kg/day. Bennett has calculated the relative infant dose from 11.7% to as high as 24% of the maternal dose.[8] Heisterberg found metronidazole levels in infant plasma to be 16% and 19% of the maternal plasma levels following doses of 600 mg/d and 1200 mg/d.[3] While these levels seem significant, it is still pertinent to remember that metronidazole is a commonly used drug in premature neonates, infants and children, and 2.3 mg/kg/d is still much less than the therapeutic dose used in infants/children (7.5-30 mg/kg/d). Thus far virtually no adverse effects have been reported.

INTRAVENOUS STUDIES

Metronidazole is approximately 98% bioavailable orally and it is rapidly absorbed. In one study of intravenous kinetics, the authors found peak plasma levels of 28.9 μg/mL in adults following a 500 mg TID dose.[5] In another study of oral and intravenous kinetics, the authors used 400 mg orally, and 500 mg intravenously.[6] Following 400 mg orally, the Cmax at 90 minutes was 17.4 μg/mL. Following 500 mg I.V., the Cmax at 90 minutes was 23.6 μg/mL. Reducing the I.V. dose to 400 mg would have given a plasma level of approximately 18.8 or an amount similar to the oral plasma level attained in the above group(17.4). From these two sets of data, it is apparent that the peak(Cmax) following an intravenous dose is only slightly higher than that obtained following oral administration. In an elegant study of plasma kinetics of oral and I.V. metronidazole (both 500 mg and 2000 mg), Loft found that the AUC (500mg dose) for oral and I.V. treatments was virtually identical (101 vs 100 μg/mL h respectively).[7] The Cmax (taken from graph) for oral and I.V. treatments were essentially the same. In another study comparing the plasma kinetics following 800 mg doses orally and I.V., Bergan[12] found that plasma levels are virtually identical at 2-3 hours after the dose. Therefore, in a breastfeeding mother receiving I.V. metronidazole, a brief interruption of breastfeeding for perhaps 1-2 hours would expose the infant to almost identical levels as obtained from the same dose given orally.

Data from older studies with rats and mice have shown that metronidazole is potentially mutagenic/carcinogenic. Thus far, no studies in humans have found it to be mutagenic, in fact the opposite seems to be the finding.[9-11] Roe suggests that metronidazole is "essentially free of cancer risk or other serious toxic side effects".[11] Age-gender stratified analysis did not reveal any association between short-term exposure to metronidazole and cancer in humans.[10]

Pregnancy Risk Category: B

Lactation Risk Category: L2

Theoretic Infant Dose: 2.3 mg/kg/day

Adult Concerns: Nausea, dry mouth, vomiting, diarrhea, abdominal discomfort. Drug may turn urine brown.

Pediatric Concerns: Numerous studies show no untoward effects. One letter to the editor suggests an infant developed diarrhea, and a case of lactose intolerance. The link to metronidazole is tenuous.

Drug Interactions: Phenytoin and phenobarbital may decrease half-life of metronidazole. Alcohol may induce disulfiram-like reactions. May increase prothrombin times when used with warfarin.

Alternatives:

Adult Dosage: 250-500 mg BID

T½ = 8.5 hours	M/P = 1.15
PHL= 25-75 hours (full term)	PB = 10%
PK = 2-4 hours	Oral = 100%
MW = 171	pKa =
Vd =	

References:

1. Erickson SH, Oppenheim Gl, Smith GH. Metronidazole in breast milk. Obstet. Gynecol. 57:48-50, 1981.
2. Passmore CM, McElnay JC, Rainey EA, D'Arcy PF. Metronidazole excretion in human milk and its effect on the suckling neonate. Br. J. Clin. Pharmac. 26:45-51, 1988.
3. Heisterberg L, Branebjerg PE. Blood and milk concentration of metronidazole in mothers and infants. J Perinat Med. 11:114-120, 1983.
4. Amon I, Amon K. Wirkstoffkonzentrationen von metronidazol bie schwangeren und postpartal. Fortschritte der antimikrobiellen und antineoplastischen. Chemotherapie, Band 2-4, 605-612.
5. Ti TY, Lee HS, Khoo YM. Disposition of intravenous metronidazole in Asian surgical patients. Antimicrob Agents Chemother. 40(10):2248-51, 1996.
6. Earl P, Sisson PR, Ingham HR. Twelve-hourly dosage schedule for oral and intravenous metronidazole. J Antimicrob Chemother. 23(4):619-21, 1989.
7. Loft S, Dossing M, Poulsen HE, Sonne J, Olesen KL, Simonsen K, Andreasen PB. Influence of dose and route of administration on disposition of metronidazole and its major metabolites. Eur J Clin Pharmacol. 30(4):467-73, 1986.
8. Bennett PN. Use of the monographs on drugs. Drugs and Human Lactation, second edition. Amsterdam: Elsevier, 1996:164-166.
9. Falagas ME, Walker AM, Jick H, Ruthazer R, Griffith J, Snydman DR. Late incidence of cancer after metronidazole use: a matched metronidazole user/nonuser study. Clin Infect Dis 26(2):384-8, 1998.
10. Fahrig R, Engelke M. Reinvestigation of in vivo genotoxicity studies in man. I. No induction of DNA strand breaks in peripheral lymphocytes after metronidazole therapy. Mutat Res 12;395(2-3):215-21, 1997.
11. Roe FJ. Toxicologic evaluation of metronidazole with particular reference to carcinogenic, mutagenic, and teratogenic potential. Surgery. 93(1 Pt 2):158-64, 1983.
12. Bergan T, Leinebo O, Blom-Hagen T, Salvesen B. Pharmacokinetics and bioavailability of metronidazole after tablets, suppositories and intravenous administration. Scand J Gastroenterol Suppl. 91:45-60, 1984.

METRONIDAZOLE TOPICAL GEL

Trade: Metrogel Topical
Can/Aus/UK: Metro-Gel, Metrogel, Metrogyl
Uses: Topical antibacterial
AAP: Not reviewed

Metronidazole topical gel is primarily indicated for acne and is a gel formulation containing 0.75% metronidazole. For metronidazole kinetics and entry into human milk see Metronidazole. Following topical application of 1 gm of metronidazole gel to the face (equivalent to 7.5 mg metronidazole base), the maximum serum concentration was only 66 nanograms/mL in only one of 10 patients (In 3 of the 10 patients, levels were undetectable).[1,2] This concentration is 100 times less than the serum concentration achieved following the oral ingestion of just one 250 mg tablet. Therefore, the topical application of metronidazole gel provides only exceedingly low plasma levels in the mother and minimal to no levels in milk.

Pregnancy Risk Category: B

Lactation Risk Category: L3

Theoretic Infant Dose:

Adult Concerns: Watery eyes if the gel is applied too close to eyes. Minor skin irritation, redness, milk dryness, burning.

Pediatric Concerns: None reported via milk. Milk levels would be exceedingly low to nil.

Drug Interactions: Although many known interactions with oral metronidazole are documented, due to minimal plasma levels of this preparation, they would be extremely remote.

Alternatives:

Adult Dosage: apply topical BID

T½ = 8.5 hours	M/P = 0.4-1.8
PHL =	PB = 10%
PK =	Oral = Complete
MW = 171	pKa =
Vd =	

References:
1. Drug Facts and Comparisons. 1996. ed. Facts and Comparisons, St. Louis.
2. Pharmaceutical Manufacturers Package Insert, 1997.

METRONIDAZOLE VAGINAL GEL

Trade: Metrogel - Vaginal
Can/Aus/UK: Metrogel
Uses: Antibiotic
AAP: Drug whose effect on nursing infants is unknown but may be of concern

Both topical and vaginal preparations of metronidazole contain only 0.75% metronidazole. Plasma levels following administration are exceedingly low.[1] This metronidazol vaginal product produces only 2% of the mean peak serum level concentration of a 500 mg oral metronidazole tablet. The maternal plasma level following use of each dose of vaginal gel averaged 237 μg/L compared to 12,785 μg/L following an oral 500 mg tablet. Milk levels following intravaginal use would probably be exceeding low.

Milk/plasma ratios, although published for oral metronidazole, may be different for this route of administration, primarily due to the low plasma levels attained with this product. Topical and intravaginal metronidazole gels are indicated for bacterial vaginosis.

Pregnancy Risk Category: B

Lactation Risk Category: L2

Theoretic Infant Dose:

Adult Concerns: Mild irritation to vaginal wall.

Pediatric Concerns: None reported.

Drug Interactions: Phenytoin and phenobarbital may decrease half-life of metronidazole. Alcohol may induce disulfiram-like reactions. May increase prothrombin times when used with warfarin.

Alternatives:

Adult Dosage: 37.5 mg BID

T½ = 8.5 hours	M/P =
PHL =	PB = 10%
PK = 6-12 hours	Oral = Complete
MW = 171	pKa =
Vd =	

References:
1. Pharmaceutical Manufacturers Package Insert, 1996.

MEXILETINE HCL

Trade: Mexitil
Can/Aus/UK: Mexitil, Novo-Mexiletine
Uses: Antiarrhythmic
AAP: Approved by the American Academy of Pediatrics for use in breastfeeding mothers

Mexiletine is an antiarrhythmic agent with activity similar to lidocaine. In a study on one patient who was receiving 600 mg/day in divided doses, the milk level at steady state was 0.8 mg/L which represented at milk/plasma ratio of 1.1.[1] Mexiletine was not detected in the infant nor were untoward effects noted. In another study on day 2 to 5 postpartum, and in a patient receiving 200 mg three times daily, the mean peak concentration of mexiletine in breastmilk was 959 μg/L and while the maternal serum was 724 μg/L.[2] Extrapolating this data, an infant ingesting 1 L of milk daily would ingest 0.95 mg of mexiletine daily, approximately 0.01 % of the daily maternal dose. In this study the milk plasma ratio varied from 0.78 to 1.89 with an average of 1.45. It is unlikely this exposure would lead to untoward side effects in a breastfeeding infant.

Pregnancy Risk Category: B

Lactation Risk Category: L2

Theoretic Infant Dose: 143.9 μg/kg/day

Adult Concerns: Arrhythmias, bradycardia, hypotension, tremors, dizziness.

Pediatric Concerns: None reported.

Drug Interactions: Aluminum, magnesium hydroxide, atropine, and narcotics may reduce the oral absorption of mexiletine. Cimetidine may increase or decreased mexiletine plasma levels. Hydantoins such as phenytoin may increase mexiletine clearance and reduce plasma levels. Rifampin may increase mexiletine clearance leading to lower levels. Mexiletine may reduce the clearance of caffeine by 50%. Serum theophylline levels may be increased significantly to toxic levels.

Alternatives:

Adult Dosage: 200 mg q 8 hours

T½ = 9.2 hours	**M/P = 1.45**
PHL =	**PB = 63%**
PK = 2-3 hours(oral)	**Oral = 90%**
MW = 179	**pKa = 8.4**
Vd = 6-12	

References:
1. Lewis AM et. al. Mexiletine in human blood and breast milk. Postgrad. Med. J. 57:546-7, 1981.
2. Timmis AD, Jackson G, Holt DW. Mexiletine for control of ventricular arrhythmias in pregnancy. Lancet 2:647-8, 1980.

MICONAZOLE

Trade: Monistat IV, Monistat 3, 7
Can/Aus/UK: Daktarin, Daktozin, Fungo, Micatin, Monistat
Uses: Antifungal for candidiasis
AAP: Not reviewed

Miconazole is an effective antifungal that is commonly used I.V., topically, and intravaginally. After intravaginal application, approximately 1% of the dose is absorbed systemically.[1,2] After topical application, there is little or no absorption (0.1%). It is unlikely that the limited absorption of miconazole from vaginal application would produce significant milk levels. Milk concentrations following oral and I.V. miconazole have not been reported. Oral absorption of miconazole is poor, only 25-30%. Miconazole is commonly used in pediatric patients less than 1 year of age.

Pregnancy Risk Category: C

Lactation Risk Category: L2

Theoretic Infant Dose:

Adult Concerns: Nausea, vomiting, diarrhea, anorexia, itching, rash, local irritation.

Pediatric Concerns: None reported via milk.

Drug Interactions: May increase warfarin anticoagulant effect. May increase hypoglycemia of oral sulfonylureas. Phenytoin levels may be increased.

Alternatives:

Adult Dosage: 200-1200 mg TID

T½ = 20-25 hours	M/P =
PHL =	PB = 91-93%
PK = Immediate(IV)	Oral = 25-30%
MW = 416	pKa =
Vd =	

References:
1. Drug Facts and Comparisons. 1995 ed. Facts and Comparisons, St. Louis.
2. McEvoy GE(ed):AHFS Drug Information, New York, NY. 1995.

MIDAZOLAM

Trade: Versed
Can/Aus/UK: Hypnovel, Versed
Uses: Short acting benzodiazepine sedative, hypnotic
AAP: Effect on nursing infants unknown but may be of concern.

Midazolam is a very short acting benzodiazepine primarily used as an induction or preanesthetic medication. The onset of action of midazolam is extremely rapid, its potency is greater than diazepam, and its metabolic elimination is more rapid. With a plasma half-life of only 1.9 hours, it is preferred for rapid induction and maintenance of anesthesia. After oral administration of 15 mg for up to 6 days postnatally in 22 women, the mean milk/plasma ratio was 0.15 and the maximum level of midazolam in breastmilk was 9 nanogram/mL, and occurred 1-2 hours after administration.[1] Midazolam and its hydroxy-metabolite were undetectable 4 hours after administration. Therefore, the amount of midazolam transferred to an infant via early milk is minimal, particularly if the baby is breastfed more than 4 hours after administration.

Pregnancy Risk Category: D

Lactation Risk Category: L3

Theoretic Infant Dose: 1.4 μg/kg/day

Adult Concerns: Sedation, respiratory depression.

Pediatric Concerns: None reported in several studies. Wait 4 hours after dose.

Drug Interactions: Theophylline may reduce the sedative effects of midazolam. Other CNS depressants may potentiate the depressant effects of midazolam. Cimetidine may increase plasma levels of midazolam.

Alternatives: Lorazepam

Adult Dosage: 1-2.5 mg once or twice

T½ = 2-5 hours	M/P = 0.15
PHL = 6.5-23 hours	PB = 97%.
PK = 20-50 min.(oral)	Oral = 27-44%
MW = 326	pKa = 6.2
Vd = 1.0-2.5	

References:
1. Matheson I, Lunde PK, and Bredesen JE. Midazolam and nitrazepam in the maternity ward: milk concentrations and clinical effects. Brit. J. Clin. Pharmacol. 30:787-93, 1990.

MILK THISTLE

Trade: Holy Thistle, Lady Thistle, Marian Thistle, Silybum, Silymarin
Can/Aus/UK:
Uses: Hepatoprotectant
AAP: Not reviewed

Milk Thistle has been used since 23 A.D. as a liver protectant.[1] Silymarin, a mixture of three isomeric flavonolignans, consists of Silybin, silicristin, and silidianin.[2] Silybin is the most biologically active and is believed to be a potent antioxidant and hepatoprotective agent. Silymarin is poorly soluble in water so aqueous preparations such as teas are ineffective. The oral bioavailability is likewise poor, only 23-47% is absorbed orally. Oral forms are generally concentrated. Silymarin effects are almost exclusively on the liver and kidney and concentrates in liver cells. It is believed to inhibit oxidative damage to cells by increasing glutathione synthesis. It is believed to also stimulate the regenerative capacity of liver cells. While it has been advocated for the stimulation of milk synthesis, little evidence of efficacy exists. No data are available concerning Silymarin transfer to human milk but some probably transfers. However, it is rather devoid of reported toxicity, with only brief GI intolerance, and mild allergic reactions.[3,4]

Pregnancy Risk Category:

Lactation Risk Category: L3

Theoretic Infant Dose:

Adult Concerns: Mild GI intolerance and allergic reactions.

Pediatric Concerns: None reported via milk.

Drug Interactions:

Alternatives:

Adult Dosage: 200-400 mg daily via extracts

T½ =	M/P =
PHL=	PB =
PK =	Oral = 23-47%
MW = 482	pKa =
Vd =	

References:
1. Foster S. Milk thistle-Silybum marianum. Botanical Series No. 305, American botanical Council, Austin, Tx 3-7, 1991.
2. Leung A, et.al. Encyclopedia of Common Natural Ingredients Used in food, Drugs, and Cosmetics. John Wiley and Sons, Inc, New York, NY 366-68, 1996.

3.   Review of Natural Products, Facts and Comparisons, 1999.
4.   Awang D. Can. Pharm. J. Oct. 403-4, 1993.

MINOCYCLINE

Trade: Minocin, Dynacin, Arestin
Can/Aus/UK: Akamin, Blemix, Minocin, Minomycin, Novo-Minocycline
Uses: Tetracycline antibiotic
AAP: Not reviewed

Minocycline is a broad spectrum tetracycline antibiotic with significant side effects in pediatric patients, including dental staining and reduced bone growth.[1,2] It is probably secreted into breastmilk in small but clinically insignificant levels. Because tetracyclines bind to milk calcium, they would have reduced absorption in the infant. However, minocycline may be absorbed to a greater degree than the older tetracyclines. Although most tetracyclines secreted into milk are generally bound to calcium, thus inhibiting their absorption, minocycline is poorly bound and may be better absorbed in a breastfeeding infant than the older tetracyclines. While the absolute absorption of older tetracyclines may be dramatically reduced by calcium salts, the newer doxycycline and minocycline analogs bind less and their overall absorption while slowed, may be significantly higher than earlier versions. A dosage of tetracycline 2 gm/day for 3 days has achieved a milk/plasma ratio of 0.6 to 0.8. In another study of 5 lactating women receiving tetracycline 500 mg PO four times daily, the breastmilk concentrations ranged from 0.43 mg/L to 2.58 mg/L. Levels in infants were below the limit of detection. Because we have many other antimicrobials with similar spectrums, the short-term use of tetracyclines in breastfeeding women is not generally recommended, but not necessarily contraindicated. There is little risk of permanent dental staining with only a brief exposure (several weeks).

Pregnancy Risk Category: D

Lactation Risk Category: L2 for acute use
                                              L4 for chronic use

Theoretic Infant Dose: 0.4 mg/kg/day

Adult Concerns: Adverse effects include GI distress, dizziness, thyroid pigmentation, vomiting, diarrhea, nephrotoxicity, photosensitivity.

Pediatric Concerns: None via breastmilk, but pediatric side effects include decreased linear bone growth and dental staining.

Drug Interactions: Absorption may be reduced or delayed when used with dairy products, calcium, magnesium, or aluminum containing antacids, oral contraceptives, iron, zinc, sodium bicarbonate, penicillins, cimetidine. Increased toxicity may result when used with methoxiflurane anesthesia. Use with warfarin anticoagulants may increase anticoagulation.

Alternatives: Doxycycline

Adult Dosage: 100 mg BID

T½ = 15-20 hours	M/P =
PHL=	PB = 76%
PK = 3 hours	Oral = 90-100%
MW = 457	pKa =
Vd =	

References:
1. Drug Facts and Comparisons. 1996. ed. Facts and Comparisons, St. Louis.
2. McEvoy GK. In: Drug Information. American Hospital Formulary Service. American Society of Health-System Pharmacists. 1995.

MINOXIDIL

Trade: Loniten, Minodyl, Rogaine
Can/Aus/UK: Apo-Gain, Loniten, Minox, Regaine, Rogaine
Uses: Antihypertensive
AAP: Approved by the American Academy of Pediatrics for use in breastfeeding mothers

Minoxidil is a potent vasodilator and antihypertensive. It is also used for hair loss and baldness. When applied topically, only 1.4% of the dose is absorbed systemically. Following a dose of 7.5 mg, minoxidil was secreted into human milk in concentrations ranging from trough levels of 0.3 μg/L at 12 hours to peak levels of 41.7-55 μg/L at 1 hour following an oral dose of 7.5 mg.[1] Long-term exposure of breastfeeding infants in women ingesting oral minoxidil may not be advisable. However, in those using topical minoxidil, the limited absorption via skin would minimize systemic levels and significantly reduce risk of transfer to infant via breastmilk. It is unlikely that the amount absorbed via topical application would produce clinically relevant concentrations in breastmilk.

Pregnancy Risk Category: C

Lactation Risk Category: L3

Theoretic Infant Dose: 8.3 μg/kg/day

Adult Concerns: Hypotension, tachycardia, headache, weight gain, skin pigmentation, rash, renal toxicity, leukopenia.

Pediatric Concerns: None reported.

Drug Interactions: Profound orthostatic hypotension when used with guanethidine. May potentiate hypotensive effect of other antihypertensives.

Alternatives:

Adult Dosage: 10-40 mg QD

T½ = 3.5-4.2 hours	M/P = 0.75-1.0
PHL =	PB = Low
PK = 2-8 hour	Oral = 90-95%
MW = 209	pKa =
Vd =	

References:
1. Valdivicso A, et. al. Minoxidil in breast milk. Ann Intern Med 102:135, 1985.

MIRTAZAPINE

Trade: Remeron
Can/Aus/UK: Zispin
Uses: Antidepressant
AAP: Not reviewed

Mirtazapine is a unique antidepressant structurally dissimilar to the SSRIs, tricyclics, or the monoamine oxidase inhibitors. Mirtazapine has little or no serotonergic-like side effects, fewer anticholinergic side effects than amitriptyline, it produces less sexual dysfunction, and has not demonstrated cardiotoxic or seizure potential in a limited number of overdose cases.[1] However, its sedative and tendency to produce weight-gain limit its usefulness, except in those patients who need sedation. No data are available on its entry into human milk. Due to its sedative properties and long half-life, its use in breastfeeding patients is not generally recommended.

Pregnancy Risk Category: C

Lactation Risk Category: L3

Theoretic Infant Dose:

Adult Concerns: Drowsiness (54%), dizziness, dry mouth, constipation, increased appetite (17%), and weight gain (12%) have been reported.

Pediatric Concerns: None reported via milk.

Drug Interactions: Enhanced impairment of cognitive function when administered with alcohol. Mirtazapine is a weak inhibitor of cytochrome P450 2D6 and others. Drugs metabolized by this enzyme system may have enhanced activity. Coadministration with benzodiazepines may reduce cognitive function.

Alternatives: Sertraline, Venlafaxine, Paroxetine

Adult Dosage: 15-45 mg daily

T½ = 20-40 hours	**M/P** =
PHL =	**PB** = 85%
PK = 2 hours	**Oral** = 50%
MW = 265	**pKa** =
Vd =	

References:
1. Pharmaceutical Manufacturers Package Insert, 1999.

MISOPROSTOL

Trade: Cytotec
Can/Aus/UK: Cytotec
Uses: Prostaglandin hormone, gastric protectant
AAP: Not reviewed

Misoprostol is a prostaglandin E1 compound that is useful in treating nonsteroidal-induced gastric ulceration. Misoprostol is absorbed orally and rapidly metabolized. Intact misoprostol is not detectable in plasma, and is rapidly metabolized to misoprostol acid which is biologically active.[1] Secretion of misoprostol in milk is unlikely due to rapid maternal metabolism. However, secretion of its active metabolite is possible and could produce diarrhea in newborns, although this has not been reported.

Pregnancy Risk Category: X

Lactation Risk Category: L3

Theoretic Infant Dose:

Adult Concerns: Diarrhea, abdominal cramps and pain, uterine bleeding and abortion.

Pediatric Concerns: None reported, but observe for diarrhea, abdominal cramps.

Drug Interactions: Levels are diminished when administered with food. Antacids reduce total bioavailability but this does not appear clinically significant.

Alternatives:

Adult Dosage: 100-200 mcg QID

T½ = 20-40 min.	M/P =
PHL =	PB = 80-90%
PK = 14-20 min.(oral)	Oral = Complete
MW = 383	pKa =
Vd =	

References:
1. Pharmaceutical Manufacturers Package Insert, 1995.

MITOXANTRONE

Trade: Novantrone
Can/Aus/UK: Novantrone, Onkotrone
Uses: Immunosuppressant for MS
AAP: Not reviewed

Mitoxantrone is an antineoplastic agent used in the treatment of relapsing multiple sclerosis. It is a DNA-reactive agent that intercalates into DNA via hydrogen bonding, causing crosslinks. It inhibits B cell, T cell and macrophage proliferation. Milk levels of 18 μg/L up to 28 days after the last administration have been reported by the manufacturer.[1] As this is a DNA-reactive agent, and it has a huge volume of distribution leading to prolonged plasma levels, it should not be used in breastfeeding mothers.

Pregnancy Risk Category: D

Lactation Risk Category: L5

Theoretic Infant Dose:

Adult Concerns: Leukopenia and thrombocytopenia are the most common adverse effects. Cardiotoxicity, nausea, vomiting, diarrhea, mucositis, hepatotoxicity, alopecia, pruritus, phlebitis have been reported. Neuropathy and paralysis of the bowel and bladder are reported.

Pediatric Concerns: None reported but extreme caution is recommended. Probably contraindicated.

Drug Interactions: Avoid vaccinations with live or attenuated vaccines (Smallpox, Rotavirus, etc).
The half-life of mitoxantrone is increased (1.8 fold) by use with valspodar.

Alternatives:

Adult Dosage: 12 mg/meter^2

T½ = 23-215 hours	M/P =
PHL=	PB = 78%
PK =	Oral = Poor
MW = 517	pKa =
Vd = 14-54	

References:
1.   Pharmaceutical manufacturers package insert, 2002.

MIVACURIUM

Trade: Mivacron
Can/Aus/UK: Mevacron, Mivacrom, Mivacron
Uses: Neuromuscular blocking agent
AAP: Not reviewed

Mivacurium is a short-acting neuromuscular blocking agent used to relax skeletal muscles during surgery.   Its duration is very short and complete recovery generally occurs in 15-30 minutes.[1,2]   No data are available on its transfer to breastmilk. However, it has an exceedingly short plasma half-life and probably poor to no oral absorption.   It is very unlikely that it would be absorbed by a breastfeeding infant.

Pregnancy Risk Category: C

Lactation Risk Category: L2

Theoretic Infant Dose:

Adult Concerns: Flushing, hypotension, weakness.

Pediatric Concerns: None reported.

Drug Interactions: Inhaled anesthetics, local anesthetics, calcium channel blockers, antiarrhythmic such as quinidine, and certain antibiotics such as amino glycosides, tetracyclines, vancomycin, and clindamycin may significantly prolong neuromuscular blockade with mivacurium.

Alternatives:

Adult Dosage: 0.1-0.15 mg/kg q 15 minutes PRN

T½ = < 30 minutes	M/P =
PHL=	PB =
PK =	Oral = Poor
MW =	pKa =
Vd =	

References:
1.   McEvoy GE(ed):AHFS Drug Information, New York, NY. 1995.

2.   Pharmaceutical Manufacturers Package Insert, 1995.

MMR VACCINE

Trade: MMR Vaccine, Measles - Mumps - Rubella
Can/Aus/UK:
Uses: Live attenuated triple virus vaccine
AAP: Not reviewed

MMR vaccine is a mixture of live, attenuated viruses from measles, mumps, and rubella strains. It is usually administered to children at 12-15 months of age. NEVER administer to a pregnant woman. Rubella, and perhaps measles and mumps virus, are undoubtedly transferred via breastmilk and have been detected in throat swabs of 56% of breastfeeding infants.[1-4] Infants exposed to the attenuated viruses via breastmilk had only mild symptoms. If medically required, MMR vaccine can be administered early postpartum.[5] See rubella.

Pregnancy Risk Category:

Lactation Risk Category: L2

Theoretic Infant Dose:

Adult Concerns: Mild symptoms, fever, flu-like symptoms.

Pediatric Concerns: Mild symptoms of rubella have been reported in one newborn infant.

Drug Interactions:

Alternatives:

Adult Dosage: 0.5 mL once

References:
1.   Buimovici-Klein E, et. al. Isolation of rubella virus in milk after postpartum immunization. J Pediatr 91:939-41, 1977.
2.   Losonsky GA et.al. Effect of immunization against rubella on lactation products. I. Development and characterization of specific immunologic reactivity in breast milk. J. Infect. Dis. 145:654, 1982.
3.   Losonsky GA, et.al. Effect of immunization against rubella on lactation products. II. Maternal-neonatal interactions. fJ. Infect. Dis. 145:661, 1982.
4.   Landes RD et.al. Neonatal rubella following postpartum maternal immunization. Pediatrics 97:465-467, 1980.
5.   Lawrence RA. In: Breastfeeding, A guide for the medical profession. Mosby, St.Louis, 1994.

MOCLOBEMIDE

Trade:
Can/Aus/UK: Apo-Moclobemide, Arima, Aurorix, Manerix
Uses: MAO inhibitor, antidepressant.
AAP: Not reviewed

Unlike older MAO inhibitors, moclobemide is a selective and reversible inhibitor of MAO-A isozyme, and thus is not plagued with the dangerous side effects of the older MAO inhibitor families. It is an effective treatment for depression.[1] In a study by Pons in 6 lactating women[2], who received a single oral dose of 300mg, the concentration of moclobemide (Cmax) was highest at 3 hours after the dose and averaged 2.7 mg/L.[2] The average (AUC) milk concentration through the 12 hour period was 0.97 mg/L hour. According to the authors, an average 3.5 kg breastfed infant would therefore be exposed to only a 0.05 mg/kg dose, which is approximately 1% of the maternal dose on a weight basis. The minimal levels of moclobemide found in milk are unlikely to product untoward effects according to the authors.

Pregnancy Risk Category:

Lactation Risk Category: L3

Theoretic Infant Dose: 0.1 mg/kg/day

Adult Concerns: Dry mouth, headache, dizziness, tremor, sweating, insomnia, and constipation.

Pediatric Concerns: None reported via milk.

Drug Interactions: Serotonergic syndrome is unlikely, but possible when admixed with SSRI antidepressants, clomipramine, fluoxetine, etc. Do not coadminister with SSRIs and tricyclic antidepressants. Do not administer with meperidine(pethidine) or dextromethorphan. Sympathomimetic hyperactivity (hypertension, headache, hyperpyrexia, arrhythmias, cerebral hemorrhage) may occur when admixed with tyramine, ephedrine, pseudoephedrine, phenylephrine, epinephrine, norepinephrine and other sympathomimetics.

Alternatives:

Adult Dosage: 450 mg/day

T½ = 1-2.2 hours	M/P = 0.72
PHL =	PB = 50%
PK = 2 hours	Oral = 80%
MW = 269	pKa = 6.3
Vd = 1-2	

References:
1.   Fulton B, and Benfield P. Moclobemide: An update of its pharmacological properties and therapeutic uses. Drugs 52:450-474, 1996.
2.   Pons G, Schoerlin MP, et.al. Moclobemide excretion in human breast milk. Br. J. Clin. Pharmacol. 29(10):27-31, 1990.

MODAFINIL

Trade: Provigil
Can/Aus/UK: Alertec, Provigil
Uses: Wakefulness-promoting agent
AAP: Not reviewed

Modafinil is a wakefulness-promoting agent used for the treatment of narcolepsy.   Although it's pharmacologic results are similar to amphetamines and methylphenidate(Ritalin),   its method of action is unknown. No data are available on its transfer into human milk. Some caution is recommended as it is small in molecular weight and very lipid soluble, both characteristics which may ultimately lead to higher milk levels.   In addition,   it apparently stimulates dopamine levels. Compounds that stimulate dopamine levels in brain often reduce prolactin secretion. Milk production may suffer but this is only supposition.

Pregnancy Risk Category: C

Lactation Risk Category: L4

Theoretic Infant Dose:

Adult Concerns: May increase incidence of headache, chest pain, palpitations, dyspnea, and transient T-wave changes on ECG. CNS changes include delusions, auditory hallucinations and sleep deprivation.   Diarrhea, dry mouth, nausea, and rhinitis have been reported.

Pediatric Concerns: None reported. Observe for reduced milk supply.

Drug Interactions: May increase plasma levels of diazepam, phenytoin and propranolol.   Caution when used with tricyclic and SSRI antidepressants.   May induce hepatic enzymes,   thus reducing circulating levels of cyclosporine, theophylline, and steroidal contraceptives.

Alternatives:

Adult Dosage: 200-400 up to twice daily

T½ = 15 hours	M/P =
PHL=	PB = 60%
PK = 2-4 hours	Oral = Complete
MW = 273	pKa =
Vd = 0.9	

References:
1.   Pharmaceutical manufacturers package insert, 2001.

MOMETASONE

Trade: Elocon, Nasonex
Can/Aus/UK:
Uses: Corticosteroid
AAP: Not reviewed

Mometasone is a corticosteroid primarily intended for intranasal and topical use. It is considered a medium-potency steroid, similar to betamethasone and triamcinolone. Following topical application to the skin, less than 0.7% is systemically absorbed over an 8 hour period.[1,2] It is extremely unlikely mometasone would be excreted into human milk in clinically relevant levels following topical or intranasal administration.

Pregnancy Risk Category: C

Lactation Risk Category: L3

Theoretic Infant Dose:

Adult Concerns: Topically only minimal side effects have been reported and include irritation, burning, stinging, and dermal atrophy. After nasal administration, common adverse effects include headache, pharyngitis, epistaxis, and cough.

Pediatric Concerns: None reported via milk.

Drug Interactions:

Alternatives:

Adult Dosage: Apply topically 2-3 times daily

References:
1.   Pharmaceutical Manufacturers Package Insert, 1999.
2.   Drug Facts and Comparisons. 1999 ed. Facts and Comparisons, St. Louis.

MONTELUKAST SODIUM

Trade: Singulair
Can/Aus/UK:
Uses: Antiasthmatic agent
AAP: Not reviewed

Montelukast is a leukotriene receptor inhibitor similar to Accolate and is used as an adjunct in the treatment of asthma.   The manufacturer reports that montelukast is secreted into animal milk, but no data are available on transfer to human milk.[1] This product is cleared for use in children aged 6 and above.   This product does not enter the CNS nor many other tissues. Although the milk levels in humans are unreported, they are probably quite low.

Pregnancy Risk Category: B

Lactation Risk Category: L3

Theoretic Infant Dose:

Adult Concerns: Abdominal pain, fever, dyspepsia, dental pain, dizziness, headache, cough and nasal congestion, some changes in liver enzymes.

Pediatric Concerns: None reported via milk

Drug Interactions: Phenobarbital may reduce plasma levels by 40%. Although unreported, other inhibitors of Cytochrome P450 may affect plasma levels.

Alternatives: Zafirlukast

Adult Dosage: 10 mg daily

T½ = 2.7-5.5 hours	M/P =
PHL=	PB = 99%
PK = 2-4 hours	Oral = 64%
MW = 608	pKa =
Vd = 0.15	

References:
1.   Pharmaceutical manufacturers package insert, 1998.

MORPHINE

Trade: Morphine
Can/Aus/UK: Anamorph, Epimorph, Kapanol, M.O.S. MS Contin, MS Contin, Morphalgin, Morphitec, Oramorph, Ordine, Sevredol, Statex
Uses: Narcotic analgesic
AAP: Approved by the American Academy of Pediatrics for use in breastfeeding mothers

Morphine is a potent narcotic analgesic. In a group of 5 lactating women[1], the highest morphine concentration in breastmilk following two epidural doses was only 82 μg/L at 30 minutes. The highest breastmilk level following 15 mg I.V./IM was only 0.5 mg/L. In another study of women receiving morphine via PCA pumps for 12-48 hours postpartum, the concentration of morphine in breastmilk ranged from 50-60 μg/L(estimated from graph).[2]   None of the infants in this study were neurobehaviorally delayed at 3 days.   Because of the poor oral bioavailability of morphine (26%) it is unlikely these levels would be clinically relevant in a stable breastfeeding infant.

However, data from Robieux[3] suggests the levels transferred to the infant are higher. In this study of a single patient, plasma levels in the breastfed infant were within therapeutic range (4 ng/mL) although the infant showed no untoward signs or symptoms. However, this case was somewhat unique in that the mother received daily morphine (50 mg PO every 6 hours) during the third trimester for severe back pain. One week postpartum, the morphine was discontinued, and then 5 days later, reinstated due to withdrawal effects in the mother. The reported concentration in foremilk and hindmilk was 100 ng/mL and 10 ng/mL respectively and the authors suggested that the dose to the infant would be 0.8 to 12% of the maternal oral dose (0.15 to 2.41 mg/day). Although this study suggests that the amount of morphine transferred in milk can be clinically relevant, the authors calculated the infant dose from the highest milk concentration and a milk intake of 150 ml/kg/day, thus the dose of morphine to the infant would have been substantially lower (53 μg/day). This study seems flawed as the plasma levels, and the doses via milk just don't correlate. That this infant showed no untoward effects, can be explained by the fact that it may have exhibited tolerance after long exposure, or that the reported analgesic-therapeutic level required in neonates is actually slightly higher than in adults, or the plasma levels assayed in this infant were in error.

Infants under 1 month of age have a prolonged elimination half-life and decreased clearance of morphine relative to older infants. The clearance of morphine and its elimination begins to approach adult values by 2 months of age.

Pregnancy Risk Category: B

Lactation Risk Category: L3

Theoretic Infant Dose: 75.0 μg/kg/day

Adult Concerns: Sedation, flushing, CNS depression, respiratory depression, bradycardia.

Pediatric Concerns: None reported via milk.

Drug Interactions: Barbiturates may significantly increase respiratory and CNS depressant effects of morphine. The admixture of cimetidine has produced CNS toxicity such as confusion, disorientation, respiratory depression, apnea, and seizures when used with narcotic analgesics. Diazepam may produce cardiovascular depression when used with opiates. Phenothiazines may antagonize the analgesic effect of morphine.

Alternatives: Codeine

Adult Dosage: 10-30 mg q 4 hours PRN

T½ = 1.5-2 hours	M/P = 1.1-3.6
PHL= 13.9 hours(neonates)	PB = 35%
PK = 0.5-1 hours	Oral = 26%
MW = 285	pKa = 8.1
Vd = 2-5	

References:
1. Feilberg VL, Rosenborg D, Broen Christensen C, et.al. Excretion of morphine in human breast milk. Acta Anaesthiol Scan. 33:426-428, 1989.
2. Wittels Bk, Scott DT, Sinatra RS. Exogenous opioids in human breast milk and acute neonatal neurobehavior: a preliminary study. Anesthesiology 73:864-869, 1990.
3. Robieux I, Koren, G, Vandenberg, H. Schneiderman, J. Morphine excretion in breast milk and resultant exposure of a nursing infant. Clin. Toxicol. 28(3):365-370,1990.

MOXIFLOXACIN

Trade: Avelox
Can/Aus/UK:
Uses: Antibiotic
AAP: Not reviewed

Moxifloxacin in a new broad spectrum fluoroquinolone antibiotic similar to ciprofloxacin and others. Fluoroquinolone antibiotics are generally contraindicated in pediatric age patients due to arthropathy, although they are occasionally used in severe infections. No studies in breastfeeding mothers are available. In rodents, milk levels were 25-40% of maternal plasma levels. The average adult human concentration over 24 hours is approximately 2 μg/mL. Assuming a low milk/plasma ratio like in rodents (0.4), an infant would likely ingest less than 120 μg/kg/day (theoretical). It is not likely that this would produce a clinical effect in an infant, but changes in colonic flora could occur.

Pregnancy Risk Category: C

Lactation Risk Category: L3

Theoretic Infant Dose:

Adult Concerns: Asthenia, moniliasis, pain, malaise, abdominal pain, cardiac palpitations, vasodilation, tachycardia, hypertension, insomnia, nervousness, confusion, dry mouth, constipation, stomatitis, arthralgia, myalgia, etc. have been reported.

Pediatric Concerns: None via milk but observe for diarrhea in infant.

Drug Interactions: Antacids, sucralfate, metal cations, and multivitamins may reduce absorption. No clinical interactions have been noted between moxifloxacin and warfarin, theophylline, digoxin, or glyburide.

Alternatives: Ofloxacin, Norfloxacin, Levofloxacin

Adult Dosage: 400 mg daily

T½ = 12 hours		M/P =	
PHL =		PB = 50%	
PK = 1-3 hours		Oral = 90%	
MW = 439		pKa =	
Vd = 2.7			

References:
1.   Pharmaceutical manufacturers package insert, 2000.

MUPIROCIN OINTMENT

Trade: Bactroban
Can/Aus/UK: Bactroban
Uses: Antibacterial ointment
AAP: Not reviewed

Mupirocin is a topical antibiotic used for impetigo, Group A beta-hemolytic strep, and strep. pyogenes. Mupirocin is only minimally absorbed following topical application. In one study, less than 0.3% of a topical dose was absorbed after 24 hours. Most remained adsorbed to the corneum layer of the skin. The drug is absorbed orally, but it is so rapidly metabolized that systemic levels are not sustained.

Pregnancy Risk Category: B

Lactation Risk Category: L1

Theoretic Infant Dose:

Adult Concerns: Rash, irritation.

Pediatric Concerns: None reported. Commonly used in pediatric patients.

Drug Interactions:

Alternatives:

Adult Dosage:

T½ = 17-36 min.		M/P =	
PHL=		PB =	
PK =		Oral = Complete	
MW = 501		pKa =	
Vd =			

References:

NABUMETONE

Trade: Relafen
Can/Aus/UK: Relafen, Relifex
Uses: Anti-inflammatory agent for arthritic pain
AAP: Not reviewed

Nabumetone is a non-steroidal anti-inflammatory agent for arthritic pain.[1] Immediately upon absorption, nabumetone is metabolized to the active metabolite. The parent drug is not detectable in plasma. It is not known if the nabumetone metabolite (6MNA) is secreted in human milk. It is known to be secreted into animal milk and has a very long half-life. NSAIDS are not generally recommended in nursing mothers, with the exception of ibuprofen. See ibuprofen as alternative.

Pregnancy Risk Category: C

Lactation Risk Category: L3

Theoretic Infant Dose:

Adult Concerns: GI distress, nausea, vomiting, diarrhea.

Pediatric Concerns: None reported via milk. Observe for GI distress.

Drug Interactions: May prolong prothrombin time when used with warfarin.   Antihypertensive effects of ACEi family may be blunted or completely abolished by NSAIDs.   Some NSAIDs may block antihypertensive effect of beta blockers, diuretics.   Used with cyclosporin, may dramatically increase renal toxicity. May increase digoxin, phenytoin, lithium levels.   May increase toxicity of methotrexate.   May increase bioavailability of penicillamine.

Probenecid may increase NSAID levels.

Alternatives: Ibuprofen

Adult Dosage: 500-1000 mg QD-BID

T½ = 22-30 hours	M/P =
PHL =	PB = 99%
PK = 2.5 - 4 hours	Oral = 38%
MW = 228	pKa =
Vd =	

References:
1. Pharmaceutical Manufacturers Package Insert, 1996.

NADOLOL

Trade: Corgard, Nadolol
Can/Aus/UK: Corgard, Novo-Nadolol, Syn-Nadolol
Uses: Antihypertensive, antiangina, beta blocker
AAP: Approved by the American Academy of Pediatrics for use in breastfeeding mothers

Nadolol is a long-acting beta adrenergic blocker used as an antihypertensive. It is secreted into breastmilk in moderately high concentrations. Following a maternal dose of 20 mg/day, breastmilk levels at 38 hours postpartum were 146 μg/L.[1] In another study of 12 women receiving 80 mg daily the mean steady-state concentrations in milk were 357 μg/L.[2] The time to maximum concentration was 6 hours. The milk/serum ratio was reported to average 4.6. A five kg infant would receive from 2-7% of the maternal dose. The authors recommended caution with the use of this beta blocker in breastfeeding patients. Due to its long half-life and high milk/plasma ratio, this would not be a preferred beta blocker.

Pregnancy Risk Category: C

Lactation Risk Category: L4

Theoretic Infant Dose: 53.6 μg/kg/day

Adult Concerns: Hypotension, nausea, diarrhea, bradycardia, apnea, depression.

Pediatric Concerns: None reported, but due to the high M:P ratio of 4.6, this product is not recommended.

Drug Interactions: Decreased effect when used with aluminum salts, barbiturates, calcium salts, cholestyramine, NSAIDs, ampicillin, rifampin, and salicylates. Beta blockers may reduce the effect of oral sulfonylureas (hypoglycemic agents). Increased toxicity/effect when used with other antihypertensives, contraceptives, MAO inhibitors, cimetidine, and numerous other products. See drug interaction reference for complete listing.

Alternatives: Propranolol, Metoprolol

Adult Dosage: 40-80 mg QD

T½ = 20-24 hours	M/P = 4.6
PHL =	PB = 30%
PK = 2-4 hours	Oral = 20-40%
MW = 309	pKa = 9.7
Vd = 1.5-3.6	

References:

1. Fox RE, et. al. Neonatal effects of maternal nadolol therapy. Am J Obstet Gynecol 152:1045-6, 1985.
2. Devlin RT, Duchin KL, et.al. Nadolol in human serum and breast milk. Br. J. Clin. Pharmacol. 12:393-6, 1981.

NAFCILLIN

Trade: Unipen, Nafcil
Can/Aus/UK: Unipen
Uses: Penicillin antibiotic
AAP: Not reviewed

Nafcillin is a penicillin antibiotic that is poorly and erratically absorbed orally.[1] The only formulations are I.V. and IM. No data are available on concentration in milk, but it is likely small. Oral absorption in the infant would be minimal. See other penicillins.

Pregnancy Risk Category: B

Lactation Risk Category: L1

Theoretic Infant Dose:

Adult Concerns: Neutropenia, hypokalemia, pseudomembranous colitis, allergic rash.

Pediatric Concerns: None reported. Observe for GI symptoms such as diarrhea. Nafcillin is frequently used in infants.

Drug Interactions: Chloramphenicol may decreased nafcillin levels. Nafcillin may inhibit efficacy of oral contraceptives. Probenecid may increase nafcillin levels. May increase anticoagulant effect of warfarin and heparin.

Alternatives:

Adult Dosage: 250-1000 mg q 4-6 hours

T½ = 0.5-1.5 hours	M/P =
PHL = 2.2-5.5 hours(neonates).	PB = 70-90%
PK = 30-60 min(IM).	Oral = 50%
MW = 436	pKa =
Vd =	

References:
1.   McEvoy GE(ed):AFHS Drug Information, New York, NY. 1995.

NALBUPHINE

Trade: Nubain
Can/Aus/UK: Nubain
Uses: Analgesic
AAP: Not reviewed

Nalbuphine is a potent narcotic analgesic similar in potency to morphine. In a group of 20 postpartum mothers who received 20 mg IM nalbuphine, the total amount of nalbuphine excreted into human milk during a 24 hour period averaged 2.3 micrograms, which is equivalent to 0.012% of the maternal dosage.[1]   The mean milk/plasma ratio using the AUC was 1.2.   According to the authors, an oral intake of 2.3 micrograms nalbuphine would not show any measurable plasma concentrations in the neonate.   Nalbuphine is both an antagonist and agonist of opiate receptors, and should not be mixed with other opiates due to interference with analgesia.

Pregnancy Risk Category: B

Lactation Risk Category: L3

Theoretic Infant Dose:

Adult Concerns: Hypotension, sedation, withdrawal syndrome, respiratory depression.

Pediatric Concerns: None reported via milk.

Drug Interactions: May reduce efficacy of other opioid analgesics. Barbiturates may increase CNS sedation.

Alternatives:

Adult Dosage: 10-20 mg q 3-6 hours PRN

T½ = 5 hours	M/P = 1,2
PHL = 0.86 hours	PB =
PK = 2-15 min.(IV, IM)	Oral = 16%
MW = 357	pKa =
Vd = 2.4-7.3	

References:
1. Wischnik A. Wetzelsberger N. Lucker PW. Elimination of nalbuphine in human milk. Arzneimittel-Forschung 38(10):1496-8, 1988.
2. Jaillon P. et.al. Pharmacokinetics of nalbuphine in infants, young healthy volunteers, and elderly patients. Clin. Pharmacol. Ther. 46:226-233, 1989.

NALIDIXIC ACID

Trade: Neggram
Can/Aus/UK: NegGram
Uses: Urinary anti-infective
AAP: Approved by the American Academy of Pediatrics for use in breastfeeding mothers

Nalidixic is an old urinary antiseptic and belongs to the fluoroquinolone family. In a group of 4 women receiving 1000 mg orally/day the concentration in breastmilk was approximately 5 mg/L.[1] Hemolytic anemia has been reported in one infant whose mother received 1 gm nalidixic acid 4 times daily. Use with extreme caution. A number of new and less toxic choices should preclude the use of this compound.[2]

Pregnancy Risk Category: B

Lactation Risk Category: L4

Theoretic Infant Dose: 75.0 μg/kg/day

Adult Concerns: Hemolytic anemia, headache, drowsiness, blurred vision, nausea, vomiting.

Pediatric Concerns: Hemolytic anemia in one infant. This is an old product that should not be used currently.

Drug Interactions: Decreased efficacy/oral bioavailability when used with antacids. Increased anticoagulation with warfarin.

Alternatives: Norfloxacin, Ofloxacin

Adult Dosage: 1 g QID

T½ = 1-2.5 hours	M/P = 0.08-0.13
PHL=	PB = 93%
PK = 1-2 hours	Oral = 60%
MW = 232	pKa =
Vd =	

References:
1. Belton EM, Jones RV. Hemolytic anemia due to nalidixic acid. Lancet 2:691, 1965.
2. Drug Facts and Comparisons. 1994 ed. Facts and Comparisons, St. Louis.

NALTREXONE

Trade: ReVia
Can/Aus/UK: Nalorex, ReVia
Uses: Narcotic antagonist
AAP: Not reviewed

Naltrexone is a long acting narcotic antagonist similar in structure to Naloxone. Orally absorbed, it has been clinically used in addicts to prevent the action of injected heroin. It occupies and competes with all opioid medications for the opiate receptor. When used in addicts, it can induce rapid and long lasting withdrawal symptoms. Although the half-life appears brief, the duration of antagonism is long lasting (24-72 hours).[1-5] Naltrexone appears relatively lipid soluble and transfers into the brain easily (brain/plasma ratio = 0.81). Breastmilk levels have not been reported.

Pregnancy Risk Category: C

Lactation Risk Category: L3

Theoretic Infant Dose:

Adult Concerns: Rapid opiate withdrawal symptoms. Dizziness, anorexia, rash, nausea, vomiting, and hepatocellular toxicity. Liver toxicity is common at doses approximately 5 times normal or less. A Narcan challenge test should be initiated in patients prior to therapy with naltrexone.

Pediatric Concerns: None reported, but not cleared for infants.

Drug Interactions: Suppresses narcotic analgesia and sedation.

Alternatives:

Adult Dosage: 50-150 mg QD

T½ = 4-13 hours	**M/P** =
PHL =	**PB** = 21%
PK = 1 hour	**Oral** = Complete
MW = 341	**pKa** =
Vd = 19 L/kg	

References:
1. Bullingham RES, McQuay HJ, Moore RA: Clinical pharmacokinetics of narcotic agonist-antagonist drugs. Clin Pharmacokinet 8:332-343, 1983.
2. Crabtree BL: Review of naltrexone, a long-acting opiate antagonist. Clin Pharm 3:273-280, 1984.
3. Ludden TM, Malspeis L, Baggott JD: Tritiated naltrexone binding in plasma from several species and tissue distribution in mice. J Pharm Sci 65:712-716, 1976.
4. Verebey K, Volavka J, Mule SJ et al: Naltrexone disposition, metabolism, and effects after acute and chronic dosing. Clin Pharmacol Ther 20:315-

328, 1976.

5. Wall ME, Brine DR, Perez-Reyes M: Metabolism and disposition of naltrexone in man after oral and intravenous administration. Drug Metab Dispos 9:369-375, 1981.

NAPROXEN

Trade: Anaprox, Naprosyn, Naproxen, Aleve
Can/Aus/UK: Anaprox, Apo-Naproxen, Inza, Naprosyn, Naxen, Proxen SR, Synflex
Uses: NSAID, analgesic for arthritis
AAP: Approved by the American Academy of Pediatrics for use in breastfeeding mothers

Naproxen is a popular NSAID analgesic. In a study done at steady state in one mother consuming 375 mg twice daily, milk levels ranged from 1.76-2.37 mg/L at 4 hours.[1,2] Total naproxen excretion in the infant's urine was only 0.26% of the maternal dose. Although the amount of naproxen transferred via milk is minimal, one should use with caution in nursing mothers because of its long half-life and its effect on infant cardiovascular system, kidneys, and GI tract. However, its short term use postpartum, or infrequent or occasional use would not necessarily be incompatible with breastfeeding. One reported case of prolonged bleeding, hemorrhage, and acute anemia in a seven-day-old infant.[3] The relative infant dose on a weight-adjusted maternal daily dose would be approximately 2.8%.

Pregnancy Risk Category: B

Lactation Risk Category: L3
 L4 for chronic use

Theoretic Infant Dose: 0.4 mg/kg/day

Adult Concerns: GI distress, gastric bleeding, hemorrhage.

Pediatric Concerns: One reported case of prolonged bleeding, hemorrhage, and acute anemia in a seven-day-old infant.

Drug Interactions: May prolong prothrombin time when used with warfarin. Antihypertensive effects of ACEi family may be blunted or completely abolished by NSAIDs. Some NSAIDs may block antihypertensive effect of beta blockers, diuretics. Used with cyclosporin, may dramatically increase renal toxicity. May increase digoxin, phenytoin, lithium levels. May increase toxicity of methotrexate. May increase bioavailability of penicillamine. Probenecid may increase NSAID levels.

Alternatives: Ibuprofen

Adult Dosage: 250-500 mg BID

T½ = 12-15 hours	M/P = 0.01
PHL = 12-15 hours	PB = 99.7%
PK = 2-4 hours	Oral = 74-99%
MW = 230	pKa = 5.0
Vd = 0.09	

References:

1. Jamali F, Stevens DR. Naproxen excretion in milk and its uptake by the infant. Drug Intell Clin Pharm. 17:910-911, 1983.
2. Jamali F, et. al. Naproxen excretion in breast milk and its uptake by sucking infant. Drug Intell Clin Pharm 16:475 (Abstr),1982.
3. Figalgo I, et.al. Anemia aguda, rectaorragia y hematuria asociadas a la ingestion de naproxen. Anales Espanoles de Pediatrica 30:317-9, 1989.

NARATRIPTAN

Trade: Amerge
Can/Aus/UK: Naramig
Uses: Migraine headaches
AAP: Not reviewed

Naratriptan is a 5-HT1D and 5-HT1B receptor stimulant, and is used for treatment of acute migraine headache.   No data are currently available on its transfer into human milk, although the manufacturer suggests it penetrates the milk of rodents.[1]   Naratriptan is a close congener of sumatriptan, only slightly better absorbed orally, and may produce few side effects in sumatriptan-sensitive patients. Some studies suggest that sumatriptan is equal to if not more effective than naratriptan.[2]   Sumatriptan has been studied in breastfeeding mothers and produces minimal milk levels. See sumatriptan.

Pregnancy Risk Category: C

Lactation Risk Category: L3

Theoretic Infant Dose:

Adult Concerns: Chest discomfort including pain, pressure, heaviness, tightness has been reported.   Nausea, dizziness, paresthesias are infrequently reported.   Cardiovascular events are rare but include hypertension, and tachyarrhythmias.

Pediatric Concerns: None reported via milk.

Drug Interactions: MAOIs can markedly increase naratriptan systemic effect and elimination including elevated plasma levels.   Ergot containing drugs have caused prolonged vasospastic reactions, do not use within 24 hours after using an ergot-containing product.   There have been rare reports of weakness, hyperreflexia, and incoordination with combined use with SSRIs such as fluoxetine, paroxetine, sertraline and fluvoxamine.

Alternatives: Sumatriptan

Adult Dosage: 1-2.5 mg q 4 hours X 2-3

T½ = 6 hours	M/P =
PHL=	PB = 31%
PK = 2-3 hours	Oral = 70%
MW = 372	pKa =
Vd = 2.42	

References:
1. Pharmaceutical Manufacturers Package Insert, 1999.
2. Dahlof C, Winter P, Whitehouse H et al: Randomized, double-blind, placebo-controlled comparison of oral naratriptan and oral sumatriptan in the acute treatment of migraine (abstract). Neurology 48(suppl):A85-A86, 1997.

NEDOCROMIL SODIUM

Trade: Tilade
Can/Aus/UK: Mireze, Tilade
Uses: Inhaled anti-inflammatory for asthmatics
AAP: Not reviewed

Nedocromil is believed to stabilize mast cells and prevent release of bronchoconstrictors in the lung following exposure to allergens. The systemic effects are minimal due to reduced plasma levels. Systemic absorption averages less than 8-17% of the total dose even after continued dosing, which is quite low.[1,2] The poor oral bioavailability of this product, and the reduced side effect profile of this family of drugs suggest that it is unlikely to produce untoward effects in a nursing infant. See cromolyn as comparison.

Pregnancy Risk Category: B

Lactation Risk Category: L2

Theoretic Infant Dose:

Adult Concerns: Poor taste. Dizziness, headache, nausea and vomiting, sore throat, and cough.

Pediatric Concerns: None reported via milk.

Drug Interactions:

Alternatives:

Adult Dosage: 3.5-4 mg QID

T½ = 3.3 hours	M/P =
PHL=	PB = 89%
PK = 28 min.	Oral = 8-17%
MW = 371	pKa =
Vd =	

References:
1.   Pharmaceutical Manufacturers Package Insert, 1996.
2.   Drug Facts and Comparisons. 1995. ed. Facts and Comparisons, St. Louis.

NEFAZODONE HCL

Trade: Serzone
Can/Aus/UK: Dutonin, Serzone
Uses: Antidepressant
AAP: Not reviewed

Nefazodone is an antidepressant similar to trazodone but structurally dissimilar from the other serotonin reuptake inhibitors.   It is rapidly metabolized to three partially active metabolites that have significantly longer half-lives (1.5 to 18 hours).[1]

In a study of one patient receiving 200 mg in the morning and 100 mg at night, the infant at 9 weeks of age (2.1 kg), was admitted for drowsiness, lethargy, failure to thrive, and poor temperature control.[2] The infant was born premature at 27 weeks.   The maximum milk concentration of nefazodone was 358 μg/L while the maternal plasma Cmax was 1270 μg/L.   The concentration of the metabolites was reported to be 83 μg/L for triazoledione, 32 μg/L for HO-Nefazodone, and 18 μg/L for m-Chlorophenylpiperazine.   The relative infant dose was calculated to be 0.45 % of the weight-adjusted maternal dose.   The AUC milk/plasma ratio ranged from 0.02 to 0.27.   Unfortunately no infant plasma samples were taken for analysis.

Dodd et.al.[3] recently reported a M/P ratio of only 0.1 for nefazodone in a patient receiving 200 mg twice daily. This is approximately one-third of the M/P ratio(0.27) reported by Yapp.   However, the Yapp study used AUC data over many points and is probably a more accurate reflection of nefazodone transfer into milk during the day.

This medication should probably not be used in breastfeeding mothers with young infants, premature infants, infants subject to apnea, or other weakened infants.

Pregnancy Risk Category: C

Lactation Risk Category: L4

Theoretic Infant Dose: 53.7 μg/kg/day

Adult Concerns: Weakness, hypotension, somnolence, dizziness, dry mouth, constipation, nausea, headache.

Pediatric Concerns: Drowsiness, lethargy, failure to thrive, and poor temperature control in one infant.

Drug Interactions: Sometimes fatal reactions may occur with MAOI. Plasma levels of astemizole and terfenadine may be increased. Clinically important increases in plasma concentrations of alprazolam and triazolam have been reported. Serum concentrations of digoxin have been increased by nefazodone by 29%. Haloperidol clearance decreased by 35%. Nefazodone may decrease propranolol plasma levels by as much as 30%.

Alternatives: Sertraline, Paroxetine, Trazedone

Adult Dosage: 150-300 mg BID

T½ = 1-4 hours	**M/P = 0.1-0.27**
PHL =	**PB = > 99%**
PK = 1 hour	**Oral = 20%**
MW = 507	**pKa = 6.6**
Vd = 0.9	

References:
1. Pharmaceutical Manufacturers Package Insert, 1996.
2. Yapp P, Ilett K, Kristensen J, Hackett LP, Paech M, Rampono J. Drowsiness and Poor Feeding in a Breast-fed Infant: Association with Nefazodone and its Metabolites. Annals of Pharmacotherapy 34:1269-1272, 2000.
3. Dodd S, Buist A, Burrows GD, Maguire KP, Norman TR. Determination of nefazodone and its pharmacologically active metabolites in human blood plasma and breast milk by high-performance liquid chromatography. J Chromatogr B Biomed Sci Appl 9;730(2):249-55,1999.

NETILMICIN

Trade: Netromycin
Can/Aus/UK: Netromycin, Nettilin
Uses: Aminoglycoside antibiotic
AAP: Not reviewed

Netilmicin is a typical aminoglycoside antibiotic (see gentamicin). Poor oral absorption limits its use to IM and I.V. administration although some studies suggest significant oral absorption in infancy.[1,2] Only small levels are believed to be secreted into human milk, although no reports exist. See gentamicin.

Pregnancy Risk Category: D

Lactation Risk Category: L3

Theoretic Infant Dose:

Adult Concerns: Kidney damage, hearing loss, changes in GI flora.

Pediatric Concerns: None reported, but observe for GI symptoms such as diarrhea.

Drug Interactions: Risk of nephrotoxicity may be increased when used with cephalosporins, enflurane, methoxiflurane, and vancomycin. Auditory toxicity may increase when used with loop diuretics. The neuromuscular blocking effects of neuromuscular blocking agents may be increased when used with aminoglycosides.

Alternatives:

Adult Dosage: 1.3-2.2 mg/kg q 8 hours

T½ = 2-2.5 hours	M/P =
PHL = 4.5-8 hours (neonates)	PB = < 10%
PK = 30-60 min.(IM)	Oral = Negligible
MW = 476	pKa =
Vd =	

References:
1. Pharmaceutical Manufacturers Package Insert, 1995.
2. McEvoy GE(ed):AHFS Drug Information, New York, NY. 1995.

NICARDIPINE

Trade: Cardene
Can/Aus/UK: Cardene
Uses: Antihypertensive, calcium channel blocker
AAP: Not reviewed

Nicardipine is a typical calcium channel blocker structurally related to nifedipine. Animal studies indicate that it is secreted to some degree in breastmilk.[1] No specific data on human milk levels are available. See verapamil, nifedipine.

Pregnancy Risk Category: C

Lactation Risk Category: L3

Theoretic Infant Dose:

Adult Concerns: Headache, peripheral edema, flushing, hypotension, bradycardia, gingival hyperplasia.

Pediatric Concerns: None reported, but no studies available. See nifedipine as alternative.

Drug Interactions: Barbiturates may reduce bioavailability of calcium channel blockers (CCB). Calcium salts may reduce hypotensive effect.

Dantrolene may increase risk of hyperkalemia and myocardial depression. H2 blockers may increase bioavailability of certain CCBs. Hydantoins may reduce plasma levels. Quinidine increases risk of hypotension, bradycardia, tachycardia. Rifampin may reduce effects of CCBs. Vitamin D may reduce efficacy of CCBs. CCBs may increase carbamazepine, cyclosporin, encainide, prazosin levels.

Alternatives: Nifedipine, Nimodipine

Adult Dosage: 5-15 mg q 1 hour PRN

T½ = 2-4 hours	M/P =
PHL =	PB = > 95%
PK = 0.5-2 hours	Oral = 35%
MW = 480	pKa =
Vd =	

References:
1. Pharmaceutical Manufacturers Package Insert, 1996.

NICOTINE PATCHES/GUM

Trade: Habitrol, NicoDerm, Nicotrol, ProStep, Nicotine Patches
Can/Aus/UK: Habitrol, NicoDerm, Nicorette, Nicotinell, Nicotinell TTS, ProStep
Uses: Nicotine withdrawal systems
AAP: Not reviewed

Nicotine and its metabolite cotinine are both present in milk. In one study of 927 mother-infant pairs, urinary cotinine levels in breast-fed infants of smoking mothers was 10-fold higher than in bottle-fed infants of smoking mothers.[1] This clearly suggests that a significant amount of nicotine transfers via milk to the infant.

Although highly variable, the blood level of nicotine in smokers approaches 44 ng/ml, whereas nicotine levels in patch users approximate 17 ng/ml, depending on the dose in the patch.[2,3] Therefore, nicotine levels in milk can be expected to be less in patch users than those found in smokers, assuming the patch is used correctly and the mother abstains from smoking. Individuals who both smoke and use the patch would have extremely high blood nicotine levels and could endanger the nursing infant. Patches should be removed at bedtime to reduce exposure of the infant and reduce side effects such as nightmares.

With nicotine gum, maternal serum nicotine levels average 30-60% of those found in cigarette smokers. While patches (transdermal systems) produce a sustained and lower nicotine plasma level, nicotine gum may produce large variations in peak levels when the gum is chewed rapidly, fluctuations similar to smoking itself. Mothers who choose to use nicotine gum and breastfeed, should be counseled to refrain from breastfeeding for 2-3 hours after using the gum product.

Nicotine is known to reduce milk production through a decrease in basal prolactin production.[3,4] One study clearly suggests that cigarette smoking significantly reduces breastmilk production at two weeks postpartum from 514 ml/day in non-smokers to 406 ml/day in smoking mothers.[5] For a complete review of nicotine and lactation see Schatz.[6]

However, the risk of nicotine via breastmilk is far less than the risk of formula feeding. Mothers should be advised to limit smoking as much as possible, and to smoke only after they have fed their infant.

Pregnancy Risk Category: X if used in overdose
D if used in last trimester

Lactation Risk Category: L3

Theoretic Infant Dose:

Adult Concerns: Tachycardia, GI distress, vomiting, diarrhea, rapid heart beat, and restlessness. Smoking during pregnancy has been associated with preterm births, decreased birth weight, and an increased risk of abortion and stillbirth . The use of nicotine during the last trimester has been associated with a decrease in fetal breathing movements, possibly resulting from decreased placental perfusion induced by nicotine. However, the use of nicotine patches instead of smoking is still preferred .

Pediatric Concerns: None reported, but observe for shock, vomiting, diarrhea, rapid heart beat, and restlessness.

Drug Interactions: Cessation of smoking may alter response to a number of medications in ex-smokers. Including are acetaminophen, caffeine, imipramine, oxazepam, pentazocine, propranolol, and theophylline. Smoking may reduce diuretic effect of furosemide. Smoking while continuing to use patches may dramatically elevate nicotine plasma levels.

Alternatives:

Adult Dosage: 7-21 mg daily

T½ = 2.0 hours(non-patch)	M/P = 2.9
PHL =	PB = 4.9%
PK = 2-4 hours	Oral = 30%
MW = 162	pKa =
Vd =	

References:
1. Mascola MA, Vaunakis HV, Tager IB, Speizer FE, and Hanrahan JP. Exposure of young infants to environmental tobacco spoke: Breast-feeding

among smoking mothers. Am.J.Public Health 88(6):893-896, 1998.
2. Pharmaceutical Manufacturers Package Insert, 1995.
3. Benowitz NL. Nicotine replacement therapy during pregnancy. JAMA 266:3174-77, 1991.
4. Matheson I, Rivrud GN. The effect of smoking on lactation and infantile colic. JAMA 261:42-43, 1989.
5. Hopkinson JM, Schanler RJ, Fraley JK, Garza C. Milk production by mothers of premature infants: influence of cigarette smoking. Pediatrics 90(6):934-8, 1992.
6. Schatz, BS. Nicotine replacement products: Implications for the breastfeeding mother. J. Human Lactation 14(2): 161-3, 1998.

NICOTINIC ACID

Trade: Nicobid, Nicolar, Niacels
Can/Aus/UK:
Uses: Vitamin B-3
AAP: Not reviewed

Nicotinic acid, commonly called niacin, is a component of two coenzymes which function in oxidation-reduction reactions essential for tissue respiration. It is converted to nicotinamide in vivo. Although considered a vitamin, large doses(2-6 gm/day) are effective in reducing serum LDL cholesterol and triglyceride, and increasing serum HDL. Niacin is transferred into milk in concentrations of 1470 μg/L. RDA for females is 10-20 mg/day.[1,2] The concentration transferred into milk following high maternal doses has not been reported, but it is presumed that elevated maternal plasma levels may significantly elevate milk levels of niacin as well. Because niacin is known to be hepatotoxic in higher doses, breastfeeding mothers should not significantly exceed the RDA.[3]

Pregnancy Risk Category: A during 1st and 2nd trimesters
                                                                C during 3rd trimester

Lactation Risk Category: L3

Theoretic Infant Dose: 220.5 μg/kg/day

Adult Concerns: Flushing, peripheral dilation, itching, nausea, bloating, flatulence, vomiting. In high doses, some abnormal liver function tests.

Pediatric Concerns: None reported via milk, but do not exceed RDA.

Drug Interactions: Niacin may produce fluctuations in blood glucose levels and interfere with oral hypoglycemics. May inhibit uricosuric effects of sylfinpyrazone and probenecid. Increased toxicity(myopathy) when used with lovastatin and other cholesterol-lowering drugs.

Alternatives:

Adult Dosage: 10-20 mg daily

T½ = 45 minutes	M/P =
PHL=	PB =
PK = 45 minutes	Oral = Complete
MW = 123	pKa = 4.85
Vd =	

References:
1. Lacy C. et.al. Drug information handbook. Lexi-Comp, Hudson(Cleveland), Oh. 1996.
2. Drug Facts and Comparisons. 1996. ed. Facts and Comparisons, St. Louis.
3. Lawrence RA. Breastfeeding. A guide for the medical profession. Mosby, St.Louis, Fourth Edition, p.132. 1994.

NIFEDIPINE

Trade: Adalat, Procardia
Can/Aus/UK: Adalat, Apo-Nifed, Nefensar XL, Nifecard, Novo-Nifedin, Nu-Nifed, Nyefax
Uses: Antihypertensive calcium channel blocker
AAP: Approved by the American Academy of Pediatrics for use in breastfeeding mothers

Nifedipine is an effective antihypertensive. It belongs to the calcium channel blocker family of drugs. Two studies indicate that nifedipine is transferred to breastmilk in varying but generally low levels. In one study in which the dose was varied from 10-30 mg three times daily, the highest concentration (53.35 μg/L) was measured at 1 hour after a 30 mg dose.[1] Other levels reported were 16.35 μg/L 60 minutes after a 20 mg dose and 12.89 μg/L 30 minutes after a 10 mg dose. The milk levels fell linearly with the milk half-lives estimated to be 1.4 hours for the 10 mg dose, 3.1 hours for the 20 dose, and 2.4 hours for the 30 mg dose. The milk concentration measured 8 hours following a 30 mg dose was 4.93 μg/L. In this study, using the highest concentration found and a daily intake of 150 mL/kg of human milk, the amount of nifedipine intake would only be 8 μg/kg/day (less than 5% of the therapeutic pediatric dose). The authors conclude that the amount ingested via breastmilk poses little risk to an infant.

In another study, concentrations of nifedipine in human milk 1 to 8 hours after 10 mg doses varied from <1 to 10.3 μg/L (median 3.5 μg/L) in six of eleven patients.[2] In this study, milk levels three days after discontinuing medication ranged from < 1 to 9.4 μg/L. The authors concluded the exposure to nifedipine through breastmilk is not significant. In a study by Penny and Lewis, following a maternal dose of 20 mg nifedipine daily for 10 days, peak breastmilk levels at 1 hour were 46 μg/L.[3] The corresponding maternal serum level was 43 μg/L. From this data the authors suggest a daily intake for an infant would be approximately 6.45 μg/kg/day.

Nifedipine has been found clinically useful for nipple vasospasm. Because of the similarity to Raynaud's Phenomonon, sustained release formulations providing 30-60 mg per day are suggested.

Pregnancy Risk Category: C

Lactation Risk Category: L2

Theoretic Infant Dose: 8.0 μg/kg/day

Adult Concerns: Headache, peripheral edema, gingival hyperplasia, hypotension. Distortion of smell and taste.

Pediatric Concerns: None reported via milk.

Drug Interactions: Barbiturates may reduce bioavailability of calcium channel blockers (CCB). Calcium salts may reduce hypotensive effect. Dantrolene may increase risk of hyperkalemia and myocardial depression. H2 blockers may increase bioavailability of certain CCBs. Hydantoins may reduce plasma levels. Quinidine increases risk of hypotension, bradycardia, tachycardia. Rifampin may reduce effects of CCBs. Vitamin D may reduce efficacy of CCBs. CCBs may increase carbamazepine, cyclosporin, encainide, prazosin levels.

Alternatives: Nimodipine

Adult Dosage: 10-20 mg TID

T½ = 1.8-7 hours	M/P = 1.0
PHL = 26.5(neonatal)	PB = 92-98%
PK = 45 min-4 hours.	Oral = 50%
MW = 346	pKa =
Vd =	

References:
1. Ehrenkranz RA, et. al. Nifedipine transfer into human milk. J Pediatr 114: 478-80, 1989.
2. Manninen AK, Juhakoski A. Nifedipine concentrations in maternal and umbilical serum, amniotic fluid, breast milk and urine of mothers and offspring. Int. J. Clin. Pharmacol. Res. 11(5):231-6, 1991.
3. Penny WJ, Lewis MJ: Nifedipine is excreted in human milk. Eur J Clin Pharmacol 1989; 36:427-428.

NIMODIPINE

Trade: Nimotop
Can/Aus/UK: Nemotop, Nimotop
Uses: Antihypertensive, calcium channel
AAP: Not reviewed

Nimodipine is a calcium channel blocker, although it is primarily used in preventing cerebral artery spasm and improving cerebral blood flow. Nimodipine is effective in reducing neurologic deficits following subarachnoid hemorrhage, acute stroke and severe head trauma. It is also useful in prophylaxis of migraine headaches.

In one study of a patient 3 days postpartum who received 60 mg every 4 hours for one week, breastmilk levels paralleled maternal serum levels with a milk/plasma ratio of approximately 0.33.[1] The highest milk concentration reported was approximately 3.5 μg/L while the maternal plasma was approximately 16 μg/L.

In another study (2), a 36 year old mother received a total dose of 46 mg I.V. over 24 hours. Nimodipine concentration in milk was much lower than in maternal serum, with a milk/serum ratio of 0.06 to 0.15. During I.V. infusion, nimodipine concentrations in milk raised initially to 2.2 μg/L and stabilized at concentrations between 0.87 and 1.6 μg/L of milk. Assuming a daily milk intake of 150 mg/kg, an infant would ingest approximately 0.063 to 0.705 μg/kg/day, or 0.008 to 0.092% of the weight-adjusted dose administered to the mother.

Pregnancy Risk Category: C

Lactation Risk Category: L2

Theoretic Infant Dose: 0.5 μg/kg/day

Adult Concerns: Hypotension, diarrhea, nausea, cramps.

Pediatric Concerns: None reported via milk in two studies.

Drug Interactions: When used with adenosine, prolonged bradycardia may result. Use with amiodarone may lead to sinus arrest and AV block. H2 blockers may increase bioavailability of nimodipine. Beta blockers may increase cardiac depression. May increase carbamazepine levels with admixed. May increase cyclosporine, digoxin, quinidine plasma levels. May increase theophylline effects. Used with fentanyl, it may increase hypotension.

Alternatives: Verapamil, Nifedipine

Adult Dosage: 60 mg q 4 hours

T½ = 9 hours	M/P = 0.06 to 0.33
PHL =	PB = 95%
PK = 1 hour	Oral = 13%
MW = 418	pKa =
Vd = 0.94	

References:

1. Tonks AM: Nimodipine levels in breast milk. NZ J Surg 65:693-694, 1995.
2. Carcas AJ. Abad-Santos F. de Rosendo JM. Frias J. Nimodipine transfer into human breast milk and cerebrospinal fluid. Annals of Pharmacotherapy. 30(2):148-50, 1996.

NISOLDIPINE

Trade: Sular
Can/Aus/UK: Syscor
Uses: Antihypertensive
AAP: Not reviewed

Nisoldipine is a typical calcium channel blocker antihypertensive.[1] No data are available on its transfer into human milk. For alternatives see nifedipine, and verapamil. Due to its poor oral bioavailability, presence of lipids which reduce its absorption, and high protein binding, it is unlikely to penetrate milk and be absorbed by the infant (undocumented).

Pregnancy Risk Category: C

Lactation Risk Category: L4

Theoretic Infant Dose:

Adult Concerns: Hypotension, bradycardia, peripheral edema.

Pediatric Concerns: None reported via milk. Observe for hypotension, sedation although unlikely.

Drug Interactions: Barbiturates may reduce bioavailability of calcium channel blockers (CCB). Calcium salts may reduce hypotensive effect. Dantrolene may increase risk of hyperkalemia and myocardial depression. H2 blockers may increase bioavailability of certain CCBs. Hydantoins may reduce plasma levels. Quinidine increases risk of hypotension, bradycardia, tachycardia. Rifampin may reduce effects of CCBs. Vitamin D may reduce efficacy of CCBs. CCBs may increase carbamazepine, cyclosporin, encainide, prazosin levels.

Alternatives: Nifedipine, Verapamil, Nimodipine

Adult Dosage: 20-40 mg QD

T½ = 7-12 hours	M/P =
PHL =	PB = 99%
PK = 6-12 hours	Oral = 5%
MW = 388	pKa =
Vd = 4	

References:
1. Pharmaceutical manufacturers package insert, 1998.

NITRAZEPAM

Trade: Mogadon
Can/Aus/UK: Alodorm, Atempol, Magadon, Mogadon, Nitrazadon, Nitrodos
Uses: Sedative, hypnotic
AAP: Not reviewed

Nitrazepam is a typical benzodiazepine (Valium family) used as a sedative. Nitrazepam is secreted into breastmilk and levels increase from day 1 to at least day 5 of therapy.[1] Oral bioavailability is good. Milk/plasma ratio 7 hours post-dose is low (0.27) . Estimated milk levels were 10-15 μg/L milk. No side-effects were reported in infants.

Pregnancy Risk Category:

Lactation Risk Category: L3

Theoretic Infant Dose: 2.3 μg/kg/day

Adult Concerns: Sedation, disorientation.

Pediatric Concerns: None reported, but observe for sedation.

Drug Interactions:

Alternatives: Alprazolam, Lorazepam

Adult Dosage: 5-10 mg QD

T½ = 30 hours	M/P = 0.27
PHL =	PB = 90%
PK = 0.5 - 5 hours	Oral = 53-94%
MW = 281	pKa = 3.2,10.8
Vd = 2-5	

References:
1. Matheson I, Lunde PK, and Bredesen JE. Midazolam and nitrazepam in the maternity ward: milk concentrations and clinical effects. Brit. J. Clin. Pharmacol. 30:787-93, 1990.

NITRENDIPINE

Trade: Baypress
Can/Aus/UK:
Uses: Calcium channel blocker, antihypertensive
AAP: Not reviewed

Nitrendipine is a typical calcium channel antihypertensive. It is secreted into breastmilk at peak concentrations ranging from 4.3 to 6.5 μg/L one to two hours after acute dosing of 10 mg.[1] After 5 days of continuous maternal dosing (20mg/day) the milk levels were approximately the same. Based on a maternal dose of 20mg/day, a newborn infant would ingest an average of 1.0-1.7 ug of nitrendipine per day (0.095% of maternal dose).

Pregnancy Risk Category:

Lactation Risk Category: L2

Theoretic Infant Dose: 1.0 μg/kg/day

Adult Concerns: Headache, hypotension, peripheral edema, cardiac arrhythmias, fatigue.

Pediatric Concerns: None reported via milk.

Drug Interactions: Barbiturates may reduce bioavailability of calcium channel blockers (CCB). Calcium salts may reduce hypotensive effect. Dantrolene may increase risk of hyperkalemia and myocardial depression. H2 blockers may increase bioavailability of certain CCBs. Hydantoins may reduce plasma levels. Quinidine increases risk of hypotension, bradycardia, tachycardia. Rifampin may reduce effects of CCBs. Vitamin D may reduce efficacy of CCBs. CCBs may increase carbamazepine, cyclosporin, encainide, prazosin levels.

Alternatives: Nifedipine, Nimodipine

Adult Dosage: 10-80 mg/day

T½ = 8-11 hours	M/P = 0.5-1.4
PHL=	PB = 98%
PK = 1-2 hours	Oral = 16-20%
MW = 360	pKa =
Vd =	

References:
1.   White WB, Yeh SC, and Krol GJ. Nitrendipine in human plasma and breast milk. Eur. J. Clin. Pharmacol. 36(5):531-4,1989.

NITROFURANTOIN

Trade: Furadantin, Macrodantin, Furan, Macrobid
Can/Aus/UK: Apo-Nitrofurantoin, Furadantin, Macrodantin, Nephronex
Uses: Urinary antibiotic
AAP: Approved by the American Academy of Pediatrics for use in breastfeeding mothers

Nitrofurantoin is an old urinary tract antimicrobial. It is secreted in breastmilk but in very small amounts. In one study of 20 women receiving 100 mg four times daily, none was detected in milk.[1]   In another group of nine nursing women who received 100-200 mg every

6 hours, nitrofurantoin was undetectable in the milk of those treated with 100 mg and only trace amounts were found in those treated with 200 mg (0.3-0.5 mg/L milk).[2] In these two patients the milk/plasma ratio ranged from 0.27 to 0.31.

In a well-done study of 4 breastfeeding mothers who ingested 100 mg nitrofurantoin with a meal, the milk/plasma ratio averaged 6.21 suggesting an active transfer into milk.[3] Regardless of an active transfer, the average milk concentration throughout the day was only 1.3 mg/L. The estimated dose an infant would ingest was 0.2 mg/kg/day or 6% of the weight-adjusted maternal dose. The therapeutic dose administered to infants is 5-7 mg/kg/day.

Use with caution in infants with G6PD or in infants less than 1 month of age with hyperbilirubinemia, due to displacement of bilirubin from albumin binding sites.

Pregnancy Risk Category: B

Lactation Risk Category: L2

Theoretic Infant Dose: 0.2 mg/kg/day

Adult Concerns: Nausea, vomiting, brown urine, hemolytic anemia, hepatotoxicity.

Pediatric Concerns: None reported via milk, however, do not use in infants with G6PD or in infants less than 1 month of age.

Drug Interactions: Anticholinergics increase nitrofurantoin bioavailability by delaying gastric emptying and increasing absorption. Magnesium salts may delay or decrease absorption. Uricosurics may increase nitrofurantoin levels by decreasing renal clearance.

Alternatives:

Adult Dosage: 50-100 mg QID

T½ = 20-58 minutes	M/P = 0.27-6.2
PHL =	PB = 20-60%
PK = Variable	Oral = 94%
MW = 238	pKa = 7.2
Vd =	

References:
1. Hosbach RE, Foster RB. Absence of nitrofurantoin from human milk. JAMA 202:1057, 1967.
2. Varsano I, et. al. The excretion of orally ingested nitrofurantoin in human milk. J Pediatr 82:886-7, 1973.
3. Gerk PM, Kuhn RJ, Desai NS, McNamara PJ. Active transport of nitrofurantoin into human milk. Pharmacotherapy. 21(6):669-75, 2001.

NITROGLYCERIN, NITRATES, NITRITES

Trade: Nitrostat, Nitrolingual, Nitrogard, Amyl Nitrite, Nitrong, Nitro-Bid, Nitroglyn, Minitran, Nitro-Dur
Can/Aus/UK: Anginine, Deponit, Nitradisc, Nitro-Dur, Nitrol, Nitrolingual Spray, Nitrong SR, Transderm-Nitro
Uses: Vasodilator
AAP: Not reviewed

Nitroglycerin is a rapid and short acting vasodilator used in angina and other cardiovascular problems including congestive heart failure. Nitroglycerin, as well as numerous other formulations (amyl nitrate, isorbide dinitrate, etc) all work by release of the nitrite and nitrate molecule. Nitrates come in numerous formulations, some for acute use (sublingual), others are more sustained (Nitro-Dur). Nitrates and Nitrites are derived from multiple sources, including medications in the form of nitroglycerin, or isorbide dinitrate, or from food and water sources. Elevated nitrate levels in drinking water in the USA is common in rural areas. Numerous cases of nitrate-induced methemoglobinemia have been reported in infants exposed to well water with high levels of nitrates when they were fed foods/formulas prepared with contaminated water. Only one case of a breastfed infant has been reported and it is questionable.[1] Thus far it is less certain that the oral ingestion of nitrates can penetrate into human milk in clinically relevant amounts.

Two studies suggest that while nitrates/nitrites are well absorbed orally in the mother (approx. 50%), little seems to be transported to human milk. In a study by Dusdieker,[2] following a mean total nitrate intake from diet and water of 46.6, 168.1, and 272 mg/day, milk levels only averaged 4.4, 5.1, and 5.2 mg/L respectively. Thus higher maternal intake did not necessarily correlate with higher milk levels. The authors conclude that mothers who ingest nitrate of 100 mg/day or less do not produce milk with elevated nitrate levels.

In a study by Green,[3] milk levels were not different from maternal plasma levels. Thus it is apparent that even at relatively high rates of ingestion, nitrate levels do not concentrate in milk, and may not be high enough to harm an infant. However, these studies were done using nitrates in water, and may not correlate with the ingestion of high and prolonged concentrations of nitrates from medications administered orally, buccally, or transcutaneously. No studies have been found comparing milk nitrates with oral nitroglycerine or isorbide dinitrate.

While it is apparent that milk levels are not high following the ingestion of oral nitrates, infants younger than 6 months are most at risk from nitrate intoxication because of their susceptibility to methemoglobinemia.[4]

In another study of 59 women living in regions with high nitrate levels, breastmilk levels of nitrates and nitrities were 2.83 mg/L and 0.46 mg/L respectively, while those living in low nitrate regions were 2.75 mg/L and 0.32 mg/L respectively.[5] They were not significantly different. Breastfeed with caution at higher doses and with prolonged exposure. Observe the infant for methemoglobinemia.

Pregnancy Risk Category: C

Lactation Risk Category: L4

Theoretic Infant Dose:

Adult Concerns: Postural hypotension, flushing, headache, weakness, drug rash, exfoliative dermatitis, bradycardia, nausea, vomiting, methemoglobinemia (overdose), sweating.

Pediatric Concerns: None are reported via milk. Observe for methemoglobinemia.

Drug Interactions: I.V. nitroglycerin may counteract the effects of heparin. Increased toxicity when used with alcohol, beta-blockers. Calcium channel blockers may increase hypotensive effect of nitrates.

Alternatives:

Adult Dosage: 1.3-6.5 mg BID

T½ = 1-4 minutes	M/P =
PHL=	PB = 60%
PK = 2-20 minutes	Oral = Complete
MW = 227	pKa =
Vd =	

References:

1. Donahoe WE. Cyanosis in infants with nitrates in drinking water as a cause. Pediatrics 3:308, 1949.
2. Dusdieker LB, Stumbo PJ, Kross BC, et al. Does increased nitrate ingestion elevate nitrate levels in human milk? Arch Pediatr Adolesc Med 150:311-4, 1996.
3. Green LC, Tannenbaum SR, Fox JG. Nitrate in human and canine milk. N Engl J Med 306:1367-8, 1982.
4. Johnson CJ, Kross BC. Continuing importance of nitrate contamination of groundwater and wells in rural areas. Am J Ind Med 18:449-56, 1990.
5. Paszkowski T, Sikorski R, Kozak A, Kowalski B, Jakubik J. [Contamination of human milk with nitrates and nitrites] Pol Tyg Lek. 13-27;44(46-48):961-3, 1989. Polish.

NITROPRUSSIDE

Trade: Nitropress
Can/Aus/UK: Nipride
Uses: Hypotensive agent
AAP: Not reviewed

Nitroprusside is a rapid acting hypotensive agent of short duration (1-10 minutes). Besides rapid hypotension, nitroprusside is converted metabolically to cyanogen (cyanide radical) which is potentially toxic. Although rare, significant thiocyanate toxicity can occur at higher doses (> 2 µg/kg/min.) and longer durations of exposure (> 1-2 days).[1] When administered orally, nitroprusside is reported to not be active, although one report suggests a modest hypotensive effect. No data are available on transfer of nitroprusside nor thiocyanate into human milk. The half-life of the thiocyanate metabolite is approximately 3 days. Because the thiocyanate metabolite is orally bioavailable, some caution is advised if the mother has received nitroprusside for more than 24 hours.[2]

Pregnancy Risk Category: C

Lactation Risk Category: L4

Theoretic Infant Dose:

Adult Concerns: Hypotension, methemoglobinemia, headache, drowsiness, cyanide toxicity, hypothyroidism, nausea, vomiting.

Pediatric Concerns: None reported but caution is urged due to thiocyanate metabolite.

Drug Interactions: Clonidine may potentiate the hypotensive effect of nitroprusside. May reduce Iodine-131 uptake and induce hypothyroidism.

Alternatives:

Adult Dosage: 0.3-10 mcg/kg/minute X 10 minutes

T½	= 3-4 minutes	M/P	=
PHL	=	PB	=
PK	= 1-2 minutes	Oral	= Poor
MW	=	pKa	=
Vd	=		

References:

1. Page IH, Corcoran AC et.al. : Cardiovascular actions of sodium nitroprusside in animals and hypertensive patients. Circulation 1:188-198, 1955.
2. Benitz WE, Malachowski N, et al: Use of sodium nitroprusside in neonates: efficacy and safety. J Pediatr 106:102-110, 1985.

NITROUS OXIDE

Trade:
Can/Aus/UK: Entonox
Uses: Anesthetic gas
AAP: Not reviewed

Nitrous oxide is a weak anesthetic gas. It provides good analgesia and a weak anesthesia. It is rapidly eliminated from the body due to rapid exchange with nitrogen via the pulmonary alveoli (within minutes).[1] A rapid recovery generally occurs in 3-5 minutes. Due to poor lipid solubility, uptake by adipose tissue is relatively poor, and only insignificant traces of nitrous oxide circulate in blood after discontinuing inhalation of the gas. No data exists on the entry of nitrous oxide into human milk. Ingestion of nitrous oxide orally via milk is unlikely. Chronic exposure may lead to elevated risks of fetal malformations, abortions, and bone marrow toxicity (particular in dental care workers).[2]

Pregnancy Risk Category:

Lactation Risk Category: L3

Theoretic Infant Dose:

Adult Concerns: Chronic exposure can produce bone marrow suppression, headaches, hypotension and bradycardia.

Pediatric Concerns: None reported via milk.

Drug Interactions:

Alternatives:

Adult Dosage: Inhalation 30% with 70% oxygen

T½ = < 3 minutes	M/P =
PHL=	PB =
PK = 15 min.	Oral = Poor
MW = 44	pKa =
Vd =	

References:
1.   General Anesthetics.   In: Drug Evaluations Annual 1995.   American Medical Association, 1995.
2.   Adriani J. General Anesthetics. In: Clinical Management of Poisoning and Drug Overdose.pp. 762-3, W.B.Saunders & Co.1983.

NIZATIDINE

Trade: Axid
Can/Aus/UK: Apo-Nizatidine, Axid, Tazac
Uses: Reduces gastric acid secretion
AAP: Not reviewed

Nizatidine is an antisecretory, histamine-2 antagonist that reduces stomach acid secretion. In one study of 5 lactating women using a dose of 150 mg, milk levels of nizatidine were directly proportional to circulating maternal serum levels, yet were very low.[1] Over a 12 hour period 96 ug (less than 0.1% of dose) was secreted into the milk. No effects on infant have been reported.

Pregnancy Risk Category: C

Lactation Risk Category: L2

Theoretic Infant Dose:

Adult Concerns: Headache, GI distress.

Pediatric Concerns: None reported.

Drug Interactions: Elevated salicylate levels may occur when nizatidine is used with high doses of salicylates.

Alternatives: Famotidine

Adult Dosage: 150-300 mg QD

T½ = 1.5 hours	M/P =
PHL =	PB = 35%
PK = 0.5-3 hours	Oral = 94%
MW = 331	pKa =
Vd =	

References:
1. Obermeyer BD, Bergstrom RF, Callaghan JT, et.al. Secretion of nizatidine into human breast milk after single and multiple doses. Clin.Pharmacol.Ther. 47:724-30,1990.

NORETHINDRONE

Trade: Aygestin, Norlutate, Micronor, Nor-q.d.
Can/Aus/UK: Brevinor, Micronor, Norethisterone, Norlutate
Uses: Progestin for oral contraceptives.
AAP: Not reviewed

Norethindrone is a typial synthetic progestational agent that is used for oral contraception and other endocrine functions. It is believed to be secreted into breastmilk in small amounts. It produces a dose-dependent suppression of lactation at higher doses, although somewhat minimal at lower doses. It may reduce lactose content and reduce overall milk volume and nitrogen/protein content, resulting in lower infant weight gain, although these effects are unlikely if doses are kept low.[1-5] Progestin-only mini pills are preferred oral contraceptives in breastfeeding mothers.

Pregnancy Risk Category: X

Lactation Risk Category: L1

Theoretic Infant Dose:

Adult Concerns: Changes in menstruation, breakthrough bleeding, nausea, abdominal pain, edema, breast tenderness.

Pediatric Concerns: None reported via milk.

Drug Interactions: Rifampin may reduce the plasma level of norethindrone possibly decreasing its effect.

Alternatives:

Adult Dosage: 0.35-5 mg QD

T½ = 4-13 hours.	M/P =
PHL=	PB = 97%
PK = 1-2 hours.	Oral = 60%
MW = 298	pKa =
Vd =	

References:

1. Kora SJ. Effect of oral contraceptives on lactation. Fertil Steril 20:419-23, 1969.
2. Miller GH & Hughes LR: Lactation and genital involution effects of a new low-dose oral contraceptive on breast-feeding mothers and their infants. Obstet Gynecol 35:44-50, 1970.
3. Karim M, Ammarr R, El-Mahgoubh S et al: Injected progestogen and lactation. Br Med J 1:200-203, 1971.
4. Lonnerdal B, Forsum E & Hambraeus L: Effect of oral contraceptives on composition and volume of breast milk. Am. J. Clin. Nutr 33:816-824, 1980.
5. Laukaran VH. The effects of contraceptive use on the initiation and duration of lactation. Int J Gynecol Obstet. 25(suppl)129-142, 1987

NORETHYNODREL

Trade: Enovid
Can/Aus/UK:
Uses: Progestational agent
AAP: Approved by the American Academy of Pediatrics for use in breastfeeding mothers

Norethynodrel is a synthetic progestational agent used in oral contraceptives. Limited or no effects on infant. May decrease volume of breastmilk to some degree if therapy initiated too soon after birth and if dose is too high.[1-3]   See norethindrone, medroxyprogesterone.

Pregnancy Risk Category: X

Lactation Risk Category: L2

Theoretic Infant Dose:

Adult Concerns: Changes in menstruation, breakthrough bleeding, nausea, abdominal pain, edema, breast tenderness.

Pediatric Concerns: None reported. May suppress lactation.

Drug Interactions:

Alternatives:

Adult Dosage:

T½ =	M/P =
PHL=	PB =
PK =	Oral =
MW = 298	pKa =
Vd =	

References:
1. Booker DE, Pahyl IR. Control of postpartum breast engorgement with oral contraceptives. Am J Obstet Gynecol 98:1099-1101, 1967.
2. Laukaran VH. The effects of contraceptive use on the initiation and duration of lactation. Int J Gynecol Obstet. 25(suppl)129-142, 1987
3. Kora SJ. Effect of oral contraceptives on lactation. Fertil Steril 20:419-23, 1969.

NORFLOXACIN

Trade: Noroxin
Can/Aus/UK: Noroxin
Uses: Fluoroquinolone antibiotic
AAP: Not reviewed

Norfloxacin is a second-generation fluoroquinolone antimicrobial. The fluoroquinolone family is known to produce arthropathy in neonatal animals, and has been reported to do so in at least three children with cystic fibrosis who received oral dosing. Pseudomembranous colitis has been reported in one breastfed infant whose mother consumed another fluoroquinolone, ciprofloxacin.[1]

Although other members in the fluoroquinolone family are secreted into breastmilk (see ciprofloxacin, ofloxacin), only limited data are available on this drug. Wise (1984)[2] has suggested that norfloxacin is not present in breastmilk. The manufacturer's product information states that doses of 200 mg do not produce detectable concentrations in milk[3], although this was a single dose. Of the fluoroquinolone family, norfloxacin, levofloxacin, or perhaps ofloxacin, may be preferred over others for use in a breastfeeding mother.

Pregnancy Risk Category: C

Lactation Risk Category: L3

Theoretic Infant Dose:

Adult Concerns: Nausea, vomiting, GI dyspepsia, depression, dizziness, pseudomembranous colitis in pediatric patients.

Pediatric Concerns: None reported via milk. Observe for diarrhea.

Drug Interactions: Decreased absorption with antacids. Quinolones cause increased levels of caffeine, warfarin, cyclosporine, theophylline. Cimetidine, probenecid, azlocillin increase norfloxacin levels. Increased risk of seizures when used with foscarnet.

Alternatives: Ofloxacin, Levofloxacin

Adult Dosage: 400 mg BID

T½ = 3.3 hours	M/P =
PHL =	PB = 20%
PK = 1-2 hours	Oral = 30-40%
MW = 319	pKa =
Vd =	

References:
1. Harmon T, Burkhart G, and Applebaum H. Perforated pseudomembranous colitis in the breast-fed infant. J. Ped. Surg. 27:744-6,1992.
2. Wise R: Norfloxacin - a review of pharmacology and tissue penetration. J Antimicrob Chemother 13:59-64, 1984.
3. Pharmaceutical Manufacturers Package Insert, 1999

NORTRIPTYLINE

Trade: Aventyl, Pamelor
Can/Aus/UK: Allegron, Apo-Nortriptyline, Aventyl, Norventyl
Uses: Tricyclic antidepressant
AAP: Drug whose effect on nursing infants is unknown but may be of concern

Nortriptyline (NT) is a tricyclic antidepressant and is the active metabolite of amitriptyline (Elavil). In one patient receiving 125 mg or nortriptyline at bedtime, milk concentrations of NT averaged 180 μg/L after 6-7 days of administration.[1] Based on these concentrations, the authors estimate that the average daily infant exposure would be 27 μg/kg/d. The relative dose in milk would be 2.3% of the maternal dose. Several other authors have been unable to detect NT in maternal milk nor the serum of infants after prolonged exposure.[2,3] So far no untoward effects have been noted.

Pregnancy Risk Category: D

Lactation Risk Category: L2

Theoretic Infant Dose: 27.0 μg/kg/day

Adult Concerns: Sedation, dry mouth, constipation, urinary retention, blurred vision.

Pediatric Concerns: None reported in several studies.

Drug Interactions: Phenobarbital may reduce effect of nortriptyline. Nortriptyline blocks the hypotensive effect of guanethidine. May increase toxicity of nortriptyline when used with clonidine. Dangerous when used with MAO inhibitors, other CNS depressants. May increase anticoagulant effect of coumadin, warfarin. SSRIs (Prozac, Zoloft,etc) should not be used with or soon after nortriptyline or other TCAs due to serotonergic crisis.

Alternatives: Imipramine

Adult Dosage: 25 mg TID-QID

T½ = 16-90 hours	M/P = 0.87-3.71
PHL =	PB = 92%
PK = 7-8.5 hours	Oral = 51%
MW = 263	pKa = 9.7
Vd = 20-57	

References:
1. Matheson I, Skjaeraasen J. Milk concentrations of flupenthixol, nortriptyline, and zuclopenthixol and between-breast differences in two patients. Eur. J. Clin. Pharmacol. 35:217-20,1988.
2. Wisner KS and Perel J. Serum nortriptyline levels in nursing mothers and

their infants. Am. J. Psychiatry 148(9):1234-1236, 1991.
3. Brixen-Rasmussen L, Halgrener J, Jergensen A. Amitriptyline and nortriptyline excretion in human breast milk. Psychopharmacology 76:94-95, 1982.

NYSTATIN

Trade: Mycostatin, Nilstat
Can/Aus/UK: Candistatin, Mycostatin, Nadostine, Nilstat, Nystan
Uses: Antifungal
AAP: Not reviewed

Nystatin is an antifungal primarily used for candidiasis topically and orally. The oral absorption of nystatin is extremely poor, and plasma levels are undetectible after oral administration.[1]   The likelihood of secretion into milk is remote due to poor maternal absorption. It is frequently administered directly to neonates in neonatal units for candidiasis. In addition, absorption into infant circulation equally unlikely. Dose: neonates= 100,000 units; children=200,000 units, 400,000-600,000 units in older children, administered four times daily. Current studies suggest that resistance to nystatin is growing and approaches 45% of candida strains.

Pregnancy Risk Category: B

Lactation Risk Category: L1

Theoretic Infant Dose:

Adult Concerns: Bad taste, diarrhea, nausea, vomiting.

Pediatric Concerns: None reported. Nystatin is commonly used in infants.

Drug Interactions:

Alternatives: Fluconazole

Adult Dosage: 500,000-1 million units TID

T½ =	M/P =
PHL=	PB =
PK =	Oral = Poor
MW =	pKa =
Vd =	

References:
1. Rothermel P, Faber M. Drugs in breast milk: a consumer's guide. Birth and Family J 2:76-78, 1975.

OCTREOTIDE ACETATE and 111-INDIUM OCTREOTIDE

Trade: Sandostatin Lar, OctreoScan
Can/Aus/UK:
Uses: Somatostatin analog
AAP: Radioactive compound that requires temporary cessation of breastfeeding.

Octreotide (Sandostatin LAR) is a long acting form consisting of microspheres containing octreotide. Octreotide is a close analog of and provides activity similar to the natural hormone somatostatin. Like somatostatin, it also suppresses LH response to GnRH, decreases splanchnic blood flow, and inhibits release of serotonin, gastrin, vasoactive intestinal peptide, secretin, motilin, and pancreatic polypeptide. It is used to treat acromegaly and carcinoid tumors. This product, if present in milk, would not likely be absorbed to any degree.

Radioactive 111-Indium Octreotide (OctreoScan):
OctreoScan® is an imaging agent that can help find primary and metastatic neuroendocrine tumors. The concentration of radioactive octreotide in breastmilk in a 10 weeks postpartum woman was measured at daily intervals for three days after injection of 5.3 mCi (196 MBq) of 111-Indium-octreotide (OctreoScan).[1] The disappearance of radiolabelled octreotide from the breastmilk exhibited a bi-exponential pattern with a maximum concentration of 14.2 nCi (0.54 kBq) per 125 ml feeding at 4 h. The maximum reading was 8.3 mrem x h(-1) (0.83 mSv x h(-1)) immediately after administration. This decreased rapidly (85%) due to rapid urinary clearance by 24 h.

Breastmilk content of radio-active octreotide and external surveys at the breast surface were determined at 3 h intervals for up to 10 days. Assuming an infant is breastfed for the first 10 days following therapy, the internal and external dose equivalents would be 22.97 mrem (0.23 mSv) and 27.86 mrem (0.28 mSv), respectively, for a total of 50.83 mrem (0.5 mSv). In this paper, the patient resumed breast-feeding on day 10, when the newborn received a total dose equivalent of 1.55 mrem (0.016 mSv). The 10 day waiting period used in this study was based on very conservative assumptions, and assumed 100% of the ingested 111-In is orally bioavailable. However, oral indium has been shown to be poorly absorbed from the gastrointestinal tract (approximately 0.15%), which suggests the infant's dose could be considerably less. The authors suggest that a briefer interruption deserves attention.

Pregnancy Risk Category: B

Lactation Risk Category: L3
L4 for radioactive product

Theoretic Infant Dose:

Adult Concerns: May inhibit gallbladder contractility and decrease bile secretion. Hypoglycemia or hyperglycemia, hypothyroidism may result. Bradycardia, arrhythmias in acromegalic patients. Numerous other adverse effects, consult package insert.

Pediatric Concerns: None reported via milk.

Drug Interactions: May reduce absorption of cyclosporin and other drugs by altering oral absorption. Patients receiving insulin, oral hypoglycemic agents, beta blockers, and other drugs may require dosage adjustment of these therapeutic agents.

Alternatives:

Adult Dosage: 50 mg TID (non-depo form)

T½ = 1.7 hours	M/P =
PHL =	PB = 65%
PK = 0.4 hours	Oral = Nil
MW = 1019	pKa =
Vd = 13.6	

References:
1. Castronovo FP Jr, Stone H, Ulanski J. Radioactivity in breast milk following 111In-octreotide. Nucl Med Commun. 21(7):695-9, 2000.

OFLOXACIN

Trade: Floxin
Can/Aus/UK: Floxin, Ocuflox, Tarivid
Uses: Fluoroquinoline antibiotic
AAP: Approved by the American Academy of Pediatrics for use in breastfeeding mothers

Ofloxacin is a typical fluoroquinolone antimicrobial. Breastmilk concentrations are reported equal to maternal plasma levels. In one study in lactating women who received 400 mg oral doses twice daily, drug concentrations in breastmilk averaged 0.05-2.41 mg/L in milk (24 hours and 2 hours post-dose respectively).[1] The drug was still detectable in milk 24 hours after a dose. The fluoroquinolone family is known to produce arthropathy in neonatal animals, and has been reported to do so in at least three children with cystic fibrosis who received high oral doses. However, it is extremely unlikely that arthropathy would ensue following the dose received via milk. The only likely risk is change in gut flora, diarrhea and a remote risk of overgrowth of C. Difficile. Ofloxacin levels in breastmilk are consistently lower (37%) than ciprofloxacin. If a fluoroquinolone is required, ofloxacin, levofloxacin, or norfloxacin are probably the better choices for breastfeeding mothers.

Pregnancy Risk Category: C

Lactation Risk Category: L3

Theoretic Infant Dose: 0.4 mg/kg/day

Adult Concerns: Nausea, vomiting, diarrhea, abdominal cramps, GI bleeding.

Pediatric Concerns: None reported, but caution recommended. Observe for diarrhea.

Drug Interactions: Decreased absorption with antacids. Quinolones cause increased levels of caffeine, warfarin, cyclosporine, theophylline. Cimetidine, probenecid, azlocillin may increase ofloxacin levels. Increased risk of seizures when used with foscarnet.

Alternatives: Norfloxacin, Trovafloxacin

Adult Dosage: 200-400 mg BID

T½ = 5-7 hours	M/P = 0.98-1.66
PHL =	PB = 32%
PK = 0.5-2 hours	Oral = 98 %
MW = 361	pKa =
Vd = 1.4	

References:
1. Giamarellou H, Kolokythas E, Petrikkos G, et.al. Pharmacokinetics of three newer quinolones in pregnant and lactating women. Amer. Jour. of Med. 87:5A-49S-51S, 1989.

OLANZAPINE

Trade: Zyprexa
Can/Aus/UK: Zyprexa
Uses: Antipsychotic
AAP: Not reviewed

Olanzapine is a typical antipsychotic agent structurally similar to clozapine and may be used for treating schizophrenia.[1] It is rather unusual in that it blocks serotonin receptors rather than dopamine receptors.

Preliminary unpublished data from Ilett et.al. suggests that the relative infant dose will be approximately 1.05 +/-0.05% of the maternal dose.[2] In a patient receiving 15 mg/d the average milk level (AUC) was 9.3 μg/L and a milk/plasma ratio of 0.35. The highest milk level observed in this patient was 18 μg/L at 6 hours after dose.

Another case of its use in a lactating women has been briefly mentioned.

No levels were reported but it did not produce complications in the infant.[3]

Pregnancy Risk Category: C

Lactation Risk Category: L3

Theoretic Infant Dose: 2.7 μg/kg/day

Adult Concerns: Agitation, dizziness, somnolence, constipation, weight gain, elevated liver enzymes.

Pediatric Concerns: None reported. Use with caution.

Drug Interactions: Ethanol may potentiate the effects of olanzapine. Fluvoxamine may inhibit olanzapine metabolism. Carbamazepine may increase clearance of olanzapine by 50%. Levodopa may antagonize the effect of olanzapine.

Alternatives: Haloperidol

Adult Dosage: 5-10 mg QD

T½ = 21-54 hours	M/P =
PHL =	PB = 93%
PK = 5-8 hours	Oral = >57%
MW =	pKa =
Vd = 14.3	

References:
1. Pharmaceutical Manufacturers Package Insert, 1997.
2. Ilett KF. Personnal communication, 2001.
3. Goldstein DJ, Corbin LA, Fung MC. Olanzapine-exposed pregnancies and lactation: early experience. J Clin Psychopharmacol. 20(4):399-403, 2000.

OLSALAZINE

Trade: Dipentum
Can/Aus/UK: Dipentum
Uses: Anti-inflammatory
AAP: Not reviewed

Olsalazine is converted to 5-aminosalicylic acid (mesalamine:5-ASA) in the gut which has anti-inflammatory activity in ulcerative colitis.[1] After oral administration, only 2.4% is systemically absorbed, while the majority is metabolized in the GI tract to 5-ASA. 5-ASA is slowly and poorly absorbed. Plasma levels are exceedingly small (1.6-6.2 mmol/L), the half-life very short, and protein binding is very high. In rodents fed up to 20 times the normal dose, olsalazine produced growth retardation in pups. In one study of a mother who received a single 500 mg dose of olsalazine, acetylated-5-ASA achieved concentrations of 0.6, 0.86, and 1.24 μmol/L in breastmilk at 10, 14, and 24 hours respectively.[2] Olsalazine, olsalazine-S, and 5-ASA were undetectable in breastmilk. While clinically significant levels in milk are remote, infants should be closely monitored for gastric changes such as diarrhea.

Pregnancy Risk Category: C

Lactation Risk Category: L3

Theoretic Infant Dose: 62.3 μg/kg/day

Adult Concerns: Watery diarrhea, dyspepsia, diarrhea, nausea, pain/cramping, headache,

Pediatric Concerns: None specifically reported with this product, but observe for diarrhea and cramping if used for longer periods.

Drug Interactions:

Alternatives:

Adult Dosage: 500 mg BID

T½ = 0.9 hours	M/P =
PHL=	PB = > 99%
PK = 1-2 hours	Oral = 2.4% (olsalazine)
MW = 346	pKa =
Vd =	

References:
1. Drug Facts and Comparisons. 1995 ed. Facts and Comparisons, St. Louis.
2. Miller LG, Hopkinson JM, Motil KJ et al: Disposition of olsalazine and metabolites in breast milk. J Clin Pharmacol 33(8):703-706, 1993.

OMEPRAZOLE

Trade: Prilosec
Can/Aus/UK: Losec, Prilosec
Uses: Reduces gastric acid secretion
AAP: Not reviewed

Omeprazole is a potent inhibitor of gastric acid secretion. In a study of one patient receiving 20 mg omeprazole daily, the maternal serum concentration was negligible until 90 minutes after ingestion and then reached 950 nM at 240 min.[1] The breastmilk concentration of omeprazole began to rise minimally at 90 minutes after ingestion, but peaked after 180 minutes at only 58 nM, or less than 7% of the highest serum level. Omeprazole milk levels were essentially flat over 4 hours of observation.

Omeprazole is extremely acid labile with a half-life of 10 minutes at pH values below 4.[2] Virtually all omeprazole ingested via milk would probably be destroyed in the stomach of the infant prior to absorption.

Pregnancy Risk Category: C

Lactation Risk Category: L2

Theoretic Infant Dose:

Adult Concerns: Headache, diarrhea, elevated liver enzymes.

Pediatric Concerns: None reported via milk in one case.

Drug Interactions: Administration of Omeprazole and clarithromycin may result in increased plasma levels of omeprazole. Omeprazole produced a 130% increase in the half-life of diazepam, reduced the plasma clearance of phenytoin by 15%, and increased phenytoin half-life by 27%. May prolong the elimination of warfarin.

Alternatives: Famotidine, Nizatidine

Adult Dosage: 20 mg BID

T½ = 1 hour	M/P =
PHL =	PB = 95%
PK = 0.5-3.5 hours	Oral = 30-40%
MW = 345	pKa =
Vd =	

References:
1.   Marshall JK, Thompson AB, Armstrong D. Omeprazole for refractory gastroesophageal reflux disease during pregnancy and lactation. Can J Gastroenterol. 12(3):225-7, 1998.
2.   Pilbrant A, Cederberg C.   Development of an oral formulation of omeprazole. Scand J Gastroenterol Suppl. 108:113-20, 1985.

ONDANSETRON

Trade: Zofran
Can/Aus/UK: Zofran
Uses: Antiemetic
AAP: Not reviewed

Ondasetron is used clinically for reducing the nausea and vomiting associated with chemotherapy. It has occasionally been used during pregnancy without effect on the fetus.[1,2]   It is available for oral and I.V. administration. Ondasetron is secreted in animal milk, but no data on humans is available. Four studies of ondasetron use in pediatric patients 4-18 years of age are available.

Pregnancy Risk Category: B

Lactation Risk Category: L2

Theoretic Infant Dose:

Adult Concerns: Headache, drowsiness, malaise, clonic-tonic seizures, and constipation.

Pediatric Concerns: None reported via milk.

Drug Interactions: The clearance and half-life of ondansetron may be changed when used with barbiturates, carbamazepine, rifampin, phenytoin.

Alternatives:

Adult Dosage: 8 mg BID

T½ = 3.6 hours.	M/P =
PHL= 2.7 hours.	PB = 70-76%
PK = 1.7 ,3.1 (IV,PO)	Oral = 56-66%
MW = 293	pKa =
Vd =	

References:
1. Pharmaceutical Manufacturers Package Insert, 1996.
2. Spratto GR, Woods AL. In: Nurse's Drug Reference. Delmar Publishers Inc. Albany, NY, 1995.

ORAL CONTRACEPTIVES

Trade: Norinyl, Norlestin, Oral Contraceptives, Ortho-Novum, Ovral
Can/Aus/UK: Brevinor, Cilest, Nornyl
Uses: Contraceptive
AAP: Approved by the American Academy of Pediatrics for use in breastfeeding mothers.

Oral contraceptives, particularly those containing estrogens, tend to reduce lactose production, hence reducing volume of milk produced.[1] Quality (fat content) may similarly be reduced, although one recent study of the fat, energy, protein, and lactose concentration in milk of mothers using oral contraceptives showed no effect of contraceptives.[4] The earlier oral contraceptives are started, the greater the negative effect on lactation.[2,3] Suppression of breastmilk production with estrogen-progestin contraceptives is well known, is more prevalent early postpartum, and is common. Although it was previously believed that waiting for 6 weeks would preclude breastfeeding problems, this is apparently not accurate. Numerous examples of supply problems have occurred months postpartum in some patients. Suggest that the mother establish a good flow (60-90 days) prior to beginning oral contraceptives. If necessary, use only LOW DOSE combination oral contraceptives with 35-50 mcg of estrogen or better, progestin-only mini pills. Suggest alternates such as progestin-only oral contraceptives (rather than Depo-Provera) so that if a supply problem occurs, the patient can easily withdraw from the medication. Use Depo-Provera in those patients who have used it previously and have not experienced breastmilk supply problems, or in those who have used progestin-only mini pills without problems. Attempt to wait for 6 weeks postpartum prior to using Depo-Provera.

The progestins and estrogens present in breastmilk are quite low, and numerous studies confirm that they have minimal or no effect on sexual development in infants.

Pregnancy Risk Category: X

Lactation Risk Category: L3

Theoretic Infant Dose:

Adult Concerns: Reduced milk production, particularly with estrogen containing preparations, but also rarely with progestin only products.

Pediatric Concerns: None reported via milk. May suppress lactation, reducing weight gain of infant.

Drug Interactions: Barbiturates, hydantoins, and rifampin, may increase the clearance of oral contraceptives resulting in decreased effectiveness of the OC. Co-administration of griseofulvin, penicillin, or tetracyclines with OC s may decrease the efficacy of oral contraceptives possibly due to altered gut metabolism. May increase or decrease anticoagulant efficacy. Co-administration with cyclosporine, or carbamazepine may result in decreased OC efficacy.

Alternatives: Norethindrone

Adult Dosage:

References:
1. Booker DE, Pahyl IR. Control of postpartum breast engorgement with oral contraceptives. Am J Obstet Gynecol 98:1099-1101, 1967.
2. Laukaran VH. The effects of contraceptive use on the initiation and duration of lactation. Int J Gynecol Obstet. 25(suppl)129-142, 1987
3. Kora SJ. Effect of oral contraceptives on lactation. Fertil Steril 20:419-23, 1969.
4. Costa TH and Dorea JG. Concentration of fat, protein, lactose and energy in milk of mothers using hormonal contraceptives. Annals of Tropical Paediatrics 12:203-9, 1992.

ORPHENADRINE CITRATE

Trade: Norflex, Banflex, Norgesic, Myotrol
Can/Aus/UK: Disipal, Norflex, Norgesic, Orfenace
Uses: Muscle relaxant
AAP: Not reviewed

Orphenadrine is an analog of Benadryl.[1] It is primarily used as a muscle relaxant, although its primary effects are anticholinergic. No data are available on its secretion into breastmilk.

Pregnancy Risk Category: C

Lactation Risk Category: L3

Theoretic Infant Dose:

Adult Concerns: Agitation, aplastic anemia, dizziness, tremor, dry mouth, nausea, constipation.

Pediatric Concerns: None reported due to limited studies.

Drug Interactions: Increased anticholinergic side effects may be noted when used with amantadine. Orphenadrine may reduce therapeutic efficacy of phenothiazine family.

Alternatives:

Adult Dosage: 100 mg BID

T½ = 14 hours.	M/P =
PHL =	PB =
PK = 2-4 hours	Oral = 95%
MW = 269	pKa =
Vd =	

References:
1. McEvoy GE(ed):AHFS Drug Information, New York, NY. 1995.

OSELTAMIVIR PHOSPHATE

Trade: Tamiflu
Can/Aus/UK: Tamiflu
Uses: Anti-viral for influenza A and B
AAP: Not reviewed

Tamiflu is indicated for the treatment of uncomplicated acute illness due to influenza A and B infection in adults who have been symptomatic for no more than 2 days. Tamiflu is an oral viral neuraminidase inhibitor, which blocks or prevents viral seeding or release from infected cells, and prevents viral aggregation. It is only moderately effective, and is believed to reduce symptoms by only 1.3 days, and only if treatment is instituted within 2 days of infection. It is approximately 75% bioavailable following oral administration. The peak maternal plasma concentration is only 551 nanograms/mL following a 75 mg oral dose. It is not known if it transfers into human milk, but the levels would likely be incredibly low due to the low maternal plasma levels. However, due to its limited efficacy (reduces length of illness by 1.3

days),   its use in breastfeeding mothers is probably not warranted, unless in high-risk patients with other severe medical conditions.

Pregnancy Risk Category: C

Lactation Risk Category: L3

Theoretic Infant Dose:

Adult Concerns: Nausea and vomiting are most common. Diarrhea, bronchitis, abdominal pain are less common.

Pediatric Concerns: None reported via milk.

Drug Interactions: None yet reported.

Alternatives:

Adult Dosage: 75 mg twice daily for 5 days.

T½ = 6-10 hours	M/P =
PHL=	PB = 42%
PK =	Oral = 75%
MW = 312	pKa =
Vd = 0.37	

References:
1.   Manufacturers Product information, Roche Laboratories, 1999.

OSMOTIC LAXATIVES

Trade: Milk Of Magnesia, Fleet Phospho-soda, Citrate Of Magnesia, Epsom Salt
Can/Aus/UK: Acilac, Citromag, Duphalac, Fleet Phosph-Soda, Sorbilax
Uses: Laxatives
AAP: Not reviewed

Osmotic or Saline laxatives comprise a large number of magnesium and phosphate compounds, but all work similarly in that they osmotically pull and retain water in the GI tract, thus functioning as laxatives. Because they are poorly absorbed, they largely stay in the GI tract and are eliminated without significant systemic absorption.[1,2]   The small amount of magnesium and phosphate salts absorbed are rapidly cleared by the kidneys.   Products considered osmotic laxatives include: Milk of Magnesia, Epsom Salts, Citrate of Magnesia, Fleets Phospho-soda, and other sodium phosphate compounds.

Because milk electrolytes and ion concentrations are tightly controlled by the maternal alveolar cell, the secretion of higher than normal levels into milk is rare and unlikely. It is not known if these products enter milk in higher levels than are normally present, but it is very unlikely.

Pregnancy Risk Category: C

Lactation Risk Category: L1

Theoretic Infant Dose:

Adult Concerns: Diarrhea, nausea, vomiting, hypocalcemia, hypermagnesemia.

Pediatric Concerns: None reported via milk.

Drug Interactions: May reduce absorption of anticoagulants such as coumarin, and dicoumarol.

Alternatives:

Adult Dosage:

References:
1.   Drug Facts and Comparisons. 1997. ed. Facts and Comparisons, St. Louis.
2.   Pharmaceutical manufacturers package insert, 1997.

OXAPROZIN

Trade: Daypro
Can/Aus/UK: Daypro
Uses: Nonsteroidal analgesic
AAP: Not reviewed

Oxaprozin belongs to the NSAID family of analgesics and is reputed to have lesser GI side effects than certain others.[1] Although its long half-life could prove troublesome in breastfed infants, it is probably poorly transferred to human milk.   No data on transfer into human milk are available, although it is known to transfer into animal milk.

Pregnancy Risk Category: C

Lactation Risk Category: L3

Theoretic Infant Dose:

Adult Concerns: Headache, nausea, abdominal pain, gastric bleeding, diarrhea, vomiting, bleeding, constipation.

Pediatric Concerns: None reported, but ibuprofen preferred in absence of data.

Drug Interactions: May prolong prothrombin time when used with warfarin. Antihypertensive effects of ACEi family may be blunted or completely abolished by NSAIDs.   Some NSAIDs may block antihypertensive effect of beta blockers, diuretics.   Used with cyclosporin, may dramatically increase renal toxicity. May increase digoxin, phenytoin, lithium levels.   May increase toxicity of methotrexate. Oxaprozin may increase bioavailability of penicillamine.

Probenecid may increase NSAID levels.

Alternatives: Ibuprofen

Adult Dosage: 600-1200 mg QD

T½ = 42-50 hours	M/P =
PHL=	PB = 99%
PK = 3-5 hours	Oral = 95%
MW = 293	pKa =
Vd =	

References:
1.   Pharmaceutical Manufacturers Package Insert, 1996.

OXAZEPAM

Trade: Serax
Can/Aus/UK: Alepam, Apo-Oxazepam, Murelax, Novoxapam, Oxanid, Serax, Serepax, Zapex
Uses: Benzodiazepine antianxiety drug
AAP: Not reviewed

Oxazepam is a typical benzodiazepine (See Valium) and is used in anxiety disorders. Of the benzodiazepines, oxazepam is the least lipid soluble, which accounts for its low levels in milk.   In one study of a patient receiving 10 mg three times daily for 3 days, the concentration of oxazepam in breastmilk was relatively constant between 24 and 30 μg/L from the evening of the first day.[1]   The milk/plasma ratio ranged from 0.1 to 0.33. Thus a breastfeeding infant would be exposed to less than 1/1000th of the maternal dose.

Pregnancy Risk Category: D

Lactation Risk Category: L3

Theoretic Infant Dose: 4.5 μg/kg/day

Adult Concerns: Sedation.

Pediatric Concerns: None reported in one study.

Drug Interactions: May increase sedation when used with CNS depressants such as alcohol, barbiturates, opioids. Cimetidine may decrease metabolism and clearance of oxazepam.   Cisapride can dramatically increase plasma levels of diazepam.   SSRIs (fluoxetine, sertraline, paroxetine) can dramatically increase benzodiazepine levels by altering clearance, thus leading to sedation . Digoxin plasma levels may be increased.

Alternatives:

Adult Dosage: 10-30 mg TID-QID

T½ = 12 hours	M/P = 0.1-0.33
PHL = 22 hours	PB = 97%
PK = 1-2 hours	Oral = 97%
MW = 287	pKa = 1.7,11.6
Vd = 0.7-1.6	

References:
1. Wretlind M. Excretion of oxazepam in breast milk. Eur. J. Clin. Pharmacol. 33:209-210, 1987.

OXCARBAZEPINE

Trade: Trileptal
Can/Aus/UK: Trileptal
Uses: Anticonvulsant
AAP: Not reviewed

Oxcarbazepine is a derivative of carbamazepine and is used in the treatment of partial seizures in adults and as adjunctive therapy in the treatment of partial seizures in children. It is rapidly metabolized to a longer half-life active metabolite 10-hydroxy-carbazepine (MHD). In a brief and somewhat incomplete study of a pregnant patient who received 300 mg three times daily while pregnant, plasma levels were studied in her infant for the first 5 days postpartum while the infant was breastfeeding.[1] While no breastmilk levels were reported, plasma levels of MHD were essentially the same as the mothers immediately after delivery, suggesting complete transfer transplacentally of the drug. However, while breastfeeding for the next 5 days, plasma levels of MHD in the infant declined significantly from approximately 7 μg/mL to 0.2 μg/mL on the fifth day. The decay of MHD concentrations in neonatal plasma during the first 4 days postpartum indicated first order elimination. The plasma MHD levels on day 5 amounted to 7% of those one day 1 postpartum (93% drop in 5 days). The authors estimated the milk/plasma ratio to be 0.5. No neonatal side effects were reported by the authors.

Pregnancy Risk Category: C

Lactation Risk Category: L3

Theoretic Infant Dose:

Adult Concerns: Cognitive symptoms include psychomotor slowing, difficulty with concentration, speech or language problems, somnolence or fatigue, ataxia and gait disturbances. Hyponatremia,

Pediatric Concerns: None reported.

Drug Interactions: Slight increases in other anticonvulsant plasma levels have been reported and include phenobarbital, phenytoin. A reduction in plasma levels of oxycarbazepine have been reported with admixed with phenobarbital, carbamazepine, phenytoin, etc. Major reductions in plasma levels of estrogens and other hormonal contraceptives has been reported and may render oral contraceptives less effective.

Alternatives: Carbamazepine

Adult Dosage: 300-600 mg BID

T½ = 9 hours MHD	**M/P = 0.5**
PHL=	**PB = 40%**
PK = 4.5 hours-	**Oral = Complete**
MW = 252	**pKa =**
Vd = 0.7	

References:
1. Bulau P, Paar WD, von Unruh GE. Pharmacokinetics of oxcarbazepine and 10-hydroxy-carbazepine in the newborn child of an oxcarbazepine-treated mother. Eur J Clin Pharmacol. 34(3):311-3, 1988.

OXYBUTYNIN

Trade: Ditropan
Can/Aus/UK: Apo-Oxybutynin, Ditropan, Oxybutyn
Uses: Anticholinergic, antispasmotic
AAP: Not reviewed

Oxybutynin is an anticholinergic agent used to provide antispasmodic effects for conditions characterized by involuntary bladder spasms, and reduces urinary urgency and frequency. It has been used in children down to 5 years of age at doses of 15 mg daily.[1]

No data on transfer of this product into human milk is available. But oxybutynin is a tertiary amine which is poorly absorbed orally (only 6%). Further, the maximum plasma levels(Cmax) generally attained are less than 31.7 nanogram/mL.[2] If one were to assume a theoretical M/P ratio of 1.0 (which is probably unreasonably high) and a daily ingestion of 1 Liter of milk, then the theoretical dose to the infant would be < 2 micrograms/day, a dose that would be clinically irrelevant to even a neonate.

Pregnancy Risk Category: B

Lactation Risk Category: L3

Theoretic Infant Dose:

Adult Concerns: Nausea, dry mouth, constipation, esophagitis, urinary hesitancy, flushing and urticaria. Palpitations, somnolence, hallucinations infrequently occur.

Pediatric Concerns: Suppression of lactation has been reported by the manufacturer.

Drug Interactions: May potentiate the anticholinergic effect of biperiden and other anticholinergics such as the tricylic antidepressants. May counteract the effects of cisapride and metoclopramide.

Alternatives:

Adult Dosage: 5 mg BID-QID

T½ = 1-2 hours	M/P =
PHL =	PB =
PK = 3-6 hours	Oral = 6%
MW = 393	pKa = 6.96
Vd =	

References:
1.   Pharmaceutical Manufacturers Package Insert, 1997.
2.   Douchamps J, Derene F, et.al. The pharmacokinetics of oxybutynin in man. Eur. J. Clin. Pharmacol. 35(5):515-20, 1988.

OXYCODONE

Trade: Tylox, Percodan, Oxycontin
Can/Aus/UK: Endone, Proladone, Supeudol
Uses: Narcotic analgesic
AAP: Not reviewed

Oxycodone is similar to hydrocodone and is a mild analgesic somewhat stronger than codeine.   Small amounts are secreted in breastmilk. Following a dose of 5-10 mg every 4-7 hours, maternal levels peaked at 1-2 hours, and analgesia persisted for up to 4 hours.[1] Reported milk levels range from <5 to 226 μg/L. Maternal plasma levels were 14-35 μg/L. At the highest concentration, an infant ingesting 1 L per day would receive less than 2% of the maternal dose.   No reports of untoward effects in infants have been found although sedation is a possibility in some infants.

Pregnancy Risk Category: B

Lactation Risk Category: L3

Theoretic Infant Dose: 33.9 μg/kg/day

Adult Concerns: Drowsiness, sedation, nausea, vomiting, constipation.

Pediatric Concerns: None reported via milk.

Drug Interactions: Cigarette smoking increases effect of codeines. Increased toxicity/sedation when used with CNS depressants, phenothiazines, tricyclic antidepressants, other opiates, guanabenz, MAO inhibitors, neuromuscular blockers.

Alternatives: Codeine

Adult Dosage: 5 mg q 6 hours

T½ = 3-6 hours	M/P = 3.4
PHL=	PB =
PK = 1-2 hours	Oral = 50%
MW = 315	pKa = 8.5
Vd = 1.8-3.7	

References:
1.   Marx CM, Pucin F, Carlson JD, et.al. Oxycodone excretion in human milk in the puerperium. Drug Intel Clin Pharm. 20:474, 1986

OXYTOCIN

Trade: Pitocin
Can/Aus/UK: Syntocinon, Syntometrine, Toesen
Uses: Labor induction
AAP: Not reviewed

Oxytocin is an endogenous nonapeptide hormone produced by the posterior pituitary, and has uterine and myoepithelial muscle cell stimulant properties, as well as vasopressive and antidiuretic effects. Prepared synthetically it is bioavailable via I.V. and intranasal applications. It is destroyed orally by chymotrypsin in the stomach of adults, and systemically by the liver. It is known to be secreted in small amounts into human milk. Takeda reported that mean oxytocin concentrations in human milk at postpartum day 1 to 5 were 4.5, 4.7, 4.0, 3.2, and 3.3 microunits/mL respectively.[1] The oral absorption in neonates is unknown, but probably minimal.

Intranasal sprays (Syntocinon) contained 40 IU/mL with a recommended typical dose being one spray (3 drops) in each nostril to induce letdown. This is roughly equivalent to 2 IU per drop or a total dose of approximately 12 IU per letdown dose. Although oxytocin is secreted in small amounts in breastmilk, no untoward effects have been noted. However, chronic use of intranasal oxytocin may lead to dependence and should be limited to the first week postpartum. See index for intranasal formulation.

Pregnancy Risk Category:

Lactation Risk Category: L2

Theoretic Infant Dose:

Adult Concerns: Hypotension, hypertension, water intoxication and excessive uterine contractions, uterine hypertonicity, spasm, etc. May induce bradycardia, arrhythmias, intracranial hemorrhage, neonatal jaundice.

Pediatric Concerns: None via breastmilk.

Drug Interactions: When used within 3-4 hours of cyclopropane,

Alternatives:

Adult Dosage: 40-80 units QD

T½ = 3-5 minutes	M/P =
PHL =	PB =
PK =	Oral = Minimal
MW = >1000	pKa =
Vd =	

References:
1. Takeda S, Kuwabara Y, and Mizuno M. Concentrations and origin of oxytocin in breast milk. Endocrinol Japon. 33(6):821-826, 1986.

PACLITAXEL

Trade: Taxol
Can/Aus/UK: Anzatax, Paxene, Taxol
Uses: Antineoplastic agent
AAP: Not reviewed

Paclitaxel is a diterpene plant product with antineoplastic activity that is derived from the bark of the western yew tree. It is an antimicrotubule agent that instead promotes assembly of dimeric tubulin, which is stable to depolymerization.[1] It is a large molecular weight, highly lipophilic agent with only minimal kinetic data available. It is not known if paclitaxel enters milk, but due to the extraordinary toxicity and lipophilicity of this compount, it would inadvisable to breastfeed while under therapy with this drug.

Pregnancy Risk Category: D

Lactation Risk Category: L5

Theoretic Infant Dose:

Adult Concerns: Anaphylaxis and severe hypersensitivity reactions including fatal dyspnea and hypotension, and angioedema have been reported. Neutropenia, leukopenia, abnormal ECG, myalgia, arthralgia, nausea, vomiting, and diarrhea.

Pediatric Concerns: None reported via milk, but extreme caution is recommended.

Drug Interactions: Increased myelosuppresion when admixed with cisplatin. Increased levels of doxorubicin when admixed with paclitaxel.

Alternatives:

Adult Dosage: 135-175 mg/m(2) q 3 weeks

T½ = 13-52 hours	**M/P** =
PHL =	**PB** = 89-98%
PK =	**Oral** =
MW = 853	**pKa** =
Vd = 688 L/sq meter	

References:
1. Pharmaceutical Manufacturers Package Insert, 1999.

PAMIDRONATE

Trade: Aredia
Can/Aus/UK:
Uses: Bisphosphonate bone-resorption inhibitor.
AAP: Not reviewed

Pamidronate is an inhibitor of bone-resorption. Although its mechanism of action is obscure, it possibly absorbs to the calcium phosphate crystal in bone and blocks dissolution (reabsorption) of this mineral component in bone, thus reducing turnover of bone calcium. A 39 year-old patient presented in the first month of pregnancy with reflex sympathetic dystrophy. Because she wished to continue breastfeeding, she was treated with monthly I.V. doses of pamidronate (30 mg). Following the first dose, breastmilk was assayed for pamidronate content. After infusion, breastmilk was pumped and collected int two portions: 0-24 h and 25-48 h. None was detected (limit of detection, 0.4 micromol/L). The authors suggested that pamidronate could be considered safe for use in lactating women. Pamidronate is poorly absorbed (0.3% to 3% of a dose) after oral administration and thus any present in milk would not likely be absorbed by the infant.

Pregnancy Risk Category: C

Lactation Risk Category: L2

Theoretic Infant Dose:

Adult Concerns: Adverse effects include fever and malaise, anemia(6%), leukopenia, thrombocytopenia, hypertension, hypocalcemia, abdominal pain, anorexia, constipation, nausea and vomiting. Numerous other side effects, consult package insert.

Pediatric Concerns: None reported via milk.

Drug Interactions: None reported.

Alternatives:

Adult Dosage: 60 to 90 milligrams as a single intravenous infusion.

T½ = 28 hours	M/P =
PHL=	PB =
PK =	Oral = 0.3% to 3%
MW = 369	pKa =
Vd =	

References:
1. Siminoski K, Fitzgerald AA, Flesch G, Gross MS.   Intravenous pamidronate for treatment of reflex sympathetic dystrophy during breast feeding. J Bone Miner Res. 15(10):2052-5, 2000.

PANTOPRAZOLE

Trade: Protonix
Can/Aus/UK: Pantoloc
Uses: Suppresses gastric acid production
AAP: Not reviewed

Pantoprazole is a proton-pump inhibitor similar to omeprazole(Prilosec). It is used primarily to suppress acid production in the stomach for treatment of gastroesophageal reflux or peptic ulcer disease.   The pharmaceutical manufacturer reports 0.02% of an administered dose is excreted into milk.[1] As with all the proton-pump inhibitors, pantoprazole is virtually unstable in an acid mileu and when presented in milk, it would be highly unstable in the infant's stomach. If any were present in milk, it would be largely degraded prior to absorption. See omeprazole for an alternative.

Pregnancy Risk Category: B

Lactation Risk Category:

Theoretic Infant Dose:

Adult Concerns: Headache, diarhea, flatulence, and rash.

Pediatric Concerns: None reported via milk.

Drug Interactions: None reported.

Alternatives: Omeprazole

Adult Dosage:

T½ = 1 hour	M/P =
PHL =	PB = 98%
PK = 2,4 hours	Oral = 77% Enteric coated
MW = 432	pKa =
Vd = 0.32	

References:
1. Fachinformation: Pantozol(R), pantoprazole. Byk-Gulden, Konstanz, 1995.

PAREGORIC

Trade:
Can/Aus/UK:
Uses: Opiate analgesic used for diarrhea.
AAP: Not reviewed

Paregoric is camphorated tincture of opium, and contains approximately 2 mg morphine per 5cc (teaspoonful) in 45% alcohol.[1] It is frequently used for diarrhea and in the past for withdrawal symptoms in neonates (Tincture of Opium is now preferred). Because the active ingredient is morphine, see morphine for breastfeeding indications. Due to its camphor content, the pediatric use of paregoric is discouraged.

Pregnancy Risk Category: B

Lactation Risk Category: L3

Theoretic Infant Dose:

Adult Concerns: Sedation, constipation, apnea, nausea, vomiting.

Pediatric Concerns: None reported. See morphine.

Drug Interactions: See morphine.

Alternatives:

Adult Dosage: 5-10 mL (2-4 mg morphine) BID-QID

T½ = 1.5-2 hours	M/P = 1.1-3.6
PHL = 13.9 hours(neonatal)	PB = 35%
PK = 0.5-1 hours	Oral = 26%
MW =	pKa =
Vd =	

References:
1. Drug Facts and Comparisons. 1995 ed. Facts and Comparisons, St. Louis.

PAROXETINE

Trade: Paxil
Can/Aus/UK: Aropax 20, Paxil, Seroxat
Uses: Antidepressant, serotonin reuptake inihibitor
AAP: Drug whose effect on nursing infants is unknown but may be of concern

Paroxetine is a typical serotonin reuptake inhibitor.   Although it undergoes hepatic metabolism,   the metabolites are not active. Paroxetine is exceedingly lipophilic and distributes throughout the body with only 1% remaining in plasma.   In one case report of a mother receiving 20 mg/day paroxetine at steady state[1], the breastmilk level at peak (4 hours) was 7.6 μg/L.   While the maternal paroxetine dose was 333 μg/kg, the maximum daily dose to the infant was estimated at 1.14 μg/kg or 0.34% of the maternal dose.

In two studies of 6 and 4 nursing mothers respectively[2], the mean dose of paroxetine received by the infants in the first study was 1.13% (range 0.5-1.7) of the weight adjusted maternal dose. The mean M/P (AUC) was 0.39 (range 0.32-0.51) while the predicted M/P was 0.22.

In the second study, the mean dose of paroxetine received by the infants was 1.25% (range 0.38-2.24%) of the weight adjusted maternal dose, with a mean M/P of 0.96 (range 0.31-3.33). The drug was not detected in the plasma of 7 of the 8 infants studied and was detected (< 4 mg/L) in only one infant. No adverse effects were observed in any of the infants.

In a recent study of 16 mothers by Stowe[3], paroxetine levels in milk were low, and varied according to maternal dose. Milk/plasma ratios varied from 0.056 to 1.3. Milk levels ranged from approximately 17 μg/L, 45 μg/L, 70 μg/L, 92 μg/L and 101 μg/L in mothers receiving a dose of 10, 20, 30, 40 and   50 mg/day respectively.   Levels of paroxetine were below the limit of detection (< 2 ng/mL) in all 16 infants.

In a study of 6 women receiving 20-40 mg/day, the milk/plasma ratio ranged from 0.39 to 1.11 but averaged 0.69 and the average estimated dose to the infants ranged from 0.7 to 2.9% of the weight-adjusted maternal dose.[4]   In a seventh patient, and based on area-under-the-curve data, the milk/plasma ratio was 0.69 at a dose of 20 mg and 0.72 at a dose of 40 mg/day. The estimated dose to the infant was 1.0% and 2.0% of the weight-adjusted maternal dose at 20 and 40 mg respectively.   Paroxetine levels in milk averaged 44.3 and 78.5 μg/L over 6 hours following 20 and 40 mg doses respectively. No adverse reactions or unusual behaviors were noted in any of the infants.

In another study of 24 breastfeeding mothers who received an average dose of 17.6 mg/d (range 10-40 mg/d) the average level of paroxetine in maternal serum and milk was 45.2 ng/mL and 19.2 μg/L, respectively.[5] The average milk/plasma ratio was 0.53. The authors estimated the average infant dose to be 2.88 μg/kg/d or 2.88% of the weight-adjusted maternal dose. All infant serum levels were below the limit of detection.

These studies generally conclude that paroxetine can be considered relatively 'safe' for breastfeeding infants as the absolute dose transferred is quite low. Plasma levels in the infant were generally undetectable. Recent data suggests that a neonatal withdrawal syndrome may occur in newborns exposed in utero to paroxetine[6], although there is significant difficulty in differentiating between withdrawal and toxicity.[7] Symptoms include jitteriness, vomiting, irritability, hypoglycemia, and necrotizing enterocolitis.

Pregnancy Risk Category: B

Lactation Risk Category: L2

Theoretic Infant Dose: 15.2 μg/kg/day

Adult Concerns: Sedation, headache, dry mouth, dizziness, nausea, insomnia, constipation, seizures.

Pediatric Concerns: Although this product has been occasionally used in breastfeeding and pregnant women, no reports of untoward effects have been found.

Drug Interactions: Decreased effect with phenobarbital and phenytoin. Increased toxicity with alcohol, cimetidine, MAO inhibitors (serotonergic syndrome). Increased effect with fluoxetine, tricyclic antidepressants, sertraline, phenothiazines, warfarin.

Alternatives: Sertraline

Adult Dosage: 20 mg QD

T½ = 21 hours.	M/P = 0.056-1.3
PHL =	PB = 95%
PK = 5-8 hours	Oral = Complete
MW = 329	pKa =
Vd = 3-28	

References:
1. Spigset O. Paroxetine level in breast milk. J. Clin Psy. 57(1):39, 1996.
2. Begg EJ, Duffull SB, Saunders DA, Buttimore RC, Ilett KF, et.al. Paroxetine in human milk. Brit. J.Clin. Pharmacol. 48(2):142-7, 1999.
3. Stowe ZN, Cohen LS, Hostetter A, Ritchie JC, et.al. Paroxetine in human milk and nursing infants. Am. J. Psychiatry, 157(2): 185-189, 2000.
4. Ohman R, Hagg S, Carleborg L, Spigset O. Excretion of paroxetine into breast milk. J Clin Psychiatry. 60(8):519-23, 1999.
5. Misri S, Kim J, Riggs KW, Kostaras X. Paroxetine levels in postpartum depressed women, breast milk, and infant serum. J Clin Psychiatry. 61(11):828-32, 2000.
6. Stiskal JA, Kulin N, Koren G, Ho T, Ito S. Neonatal paroxetine

withdrawal syndrome. Arch Dis Child Fetal Neonatal Ed. 84(2):F134-5, 2001.

7. Isbister GK, Dawson A, Whyte IM, Prior FH, Clancy C, Smith AJ. Neonatal paroxetine withdrawal syndrome or actually serotonin syndrome? Arch Dis Child Fetal Neonatal Ed. 2001

PEMOLINE

Trade: Cylert
Can/Aus/UK: Cylert, Kethamed, Ronyl
Uses: CNS stimulant for attention deficit disorder.
AAP: Not reviewed

Pemoline is a specialized CNS stimulate qualitatively similar to amphetamine and Ritalin.[1] At present there are no data available on its transfer into human milk, but it is likely due to its low molecular weight. Maternal peak level occurs 2-4 hours after dose. Serum half-life in children (5-12 yrs) is less than that of adults.

Pregnancy Risk Category: C

Lactation Risk Category: L4

Theoretic Infant Dose:

Adult Concerns: Agitation, excitement, elevated liver enzymes, weight loss, insomnia, tachycardia.

Pediatric Concerns: None reported, but observe for agitation, excitement, insomnia.

Drug Interactions: May reduce effect of insulin. Increased toxicity when used with other CNS depressants, CNs stimulants.

Alternatives:

Adult Dosage: 50-200 mg QD

T½ = 12 hours	M/P =
PHL = 7-8.6 hours	PB = 50%.
PK = 2-4 hours	Oral = Complete
MW = 176	pKa = 10.5
Vd = 0.22-0.59	

References:
1. Drug Facts and Comparisons. 1995 ed. Facts and Comparisons, St. Louis.

PENCICLOVIR

Trade: Denavir
Can/Aus/UK: Vectavir
Uses: Antiviral agent.
AAP: Not reviewed

Penciclovir is an antiviral agent for the treatment of cold sores (herpes simplex labialis) of the lips and face, and occasionally for herpes zoster(Shingles).[1]   Following topical administration, plasma levels are undetectable.[2]   Because oral bioavailability is nil, and maternal plasma levels are undetectable following topical therapy,   it is extremely unlikely that detectable amounts would transfer into human milk or be absorbable by an infant.

Pregnancy Risk Category: B

Lactation Risk Category: L3

Theoretic Infant Dose:

Adult Concerns: Following topical application only mild erythema was occasionally observed.

Pediatric Concerns: None reported.

Drug Interactions: None reported.

Alternatives:

Adult Dosage: topical application q 2 hours

T½ = 2.3 hours	M/P =
PHL =	PB = < 20%
PK =	Oral = 1.5%
MW =	pKa =
Vd =	

References:
1. Vere Hodge RA & Perkins RM: Mode of action of 9-(4-hydroxy-3-hydroxymethylbut-1-yl) guanine (BRL 39123)   against herpes simplex virus in MRC-5 cells. Antimicrob Agents Chemother 33:223-229, 1989.
2. Pharmaceutical Manufacturers Package Insert, 1998.

PENICILLAMINE

Trade: Cuprimine, Depen
Can/Aus/UK: Cuprimine, D-Penamine, Depen, Distamine, Pendramine
Uses: Used in arthritis, autoimmune syndromes
AAP: Not reviewed

Penicillamine is a potent chelating agent used to chelate copper, iron, mercury, lead and other metals. It is also used to suppress the immune response in rheumatoid arthritis and other immunologic syndromes. It is extremely dangerous during pregnancy. Safety has not been established during lactation. Penicillamine is a potent drug that requires constant observation and care by attending physicians. Recommend discontinuing lactation if this drug is mandatory.[1]

Pregnancy Risk Category: D

Lactation Risk Category: L4

Theoretic Infant Dose:

Adult Concerns: Anorexia, nausea, vomiting, diarrhea, alteration of taste, elevated liver enzymes, kidney damage.

Pediatric Concerns: None reported, but caution is recommended.

Drug Interactions: An increased risk of serious hematologic and renal reactions may occur if used with gold therapy, antimalarial, or other cytotoxic drugs. The absorption of penicillamine is decreased by 35% when used with iron salts. The absorption of penicillamine is decreased by 66% when used with antacids. Digoxin plasma levels may be reduced.

Alternatives:

Adult Dosage: 250-500 mg QID

T½ = 1.7-3.2 hours	M/P =	
PHL =	PB =	
PK = 1 hour	Oral = Complete	
MW = 149	pKa =	
Vd =		

References:
1. Ostensen M, Husby G. Antirheumatic drug treatment during pregnancy and lactation. Scand J Rheumatol 14:1-7, 1985.

PENICILLIN G

Trade: Pfizerpen
Can/Aus/UK: Ayercillin, Bicillin L-A, Crystapen, Megacillin
Uses: Antibiotic
AAP: Approved by the American Academy of Pediatrics for use in breastfeeding mothers

Penicillins generally penetrate into breastmilk in small concentrations which is largely determined by class. Following IM doses of 100,000 units, the milk/plasma ratios varied between 0.03 - 0.13.[1,2] Milk levels varied from 7 units to 60 units/L. Possible side effects in infants would include alterations in GI flora or allergic responses in a hypersensitive infant. Compatible with breastfeeding in non-hypersensitive infants.

Pregnancy Risk Category: B

Lactation Risk Category: L1

Theoretic Infant Dose:

Adult Concerns: Changes in GI flora, allergic rashes.

Pediatric Concerns: None reported via milk, but observe for changes in GI flora, diarrhea.

Drug Interactions: Probenecid may increase penicillin levels. Tetracyclines may decrease penicillin effectiveness.

Alternatives:

Adult Dosage: 1.2-2.4 million units QD

T½ = <1.5 hours	M/P = 0.03-0.13
PHL =	PB = 60-80%
PK = 1-2 hours	Oral = 15-30%
MW = 372	pKa =
Vd =	

References:
1. Matsuda S. Transfer of antibiotics into maternal milk. Biol Res Pregnancy Perinatol 5:57-60, 1984.
2. Greene H, Burkhart B, Hobby G. Excretion of penicillin human milk following partiturition. Am. J. Obstet. Gynecol. 51:732, 1946.

PENTAZOCINE

Trade: Talwin, Talacen
Can/Aus/UK: Fortral, Talwin
Uses: Analgesic
AAP: Not reviewed

Pentazocine is a synthetic opiate and is also an opiate antagonist. Once absorbed it undergoes extensive hepatic metabolism and only small amounts achieve plasma levels.[1] It is primarily used as a mild analgesic. No data are available on transfer into breastmilk.

Pregnancy Risk Category: B

Lactation Risk Category: L3

Theoretic Infant Dose:

Adult Concerns: Sedation, respiratory depression, nausea, vomiting, dry mouth, taste alteration.

Pediatric Concerns: None reported due to limited studies.

Drug Interactions: May reduce the analgesic effect of other opiate agonists such as morphine.   Increased toxicity when used with tripelennamine can be lethal. Increased toxicity when used with CNS depressants such as phenothiazines, sedatives, hypnotics, or alcohol.

Alternatives:

Adult Dosage: 50-100 mg q 3-4 hours PRN

T½ = 2-3 hours	**M/P =**
PHL=	**PB = 60%**
PK = 1-3 hours	**Oral = 18%**
MW = 285	**pKa = 9.0**
Vd = 4.4-7.8	

References:
1.   McEvoy GE(ed):AHFS Drug Information, New York, NY. 1995.

PENTOBARBITAL

Trade: Nembutal
Can/Aus/UK: Barhopen, Carbrital, Lethobarb, Nembutal, Nova Rectal, Novo-Pentobarb
Uses: Sedative, hypnotic.
AAP: Not reviewed

Pentobarbital is a short acting barbiturate primarily used at a sedative. Following a dose of 100 mg for 3 days, the concentration of pentobarbital 19 hours after the last dose was 0.17 mg/L.[1] The effect of short acting barbiturates on the breastfed infant is unknown but significant tolerance and addiction can occur.[2-4] Use caution if used in large amounts. No reported harmful effects breastfeeding infants.

Pregnancy Risk Category: D

Lactation Risk Category: L3

Theoretic Infant Dose: 25.5 μg/kg/day

Adult Concerns: Sedation, respiratory arrest, tachycardia, physical dependence.

Pediatric Concerns: None reported, but observe for sedation, dependence.

Drug Interactions: Barbiturates may decrease the antimicrobal activity of metronidazole. Phenobarbital may significantly reduce the serum levels and half-life of quinidine. Barbiturates decrease theophylline levels.   The clearance of verapamil may be increased and its bioavailability decreased.

Alternatives:

Adult Dosage: 20-40 mg BID-QID

T½ = 15-50 hours	M/P =
PHL =	PB = 35-45%
PK = 30-60 min.(oral)	Oral = 95%
MW = 248	pKa = 7.9
Vd = 0.5-1.0	

References:

1. Wilson Jt. et.al. Drug excretion in human breastmilk: principles, pharmacokinetics, and projected consequences. Clin. Pharmacokinet. 5:1-66, 1980.
2. Tyson RM, Shrader EA, Perlman HH. Drugs transmitted through breast milk. II Barbiturates. J Pediatr. 14:86-90, 1938.
3. Kaneko S, Sato T, Suzuki K. The levels of anticonvulsants in breast milk. Br J Clin Pharmacol. 7:624-627,1979.
4. Horning, MG et.al. Identification and quantification of drugs and drug metabolites in human breast milk using GC-MS-COM methods. Milk and Lactation Mod. Probl. Paediat. 15:73-79, 1975.

PENTOSAN POLYSULFATE

Trade: Elmiron
Can/Aus/UK: Elmiron
Uses: Urinary tract analgesic
AAP: Not reviewed

Pentosan polysulfate is a negatively-charged synthetic sulfated polysaccharide with Heparin-like properties although it is used as a urinary tract analgesic. It is structurally related to dextran sulfate with a molecular weight of 4000-6000 daltons. Pentosan adheres to the bladder wall mucosa and may act as a buffer to control cell permeability preventing irritating solutes in the urine from reaching the cell membrane.[1,2] Although no data are available on its transfer into human milk, its large molecular weight and its poor oral bioavailability would largely preclude the transfer and absorption of clinically relevant amounts in breastfed infants.

Pregnancy Risk Category: B

Lactation Risk Category: L2

Theoretic Infant Dose:

Adult Concerns: Alopecia areata. Weak anticoagulant (1/15 th activity of heparin). Mildly hepatotoxic. Headache, depression, insomnia, pruritus, urticaria, diarrhea, nausea, vomiting, etc. have been reported.

Pediatric Concerns: None reported via milk.

Drug Interactions: May increase bleeding time when used with cisapride.

Alternatives:

Adult Dosage: 100 mg TID

T½ = < 5 hours	M/P =
PHL =	PB =
PK = 3 hours	Oral = 3%
MW = 6000	pKa =
Vd =	

References:

1. Wagner WH: Hoe/Bay 946 - a new compound with activity against the AIDS virus Arzneimittelforschung 39:112-113, 1989.
2. Asmal AC, Leary WP, Carboni J et al: The effects of sodium pentosan polysulfate on peripheral metabolism. S Afr Med J 49:1091-1094, 1975

PENTOXIFYLLINE

Trade: Trental
Can/Aus/UK: Apo-Pentoxifylline, Trental
Uses: Reduces blood viscosity
AAP: Not reviewed

Pentoxifylline and its metabolites improve the flow properties of blood by decreasing its viscosity. It is a methylzanthine derivative similar in structure to caffeine and is extensively metabolized, although the metabolites do not have long half-lives. In a group of 5 breastfeeding women who received a single 400 mg dose, the mean milk/plasma ratio was 0.87 for the parent compound.[1] The milk/plasma ratios for the metabolites were lower, 0.54, 0.76 and 1.13. Average milk concentration at 2 hours following the dose was 73.9 μg/L.

Pregnancy Risk Category: C

Lactation Risk Category: L2

Theoretic Infant Dose: 11.1 μg/kg/day

Adult Concerns: Bleeding. Dyspepsia, bloating, diarrhea, nausea, vomiting, bad taste, dyspnea.

Pediatric Concerns: None reported.

Drug Interactions: Bleeding, and prolonged prothrombin times when used with coumarins. Use with other theophylline containing products leads to increased theophylline plasma levels.

Alternatives:

Adult Dosage: 400 mg TID

T½ = 0.4-1.6 hours	**M/P =**
PHL =	**PB =**
PK = 1 hour	**Oral = Complete**
MW = 278	**pKa =**
Vd =	

References:

1.   Witter FR, Smith RV. The excretion of pentoxifylline and its metabolites into human breast milk. Am. J. Obstet. Gynecol. 151:1094-97, 1985.

PERMETHRIN

Trade: Nix, Elimite, A-200, Pyrinex, Pyrinyl, Acticin
Can/Aus/UK: Lyclear, Nix, Pyrifoam, Quellada
Uses: Insecticide, scabicide
AAP: Not reviewed

Permethrin is a synthetic pyrethroid structure of the natural ester pyrethrum, a natural insecticide, and used to treat lice, mites and fleas. Permethrin absorption through the skin following application of a 5% cream is reported to be less than 2%.[1]   Permethrin is rapidly metabolized by serum enzymes to inactive metabolites and rapidly excreted in the urine. Overt toxicity is very low. It is not known if permethrin is secreted in human milk, although it has been found in animal milk after injection of significant quantities I.V.. In spite of its rapid metabolism, some residuals are sequestered in fat tissue.

To use, recommend that the hair be washed with detergent, then saturated with permethrin liquid for 10 minutes before rinsing with water.   One treatment is all that is required.   At 14 days, a second treatment may be required if viable lice are seen. Elimite cream is generally recommended for scabies infestations, and should be applied head to toe for 8-12 hours. Reapplication may be needed in 7 days if live mites appear.

Pregnancy Risk Category: B

Lactation Risk Category: L2

Theoretic Infant Dose:

Adult Concerns: Itching, rash, skin irritation. Dyspnea has been reported in one patient.

Pediatric Concerns: Pruritus, skin irritation, burning.

Drug Interactions:

Alternatives:

Adult Dosage:

T½ =	M/P =
PHL =	PB =
PK =	Oral =
MW = 391	pKa =
Vd =	

References:
1. Pharmaceutical Manufacturers Package Insert, 1996.

PERPHENAZINE and AMITRIPTYLINE

Trade: Triavil, Etrafon
Can/Aus/UK:
Uses: Phenothiazine antipsychotic and antidepressant
AAP: Drug whose effect on nursing infants is unknown but may be of concern

Commonly combined in the USA with amitriptyline it is called Etrafon or Triavil. For information on amitriptyline see individual monograph.

Perphenazine is a phenothiazine derivative used as an antipsychotic or sedative.   In a study of one patient receiving either 16, or 24 mg/day of perphenazine divided in two doses at 12 hour intervals, milk levels were 2.1 μg/L and 3.2 μg/L respectively.[1] The authors estimated the dose to the infant at 1.06 ug (0.3 μg/kg) or 1.59 ug (0.45 μg/kg) respective of dose. Serum perphenazine levels in the mother drawn 12 hours after doses of 16 or 24 mg/d were 2.0 and 4.9 ng/mL respectively. Hence milk/plasma ratios were approximately 1.1 and 0.7 respective of the dose.   The authors estimate the dose to be approximately 0.1% of the weight-adjusted maternal dose. The authors report that during a 3 month exposure,   the infant thrived and had no adverse response to the medication.

Pregnancy Risk Category: C

Lactation Risk Category: L3

Theoretic Infant Dose: 0.5 μg/kg/day

Adult Concerns: Sedation, extrapyramidal symptoms, tardive dyskinesia, anticholinergic symptoms, postural hypotension, obstructive jaundice.

Pediatric Concerns: None reported via milk. Observe for sedation. Rate of SIDS may be increased in infants exposed to phenothiazines.

Drug Interactions: Anticholinergics used to control extrapyramidal side effects may reduce oral absorption of perphenazine, and antagonize the behavioral and antipsychotic effects of the drug.   They may also enhance the anticholinergic side effects.

Enhanced cardiotoxicity with cisapride.   Check drug reference for numerous others.

Alternatives:

Adult Dosage: 12-64 mg daily

T½ = 8-12 hours	M/P = 1.1
PHL=	PB =
PK = 3 hours	Oral = Complete
MW = 403	pKa = 7.8
Vd = 10-35	

References:
1.   Olesen OV, Bartels U, Poulsen JH. Perphenazine in breast milk and serum. Am J Psychiatry. 147(10):1378-9, 1990.

PHENAZOPYRIDINE HCL

Trade: Pyridium, Eridium, Azo-standard
Can/Aus/UK: Phenazo, Pyridium, Pyronium, Uromide
Uses: Urinary tract analgesic
AAP: Not reviewed

Phenazopyridine is an azo dye that is rapidly excreted in the urine, where it exerts a topical analgesic effect on urinary tract mucosa.[1] Pyridium is only moderately effective and produces a reddish-orange discoloration of the urine. It may also ruin contact lenses. It is not known if pyridium transfers into breastmilk but it probably does to a limited degree. This product, due to limited efficacy, should probably not be used in lactating women although it is doubtful that it would be harmful to an infant.   This product is highly colored and can stain clothing. Stains can be removed by soaking in a solution of 0.25% sodium dithionite.

Pregnancy Risk Category: B

Lactation Risk Category: L3

Theoretic Infant Dose:

Adult Concerns: Anemia, nausea, vomiting, diarrhea, colored urine, methemoglobinemia, hepatitis, GI distress,

Pediatric Concerns: None reported via lactation.

Drug Interactions:

Alternatives:

Adult Dosage: 100-200 mg TID

T½ =	M/P =
PHL=	PB =
PK =	Oral = Complete
MW = 250	pKa =
Vd =	

References:
1. Drug Facts and Comparisons. 1994 ed. Facts and Comparisons, St. Louis.

PHENCYCLIDINE

Trade: PCP, Angel Dust
Can/Aus/UK:
Uses: Hallucinogen
AAP: Contraindicated by the American Academy of Pediatrics in Breastfeeding Mothers

Phencyclidine, also called Angel Dust, is a potent and extremely dangerous hallucinogen. High concentrations are secreted into breastmilk (>10 times plasma level) of mice.[1] Continued secretion into milk occurs over long period of time (perhaps months). One patient who consumed PCP 41 days prior to lactating had a milk level of 3.90 μg/L.[2] EXTREMELY DANGEROUS TO NURSING INFANT. PCP is stored for long periods in adipose tissue. Urine samples are positive for 14-30 days in adults and probably longer in infants. The infant could test positive for PCP long after maternal exposure, particularly if breastfeeding. Definitely contraindicated.

Pregnancy Risk Category: X

Lactation Risk Category: L5

Theoretic Infant Dose:

Adult Concerns: Hallucinations, psychosis.

Pediatric Concerns: Significant concentrations would likely transfer to infant. Extremely dangerous.

Drug Interactions:

Alternatives:

Adult Dosage:

T½ = 24-51 hours	M/P = > 10
PHL=	PB = 65%
PK = Immediate	Oral = Complete
MW = 243	pKa = 8.5
Vd = 5.3-7.5	

References:

1. Nicholas JM, Liqshitz J, Schreiber EC, et.al. Phencyclidine. Its transfer across the placenta as well as into breast milk. Am J Obstet Gynecol 143:143-146, 1982.
2. Kaufman KR, Petrucha RA, Pitts FN, Weekes ME. PCP in amniotic fluid and breast milk: case report. J. Clin. Psychiatry 44:269, 1983.

PHENOBARBITAL

Trade: Luminal
Can/Aus/UK: Barbilixir, Gardenal, Phenobarbitone
Uses: Long acting barbiturate sedative, anticonvulsant
AAP: Drugs associated with significant side effects and should be given with caution

Phenobarbital is a long half-life barbiturate frequently used as an anticonvulsant in adults and during the neonatal period. Its long half-life in infants may lead to significant accumulation and blood levels higher than mother, although this is infrequent. During the first 3-4 weeks of life, phenobarbital is poorly absorbed by the neonatal GI tract. However, protein binding by neonatal albumin is poor, 36-43%, as compared to the adult, 51%. Thus, the volume of distribution is higher in neonates and the tissue concentrations of phenobarbital may be significantly higher. The half-life in premature infants can be extremely long (100-500 hours) and plasma levels must be closely monitored. Although varied, milk/plasma ratios vary from 0.46 to 0.6.[1-3] In one study, following a dose of 30 mg four times daily, the milk concentration of phenobarbital averaged 2.74 mg/L 16 hours after the last dose.[3] The dose an infant would receive was estimated at 2-4 mg/day.[4] Phenobarbital should be administered with caution and close observation of infant is required, including plasma drug levels. One should generally expect the infant's plasma level to be approximately 30-40% of the maternal level.

Pregnancy Risk Category: D

Lactation Risk Category: L3

Theoretic Infant Dose: 0.4 mg/kg/day

Adult Concerns: Drowsiness, sedation, ataxia, respiratory depression, withdrawal symptoms.

Pediatric Concerns: Phenobarbital sedation has been reported, but is infrequent. Expect infant plasma levels to approximate one-third (or lower) of maternal plasma level. Withdrawal symptoms have been reported.

Drug Interactions: Barbiturates may decrease the antimicrobal activity of metronidazole. Phenobarbital may significantly reduce the serum levels and half-life of quinidine. Barbiturates decrease theophylline levels. The clearance of verapamil may be increased and its bioavailability decreased.

Alternatives:

Adult Dosage: 100-200 mg QD

T½ = 53-140 hours	M/P = 0.4-0.6
PHL = 36-144 hours	PB = 51%
PK = 8-12 hours	Oral = 80% (Adult)
MW = 232	pKa = 7.2
Vd = 0.5-0.6	

References:
1. Tyson RM, Shrader EA, Perlman HH. Drugs transmitted through breast milk. II Barbiturates. J Pediatr. 14:86-90, 1938.
2. Kaneko S, Sato T, Suzuki K. The levels of anticonvulsants in breast milk. Br J Clin Pharmacol. 7:624-627,1979.
3. Nau H, et.al. Anticonvulsants during pregnancy and lactation. Clin. Pharmacokinetics 7:508-543, 1982.
4. Horning MG, Stillwell WG et.al. Identification and quantification of drugs and drug metabolites in human breast milk using GC-MS-COM methods. Mod. Probl. Paediatr. 15:73-79, 1975.

PHENTERMINE

Trade: Fastin, Zantryl, Ionamin, Adipex-p
Can/Aus/UK: Duromine, Ionamin, Ponderax caps
Uses: Appetite suppressant
AAP: Not reviewed

Phentermine is an appetite suppressant structurally similar to the amphetamine family. As such it frequently produces CNS stimulation.[1] No data are available on transfer to human milk. This product has a very small molecular weight (149) and would probably transfer into human milk in significant quantities and could product stimulation, anorexia, tremors, and other CNS side effects in the newborn. The use of this product in breastfeeding mothers would be difficult to justify and is not advised.

Pregnancy Risk Category: C

Lactation Risk Category: L4

Theoretic Infant Dose:

Adult Concerns: Hypertension, tachycardia, palpitations, nervousness, tremulousness, insomnia, dizziness, depression, headache, cerebral infarct, paranoid psychosis, heat stroke, nausea, vomiting, physical dependence as evidenced by withdrawal syndrome.

Pediatric Concerns: Growth impairment has been reported from direct use of phentermine in children age 3-15 years.

Drug Interactions: Decreased effect of guanethidine, CNS depressants. Increased toxicity of MAO inhibitors, other stimulants.

Alternatives:

Adult Dosage: 8 mg TID

T½ = 7-20 hours		M/P =	
PHL =		PB =	
PK = 8 hours		Oral = Complete	
MW = 149		pKa =	
Vd =			

References:
1. Silverstone T: Appetite suppressants: a review. Drugs 43:820-836, 1992.

PHENYLEPHRINE

Trade: Neo-synephrine, Ak-dilate, Vicks Sinex Nasal
Can/Aus/UK: Albalone, Dionephrine, Fenox, Mydfrin
Uses: Decongestant
AAP: Not reviewed.

Phenylephrine is a sympathomimetic most commonly used as a nasal decongestant due to its vasoconstrictive properties, but also for treatment of ocular uveitis, inflammation and glaucoma, as a mydriatic agent to dilate the pupil during examinations, and for cardiogenic shock.[1] Phenylephrine is a potent adrenergic stimulant and systemic effects (tachycardia, hypertension, arrhythmias), although rare, have occurred following ocular administration in some sensitive individuals. Phenylephrine is most commonly added to cold mixtures and nasal sprays for use in respiratory colds, flu and congestion. Numerous pediatric formulations are in use and it is generally considered safe in pediatric patients.

No data are available on its secretion into human milk. It is likely that small amounts will probably be transferred, but due to the poor oral bioavailability (<38%), it is not likely that it would produce clinical effects in a breastfed infant unless the maternal doses were quite high.

Pregnancy Risk Category: C

Lactation Risk Category: L3

Theoretic Infant Dose:

Adult Concerns: Local ocular irritation, transient tachycardia, hypertension, and sympathetic stimulation.

Pediatric Concerns: None reported via milk.

Drug Interactions: Concomitant use with other sympathomimetics may exacerbate cardiovascular effects of phenylephrine. This includes albuterol, amitriptyline, other tricyclic antidepressants, MAO inhibitors, furazolidone, guanethidine, and others. Increased effect when used with oxytocic drugs.

Alternatives: Pseudoephedrine

Adult Dosage: 1-10 mg IM

T½ = 2-3 hours	M/P =
PHL =	PB =
PK = 10-60 minutes	Oral = 38%
MW = 203	pKa =
Vd = 0.57	

References:
1. Pharmaceutical manufacturers package insert, 1997.

PHENYLPROPANOLAMINE

Trade: Dexatrim, Acutrim
Can/Aus/UK: Caldomine-DH, Dimetapp, Eskornade
Uses: Adrenergic, nasal decongestant, anorexiant.
AAP: Not reviewed

Phenylpropanolamine is an adrenergic compound frequently used in nasal decongestants, and also diet pills. It produces significant constriction of nasal mucosa, and is a common ingredient in cold preparations. No data are available on its secretion into human milk, but due to its low molecular weight, and its rapid entry past the blood-brain-barrier, it should be expected. It has recently been withdrawn from the US market.

Pregnancy Risk Category: C

Lactation Risk Category: L2

Theoretic Infant Dose:

Adult Concerns: Hypertension, bradycardia, AV block, arrhythmias, paranoia, seizures, psychosis, tremor, excitement, insomnia, seizures, anorexia and physical dependence.

Pediatric Concerns: None reported via milk but observe for excitement, loss of appetite, insomnia.

Drug Interactions: Hypertensive crisis when admixed with MAO inhibitors. Increased toxicity (pressor effects) with beta blockers. Decreased effect of antihypertensives.

Alternatives:

Adult Dosage: 12.5-25 mg q 4-6 hours

T½ = 5.6 hours.	M/P =
PHL =	PB = Low
PK = 1 hour	Oral = 100%
MW = 188	pKa = 9.1
Vd = 4.5	

References:

PHENYTOIN

Trade: Dilantin
Can/Aus/UK: Dilantin, Epanutin, Novo-Phenytoin
Uses: Anticonvulsant
AAP: Approved by the American Academy of Pediatrics for use in breastfeeding mothers

Phenytoin is an old and efficient anticonvulsant. It is secreted in small amounts into breastmilk. The effect on infant is generally considered minimal if the levels in the maternal circulation are kept in low-normal range (10 μg/ml). Phenytoin levels peak in milk at 3.5 hours

In one study of 6 women receiving 200-400 mg/day, plasma concentrations varied from 12.8 to 78.5 μmol/L, while their milk levels ranged from 0.8 to 11.7 μmol/L.[1] The milk/plasma ratios were low, ranging from 0.06 to 0.18. In only two of these infants were plasma concentrations of phenytoin detectible (0.46 and 0.72 μmol/L). No untoward effects were noted in any of these infants.

Others have reported milk levels of 6 μg/mL[2], or 0.8 μg/mL.[3] Although the actual concentration in milk varies significantly between studies, the milk/plasma ratio appears relatively similar, at 0.13 to 0.45. Breastmilk concentrations varied from 0.26 to 1.5 mg/L depending on the maternal dose. The neonatal half-life of phenytoin is highly variable for the first week of life. Monitoring of the infants' plasma may be useful although it is not definitely required. All of the current studies indicate rather low levels of phenytoin in breastmilk and minimal plasma levels in breastfeeding infants.

Pregnancy Risk Category: D

Lactation Risk Category: L2

Theoretic Infant Dose: 0.9 mg/kg/day

Adult Concerns: Sedation, hypertrophied gums, ataxia, liver toxicity.

Pediatric Concerns: Only one case of methemoglobinemia, drowsiness, and poor sucking has been reported. Most other studies suggest no problems.

Drug Interactions: Increased effects of phenytoin may occur when used with: amiodarone, benzodiazepines, chloramphenicol, cimetidine, disulfiram, ethanol, fluconazole(azoles), isoniazid, metronidazole, omeprazole, sulfonamides, valproic acid, TCAs, ibuprofen. Decreased effects of phenytoin may occur when used with: barbiturates, carbamazepine, rifampin, antacids, charcoal, sucralfate, folic acid, loxapine, nitrofurantoin, pyridoxine. May others have been reported, please consult more complete reference.

Alternatives:

Adult Dosage: 300 mg QD

T½ = 6-24 hours	M/P = 0.18-0.45
PHL = 20-160 h (premature)	PB = 89%
PK = 4-12 hours	Oral = 70-100%
MW = 252	pKa = 8.3
Vd = 0.5-0.8	

References:
1. Steen B, Rane A. Lonnerholm G, et.al. Phenytoin excretion in human breast milk and plasma levels in nursed infants. Ther Drug Monit 4:331-334, 1982.
2. Svensmark, O and Schiller PJ. 5,5-Diphenylhydantoin blood level after oral or intravenous dosage in man. Acta. Pharmac. Tox 16:331-346, 1960.
3. Kaneko S, Sato T, Suzuki K. The levels of anticonvulsants in breast milk. Br J Clin Pharmacol. 7:624-627,1979.

PHYTONADIONE

Trade: Phytonadione, AquaMephyton, Konakion, Mephyton, Vitamin K1

Can/Aus/UK: Konakion

Uses: Vitamin K1

AAP: Approved by the American Academy of Pediatrics for use in breastfeeding mothers

Vitamin K1 is often used to reverse the effects of oral anticoagulants and to prevent hemorrhagic disease of the newborn (HDN).[1-3] The use of vitamin K has long been accepted primarily because it reduces the decline of the vitamin K dependent coagulation factors II, VII, IX, and

X.   A single IM injection of 0.5 to 1 mg or an oral dose of 1-2 mg during the neonatal period is recommended by the AAP.   Although controversial, it is generally recognized that exclusive breastfeeding may not provide sufficient vitamin K1 to provide normal clotting factors,   particularly in the premature infant, or those with malabsorptive disorders. Vitamin K concentration in breastmilk is normally low (<5-20 ng/ml), and most infants are born with low coagulation factors (30-60%) of normal.   Although vitamin K is transferred to human milk, the amount may not be sufficient to prevent hemorrhagic disease of the newborn. Vitamin K requires the presence of bile and other factors for absorption, and neonatal absorption may be slow or delayed due to the lack of requisite gut factors.

Pregnancy Risk Category: C

Lactation Risk Category: L1

Theoretic Infant Dose: 3.0 ng/kg/day

Adult Concerns: Adverse effects include hemolytic anemia, thrombocytopenia,   thrombosis,   hypotension,   prothrombin abnormalities, pruritus, and cutaneous reactions. Anaphylaxis.

Pediatric Concerns: Vitamin K transfer to milk is low.

Drug Interactions: Decreased effect when used with coumarin/warfarin anticoagulants.

Alternatives:

Adult Dosage: 65 ug daily

T½ =	M/P =
PHL = 26-193 hours	PB =
PK = 12 hours	Oral = Complete
MW = 450	pKa =
Vd =	

References:

1.   Olsen JA: Recommended dietary intakes of vitamin K in humans. Am J Clin Nutr 45:687-692, 1987.
2.   Lane PA, Hathaway WE. Vitamin K in infancy. J. Pediatr. 106:351-359, 1985.
3.   Committee on Nutrition, American Academy of Pediatrics. Vitamin and mineral supplement needs in normal children in the United States. Pediatrics 66:1015-21, 1980.

PILOCARPINE

Trade: Isopto Carpine, Pilocar, Akarpine, Ocusert Pilo
Can/Aus/UK: Minims Pilocarpine, Ocusert-Pilo
Uses: Intraocular hypotensive
AAP: Not reviewed .

Pilocarpine is a direct acting cholinergic agent used primarily in the eyes for treatment of open-angle glaucoma. The ophthalmic dose is approximately 1 mg or less per day, while the oral adult dose is approximately 15-30 mg daily.[1,2] It is not known if pilocarpine enters milk, but it probably does in low levels due to its minimal plasma level. It is not likely that an infant would receive a clinical dose via milk, but this is presently unknown. Side effects would largely include diarrhea, gastric upset, excessive salivation and other typical cholinergic symptoms.

Pregnancy Risk Category: C

Lactation Risk Category: L3

Theoretic Infant Dose:

Adult Concerns: Common side effects from ophthalmic use include burning or itching, blurred vision, poor night vision, headaches. Following oral use, excessive sweating may occur.

Pediatric Concerns: None reported via milk but observe for vomiting, epigastric distress, abdominal cramping and diarrhea.

Drug Interactions: A decreased response when added with anticholinergic agents. Diprivan and pilocarpine may increase myopia and increase blurred vision. Sulfacetamide ophthalmic solutions may precipitate pilocarpine prior to absorption and should not be used together.

Alternatives:

Adult Dosage: 5-10 mg TID

T½ = 0.76-1.55 Hours	M/P =
PHL =	PB = 0%
PK = 1.25 hours	Oral = Good
MW = 208	pKa = 7.15
Vd =	

References:
1. Drug Facts and Comparisons. 1999 ed. Facts and Comparisons, St. Louis.
2. Pharmaceutical Manufacturers Package Insert, 1999.

PIMOZIDE

Trade: Orap
Can/Aus/UK: Orap
Uses: Potent tranquilizer
AAP: Not reviewed

Pimozide is a potent neuroleptic agent primarily used for Tourette's syndrome and chronic schizophrenia which induces a low degree of sedation.[1,2] No data are available on the secretion of pimozide into breastmilk. Must weigh benefit to mother with possible dangers to child. Suggest extreme caution.

Pregnancy Risk Category: C

Lactation Risk Category: L4

Theoretic Infant Dose:

Adult Concerns: Extrapyramidal symptoms, anorexia, weight loss, GI distress, seizures.

Pediatric Concerns: None reported but caution is urged. No pediatric studies are found.

Drug Interactions: Increases toxicity of alfentanil, CNS depressants, guanabenz, and MAO inhibitors. Do not use with macrolide antibiotics such as clarithromycin, erythromycin, azithromycin and dirithromycin, due to two reported deaths.

Alternatives:

Adult Dosage: 7-16 mg QD

T½ = 55 hours	M/P =
PHL = 66 hours	PB =
PK = 6-8 hours	Oral = >50%
MW = 462	pKa =
Vd =	

References:
1. Pharmaceutical Manufacturers Package Insert, 1996.
2. Drug Facts and Comparisons. 1995 ed. Facts and Comparisons, St. Louis.

PIOGLITAZONE

Trade: Actos
Can/Aus/UK:
Uses: Oral antidiabetic agent
AAP: Not reviewed

Pioglitazone is a thiazolindinedione family oral antidiabetic agent similar to troglitazone and rosiglitazone. It acts primarily by increasing insulin sensitivity. In essence, the insulin receptor is activated reducing insulin resistance. This family also decreases hepatic gluconeogenesis and increases insulin-dependent muscle glucose uptake. They do not increase the release or secretion of insulin. No data are available on its entry into human milk.

Pregnancy Risk Category: C

Lactation Risk Category: L3

Theoretic Infant Dose:

Adult Concerns: Hypoglycemia, upper respiratory tract infection, headache, sinusitis, myalgia, elevated liver enzymes. Elevated CPK. Edema, anemia, and pharyngitis have been reported but are rare.

Pediatric Concerns: None reported via milk, but no data are available.

Drug Interactions: May reduce plasma levels of oral contraceptives, estrogens and progestins, by 30% which could lead to loss of contraception.

Alternatives:

Adult Dosage: 15-30 mg once daily.

T½ = 16-24 hours	M/P =
PHL=	PB = >99%
PK = 2 hours	Oral =
MW = 392	pKa =
Vd = 0.63	

References:
1. Pharmaceutical Manufacturer package insert, 2000.

PIPERACILLIN

Trade: Zosyn, Pipracil
Can/Aus/UK: Pipracil, Pipril, Tazocin
Uses: Penicillin antibiotic.
AAP: Not reviewed

Piperacillin is an extended-spectrum penicillin, it is not absorbed orally, and must be given IM or I.V.. Piperacillin when combined with tazobactam sodium is called Zosyn.[1] Tazobactam is a penicillin-like inhibitor of the enzyme beta lactamase and has few clinical effects. Concentrations of piperacillin secreted into milk are believed to be extremely low.[2] Its poor oral absorption would limit its absorption.

Pregnancy Risk Category: B

Lactation Risk Category: L2

Theoretic Infant Dose:

Adult Concerns: Allergic skin rash, blood dyscrasias, diarrhea, nausea, vomiting, kidney toxicity, changes in GI flora.

Pediatric Concerns: None reported via milk.

Drug Interactions: Tetracyclines may reduce penicillin effectiveness. Probenecid may increase penicillin levels.

Alternatives:

Adult Dosage: 4-5 g BID-TID

T½ = 0.6-1.3 hours	M/P =
PHL = 3.6 hours(neonate)	PB = 30 %
PK = 30 - 50 min.	Oral = Poor
MW = 518	pKa =
Vd =	

References:
1. Pharmaceutical Manufacturers Package Insert, 1996.
2. Chaplin S, Sanders GL , Smith JM. Drug excretion in human breast milk. Adv Drug React Ac Pois Rev 1:255-287, 1982.

PIRBUTEROL ACETATE

Trade: Maxair
Can/Aus/UK: Evirel, Maxair
Uses: Bronchodilator for asthmatics
AAP: Not reviewed

Pirbuterol is a classic beta-2 drug (similar to albuterol) for dilating pulmonary bronchi in asthmatic patients. It is administered by inhalation, and occasionally orally.[1] Plasma levels are all but undetectable with normal inhaled doses. No data exists on levels in milk, but they would probably be minimal if administered via inhalation. Oral preparations would provide much higher plasma levels and would be associated with a higher risk for breastfeeding infants.

Pregnancy Risk Category: C

Lactation Risk Category: L2

Theoretic Infant Dose:

Adult Concerns: Irritability, tremors, dry mouth, excitement, palpitations, and tachycardia.

Pediatric Concerns: None reported via milk, but observe for irritability, tremors.

Drug Interactions: Decreased effect when used with beta blockers. Increased toxicity with other beta agonists, MAOi, and TCAs.

Alternatives:

Adult Dosage: 0.2-0.4 mg q 4-6 hours

T½ = 2-3 hours.	M/P =
PHL=	PB =
PK = 5 min.(Aerosol)	Oral = Complete
MW = 240	pKa =
Vd =	

References:
1. Pharmaceutical Manufacturers Package Insert, 1993, 1994.

PIROXICAM

Trade: Feldene
Can/Aus/UK: Apo-Piroxicam, Candyl, Feldene, Mobilis, Novo-Pirocam, Pirox
Uses: Non-steroidal analgesic for arthritis
AAP: Approved by the American Academy of Pediatrics for use in breastfeeding mothers

Piroxicam is a typical nonsteroidal anti-inflammatory commonly used in arthritics. In one patient taking 40 mg/day breastmilk levels were 0.22 mg/L at 2.5 hours after dose.[1] In another study of long-term therapy in four lactating women receiving 20 mg/day, the mean piroxicam concentration in breastmilk was 78 μg/L which is approximately 1-3% of the maternal plasma concentration.[2] The daily dose ingested by the infant was calculated to average 3.5% of the weight-adjusted maternal dose of piroxicam. Even though piroxicam has a very long half-life, this report suggests its use to be safe in breastfeeding mothers.

Pregnancy Risk Category: B

Lactation Risk Category: L2

Theoretic Infant Dose: 11.7 μg/kg/day

Adult Concerns: Gastric distress, GI bleeding, constipation, vomiting, edema, dizziness, liver toxicity.

Pediatric Concerns: None reported via milk in several studies.

Drug Interactions: May prolong prothrombin time when used with warfarin. Antihypertensive effects of ACEi family may be blunted or completely abolished by NSAIDs. Some NSAIDs may block antihypertensive effect of beta blockers, diuretics. Used with cyclosporin, may dramatically increase renal toxicity. May increase digoxin, phenytoin, lithium levels. May increase toxicity of methotrexate. May increase bioavailability of penicillamine. Probenecid may increase NSAID levels.

Alternatives: Ibuprofen

Adult Dosage: 20 mg QD

T½ = 30-86 hours	M/P = 0.008-.013
PHL=	PB = 99.3%.
PK = 3-5 hours	Oral = Complete
MW = 331	pKa = 5.1a1.8b
Vd = 0.31	

References:

1. Ostensen M. Piroxicam in human breastmilk. Eur. J. Clin. Pharmacol. 25:829-30, 1983.
2. Ostensen M, Matheson I, Laufen H. Piroxicam in breast milk after long-term treatment. Eur J Clin Pharmacol 35:567-569, 1988.

POLIO VACCINE, ORAL

Trade: Vaccine - Live Oral Trivalent Polio
Can/Aus/UK:
Uses: Vaccine
AAP: Not reviewed

Oral polio vaccine is a mixture of three, live, attenuated oral polio viruses.[1] Human milk contains oral polio antibodies consistent with that of the maternal circulation.[2] Early exposure of the infant may reduce production of antibodies in the infant later on. Immunization of infant prior to 6 weeks of age is not recommended due to reduced antibody production. At this age, the effect of breastmilk antibodies on the infant's development of antibodies is believed minimal. Wait until infant is 6 weeks of age before immunizing mother.

Pregnancy Risk Category: C

Lactation Risk Category: L2

Theoretic Infant Dose:

Adult Concerns: Rash, fever.

Pediatric Concerns: None reported via milk.

Drug Interactions: May have inadequate response when used with immunosuppressants. Cholera vaccine may reduce seroconversion rate when coadministered, wait at least 30 days.

Alternatives:

Adult Dosage:

References:
1. Pharmaceutical Manufacturers Package Insert, 1996.
2. Adcock E, Greene H. Poliovirus antibodies in breast-fed infants. The Lancet 1:662-663, 1971.

POLYETHYLENE GLYCOL-ELECTROLYTE SOLUTIONS

Trade: GoLytely, Col-lav, Colovage, Colyte, Ocl
Can/Aus/UK: PegLyte
Uses: Bowel evacuant
AAP: Not reviewed

PEG-ES is a polyethylene glycol-3350 saline laxative.[1] It is a non-absorbable solution used as an osmotic agent to cleanse the bowel. It is completely non-absorbed from the adult GI tract and would not likely penetrate human milk. This product is often used in children and infants prior to GI surgery. Although no data are available on transfer into human milk, it is highly unlikely that enough maternal absorption would occur to produce milk levels.

Pregnancy Risk Category: C

Lactation Risk Category: L3

Theoretic Infant Dose:

Adult Concerns: Diarrhea, bad taste, intestinal fullness. Do not use in GI obstruction, gastric retention, bowel preformation, toxic colitis, megacolon or ileus.

Pediatric Concerns: None reported via milk.

Drug Interactions: Due to intense diarrhea produced, it would dramatically reduce oral absorption of any other orally administered medicine.

Alternatives:

Adult Dosage: 240 mL q 10 minutes up to 4 L

T½ =		M/P =	
PHL =		PB =	
PK =		Oral = None	
MW =		pKa =	
Vd =			

References:
1. Drug Facts and Comparisons. 1996. ed. Facts and Comparisons, St. Louis.

POTASSIUM IODIDE

Trade:
Can/Aus/UK:
Uses: Antithyroid agent, Expectorant
AAP: Not reviewed

Potassium iodide is frequently used to suppress thyroxine secretion in hyperthyroid patients.   Iodide salts are known to be secreted into milk in high concentrations.[1,2]   Milk/plasma ratios as high at 23 have been reported. Iodides are sequestered in the thyroid gland at high levels and can potentially cause severe thyroid depression in a breastfed infant.[1] Use with extreme caution if at all. Combined with the fact that it is a poor expectorant and that it is concentrated in breastmilk, it is not recommended in breastfeeding mothers.

Pregnancy Risk Category: D

Lactation Risk Category: L4

Theoretic Infant Dose:

Adult Concerns: Thyroid depression, goiter, GI distress, rash, GI bleeding, fever, weakness.

Pediatric Concerns: Thyroid suppression may occur. Do not use doses higher than RDA.

Drug Interactions:

Alternatives:

Adult Dosage: 5-10 mg QD

T½ =	M/P = 23
PHL=	PB =
PK =	Oral = Complete
MW = 166	pKa =
Vd =	

References:
1.   Delange F, Chanoine JP, Abrassart C, et.al. Topical iodine, breastfeeding, and neonatal hypothyroidism. Arch Dis Child. 63: 106-107, 1988.
2.   Postellon DC, Aronow R. Iodine in mother's milk. JAMA 247:463, 1982.

POVIDONE IODIDE

Trade: Betadine, Iodex, Operand, Pharmadine
Can/Aus/UK: Betadine, Isodine, Minidine, Proviodine, Viodine
Uses: Special chelated iodine antiseptic
AAP: Not reviewed

Povidone iodide is a chelated form of iodine. It is primarily used as an antiseptic and antimicrobial. When placed on the adult skin, very little is absorbed. When used intravaginally, significant and increased plasma levels of iodine have been documented. In a study of 62 pregnant women who used povidone-iodine douches, significant increases in plasma iodine were noted, and a seven fold increase in fetal thyroid iodine content was reported.[1] Topical application to infants has resulted in significant absorption through the skin. Once plasma levels are attained in the mother, iodide rapidly sequester in human milk at high milk/plasma ratios.[2,3] See potassium iodide. High oral iodine intake in mothers is documented to produce thyroid suppression in breastfed infants.[2] Use with extreme caution or not at all. Repeated use of povidone iodide is not recommended in nursing mothers or their infants.

Pregnancy Risk Category: D

Lactation Risk Category: L4

Theoretic Infant Dose:

Adult Concerns: Iodine toxicity, hypothyroidism, goiter, neutropenia.

Pediatric Concerns: Transfer of absorbed iodine could occur leading to neonatal thyroid suppression. Avoid if possible.

Drug Interactions:

Alternatives:

Adult Dosage:

T½ =	M/P = >23
PHL =	PB =
PK =	Oral = Complete
MW =	pKa =
Vd =	

References:
1. Mahillon I, Peers W, Bourdoux P, Ermans AM, Delange F. Effect of vaginal douching with povidone-iodine during early pregnancy on the iodine supply to mother and fetus. Biol Neonate. 56(4):210-7, 1998.
2. Delange F, Chanoine JP, Abrassart C, et.al. Topical iodine, breastfeeding, and neonatal hypothyroidism. Arch Dis Child. 63: 106-107, 1988.
3. Postellon DC, Aronow R. Iodine in mother's milk. JAMA 247:463, 1982.

PRAVASTATIN

Trade: Pravachol
Can/Aus/UK: Lipostat, Pravachol
Uses: Lowers blood cholesterol
AAP: Not reviewed

Pravastatin belongs to the HMG-CoA reductase family of cholesterol lowering drugs.[1]   Small amounts are believed to be secreted into human milk but the levels were unreported. The effect on an infant is unknown, but it could reduce cholesterol synthesis. Atherosclerosis is a chronic process and discontinuation of lipid-lowering drugs during pregnancy and lactation should have little to no impact on the outcome of long-term therapy of primary hypercholesterolemia. Cholesterol and other products of cholesterol biosynthesis are essential components for fetal and neonatal development and the use of cholesterol-lowering drugs would not be advisable under any circumstances.

Pregnancy Risk Category: X

Lactation Risk Category: L3

Theoretic Infant Dose:

Adult Concerns: Leukopenia, elevated liver enzymes, depression, neuropathy, etc.

Pediatric Concerns: None reported via milk but studies are limited.

Drug Interactions: The anticoagulant effect of warfarin may be increased. Use with bile acid sequestrants may reduce pravastatin bioavailability by 50%. May increased toxicities of cyclosporine. Concurrent use of niacin may increase risk of severe myopathy.

Alternatives:

Adult Dosage: 10-20 mg QD

T½ = 77 hours	M/P =
PHL=	PB = 50%
PK = 1-1.5 hours	Oral = 17%
MW = 446	pKa =
Vd =	

References:
1.   Pharmaceutical Manufacturers Package Insert, 1996.

PRAZEPAM

Trade: Centrax
Can/Aus/UK: Centrax
Uses: Antianxiety agent
AAP: Drug whose effect on nursing infants is unknown but may be of concern

Prazepam is a typical benzodiazepine that belongs to Valium family. It has a long half-life in adults. Peak plasma level occurs 6 hours post-dose.[1] An active metabolite with a longer half-life is produced. No data are available on transfer into human milk. Most benzodiazepines have high milk/plasma ratios and transfer into milk readily. Observe infant closely for sedation. See diazepam.

Pregnancy Risk Category: D

Lactation Risk Category: L3

Theoretic Infant Dose:

Adult Concerns: Sedation, hypotension, depression.

Pediatric Concerns: None reported via milk, but benzodiazepines may induce sedation in breastfed infants.

Drug Interactions: May decrease effect of levodopa. May produce increased toxicity when used with other CNS depressants, disulfiram, cimetidine, anticoagulants, and digoxin.

Alternatives: Lorazepam, Alprazolam

Adult Dosage: 10 mg TID

T½ = 30-100 hours	M/P =
PHL =	PB = >70%
PK = 6 hours	Oral = Complete
MW = 325	pKa = 2.7
Vd = 12-14	

References:
1. Drug Facts and Comparisons. 1995 ed. Facts and Comparisons, St. Louis.

PRAZIQUANTEL

Trade: Biltricide
Can/Aus/UK: Biltricide
Uses: Anthelmintic
AAP: Not reviewed

Praziquantel is a trematodicide used for treatment of schistosome infections and infestations of liver flukes. One study suggests that milk levels are 25% of plasma levels.[1] From a number of studies, the mean peak serum level ranges from 1.007 to 1.625 mg/L. The prior data would suggest that milk levels would be at most 0.4 mg/L. Because praziquantel is a one-time dose, and because it has few untoward effects, it is unlikely that this dose would be detrimental to a breastfed infant. However, the manufacturer recommends an interruption of breastfeeding for 72 hours, which is probably excessive since the plasma levels drop by 95% with about 10 hours.[1]

Pregnancy Risk Category: B

Lactation Risk Category: L3

Theoretic Infant Dose: 60.0 μg/kg/day

Adult Concerns: Fever, dizziness, headache, abdominal pain, drowsiness and malaise.

Pediatric Concerns: None reported via milk.

Drug Interactions: May increase levels of albendazole with admixed. Carbamazepine, dexamethasone, and phenytoin may decrease praziquantel AUC significantly. Cimetidine may increase plasma levels by 300%.

Alternatives:

Adult Dosage: 10-25 mg/kg BID-TID X 1 day

T½ = 0.8-3 hours	M/P = 0.25%
PHL =	PB = 80%
PK = 1-3 hours	Oral = 80%
MW = 312	pKa =
Vd =	

References:
1. Leopold G, Ungenthum W, et.al. Clinical pharmacology in normal volunteers of praziquantel, a new drug against schistosomes and cestodes. Eur. J. Clin. Pharmacol. 14:281-291, 1978.

PRAZOSIN

Trade: Prazosin, Minipress
Can/Aus/UK: Apo-Prazo, Hypovasl, Minipress, Novo-Prazin, Pressin
Uses: Strong antihypertensive
AAP: Not reviewed

Prazosin is a selective alpha-1-adrenergic antagonist used to control hypertension. It is structurally similar to doxazosin and terazosin.[1,2]

antihypertensives may reduce breastmilk production and prazosin may do likewise. Others in this family (doxazosin) are known to concentrate in milk. Exercise extreme caution when administering to nursing mothers.

Pregnancy Risk Category: C

Lactation Risk Category: L4

Theoretic Infant Dose:

Adult Concerns: Leukopenia, tachycardia, hypotension, dizziness, fainting, headache, edema, diarrhea, urinary frequency.

Pediatric Concerns: None reported via milk, but some in this family are concentrated in milk. Observe extreme caution.

Drug Interactions: Beta blockers may enhance acute postural hypotensive reaction. The antihypertensive action of prazosin may be decreased by NSAIDs. Verapamil appears to increase serum prazosin levels. The antihypertensive effect of clonidine may be decreased when used with Prazosin.

Alternatives:

Adult Dosage: 3-7.5 mg BID

T½ = 2-3 hours	M/P =
PHL =	PB = 97%
PK = 2-3 hours	Oral =
MW = 383	pKa = 6.5
Vd = 0.6	

References:
1. Drug Facts and Comparisons. 1994 ed. Facts and Comparisons, St. Louis.
2. Pharmaceutical Manufacturers Package Insert, 1993, 1994.

PREDNICARBATE

Trade: Dermatop
Can/Aus/UK:
Uses: High potency steroid ointment
AAP: Not reviewed

Prednicarbate is a high potency steroid ointment. Its absorption via skin surfaces is exceedingly low, even in infants. Its oral absorption is not reported, but would probably be equivalent to prednisolone, or high. If recommended for topical application on the nipple, other less potent steroids should be suggested, including hydrocortisone or triamcinolone. If applied to the nipple, only extremely small amounts should be applied.

Pregnancy Risk Category: C

Lactation Risk Category: L3

Theoretic Infant Dose:

Adult Concerns: Symptoms of adrenal steroid suppression, fluid retention, gastric erosions.

Pediatric Concerns: None reported via milk.

Drug Interactions:

Alternatives:

Adult Dosage:

T½ =		M/P =	
PHL =		PB =	
PK =		Oral =	
MW = 488		pKa =	
Vd =			

References:

PREDNISONE

Trade: Deltasone, Meticorten, Orasone
Can/Aus/UK: Apo-Prednisone, Decortisyl, Deltasone, Econosone, Novo-Prednisone, Panafcort, Sone
Uses: Corticosteroid
AAP: Approved by the American Academy of Pediatrics for use in breastfeeding mothers

Prednisone is rapidly absorbed and metabolized to the active form, prednisolone. It is known to be secreted into human milk in very small amounts. Studies currently suggest that prednisolone levels in milk most closely correlate with the 'free' fraction of prednisolone in the mother's plasma. Thus as the doses increase, the free fraction increases at a more rapid rate. At doses of 10-20 mg, the milk/plasma ratio was 0.1, while at doses of > 30 to 80 mg, the milk/plasma ratio was elevated to 0.2 .[1] Based on the data from a patient receiving 80 mg per day, the amount an infant would ingest would be approximately 10 μg/kg, which is only 10% more than endogenous corticosteroid secretion anyway. Introduction of a 4 hour wait following administration would significantly lower risk.

Two hours after a 10 mg oral dose of prednisone, the concentration of prednisolone and prednisone were 1.6 μg/L and 26.7 μg/L respectively.[2] Using this data, an infant consuming 1 liter of milk daily would ingest 28.3 ug of the two steroids, an amount that would be clinically insignificant. In a mother receiving a high dose of 120 mg/day of prednisone, breastmilk levels of steroid ranged from 54.1 to 627 μg/L at 30 min. and 2 hours respectively.[3] Assuming the infant nursed 120 cc every 4 hours, total possible ingestion would be 47 μg, an amount that would not be hazardous.

Doses of 80 mg/day in mothers produce insignificant absorption in infant (< 0.1% of dose). In small doses, steroids are not contraindicated in nursing mothers. Whenever possible use low-dose alternatives such as aerosols or inhalers. Following administration, wait at least 4 hours if possible prior to feeding infant to reduce exposure.

Pregnancy Risk Category: B

Lactation Risk Category: L2
                                          L4 for chronic high doses

Theoretic Infant Dose: 4.2 μg/kg/day

Adult Concerns: In pediatrics: shortened stature, GI bleeding, GI ulceration, edema, osteoporosis.

Pediatric Concerns: None reported via breastmilk. Limit dose and length of exposure if possible. High doses and durations may inhibit epiphyseal bone growth, induce gastric ulcerations, glaucoma, etc. Use inhaled or intranasal forms when possible to limit exposure.

Drug Interactions: Barbiturates may significantly reduce the effects of corticosteroids. Cholestyramine may reduce absorption of prednisone. Oral contraceptives may reduce half-life and concentration of steroids. Ephedrine may reduce the half-life and increase clearance of certain steroids. Phenytoin may increase clearance. Corticosteroid clearance may be decreased by ketaconazole. Certain macrolide antibiotics may significantly decrease clearance of steroids. Isoniazid serum concentrations may be decreased.

Alternatives:

Adult Dosage: 5-60 mg QD

T½ = 3 hours(elim.)	M/P =
PHL =	PB = 70%
PK = 1-2 hours	Oral = 92%
MW = 358	pKa =
Vd =	

References:
1. Ost L et.al. Prednisolone excretion in human milk. J. Pediatr. 106(6):1008-11, 1985.
2. Katz FH, Duncan BR. Entry of prednisone in human milk. N. Eng. J. Med. 293:1154, 1975.
3. Berlin CM. Kaiser DG, Demers L. Excretion of prednisone and prednisolone in human milk. Pharmacologist 21:264, 1979.

PRIMAQUINE PHOSPHATE

Trade:
Can/Aus/UK: Primacin, Primaquine phosphate
Uses: Antimalarial
AAP: Not reviewed

Primaquine is a typical antimalarial medication that is primarily used as chemoprophylaxis after the patient has returned from the region of exposure with the intention of preventing relapses of plasmodium vivax, and or ovale. It is used in pediatric patients at a dose of 0.3 mg/kg/day for 14 days.[1-3]   No data are available on its transfer into human milk. Maternal plasma levels are rather low, only 53-107 nanogram/mL, suggesting that milk levels might be rather low as well.

Pregnancy Risk Category: C

Lactation Risk Category: L3

Theoretic Infant Dose:

Adult Concerns: Blood dyscrasias including granulocytopenia, anemia, leukocytosis, methemoglobinemia. Arrhythmia, hypertension, abdominal pain, cramps, visual (ocular) disturbances.

Pediatric Concerns: None reported from milk.

Drug Interactions: Elevated risk of blood dyscrasias with aurothioglucose. May reduce plasma levels of oral contraceptives.

Alternatives:

Adult Dosage: 15 mg daily

T½ = 4-7 hours	M/P =
PHL=	PB =
PK = 1-2 hours	Oral = 96%
MW = 259	pKa =
Vd =	

References:
1.   Mihaly GW, Ward SA, Edwards G et al: Pharmacokinetics of primaquine in man: identification of the carboxylic acid derivative as a major plasma metabolite. Br J Clin Pharmacol 17:441-446, 1984.
2.   Mihaly GW, Ward SA, Edwards G et al: Pharmacokinetics of primaquine in man. I. Studies of the absolute bioavailability and effects of dose size. Br J Clin Pharmacol 19:745-750, 1985.
3.   Bhatia SC, Saraph YS, Revankar SN et al: Pharmacokinetics of primaquine in patients with p vivax malaria. Eur J Clin Pharmacol 31:205-210, 1986.

PRIMIDONE

Trade: Myidone, Mysoline
Can/Aus/UK: Apo-Primidone, Misolyne, Mysoline, Sertan
Uses: Anticonvulsant
AAP: Drugs associated with significant side effects and should be given with caution

Primidone is metabolized in adults to several derivatives including phenobarbital. After chronic therapy, levels of phenobarbital rise to a therapeutic range. Hence, problems for the infant would not only include primidone, but subsequently, phenobarbital. In one study of 2 women receiving primidone, the steady-state concentrations of primidone in neonatal serum via ingestion of breastmilk were 0.7 and 2.5 μg/ml.[1] The steady-state phenobarbital levels in neonatal serum were between 2.0 to 13.0 μg/ml. The calculated dose of phenobarbital per day received by each infant ranged from 1.8 to 8.9 mg/day. Some sedation has been reported, particularly during the neonatal period. See phenobarbital.

Pregnancy Risk Category: D

Lactation Risk Category: L3

Theoretic Infant Dose: 0.4 mg/kg/day

Adult Concerns: Sedation, apnea, reduced suckling.

Pediatric Concerns: Some sedation, during neonatal period.

Drug Interactions: Acetazolamide may decrease primidone plasma levels. Co-administration of carbamazepine may lower primidone and phenobarbital concentrations and elevate carbamazepine concentrations. Use of phenytoin may reduce primidone concentrations. Primidone concentrations may be increased when used with isoniazid. The clearance of primidone may be decreased with nicotinamide.

Alternatives:

Adult Dosage: 250 mg TID

T½ = 10-21 h (primidone)	M/P = 0.72
PHL =	PB = <20%
PK = 0.5-5 hours.	Oral = 90%
MW = 218	pKa =
Vd = 0.5-1.0	

References:
1. Kuhnz W, Koch S, Helge H et.al. Primidone and phenobarbital during lactation period in epileptic women: total and free drug serum levels in the nursed infants and their effects on neonatal behavior. Dev Pharmacol Ther 11:147-154,1988.

PROCAINAMIDE

Trade: Pronestyl, Procan
Can/Aus/UK: Apo-Procainamide, Procan SR, Pronestryl, Pronestyl
Uses: Antiarrhythmic
AAP: Approved by the American Academy of Pediatrics for use in breastfeeding mothers

Procainamide is an antiarrhythmic agent. Procainamide and its active metabolite are secreted into breastmilk in moderate concentrations. In one patient receiving 500 mg four times daily, the breastmilk levels of procainamide at 0, 3, 6, 9, and 12 hours were 5.3, 3.9, 10.2, 4.8, and 2.6 mg/L respectively.[1] The milk/serum ratio varied from 1.0 at 12 hours to 7.3 at 6 hours post-dose (mean = 4.3). The milk levels averaged 5.4 mg/L for parent drug and 3.5 mg/L for metabolite. Although levels in milk are still too small to provide significant blood levels in an infant, one should use with caution. Only 1-2% of the maternal dose appeared in milk daily.

Pregnancy Risk Category: C

Lactation Risk Category: L3

Theoretic Infant Dose: 1.3 mg/kg/day

Adult Concerns: Nausea, vomiting, liver toxicity, blood dyscrasias, hypotension,

Pediatric Concerns: None reported via milk. Observe for liver toxicity, hypotension, but very unlikely.

Drug Interactions: Propranolol may increase procainamide serum levels. Cimetidine and ranitidine appear to increase bioavailability of procainamide. Use with lidocaine may increase cardiodepressant action of procainamide.

Alternatives:

Adult Dosage: 500-1000 mg q 4-6 hours

T½ = 3.0 hours	M/P = 1-7.3
PHL = 13.5 hours(neonate)	PB = 16%
PK = 0.75-2.5 hours	Oral = 75-90%
MW = 271	pKa = 9.2
Vd = 3.3-4.8	

References:
1. Pittard WB III, Glazier H. Procainamide excretion in human milk. J. Pediatr. 102:631-3, 1983.

PROCAINE HCL

Trade: Novocaine
Can/Aus/UK:
Uses: Local anesthetic
AAP: Not reviewed

Procaine is an ester-type local anesthetic with low potential for systemic toxicity and short duration of action.[1] Procaine is generally used for infiltration or local anesthesia, peripheral nerve block or rarely spinal anesthesia. Procaine is rapidly metabolized by plasma pseudocholinesterase to p-aminobenzoic acid.[2] No data are available on its transfer to human milk, but it is unlikely. Most other local anesthetics (see bupivacaine, lidocaine) penetrate milk only poorly and it is likely that procaine, due to its brief plasma half-life, would produce even lower milk levels. Due to its ester bond, it would be poorly bioavailable.

Pregnancy Risk Category: C

Lactation Risk Category: L3

Theoretic Infant Dose:

Adult Concerns: High plasma concentrations of procaine due to excessive dosage, or inadvertent intravascular injection may result in systemic adverse effects involving the cardiovascular and central nervous systems including nervousness, drowsiness, or blurred vision. Allergic reactions due to the p-aminobenzoic acid metabolite have been reported and may produce urticaria and edema.

Pediatric Concerns: None reported via milk.

Drug Interactions:

Alternatives:

Adult Dosage: 350-600 mg X 1

T½ = 7.7 minutes	M/P =
PHL =	PB = 5.8%
PK =	Oral = Poor
MW = 236	pKa = 9.1
Vd =	

References:
1. Drug Facts and Comparisons. 1999 ed. Facts and Comparisons, St. Louis.
2. McEvoy GE(ed):AFHS Drug Information, New York, NY. 1999

PROCHLORPERAZINE

Trade: Compazine
Can/Aus/UK: Buccastem, Nu-Prochlor, Prorazin, Stemetil
Uses: Antiemetic, tranquilizer-sedative
AAP: Not reviewed

Prochlorperazine is a phenothiazine primarily used as an antiemetic in adults and pediatric patients.[1]   There are no data yet concerning breastmilk levels but other phenothiazine derivatives enter milk in small amounts.   Because infants are extremely hypersensitive to these compounds, suggest caution in younger infants. This product may also increase prolactin levels.[2]   See promethazine as a safer alternative.

Pregnancy Risk Category: C

Lactation Risk Category: L3

Theoretic Infant Dose:

Adult Concerns: Sedation, extrapyramidal effects, seizures, weight gain, liver toxicity.

Pediatric Concerns: None reported via milk, but caution is recommended.

Drug Interactions: May have increased toxicity when used with other CNS depressants, anticonvulsants. Epinephrine may cause hypotension.

Alternatives: Promethazine

Adult Dosage: 5-10 mg TID-QID

T½ = 10-20 hours	M/P =
PHL =	PB = 90%
PK = 3.4-9.9(oral)	Oral = Complete
MW = 374	pKa =
Vd =	

References:
1.   Drug Facts and Comparisons. 1995 ed. Facts and Comparisons, St. Louis.
2.   McEvoy GE(ed):AHFS Drug Information, New York, NY. 1995.

PROGESTERONE

Trade: Crinone, Prometrium
Can/Aus/UK: Crinone, Cyclogest, Gesterol, Gestone
Uses: Progestational agent
AAP: Approved by the American Academy of Pediatrics for use in breastfeeding mothers

Progesterone is a naturally occurring steroid that is secreted by the ovary, placenta, and adrenal gland. The major problem with progesterone is its route of administration. Oral administration is hampered by rapid and extensive intestinal and liver metabolism leading to poorly sustained serum concentrations and poor bioavailability.[1] As progesterone is virtually unabsorbed orally, the vaginal route has become the most established way to deliver natural progesterone because it is easily administered, avoids liver first-pass metabolism, and has no systemic side-effects. Absorption through the vagina produces higher uterine levels and is called the 'uterine first-pass effect'. Thus fewer systemic effects are noted.

With the use of progesterone in breastfeeding mothers, two principles are of paramount interest: 1) What effect does it have on milk production, and the components of milk? 2) Does it transfer into milk in high enough levels to affect the infant directly? In general there is significant confusion in the literature as to the effect of progestins on milk composition, but the compositional changes do not appear major, volume is normal or higher, and some authors report minor changes in lipid and protein content.[2-5] However, the majority of the studies are with other progestins (e.g. medroxyprogesterone). Shaaban studied the effect of an intravaginal progesterone ring(10 mg/d) in 120 women and found no changes in growth and development of the infant, or breastfeeding performance of the study participants.[6] The author suggests the ring adds a measure of safety, since the amount of steroid present in milk would be effectively absorbed from the infant's gut.

The effect on the nursing infant is generally unknown, but it is believed minimal to none as natural progesterone is poorly bioavailable to the infant via milk.

Pregnancy Risk Category: X

Lactation Risk Category: L3

Theoretic Infant Dose:

Adult Concerns: Bloating, cramps, pain, dizziness, headache, nausea, breast pain, constipation, diarrhea, nausea, somnolence, breast enlargement.

Pediatric Concerns: None reported, not bioavailable.

Drug Interactions: May increase estrogen levels when co-administered with estrogen-containing tablets. Increased doxorubicin-induced neutropenia when co-administered. Ketoconazole may increase levels of progesterone.

Alternatives:

Adult Dosage: 90 mg daily

T½ = 13-18 hours	M/P =
PHL=	PB = 99%
PK = 6 hours	Oral = Low
MW = 314	pKa =
Vd =	

References:
1. Levy T, Gurevitch S, Bar-Hava I, Ashkenazi J, Magazanik A, Homburg R, Orvieto R, Ben-Rafael Z. Pharmacokinetics of natural progesterone administered in the form of a vaginal tablet. Hum Reprod. 14(3):606-10, 1999.
2. Naqvi HM, Baseer A. Milk composition changes--a simple and non-invasive method of detecting ovulation in lactating women. J Pak Med Assoc. 51(3):112-5, 2001.
3. Rodriguez-Palmero M, Koletzko B, Kunz C, Jensen R. Nutritional and biochemical properties of human milk: II. Lipids, micronutrients, and bioactive factors. Clin Perinatol. 26(2):335-59, 1999.
4. Costa TH, Dorea JG. Concentration of fat, protein, lactose and energy in milk of mothers using hormonal contraceptives. Ann Trop Paediatr. 12(2):203-9, 1992.
5. Sas M, Gellen JJ, Dusitsin N, Tunkeyoon M, Chalapati S, Crawford MA, Drury PJ, Lenihan T, Ayeni O, Pinol A. An investigation on the influence of steroidal contraceptives on milk lipid and fatty acids in Hungary and Thailand. WHO Special Programme of Research, Development and Research Training in Human Reproduction. Task Force on oral contraceptives. Contraception. 33(2):159-78, 1986.
6. Shaaban MM. Contraception with progestogens and progesterone during lactation. J Steroid Biochem Mol Biol. 40(4-6):705-10, 1991.

PROMETHAZINE

Trade: Phenergan
Can/Aus/UK: Avomine, Histanil, PMS Promethazine, Phenergan
Uses: Phenothiazine used as antihistamine
AAP: Not reviewed

Promethazine is a phenothiazine that is primarily used for nausea, vomiting, and motion sickness. It has been used safely for many years in adult and pediatric patients for vomiting, particularly associated with pregnancy. No data are available on the transfer of promethazine into milk, but small amounts probably do transfer. However, this product has been safely used in many pediatric conditions, and it is unlikely to produce untoward effects in older infants. Observe for sedation, particularly in younger infants. Long term followup (6 years) has found no untoward effects on development[1]

Pregnancy Risk Category: C

Lactation Risk Category: L2

Theoretic Infant Dose:

Adult Concerns: Sedation, apnea, extrapyramidal symptoms.

Pediatric Concerns: None reported via breastmilk.

Drug Interactions: Epinephrine may cause significant decrease in blood pressure.

Alternatives:

Adult Dosage: 12.5-25 mg q 4-6 hours

T½ = 12.7 hours	**M/P =**
PHL =	**PB = 76-80%**
PK = 2.7	**Oral = 25%**
MW = 284	**pKa = 9.1**
Vd = 9-19	

References:
1. Kris EB. Children born to mothers maintained on pharmacotherapy during pregnancy and postpartum. Recent Adv. Biol. Psychiatry 4:180-7,1962.

PROPAFENONE

Trade: Rythmol
Can/Aus/UK: Arythmol
Uses: Antiarrhythmic agent
AAP: Not reviewed

Propafenone is a class 1C antiarrhythmic agent with structural similarities to propranolol. In a mother receiving 300 mg three times daily and at 3 days postpartum, maternal serum levels of propafenone and 5-OH-propafenone(active metabolite) were 219 μg/L and 86 μg/L respectively. The breastmilk level of parafenone and 5-OH-propafenone was 32 μg/L and 47 μg/L respectively. The milk/plasma ratios for drug and metabolite were 0.15 and 0.54 respectively. The authors estimate that the daily intake of drug and active metabolite in their infant (3.3 kg) would have been 16 ug and 24 ug per day respectively.

Pregnancy Risk Category: C

Lactation Risk Category: L2

Theoretic Infant Dose: 7.1 μg/kg/day

Adult Concerns: Adverse effects include dizziness, unusual taste, first degree AV block, intraventricular conduction delay, nausea and/or vomiting, and constipation. In addition, dyspnea, CHF and proarrhythmia has been reported. Less frequently, hepatotoxicity, agranulocytosis, leukopenia, and positive ANA have been reported. Other side effects include sexual dysfunction.

Pediatric Concerns: None reported via milk. Levels are quite low.

Drug Interactions: Increased levels with cimetidine, beta blockers, quinidine, warfarin, cyclosporin and other drugs metabolized by this enzyme.
Rifampin may reduce levels of propafenone.

Alternatives:

Adult Dosage: 150-225 mg TID

T½ = 2-10 hours	M/P = 0.15
PHL =	PB = 85-97%
PK = 2-3 hours	Oral = 12%
MW =	pKa =
Vd = 4	

References:
1. Libardoni M, Piovan D, Busato E, Padrini R. Transfer of propafenone and 5-OH-propafenone to foetal plasma and maternal milk. Br J Clin Pharmacol. 32(4):527-8, 1991.

PROPOFOL

Trade: Diprivan
Can/Aus/UK: Diprivan
Uses: Preanesthetic sedative
AAP: Not reviewed

Propofol is an I.V. sedative hypnotic agent for induction and maintenance of anesthesia. It is particularly popular in various pediatric procedures. Although the terminal half-life is long, it is rapidly distributed out of the plasma compartment to other peripheral compartments (adipose) so that anesthesia is short (3-10 minutes). Propofol is incredibly lipid soluble. However, only very low concentrations of propofol have been found in breastmilk. In one study of 3 women who received propofol 2.5 mg/kg I.V. followed by a continuous infusion, the breastmilk levels ranged from 0.04 to 0.74 mg/L.[1] The second breastmilk level obtained 24 hours after delivery contained only 6% of the 4-hour sample. Similar levels (0.12-0.97 mg/L) were noted by Schmitt in colostrum samples obtained 4-8 hours after induction with propofol.[2] From these data it is apparent that only minimal levels of propofol is transferred to human milk. No data are available on the oral absorption of propofol. Propofol is rapidly cleared from the neonatal circulation.[1]

Pregnancy Risk Category: B

Lactation Risk Category: L2

Theoretic Infant Dose: 111.0 μg/kg/day

Adult Concerns: Sedation, apnea.

Pediatric Concerns: None reported in several studies.

Drug Interactions: Anaphylactoid reactions when used with atracurium. May potentiate the neuromuscular blockade of vecuronium. May be additive with other CNS depressants. Theophylline may antagonize the effect of propofol.

Alternatives: Midazolam

Adult Dosage: 6-12 mg/kg/hour

T½ = 1-3 days.	M/P =
PHL=	PB = 99%
PK = Instant(IV)	Oral =
MW = 178	pKa = 11.0
Vd = 60	

References:
1. Dailland P, Cockshott ID, et al: Intravenous propofol during cesarean section: placental transfer, concentrations in breast milk, and neonatal effects. A preliminary study. Anesthesiology 71:827-834, 1989
2. Schmitt JP, Schwoerer D, et.al. Passage of propofol in the colostrum. Preliminary data. Ann. Fr. Anesth. Reanim 6:267-268, 1987.

PROPOXYPHENE

Trade: Darvocet-n, Propacet, Darvon
Can/Aus/UK: Capadex, Darvon-N, Dextropropoxyphene, Di-Gesic, Doloxene, Novo-Propoxyn, Paradex, Progesic
Uses: Mild narcotic analgesic
AAP: Approved by the American Academy of Pediatrics for use in breastfeeding mothers

Propoxyphene is a mild narcotic analgesic similar in efficacy to aspirin. The amount secreted into milk is extremely low and is generally too low to produce effects in infant (< 1 mg/day).[1]   Maternal plasma levels peak at 2 hours Propoxyphene is metabolized to norpropoxyphene (which has weaker CNS effects).   AHL= 6-12 hours (propoxyphene), 30-36 hours (norpropoxyphene). Thus far, no reports of untoward effects in infants have been reported.

Pregnancy Risk Category: C

Lactation Risk Category: L2

Theoretic Infant Dose:

Adult Concerns: Nausea, respiratory depression, sedation, agitation, seizures, anemia, liver toxicity, withdrawal symptoms.

Pediatric Concerns: None reported but observe for sedation.

Drug Interactions: Additive sedation may occur when used with CNS depressants such as barbiturates. Carbamazepine levels may be increased. Use with cimetidine may produce CNS toxicity such as confusion, disorientation, apnea, seizures.

Alternatives: Ibuprofen, Acetaminophen

Adult Dosage: 65 mg q 4 hours PRN

T½ = 6-12 h (propoxyphene)	M/P =
PHL =	PB = 78%
PK = 2 hours	Oral = Complete
MW = 339	pKa = 6.3
Vd = 12-26	

References:
1. Catz C, Gulacoia G. Drugs and breast milk. Pediatr Clin North Am 19:151-66, 1972.

PROPRANOLOL

Trade: Inderal
Can/Aus/UK: Cardinol, Deralin, Detensol, Inderal, Novo-Pranol
Uses: Beta-blocker, antihypertensive
AAP: Approved by the American Academy of Pediatrics for use in breastfeeding mothers

Propranolol is a popular beta blocker used in treating hypertension, cardiac arrhythmia, migraine headache, and numerous other syndromes. In general, the maternal plasma levels are exceeding low, hence the milk levels are low as well. Milk/plasma ratios are generally less than one. In one study of 3 patients, the average milk concentration was only 35.4 μg/L after multiple dosing intervals. The milk/plasma ratio varied from 0.33 to 1.65.[1] Using this data, the authors suggest that an infant would receive only 70 μg/Liter of milk per day, which is < 0.1% of the maternal dose. In another study of a patient receiving 20 mg twice daily, milk levels varied from 4 to 20 μg/L with an estimated average dose to infant of 3 μg/day.[2] In another patient receiving 40 mg four times daily, the peak concentration occurred at 3 hours after dosing.[3] Milk levels varied from zero to 9 μg/L. After a 30 day regimen of 240 mg/day propranolol, the pre-dose and postdose concentration in breastmilk was 26 and 64 μg/L, respectively.[3] No symptoms or signs of beta blockade were noted in this infant.

The above amounts in milk would likely be clinically insignificant. Long term exposure has not been studied, and caution is urged. Of the beta blocker family, propranolol is probably preferred in lactating women.

Pregnancy Risk Category: C

Lactation Risk Category: L3

Theoretic Infant Dose: 5.3 μg/kg/day

Adult Concerns: Bradycardia, asthmatic symptoms, hypotension, sedation, weakness, hypoglycemia.

Pediatric Concerns: None reported via breastmilk in numerous studies.

Drug Interactions: Decreased effect when used with aluminum salts, barbiturates, calcium salts, cholestyramine, NSAIDs, ampicillin, rifampin, and salicylates. Beta blockers may reduce the effect of oral sulfonylureas (hypoglycemic agents). Increased toxicity/effect when used with other antihypertensives, contraceptives, MAO inhibitors, cimetidine, and numerous other products. See drug interaction reference for complete listing.

Alternatives: Metoprolol

Adult Dosage: 160-240 mg QD

T½ = 3-5 hours	M/P = 0.5
PHL =	PB = 90%
PK = 60-90 min.	Oral = 30%
MW = 259	pKa = 9.5
Vd = 3-5	

References:
1. Smith MT, et.al. Propranolol, propranolol glucoronide, and naphthoxylacetic acid in breast milk and plasma. Ther Drug Monit. 5:87-93,1983.
2. Taylor EA, Turner P. Anti-hypertensive therapy with propranolol during pregnancy and lactation. Postgrad Med J. 57:427-430, 1981.
3. Bauer JH, Pape B, Zajicek J et.al. Propranolol in human plasma and breast milk. Am J Cardiol. 43:860-863,1979.

PROPYLTHIOURACIL

Trade: PTU
Can/Aus/UK: Propyl-Thyracil
Uses: Antithyroid
AAP: Approved by the American Academy of Pediatrics for use in breastfeeding mothers

Propylthiouracil reduces the production and secretion of thyroxine by the thyroid gland. Only small amounts are secreted into breastmilk. Reports thus far suggest that levels absorbed by infant are too low to produce side effects.[1]   In one study of nine patients given 400 mg doses, mean serum and milk levels were 7.7 mg/L and 0.7 mg/L respectively, which correlated to only 0.025% of the maternal dose.[2] No changes in infant thyroid have been reported. PTU is the best of antithyroid medications for use in lactating mothers. Monitor infant thyroid function (T4, TSH) carefully during therapy.

Pregnancy Risk Category: D

Lactation Risk Category: L2

Theoretic Infant Dose: 105.0 μg/kg/day

Adult Concerns: Hypothyroidism, liver toxicity, aplastic anemia, anemia.

Pediatric Concerns: None reported, but observed closely for thyroid function.

Drug Interactions: Activity of oral anticoagulants may be potentiated by PTU associated anti-vitamin K activity.

Alternatives:

Adult Dosage: 100 mg TID

T½ = **1-2 hours**	**M/P = 0.1**
PHL=	**PB** = **80%**
PK = **1-1.5 hours**	**Oral** = **50-95%**
MW = **170**	pKa =
Vd =	

References:
1. Cooper DS. Antithyroid drugs: to breast-feed or not to breast-feed. Am J Obstet Gynecol 157:234-235,1987.
2. Kampmann JP, et.al. Propylthiouracil in human milk. Lancet 1:736-8, 1980.

PSEUDOEPHEDRINE

Trade: Sudafed, Halofed, Novafed, Actifed
Can/Aus/UK: Balminil, Contac, Eltor, Pseudofrin, Sudafed
Uses: Decongestant
AAP: Approved by the American Academy of Pediatrics for use in breastfeeding mothers

Pseudoephedrine is an adrenergic compound primarily used as a nasal decongestant. It is secreted into breastmilk but in low levels. In a study of 3 lactating mothers who received 60 mg of pseudoephedrine, the milk/plasma ratio was as high as 2.6-3.9.[1]   The average pseudoephedrine milk level over 24 hours was 264 μg/L.   The calculated dose that would be absorbed by the infant was still very low (0.4 to 0.6% of the maternal dose). Preliminary studies from our laboratories suggest that in some mothers, a significant reduction in milk volume and prolactin levels may result following exposure to pseudoephedrine.[2] While the amount of pseudoephedrine in milk is not clinically relevant, the reduction in milk production is concerning. Caution is recommended.

Pregnancy Risk Category: C

Lactation Risk Category: L3 for acute use
L4 for chronic use

Theoretic Infant Dose: 39.6 μg/kg/day

Adult Concerns: Irritability, agitation, anorexia, stimulation, insomnia, hypertension, tachycardia.

Pediatric Concerns: One case of irritability via milk. This product is commonly used in infants with minimal problems.

Drug Interactions: May have increased toxicity when used with MAOI.

Alternatives:

Adult Dosage: 60 mg q 4-6 hours

T½ = < 4 hours	M/P = 2.6-3.3
PHL=	PB =
PK = 0.5-1 hours	Oral = 90%
MW = 165	pKa = 9.7
Vd =	

References:
1. Findlay JWA, et. al. Pseudoephedrine and triprolidine in plasma and breast milk of nursing mothers. Br J Clin Pharmacol 18:901-6, 1984.
2. Hale TW, Hartmann PE, Ilett KF. Personnal communication, 2002.

PYRANTEL

Trade: Pin-rid, Reese's Pinworm, Antiminth, Pin-x
Can/Aus/UK: Combantrin, Early Bird
Uses: Anthelmintic
AAP: Not reviewed

Pyrantel is an anthelmintic used to treat pinworm, hookworm, and round worm infestations. It is only minimally absorbed orally, with the majority being eliminated in feces. Peak plasma levels are generally less than 0.05 to 0.13 μg/mL and occur prior to 3 hours. Reported side effects are few and minimal. No data on transfer of pyrantel in human milk are available, but due to minimal oral absorption, and low plasma levels, it is unlikely that breastmilk levels would be clinically relevant. Generally it is administered as a single dose.

Pregnancy Risk Category: C

Lactation Risk Category: L3

Theoretic Infant Dose:

Adult Concerns: Side effects are generally minimal and include headache, dizziness, somnolence, insomnia, nausea, vomiting, abdominal cramps, diarrhea and pain. Only moderate changes in liver enzymes have been noted, without serious hepatotoxicity.

Pediatric Concerns: None reported via milk.

Drug Interactions: Pyrantel and piperazine should not be mixed because they are antagonistic. Pyrantel increases theophylline plasma levels.

Alternatives:

Adult Dosage: 11 mg/kg X 2 over two weeks

T½ =		M/P =	
PHL =		PB =	
PK = < 3 hours		Oral = < 50%	
MW = 206		pKa =	
Vd =			

References:

PYRAZINAMIDE

Trade: Pyrazinamide, D-50, Mk-56
Can/Aus/UK: PMS-pyrazinamide, Tebrazid, Zinamide
Uses: Antitubercular antibiotic
AAP: Not reviewed

Pyrazinamide is a typical antituberculosis antibiotic used as first-line therapy in tuberculosis infections. In one patient three hours following an oral dose of 1000 mg, peak milk levels were 1.5 mg/Liter of milk.[1] Peak maternal plasma levels at 2 hours were 42 μg/mL.

Pregnancy Risk Category: C

Lactation Risk Category: L3

Theoretic Infant Dose: 0.2 mg/kg/day

Adult Concerns: The most common side effect is hepatotoxicity, nausea and vomiting. Transient increases in liver enzymes, including fever, anorexia, malaise, jaundice, and liver tenderness have been reported. Hyperuricemia including gout has been reported. Maculopapular rashes, arthralgia, acne and numerous other side effects have been noted.

Pediatric Concerns: None reported via milk.

Drug Interactions:

Alternatives:

Adult Dosage: 15-30 mg/kg daily

T½ = 9-10 hours	M/P =
PHL =	PB = 17%
PK = 2 hours	Oral = Complete
MW = 123	pKa =
Vd =	

References:
1. Holdiness MR. Antituberculosis drugs and breast-feeding. Arch. Intern. Med. 144:1888- , 1984.

PYRIDOSTIGMINE

Trade: Mestinon, Regonol
Can/Aus/UK: Mestinon, Regonol
Uses: Anticholinesterase muscle stimulant
AAP: Approved by the American Academy of Pediatrics for use in breastfeeding mothers

Pyridostigmine is a potent cholinesterase inhibitor used in myasthenia gravis to stimulate muscle strength. In a group of 2 mothers receiving from 120-300 mg/day, breastmilk concentrations varied from 5 to 25 μg/Liter.[1] The calculated milk/plasma ratios varied from 0.36 to 1.13. No cholinergic side effects were noted and no pyridostigmine was found in the infants plasma.

Because the oral bioavailability is so poor (10-20%), the actual dose received by the breastfed infant would be significantly less than the above concentrations. Please note the dosage is highly variable and may be as high as 600 mg/day in divided doses. The authors estimated total daily intake at 0.1% or less of the maternal dose.

Pregnancy Risk Category: C

Lactation Risk Category: L2

Theoretic Infant Dose: 3.8 μg/kg/day

Adult Concerns: Nausea, vomiting, salivation, sweating, weakness, asthmatic symptoms, muscle cramps, fasciculations, constricted pupils.

Pediatric Concerns: None reported in one study of two infants.

Drug Interactions: Increased effect of neuromuscular blockers such as succinylcholine. Increased toxicity with edrophonium.

Alternatives:

Adult Dosage: 60-180 mg BID-QID

T½ = 3.3 hours	M/P = 0.36-1.13
PHL =	PB = 0%
PK = 1-2 hours	Oral = 10-20%
MW = 261	pKa =
Vd =	

References:
1. Hardell LI, et.al. Pyridostigmine in human breast milk. Br. J. Clin. Pharmacol. 14:565-7, 1982.

PYRIDOXINE

Trade: Vitamin B-6, Hexa-betalin
Can/Aus/UK: Complement continus, Hexa-Betalin, Pyroxin
Uses: Vitamin B-6
AAP: Approved by the American Academy of Pediatrics for use in breastfeeding mothers

Pyridoxine is vitamin B-6. The recommended daily allowance for non-pregnant women is 1.6 mg/day. Pyridoxine is secreted in milk in direct proportion to the maternal intake and concentrations in milk vary from 123 to 314 ng/ml depending on the study. Pyridoxine is required in slight excess during pregnancy and lactation and most prenatal vitamin supplements contain from 12-25 mg/day. Very high doses (600 mg/day) suppress prolactin secretion and therefore production of breastmilk.[1,2] Although this data has been refuted in two studies where high doses of pyridoxine failed to suppress prolactin levels or lactation.[3,4]

However, it is advisable to not use in excess of 25 mg/day. One study clearly indicates that pyridoxine readily transfers into breastmilk and that B-6 levels in milk correlate closely with maternal intake.[5] Breastfeeding mothers who are deficient in pyridoxine should be supplemented with modest amounts (< 25 mg/day).

Pregnancy Risk Category: A

Lactation Risk Category: L2
                           L4 in high doses

Theoretic Infant Dose: 47.1 μg/kg/day

Adult Concerns: Reduced milk production, sensory neuropathy, GI distress, sedation.

Pediatric Concerns: Excessive oral doses have been reported to produce sedation,   hypotonia and respiratory distress in infants, although none have been reported via breastmilk.

Drug Interactions: Decreased serum levels with levodopa, phenobarbital, and phenytoin.

Alternatives:

Adult Dosage: 1.6 mg QD

T½ = 15-20 days	**M/P =**
PHL =	**PB =**
PK = 1-2 hours	**Oral = Complete**
MW = 205	**pKa =**
Vd =	

References:
1. Marcus RG Suppression of lactation with high doses of pyridoxine. S Afr Med J. 49:2155-2156, 1975.
2. Foukas MD. An antilactogenic effect of pyridoxine. J Obstet Gynaecol Br Commonw 80:718-20, 1973.
3. de Waal JM, Steyn AF, Harms JH, Slabber CF, Pannall PR. Failure of pyridoxine to suppress raised serum prolactin levels. S Afr Med J. 25;53(8):293-4, 1978.
4. Canales ES, Soria J, Zarate A, Mason M, Molina M. The influence of pyridoxine on prolactin secretion and milk production in women. Br J Obstet Gynaecol.83(5):387-8, 1976.
5. Kang-Yoon SA, et.al. Vitamin B-6 status of breast-fed neonates: influence of pyridoxine spplementation on mothers and neonates. Amer. J. Clin. Nutr. 56:548-58,1992.

PYRIMETHAMINE

Trade: Daraprim
Can/Aus/UK: Daraprim, Fansidar, Maloprim
Uses: Antimalarial, folic acid antagonist
AAP: Approved by the American Academy of Pediatrics for use in breastfeeding mothers

Pyrimethamine is a folic acid antagonist that has been used for prophylaxis of malaria. Maternal peak plasma levels occur 2-6 hours post-dose.[1] Pyrimethamine is secreted into human milk. In a group of mothers receiving 25, 50, and 75 mg/day of pyrimethamine for 10 days, the peak concentration was 3.3 mg/L.[2] An infant would receive an estimated dose of 3-4 mg in a 48 hour period (following 75 mg maternal dose). A number of reports of carcinogenesis in adults are available and indicate that infants should not be exposed to this medication.

Pregnancy Risk Category: C

Lactation Risk Category: L4

Theoretic Infant Dose: 0.5 mg/kg/day

Adult Concerns: Anemia, blood dyscrasias, folate deficiency states, carcinogenesis, insomnia, headache, anorexia, vomiting, megaloblastic anemia, leukopenia.

Pediatric Concerns: None reported, but possible carcinogenesis may preclude its use in breastfed infants.

Drug Interactions: Use of pyrimethamine with other antifolate drugs(methotrexate, sulfonamides, TMP-SMZ) may increase the risk of bone marrow suppression and folate deficiency states.

Alternatives:

Adult Dosage: 25 mg q week

T½ = 96 hours	M/P = 0.2-0.43
PHL=	PB = 87%
PK = 2-6 hours	Oral = Complete
MW = 249	pKa =
Vd =	

References:
1. Pharmaceutical Manufacturers Package Insert, 1996.
2. Clyde DF, Shute GT. Transfer of pyrimethamine in human milk. J. Trop. Med. and Hyg. 59:277-284, 1956.

QUAZEPAM

Trade: Doral, Dormalin
Can/Aus/UK:
Uses: Sedative, hypnotic
AAP: Drug whose effect on nursing infants is unknown but may be of concern

Quazepam is a long half-life benzodiazepine (Valium-like) medication used as a sedative and hypnotic. It is selectively metabolized to several metabolites that have even longer half-lives. In a study of four breastfeeding mothers, the amount of quazepam transferred into milk through 48 hours was 11.59 μg, corresponding to 0.08% of the dose.[1] During the same time period, only 4.02 ug of 2-oxoquazepam was transferred. Through 48 hours, only 17.1 ug quazepam equivalents, or 0.11% of the administered dose was excreted into breastmilk. Although this study was not at steady state, using standard algorithms the authors estimate that the daily dose to infant following daily usage would be approximately 28.7 ug quazepam equivalents, or 0.19% of the maternal dose.

Pregnancy Risk Category: X

Lactation Risk Category: L2

Theoretic Infant Dose:

Adult Concerns: Drowsiness, sedation.

Pediatric Concerns: None reported via breastmilk. Observe for sedation.

Drug Interactions: May increase sedation when used with CNS depressants such as alcohol, barbiturates, opioids. Cimetidine may decrease metabolism and clearance of benzodiazepines. Valproic may displace BZs from binding sites, thus increasing sedative effects. SSRIs (fluoxetine, sertraline, paroxetine) can dramatically increase BZs levels by altering clearance, thus leading to sedation .

Alternatives: Lorazepam, Alprazolam

Adult Dosage: 15 mg daily

T½ = 39 hours	M/P = 4.19
PHL=	PB = >95%.
PK = 2 hours	Oral = Complete
MW = 387	pKa =
Vd =	

References:
1. Hilbert JM, Symchowicz S,Zampaglione N. Excretion of quazepam into human breast milk. J Clin Pharmacol 24:457-462, 1984.

QUETIAPINE FUMARATE

Trade: Seroquel
Can/Aus/UK:
Uses: Antipsychotic drug
AAP: Not reviewed

Quetiapine(Seroquel) is indicated for the treatment of psychotic disorders.[1] It works similarly to other antipsychotic agents by inhibiting dopamine and serotonin receptors. It has some affinity for histamine receptors, which may account for its sedative properties. It has been shown to increase the incidence of seizures, prolactin levels, and to lower thyroid levels in adults. At present, there are no data on the transmission of quetiapine into human milk but it has been found in rodent milk. Until we know more, this product should be considered risky for breastfeeding women.

Pregnancy Risk Category: C

Lactation Risk Category: L4

Theoretic Infant Dose:

Adult Concerns: The side effects of quetiapine are similar to other anti-psychotic drugs and include sedation, tardive dyskinesia, seizures, priapism, hypothermia, dysphagia, hyperprolactinemia, orthostatic hypotension, cataracts, and hypothyroidism.

Pediatric Concerns: None reported via milk, but caution is recommended.

Drug Interactions: Phenytoin increases clearance of quetiapine significantly (5X). Other drugs which increase clearance include: cimetidine, thioridazine, and other P450 3a inhibitors. Lorazepam levels may be reduced by 20% when used with quetiapine.

Alternatives:

Adult Dosage: 300-400 mg daily

T½ = 6 hours	M/P =
PHL =	PB = 83%
PK = 1.5 hours	Oral = 100%
MW = 883	pKa =
Vd = 10	

References:
1. Pharmaceutical Manufacturers Package Insert, 1999.

QUINACRINE

Trade: Atabrine
Can/Aus/UK:
Uses: Antimalarial, giardiasis
AAP: Not reviewed

Quinacrine was once used for malaria, but has been replaced by other preparations. It is primarily used for giardiasis.[1,2] Small to trace amounts are secreted into milk. No known harmful effects except in infants with G6PD deficiencies. However, quinacrine is eliminated from the body very slowly, requiring up to 2 months for complete elimination. Quinacrine levels in liver are extremely high. Accumulation in infant is likely due to slow rate of excretion. Extreme caution is urged.

Pregnancy Risk Category: C

Lactation Risk Category: L4

Theoretic Infant Dose:

Adult Concerns: GI distress, liver toxicity, seizures, aplastic anemia, retinopathy.

Pediatric Concerns: None reported via milk, but accumulation may occur after prolonged exposure. Use with caution.

Drug Interactions: Primaquine toxicity is increased by quinacrine. Concomitant use is contraindicated.

Alternatives:

Adult Dosage: 100 mg TID

T½ = >5 days	M/P =
PHL =	PB = High
PK = 1-3 hours	Oral = Complete
MW = 400	pKa =
Vd =	

References:
1. Drug Facts and Comparisons. 1994 ed. Facts and Comparisons, St. Louis.
2. McEvoy GE(ed):AHFS Drug Information, New York, NY. 1992, pp 417-26.

QUINAPRIL

Trade: Accupril, Accuretic
Can/Aus/UK: Accupril, Accupro, Asig
Uses: ACE inhibitor, antihypertensive
AAP: Not reviewed

Quinapril is an angiotensin converting enzyme inhibitor (ACE) used as an antihypertensive. Accuretic products also contain the diuretic hydrochlorothiazide. Once in the plasma compartment, quinapril is rapidly converted to quinaprilat, the active metabolite. In a study of 6 women who received 20 mg/d the M/P ratio for quinapril was 0.12.[1] Quinapril was not detected in milk after 4 h. No quinaprilat was detected in any of the milk samples. The estimated 'dose' of quinapril that would be received by the infant was 1.6% of the maternal dose, adjusted for respective weights. The authors suggest that quinapril appears to be 'safe' during breastfeeding although as always, the risk:benefit ratio should be considered when it is to be given to a nursing mother.

ACE inhibitors are generally contraindicated during pregnancy due to increased fetal morbidity with ACE inhibitors. Newborns are especially susceptible to ACE inhibitors and they should probably be avoided during the first two weeks postpartum in normal infants.

Pregnancy Risk Category: D

Lactation Risk Category: L2
                               L4 if used early postpartum

Theoretic Infant Dose:

Adult Concerns: Cough, hypotension, nausea, vomiting.

Pediatric Concerns: None reported in one study.

Drug Interactions: Probenecid increases plasma levels of ACEi. ACEi and diuretics have additive hypotensive effects. Antacids reduce bioavailability of ACE inhibitors. NSAIDS reduce hypotension of ACE inhibitors. Phenothiazines increase effects of ACEi. ACEi increase digoxin and lithium plasma levels. May elevate potassium levels when potassium supplementation is added.

Alternatives: Captopril, Enalapril

Adult Dosage: 20-80 mg QD

T½ = 2 hours	**M/P =**
PHL=	**PB = 97%**
PK = 2 hour	**Oral = Complete**
MW = 474	**pKa =**
Vd =	

References:
1.   Begg EJ, Robson RA, Gardiner SJ, Hudson LJ, Reece PA, Olson SC, Posvar EL, Sedman AJ. Quinapril and its metabolite quinaprilat in human milk. Br J Clin Pharmacol. 51(5):478-81, 2001.

QUINIDINE

Trade: Quinaglute, Quinidex
Can/Aus/UK: Apo-Quinidine, Cardioquin, Kiditard, Kinidin Durules, Novo-Quinidin
Uses: Antiarrhythmic agent
AAP: Approved by the American Academy of Pediatrics for use in breastfeeding mothers

Quinidine is used to treat cardiac arrhythmias. Three hours following a dose of 600 mg, the level of quinidine in the maternal serum was 9.0 mg/L and the concentration in her breastmilk was 6.4 mg/L.[1] Subsequently, a level of 8.2 mg/L was noted in breastmilk. An infant ingesting 1 Liter of milk daily, would receive approximately 1% of the total maternal dose which is below the normal therapeutic dosage used in infants. Quinidine is selectively stored in the liver, long-term use could expose an infant to liver toxicity. Monitor liver enzymes.

Pregnancy Risk Category: C

Lactation Risk Category: L2

Theoretic Infant Dose: 1.2 mg/kg/day

Adult Concerns: Blood dyscrasias, hypotension, thrombocytopenia, depression, fever.

Pediatric Concerns: None reported, but observe for changes in liver function.

Drug Interactions: Quinidine levels may be elevated with amiodarone, certain antacids, cimetidine, verapamil. Digoxin plasma levels may be increased with quinidine. Quinidine may increase anticoagulant levels with used with warfarin.   Quinidine levels or effect may be reduced when used with barbiturates, nifedipine, rifampin, sucralfate, or phenytoin. Effects of procainamide may be dangerously increased when used with quinidine.   Clearance of TCAs may be decreased by quinidine.

Alternatives:

Adult Dosage: 200-400 mg TID-QID

T½ = 6-8 hours	M/P = 0.71
PHL=	PB = 87%
PK = 1-2 hours	Oral = 80%
MW = 324	pKa = 4.2,8.3
Vd = 1.8-3.0	

References:
1.   Hill LM, Malkasian GD Jr. The use of quinidine sulfate throughout pregnancy. Obstet Gynecol 54:366-8, 1979.

QUININE

Trade: Quinamm
Can/Aus/UK: Biquinate, Myoquin, Novo-Quinine, Quinate, Quinbisul
Uses: Antimalarial
AAP: Approved by the American Academy of Pediatrics for use in breastfeeding mothers

Quinine is a cinchona alkaloid primarily used in malaria prophylaxis and treatment. Small to trace amounts are secreted into milk. No reported harmful effects have been reported except in infants with G6PD deficiencies.   In a study of 6 women receiving 600-1300 mg/day, the concentration of quinine in breastmilk ranged from 0.4 to 1.6 mg/L at 1.5 to 6 hours postdose.[1]   The authors suggest these levels are clinically insignificant.   In another study, with maternal plasma concentrations of 0.5 to 8 mg/L, the milk/plasma ratio ranged from 0.11 to 0.53.[2]   The total daily consumption by a breastfed infant was estimated to be 1-3 mg/day.

Pregnancy Risk Category: D

Lactation Risk Category: L2

Theoretic Infant Dose: 1.2 mg/kg/day

Adult Concerns: Blood dyscrasias, thrombocytopenia, retinal toxicity, tongue discoloration, kidney damage.

Pediatric Concerns: None reported via breastmilk in several studies.

Drug Interactions: Aluminum containing antacid may delay or decrease absorption. Quinine may depress vitamin K dependant clotting factors. Therefore increasing warfarin effects. Cimetidine may reduce quinine clearance. Digoxin serum levels may be increased. Do not use with mefloquine.

Alternatives:

Adult Dosage: 650 mg q 8 hours

T½ = 11 hours	**M/P = 0.11-0.53**
PHL=	**PB = 93%**
PK = 1-3 hours	**Oral = 76%**
MW = 324	**pKa = 4.3,8.4**
Vd = 1.8-3.0	

References:
1.   Terwillinger WG, Hatcher RA. The elimination of morphine and quinine in human milk. Surg. Gynecol. Obstet. 58:823, 1934.
2.   Phillips RE, Looareesuwan S, White NJ et.al. Quinine pharmacokinetics and toxicity in pregnant and lactating women with falciparum malaria. Br J Clin Pharmacol 21:677-683, 1986.

QUINUPRISTIN AND DALFOPRISTIN

Trade: Synercid
Can/Aus/UK:
Uses: Antimicrobial
AAP: Not reviewed

Synercid is a streptogramin antibacterial agent for intravenous use only. It is indicated for the treatment of vancomycin-resistant enterococcus faecium, as well as for treatment of susceptible staph aureus. It has some use against methicillin-resistant organisms. No data are available on its transfer to human milk. However, due to its acidity and large molecular weight, milk levels will probably be low.

Pregnancy Risk Category: B

Lactation Risk Category: L3

Theoretic Infant Dose:

Adult Concerns: This product is well-tolerated. Infusion site problems such as pain and erythema have been reported. Headache, GI disturbances, and elevated liver enzymes report. Arthalagia, myalgia have been reported.

Pediatric Concerns: None reported via milk.

Drug Interactions: Synercid inhibits cytochrome P450 3A4. Thus numerous interactions with other drugs metabolized by this enzyme. A partial list includes: cyclosporin, midazolam, nifedipine, and terfenadine. Check numerous other drug interactions with alternate drug source.

Alternatives:

Adult Dosage: 7.5 mg/kg q 8 h

T½ = 1-3 hours	M/P =
PHL=	PB = 32%q + 56%d
PK = 1 hour	Oral = Nil
MW = 1022	pKa =
Vd = 0.45q and 0.24d	

References:
1. Pharmaceutical manufacturers package insert, 2002.

RABEPRAZOLE

Trade: Aciphex
Can/Aus/UK:
Uses: Antisecretory, antacid
AAP: Not reviewed

Rabeprazole is an antisecretory proton pump inhibitor similar to omeprazole(Prilosec). Rodent studies suggest a high milk/plasma ratio but as we know, these do not correlate well with humans. No data are available in humans. Further, rabeprazole is only 52% bioavailable in adults when enteric coated due to its instability in gastric acids. As presented in milk, it would be virtually destroyed in the infants stomach prior to absorption.

Pregnancy Risk Category: B

Lactation Risk Category: L3

Theoretic Infant Dose:

Adult Concerns: Asthenia, fever, allergies, malaise, chest pain, photosensitivity. Myalgia, arthritis, leg cramps and bone pain have been reported.

Pediatric Concerns: None reported via milk.

Drug Interactions: None are reported.

Alternatives: Omeprazole

Adult Dosage: 20 mg daily

T½ = 1-2 hours	M/P =
PHL=	PB = 96.3
PK = 2-5 hours	Oral = 52%(enteric)
MW = 381	pKa =
Vd =	

References:
1. Pharmaceutical manufacturers package insert, 2000.

RABIES INFECTION

Trade: Rabies Infection
Can/Aus/UK:
Uses: Viral infection
AAP: Not reviewed

Rabies is an acute rapidly progressing illness caused by an RNA-containing virus that is usually fatal. Infection is via other warm-blooded mammals. Incubation is prolonged and can be up to 4-6 weeks.[1] The virus multiplies locally, passes into local neurons and progressively ascends to the central nervous system. The virus is seldom found in the plasma compartment. The issue of breastfeeding following exposure to an animal bite is contentious and somewhat obscure. Person to person transmission has not been documented, nor has there been documentation of transmission of the rabies virus into human milk.[2,3] If a breastfeeding women is exposed to the rabies virus, she should receive the human rabies immune globulin and begin the vaccination series.[4] Most sources agree that once immunization has begun, the mother can continue breastfeeding. For a thorough review, see reference 4.

Pregnancy Risk Category:

Lactation Risk Category:

Theoretic Infant Dose:

Adult Concerns:

Pediatric Concerns: None reported.

Drug Interactions:

Alternatives:

Adult Dosage:

References:
1. American Academy of Pediatrics. In: Pickering LK, ed. 2000 Red Book: Report of the Committee on Infectious Diseases. 25th ed. Elk Grove Village, IL: American Academy of Pediatrics;2000:475-482.
2. Lawrence RA, Lawrence RM. Breastfeeding: a Guide for the Medical Profession. 5th ed. St. Louis: Mosby; 1999:604-5.
3. Hall TG, ed. Diseases Transmitted from Animal to Man. Springfield, Il: Thomas 1963; 293-7
4. Merewood A, Philipp B. Breastfeeding: Conditions and Diseases. 1st ed. Amarillo: Pharmasoft Publishing; 2001, 164-5.

RABIES VACCINE

Trade: Imovax Rabies Vaccine
Can/Aus/UK:
Uses: Vaccination for rabies.
AAP: Not reviewed

Rabies vaccine is prepared from inactivated rabies virus. No data are available on transmission to breastmilk. Even if transferred to breastmilk, it is unlikely to produce untoward effects.[1]

Pregnancy Risk Category:

Lactation Risk Category: L3

Theoretic Infant Dose:

Adult Concerns: Rash, anaphylactoid reactions, nausea, vomiting, diarrhea, etc.

Pediatric Concerns:

Drug Interactions:

Alternatives:

Adult Dosage: 1 mL X 3 over 21-28 days

References:
1. Pharmaceutical Manufacturers Package Insert, 1995.

RADIOACTIVE SODIUM

Trade: Radioactive Sodium
Can/Aus/UK:
Uses: Radioactive tracer
AAP: Radioactive compound that requires temporary cessation of breastfeeding.

Radioactivity in milk is present for up to 96 hours.[1] It reaches a peak at 2 hours. Pump and discard milk until radioactivity is depleted, approximately 16 days.

Pregnancy Risk Category:

Lactation Risk Category: L5

Theoretic Infant Dose:

Adult Concerns:

Pediatric Concerns: None reported via milk, but radiation exposure is possible.

Drug Interactions:

Alternatives:

Adult Dosage:

T½ =	M/P =
PHL =	PB =
PK = < 2 hours	Oral =
MW =	pKa =
Vd =	

References:
1. Pommerenke WT, and Hahn PF. Secretion of radioactive sodium in human milk. Proc. Soc. Exp. Biol. Med. 52:223, 1943.

RADIOPAQUE AGENTS

Trade: Omnipaque, Conray, Cholebrine, Telepaque, Oragrafin, Bilivist, Hypaque, Optiray, Contrast Agents
Can/Aus/UK:
Uses: Radio-contrast agents
AAP: Some approved by the American Academy of Pediatrics for use in breastfeeding mothers

Radiocontrast or radiopaque agents are opaque to X-rays, and are used to visualize blood vessels in various tissues. Barium sulfate was one of the original agents used, while organic iodinated compounds are used primarily in CAT scans and for various X-ray procedures. While iodinated products in general are contraindicated in breastfeeding mothers due to the high milk transfer of iodine, in these products the iodine is covalently bound to the organic molecule and is metabolically stable and essentially not bioavailable. For the most part, these organic radiocontrast agents are rapidly excreted without significant metabolism and the amount of elemental iodine released is minimal.[1] Virtually all of these agents have very short plasma half-lives (< 1 h), and for those studied, milk concentrations are extremely low (see table below).[2-6] Of the minimal amount in milk, virtually none is bioavailable to the infant as these agents are largely unabsorbed orally. According to several manufacturers, less than 0.005% of the iodine is free. These contrast agents are in essence pharmacologically inert, not metabolized, unabsorbed, and are rapidly excreted by the kidney (80-90% with 24 hours). **See radiocontrast tables in index.**

Pregnancy Risk Category:

Lactation Risk Category: L2

Theoretic Infant Dose:

Adult Concerns: GI distress, rash, anaphylaxis.

Pediatric Concerns: None reported via milk. Commonly used in pediatric patients for diagnostic purposes.

Drug Interactions:

Alternatives:

Adult Dosage:

T½ = 20-90 min.	M/P =
PHL –	PB = 0-10%
PK = < 1 hour	Oral = Minimal
MW =	pKa =
Vd =	

References:
1. Pharmaceutical Manufacturers Package Insert, 1993, 1994.
2. Nielsen ST, Matheson I, Rasmussen JN, et al. Excretion of iohexol and metrizoate in human breast milk. Acta Radiol 28(5):523-6, 1987.
3. Holmdahl KH. Cholecystography during lactation. Acta Radiol 45:305-7, 1956.
4. Ilett KF, Hackett LP, Paterson JW, et al. Excretion of metrizamide in milk [letter]. Br J Radiol 54(642):537-8, 1981.
5. Rofsky NM, Weinreb JC, Litt AW. Quantitative analysis of gadopentetate dimeglumine excreted in breast milk. J Magn Reson Imaging 3(1):131-2, 1993.
6. Fitz-John TP, et.al. Intravenous urography during lactation. Br. J. Radiol 55:603-5, 1982.

RAMIPRIL

Trade: Altace
Can/Aus/UK: Altace, Ramace, Tritace
Uses: ACE inhibitor, antihypertensive
AAP: Not reviewed

Ramipril is rapidly metabolized to ramiprilat which is a potent ACE inhibitor with a long half-life. It is used in hypertension. ACE inhibitors can cause increased fetal and neonatal morbidity and should not be used in pregnant women. Ingestion of a single 10 mg oral dose produced an undetectable level in breastmilk.[1,2] However, animal studies have indicated that ramiprilat is transferred into milk in concentrations about one-third of those found in serum. Only 0.25% of the total dose is estimated to penetrate into milk. However, caution should be exercised in using ACE inhibitors in lactating women, because neonates are very sensitive to these compounds.

Pregnancy Risk Category: D

Lactation Risk Category: L3
                              L4 if used in neonatal period

Theoretic Infant Dose:

Adult Concerns: Hypotension, cough, nausea, vomiting, dizziness.

Pediatric Concerns: None reported via milk. Observe for hypotension.

Drug Interactions: Probenecid increases plasma levels of ACEi. ACEi and diuretics have additive hypotensive effects. Antacids reduce bioavailability of ACE inhibitors. NSAIDS reduce hypotension of ACE inhibitors. Phenothiazines increase effects of ACEi. ACEi increase digoxin and lithium plasma levels. May elevate potassium levels when potassium supplementation is added.

Alternatives: Captopril, Enalapril

Adult Dosage: 2.5-20 mg QD

T½ = 13-17 hours	M/P =
PHL =	PB = 56%
PK = 2-4 hours	Oral = 60%
MW = 417	pKa =
Vd =	

References:
1. Pharmaceutical Manufacturers Package Insert, 1996.
2. Ball SG, Robertson JIS. Clinical pharmacology of ramipril. Am J Cardiol 59:23D-27D, 1987.

RANITIDINE

Trade: Zantac
Can/Aus/UK: Apo-Ranitidine, Novo-Ranidine, Nu-Ranit, Zantac
Uses: Reduces gastric acid secretion
AAP: Not reviewed

Ranitidine is a prototypical histamine-2 blocker used to reduce acid secretion in the stomach. It has been widely used in pediatrics without significant side effects primarily for gastroesophageal reflux (GER). Following a dose of 150 mg for four doses, concentrations in breastmilk were 0.72, 2.6, and 1.5 mg/L at 1.5, 5.5 and 12 hours respectively.[1] The milk/serum ratios varied from 6.81, 8.44 to 23.77 at 1.5, 5.5 and 12 hours respectively. Although the milk/plasma ratios are quite high, using this data an infant consuming 1 L of milk daily would ingest less than 2.6 mg/24 hours. This amount is quite small considering the pediatric dose currently recommended is 2-4 mg/kg/24 hours. See nizatidine or famotidine for alternatives.

Pregnancy Risk Category: B

Lactation Risk Category: L2

Theoretic Infant Dose: 0.4 mg/kg/day

Adult Concerns: Side effects are generally minimal and include headache, GI distress, dizziness.

Pediatric Concerns: None reported via milk. Although ranitidine is concentrated in milk, the overall dose is less than therapeutic.

Drug Interactions: Ranitidine may decrease the renal clearance of procainamide. May decrease oral absorption of diazepam. Ranitidine may increase the hypoglycemic effect of glipizide or glyburide. Ranitidine may reduce warfarin clearance, thus increasing anticoagulation.

Alternatives: Famotidine, Nizatidine

Adult Dosage: 150 mg BID

T½ = 2-3 hours	M/P = 1.9-6.7
PHL =	PB = 15%
PK = 1-3 hours	Oral = 50%
MW = 314	pKa = 2.3,8.2
Vd = 1.6-2.4	

References:
1. Kearns GL, McConnell RF, Trang JM, et.al. Appearance of ranitidine in breast milk following multiple dosing. Clin Pharm 4:322-324, 1985.

REMIFENTANIL

Trade: Ultiva
Can/Aus/UK: Ultiva
Uses: Opioid analgesic
AAP: Not reviewed

Remifentanil is a new opioid analgesic similar in potency and use as fentanyl. It is primarily metabolized by plasma and tissue esterases (in adults and neonates) and has an incredibly short elimination half-life of only 10-20 minutes, with an effective biological half-life of only 3 to 10 minutes.[1] Unlike other fentanyl analogs, the half-life of remifentanil does not increase with prolonged administration. Although remifentanil has been found in rodent milk, no data are available on its transfer into human milk. It is cleared for use in children > 2 years of age. As an analog of fentanyl, breastmilk levels should be similar and probably exceedingly low. In addition, remifentanil metabolism is not dependent on liver function, and should be exceedingly short even in neonates. Due to its kinetics and brief half-life, and its poor oral bioavailability, it is unlikely this product will produce clinically relevant levels in human breastmilk.

Pregnancy Risk Category: C

Lactation Risk Category: L3

Theoretic Infant Dose:

Adult Concerns: Nausea, hypotension, sedation, vomiting, bradycardia.

Pediatric Concerns: None reported via milk. Not orally bioavailable.

Drug Interactions: May potentiate the effects of other opioids.

Alternatives:

Adult Dosage: 0.25-0.4 mcg/kg/minute

T½ = 10-20 minutes	M/P =
PHL =	PB = 70%
PK =	Oral = Poor
MW = 412	pKa = 7.07
Vd = 0.1	

References:
1. Pharmaceutical manufacturers package insert, 1997.

REPAGLINIDE

Trade: Prandin
Can/Aus/UK: Gluconorm, Novonorm
Uses: Antidiabetic agent
AAP: Not reviewed

Repaglinide is a non-sulfonyluric hypoglycemic agent that lowers blood glucose levels in Type 2 non-insulin dependent diabetics by stimulating the release of insulin from functional beta cells. No data are available on its transfer to human milk, but rodent studies suggest that it may transfer into milk and induce hypoglycemic and skeletal changes in young animals via milk. Unfortunately, no dosing regimens were mentioned in these studies so it is not known if normal therapeutic doses would produce such changes in humans. Dosing of repaglinide is rather unique, with doses taken prior to each meal due to its short half-life, and according to the need of each patient. At this point, we do not know if it is safe for use in breastfeeding patients. But if it is used, the infant should be closely monitored for hypoglycemia, and should not be fed until at least several hours after the dose to reduce exposure.

Pregnancy Risk Category: C

Lactation Risk Category: L4

Theoretic Infant Dose:

Adult Concerns: In adults, hypoglycemia and headache were the most common side effects.

Pediatric Concerns: Hypoglycemia in animal studies via milk, but doses were not mentioned.

Drug Interactions: Metabolism and increased effect may occur when used with azole antifungals such as ketoconazole, itraconazole and other drugs which inhibit liver enzymes such as erythromycin. Decreased effect may result following use of rifampin, troglitazone, barbiturates and carbamazepine. Reduced protein binding and increased effect may result when repaglinide is used with NSAIDs, salicylates, sulfonamides, etc. Numerous other drugs may interfere with the hypoglycemic effect...check a drug interaction reference for a complete listing.

Alternatives:

Adult Dosage: 0.5-4 mg BID-QID

T½ = 1 hour	M/P =
PHL =	PB = 98%
PK = 1 hour	Oral = 56%
MW =	pKa =
Vd = 31	

References:
1. Pharmaceutical Manufacturers Package Insert, 1999.
2. Drug Facts and Comparisons. 1999 ed. Facts and Comparisons, St. Louis.

RESERPINE

Trade: Raudixin, Serpasil
Can/Aus/UK: Abicol, Adelphane, Serpasil
Uses: Antihypertensive
AAP: Not reviewed

Reserpine is an old and seldom used antihypertensive. Reserpine is known to be secreted into human milk, although the levels are unreported.[1-3] Increased respiratory tract secretions, severe nasal congestion, cyanosis, and loss of appetite can occur. Some reports suggest no observable effect but should use with extreme caution if at all. Because safer, more effective products are available, reserpine should be avoided in lactating patients.

Pregnancy Risk Category: C

Lactation Risk Category: L4

Theoretic Infant Dose:

Adult Concerns: Hypotonia, sedation, hypotension, nasal congestion, diarrhea, nausea, vomiting.

Pediatric Concerns: None reported via milk, but observe for nasal stuffiness, sedation, hypotonia. Use with caution.

Drug Interactions: Reserpine may decrease the effect of other sympathomimetics. May increased effect of MAOI and tricyclic antidepressants.

Alternatives:

Adult Dosage: 125-250 mcg QD-BID

T½ = 50-100 hours.	**M/P** =
PHL =	**PB** = 96%
PK = 2 hours	**Oral** = 40%
MW = 609	**pKa** =
Vd =	

References:
1. O'Brien, T. Excretion of drugs in human milk. Am.J. Hosp. Pharm. 31:844-854, 1974.
2. Vorherr, H. Drug excretion in breast milk. Postgrad. Med. 56:97-104, 1974.
3. Anderson PO: Drugs and breast feeding - A review. Intell Clin Pharm 11:208, 1977.

RHO (D) IMMUNE GLOBULIN

Trade: Rhogam, Gamulin Rh, Hyprho-d, Mini-gamulin Rh
Can/Aus/UK:
Uses: Immune globulin
AAP: Not reviewed

RHO(D) immune globulin is an immune globulin prepared from human plasma containing high concentrations of Rh antibodies. Only trace amounts of anti-Rh are present in colostrum and none in mature milk in women receiving large doses of Rh immune globulin. No untoward effects have been reported. Most immunoglobulins are destroyed in the gastric acidity of the newborn infant. Rh immune globulins are not contraindicated in breastfeeding mothers.[1]

Pregnancy Risk Category:

Lactation Risk Category: L2

Theoretic Infant Dose:

Adult Concerns: Infrequent allergies, discomfort at injection site.

Pediatric Concerns: None reported via milk.

Drug Interactions:

Alternatives:

Adult Dosage: 300 mcg X 1-2

T½ = 24 days.	M/P =
PHL=	PB =
PK =	Oral = None
MW =	pKa =
Vd =	

References:
1. Lawrence RA. Breastfeeding, A guide for the medical profession. Mosby, St. Louis, 1994.

RIBAVIRIN

Trade: Virazole, Rebetol
Can/Aus/UK: Virazide, Virazole
Uses: Antiviral agent.
AAP: Not reviewed

Ribavirin is a synthetic nucleoside used as an antiviral agent and is effective in a wide variety of viral infections.[1]   It has heretofore been used acutely in respiratory syncytial virus infections in infants without major complications. However, its current use in breastfeeding patients for treatment of Hepatitis C infcctions when combined with interferon alfa (Rebetron) for periods up to one year may be more problematic as high concentrations of ribavirin could accumulate in the breastfed infant. No data are available on its transfer to human milk, but it is probably low and its oral bioavailability is low as well. However, ribavirin concentrates in peripheral tissues and in the red blood cells in high concentrations over time (Vd= 802).[2] Its elimination half-life at steady state averages 298 hours, which reflects slow elimination from non-plasma compartments. Red cell concentrations on average are 60 fold higher than plasma levels and may account for the occasional hemolytic anemia. It is likely the acute exposure of a breastfed infant would produce minimal side effects. However, chronic exposure over 6-12 months may be more risky, so caution is recommended.

Pregnancy Risk Category: X

Lactation Risk Category: L4

Theoretic Infant Dose:

Adult Concerns: Rash, conjunctivitis, hemolytic anemia, congestive heart failure, seizures, asthenia, hypotension, bradycardia, reticulocytosis, bronchospasm, pulmonary edema, etc. Ribavirin may be a potent teratogen. Nursing personnel exposed to inhaled ribavirin should avoid environmental exposure.

Pediatric Concerns: None yet reported via breastmilk.

Drug Interactions:

Alternatives:

Adult Dosage: 12.5 L mist/minute (190 mcg/L) 12-18 hours QD

T½ = 298 hours(SS)	M/P =
PHL=	PB = 0%
PK = 1.5 hours	Oral = 44%
MW = 244	pKa =
Vd = 40.4	

References:
1.   Pharmaceutical Manufacturers Package Insert, 1999.
2.   Lertora JJL, Rege AB, Lacour JT et al: Pharmacokinetics and long-term tolerance to ribavirin in asymptomatic patients infected with human immunodeficiency virus. Clin Pharmacol Ther 50:442-449,1991.

RIBAVIRIN + INTERFERON ALFA-2B

Trade: Rebetron
Can/Aus/UK:
Uses: Antivirals for Hepatitis C treatment
AAP: Not reviewed

Rebetron is a combination product containing the antiviral Ribavirin and the immunomodulator drug called interferon alfa-2b. This new combination product is indicated for the long-term treatment of hepatitis C. The typical dose for an individual < 75 kg consists of 1000 mg ribavirin daily in divided doses and 3 million units of interferon three times weekly.

Ribavirin is a synthetic nucleoside used as an antiviral agent and is effective in a wide variety of viral infections. It has heretofore been used acutely in respiratory syncytial virus infections in infants without major complications. However, its current use in breastfeeding patients for treatment of Hepatitis C infections when combined with interferon alfa (Rebetron) for periods up to one year may be more problematic as high concentrations of ribavirin could accumulate in the breastfed infant over time. No data are available on its transfer to human milk, but it is probably low and its oral bioavailability is low as well. However, ribavirin concentrates in peripheral tissues and in the red blood cells in high concentrations over time (Vd= 802).[1] Its elimination half-life at steady state averages 298 hours, which reflects slow elimination from nonplasma compartments. Red cell concentrations on average are 60 fold higher than plasma levels and may account for the occasional hemolytic anemia. It is likely the acute exposure of a breastfed infant would produce minimal side effects. However, chronic exposure over 12 months may be more risky, so caution is recommended.

Very little is known about the secretion of interferons in human milk, although some interferons are known to be secreted normally and may contribute to the antiviral properties of human milk. However, interferons are large in molecular weight (16-28,000 daltons) which would limit their transfer into human milk. Following treatment with a massive dose of 30 million units I.V. of interferon alpha in a breastfeeding patient, the amount of interferon alpha transferred into human milk was 894, 1004, 1551, 1507, 788, 721 IU at 0 (baseline), 2, 4, 8, 12, and 24 hours respectively.[2] Hence, even following a massive dose, no change in breastmilk levels were noted. One thousand international units is roughly equivalent to 500 nanograms of interferon. So it is unlikely that the interferon in Rebetron would transfer to milk or the infant in amounts clinically relevant.

Rebetron is extremely dangerous to a fetus and is extremely teratogenic at doses even 1/20th of the above therapeutic doses. Pregnancy must be strictly avoided if this product is used in either the male or female partner. Due to the long half-life of this product, pregnancy should be avoided for at least 6 months following use.

Pregnancy Risk Category: X

Lactation Risk Category: L4

Theoretic Infant Dose:

Adult Concerns: Anemia, insomnia, depression and irritability are common.   Headache, fatigue, rigors, fever, flu-like symptoms, dizziness, nausea, myalgia, insomnia and numerous other symptoms are typical.

Pediatric Concerns: None reported via breastmilk, but caution is recommended.

Drug Interactions:

Alternatives:

Adult Dosage:

T½ = 298 hours	**M/P =**
PHL=	**PB =**
PK =	**Oral =**
MW =	**pKa =**
Vd =	

References:
1. Lertora JJL, Rege AB, Lacour JT et al: Pharmacokinetics and long-term tolerance to ribavirin in asymptomatic patients infected with human immunodeficiency virus. Clin Pharmacol Ther 50:442-449,1991.
2. Kumar, A. and Hale, T. Excretion of human interferon alpha-n3 into human milk. In press. 1999.

RIBOFLAVIN

Trade: Vitamin B-2
Can/Aus/UK: Abdec, Accomin
Uses: Vitamin B2
AAP: Approved by the American Academy of Pediatrics for use in breastfeeding mothers

Riboflavin is a B complex vitamin, also called Vitamin B-2. Riboflavin is absorbed by the small intestine by a well established transport mechanism. It is easily saturable, so excessive levels are not absorbed. Riboflavin is transported into human milk in concentrations proportional to dietary intake, but generally averaged 400 ng/ml.[1] Maternal supplementation is permitted if dose is small (2 mg/day). No untoward effects have been reported.

Pregnancy Risk Category: A

Lactation Risk Category: L1

Theoretic Infant Dose: 60.0 ng/kg/day

Adult Concerns: Yellow colored urine.

Pediatric Concerns: None reported via milk.

Drug Interactions:

Alternatives:

Adult Dosage: 1-4 mg QD

T½ = 14 hours.	**M/P** =
PHL =	**PB** =
PK = Rapid	**Oral** = Complete
MW = 376	**pKa** =
Vd =	

References:
1. Deodhar AD. Studies on human lactation. Part III. Effect of dietary vitamin supplementation on vitamin contents of breast milk. Acta Paediatr Scand 53:42-6, 1964.

RIFAMPIN

Trade: Rifadin, Rimactane
Can/Aus/UK: Rifadin, Rifampicin, Rimactane, Rimycin, Rofact
Uses: Antitubercular drug
AAP: Approved by the American Academy of Pediatrics for use in breastfeeding mothers

Rifampin is a broad spectrum antibiotic, with particular activity against tuberculosis. It is secreted into breastmilk in very small levels. One report indicates that following a single 450 mg oral dose, maternal plasma levels averaged 21.3 mg/L and milk levels averaged 3.4 - 4.9 mg/L.[1] Vorherr reported that after a 600 mg dose of rifampin, peak plasma levels were 50 mg/L while milk levels were 10-30 mg/L.[2] Only 0.05% of the maternal dose appeared in breastmilk.

Pregnancy Risk Category: C

Lactation Risk Category: L2

Theoretic Infant Dose: 4.5 mg/kg/day

Adult Concerns: Hepatitis, anemia, headache, diarrhea, pseudomembranous colitis.

Pediatric Concerns: None reported via milk.

Drug Interactions: Rifampin is known to reduce the plasma level of a large number of drugs including: acetaminophen, anticoagulants, barbiturates, benzodiazepines, beta blockers, contraceptives, corticosteroids, cyclosporine, digitoxin, phenytoin, methadone, quinidine, sulfonylureas, theophylline, verapamil, and a large number of others.

Alternatives:

Adult Dosage: 600 mg QD

T½ = 3.5 hours	M/P = 0.16-0.23
PHL = 2.9 hours	PB = 80%
PK = 2-4 hours	Oral = 90-95%
MW = 823	pKa =
Vd =	

References:
1. Lenzi E, Santuari S: Preliminary observations on the use of a new semi-synthetic rifamycin derivative in gynecology and obstetrics. Atti Accad Lancisiana Roma 13:(suppl 1): 87-94,1969.
2. Vorherr H. Drug excretion in breast milk. Postgrad Med 56:97-104, 1974.

RIMANTADINE HCL

Trade: Flumadine
Can/Aus/UK:
Uses: Antiviral, anti-influenza A
AAP: Not reviewed

Rimantadine is an antiviral agent primarily used for influenza A infections. It is concentrated in rodent milk.[1] Levels in animal milk 2-3 hours after administration were approximately twice those of the maternal serum, suggesting a milk/plasma ratio of about 2. Manufacturer alludes to toxic side effects but fails to state them. No side effects yet reported in breastfeeding infants. Rimantadine is, however, indicated for prophylaxis of influenza A in pediatric patients > 1 year of age.

Pregnancy Risk Category: C

Lactation Risk Category: L3

Theoretic Infant Dose:

Adult Concerns: Gastrointestinal distress, nervousness, fatigue, and sleep disturbances.

Pediatric Concerns: None reported via milk.

Drug Interactions: The use of acetaminophen significantly reduces rimantadine plasma levels by 11%. Peak plasma levels of rimantadine were reduce 10% by aspirin. Rimantadine clearance was reduced by 16% when used with cimetidine.

Alternatives:

Adult Dosage: 100 mg BID

T½ = 25.4 hours	M/P = 2
PHL =	PB = 40%
PK = 6 hours	Oral = 92%
MW = 179	pKa =
Vd =	

References:
1. Pharmaceutical Manufacturers Package Insert, 1996.

RISEDRONATE

Trade: Actonel
Can/Aus/UK: Actonel
Uses: Prevents bone resorption
AAP: Not reviewed

Risedronate is a bisphosphonate that slows the dissolution of hydroxyapatite crystals in the bone, thus reducing bone calcium loss in certain syndromes such as Paget's syndrome. Its penetration into milk is possible due to its small molecular weight, but it has not yet been reported except in rats. However, due to the presence of fat and calcium in milk, its oral bioavailability in infants would be exceedingly low. However, the presence of this product in an infant's growing bones is concerning, and due caution is recommended.

Pregnancy Risk Category: C

Lactation Risk Category: L3

Theoretic Infant Dose:

Adult Concerns: Nausea, diarrhea, flatulence, gastritis, arthralgia have been reported.

Pediatric Concerns: None via milk.

Drug Interactions: Oral products containing calcium or magnesium will significantly reduce oral bioavailability. Take on empty stomach.

Alternatives:

Adult Dosage: 30 mg/d for 2 months

T½ = 480 hours	M/P =
PHL =	PB = 24%
PK = 1 hour	Oral = 0.63%
MW = 305	pKa =
Vd = 6.3	

References:
1. Pharmaceutical manufacturers package insert, 2002.

RISPERIDONE

Trade: Risperdal
Can/Aus/UK: Risperdal
Uses: Antipsychotic
AAP: Not reviewed

Risperidone is a potent antipsychotic agent belonging to a new chemical class and is a dopamine and serotonin antagonist.   Risperidone is metabolized to an active metabolite, 6-hyrdoxyrisperidone. In a study of one patient receiving 6 mg/day of risperidone at steady state, the peak plasma level of approximately 130 μg/L occurred 4 hours after an oral dose.[1] Peak milk levels of risperidone and 9-hydroxyrisperidone were approximately 12 μg/L and 40 μg/L respectively.   The estimated daily dose of risperidone and metabolite (risperidone equivalents) was 4.3% of the weight-adjusted maternal dose.   The milk/plasma ratios calculated from areas under the curve over 24 hours were 0.42 and 0.24 respectively for risperidone and 6-hydroxyrisperidone.

Pregnancy Risk Category: C

Lactation Risk Category: L3

Theoretic Infant Dose: 7.8 μg/kg/day

Adult Concerns: Risks include neuroleptic malignant syndrome, tardive dyskinesia, myocardial arrhythmias, orthostatic hypotension, seizures, hyperprolactinemia, somnolence.   Galactorrhea has been reported.

Pediatric Concerns: None reported via milk.

Drug Interactions: Do not use with alcohol. May enhance the hypotensive response of other antihypertensives. May antagonize the effect of levodopa. Carbamazepine or clozapine may increase clearance of risperidone.

Alternatives:

Adult Dosage: 3 mg BID

T½ = 3-20 hours	M/P = 0.42
PHL =	PB = 90%
PK = 3-17 hours	Oral = 70-94%
MW = 410	pKa =
Vd =	

References:

1. Hill RC, McIvor RJ, Wojnar-Horton RE, Hackett LP, Ilett KF: Risperidone distribution and excretion into human milk; a case report and estimated infant exposure during breast-feeding. J. Clin. Psychopharmacol. J.Clin. Psychopharmacol 20(2):285-6,2000.

RITODRINE

Trade: Pre-par, Yutopar
Can/Aus/UK: Yutopar
Uses: Adrenergic agent
AAP: Not reviewed

Ritodrine is primarily used to reduce uterine contractions in premature labor due to its beta-2 adrenergic effect on uterine receptors.[1] No data are available on its transfer to human milk.

Pregnancy Risk Category: B

Lactation Risk Category: L3

Theoretic Infant Dose:

Adult Concerns: Fetal and maternal tachycardia, hypertension, lethargy, sleepiness, ketoacidosis, pulmonary edema.

Pediatric Concerns: None reported via milk.

Drug Interactions: Use cautiously with steroids due to pulmonary edema. Acebutolol and other beta blockers would block efficacy of ritodrine. Use with atropine may lead to systemic exaggerated. hypertension. Use with bupivacaine has lead to extreme hypotension. Numerous other interactions are listed, please review.

Alternatives:

Adult Dosage: 10-20 mg q 4-6 hours

T½ = 15 hours	M/P =
PHL =	PB = 32%
PK = 40-60 minutes	Oral = 30%
MW = 287	pKa = 9
Vd = 0.7	

References:
1.   Gandar R et al.   Serum level of ritodrine in man. Eur J Clin Pharmacol 17:117-122, 1980.

RIZATRIPTAN

Trade: Maxalt
Can/Aus/UK: Maxalt
Uses: Antimigraine
AAP: Not reviewed

Rizatriptan is a selective serotonin receptor agonist, similar in effect to sumatriptan.[1]   It is primarily indicated for acute migraine headache treatment. No data are available on its transfer into human milk, but it is concentrated in rodent milk (M/P=5). Until we have clear breastmilk data , the kinetics of this drug may predispose to higher milk levels and sumatriptan may be preferred.

Pregnancy Risk Category: C

Lactation Risk Category: L3

Theoretic Infant Dose:

Adult Concerns: Do not use in patients with ischemic heart disease, coronary artery vasospasm, or significant underlying cardiac disease. Rizatriptan should not be used within 24 hours of an ergot alkaloid, dihydroergotamine, or methysergide. Side effects include chest pain, paresthesia, dry mouth, nausea, dizziness, and somnolence.

Pediatric Concerns: None reported via milk, but caution is recommended.

Drug Interactions: Plasma levels may be increased when used with a MAO inhibitor, or shortly thereafter.   Concurrent use of propranolol produced a 70% increase in plasma level of rizatriptan. No interactions were noted with nadolol or metoprolol.

Alternatives: Sumatriptan

Adult Dosage: 5-10 mg orally, repeat only after 2 hours

T½ = 2-3 hours	M/P =
PHL=	PB = 14%
PK = 1-1.5 hours	Oral = 45%
MW = 269	pKa =
Vd = 2	

References:
1.   Pharmaceutical Manufacturers Package Insert, 1999.

ROFECOXIB

Trade: Vioxx
Can/Aus/UK: Vioxx
Uses: NSAID analgesic
AAP: Not reviewed

Rofecoxib is a new NSAID useful for pain relief in arthritic patients. It is one of the newer Cyclooxigenase-2 (COX-2) inhibitors. The COX-2 inhibitors claim to reduce GI symptoms in users as they do not inhibit the COX-1 enzyme in the gastrointestinal tract. The manufacturer reports that in rodents, the milk/plasma ratio was approximately 1, but this was using doses as high as 6-18 times that used in humans. It is not known if this drug is secreted into human milk. Using the reported area under the curve(AUC) for this product following a 25 mg dose, and a theoretical but high milk/plasma ratio of 1.0, then the estimated concentration in milk would be 136 ng/mL and the estimated dose to the infant over 24 hours would be 20.4 μg/kg which is less than 5% of the maternal dose. These estimates are probably high.

Pregnancy Risk Category: C

Lactation Risk Category: L3

Theoretic Infant Dose:

Adult Concerns: Abdominal pain, fatigue, dizziness, diarrhea, headache,

Pediatric Concerns: None reported via milk but observe for GI cramping, distress, diarrhea.

Drug Interactions: May reduce efficacy of ACE inhibitors with elevation of blood pressure. Increased plasma concentrations of rofecoxib result when coadministered with cimetidine. May increase lithium levels, and reduce the efficacy of diuretics. May increase plasma concentrations of methotrexate by 23%. Rifampin may increase rofecoxib plasma levels by 50%. When added to warfarin therapy, may increase INR by 8%.

Alternatives: Ibuprofen

Adult Dosage: 12.5 to 25 mg once daily.

T½ = 17 hours	M/P =
PHL =	PB = 87%
PK = 2-3 hours	Oral = 93%
MW = 314	pKa =
Vd = 1.3 L/kg	

References:
1. Pharmaceutical Manufacturers Package Insert, 1999.

ROSIGLITAZONE

Trade: Avandia
Can/Aus/UK:
Uses: Oral antidiabetic agent
AAP: Not reviewed

Rosiglitazone is an oral antidiabetic agent which acts primarily by increasing insulin sensitivity. In essence, the insulin receptor is activated reducing insulin resistance. It also decreases hepatic gluconeogenesis and increases insulin-dependent muscle glucose uptake. It does not increase the release of or secretion of insulin. No data are available on its entry into human milk. The maximum plasma concentration following a 2 mg dose is only 156 nanograms/mL.[1] Assuming a dose of 2 mg every 12 hours, and a theoretical Milk/Plasma ratio of 1.0 (which is probably high), then an infant would likely ingest about 23.4 μg/kg/day via milk. In a 5 kg infant, this would be approximately 2.8% of the maternal dose.

Pregnancy Risk Category: C

Lactation Risk Category: L3

Theoretic Infant Dose: 23.4 μg/kg/day

Adult Concerns: Elevated liver enzymes in small percentage of patients. Hypoglycemia, increased body weight gain, edema, anemia.

Pediatric Concerns: None via milk, but it has not been studied.

Drug Interactions: Metformin may enhance hypoglycemic effect. Rosiglitazone may reduce effectiveness of oral contraceptives containing estrogen and progestins by reducing plasma levels of these hormones. These changes could result in loss of contraception. Consider a higher dose contraceptive. Rosiglitazone may reduce cyclosporine levels.

Alternatives:

Adult Dosage: 2-8 mg daily

T½ = 3-4 hours	M/P =
PHL =	PB = 99.8%
PK = 1 hour	Oral = 99%
MW = 357	pKa = 6.8
Vd = 0.25	

References:
1. Pharmaceutical Manufacturers package insert, 2000.

RUBELLA VIRUS VACCINE, LIVE

Trade: Meruvax, Rubella Vaccine, Measles Vaccine
Can/Aus/UK:
Uses: Live attenuated (measles) vaccine
AAP: Not reviewed

Rubella virus vaccine contains a live attenuated virus. The American College of Obstetricians and Gynecologists and the CDC currently recommend the early postpartum immunization of women who show no or low antibody titers to rubella. At least four studies have found rubella virus to be transferred via milk although presence of clinical symptoms was not evident.[1-3] Rubella virus has been cultured from the throat of one infant, while another infant was clinically ill with minor symptoms and serologic evidence of rubella infection.[4] In general, the use of rubella virus vaccine in mothers of full-term, normal infants has not been associated with untoward effects and is generally recommended.[5]

Pregnancy Risk Category: X

Lactation Risk Category: L2

Theoretic Infant Dose:

Adult Concerns: Burning, stinging, lymphadenopathy, rash, malaise, sore throat, etc.

Pediatric Concerns: One case report of rash, vomiting, and mild rubella infection.

Drug Interactions: Immunosuppressants and immune globulins may reduce immunogenicity. Concurrent use of interferon may reduce antibody response.

Alternatives:

Adult Dosage: 0.5 mL X 1

References:
1. Buimovici-Klein E, et. al. Isolation of rubella virus in milk after postpartum immunization. J Pediatr 91:939-41, 1977.
2. Losonsky GA et.al. Effect of immunization against rubella on lactation products. I. Development and characterization of specific immunologic reactivity in breast milk. J. Infect. Dis. 145:654, 1982.
3. Losonsky GA, et.al. Effect of immunization against rubella on lactation products. II. Maternal-neonatal interactions. J. Infect. Dis. 145:661, 1982.
4. Landes RD et.al. Neonatal rubella following postpartum maternal immunization. Pediatrics 97:465-467, 1980.
5. Lawrence RA. In: Breastfeeding, A guide for the medical profession. Mosby, St.Louis, 1994.

SACCHARIN

Trade: Saccharin
Can/Aus/UK:
Uses: Sweetener
AAP: Not reviewed

In one group of 6 women who received 126 mg (per 12 oz drink) every 6 hours for 9 doses, milk levels varied greatly from < 200 μg/L after 1dose to 1.765 mg/L after 9 doses.[1]   Under these dosing conditions, saccharin levels appear to accumulate over time. Half-life in serum and milk were 4.84 hours and 17.9 hours respectively after 3 days. Even after such doses, these milk levels are considered minimal. Moderate intake should be compatible with nursing.

Pregnancy Risk Category: C

Lactation Risk Category: L3

Theoretic Infant Dose: 0.3 mg/kg/day

Adult Concerns:

Pediatric Concerns: None reported via milk.

Drug Interactions:

Alternatives:

Adult Dosage:

T½ = **4.84 hours**	**M/P** =
PHL =	**PB** =
PK =	**Oral** = **Complete**
MW = 183	**pKa** =
Vd =	

References:
1. Egan PC, Marx CM, et.al. Saccharin excretion in mature human milk. Drug Intell. Clin. Pharm. 18:511, 1984.

SAGE

Trade: Sage, Dalmatian, Sage, Spanish
Can/Aus/UK:
Uses: Herbal product
AAP: Not reviewed

Salvia officinalis L.(Dalmatian sage) and Salvia lavandulaefolia Vahl (Spanish sage) are most common of the species. Extracts and teas have been used to treat digestive disorders (antispasmodic), as an antiseptic and astringent, for treating diarrhea, gastritis, sore throat and other maladies.[1] The dried and smoked leaves have been used for treating asthma symptoms. These uses are largely unsubstantiated in the literature.

Sage extracts have been found to be strong antioxidants and with some antimicrobial properties (staph. aureus) due to the phenolic acid salvin content. Sage oil has antispasmodic effects in animals and this may account for its moderating effects on the GI tract. For the most part, Sage is relatively nontoxic, and nonirritating. Ingestion of significant quantities may lead to cheilitis, stomatitis, dry mouth or local irritation.[2]

Due to drying properties and pediatric hypersensitivity to anticholinergics, sage should be used with some caution in breastfeeding mothers.

Pregnancy Risk Category:

Lactation Risk Category: L4

Theoretic Infant Dose:

Adult Concerns: Observe for typical anticholinergic effects such as cheilitis, stomatitis, dry mouth or local irritation.

Pediatric Concerns: None reported but observe for dry mouth, stomatitis, cheilitis.

Drug Interactions:

Alternatives:

Adult Dosage:

References:
1. Leung AY. Encyclopedia of Common Natural Ingredients used in food, drugs, and cosmetics. New York, NY: J. Wiley and Sons, 1980.
2. Bissett NG. In: Herbal Drugs and Phytopharmaceuticals. Medpharm Scientific Publishers, CRC Press, Boca Raton, 1994.

SALMETEROL XINAFOATE

Trade: Serevent
Can/Aus/UK: Serevent
Uses: Long acting beta adrenergic bronchodilator
AAP: Not reviewed

Salmeterol is a long acting beta-2 adrenergic stimulant used as a bronchodilator in asthmatics. Maternal plasma levels of salmeterol after inhaled administration are very low (85-200 pg/ml), or undetectable.[1] Studies in animals have shown that plasma and breastmilk levels are very similar. Oral absorption of both salmeterol and the xinafoate moiety are good. The terminal half-life of salmeterol is 5.5 hours, xinafoate is 11 days. No reports of use in lactating women are available.

Pregnancy Risk Category: C

Lactation Risk Category: L2

Theoretic Infant Dose: 0.3 μg/kg/day

Adult Concerns: Tremor, dizziness, hypertension.

Pediatric Concerns: None reported via milk, but studies are limited.

Drug Interactions: Use with MAOI may result in severe hypertension, severe headache, and hypertensive crisis. Tricyclic antidepressants may potentiate the pressure response. The pressor response of salmeterol may be reduced by lithium.

Alternatives:

Adult Dosage: 50 ug BID

T½ = 5.5 hours	M/P = 1.0
PHL =	PB = 98%
PK = 10 - 45 min.	Oral = Complete
MW =	pKa =
Vd =	

References:
1. Pharmaceutical Manufacturers Package Insert, 1996.

SCOPOLAMINE

Trade: Transderm Scope
Can/Aus/UK: Benacine, Buscopan, Scopoderm TTS, Transderm-V
Uses: Anticholinergic
AAP: Approved by the American Academy of Pediatrics for use in breastfeeding mothers

Scopolamine is a typical anticholinergic used primarily for motion sickness, and preoperatively to produce amnesia and decrease salivation.[1-3] Scopolamine is structurally similar to atropine, but is known for its prominent CNS effects including reducing motion sickness. There are no reports on its transfer into human milk, but due to its poor oral bioavailability, it is generally believed to be minimal.

Pregnancy Risk Category: C

Lactation Risk Category: L3

Theoretic Infant Dose:

Adult Concerns: Blurred vision, dry mouth, drowsiness, constipation, confusion, drowsiness, bradycardia, hypotension, dermatitis.

Pediatric Concerns: None via milk. Observe for anticholinergic symptoms such as drowsiness, dry mouth.

Drug Interactions: Decreased effect of acetaminophen, levodopa, ketoconazole, digoxin. GI absorption of the following drugs may be altered: ketoconazole, digoxin, potassium supplements, acetaminophen, levodopa.

Alternatives:

Adult Dosage: 0.3-0.6 mg once

T½ = 2.9 hours	M/P =
PHL =	PB =
PK = 1 hour	Oral = 27%
MW = 303	pKa = 7.55
Vd = 1.4	

References:
1. Lacy C. et.al. Drug information handbook. Lexi-Comp, Hudson(Cleveland), Oh. 1996.
2. Drug Facts and Comparisons. 1996. ed. Facts and Comparisons, St. Louis.
3. Pharmaceutical Manufacturers Package Insert, 1997.

SECOBARBITAL

Trade: Seconal
Can/Aus/UK: Novo-Secobarb, Seconal, Seconal sodium
Uses: Short acting barbiturate sedative
AAP: Approved by the American Academy of Pediatrics for use in breastfeeding mothers

Secobarbital is a sedative, hypnotic barbiturate. It is probably secreted into breastmilk, although levels are unknown, and may be detectable in milk for 24 hours or longer.[1-3] Recommend mothers delay breastfeeding for 3-4 hours to reduce possible transfer to infant if exposure to this barbiturate is required.

Pregnancy Risk Category: D

Lactation Risk Category: L3

Theoretic Infant Dose:

Adult Concerns: Respiratory depression, sedation, addiction.

Pediatric Concerns: None reported via milk, but observer for sedation.

Drug Interactions:

Alternatives:

Adult Dosage: 100 mg QD

T½	= 15-40 hours	M/P	=
PHL	=	PB	= 30-45%
PK	= 2-4 hours	Oral	= 90%
MW	= 260	pKa	= 7.9
Vd	= 1.6-1.9		

References:
1. Tyson RM, Shrader EA, Perlman HH. Drugs transmitted through breast milk. II Barbiturates. J Pediatr. 14:86-90, 1938.
2. Kaneko S, Sato T, Suzuki K. The levels of anticonvulsants in breast milk. Br J Clin Pharmacol. 7:624-627,1979.
3. Wilson JT. Drug excretion in human breast milk: principles, pharmacokinetics and projected consequences. Clin Pharmacokinet 5:1-66, 1980.

SELENIUM SULFIDE

Trade: Selsun, Exsel, Head And Shoulders, Selsun Blue
Can/Aus/UK:
Uses: Topical antimicrobial
AAP: Not reviewed

Selenium sulfide is an anti-infective compound with mild antibacterial and antifungal activity. It is commonly used for Tinea Versicolor, and seborrheic dermatitis such as dandruff. Selenium is not apparently absorbed significantly through intact skin, but is absorbed by damaged skin or open lesions.[1] There are no data on its transfer into human milk. If used properly on undamaged skin, it is very unlikely that enough would be absorbed systemically to produce untoward effects in a breastfed infant. Do not apply directly to nipple as enhanced absorption by the infant could occur.

Pregnancy Risk Category:

Lactation Risk Category: L3

Theoretic Infant Dose:

Adult Concerns: Changes in hair color and loss of hair have been reported. Extensive washing of hair reduces the incidence of these problems. Extensive systemic absorption can occur with application to broken skin. Nausea, vomiting, diarrhea.

Pediatric Concerns: None reported via milk. Do not apply directly to nipple.

Drug Interactions:

Alternatives: Topical Clotrimazole, Itraconazole

Adult Dosage: Apply topic twice weekly

References:
1.   McEvoy GE(ed):AFHS Drug Information, New York, NY. 1999.

SENNA LAXATIVES

Trade: Senokot, Senexon, Ex Lax, Senna-gen, Black-draught, Fletcher's Castoria, Agoral
Can/Aus/UK:
Uses: Laxative
AAP: Approved by the American Academy of Pediatrics for use in breastfeeding mothers

Senna is a potent, proven laxative. Anthraquinones, its key ingredient, are believed to increase bowel activity due to secretion of anthraquinones into the colon. Side effects such as abdominal cramping and colic are unpredictable with homemade varieties of this plant, so most sources recommend taking a standardized formulation commonly available. This product is only recommended for short use, such as 10 days.   Do not use for intestinal obstruction, or appendicitis, or abdominal pain of unknown origin. Senna laxatives are occasionally used in postpartum women to alleviate constipation. In one study of 23 women who received Senokot (100mg containing 8.602 mg of Sennosides A and B), no sennoside A or B was detectable in their milk. [1]   Of 15 mothers reporting loose stools, two infants had loose stools.

Pregnancy Risk Category:

Lactation Risk Category: L3

Theoretic Infant Dose:

Adult Concerns: Diarrhea, abdominal cramps, dark colored urine, chronic diarrhea, fluid loss.

Pediatric Concerns: Several infants had loose stools although no drug was detected in milk.

Drug Interactions:

Alternatives:

Adult Dosage: 100 mg daily.

References:
1.   Werthmann, MW and Krees S.   Quantitative excretion of Senokot in human breast milk. Med Ann Dist Columbia. Jan;42(1):4-5, 1973.

SERTRALINE

Trade: Zoloft
Can/Aus/UK: Lustral, Zoloft
Uses: Antidepressant
AAP: Drug whose effect on nursing infants is unknown but may be of concern

Sertraline is a typical serotonin reuptake inhibitor similar to Prozac and Paxil, but unlike Prozac, the longer half-life metabolite of sertraline is only marginally active. In one study of a single patient taking 100 mg of sertraline daily for 3 weeks postpartum, the concentration of sertraline in milk was 24, 43, 40, and 19 μg/Liter of milk at 1, 5, 9, and 23 hours respectively following the dose.[1]   The maternal plasma levels of sertraline after 12 hours was 48 ng/ml.   Sertraline plasma levels in the infant at three weeks were below the limit of detection (< 0.5 ng/ml) at 12 hours post-dose.   Routine pediatric evaluation after 3 months revealed a neonate of normal weight who had achieved the appropriate developmental milestones.

In another study of 3 breastfeeding patients who received 50-100 mg sertraline daily, the maternal plasma levels ranged from 18.4 to 95.8 ng/mL, whereas the plasma levels of sertraline and its metabolite, desmethylsertraline, in the three breastfed infants was below the limit of detection (< 2 ng/mL).[2]   Milk levels were not measured. Desmethylsertraline is poorly active, less than 10% of the parent sertraline.

Another recent publication reviewed the changes in platelet serotonin levels in breastfeeding mothers and their infants who received up to 100 mg of sertraline daily.[3]   Mothers treated with sertraline had significant decreases in their platelet serotonin levels, which is expected. However, there was no change in platelet serotonin levels in breastfed infants of mothers consuming sertraline, suggesting that only minimal amounts of sertraline are actually transferred to the infant. This confirms other studies.

Studies by Stowe of eleven mother/infant pairs (maternal dose = 25-150 mg/day) further suggest minimal transfer of sertraline into human milk.[4] From this superb study, the concentration of sertraline peaked in the milk at 7-8 hours, and the metabolite (desmethylsertraline) at 5-11 hours.   The reported concentrations of sertraline and desmethylsertraline in breastmilk were 17-173 ng/ml, and 22-294 ng/ml, respectively.   The reported dose of sertraline to the infant via milk varied from undetectable (5 of 11) to 0.124 mg/day in one infant. The infant's serum concentration of sertraline varied from undetectable to 3.0 ng/ml, but was undetectable in 7 of 11patients.   No developmental abnormalities were noted in any of the infants studied. Sertraline is a potent inhibitor of 5-HT transporter function both in the CNS and platelets.   One recent study assessed the effect of sertraline on platelet 5-HT transporter function in 14 breastfeeding mothers (dose = 25-200 mg/d) and their infants, to determine if even low levels of sertraline exposure could perhaps lead to changes in the infant's blood platelet 5-HT levels and therefore CNS serotonin levels.[5] While a significant reduction in platelet levels of 5-HT were noted in the mothers, no changes in 5-HT levels were noted in the 14 infants. Thus it appears that at typical clinical doses, maternal sertraline has a minimal effect on platelet 5-HT transport in breastfeeding infants.

These studies generally confirm that the transfer of sertraline and its metabolite to the infant is minimal, and that attaining clinically relevant plasma levels in infants is remote at maternal doses less than 150 mg/day. A thorough review of antidepressant use in breastfeeding mothers is available.[6]

Pregnancy Risk Category: B

Lactation Risk Category: L2

Theoretic Infant Dose: 26.0 ng/kg/day

Adult Concerns: Diarrhea, nausea, tremor, and increased sweating.

Pediatric Concerns: Of the cases reported in the literature, only one infant developed benign neonatal sleep at age 4 months which spontaneous resolved at 6 months. Its relationship, if any, to sertraline is unknown.

Drug Interactions: All SSRIs inhibit Cytochrome P450 enzymes and may inhibit metabolism of desipramine, dextromethorphan, encainide, haloperidol, metoprolol, etc. May induce serotonergic hyperstimulation when added too soon after MAO inhibitors, tricyclic antidepressants, and lithium. May displace warfarin from binding sites increasing anticoagulation.

Alternatives: Paroxetine

Adult Dosage: 50-200 mg QD

T½ = 26-65 hours	M/P = 0.89
PHL =	PB = 98%
PK = 7-8 hours	Oral = Complete
MW = 306	pKa =
Vd = 20	

References:
1. Altshuler LL. Breastfeeding and Sertraline: A 24 hours Analysis. J. Clin Psychiatry 56(6):243-245, 1995.
2. Mammen OK, Perel JM et.al: Sertraline and norsertraline levels in three breastfed infants. J. Clin. Psychiatry 58(3): 100-103, 1997.
3. Epperson, CN et.al. Sertraline and Breastfeeding. NEJM 336(16):1189-90,1997.
4. Stowe, ZN, Owens, MJ, Landry,JC. et.al. Sertraline and desmethylsertraline in human breast milk and nursing infants. Am.J.Psychiatry 154(9):1255-1260, 1997.

5. Epperson N, Czarkowski KA, Ward-O'Brien D, Weiss E, Gueorguieva R, Jatlow P, Anderson GM. Maternal sertraline treatment and serotonin transport in breast-feeding mother-infant pairs. Am J Psychiatry. 158(10):1631-7, 2001.
6. Wisner KL, Perel JM, Findling RL: Antidepressant treatment during breast-feeding. Am J Psychiatry 153(9): 1132-1137, 1996.

SIBUTRAMINE

Trade: Meridia
Can/Aus/UK: Meridia
Uses: Appetite suppressant
AAP: Not reviewed

Sibutramine is a nonamphetamine appetite suppressant. Due to its effect on serotonin and norepinephrine reuptake, it is considered an antidepressant as well.   Sibutramine is rather small in molecular weight, active in the CNS, extremely lipid soluble, and has two 'active' metabolites with long half-lives (14-16 hours).[1-3] Although no data are available on its transfer into human milk, the pharmacokinetics of this drug theoretically suggest that it might have a rather high milk/plasma ratio and could enter milk in significant levels. Until we know more, a risk assessment may not support the use of this product in breastfeeding mothers.

Pregnancy Risk Category: C

Lactation Risk Category: L4

Theoretic Infant Dose:

Adult Concerns: Adult side effects include headache, insomnia, back pain, flu-like syndrome, abdominal pain, seizures (rarely), and elevated liver enzymes.   Cardiovascular events include tachycardia, hypertension.

Pediatric Concerns: None reported via milk.   Caution is recommended.

Drug Interactions: Use of Sibutramine with drugs that may increase blood pressure (decongestants, cough and cold remedies) could be hazardous. Do not use with MAO inhibitors. Do not admix with drugs that inhibit cytochrome P450 enzymes in the liver (ketoconazole, cimetidine, erythromycin (minor effect).

Alternatives:

Adult Dosage: 5-15 mg daily

T½ = 12.5-21.8 hours	M/P =
PHL =	PB = 94%
PK = 3-4 hours	Oral = 77%
MW = 334	pKa =
Vd =	

References:
1. Lean MEJ: Sibutramine–a review of clinical efficacy. Int J Obesity 21(suppl 1):S30-S36, 1997.
2. Stock MJ: Sibutramine: a review of the pharmacology of a novel anti-obesity agent. Int J Obesity 21(1):S25-S29, 1997.
3. Pharmaceutical Manufacturers package insert, 1998.

SILDENAFIL

Trade: Viagra
Can/Aus/UK: Viagra
Uses: For erectile dysfunction
AAP: Not reviewed

Sildenafil is an inhibitor of nitrous oxide metabolism, thus increasing levels of nitrous oxide, smooth muscle relaxation, and an increased flow of blood in the corpus cavernosum of the penis.[1] While not currently indicated for women, illicit use is increasing. No data are available on the transfer of sildenafil into human milk, but it is unlikely that significant transfer will occur due to its larger molecular weight, and short half-life. However, caution is recommended in breastfeeding mothers. While not reported, persistent abnormal erections (priapism) could potentially occur in male infants.

Pregnancy Risk Category: B

Lactation Risk Category: L3

Theoretic Infant Dose:

Adult Concerns: Changes in visual color perception is common. Other side effects include headache, flushing, dyspepsia, nasal congestion, and hypotension.

Pediatric Concerns: None reported via milk. If used, observe for priapism in male infants.

Drug Interactions: Do not admix with any form of nitrate, including nitroglycerine. Because it is metabolized by cytochrome P450 CYP3A4 and 2C9, increased plasma levels may result when admixed with azole antifungals, erythromycins, cimetidine and other such enzyme inhibitors.

Alternatives:

Adult Dosage: 50 mg daily

T½ = 4 hours	M/P =
PHL=	PB = 96%
PK = 60 minutes	Oral = 40%
MW = 666	pKa =
Vd = 1.5	

References:
1. Pharmaceutical Manufacturers Package Insert, 1999.

SILICONE BREAST IMPLANTS

Trade:
Can/Aus/UK:
Uses: Silicone mammoplasty
AAP: Not reviewed

Augmentation mammoplasty with silicone implants is no longer available in the USA. In general, placement of the implant behind the breast seldom produces interruption of vital ducts, nerve supply, or blood supply. Most women have been able to breastfeed. Breast reduction surgery, on the other hand, has been found to produce significant interruption of the nervous supply (particularly the ductile tissue), leading to a reduced ability to lactate.

Silicone transfer to breastmilk has been studied in one group of 15 lactating mothers with bilateral silicone breast implants.[1] Silicon levels were measured in breastmilk, whole blood, cow's milk, and 26 brands of infant formula. Comparing implanted women to controls, mean silicon levels were not significantly different in breastmilk (55.45 +/- 35 and 51.05 +/- 31 ng/ml, respectively) or in blood (79.29 +/- 87 and 103.76 +/- 112 ng/ml, respectively. Mean silicon level measured in store-bought cow's milk was 708.94 ng/ml, and that for 26 brands of commercially available infant formula was 4402.5 ng/ml (ng/ml = parts per billion). The authors concluded that lactating women with silicone implants are similar to control women with respect to levels of silicone in their breastmilk and blood. From these studies, silicon levels are 10 times higher in cow's milk and even higher in infant formulas.

It is not known for certain if ingestion of leaking silicone by a nursing infant is dangerous. Although one article has been published showing esophageal strictures, it has subsequently been recalled by the author. Silicone by nature is extremely inert and is unlikely to be absorbed in the GI tract by a nursing infant although good studies are lacking. Silicone is a ubiquitous substance, found in all foods, liquids, etc.

Pregnancy Risk Category:

Lactation Risk Category: L3

Theoretic Infant Dose:

Adult Concerns:

Pediatric Concerns: None reported via milk.

Drug Interactions:

Alternatives:

Adult Dosage: N/A

References:
1.   Semple JL, Lugowski SJ, Baines CJ; Smith DC; McHugh A. Breast milk contamination and silicone implants: Preliminary results using silicon as a proxy measurement for Silicone. Plast. Reconstr. Surg. 102(2):528-33, 1988.

SILVER SULFADIAZINE

Trade: Silvadene, SSD Cream, Thermazene
Can/Aus/UK: Dermazin, Flamazine, SSD, Silvazine
Uses: Topical antimicrobial cream
AAP: Not reviewed

Silver sulfadiazine is a topical antimicrobial cream primarily used for reducing sepsis in burn patients. The silver component is not absorbed from the skin.[1] Sulfadiazine is partially absorbed. After prolonged therapy of large areas, sulfadiazine levels in plasma may approach therapeutic levels. Although sulfonamides are known to be secreted into human milk, they are not particularly problematic except in the newborn period when they may produce kernicterus.

Pregnancy Risk Category: B

Lactation Risk Category: L3

Theoretic Infant Dose:

Adult Concerns: Allergic rash, renal failure, crystalluria.

Pediatric Concerns: None reported, but studies are limited. Observe caution during the neonatal period.

Drug Interactions:

Alternatives:

Adult Dosage:

T½ = 10 hours(sulfa)	**M/P =**
PHL =	**PB =**
PK =	**Oral = Complete**
MW =	**pKa =**
Vd =	

References:
1. McEvoy GE(ed):AHFS Drug Information, New York, NY. 1995.

SIMVASTATIN

Trade: Zocor
Can/Aus/UK: Lipex, Zocor
Uses: Reduces cholesterol
AAP: Not reviewed

Simvastatin is an HMG-CoA reductase inhibitor that reduces the production of cholesterol in the liver. Like lovastatin, simvastatin reduces blood cholesterol levels. Others in this family are known to be secreted into human and rodent milk, but no data are available on simvastatin.[1] It is likely that milk levels will be low, since less than 5% of simvastatin reaches the plasma, most being removed first-pass by the liver. Atherosclerosis is a chronic process and discontinuation of lipid-lowering drugs during pregnancy and lactation should have little to no impact on the outcome of long-term therapy of primary hypercholesterolemia. Cholesterol and other products of cholesterol biosynthesis are essential components for fetal and neonatal development and the use of cholesterol-lowering drugs would not be advisable under any circumstances.

Pregnancy Risk Category: X

Lactation Risk Category: L3

Theoretic Infant Dose:

Adult Concerns: GI distress, headache, hypotension, elevated liver enzymes.

Pediatric Concerns: None reported.

Drug Interactions: Increased toxicity when added to gemfibrozil (myopathy, myalgia, etc), clofibrate, niacin (myopathy), erythromycin, cyclosporine, oral anticoagulants (elevated bleeding time).

Alternatives:

Adult Dosage: 5-10 mg QD

T½ = Long	M/P =
PHL=	PB = 95%
PK = 1.3-2.4 hours	Oral = Poor
MW = 419	pKa =
Vd =	

References:
1. Drug Facts and Comparisons. 1995 ed. Facts and Comparisons, St. Louis.

SIROLIMUS

Trade: Rapamune, Rapamycin, Nsc-226080
Can/Aus/UK: Rapamune
Uses: Immunosuppressant
AAP: Not reviewed

Sirolimus is an immunosuppressant sometimes used in combination with cyclosporin in renal transplants. No data are available on its transfer to human milk. Average plasma levels are quite low (264 ng x hr/mL) and the drug is strongly attached to cellular components and plasma levels are low. It is not likely it will penetrate milk in levels that are significant. However, it is a potent inhibitor of the enzyme 70 K S6 kinase, which is stimulated in breast tissue by prolactin. This agent, in rodent mammary tissue, strongly inhibits milk component production.[1] It could potentially suppress milk production in lactating mothers and caution is recommended.

Pregnancy Risk Category: C

Lactation Risk Category: L4

Theoretic Infant Dose:

Adult Concerns: Anemia, thrombocytopenia, leukopenia, hypertension, headache, hyperlipidemia, hypophosphatemia, urinary tract infection, interstitial pneumonitis.

Pediatric Concerns: None via milk, but reduced milk production could occur.

Drug Interactions: Drugs which inhibit cytochrome P450 3A4 may significantly increase levels of sirolimus. These include: bromocriptine, carbamazepine, cimetidine, cisapride, clarithromycin, clotrimazole, danazol, diltiazem, erythromycin, fluconazole, fosphenytoin, metoclopramide, etc. Co-administration with cyclosporine may increase levels of sirolimus. Numerous other drug-drug contraindications may exist, consult drug interaction reference.

Alternatives:

Adult Dosage: 2 mg/d

T½ = 57-63 hours	M/P =	
PHL =	PB =	
PK = 1-3 hours	Oral = 15%	
MW = 914	pKa =	
Vd = 12		

References:
1.　Hang J, Rillema JA.　Effect of rapamycin on prolactin-stimulated S6 kinase activity and milk product formation in mouse mammary explants. Biochim Biophys Acta. 11;1358(2):209-14, 1997.

SOMATREM, SOMATROPIN

Trade: Human Growth Hormone, Nutropin, Humatrope, Growth Hormone, Saizen
Can/Aus/UK: Genotropin, Humatrope, Norditropin, Protropin, Somatropin
Uses: Human growth hormone
AAP: Not reviewed

Somatrem and somatropin are purified polypeptide hormones of recombinant DNA origin.　It is a large protein. They are structurally similar or identical to human growth hormone (hGH).　One study in 16 women indicates that hGH treatment for 7 days stimulated breastmilk production by 18.5% (verses 11.6% in controls) in a group of normal lactating women.[1]　No adverse effects were noted.　Leukemia has occurred in a small number of children receiving hGH, but the relationship is uncertain.　Because it is a peptide of 191 amino acids and its molecular weight is so large,　its transfer into milk is very unlikely. Further,　its oral absorption would be minimal to nil.

Pregnancy Risk Category: C

Lactation Risk Category: L3

Theoretic Infant Dose:

Adult Concerns:

Pediatric Concerns: None reported via milk.　Absorption is very unlikely.

Drug Interactions:

Alternatives:

Adult Dosage: 0.1-0.3 mg/kg q week

T½ =	M/P =
PHL=	PB =
PK = 7.5 hours	Oral = Poor
MW = 22,124	pKa =
Vd =	

References:
1.　Milsom SR, et.al. Growth hormone stimulates galactopoiesis in healthy lactating women. Acta Endocrinologica 127:337-43, 1992.

SOTALOL

Trade: Betapace
Can/Aus/UK: Apo-Sotalol, Cardol, Rylosol, Sotacor
Uses: Antihypertensive, beta-blocker
AAP: Approved by the American Academy of Pediatrics for use in breastfeeding mothers

Sotalol is a typical beta blocker antihypertensive with low lipid solubility. It is secreted into milk in high levels. Sotalol concentrations in milk ranged from 4.8 to 20.2 mg/L (mean= 10.5 mg/L) in 5 mothers.[1] The mean maternal dose was 433 mg/day. Although these milk levels appear high, no evidence of toxicity was noted in 12 infants.

Pregnancy Risk Category: B

Lactation Risk Category: L3

Theoretic Infant Dose: 3.0 mg/kg/day

Adult Concerns: Bradycardia, hypotension, sedation, poor sucking.

Pediatric Concerns: None reported via milk, but observe for sedation, bradycardia, hypotension, weakness.

Drug Interactions: Decreased effect when used with aluminum salts, barbiturates, calcium salts, cholestyramine, NSAIDs, ampicillin, rifampin, and salicylates. Beta blockers may reduce the effect of oral sulfonylureas (hypoglycemic agents). Increased toxicity/effect when used with other antihypertensives, contraceptives, MAO inhibitors, cimetidine, and numerous other products. See drug interaction reference for complete listing.

Alternatives: Propranolol, Metoprolol

Adult Dosage: 80-160 mg BID

T½ = 12 hours	M/P = 5.4
PHL =	PB = 0%
PK = 2.5 - 4 hours	Oral = 90-100%
MW = 272	pKa = 8.3,9.8
Vd = 1.6-2.4	

References:

1. O'Hare MF, Murnaghan GA, et.al. Sotalol asa hypotensive agent in pregnancy. Br. J. Obstet. Gynaecol. 87:814-20, 1980.

SPIRONOLACTONE

Trade: Aldactone
Can/Aus/UK: Aldactone, Novospiroton, Spiractin
Uses: Potassium sparing diuretic
AAP: Approved by the American Academy of Pediatrics for use in breastfeeding mothers

Spironolactone is metabolized to canrenone, which is known to be secreted into breastmilk. In one mother receiving 25 mg of spironolactone, at 2 hours postdose the maternal serum and milk concentrations of canrenone were 144 and 104 μg/L respectively.[1] At 14.5 hours, the corresponding values for serum and milk were 92 and 47 μg/L respectively. Milk/plasma ratios varied from 0.51 at 14.5 hours, to 0.72 at 2 hours. The estimated dose an infant would ingest was 0.2% of maternal dose/day.

Pregnancy Risk Category: D

Lactation Risk Category: L2

Theoretic Infant Dose: 15.6 μg/kg/day

Adult Concerns: Nausea, vomiting, elevated serum potassium, hepatitis.

Pediatric Concerns: None reported via milk, but suppression of milk supply is possible but unlikely.

Drug Interactions: Use with anticoagulants may reduce the anticoagulant effect. Use with potassium preparations may increase potassium levels in plasma. Use with ACE inhibitors may elevate serum potassium levels. The diuretic effect of spironolactone may be decreased by use with salicylates.

Alternatives:

Adult Dosage: 50-100 mg QD

T½ = 10-35 hours	M/P = 0.51-0.72
PHL =	PB = >90%
PK = 1-2 hours	Oral = 70%
MW = 417	pKa =
Vd =	

References:
1. Phelps DL, Karim A. Spironolactone: relationship between concentrations of dethioacetylated metabolite in human serum and milk. J. Pharm. Sci. 66:1203, 1977.

ST. JOHN'S WORT

Trade: St. John's Wort, Saint John's Wort
Can/Aus/UK:
Uses: Antidepressant
AAP: Not reviewed

St. John's Wort (hypericum perforatum L.) consists of the whole fresh or dried plant or its components containing not less than 0.04% naphthodianthrones of the hypericin group. Hypericum contains many biologically active compounds and most researchers consider its effect due to a combination of constituents rather than any single component.[1] However, the naphthodianthrones hypericin and pseudohypericin, and numerous flavonoids have stimulated the most interest as antidepressants and antivirals. Following doses of (3 x 300 mg/day), peak steady state concentrations of hypericin and pseudohypericin were 8.5 ng/mL and 5.8 ng/mL respectively.[2] Concentrations in brain appear to be the least of all compartments. Hypericum has become increasingly popular for the treatment of depression following results from numerous studies showing efficacy. However, large well-controlled studies are currently underway and the efficacy of SJW will be further tested in the coming years.

In vitro studies have indicated that hypericin inhibits monoamine oxidase (MAO) and catechol-o-methyltransferase (COMT), the enzymes responsible for the breakdown of neurotransmitters.[3] MAO inhibitors have in the past been subject to severe restrictions due to their dangers. Thus far, the amount of hypericin present in human tissues, does not appear to inhibit MAO in adults, although no data are available on MAO inhibition in infants. Hypericin is presently in Phase I clinical trials as an antiviral agent as well, with potential use in herpes, HIV, and other viral infections. Although there is great interest in this phytomedicine, a number of deficiencies in the clinical trails have been pointed out.[4,5] They include poorly characterized depressed patient populations, heterogeneity of diagnoses, etc, but a number of current studies underway should clarify these deficiencies.

At present there is no data on the transfer of hypericum compounds into human milk. Its poor penetration into the CNS could be used to suggest that it penetrates milk poorly as well, since these compartments are similar. Due to the long half-life, some would be expected to transfer into milk and subsequently the infant. At this time, due to the availability of better studied products such as sertraline (Zoloft) and paroxetine (Paxil) which do not apparently pose a great significant risk to the breastfed infant, these products should be preferentially used in postpartum depression.

Several new studies show that St. John's Wort may significantly stimulate Cytochrome P450 3A4, which is a major drug metabolizing enzyme in the liver.[6-11] Following such induction, major reductions

(50% or more) in plasma levels of a number of important drugs have been reported and include: cyclosporin, midazolam, indinavir, and possibly numerous other drugs. Patients taking anticonvulsants, and other critically important drugs should be advised about the possible interaction with these medications leading to major reductions in plasma levels. Patients should always advise their physicians of their use of St. John's Wort. Caution, because of uterotonic effects, hypericum should not be used in pregnant patients.

Pregnancy Risk Category:

Lactation Risk Category: L3

Theoretic Infant Dose:

Adult Concerns: Caution, because of uterotonic effects, hypericum should not be used in pregnant patients. Dry mouth, dizziness, constipation, and confusion have been infrequently reported. Overt toxicity is generally considered quite low. Photosensitization in fair-skinned people has been noted. No teratogenic effects has been documented.

Pediatric Concerns: None reported. Caution is urged.

Drug Interactions: May prolong narcotic-induced sedation and sleeping times. May reduce barbiturate-induced sleeping times. A recent report in Lancet suggests St. John's wort may induce the cytochrome P-450 enzyme system. The data indicates an interaction between St. John's wort and the HIV-1 protease inhibitor, Indinavir, where indinavir AUC was reduced by a mean of 57%. In addition, trough concentrations of indinavir at 8 hours were reduced by 81%. Another report indicates acute rejection episodes in two heart transplant patients who had initiated St. John's wort for depression. Although each patient recovered after the St. John's wort was discontinued, this again implicates P-450 induction activity of St. John's wort. SJW may decrease digoxin plasma levels (AUC) by 25%, and theophylline levels significantly.

Alternatives: Sertraline, Paroxetine

Adult Dosage: 300mg TID dry-powdered (0.3% hypericin)

T½ = 26.5 hours	M/P =
PHL=	**PB =**
PK = 5.9 hours	**Oral =**
MW = 504	**pKa =**
Vd =	

References:
1. St. John's Wort. In Upton, R, editor:American Herbal Pharmacopoeia and Therapeutic Compendium, 1997.
2. Stock S, Holzl J. Pharmacokinetic tests of [14C]-labeled hypericin and pseudohypericin from Hypericum perforatum and serum kinetics of hypericin in man. Planta Medica 57(suppl 2):A61, 1991.

3. Bladt S, Wagner H. Inhibition of MAO by fractions and constituents of Hypericum extract. J. Geriatric Psychiatry Neurology 7:S57-59, 1994.
4. Ernst E. St. John's Wort, an anti-depressant? A systematic, criteria-based review. Phytomedicine 2:47-71, 1995.
5. Linde K, et.al. St. John's wort for depression-an overview and meta-analysis of randomized clinical trials. British Med. J. 313:253-258, 1996.
6. Durr D, Stieger B, Kullak-Ublick GA, et al. St John's Wort induces intestinal P-glycoprotein/MDR1 and intestinal and hepatic CYP3A4. Clin Pharmacol Ther 68:598-604,2000.
7. Barone GW, Gurley BJ, Ketel BL, et al. Drug interaction between St. John's wort and cyclosporine. Ann Pharmacother 34:1013-6,2000.
8. Obach RS. Inhibition of human cytochrome P450 enzymes by constituents of St. John's Wort, an herbal preparation used in the treatment of depression. J Pharmacol Exp Ther 294:88-95,2000.
9. Roby CA, Anderson GD, Kantor E, et al. St John's Wort: effect on CYP3A4 activity. Clin Pharmacol Ther 67:451-7,2000.
10. De Smet PA, Touw DJ. Safety of St John's wort (Hypericum perforatum). Lancet 355:575-6, 2000.

STREPTOMYCIN

Trade:
Can/Aus/UK: Streptobretin, Streptotriad
Uses: Antibiotic
AAP: Approved by the American Academy of Pediatrics for use in breastfeeding mothers

Streptomycin is an aminoglycoside antibiotic from the same family as gentamycin. It is primarily administered IM or I.V. although it is seldom used today with exception of the treatment of tuberculosis. One report suggests that following a 1 g dose (IM), levels in breastmilk were 0.3 to 0.6 mg/L (2-3% of plasma level).[1] Another report suggests that only 0.5% of a 1 gm IM dose is excreted in breastmilk within 24 hours.[2] Because the oral absorption of streptomycin is very poor, absorption by infant is probably minimal (unless premature or early neonate).

Pregnancy Risk Category: D

Lactation Risk Category: L3

Theoretic Infant Dose: 0.1 mg/kg/day

Adult Concerns: Deafness, anemia, kidney toxicity.

Pediatric Concerns: None reported via milk, but observe for changes in GI flora.

Drug Interactions: Increased toxicity when used with certain penicillins, cephalosporins, amphotericin B, loop diuretics, and neuromuscular blocking agents.

Alternatives:

Adult Dosage: 1-2 g QD

T½ = 2.6 hours	M/P = 0.12-1.0
PHL = 4-10 hours(neonates)	PB = 34%
PK = 1-2 hours(IM)	Oral = Poor
MW = 582	pKa =
Vd =	

References:
1. Wilson, J. Drugs in Breast Milk. New York: ADIS Press, 1981.
2. Snider DE, Powell KE. Should women taking antituberculosis drugs breast-feed? Arch Inter Med. 144:589-590, 1984.

STRONTIUM-89 CHLORIDE

Trade: Metastron
Can/Aus/UK:
Uses: Radioactive product for bone pain
AAP: Not reviewed

Metastron behaves similarly to calcium. It is rapidly cleared from plasma and sequestered into bone where its radioactive emissions relieve metastatic bone pain.[1] Radioactive half-life is 50.5 days. Transfer into milk is unreported but likely. This radioactive product is too dangerous to use in lactating mothers.

Pregnancy Risk Category: D

Lactation Risk Category: L5

Theoretic Infant Dose:

Adult Concerns: Severe bone marrow suppression, septicemia.

Pediatric Concerns: None reported via milk. But this product is probably too dangerous to use with breastfed infants.

Drug Interactions:

Alternatives:

Adult Dosage: 4 mCi q 90 days

T½ = 50.5 days.	M/P =
PHL =	PB =
PK = Immediate(IV)	Oral =
MW = 159	pKa =
Vd =	

References:
1. Drug Facts and Comparisons. 1995 ed. Facts and Comparisons, St. Louis.

SUCCIMER

Trade: Chemet
Can/Aus/UK:
Uses: Lead Chelator for lead poisoning
AAP: Not reviewed

Succimer is a chelating agent containing dimercaptosuccinic acid. It is commonly used to chelate and increase the urinary excretion of lead.[1] While removing lead is important, some chelators (EDTA) are noted for increasing the plasma levels of lead and promoting its migration to neural and other tissues. In the instance of a breastfeeding woman, this could theoretically increase milk lead levels. However, succimer as studied in rodents has been found to increase the urinary elimination of lead without redistribution of lead to other compartments (this would theoretically include milk).[2] While we do not have studies of succimer transfer into human milk, due to its low pKa of succimer, it is unlikely that lead, chelated to succimer, would transfer into human milk. But this is not known for sure. Clinical studies in succimer-treated patients indicate that lead levels reach their lowest point after 4-5 days of therapy with succimer.[3] If breastfeeding patients were to pump and discard milk for 5 days while under therapy with succimer, it would significantly remove the risk of lead transfer into milk(if this occurs?). However, more data are required before breastfeeding can be recommended following the use of succimer.

Pregnancy Risk Category: C

Lactation Risk Category:

Theoretic Infant Dose:

Adult Concerns: Nausea, vomiting, diarrhea, appetite loss, thrombocytosis, intermittent eosinophilia, arrhythmias, neutropenia, drowsiness, dizziness, neuropathies, headache, rash, and paresthesias.

Pediatric Concerns: None reported.

Drug Interactions:

Alternatives:

Adult Dosage: 30 milligrams/kilogram/day for 5 days

T½ = 2 -48 hours	**M/P =**
PHL =	**PB =**
PK = 1-2 hours	**Oral = Complete**
MW = 182	**pKa = 3.0**
Vd =	

References:
1. Pharmaceutical manufacturers package insert, 2001.

2.   Graziano JH, Lolacono NJ, Moulton T, Mitchell ME, Slavkovich V, Zarate
      C.   Controlled study of meso-2,3-dimercaptosuccinic acid for the
      management of childhood lead intoxication. J Pediatr. 120(1):133-9,
      1992.
3.   Graziano JH, Lolacono NJ, Meyer P. Dose-response study of oral 2,3-
      dimercaptosuccinic acid in children with elevated blood lead
      concentrations. J Pediatr. 113(4):751-7, 1988.

SUCRALFATE

Trade: Carafate
Can/Aus/UK: Antepsin, Carafate, Novo-Sucralate, Nu-Sucralfate, SCF, Sulcrate, Ulcyte
Uses: For peptic ulcers
AAP: Not reviewed

Sucralfate is a sucrose aluminum complex used for stomach ulcers. When administered orally sucralfate forms a complex that physically covers stomach ulcers.[1]   Less than 5% is absorbed orally. At these plasma levels it is very unlikely to penetrate into breastmilk.

Pregnancy Risk Category: B

Lactation Risk Category: L2

Theoretic Infant Dose:

Adult Concerns: Constipation.

Pediatric Concerns: None reported via milk. Absorption is very unlikely.

Drug Interactions: The use of aluminum containing antacids and sucralfate may increase the total body burden of aluminum. Sucralfate may reduce the anticoagulant effect of warfarin. Serum digoxin levels may be reduced.   Phenytoin absorption may be decreased. Ketaconazole bioavailability may be decreased. Serum quinidine levels may be reduced. Bioavailability of the fluoroquinolone family may be decreased.

Alternatives:

Adult Dosage: 1 g QID

T½ =		**M/P** =
PHL=		**PB** =
PK =		**Oral** = < 5%
MW = 2087		**pKa** =
Vd =		

References:
1.   Drug Facts and Comparisons. 1995 ed. Facts and Comparisons, St. Louis.

SULCONAZOLE NITRATE

Trade: Exelderm
Can/Aus/UK: Exelderm
Uses: Antifungal cream
AAP: Not reviewed

Exelderm is a broad spectrum antifungal topical cream.[1] Although no data exist on transfer into human milk, it is unlikely that the degree of transdermal absorption would be high enough to produce significant milk levels. Only 8.7% of the topically administered dose is transcutaneously absorbed.

Pregnancy Risk Category: C

Lactation Risk Category: L3

Theoretic Infant Dose:

Adult Concerns: Rash, skin irritation, burning, stinging.

Pediatric Concerns: None reported via milk.

Drug Interactions:

Alternatives:

Adult Dosage: Topical

References:
1. Pharmaceutical Manufacturers Package Insert, 1996.

SULFAMETHOXAZOLE

Trade: Gantanol
Can/Aus/UK: Apo-Methoxazole, Bactrim, Gantanol, Resprim, Septrin
Uses: Sulfonamide antibiotic
AAP: Not reviewed

Sulfamethoxazole is a common and popular sulfonamide antimicrobial. It is secreted in breastmilk in small amounts.[1] It has a longer half-life than other sulfonamides. Use with caution in weakened infants and premature infants or neonates with hyperbilirubinemia. Gantrisin (Sulfisoxazole) is considered the best choice of sulfonamides due to reduced transfer to infant. Compatible but exercise caution. PHL= 14.7-36.5 hours (neonate), 8-9 hours (older infants).

Pregnancy Risk Category: C

Lactation Risk Category: L3

Theoretic Infant Dose:

Adult Concerns: Anemia, blood dyscrasias, allergies.

Pediatric Concerns: None reported via milk, but use with caution in hyperbilirubinemic neonates and in infants with G6PD.

Drug Interactions: Decreased effect with peraminobenzoic acid or PABA metabolites of drugs such as procaine and tetracaine. Increased effect of oral anticoagulants, oral hypoglycemic agents, and methotrexate.

Alternatives:

Adult Dosage: 1-2 g BID

T½ = 10.1 hours	M/P = 0.06
PHL = 14.7-36.5 h (neonate)	PB = 62%
PK = 1-4 hours	Oral = Complete
MW = 253	pKa =
Vd =	

References:
1. Rasmussen F. Mammary excretion of sulfonamides. Acta Pharmacol Toxicol 15:138-148, 1958.

SULFASALAZINE

Trade: Azulfidine
Can/Aus/UK: PMS Sulfasalazine, SAS-500, Salazopyrin
Uses: Anti-inflammatory for ulcerative colitis
AAP: Drugs associated with significant side effects and should be given with caution

Sulfasalazine is a conjugate of sulfapyridine and 5-Aminosalicylic acid and is used as an anti-inflammatory for ulcerative colitis. Only one-third of the dose is absorbed by the mother. Most stays in the GI tract. Secretion of 5-aminosalicylic acid (active compound) and its inactive metabolite (acetyl -5-ASA) into human milk is very low.

In one study of 12 women receiving 1 to 2 grams/day of sulfasalazine, the amount of sulfasalazine in milk in patients receiving 1 gm/day was far less than 1 mg/L, and approximately 0.5 to 2 mg/L in those receiving 2 gm/day.[1] In this study, small milk levels were found in only 2 women. It was estimated by the authors that breastfed infants would receive approximately 3-4 mg/kg/day of sulfapyridine. This very small amount may be regarded as negligible in considering kernicterus, since sulfapyridine and sulfadiazine are known to have a poor bilirubin-displacing capacity.

Berlin reports that sulfasalazine itself was not present in milk, however, sulfapyridine concentrations in milk ranged from 3.2 to 13.0 mg/L.[2]

However, one reported case of toxicity which may have been an idiosyncratic allergic response.[3] Use with some caution.

Pregnancy Risk Category: B

Lactation Risk Category: L3

Theoretic Infant Dose: 0.2 mg/kg/day

Adult Concerns: Watery diarrhea, GI distress, nausea, vomiting, rapid breathing.

Pediatric Concerns: Only one reported case of hypersensitivity. Most studies show minimal effects via milk. Observe for diarrhea, GI discomfort.

Drug Interactions: Decreased effect when used with iron, digoxin, and paraminobenzoic acid containing drugs. Decreased effect of oral anticoagulants, methotrexate, and oral hypoglycemic agents.

Alternatives:

Adult Dosage: 500 mg q 6 hours

T½ = 7.6 hours	M/P = 0.09-0.17
PHL =	PB =
PK = Prolonged	Oral = Poor
MW = 398	pKa =
Vd =	

References:
1. Jarnerot G, Into-Malmberg MB. Sulphasalazine treatment during breast feeding. Scand J Gastroenterol 14:869-71, 1979.
2. Berlin CM Jr, Yaffe SJ. Disposition of salicylazosulfapyridine (Azulfidine) and metabolites in human breast milk. Dev Pharmacol Ther. 1(1):31-9, 1980.
3. Branski D, et. al. Bloody diarrhea-A possible complication of sulfasalazine transferred through human breast milk. J Pediatr Gastroenterol Nutr 5:316-7, 1986.

SULFISOXAZOLE

Trade: Gantrisin, Azo-Gantrisin
Can/Aus/UK: Novo-Soxazole, Sulfizole
Uses: Sulfonamide antibiotic
AAP: Approved by the American Academy of Pediatrics for use in breastfeeding mothers

Sulfisoxazole is a popular sulfonamide antimicrobial. It is secreted in breastmilk in small amounts, although the actual levels are somewhat controversial.[1] Kauffman (1980) reports the total amount of sulfisoxazole recovered over 48 hours following a dose of 1 gm every

6 hours (total=4gm) was 0.45% of the total dose.[2] The milk/plasma ratio was quite low for sulfisoxazole, only 0.06, and for n-acetyl sulfisoxazole, 0.22.   The infant secreted 1,104 ug total sulfisoxazole in his urine over 24 hours, compared to the 1,142 ug secreted in milk. Less than 1% of the maternal dose is secreted into human milk. This is probably insufficient to produce problems in a normal newborn. Sulfisoxazole appears to be best choice with lowest milk/plasma ratio. Use with caution in weakened infants or those with hyperbilirubinemia.

Pregnancy Risk Category: C

Lactation Risk Category: L2

Theoretic Infant Dose:

Adult Concerns: Elevated bilirubin, rash.

Pediatric Concerns: None reported via milk. Use with caution in hyperbilirubinemic neonates and in infants with G6PD.

Drug Interactions: The anesthetic effects of thiopental may be enhanced with sulfisoxazole. Cyclosporine concentrations may be decreased by sulfonamides. Serum phenytoin levels may be increased. The risk of methotrexate induced bone marrow suppression may be enhanced. Increased sulfonylurea half-lives and hypoglycemia when used with sulfonamides.

Alternatives:

Adult Dosage: 1-4 g q 4-6 hours

T½ = 4.6-7.8 hours	M/P = 0.06	
PHL=	PB = 91%	
PK = 2-4 hours	Oral = 100%	
MW = 267	pKa =	
Vd =		

References:
1.   Rasmussen F. Mammary excretion of sulfonamides. Acta Pharmacol Toxicol 15:138-148, 1958.
2.   Kauffman RE, O'Brien C, Gilford P. Sulfisoxazole secretion into human milk. J. Pediatr. 97:839-41, 1980.

SULPIRIDE

Trade:
Can/Aus/UK: Dolmatil, Sulparex, Sulpitil
Uses: Antidepressant, antipsychotic
AAP: Not reviewed

Sulpiride is a selective dopamine antagonist used as an antidepressant and antipsychotic. Sulpiride is a strong neuroleptic antipsychotic drug, however several studies using smaller doses have found it to significantly increase prolactin levels and breastmilk production in smaller doses that do not produce overt neuroleptic effects on the mother.[1]   In a study with 14 women who received sulpiride (50 mg three times daily), and in a subsequent study with 36 breastfeeding women, Ylikorkala found major increases in prolactin levels and significant, but only moderate increases in breastmilk production.[2,3] In a group of 20 women who received 50 mg twice daily[4], breastmilk samples were drawn 2 hours after the dose.   The concentration of sulpiride in breastmilk ranged from 0.26 to 1.97 mg/L. No effects on breastfed infants were noted.   The authors concluded that sulpiride, when administered early in the postpartum period, is useful in promoting initiation of lactation.

In a study by McMurdo, sulpiride was found to be a potent stimulant of maternal plasma prolactin levels.[5] Interestingly, it appears that the prolactin response to sulpiride is not dose-related, and reached a maximum at 3-10 mg and thereafter, further increased doses did not further increase prolactin levels. Sulpiride is not available in the USA.

Pregnancy Risk Category:

Lactation Risk Category: L2

Theoretic Infant Dose: 0.3 mg/kg/day

Adult Concerns: Tardive dyskinesia, extrapyramidal symptoms, sedation, neuroleptic malignant syndrome, cholestatic jaundice.

Pediatric Concerns: None reported via milk.

Drug Interactions: Antacids and sucralfate may reduce absorption of sulpiride. Increased risk of seizure may result from use of tramadol or zotepine with sulpiride.

Alternatives: Metoclopramide, Domperidone

Adult Dosage: 50 mg BID

T½ = 6-8 hours	M/P =
PHL=	PB =
PK = 2-6 hours	Oral = 27-34%
MW = 341	pKa =
Vd = 2.7	

References:
1.   Wiesel FA, Alfredsson G, Ehrnebo M et al: The pharmacokinetics of intravenous and oral sulpiride in healthy human subjects. Eur J Clin Pharmacol 17:385-391, 1980
2.   Ylikorkala O, Kauppila A, Kivinen S et al: Sulpiride improves inadequate lactation. Br Med J 285:249-251, 1982.
3.   Ylikorkala O, Kauppila A, Kivinen S et al: Treatment of inadequate lactation with oral sulpiride and buccal oxytocin. Obstet Gynecol 1984; 63:57-60.
4.   Aono T, Shioji T, et.al. Augmentation of puerperal lactation by oral administration of sulpiride. J. Clin. Endo. Metabol. 48(3): 478-482, 1979.

5. McMurdo ME, Howie PW, Lewis M, Marnie M, McEwen J, McNeilly AS.
    Prolactin response to low dose sulpiride. Br J Clin Pharmacol. 24(2):133-7,
    1987.

SUMATRIPTAN SUCCINATE

Trade: Imitrex
Can/Aus/UK: Imigran, Imitrex
Uses: Anti-migraine medication.
AAP: Approved by the American Academy of Pediatrics for
use in breastfeeding mothers

Sumatriptan is a 5-HT (Serotonin) receptor agonist and a highly
effective new drug for the treatment of migraine headache. It is not an
analgesic, rather it produces a rapid vasoconstriction in various regions
of the brain, thus temporarily reducing the cause of migraines.

In one study using 5 lactating women, each were given 6 mg
subcutaneous injections and samples drawn for analysis over 8 hours.[1]
The highest breastmilk levels were 87.2 μg/L at 2.6 hours post-dose
and rapidly disappeared over the next 6 hours. The mean total recovery
of sumatriptan in milk over the 8 hour duration was only 14.4 ug. On
a weight-adjusted basis this concentration in milk corresponded to a
mean infant exposure of only 3.5% of the maternal dose. Further,
assuming an oral bioavailability of only 14%, the weight-adjusted dose
an infant would absorb would be approximately 0.49% of the maternal
dose. The authors suggest that continued breastfeeding following
sumatriptan use would not pose a significant risk to the sucking infant.

The maternal plasma half-life is 1.3 hours, the milk half-life is 2.22
hours. Although the milk/plasma ratio was 4.9 (indicating significant
concentrating mechanisms in milk), the absolute maternal plasma levels
were small, hence the absolute milk concentrations were low.

Pregnancy Risk Category: C

Lactation Risk Category: L3

Theoretic Infant Dose: 13.1 μg/kg/day

Adult Concerns: Flushing, hot tingling sensations.

Pediatric Concerns: None reported via milk.

Drug Interactions: MAOIs can markedly increase sumatriptan
systemic effect and elimination including elevated sumatriptan plasma
levels. Ergot containing drugs have caused prolonged vasospastic
reactions. There have been rare reports of weakness, hyperreflexia, and
incoordination with combined use with SSRIs such as fluoxetine,
paroxetine, sertraline and fluvoxamine.

Alternatives: Zolmitripan

Adult Dosage: 25-100 mg BID-TID

T½ = 1.3 hours	M/P = 4.9
PHL =	PB = 14-21%
PK = 12 min.(IM)	Oral = 10-15%
MW = 413	pKa =
Vd =	

References:
1. Wojnar-Horton RE, Hackett LP, Yapp P, Dusci LJ, Paech M and Ilett KF. Distribution and excretion of sumatriptan in human milk. Brit. J. Clin. Pharmacol. 41:217-221, 1995.

TACROLIMUS

Trade: Prograf, Protopic
Can/Aus/UK: Protopic
Uses: Immunosuppressant
AAP: Not reviewed

Tacrolimus is an immunosuppressant formerly known as SK506. It is used to reduce rejection of transplanted organs including liver and kidney.[1] In one report of 21 mothers who received tacroliumus while pregnant, milk concentrations in colostrum averaged 0.79 ng/mL and varied from 0.3 to 1.9 nanograms/mL.[2] Maternal doses (PO) ranged from 9.8 to 10.3 mg/day. Milk/blood ratio averaged 0.54. Using this data and an average daily milk intake of 150 mL/kg, the average dose to the infant per day via milk would be < 0.1 μg/kg/day. Because the oral bioavailability is poor (<32%), an infant would likely ingest less than 100 ng/kg/day. The usual pediatric dose (PO) for preventing rejection varies from 0.15 to 0.20 mg/kg/day (equivalent to 150,000-200,000 nanograms/kg/day).

Recently the FDA has approved a topical form of tacrolimus (Protopic) for use in moderate to severe eczema, in those for whom standard eczema therapies are deemed inadvisable because of potential risks, or who are not adequately treated by, or who are intolerant of standard eczema therapies. Absorption via skin is minimal. In a study of 46 adult patients after multiple doses, plasma levels ranged from undetectable to 20 ng/mL, with 45 of the patients have peak blood concentrations less than 5 ng/mL.[1] In another study, the peak blood levels averaged 1.6 ng/mL, which is significantly less than the therapeutic range in kidney transplantation(7-20 ng/mL). While the absolute transcutaneous bioavailability is unknown it is apparently very low. Combined with the poor oral bioavailability of this product, it is not likely a breastfed infant will receive enough following topical use (maternal) to produce adverse effects.

Pregnancy Risk Category: C

Lactation Risk Category: L3

Theoretic Infant Dose: 0.1 μg/kg/day

Adult Concerns: Edema, renal shutdown.

Pediatric Concerns: None reported.

Drug Interactions: Drugs that may increase tacrolimus levels include: calcium channel blockers, azole antifungals, macrolide antibiotics(erythromycin, clarithromycin), cisapride, metoclopramide, bromocriptine, cimetidine, cyclosporine, danazol, methylprednisolone, protease inhibitors. Drugs that may decrease tacrolimus blood levels include: carbamazepine, phenobarbital, phenytoin, rifabutin, rifampin.

Alternatives:

Adult Dosage: 0.15-0.3 mg/kg QD

T½ = 34.2 hours	**M/P = 0.54**
PHL = 11.5 hours	**PB = 99%**
PK = 1,6 hours	**Oral = 14-32%**
MW = 822	**pKa =**
Vd = 2.6	

References:
1. Pharmaceutical manufacturers package insert, 2001.
2. Jain A, Venkataramanan R, et.al. Pregnancy after liver transplantation under tacrolimus. Transplantation 64(4):559-565.

TAMOXIFEN

Trade: Nolvadex
Can/Aus/UK: Apo-Tamox, Eblon, Genox, Noltam, Nolvadex, Tamofen, Tamone, Tamoxen
Uses: Anti-estrogen, anticancer
AAP: Not reviewed

Tamoxifen is an nonsteroidal antiestrogen. It attaches to the estrogen receptor and produces only minimal stimulation, thus it prevents estrogen from stimulating the receptor. Aside from this, it also produces a number of other effects within the cytoplasm of the cell and some of its anticancer effects may be mediated by its effects at sites other than the estrogen receptor.

Tamoxifen is metabolized by the liver and has an elimination half-life of greater than 7 days(range 3-21 days).[1] It is well absorbed orally, and the highest tissue concentrations are in the liver (60 fold). It is 99% protein bound and normally reduces plasma prolactin levels significantly (66% after 3 months). At present, there is no data on its transfer into breastmilk, however it has been shown to inhibit lactation early postpartum in several studies. In one study, doses of 10-30 mg twice daily early postpartum, completely inhibited postpartum engorgement and lactation.[2] In a second study, tamoxifen doses of 10 mg four times daily significantly reduced serum prolactin and inhibited milk production as well.[3] We do not know the effect of tamoxifen on established milk production.

Tamoxifen is potentially teratogenic (category D) and should never be used in pregnant women (Note: it is useful in conjunction with clomiphene to stimulate ovulation...short term use only). It has a pKa of 8.85 which may suggest some trapping in milk compared to the maternal plasma levels.

This product has a very long half-life, and the active metabolite is concentrated in the plasma (2 fold). This drug has all the characteristics that would suggest a concentrating mechanism in breastfed infants over time. Its prominent effect on reducing prolactin levels will inhibit early lactation, and may ultimately inhibit established lactation. In this instance, the significant risks to the infant from exposure to tamoxifen probably outweigh the benefits of breastfeeding. Mothers receiving tamoxifen should not breastfeed until we know more about the levels transferred into milk, and the plasma/tissue levels found in breastfed infants.

Pregnancy Risk Category: D

Lactation Risk Category: L5

Theoretic Infant Dose:

Adult Concerns: Hot flashes, nausea, vomiting, vaginal bleeding/discharge, menstrual irregularities, amenorrhea.

Pediatric Concerns: None reported but caution is urged.

Drug Interactions: Increased anticoagulant effect when used with coumarin-type anticoagulants. Tamoxifen is a potent inhibitor of drug metabolizing enzymes in the liver, observe for elevated levels of many drugs.

Alternatives:

Adult Dosage: 10-20 mg BID

T½ = > 7 days	M/P =
PHL =	PB = 99%
PK = 2-3 hours	Oral = Complete
MW = 371	pKa = 8.85
Vd =	

References:
1. Pharmaceutical Manufacturers Package Insert, 1997.
2. Shaaban MM. Suppression of lactation by an antiestrogen, tamoxifen.

Eur. J. Obstet. Gynecol. Reprod. Biol. 4:167-169, 1975.
3. Massala A, Delitala G, et.al. Inhibition of lactation and inhibition of prolactin release after mechanical breast stimulation in puerperal women given tamoxifen or placebo. Br. J. Obstet. Gynecol. 85:134-137, 1978.

TAZAROTENE

Trade: Tazorac
Can/Aus/UK: Zorac
Uses: Anti-psoriatic
AAP: Not reviewed

Tazarotene is a specialized retinoid for topical use. Applied daily, it is indicated for treatment of stable plaque psoriasis of up to 20% of the body surface area. Only 2-3% of the topically applied drug is absorbed transcutaneously.

Tazarotene is used for the topical treatment of stable plaque psoriasis and acne. Following topical application, tazarotene is converted to an active metabolite; transcutaneous absorption is minimal (<1%).[1] Little compound could be detected in the plasma. However, systemic absorption is a function of the surface area. When applied to large surface areas, systemic absorption is increased. Data on transmission to breastmilk are not available. The manufacturer reports some is transferred to rodent milk, but it has not been tested in humans.

Pregnancy Risk Category: X

Lactation Risk Category:

Theoretic Infant Dose:

Adult Concerns: Hypertriglyceridemia, peripheral edema, pruritus, erythema, burning, contact dermatitis have been reported.

Pediatric Concerns: None via milk.

Drug Interactions: Do not use concomitantly with drying agents.

Alternatives:

Adult Dosage:

T½ = 1-2 hours	M/P =
PHL=	PB =
PK = 9 hours	Oral =
MW = 351	pKa =
Vd =	

References:
1. Pharmaceutical manufacturers package insert, 2002.

TEA TREE OIL

Trade: Tea Tree Oil
Can/Aus/UK:
Uses: Antibacterial, antifungal
AAP: Not reviewed

Tee tree oil, as derived from Melaleuca alternifolia, has recently gained popularity for its antiseptic properties. The essential oil, derived by steam distillation of the leaves, contains terpin-4-ol in concentrations of 40% or more.[1] TTO is primarily noted for its antimicrobial effects without irritating sensitive tissues. It is antimicrobial when tested against Candida albicans, E. coli, S. Aureus, Staph. epidermidis, and pseudomonas aeruginosa. In several reports it is suggested to have antifungal properties equivalent to tolnaftate, and clotrimazole. Although the use of TTO in adults is mostly nontoxic, the safe use in infants is unknown. Use directly on the nipple should be minimized.

Pregnancy Risk Category:

Lactation Risk Category: L3

Theoretic Infant Dose:

Adult Concerns: Toxic effects include allergic eczema. Petechial body rash and leukocytosis in one individual who ingested ½ teaspoonful orally. Ataxia and drowsiness following oral ingestion of < 10 cc by a 17 month old infant.

Pediatric Concerns: None reported via milk.

Drug Interactions:

Alternatives:

Adult Dosage:

References:
1.   Review of Natural Products. Facts and Comparisons, St. Louis, Mo. 1997.

TECHNETIUM TC 99M SESTAMIBI

Trade: Cardiolite, Sestamibi
Can/Aus/UK:
Uses: Imaging agent
AAP: Radioactive compound that requires temporary cessation of breastfeeding.

Technetium 99M sestamibi is a myocardial imaging agent that is also sometimes used as an oncologic imaging agent. The radioactive technetium-99 ion is chelated to the sestamibi molecule. It is used as an alternative to Thallium-201 imaging.[1]   Sestamibi is largely distributed to the myocardium and is a function of myocardial viability.[2]

Technetium is a weak gamma emitter with a radioactive half-life of only 6.02 hours. The biological half-life of this product is approximately 6 hours, but the effective half-life (both biological and radioactive) is only about 3 hours. Transfer of significant amounts of sestamibi into human milk is yet unreported, but is rather unlikely as sestamibi binds irreversible to myocardial tissue and does not redistribute to other tissues to a significant degree.   Other forms of TC-99 have been reported to enter milk, but entry would be largely determined by the chemical form, not the radioactive agent.[3]   For current Nuclear Regulatory Commission breastfeeding guidelines consult table in appendix.

Pregnancy Risk Category: C

Lactation Risk Category: L4

Theoretic Infant Dose:

Adult Concerns: Dysgeusia, headache, flushing, angina, hypersensitivity, hypertension.

Pediatric Concerns: It is not known if the sestamibi chelate is transferred into human milk. But Technetium salts in general do transfer. Pump and dump for 24-30 hours or until all radioactive is gone.

Drug Interactions:

Alternatives:

Adult Dosage: 10-30 mCi X 1

T½ = 6 hours	M/P =
PHL =	PB = < 1%
PK =	Oral = Complete
MW =	pKa =
Vd =	

References:

1.   Berman DS: Introduction - Technetium-99m myocardial perfusion imaging agents and their relation to thallium-201. Am J Cardiol 66:1E-4E, 1990.
2.   Berman DS, Kiat H & Maddahi J: The new Tc-99m myocardial perfusion imaging agents: Tc-99m sestamibi and Tc-99m teboroxime. Circulation 84(suppl):7-21, 1991.
3.   Maisels MJ & Gilcher RO: Excretion of technetium in human milk. Pediatrics 71:841-842, 1983.

TECHNETIUM-99M

Trade: Technetium-99m
Can/Aus/UK:
Uses: Radioactive imaging
AAP: Radioactive compound that requires temporary cessation of breastfeeding.

Radioactive technetium-99M (Tc-99m) is present in milk for at least 15 hours to 3 days and significant quantities have been reported in the thyroid and gastric mucosa of infants ingesting milk from treated mothers.   Technetium is one of the halide elements and is handled, biologically, much like iodine. Like iodine, it concentrates in thyroid tissues, the stomach, and breastmilk of nursing mothers.   It has a radioactive half-life of 6.02 hours. Following a dose of 15 mCi of Tc-99m for a brain scan, the concentration of Tc-99m in breastmilk at 4, 8.5, 20, and 60 hours was 0.5 μCi, 0.1 μCi, 0.02 μCi, and 0.006 μCi respectively.[1]   In another study, following a dose of 10 mCi of NaTcO4, breastmilk levels were 5.7, 1.5, 0.015 μCi/mL at 3.25, 7.5, and 24 hours respectively.[2]   The estimated dose to infant was 1,036, 284, and 2.7 μCi/180 mL milk. These authors recommended pumping and dumping of milk for 48 hours.   Technetium-99m is used in many salt and chemical forms, but the radioactivity and decay are the same although the concentration in milk may be influenced by the salt form.

In another study using Technetium MAG3 in two mothers receiving 150 MBq of radioactivity, the total percent of ingested radioactivity ranged from 0.7 to 1.6% of the total.[3]   These authors suggested that the DTPA salt of technetium would produce the least breastmilk levels and would be preferred in breastfeeding mothers. The NRC table in the appendix suggests a duration of interruption of breastfeeding of 12 to 24 hours for 12 and 30 mCi respectively, but this depends on the salt form used.

Pregnancy Risk Category: C

Lactation Risk Category: L4

Theoretic Infant Dose:

Adult Concerns:

Pediatric Concerns: None reported, but may be transferred to infant thyroid. Pump and dump for a minimum of 48 hours.

Drug Interactions:

Alternatives:

Adult Dosage: 15-20 mCi X 1

T½ = <6 hours	M/P =
PHL =	PB =
PK =	Oral = Complete
MW =	pKa =
Vd =	

References:
1. Rumble WF, Aamodt RL, et.al. Accidental ingestion of Tc-99m in breast milk by a 10-week old child. J Nucl Med 19:913-915, 1978.
2. Maisels MJ, Gilcher RO. Excretion of technetium in human milk. Pediatrics 71:841-842, 1983.
3. Evans JL, Mountford, AN, Herring AN, and Richardson, MA. Secretion of radioactivity in breast milk following administration of 99Tcm-MAG3. Nuc. Med. Comm. 14:108-111,1993.

TELMISARTAN

Trade: Micardis, Micardis HCT
Can/Aus/UK: Micardis
Uses: Angiotensin II receptor antagonist
AAP: Not reviewed

Telmisartan is a potent antihypertensive that blocks the angiotensin II receptor site. Micardis HCT also contains hydrochlorothiazide 12.5 mg. This agent should never be used in pregnant patients, as fetal demise has been reported with similar agents in this class. No data are available on its use in lactating mothers. However, its use early postpartum in lactating mothers is not recommended due to the sensitivity of newborns to antihypertensives of this family (ACE and AT_1 antagonists).

Pregnancy Risk Category: C during 1st and 2nd trimesters
D during 3rd trimester

Lactation Risk Category: L3
L4 if used in neonatal period

Theoretic Infant Dose:

Adult Concerns: UTI infection, back pain, sinusitis and diarrhea have been reported. Flu-like symptoms, myalgia, coughing, hypotension have been reported.

Pediatric Concerns: None reported, but use early postpartum is not recommended.

Drug Interactions: When coadministered with digoxin, a 50% increase in digoxin peak plasma levels occurred, and a 13-20% increase in trough levels.

Alternatives:

Adult Dosage: 40 mg daily

T½ = 24 hours	M/P =
PHL=	PB = 99.5%
PK = 1 hour	Oral = 42-58%
MW = 514	pKa =
Vd = 7.14	

References:
1.   Pharmaceutical manufacturers package insert, 2002.

TEMAZEPAM

Trade: Restoril
Can/Aus/UK: Euhypnos, Noctume, Normison, PMS-Temazepam, Restoril, Temaze, Temtabs
Uses: Short acting benzodiazepine (Valium-like) hypnotic
AAP: Drug whose effect on nursing infants is unknown but may be of concern

Temazepam is a short acting benzodiazepine that belongs to the Valium family primarily used as a nighttime sedative.   In one study the milk/plasma ratio varied from <0.09 to   < 0.63 (mean=0.18).[1] Temazepam is relatively water soluble and therefore particians poorly into breastmilk. Levels of temazepam were undetectable in the infants studied, although these studies were carried out 15 hours post-dose. Although the study shows low neonatal exposure to temazepam via breastmilk, the infant should be monitored carefully for sleepiness and poor feeding.

Pregnancy Risk Category: X

Lactation Risk Category: L3

Theoretic Infant Dose:

Adult Concerns: Sedation.

Pediatric Concerns: None reported via milk, but observe for sedation, poor feeding.

Drug Interactions: Increased effect when used with other CNS depressants.

Alternatives: Lorazepam, Alprazolam

Adult Dosage: 7.5-30 mg QD

T½ = 9.5-12.4 hours	M/P = 0.18
PHL=	PB = 96%
PK = 2-4 hours	Oral = 90%
MW = 301	pKa = 1.3
Vd = 0.8-1.0	

References:
1.   Lebedevs TH, et.al. Excretion of temazepam in breast milk [letter]. Brit. J. Clin. Pharmacol. 33:204-6,1992.

TERAZOSIN HCL

Trade: Hytrin
Can/Aus/UK: Hytrin
Uses: Antihypertensive
AAP: Not reviewed

Terazosin is an antihypertensive that belongs to the alpha-1 blocking family. This family is generally very powerful, produces significant orthostatic hypotension, and other side effects.[1]   As such, for the past 20 years, these drugs have always been used as the STEP II drugs used in hypertension, whereas the beta blockers, ACE inhibitors, calcium channel blockers, and thiazide diuretics have always been used first (STEP I). If the STEP I drugs don't work, then the physician employs a STEP II drug.

Terazosin has rather powerful effects on the prostate and testes producing testicular atrophy in some animal studies (particularly newborn) and is therefore not preferred in pregnant or in lactating women. No data are available on transfer into human milk. Use caution.

Pregnancy Risk Category: C

Lactation Risk Category: L4

Theoretic Infant Dose:

Adult Concerns: Hypotension, bradycardia, sedation.

Pediatric Concerns: None reported, but extreme caution is recommended.

Drug Interactions: Decreased antihypertensive effect when used with NSAIDs. Increased hypotensive effects when used with diuretics and other antihypertensive beta blockers.

Alternatives:

Adult Dosage: 1-10 mg QD

T½ = 9-12 hours	M/P =
PHL=	PB = 94%
PK = 1-2 hours	Oral = 90%
MW = 423	pKa =
Vd =	

References:
1. Pharmaceutical Manufacturers Package Insert, 1995.

TERBINAFINE

Trade: Lamisil
Can/Aus/UK: Lamisil
Uses: Antifungal
AAP: Not reviewed

Terbinafine is an antifungal agent primarily used for tinea species such as athlete's foot and ringworm. Systemic absorption following topical therapy is minimal.[1]   Following an oral dose of 500 mg in two volunteers, the total dose of terbinafine secreted in breastmilk during the 72 hour post-dosing period was 0.65 mg in one mother and 0.15 mg in another..[2] The total excretion of terbinafine in breastmilk ranged from 0.13% to 0.03 % of the total maternal dose, respectively.   Topical absorption through the skin is minimal.[3]

Pregnancy Risk Category: B

Lactation Risk Category: L2

Theoretic Infant Dose:

Adult Concerns: Topical: burning, pruritus. Oral: fatigue, headache, GI distress, elevated liver enzymes, alopecia.

Pediatric Concerns: None reported via milk.

Drug Interactions: Terbinafine clearance is decreased 33% by cimetidine, and 16% by terfenadine. Terbinafine increases clearance of cyclosporin(15%).   Rifampin increases terbinafine clearance by 100%.

Alternatives: Fluconazole

Adult Dosage: 250 mg QD

T½ = 26 hours.	M/P =
PHL =	PB = 99%
PK = 1-2 hours.	Oral = 80%
MW = 291	pKa =
Vd = >28	

References:
1. Pharmaceutical Manufacturers Package Insert, 1996.
2. Drug Facts and Comparisons. 1996. ed. Facts and Comparisons, St. Louis.
3. Birnbaum JE: Pharmacology of the allylamines. J Am Acad Dermatol 23:782-785, 1990.

TERBUTALINE

Trade: Bricanyl, Brethine
Can/Aus/UK: Bricanyl
Uses: Bronchodilator for asthma
AAP: Approved by the American Academy of Pediatrics for use in breastfeeding mothers

Terbutaline is a popular Beta-2 adrenergic used for bronchodilation in asthmatics. It is secreted into breastmilk but in low quantities. Following doses of 7.5 to 15 mg/day of terbutaline, milk levels averaged 3.37 μg/L.[1] Assuming a daily intake of 165 ml milk, these levels would suggest a daily intake of less than 0.5 μg/kg/day which corresponds to 0.2 to 0.7% of maternal dose.

In another study of a patient receiving 5 mg three times daily, the mean milk concentrations ranged from 3.2 to 3.7 μg/L.[2] The author calculated the daily dose to infant at 0.4-0.5 μg/kg body weight. Terbutaline was not detectable in the infant's serum. No untoward effects have been reported in breastfeeding infants.

Pregnancy Risk Category: B

Lactation Risk Category: L2

Theoretic Infant Dose: 0.5 μg/kg/day

Adult Concerns: Tremors, nervousness, tachycardia.

Pediatric Concerns:

Drug Interactions: Decreased effect when used with beta blockers. May increase toxicity when used with MAOI and TCAs.

Alternatives:

Adult Dosage: 5 mg TID

T½ = 14 hours	M/P = < 2.9
PHL =	PB = 20%
PK = 5-30 min.	Oral = 33-50%
MW = 225	pKa = ?
Vd = 1-2	

References:
1. Lindberberg C, et.al. Transfer of terbutaline into breast milk. Eur. J. Respir. Dis. 65:87, 1984.
2. Lonnerholm G, Lindstrom B. Terbutaline excretion into breast milk. Br J Clin Pharmacol. 13:729-730,1982.

TERCONAZOLE

Trade: Terazol 3, Terazol 7
Can/Aus/UK: Terazol
Uses: Antifungal, vaginal.
AAP: Not reviewed

Terconazole is an antifungal primarily used for vaginal candidiasis. It is similar to fluconazole and itraconazole. When administered intravaginally, only a limited amount (5 -16%) is absorbed systemically (mean peak plasma level = 6 ng/ml).[1,2] It is well absorbed orally. Even at high doses, the drug is not mutagenic, nor fetotoxic. At high doses, terconazole is known to enter breastmilk in rodents, although no data are available on human milk. The milk levels are probably too small to be clinically relevant.

Pregnancy Risk Category: C

Lactation Risk Category: L3

Theoretic Infant Dose:

Adult Concerns: Vaginal burning, itching, flu-like symptoms.

Pediatric Concerns: None reported due to minimal studies.

Drug Interactions:

Alternatives: Fluconazole

Adult Dosage: 5 g QD

T½ = 4-11.3 hours	M/P =
PHL =	PB =
PK =	Oral = Complete
MW = 532	pKa =
Vd =	

References:
1. Pharmaceutical Manufacturers Package Insert, 1996.
2. McEvoy GE(ed):AHFS Drug Information, New York, NY. 1995.

TETRACYCLINE

Trade: Achromycin, Sumycin, Terramycin
Can/Aus/UK: Achromycin, Aureomycin, Mysteclin, Tetrachel, Tetracyn, Tetrex
Uses: Antibiotic
AAP: Approved by the American Academy of Pediatrics for use in breastfeeding mothers

Tetracycline is a broad spectrum antibiotic with significant side effects in pediatric patients, including dental staining and reduced bone growth.   It is secreted into breastmilk in extremely small levels. Because tetracyclines bind to milk calcium they would have reduced oral absorption in the infant.

Posner reports that in a patient receiving 500 mg four times daily, the average concentration of tetracycline in milk was 1.14 mg/L.[1]   The maternal plasma level was 1.92 mg/L and the milk/plasma ratio was 0.59.   The absolute dose to the infant ranged from 0.17 to 0.39 mg/kg/day.   None was detected in the plasma compartment of the infant (limit of detection 0.05 mg/L).

In a mother receiving 275 mg/d, milk levels averaged 1.25 mg/L with a maximum of 2.51 mg/L.[2] None was detected in the infants plasma. In another study of 2-3 patients receiving a single 150 mg/d dose, milk levels ranged from 0.3 to 1.2 mg/L at 4 hours(Cmax). The maximum reported milk level was 1.2 mg/L.[3] A milk/plasma ratio of 0.58 was reported.

Without doubt, the short-term exposure of infants to tetracyclines (via milk) is not contraindicated(< 3 weeks). However, this author does not recommend the long-term exposure of breastfeeding infants to tetracyclines, such as with their daily use for acne.   The absorption of even small amounts over a prolonged period could result in dental staining.

Pregnancy Risk Category: D

Lactation Risk Category: L2

Theoretic Infant Dose: 0.2 mg/kg/day

Adult Concerns: Pediatric: dental staining, decreased bone growth, altered GI flora.

Pediatric Concerns: None reported via milk. Poor oral absorption of tetracyclines generally limits effects. Avoid long-term exposure.

Drug Interactions: Absorption may be reduced or delayed when used with dairy products, calcium, magnesium, or aluminum containing antacids, oral contraceptives, iron, zinc, sodium bicarbonate, penicillins, cimetidine.   Increased toxicity may result when used with methoxyflurane anesthesia. Use with warfarin anticoagulants may increase anticoagulation.

Alternatives:

Adult Dosage: 500 mg QID

T½ = 6-12 hours	M/P = 0.58-1.28
PHL =	PB = 25%
PK = 1.5-4 hours	Oral = 75%
MW = 444	pKa =
Vd =	

References:

1. Posner AC, Prigot A & Konicoff NG: Further observations on the use of tetracycline hydrochloride in prophylaxis and treatment of obstetric infections. Antibiotics Annual 1954-1955. In: Medical Encyclopedia, New York 594-598, 1955.
2. Graf von H, Riemann S. Untersuchungen uber die konzentration von pyrrolidino-methyl-tetracyclin in der muttermilch. Dtsch Med Wochenschr 84:1694-1696, 1959.
3. Matsuda S. Transfer of antibiotics into maternal milk. Biol Res Pregnancy Perinatol. 5(2):57-60, 1984.

THALLIUM-201

Trade: Thallium-201
Can/Aus/UK:
Uses: Radioactive tracer
AAP: Not reviewed

Thallium-201 in the form of thallous chloride is used extensively for myocardial perfusion imaging to delineate ischemic myocardium. Following infusion, almost 85% of the administered dose is extracted into the heart on the first pass. Less than 5% of the dose remains free in the plasma in as little as 5 minutes after administration.   Whereas Thallium-201 has a radioactive half-life of only 73 hours, the whole-body half-life of the Thallium ion is about 10 days. Most all radiation will be decayed in 5-6 half-lives (15 days).   In a study of one breastfeeding patient who received 111MBq (3 mCi) for a brain scan, the amount of Thallium-201 in breastmilk at 4 hours was 326 Bq/mL, and subsequently dropped to 87 Bq/mL after 72 hours.[1]   Even without interrupting breastfeeding, the infant would have received less than the NCRP radiation safety guideline dose for infrequent exposure for a 1 year old infant.   However, a brief interruption of breastfeeding was nevertheless recommended. The length of interrupted breastfeeding is dependent on age of infant and dose of Thallium. With an interruption time varying from 2, 24, 48, to 96 hours, the respective Thallium dose to the infant would be 0.442, 0.283, 0.197, and 0.101 MBq compared to the maternal dose of 111 MBq.

In another study[2] of a breastfeeding mother who received 111 MBq (3 mCi),   the calculated dose an infant (without any interruption of breastfeeding and assuming the consumption of 1000 mL of milk daily) would receive is approximately 0.81 MBq which is presently less than the maximal allowed radiation dose (NCRP) for an infant. The authors therefore recommend that breastfeeding be discontinued for at least 24-48 hours following the administration of 111 MBq of Thallium-201. The amount of infant exposure from close contact with the mother was also measured and found to be very small in comparison to the orally ingested dose via milk. A brief interruption of breastfeeding for 24-48 hours would dramatically reduce overall exposure of the infant although the Nuclear Regulatory Commission recommends interruption of breastfeeding for 2 weeks (with dose=110 Mbq). See NRC table in appendix.

Pregnancy Risk Category:

Lactation Risk Category: L4

Theoretic Infant Dose:

Adult Concerns:

Pediatric Concerns: None reported in one case, but a brief interruption (depending on dose) is advised.

Drug Interactions:

Alternatives:

Adult Dosage: 37-148 mCi

T½ = 73 hours	M/P =
PHL =	PB =
PK = < 60 minutes	Oral =
MW =	pKa =
Vd =	

References:
1.   Johnston RE, Mukherji SK, et.al. Radiation dose from breastfeeding following administration of Thallium-201. J. Nucl. Med. 12:2079-2082, 1996.
2.   Murphy PH, Beasley CW, et.al. Thallium-201 in human milk: Observations and radiological consequences. Health Physics 56(4):539-541, 1989.

THEOPHYLLINE

Trade: Aminophylline, Quibron, Theo-dur
Can/Aus/UK: Austyn, Nuelin, Pulmophylline, Quibron-T/SR, Theo-Dur
Uses: Bronchodilator
AAP: Approved by the American Academy of Pediatrics for use in breastfeeding mothers

Theophylline is a methylzanthine bronchodilator. It has a prolonged half-life in neonates which may cause retention. Milk concentrations are approximately equal to the maternal plasma levels. If a mother is maintained at 10-20 μg/ml, the milk concentrations are closely equivalent. Estimates generally indicate that less than 1% of dose is absorbed by infant. Assuming maternal plasma levels of 10-20 μg/mL, the theophylline levels in a neonate would range from 0.9 to 3.6 μg/mL.[1] Levels in older infants would be correspondingly lower. Older infants (> 6 months) have drug kinetics similar to mother, which would reduce infant serum levels. Use of prolonged release forms by mother may alter adult half-life. Generally considered compatible with breastfeeding.

Pregnancy Risk Category: C

Lactation Risk Category: L3

Theoretic Infant Dose:

Adult Concerns: Irritability, nausea, vomiting, tachycardia, seizures.

Pediatric Concerns: None reported via milk. Observe for nausea, vomiting, irritability.

Drug Interactions: Numerous drug interactions exist. Agents that decrease theophylline levels include barbiturates, phenytoin, ketoconazole, rifampin, cigarette smoking, carbamazepine, isoniazid, loop diuretics, and others. Agents that increase theophylline levels include allopurinol, beta blockers, calcium channel blockers, cimetidine, oral contraceptives, corticosteroids, disulfiram, ephedrine, influenza virus vaccine, interferon, macrolides, mexiletine, quinolones, thiabendazole, thyroid hormones, carbamazepine, isoniazid, and loop diuretics.

Alternatives:

Adult Dosage: 3 mg/kg q 8 hours

T½ = 3-12.8 hours	M/P = 0.67
PHL = 30 hours	PB = 56%
PK = 1-2 hours(oral)	Oral = 76%
MW = 180	pKa = 8.6
Vd = 0.3-0.7	

References:
1. Stec GP, Grenberger P, Ruo TI, et.al. Kinetics of theophylline transfer to breastmilk. Clin Pharmacol Ther. 28:404-408, 1980.

THIABENDAZOLE

Trade: Mintezol
Can/Aus/UK: Mintezol
Uses: Anthelmintic, antiparasitic
AAP: Not reviewed

Thiabendazole is an antiparasitic agent for the treatment of roundworm, pinworm, hookworm, whipworm, and other parasitic infections. After absorption it is completely eliminated from the plasma by 48 hours, although most is excreted by 24 hours. Can be used in children. Although it is effective in pinworms, other agents with less side effects are preferred. No reports on its transfer to breastmilk have been found.

Pregnancy Risk Category: C

Lactation Risk Category: L3

Theoretic Infant Dose:

Adult Concerns: Hypotension, nausea, vomiting, psychotic reactions (seizures, hallucinations, delirium), rash, pruritus, intrahepatic cholestasis. Transient milk hepatitis.

Pediatric Concerns: None reported.

Drug Interactions: May increase theophylline and other xanthines levels by 50%.

Alternatives: Pyrantel

Adult Dosage: 1.5 g BID

T½ =	M/P =
PHL=	PB =
PK = **1-2 hours**	Oral = **Complete**
MW = **201**	pKa =
Vd =	

References:

THIOPENTAL SODIUM

Trade: Pentothal
Can/Aus/UK: Intraval, Pentothal
Uses: Barbiturate anesthetic agent
AAP: Approved by the American Academy of Pediatrics for use in breastfeeding mothers

Thiopental is an ultra short acting barbiturate sedative. Used in the induction phase of anesthesia, it rapidly redistributes from the brain to adipose and muscle tissue, hence the plasma levels are small, and the sedative effects are virtually gone in 20 minutes. Thiopental sodium is secreted into milk in low levels. In a study of two groups of 8 women who received from 5.0 to 5.4 mg/kg thiopental sodium, the maximum concentration in breastmilk 0.9 mg/L in mature milk and in colostrum was 0.34 mg/L.[1] The milk/plasma ratio was 0.3 for colostrum and 0.4 for mature milk. The maximum daily dose to infant would be 0.135 mg/kg, or approximately 3% of the adult dose.

Pregnancy Risk Category: C

Lactation Risk Category: L3

Theoretic Infant Dose: 0.1 mg/kg/day

Adult Concerns: Hemolytic anemia has been reported. Respiratory depression, renal failure, delirium, nausea, vomiting, pruritus.

Pediatric Concerns: None reported in a study of 16 women receiving induction doses.

Drug Interactions: Increased depression when used with CNS depressants (especially opiates and phenothiazines), and with salicylates or sulfisoxazole.

Alternatives:

Adult Dosage: 50-100 mg X 2

T½ = 3-8 hours	M/P = 0.3-0.4
PHL = 15 hours	PB = 60-96%
PK = 1-2 minutes	Oral = Variable
MW = 264	pKa =
Vd = 1.4	

References:

1. Anderson LW, Qvist T, et al: Concentrations of thiopentone in mature breast milk and colostrum following an induction dose. Acta Anaesth Scand. 31(1):30-2, 1987.

THIORIDAZINE

Trade: Mellaril
Can/Aus/UK: Aldazine, Apo-Thioridazine, Mellaril, Melleril, Novo-Ridazine
Uses: Antipsychotic
AAP: Not reviewed

Thioridazine is a potent phenothiazine tranquilizer. It has a high volume of distribution, and long half-life. No data are available on its secretion into human milk, but it should be expected.[1] Pediatric indications (2-12 years of age) are available.

Pregnancy Risk Category: C

Lactation Risk Category: L4

Theoretic Infant Dose:

Adult Concerns: Blood dyscrasias, arrhythmias, sedation, gynecomastia, nausea, vomiting, constipation, dry mouth, retinopathy.

Pediatric Concerns: None reported due to limited studies.

Drug Interactions: Alcohol may enhance CNS depression. Aluminum salts may reduce GI absorption. Other anticholinergics may reduce the therapeutic actions the phenothiazines. Barbiturates may reduce phenothiazine plasma levels. Bromocriptine effectiveness may be inhibited by phenothiazines. Propranolol and phenothiazines may result in increased plasma levels of both drugs. Tricyclic antidepressant concentrations, serum concentrations may be increased the phenothiazines. Valproic acid clearance may be decreased.

Alternatives:

Adult Dosage: 100-400 mg QD

T½ = 21-24 hours		M/P =	
PHL=		PB =	
PK =		Oral = Complete	
MW = 371		pKa = 9.5	
Vd = 18			

References:
1. O'Brien, T. Excretion of drugs in human milk. Am.J. Hosp. Pharm. 31:844-854, 1974.

THIOTHIXENE

Trade: Navane
Can/Aus/UK: Navane
Uses: Antipsychotic agent
AAP: Not reviewed

Thiothixene is an antipsychotic agent similar in action to the phenothiazines, butyrophenones (Haldol), and chlorprothixene. There are no data on its transfer into human milk. Of this family, thiothixene has a rather higher risk of extrapyramidal symptoms, and lowered seizure threshold.[1,2] Only two agents in these families have been studied with respect to milk levels, haloperidol and chlorpromazine, both produced rather low milk levels. However these agents generally have long half-lives and some concern exists for long-term exposure. Observe infant for sedation, seizures, or jerks.

Pregnancy Risk Category: C

Lactation Risk Category: L4

Theoretic Infant Dose:

Adult Concerns: Decreases seizure threshold. Sedation, lethargy, extrapyramidal jerking motion.

Pediatric Concerns: None via milk.

Drug Interactions: Thiothixene may be additive when coadministered with other sedative drugs, alcohol, anticholinergics, and hypotensive agents. Aluminum salts may reduce oral absorption of phenothiazines. Anticholinergics may reduce efficacy of thiothixene. Thiothixene may increase tricyclic antidepressant plasma levels.

Alternatives: Haloperidol

Adult Dosage: 5-15 mg TID-QID

T½ = 34 hours	M/P =
PHL =	PB =
PK = 1-2 hours	Oral = Complete
MW = 443	pKa =
Vd =	

References:
1. Drug Facts and Comparisons. 1999 ed. Facts and Comparisons, St. Louis.
2. McEvoy GE(ed):AFHS Drug Information, New York, NY. 1999.

THYROID SCAN

Trade: Thyroid Scan
Can/Aus/UK:
Uses: Radiographic scan of thyroid gland
AAP: Not reviewed

Thyroid scanning with radioiodine (I-131) or technetium ^{99}m is useful in delineating structural abnormalities of the thyroid, eg, to distinguish Grave's disease from multinodular goiter and a single toxic adenoma or to determine the functional state of a single nodule ("hot" vs "cold").

In one procedure, the radiologist uses radioactive Technetium-^{99}m pertechnetate which has a short half-life of 6.7 hours. At least 97% of the radioactivity would be decayed in 5 half-lives (33.5 hours), after which it would be presumably safe to breastfeed.

In the second procedure (an uptake scan), radioactive Iodine-131 is used. The radioactive half-life of I-131 is 8.1 days. Five half-lives in this situation is 40.5 days. Although the biologic half-life of iodine would be less than the 40.5 days, it is not known with certainty how long is required before breastmilk samples are at background levels. For safety in this case, breastmilk samples should be counted by a gamma counter prior to reinstituting breastfeeding. I-131 is sequestered in high concentrations in breastmilk, and breastmilk levels could be exceedingly high. Excessive exposure of the infants thyroid to I-131 is exceedingly dangerous.[1-6] See NRC table in appendix.

Pregnancy Risk Category:

Lactation Risk Category: L4

Theoretic Infant Dose:

Adult Concerns: High milk radioactive levels.

Pediatric Concerns: Possible thyroid suppression is possible if high levels of I-131 are used. Count breastmilk samples to determine radiation levels.

Drug Interactions:

Alternatives:

Adult Dosage:

References:
1. American Academy of Pediatrics, Committee on Drugs. Transfer of drugs and other chemicals into human milk. Pediatrics 93(1):137-150, 1994.
2. Palmer, KE. Excretion of 125-I in breast milk following administration of labelled fibrinogen. Br. J. Radiol. 52:672, 1979
3. Karjalainen, P, et.al. The amount and form of radioactivity in human milk after lung scanning, renography and placental localization by 131-I labelled tracers. Acta Obstet Gynecol Scand 50:357, 1971.
4. Hedrick WR. et.al. Radiation dosimetry from breast milk excretion of radioiodine and pertechnetate. J. Nucl. Med. 27:1569, 1986.
5. Romney B, Nickoloff EL, Esser PD. Excretion of radioiodine in breast milk. J. Nucl. Med. 30:124-6,1989.
6. Robinson PS, Barker P, Campbell A, et.al. Iodine-131 in breast milk following therapy for thyroid carcinoma. J. Nuci. Med. 35:1797-1801, 1994.

THYROTROPIN

Trade: Thyrotropin, Tsh, Thyrogen
Can/Aus/UK: Thytropar
Uses: Excess TSH, Thyrotropin, hypothyroidism
AAP: Not reviewed

Thyroid stimulating hormone (Thyrotropin, TSH) is known to be secreted into breastmilk. TSH is extremely elevated in hypothyroid mothers and could presumably cause a hyperthyroid condition in the breastfeeding infant. The level of TSH secreted into milk was determined in a hyperthyroid mother (Plasma TSH=110 mU/L).[1] The breastmilk TSH was low (Milk TSH= 1.4 mU/L) suggesting that human breastmilk does not contain excessive amounts of TSH in the presence of severe maternal hypothyroidism, and that breastfeeding is permissible in hypothyroid mothers.

Pregnancy Risk Category: C

Lactation Risk Category: L1

Theoretic Infant Dose:

Adult Concerns: Elevated thyroxine levels in breastfeeding infant.

Pediatric Concerns: None reported via milk.   Breastfeeding by hyperthyroid mother is permissible.

Drug Interactions:

Alternatives:

Adult Dosage: 10 units daily

T½ =	M/P =
PHL=	PB =
PK =	Oral = Poor
MW =	pKa =
Vd =	

References:
1.   Robinson P, Hoad K. Thyrotropin in human breast milk. Aust. NZ. J. Med. 24:68, 1994.

TIAGABINE

Trade: Gabitril
Can/Aus/UK: Gabitril
Uses: Anticonvulsant
AAP: Not reviewed

Tiagabine is a GABA inhibitor useful for the treatment of partial epilepsy.[1]   No data are available on its transfer to human milk. It has been used in pediatric patients 3-10 years of age.   Use in women who are breastfeeding only if the benefits clearly outweigh the risks.

Pregnancy Risk Category: C

Lactation Risk Category: L4

Theoretic Infant Dose:

Adult Concerns: Asthenia, sedation, dizziness, headache, mild memory impairment, and abdominal pain and nausea have been reported.

Pediatric Concerns: None reported via milk.

Drug Interactions: Enhanced clearance of tiagabine has been reported when coadministered with carbamazepine, fosphenytoin, phenytoin, primidone, and phenobarbital. Valproic acid produces a 10% drop in tiagabine plasma levels but with a significant drop in plasma protein binding (may enhance the effect).

Alternatives:

Adult Dosage: 32-56 mg daily

T½ = 7-9 hours		M/P =	
PHL = 3.2-5.7 hours		PB = 95%	
PK = 45 minutes		Oral = 90%	
MW =		pKa =	
Vd =			

References:
1. Pharmaceutical Manufacturers Package Insert, 1999.

TICARCILLIN

Trade: Ticarcillin, Ticar, Timentin
Can/Aus/UK: Tarcil, Ticar, Ticillin
Uses: Penicillin antibiotic
AAP: Approved by the American Academy of Pediatrics for use in breastfeeding mothers

Ticarcillin is an extended-spectrum penicillin, used only IM or I.V., and is not appreciably absorbed via oral ingestion.[1,2] In a study of 2-3 patients who received 1000 mg I.V., only trace amounts were detected in milk and were too low to measure.[3] In a study of 10 patients who received 5 g TID I.V., the amount of ticarcillin in milk ranged from 2-2.5 mg/L.[4] Twelve hours after discontinuing ticarcillin, it was undetectable in milk. As with many penicillins only minimal levels are secreted into milk. Poor oral absorption would limit exposure of breastfeeding infant. May cause changes in GI flora and possibly fungal overgrowth. Timentin is ticarcillin with clavulanate added.

Pregnancy Risk Category: B

Lactation Risk Category: L2

Theoretic Infant Dose:

Adult Concerns: Neutropenia, anemia, kidney toxicity. Changes in GI flora, diarrhea, candida overgrowth.

Pediatric Concerns: None reported via milk. Observe for changes in GI flora, diarrhea.

Drug Interactions: Probenecid may increase penicillin levels. Tetracyclines may decrease penicillin effectiveness.

Alternatives:

Adult Dosage: 150-300 mg QD

T½ = 0.9-1.3 hours	M/P =
PHL = 3.5 - 5.6 hours(neonate)	PB = 54%
PK = 0.5 - 1.25 hours (IM)	Oral = Poor
MW = 384	pKa =
Vd =	

References:
1. Drug Facts and Comparisons. 1995 ed. Facts and Comparisons, St. Louis.
2. Pharmaceutical Manufacturers Package Insert, 1995.
3. Matsuda S. Transfer of antibiotics into maternal milk. Biol Res Pregnancy Perinatol. 5(2):57-60, 1984.
4. von Kobyletzki D, Dalhoff A, Lindemeyer H, Primavesi CΛ. Ticarcillin serum and tissue concentrations in gynecology and obstetrics. Infection. 11(3):144-9, 1983.

TICLOPIDINE

Trade: Ticlid
Can/Aus/UK: Apo-ticlopidine, Ticlid, Tilodene
Uses: Inhibits platelet aggregation
AAP: Not reviewed

Ticlopidine is useful in preventing thromboembolic disorders, increased cardiovascular mortality, stroke, infarcts, and other clotting disorders. Ticlopidine is reported to be excreted into rodent milk.[1] No data are available on penetration into human breastmilk. However it is highly protein bound, and the levels of ticlopidine in plasma are quite low. The manufacturer recommends against use in breastfeeding mothers.

Pregnancy Risk Category: B

Lactation Risk Category: L4

Theoretic Infant Dose:

Adult Concerns: Bleeding, neutropenia, maculopapular rash.

Pediatric Concerns: None reported via milk, but caution is recommended.

Drug Interactions: Antacids may reduce absorption of ticlopidine. Chronic cimetidine administration has reduced the clearance of ticlopidine by 50%. Use of aspirin may alter platelet aggregation. Digoxin plasma levels may be slightly decreased by 15%. Theophylline elimination half-life was significantly increased from 8-10 hours.

Alternatives:

Adult Dosage: 250 mg BID

T½ = 12.6 hours	M/P =
PHL =	PB = 98%
PK = 2 hours	Oral = 80%
MW = 264	pKa =
Vd =	

References:
1. Pharmaceutical Manufacturers Package Insert, 1996.

TIMOLOL

Trade: Blocadren
Can/Aus/UK: Apo-Timol, Betim, Blocadren, Novo-Timol, Tenopt, Timoptic, Timoptol, Timpilo
Uses: Beta blocker for hypertension and glaucoma
AAP: Approved by the American Academy of Pediatrics for use in breastfeeding mothers

---

Timolol is a beta blocker used for treating hypertension and glaucoma. It is secreted into milk. Following a dose of 5 mg three times daily, milk levels averaged 15.9 μg/L.[1] Both oral and ophthalmic drops produce modest levels in milk. Breastmilk levels following ophthalmic use of 0.5% timolol drops was 5.6 μg/L at 1.5 hours after the dose.[2] Untoward effects on infant have not been reported. These levels are probably too small to be clinically relevant.

Pregnancy Risk Category: C

Lactation Risk Category: L2

Theoretic Infant Dose: 2.4 μg/kg/day

Adult Concerns: Hypotension, bradycardia, depression, sedation.

Pediatric Concerns: None reported via milk, but observe for hypotension, weakness, hypoglycemia, sedation, depression.

Drug Interactions: Decreased effect when used with aluminum salts, barbiturates, calcium salts, cholestyramine, NSAIDs, ampicillin, rifampin, and salicylates. Beta blockers may reduce the effect of oral sulfonylureas (hypoglycemic agents). Increased toxicity/effect when used with other antihypertensives, contraceptives, MAO inhibitors, cimetidine, and numerous other products. See drug interaction reference for complete listing.

Alternatives: Propranolol, Metoprolol

Adult Dosage: 10-20 mg BID

T½ = 4 hours	M/P = 0.8
PHL =	PB = 10%
PK = 1-2 hours	Oral = 50%
MW = 316	pKa = 8.8
Vd = 1-3	

References:
1.   Fidler J, et. al. Excretion of oxprenolol and timolol in breast milk. Br J Obstet Gynaecol 90:961-5, 1983.
2.   Lustgarten JS, Podos SM. Topical timolol and the nursing mother. Arch Ophthalmol 101:1381-2, 1983.

TINZAPARIN SODIUM

Trade: Innohep
Can/Aus/UK: Innohep
Uses: Anticoagulant
AAP: Not reviewed

Tinzaparin is a low molecular weight heparin with antithrombotic properties used for the treatment of deep vein thrombosis. No data are available on its transfer to milk. However, due to its protein nature and its large molecular weight, breastmilk levels would be expected to be quite low. Some breastfeeding data are available for a similar product, dalteparin. With dalteparin, levels in milk were extraordinarily low.

Pregnancy Risk Category: B

Lactation Risk Category: L3

Theoretic Infant Dose:

Adult Concerns: Thrombocytopenia, hypersensitivity, prolonged bleeding times, chest pain, urinary infection, headache.

Pediatric Concerns: None reported.

Drug Interactions: Because of increased risk of bleeding, do not use with other anticoagulants, platelet inhibitors, NSAIDs, and thrombolytics.

Alternatives: Dalteparin, Enoxaparin

Adult Dosage: 175 IU/kg/d

T½ = 3.4 hours	M/P =
PHL=	PB =
PK = 3.7 hours S.C.	Oral = Nil
MW = 7500	pKa =
Vd = 0.07	

References:
1.   Pharmaceutical manufacturers package insert, 2002.

TIZANIDINE

Trade: Zanaflex
Can/Aus/UK:
Uses: Muscle relaxant
AAP: Not reviewed

Tizanidine is a centrally acting muscle relaxant. It has demonstrated efficacy in the treatment of tension headache and spasticity associate with multiple sclerosis. It is not known if it is transferred into human milk although the manufacturer states that due to its lipid solubility, it likely penetrates milk.[1] This product has a long half-life, high lipid solubility, and significant CNS penetration, all factors that would increase milk penetration.   While the half-life of the conventional formulation is only 4-8 hours, the half-life of the sustained release formulation is 13-22 hours.[2]   Further, 48% of patients complain of sedation. Use caution if used in a breastfeeding mother.

Pregnancy Risk Category: C

Lactation Risk Category: L4

Theoretic Infant Dose:

Adult Concerns: Hypotension (49%), sedation (48%), dry mouth, asthenia, dizziness, and other symptoms have been reported.   Nausea and vomiting have been reported. A high risk of elevated liver enzymes (5%).

Pediatric Concerns: None reported via milk, but caution is recommended.

Drug Interactions: Alcohol may increase plasma levels of tizanidine by 20%.   Oral contraceptives may significantly (50%) reduce clearance of tizanidine.

Alternatives:

Adult Dosage: 8 mg q 6 hours PRN

T½ = 13-22 hours	M/P =
PHL =	PB = 30%
PK = 1.5 hours	Oral = 40%
MW =	pKa =
Vd = 2.4	

References:
1. Pharmaceutical Manufacturers Package Insert, 1999.
2. Wagstaff AJ and Bryson HM. Tizanidine: a review of its pharmacology, clinical efficacy and tolerability in the management of spasticity associated with cerebral and spinal disorders. Drugs 53(3):435-452, 1997.

TOBRAMYCIN

Trade: Nebcin, Tobrex
Can/Aus/UK: Nebcin, Tobi, Tobralex, Tobrex
Uses: Ophthalmic antibiotic
AAP: Not reviewed

Tobramycin is an aminoglycoside antibiotic similar to gentamicin.[1] Although small levels of tobramycin are known to transfer into milk, they probably pose few problems. In one study of 5 patients, following an 80 mg IM dose, tobramycin levels in milk ranged from undetectable to 0.5 μg/ml.[2] Tobramycin is poorly absorbed orally and would be unlikely to produce significant levels in an infant.

Pregnancy Risk Category: C

Lactation Risk Category: L3

Theoretic Infant Dose: 0.1 μg/kg/day

Adult Concerns: Changes in GI flora.

Pediatric Concerns:

Drug Interactions: Increased toxicity when used with certain penicillins, cephalosporins, amphotericin B, loop diuretics, and neuromuscular blocking agents.

Alternatives:

Adult Dosage: 1 mg/kg q 8 hours

T½ = 2-3 hours	M/P =
PHL = 4.6 hours(neonates)	PB = <5%
PK = 30-90 min.(IM)	Oral =
MW = 468	pKa = ?
Vd = 0.22-0.31	

References:
1. Pharmaceutical Manufacturers Package Insert, 1996.
2. Takase Z. Laboratory and clinical studies on tobramycin in the field of obstetrics and gynecology. Chemotherapy(Tokyo) 23:1402, 1975.

TOLBUTAMIDE

Trade: Oramide, Orinase
Can/Aus/UK: Apo-Tolbutamide, Glyconon, Mobenol, Novo-Butamide, Orinase, Rastinon
Uses: Antidiabetic
AAP: Approved by the American Academy of Pediatrics for use in breastfeeding mothers

Tolbutamide is a short-acting sulfonylurea used to stimulate insulin secretion in type II diabetics.   Only low levels are secreted into breastmilk. Following a dose of 500 mg twice daily, milk levels in two patients were 3 and 18 μg/L respectively.[1]   Maternal serum levels averaged 35 and 45 μg/L. An infant consuming 1 L of milk daily would only ingest 1.8% of the maternal dose daily. Observe infant closely for jaundice and hypoglycemia. Use only with close observation and caution. See chlorpropamide.

Pregnancy Risk Category: D

Lactation Risk Category: L3

Theoretic Infant Dose: 2.7 μg/kg/day

Adult Concerns: Hypoglycemia, nausea, dyspepsia.

Pediatric Concerns: None reported via milk.

Drug Interactions: The hypoglycemic effect may be enhanced by : anticoagulants, chloramphenicol, clofibrate, fenfluramine, fluconazole, H2 antagonists, magnesium salts, methyldopa, MAO inhibitors, probenecid, salicylates, TCAs, sulfonamides. The hypoglycemic effect may be reduced by: beta blockers, cholestyramine, diazoxide, phenytoin, rifampin, thiazide diuretics.

Alternatives:

Adult Dosage: 250-2000 mg QD

T½ = 4.5-6.5 hours	M/P = 0.09-0.4
PHL=	PB = 93%
PK = 3.5 hours	Oral = Complete
MW = 270	pKa = 5.3
Vd = 0.10-0.15	

References:
1.   Moiel RH, Ryan JR. Tolbutamide (Orinase) in human breast milk. Clin Pediatr 6:480, 1967.

TOLMETIN SODIUM

Trade: Tolectin
Can/Aus/UK: Tolectin
Uses: Non-steroidal analgesic, used for arthritis, etc.
AAP: Approved by the American Academy of Pediatrics for use in breastfeeding mothers

Tolmetin is a standard non-steroidal analgesic. Tolmetin is known to be distributed into milk but in small amounts. In one patient given 400 mg, the milk level at 0.67 hours was 0.18 mg/L.[1] The estimate of dose per day an infant would receive is 115 μg/Liter of milk. Tolmetin is sometimes used in pediatric rheumatoid patients (>2 yrs).

Pregnancy Risk Category: C

Lactation Risk Category: L3

Theoretic Infant Dose: 27.0 μg/kg/day

Adult Concerns: GI distress, bleeding, vomiting, nausea, edema.

Pediatric Concerns: None reported via milk.

Drug Interactions: May prolong prothrombin time when used with warfarin. Antihypertensive effects of ACEi family may be blunted or completely abolished by NSAIDs. Some NSAIDs may block antihypertensive effect of beta blockers, diuretics. Used with cyclosporin, may dramatically increase renal toxicity. May increase digoxin, phenytoin, lithium levels. May increase toxicity of methotrexate. May increase bioavailability of penicillamine. Probenecid may increase NSAID levels.

Alternatives: Ibuprofen

Adult Dosage: 200-600 mg TID

T½ = 1-1.5 hours	M/P = 0.0055
PHL =	PB = 99%
PK = 0.5-1 hour	Oral = Complete
MW = 257	pKa = 3.5
Vd = ?	

References:
1.   Sagraves R, Waller ES, Goehours HR. Tolmetin in breast milk. Drug Intell. Clin. Pharm. 19:55-6, 1985.

TOLTERODINE

Trade: Detrol
Can/Aus/UK: Detrol, Detrusitol
Uses: Urinary incontinence
AAP: Not reviewed

Tolterodine is a muscarinic anticholinergic agent similar in effect to atropine, but is more selective for the urinary bladder.[1] Tolterodine levels in milk have been reported in mice, where offspring exposed to extremely high levels had slightly reduced body weight gain, but no other untoward effects. While it is more selective for the urinary bladder, preclinical trials still showed adverse effects including blurred vision, constipation, and dry mouth in adults. While we have no data on human milk, it is unlikely concentrations will be high enough to produce untoward effects in infants. However, the infant should be monitored for classic anticholinergic symptoms including dry mouth, constipation, poor tearing, etc.

Pregnancy Risk Category: C

Lactation Risk Category: L3

Theoretic Infant Dose:

Adult Concerns: Blurred vision, constipation, and dry mouth in adults.

Pediatric Concerns: None by milk, but observe for anticholinergic symptoms such as dry mouth, constipation, poor tearing, poor urinary output.

Drug Interactions: Fluoxetine reduces metabolism of tolterodine significantly and may increase plasma levels by 4.8 fold.

Alternatives:

Adult Dosage: 2 mg BID

T½ = 1.9-3.7 hours	**M/P** =
PHL =	**PB** = 96%
PK = 1-2 hours	**Oral** = 77%
MW =	**pKa** =
Vd = 1.6	

References:
1. Pharmaceutical manufacturers package insert, 2000.

TOPIRAMATE

Trade: Topamax
Can/Aus/UK: Topamax
Uses: Anticonvulsant
AAP: Not reviewed

Topiramate is a new anticonvulsant used in controlling refractory partial seizures. Very little is known about this new product except that it is secreted in the milk of rodents in unreported amounts.[1-3]

In a group of 2 women receiving topiramate(dose unreported) at three weeks postpartum, the maternal serum levels were 6.3 and 17 μmol/L, and milk levels were 7.6 and 15 μmol/L respectively.[4] Thus the milk/plasma ratio varied from 0.9 to 1.2. Infant serum levels reported were 1.4 and 1.6 μmol/L respectively. Maternal/infant serum ratios were much lower at 0.1 to 0.2.

Topiramate has become increasingly popular due to its fewer adverse side effects. The fact that the plasma levels found in breastfeeding infants were significantly less than in maternal plasma, the risk of using this product in breastfeeding mothers is probably acceptable. Close observation for sedation is advise.

Pregnancy Risk Category: C

Lactation Risk Category: L3

Theoretic Infant Dose:

Adult Concerns: Topiramate induces a significant Cognitive dysfunction, particularly in older patients. Paresthesias, sedation, weight loss(7%), diarrhea.

Pediatric Concerns: None reported in two cases.

Drug Interactions:

Alternatives:

Adult Dosage: 200 mg BID

T½ = 18-24 hours	M/P = 1.2
PHL =	PB = 15%
PK = 1.5-4 hours	Oral = 75%
MW =	pKa =
Vd = 0.7	

References:
1. Patsalos PN and Sander J: Newer antiepileptic drugs: towards an improved risk-benefit ratio. Drug Safety 11:37-67,1994.
2. Bialer M: Comparative pharmacokinetics of the newer antiepileptic drugs. Clin Pharmacokinet 24:441-452, 1993.

3. Britton JW and So EL: New antiepileptic drugs: prospects for the future. J Epilepsy 8:267-281, 1995.
4. Ohman J, Vitols S, Soderfeldt B, Tomson T.   Pharmacokinetics of topiramate in pregnancy and lactation-transplacentar transfer and excretion in breast-milk.   Fifth Eilat Conference on Antiepileptic Drugs, Eilat, Israel, June 2000.

TORSEMIDE

Trade: Demadex
Can/Aus/UK: Demadex, Torem
Uses: Potent Loop diuretic
AAP: Not reviewed

Torsemide is a potent loop diuretic generally used in congestive heart failure and other conditions which require a strong diuretic.[1]   There are no reports of its transfer into human milk. Its extraordinary high protein binding would likely limit its transfer into human milk. As with many diuretics, reduction of plasma volume and hypotension may adversely reduce milk production although this is rare. See furosemide.

Pregnancy Risk Category: B

Lactation Risk Category: L3

Theoretic Infant Dose:

Adult Concerns: Hypotension, hypokalemia, volume depletion, headache, excessive urination, dizziness.

Pediatric Concerns: None reported. Renal calcification have been reported with other loop diuretics in premature infants, but not via milk supply.

Drug Interactions: When used with salicylates, elevated plasma salicylate levels may occur. Coadministration with other NSAIDS may increase the risk of renal dysfunction. Cholestyramine administration reduces bioavailability of torsemide. Use caution in using with lithium.

Alternatives: Furosemide

Adult Dosage: 5-10 mg QD

T½ = 3.5 hours	M/P =
PHL=	PB = >99%
PK = 1 hour	Oral = 80%
MW = 348	pKa =
Vd = 0.21	

References:
1. Pharmaceutical Manufacturers Package Insert, 1997.

TRAMADOL and ACETAMINOPHEN

Trade: Ultracet
Can/Aus/UK:
Uses: Analgesic
AAP: Not reviewed

Ultracet is the combination of 37.5 mg of tramadol(Ultram) and 325 mg acetaminophen. See individual monographs.

TRAMADOL HCL

Trade: Ultram, Ultracet
Can/Aus/UK: Dromadol, Nycodol, Tramake, Tramal, Zamadol, Zydol
Uses: Analgesic
AAP: Not reviewed

Tramadol is a new class analgesic that most closely resembles the opiates, although it is not a controlled substance and appears to have reduced addictive potential.[1] It appears to be slightly more potent than codeine. After oral use, its onset of analgesia is within 1 hour and reaches a peak in 2-3 hours. Following a single I.V. 100 mg dose of tramadol, the cumulative excretion in breastmilk within 16 hours was 100 ug of tramadol (0.1% of the maternal dose) and 27 ug of the M1 metabolite.

Pregnancy Risk Category: C

Lactation Risk Category: L3

Theoretic Infant Dose:

Adult Concerns: Sedation, respiratory depression, nausea, vomiting, constipation.

Pediatric Concerns: None reported via milk. Observe for sedation.

Drug Interactions: Use with carbamazepine dramatically increases tramadol metabolism and reduces plasma levels. Use with MAOI may increase toxicity.

Alternatives: Codeine

Adult Dosage: 50-100 mg q 4-6 hours PRN

T½ = 7 hours	M/P = 0.1
PHL =	PB = 20%
PK = 2 hours	Oral = 60%
MW = 263	pKa =
Vd =	

References:
1. Pharmaceutical Manufacturers Package Insert, 1996.

TRAZODONE

Trade: Desyrel
Can/Aus/UK: Apo-Trazodone, Desyrel, Molipaxin, Novo-Trazodone, Trazorel
Uses: Antidepressant, serotonin reuptake inhibitor
AAP: Drug whose effect on nursing infants is unknown but may be of concern

Trazodone is an antidepressant whose structure is dissimilar to the tricyclics and to the other antidepressants. In six mothers who received a single 50 mg dose, the milk/plasma ratio averaged 0.14.[1] Peak milk concentrations occurred at 2 hours. On a weight basis, an adult would receive 0.77 mg/kg whereas a breastfeeding infant, using this data, would consume only 0.005 mg/kg. About 0.6 % of the maternal dose was ingested by the infant.

Pregnancy Risk Category: C

Lactation Risk Category: L2

Theoretic Infant Dose: 5 μg/kg/day

Adult Concerns: Dry mouth, sedation, hypotension, blurred vision.

Pediatric Concerns: None reported via milk.

Drug Interactions: May enhance the CNS depressant effect of alcohol, barbiturates, and other CNS depressants. Digoxin serum levels may be increased. Use caution when administering with MAOI. Phenytoin serum levels may be increased. Use with warfarin may increase anticoagulant effect.

Alternatives:

Adult Dosage: 150-400 mg QD

T½ = 4-9 hours	M/P = 0.142
PHL =	PB = 85-95%
PK = 1-2 hours	Oral = 65%
MW = 372	pKa =
Vd = 0.9-1.5	

References:
1.   Verbeeck RK, Ross SG, and McKenna EA. Excretion of trazodone in breast milk. Br.J.Clin.Pharmacol. 22:367-370,1986.

TRETINOIN

Trade: Retin - A, Renova
Can/Aus/UK: Renova, Retin-A, Stieva-A, Vesanoid, Vitamin A Acid
Uses: Topically for acne
AAP: Not reviewed

Tretinoin is a retinoid derivative similar to Vitamin A.   It is primarily used topically for acne and wrinkling, and sometimes administered orally for leukemias and psoriasis. Used topically, tretinoin stimulates epithelial turnover and reduces cell cohesiveness.[1]   Blood concentrations are essentially zero.   Absorption of Retin-A via topical sources is reported to be minimal, and breastmilk would likely be minimal to none.[2]   However, if it is used orally, transfer into milk is likely and should be used with great caution in a breastfeeding mother.

Pregnancy Risk Category: B for topical Retin-A
C for topical Renova
D for oral

Lactation Risk Category: L3

Theoretic Infant Dose:

Adult Concerns: Leukocytosis, dry skin, skin irritation, blistering, scaling, pigmentary changes, nausea, vomiting.   Side effects of oral use are similar to hypervitaminosis A, and include headache, increased CSF pressure,   anorexia,   nausea.   scaling   of   skin,   fatigue, hepatosplenomegaly.

Pediatric Concerns: None reported via milk.

Drug Interactions: Use other topical medications such as sulfur, resorcinol ,benzoyl peroxide or salicylic acid with caution due to accelerated skin irritation.

Alternatives:

Adult Dosage: 27.5 mg/meter^2 BID

T½ = 2 hours	M/P =
PHL =	PB =
PK =	Oral = 70%
MW = 300	pKa =
Vd = 0.44	

References:
1. Zbinden G. Investigation on the toxicity of tretinoin administered systemically to animals. Acta Derm Verereol Suppl(Stockh) 74:36-40,1975.
2. Lucek RW, Colburn WA: Clinical pharmacokinetics of the retinoids. Clin Pharmacokinet 10:38-62, 1985.

TRIAMCINOLONE ACETONIDE

Trade: Nasacort, Azmacort, Tri-nasal
Can/Aus/UK: Adcortyl, Aristocort, Azmacort, Kenalog, Kenalone, Nasacort, Triaderm
Uses: Corticosteroid
AAP: Not reviewed

Triamcinolone is a typical corticosteroid (see prednisone) that is available for topical, intranasal, injection, inhalation, and oral use. When applied topically to the nose (Nasacort) or to the lungs (Azmacort) only minimal doses are used and plasma levels are exceedingly low to undetectable.[1] Although no data are available on triamcinolone secretion into human milk, it is likely that the milk levels would be exceedingly low and not clinically relevant when administered via inhalation or intranasally. While the oral adult dose is 4-48 mg/day, the inhaled dose is 200 micrograms three times daily, and the intranasal dose is 220 micrograms/day. See prednisone for more breastfeeding data.

Pregnancy Risk Category: C

Lactation Risk Category: L3

Theoretic Infant Dose:

Adult Concerns: Intranasal and inhaled: nasal irritation, dry mucous membranes, sneezing, throat irritation, hoarseness, candida overgrowth.

Pediatric Concerns: None reported via milk. Observe growth rate.

Drug Interactions:

Alternatives:

Adult Dosage: 200 mcg TID-QID

T½ = 88 minutes	M/P =
PHL =	PB =
PK =	Oral = Complete
MW = 434	pKa =
Vd =	

References:
1. Pharmaceutical Manufacturers Package Insert, 1996.

TRIAMTERENE

Trade: Dyazide
Can/Aus/UK: Dyazide, Dyrenium, Hydrene
Uses: Diuretic
AAP: Not reviewed

Triamterene is a potassium-sparing diuretic, commonly used in combination with thiazide diuretics such as hydrochlorothiazide (Dyazide). Plasma levels average 26-30 nanograms/mL.[1] No data are available on the transfer of triamterene into human milk, but it is known to transfer into animal milk. Because of the availability of other less dangerous diuretics, triamterene should be used as a last resort in breastfeeding mothers.

Pregnancy Risk Category: B

Lactation Risk Category: L3

Theoretic Infant Dose:

Adult Concerns: Leukopenia, hyperkalemia, diarrhea, nausea, vomiting, hepatitis.

Pediatric Concerns: None reported via milk.

Drug Interactions: Hyperkalemia when administered with potassium supplements. Triamterene may reduce clearance of amantadine. May increase plasma potassium levels when administered with amiloride, or ACE inhibitors, cyclosporine. May reduce clearance of lithium. Enhanced bone marrow suppression when administered with methotrexate. Use with spironolactone may result in hyperkalemia.

Alternatives: Hydrochlorthiazide

Adult Dosage: 25-100 mg daily

T½ = 1.5-2.5 hours	M/P =
PHL = 4.3 hours	PB = 55%
PK = 1.5-3 hours	Oral = 30-70%
MW = 253	pKa =
Vd =	

References:
1.   Mutschler E, Gilfrich HJ, Knauf H et al: Pharmacokinetics of triamterene. Clin Exper Hyper-theory Pract A5:249-269, 1983.

TRIAZOLAM

Trade: Halcion
Can/Aus/UK: Apo-Triazo, Halcion, Novo-Triolam
Uses: Benzodiazepine (Valium-like) hypnotic
AAP: Not reviewed

Triazolam is a typical benzodiazepine used as a nighttime sedative. Animal studies indicate that triazolam is secreted into milk, although levels in human milk have not been reported.[1]   As with all the benzodiazepines, some penetration into breastmilk is likely.

Pregnancy Risk Category: X

Lactation Risk Category: L3

Theoretic Infant Dose:

Adult Concerns: Sedation, addiction.

Pediatric Concerns: None reported for triazolam, but side effects for benzodiazepines include sedation, depression.

Drug Interactions: See diazepam.

Alternatives: Lorazepam, Alprazolam

Adult Dosage: 0.125-0.25 mg QD

T½ = 1.5-5.5 hours	M/P =
PHL =	PB = 89%
PK = 0.5-2 hours	Oral = 85%
MW = 343	pKa =
Vd = 1.1-2.7	

References:
1.   Drug Facts and Comparisons. 1995 ed. Facts and Comparisons, St. Louis.

TRIMEPRAZINE

Trade: Temaril
Can/Aus/UK: Panectyl, Vallergan
Uses: Antihistamine, antipruritic.
AAP: Not reviewed

Trimeprazine is an antihistamine from the phenothiazine family used for itching. It is secreted into human milk, but in very low levels.[1]   Exact data are not available.

Pregnancy Risk Category: C

Lactation Risk Category: L3

Theoretic Infant Dose:

Adult Concerns: Sedation, hypotension, bradycardia.

Pediatric Concerns: None reported, but as with other antihistamines, observe for sedation.

Drug Interactions:

Alternatives:

Adult Dosage: 5 mg BID

T½ = 5 hours.	M/P =
PHL=	PB =
PK = 3.5 hours.	Oral = 70%
MW = 298	pKa =
Vd =	

References:
1.   O'Brien, T. Excretion of drugs in human milk. Am.J. Hosp. Pharm. 31:844-854, 1974.

TRIMETHOBENZAMIDE

Trade: Tigan, Trimazide, Tebamide, T-gen, Arrestin, Ticon
Can/Aus/UK:
Uses: Antiemetic, antivertigo
AAP: Not reviewed

Trimethobenzamide is an older generation antiemetics whose use has been supplanted by newer more effective agents. It is most commonly used in suppository form in adults, and rarely in infants. Maternal plasma levels following a 500 mg oral dose are 1-2 mcg/mL. No data are available on breastmilk levels. But if one were to assume a milk plasma ratio of 1.0(which is probably high), then the theoretical infant dose would only be about 0.3 mg/kg/day, which is far less than the oral dose of 300-400 mg/day used in 15 kg infants. It is unlikely the amount of trimethobenzamide present in breastmilk would produce a clinical effect in an infant.

Pregnancy Risk Category: C

Lactation Risk Category: L4

Theoretic Infant Dose:

Adult Concerns: Extrapyramidal symptoms, drowsiness, depression, dizziness, headache, vertigo, blood dyscrasias have been reported following higher oral/IM/rectal doses.

Pediatric Concerns: None reported via milk.

Drug Interactions:

Alternatives: Ondansetron

Adult Dosage: 250 mg TID-QID

T½ = Short	M/P =	
PHL =	PB =	
PK =	Oral = Good	
MW =	pKa =	
Vd =		

References:
1.   Drug Facts and Comparisons. 1999 ed. Facts and Comparisons, St. Louis.

TRIMETHOPRIM

Trade: Proloprim, Trimpex
Can/Aus/UK: Alprim, Ipral, Monotrim, Proloprim, Tiempe, Triprim
Uses: Antibiotic
AAP: Approved by the American Academy of Pediatrics for use in breastfeeding mothers

Trimethoprim is an inhibitor of folic acid production in bacteria.   In one study of 50 patients,   average milk levels were 2.0 mg/L.[1] Milk/plasma ratio was 1.25. In another group of mothers receiving 160 mg 2-4 times daily, concentrations of 1.2 to 5.5 mg/L were reported in milk.   Because it may interfere with folate metabolism, use with caution. However, trimethoprim apparently poses few problems in full term or older infants.[2]   PHL= 14.7-40 hours (neonate), 5-6 hours (older infants).

Pregnancy Risk Category: C

Lactation Risk Category: L3

Theoretic Infant Dose: 0.8 mg/kg/day

Adult Concerns: Rash, pruritus nausea, vomiting, anorexia, altered taste sensation.

Pediatric Concerns:

Drug Interactions: May increase phenytoin plasma levels.

Alternatives:

Adult Dosage: 200 mg QD

T½ = 8-10 hours	M/P = 1.25
PHL = 14.7-40 hours (neonate)	PB = 44%
PK = 1-4 hours	Oral = Complete
MW = 290	pKa =
Vd =	

References:
1. Miller RD, Salter AJ. The passage of trimethoprim/sulphamethoxazole into breast milk and its significance. In Daikos GK, ed. Progress in Chemotherapy,Proceedings of the Eighth International Congress of Chemotherapy, Athens, 1973. Athens:Hellenic Society for Chemotherapy, 687-91, 1974.
2. Pagliaro and Levin (Eds): Problems in Pediatric Drug Therapy. Drug Intelligence Publications, Hamilton, IL, 1979.

TRIPELENNAMINE

Trade: PBZ, Colrex, Tromide
Can/Aus/UK: Pyrabenzamine
Uses: Antihistamine
AAP: Not reviewed

Tripelennamine is an older class of antihistamine. This product is generally not recommended in pediatric patients, particularly neonates due to increased sleep apnea.[1] The drug has been shown to be secreted into milk of animals.[2] No human data exist.

Pregnancy Risk Category: B

Lactation Risk Category: L4

Theoretic Infant Dose:

Adult Concerns: Sleep apnea in children, peptic ulcer, sedation, dry mouth, GI distress.

Pediatric Concerns: None reported, but observe for sedation, sleep apnea.

Drug Interactions: Increased sedation when used with CNS depressants, other antihistamines, alcohol, MAO inhibitors.

Alternatives:

Adult Dosage: 25-50 mg q 4-6 hours

T½ = 2-3 hours	M/P =
PHL =	PB =
PK = 2 - 3 hours	Oral = Complete
MW = 255	pKa = 4.2,8.7
Vd = 9-12	

References:
1. O'Brien, T. Excretion of drugs in human milk. Am.J. Hosp. Pharm. 31:844-854, 1974.
2. Pharmaceutical Manufacturers Package Insert, 1996.

TRIPROLIDINE

Trade: Actidil, Actacin
Can/Aus/UK: Actifed, Codral, Pro-actidil
Uses: Antihistamine
AAP: Approved by the American Academy of Pediatrics for use in breastfeeding mothers

Triprolidine is an antihistamine. It is secreted into milk but in very small levels and is marketed with pseudoephedrine as Actifed. The average concentration in milk ranged from 1.2 to 4.4 μg/L over 24 hours.[1] The estimated dose an infant would receive was 0.001-0.004 mg/24 hours which is 0.06 to 0.2% of the maternal dose. These doses are far too low to be clinically relevant.

Pregnancy Risk Category: C

Lactation Risk Category: L1

Theoretic Infant Dose: 0.7 μg/kg/day

Adult Concerns: Sedation, dry mouth, anticholinergic side effects.

Pediatric Concerns: None reported. Observe for sedation.

Drug Interactions: Increased sedation when used with CNS depressants, other antihistamines, alcohol, MAO inhibitors.

Alternatives:

Adult Dosage: 2.5 mg q 4-6 hours

T½ = 5 hours	M/P = 0.5-1.2
PHL=	PB =
PK = 2 hours	Oral = Complete
MW = 278	pKa =
Vd =	

References:
1. Findlay JWA, et.al. Pseudoephedrine and tripolidine in plasma and breast milk of nursing mothers. Br J Clin Pharmac 18:901-6,1984.

TROVAFLOXACIN MESYLATE

Trade: Trovan, Alatrofloxacin
Can/Aus/UK:
Uses: Antibiotic
AAP: Not reviewed

Trovafloxacin mesylate is a synthetic broad-spectrum antibiotic for oral use.   The I.V. formula is called alatrofloxacin mesylate which is metabolized to trovafloxacin in vivo.   Trovafloxacin is a fluoroquinolone antibiotic similar to ciprofloxacin, norfloxacin and others.   Trovafloxacin was found in measurable but low concentrations in breastmilk of three breastfeeding mothers.[1] Following an I.V. dose of 300 mg trovafloxacin equivalent, and repeated oral 200 mg doses of trovafloxacin mg daily, breastmilk levels averaged 0.8 mg/L and ranged from 0.3 to 2.1 mg per liter of milk.   This would average less than 0.4% of the maternal dose.   New data on this antibiotic documents a higher risk of hepatotoxicity and its use is restricted.

Pregnancy Risk Category: C

Lactation Risk Category: L4

Theoretic Infant Dose: 120.0 μg/kg/day

Adult Concerns: Dizziness, nausea, headache, vomiting, diarrhea have been reported.

Pediatric Concerns: None reported via milk. Only small amounts are secreted in milk.

Drug Interactions: Antacids, Morphine, Sucralfate, and iron significantly reduce oral absorption.

Alternatives: Norfloxacin, Ofloxacin

Adult Dosage: 200-300 mg daily

T½ = 12.2 hours	**M/P =**
PHL=	**PB = 76%**
PK = 1.2 hours	**Oral = 88%**
MW = 512	**pKa =**
Vd = 1.3	

References:
1.   Pharmaceutical manufacturers package insert, 1998.

TUBERCULIN PURIFIED PROTEIN DERIVATIVE

Trade: Tubersol, Aplisol, Sclavo
Can/Aus/UK:
Uses: Tuberculin skin test
AAP: Not reviewed

Tuberculin (also called Mantoux, PPD, Tine test) is a skin-test antigen derived from the concentrated, sterile, soluble products of growth of M. Tuberculosis or M. bovis. Small amounts of this purified product when placed intradermally, produce a hypersensitivity reaction at the place of injection in those individuals with antibodies to M. tuberculosis.[1,2] Preliminary studies also indicate that breastfed infants may passively acquire sensitivity to mycobacterial antigens from mothers who are sensitized. There are no contraindications to using PPD tests in breastfeeding mothers as the proteins are sterilized and unlikely to penetrate milk.

Pregnancy Risk Category: C

Lactation Risk Category: L2

Theoretic Infant Dose:

Adult Concerns: Local vesiculation, irritation, bruising, and rarely hypersensitivity.

Pediatric Concerns: None via milk.

Drug Interactions:

Alternatives:

Adult Dosage: 5 units X 1

References:
1. Drug Facts and Comparisons. 1999 ed. Facts and Comparisons, St. Louis.
2. McEvoy GE(ed):American Hospital Formulary Service Drug Information, New York, NY. 1999.

TYPHOID VACCINE

Trade: Vivotif Berna, Typhim Vi
Can/Aus/UK: Vivotif Berna
Uses: Vaccination
AAP: Approved by the American Academy of Pediatrics for use in breastfeeding mothers

Typhoid vaccine promotes active immunity to typhoid fever. It is available in an oral form (Ty21a) which is a live attenuated vaccine for oral administration.[1] The parenteral (injectable) form is derived from acetone-treated killed and dried bacteria, phenol-inactive bacteria, or a special capsular polysaccharide vaccine extracted from killed S. typhi Ty21a strains. Due to a limited lipopolysaccharide coating, the Ty21a strains are limited in their ability to produce infection.

No data are available on its transfer into human milk. If immunization is required, a killed species would be preferred, as infection of the neonate would be possible.

Pregnancy Risk Category: C

Lactation Risk Category:

Theoretic Infant Dose:

Adult Concerns: Following oral administration, nausea, abdominal cramps, vomiting, urticaria. IM preparations may produce soreness at injection site, tenderness, malaise, headache, myalgia, fever.

Pediatric Concerns: None reported, but killed species suggested.

Drug Interactions: Use cautiously in patients receiving anticoagulants. Do not coadminister with plague vaccine. Do not administer the live-attenuated varieties to immunocompromised patients. Phenytoin may reduce antibody response to this product. Do not use with sulfonamides.

Alternatives:

Adult Dosage: 0.5 mL X 2 over 4 weeks

References:
1. Pharmaceutical Manufacturers package insert, 2000.

UROFOLLITROPIN

Trade: Metrodin, Fertinex
Can/Aus/UK: Fertinorm HP, Metrodin
Uses: FSH, follicle stimulating hormone
AAP: Not reviewed

Urofollitropin is a preparation of gonadotropin (FSH) extracted from the urine of postmenopausal women.[1-3] FSH is a large molecular weight peptide (34,000 daltons). Urofollitropin differs only slightly from pituitary FSH. In the female, FSH induces growth of the Graafian follicle in the ovary preparatory to the release of the ovum. Approximately 15 ug is secreted daily by the pituitary in normal individuals. It is not known if urofollitropin is secreted into human milk, but it is extremely unlikely due to its large molecular weight. Further, it would be largely destroyed in the infants' stomach and oral absorption by the infant would be extremely unlikely.

Pregnancy Risk Category: X

Lactation Risk Category: L3

Theoretic Infant Dose:

Adult Concerns: Pulmonary and vascular complications, ovarian hyperstimulation, abdominal pain, fever and chills, abdominal pain, nausea, vomiting, diarrhea, pain at injection site, bruising. Ovarian hyperstimulation.

Pediatric Concerns: None reported via milk.

Drug Interactions: Urofollitropin does not effect prolactin levels.

Alternatives:

Adult Dosage: 75 units daily

T½ = 3.9 and 70.4 hours	M/P =
PHL=	PB =
PK = 6-18 hours	Oral = None
MW = 34,000	pKa =
Vd = 0.06, 1.08	

References:

Sharma V, Riddle A, et al: Studies on folliculogenesis and in vitro fertilization outcome after the administration of follicle-stimulating hormone at different times during the menstrual cycle. Fertil Steril 51:298-3, 1989.

JM, Harsoulis P, et al: Infusions of hFSH and hLH in normal men: of human follicle stimulating hormone. Acta Endocrinologica 3, 1976.

3.   Yen SSC, Llerena LA, Pearson OH et al: Disappearance rates of endogenous follicle-stimulating hormone in serum following surgical hypophysectomy in man. J Clin Endocrinol 30:325-329, 1970.

URSODIOL

Trade: Actigall
Can/Aus/UK: Combidol, Destolit, Lithofalk, Urdox, Urso, Ursogal
Uses: Bile acid for dissolving gall stones
AAP: Not reviewed

Ursodiol (ursodeoxycholic acid) is a bile salt found in small amounts in humans that is used to dissolve cholesterol gallstones. It is almost completely absorbed orally via the portal circulation and is extracted almost completely by the liver. Ursodiol suppresses hepatic synthesis and excretion of cholesterol. Following extraction by the liver, it is conjugated with glycine or taurine and is resecreted into the hepatic bile duct. Only trace amounts are found in the plasma and it is not likely significant amounts would be present in milk.[1] While no breastfeeding data are available, only small amounts of bile salts are known to be present in milk.[2] It is not likely with the low levels of ursodiol in the maternal plasma, that clinically relevant amounts would enter milk.

Pregnancy Risk Category: B

Lactation Risk Category: L3

Theoretic Infant Dose:

Adult Concerns: Insomnia, headache, abdominal pain, flatulence, cholecystitis, constipation, diarrhea(rare), nausea, vomiting.

Pediatric Concerns: None via breastmilk.

Drug Interactions: Cholestyramine, antacids, charcoal and colestipol may interfere with GI absorption.

Alternatives:

Adult Dosage: 8-10 mg/kg/day in 3 divided doses

$T\frac{1}{2}$ =	M/P =
PHL=	PB =
PK =	Oral = 90%
MW = 392	pKa =
Vd =	

References:
1.   Bachrach WH, Hofmann AF: Ursodeoxycholic acid in cholesterol cholelithiasis (Part I). Dig Dis Sci 27:737-

2.   Forsyth JS, Ross PE, Bouchier IAD. Bile salts in breast milk. Eur. J. Pediatr. 140:126, 1983.

VALACYCLOVIR

Trade: Valtrex
Can/Aus/UK: Valaciclovir, Valtrex
Uses: Antiviral, for herpes simplex
AAP: Not reviewed

Valacyclovir is a prodrug that is rapidly metabolized in the plasma to acyclovir. Acyclovir is the active drug that is primarily used as an antiviral for herpes simplex and other viral infections.[1] Valacyclovir has much better oral absorption that the parent drug, acyclovir. Acyclovir milk levels are quite low. See acyclovir for more data.

Pregnancy Risk Category: B

Lactation Risk Category: L1

Theoretic Infant Dose:

Adult Concerns: Nausea, vomiting, diarrhea, sore throat, edema, and skin rashes.

Pediatric Concerns: None reported via milk.

Drug Interactions:

Alternatives: Acyclovir

Adult Dosage: 500-1000 mg BID-TID

T½ = 2.5-3 hours	M/P = 0.6-4.1
PHL = 3.2 hours(neonates)	PB = 9-33%
PK = 1.5 hours	Oral = 54%
MW =	pKa =
Vd =	

References:
     Pharmaceutical Manufacturers Package Insert, 1995.

LERIAN OFFICINALIS

Valerian Root
s/UK:
rbal sedative
reviewed

most commonly used as a sedative/hypnotic. Of the

numerous chemicals present in the root, the most important chemical group appears to be the valepotriates. This family consists of at least a dozen or more related compounds, and is believed responsible for the sedative potential of this plant, although it is controversial. The combination of numerous components may inevitability account for the sedative response. Controlled studies in man have indicated a sedative/hypnotic effect with fewer night awakenings and significant somnolence.[1-3] The toxicity of valerian root appears to be low, with only minor side effects reported. However, the valepotriates have been found to be cytotoxic, with alkylating activity similar to other nitrogen mustard-like anticancer agents. Should this prove to be so in vivo, it may preclude the use of this product in humans. No data are available on the transfer of valerian root compounds into human milk. However, the use of sedatives in breastfeeding mothers is generally discouraged, due to a possible increased risk of SIDS.

Pregnancy Risk Category:

Lactation Risk Category: L3

Theoretic Infant Dose:

Adult Concerns: Ataxia, hypothermia, muscle relaxation. Headaches, excitability, cardiac disturbances.

Pediatric Concerns: None reported via human milk.

Drug Interactions:

Alternatives:

Adult Dosage:

References:
1. Leathwood PD, et.al. Aqueous extract of valerian root improves sleep quality in man. Pharmacal. Biochem. Behav. 17:65, 1982.
2. Von Eickstedt KW, et.al. Psychopharmacologic effects of valepotriates. Arzneimittelforschung 19:316, 1969.
3. Leathwood PD, Chaufard F. Aqueous extract of valerian reduces sleep latency to fall asleep in man. Planta Med 51:144, 1985.

VALPROIC ACID

Trade: Depakene, Depakote
Can/Aus/UK: Convulex, Depakene, Deproic, Epilim, Novo-Valproic, Valpro
Uses: Anticonvulsant
AAP: Approved by the American Academy of Pediatrics for use in breastfeeding mothers

Valproic acid is a popular anticonvulsant used in grand mal, petit m. myoclonic, and temporal lobe seizures. In a study of 16 patie. receiving 300-2400 mg/d, valproic acid concentrations ranged from to 3.9 mg/L(mean=1.9 mg/L). [1]   The milk/plasma ratio averaged 0.05.

In a study of 1 patient receiving 250 mg twice daily, milk levels ranged from 0.18 to 0.47 mg/L. The milk/plasma ratio ranged from 0.01 to 0.02.[2]   Alexander reports milk levels of 5.1 mg/L following a larger dose of up to 1600 mg/d. [3]

In a study of 6 women receiving 9.5 to 31 mg/kg/d valproic acid, milk levels averaged 1.4 mg/L while serum levels averaged 45.1 mg/L.[4] The average milk/serum ratio was 0.027.

Most authors agree that the amount of valproic acid transferring to the infant via milk is low. Breastfeeding would appear safe. However the infant should be closely monitored for liver and platelet changes.

Pregnancy Risk Category: D

Lactation Risk Category: L2

Theoretic Infant Dose: 0.8 mg/kg/day

Adult Concerns: Sedation, thrombocytopenia, tremor, nausea, diarrhea, liver toxicity.

Pediatric Concerns: None reported via milk. Observe infant for changes in liver enzymes, clinical status, and platelet levels.

Drug Interactions: Valproic acid levels may be reduced by charcoal, rifampin, carbamazepine, clonazepam, lamotrigine, phenytoin. Valproic acid levels may be increased when used with chlorpromazine, cimetidine, felbamate, salicylates, alcohol. Valproic acid use may increase levels or the effect of barbiturates, warfarin, benzodiazepines, clozapine.

Alternatives:

Adult Dosage: 10-30 mg/kg QD

T½ = 14 hours	M/P = 0.42
PHL = 10-67 hours(neonate)	PB = 94%
PK = 1-4 hours	Oral = Complete
MW = 144	pKa = 4.8
Vd = 0.1-0.4	

References:
von Unruh GE, Froescher W, Hoffmann F, Niesen M. Valproic acid in breast milk: how much is really there? Ther Drug Monit. 6(3):272-6, 1984.

Dickinson RG, Harland RC, Lynn RK, Smith WB, Gerber N. Transmission valproic acid (Depakene) across the placenta: half-life of the drug in her and baby. J Pediatr. 1979 May;94(5):832-5.

nder FW. Sodium valproate and pregnancy. Arch Dis Child. 0, 1979.

4. Nau H, Rating D, Koch S, Hauser I, Helge H. Valproic acid and its metabolites: placental transfer, neonatal pharmacokinetics, transfer via mother's milk and clinical status in neonates of epileptic mothers. J Pharmacol Exp Ther. 219(3):768-77, 1981.

VALSARTAN

Trade: Diovan
Can/Aus/UK: Diovan
Uses: Antihypertensive
AAP: Not reviewed

Valsartan is a new angiotensin II receptor antagonist used to treat hypertension. While it is believed to enter the milk of rodents, no human data are available.[1,2] Because newborn infants may be more susceptible to hypotension from this product (and the ACE inhibitors), use caution in breastfeeding mothers.

Pregnancy Risk Category: C during 1st trimester
                                                   D during 2nd and 3rd

Lactation Risk Category: L4

Theoretic Infant Dose:

Adult Concerns: Occcasional increase in liver enzymes. Small decreases in hemoglobin have been reported. Significant increases (> 20%) in serum potassium levels have been reported. Dizziness, insomnia, viral infection, cough, diarrhea, etc. have been reported.

Pediatric Concerns: None via milk, but caution is recommended.

Drug Interactions: May significantly increase digoxin levels by 49%.

Alternatives:

Adult Dosage: 80-320 mg QD

T½ = 9 hours	M/P =
PHL =	PB = 97%
PK = 2-4 hours	Oral = 23%
MW =	pKa =
Vd = 0.24	

References:
1.   Pharmaceutical Manufacturers Package Insert, 1999.
2.   McEvoy GE(ed):AFHS Drug Information, New York, NY. 1999.

VANCOMYCIN

Trade: Vancocin
Can/Aus/UK: Vancocin, Vancoled
Uses: Antibiotic
AAP: Not reviewed

Vancomycin is an antimicrobial agent. Only low levels are secreted into human milk. Milk levels were 12.7 mg/L four hours after infusion in one woman receiving 1 gm every 12 hours for 7 days.[1]   Its poor absorption from the infants GI tract would limit its systemic absorption. Low levels in infant could provide alterations of GI flora.   PHL= 5.9-9.8 hours (neonates), 4.1 hours (older).

Pregnancy Risk Category: C

Lactation Risk Category: L1

Theoretic Infant Dose: 1.9 mg/kg/day

Adult Concerns: Alteration of GI flora, neutropenia, hypotension, kidney and hearing damage.

Pediatric Concerns: None reported via milk.

Drug Interactions: When used with aminoglycosides, risk of nephrotoxicity may be increased. Use with anesthetics may produce erythema and histamine-like flushing in children. May increase risk of neuromuscular blockade when used with neuromuscular blocking agents.

Alternatives:

Adult Dosage: 125-500 mg q 6 hours

T½ = 5.6 hours	**M/P =**
PHL = 5.9-9.8 hours(neonates)	**PB = 10-30%**
PK =	**Oral = Minimal**
MW = 1449	**pKa =**
Vd = 0.3-0.7	

References:
1.   Reyes MP, et. al. Vancomycin during pregnancy: does it cause hearing loss or nephrotoxicity in the infant? Am J Obstet Gynecol 161:977-81, 1989.

VARICELLA VIRUS VACCINE

Trade: Varivax
Can/Aus/UK:
Uses: Vaccination for Varicella(Chickenpox)
AAP: Not reviewed

A live attenuated varicella vaccine (Varivax - Merck) was recently approved for marketing by the US Food and Drug Administration. Although effective, it does not apparently provide the immunity attained from infection with the parent virus and may not provide life-long immunity. The Oka/Merck strain used in the vaccine is attenuated by passage in human and embryonic guinea pig cell cultures. It is not known if the vaccine-acquired VZV is secreted in human milk, nor its infectiousness to infants. Interestingly, in two women with varicella-zoster infections, the virus was not culturable from milk.[1] Mothers of immunodeficient infants should not breastfeed following use of this vaccine. Recommendations for Use: Varicella vaccine is only recommended for children > 1 year of age up to 12 years of age with no history of varicella infection. Both the AAP[2] and the Center for Disease Control approve the use of varicella-zoster vaccines in breastfeeding mothers, if the risk of infection is high.

Pregnancy Risk Category: C

Lactation Risk Category: L2

Theoretic Infant Dose:

Adult Concerns: Tenderness and erythema at the injection site in about 25% of vaccines and a sparse generalized maculopapular rash occurring within one month after immunization in about 5%. Spread of the vaccine virus to others has been reported. Susceptible, immunodeficient individuals should be protected from exposure.

Pediatric Concerns: None reported via milk, but no studies are available. Immunocompromised infants should not be exposed to this product.

Drug Interactions:

Alternatives:

Adult Dosage: 0.5 mL X 2 over 4-8 weeks

References:
1. Frederick IB, White RJ, et.al. Excretion of varicella-herpes zoster virus in breast milk. Am. J. Obstet. Gynecol. 154:1116-7, 1986.
2. American Academy of Pediatrics. Committee on Infectious Diseases. Red Book 1997.

VARICELLA-ZOSTER VIRUS

Trade: Chickenpox
Can/Aus/UK:
Uses: Chickenpox
AAP: Not reviewed

Chickenpox virus has been reported to be transferred via breastmilk in one 27 year old mother who developed chickenpox postpartum.[1] Her 2 month old son also developed the disease 16 days after mother. Chickenpox virus was detected in the mother's milk and may suggest that transmission can occur via breastmilk. However, in a study of 2 breastfeeding patients who developed varicella-herpes zoster infections, in neither case was the virus isolated and cultured from their milk.[2] According to the American Academy of Pediatrics, neonates born to mothers with active varicella should be placed in isolation at birth and, if still hospitalized, until 21 or 28 days of age, depending on whether they received VZIG (Varicella Zoster Immune Globulin).[3] Candidates for VZIG include: immunocompromised children, pregnant women, newborn infant whose mother has onset of VZV within 5 days before or 48 hours after delivery. For an excellent review of VZV and breastfeeding see Merewood and Philipp.[4]

Pregnancy Risk Category:

Lactation Risk Category: L4

Theoretic Infant Dose:

Adult Concerns:

Pediatric Concerns: Varicella-zoster virus transfers into human milk. Infants should not breastfeed unless protected with VZIG.

Drug Interactions:

Alternatives:

Adult Dosage:

References:
1. Yoshida M, et.al. Case report: detection of varicella-zoster virus DNA in maternal breast milk. J. Med. Virol. 38:108, 1992.
2. Frederick IB, White RJ, Braddock SW. Excretion of varicella-herpes zoster virus in breast milk. Am J Obstet Gynecol. 154(5):1116-7, 1986.
3. Report of the Committee on Infectious Diseases. American Academy of Pediatrics Red Book. 1994.
4. Merewood A, and Philipp BL. Breastfeeding: Conditions and Diseases. Amarillo:Pharmasoft Publishing, 2001:242-245.

VASOPRESSIN

Trade: Pitressin
Can/Aus/UK: Pitresin, Pitressin, Pressyn
Uses: Antidiuretic hormone
AAP: Not reviewed

Vasopressin, also known as the antidiuretic hormone, is a small peptide (8 amino acids) that is normally secreted by the posterior pituitary.[1] It reduces urine production by the kidney. Although it probably passes to some degree into human milk, it is rapidly destroyed in the GI tract by trypsin, and must be administered by injection or intranasally. Hence, oral absorption by a nursing infant is very unlikely. Desmopressin is virtually identical and milk levels have been reported to be very low. See desmopressin.

Pregnancy Risk Category: B

Lactation Risk Category: L3

Theoretic Infant Dose:

Adult Concerns: Increased blood pressure, water retention and edema, sweating, tremor, and bradycardia.

Pediatric Concerns: None reported via milk.

Drug Interactions:

Alternatives:

Adult Dosage: 5-10 units BID-QID PRN

T½ = 10-20 minutes.	M/P =
PHL=	PB =
PK = 1 hour.	Oral = None
MW =	pKa =
Vd =	

References:
1. McEvoy GE(ed):AHFS Drug Information, New York, NY. 1995.

VENLAFAXINE

Trade: Effexor
Can/Aus/UK: Efexor, Effexor
Uses: Antidepressant, SSRI
AAP: Not reviewed

Venlafaxine is a new serotonin reuptake inhibitor antidepressant. It inhibits both serotonin reuptake and norepinephrine reuptake. Somewhat similar in mechanism to other antidepressants such as Prozac. Fewer anticholinergic side-effects.

In an excellent study of three mothers (mean age = 34.5 years, 84.5 kg) receiving venlafaxine (225-300 mg/d), the mean milk/plasma ratios for venlafaxine (V) and O-desmethylvenlafaxine (ODV) were 2.5 and 2.7, respectively.[1] The mean maximum concentrations of V and ODV in milk were 1.16 mg/L and 0.796 mg/L. The Cmax for milk was 2.25 hours. The mean infant exposure was 3.2% for V and 3.2% for ODV of the weight-adjusted maternal dose. V was detected in the plasma of one of seven infants, while ODV was detected in four of the seven infants. The infants were healthy and showed no acute adverse effects.

Pregnancy Risk Category: C

Lactation Risk Category: L3

Theoretic Infant Dose: 647.9 μg/kg/day

Adult Concerns: Nausea/vomiting, somnolence, dry mouth, dizziness, headache, weakness.

Pediatric Concerns: None reported via milk, but no studies are available.

Drug Interactions: Serious, sometimes fatal reactions when used with MAO inhibitors, or if used within 7-14 days of their use.

Alternatives: Sertraline, Paroxetine

Adult Dosage: 75 mg TID

T½ = 5 hours(venlafaxine)	M/P =
PHL=	PB = 27%
PK = 2.25 milk	Oral = 92%
MW = 313	pKa = 9.4
Vd = 4-12	

References:
1. Illett KF, Kristensen JH, Hackett LP, Paech M, et.al. Distribution of venlafaxine and its O-desmethyl metabolite in human milk and their effects in breastfed infants. Br J Clin Pharmacol 53:17-22, 2002.

VERAPAMIL

Trade: Calan, Isoptin, Covera-HS
Can/Aus/UK: Anpec, Apo-Verap, Berkatens, Cordilox, Isoptin, Novo-Veramil, Univer, Veracaps SR
Uses: Calcium channel blocker for hypertension
AAP: Approved by the American Academy of Pediatrics for use in breastfeeding mothers

Verapamil is a typical calcium channel blocker used as an antihypertensive. It is secreted into milk but in very low levels, which are highly controversial.   Anderson reports that in one patient receiving 80 mg three times daily the average steady-state concentrations of verapamil and norverapamil in milk were 25.8 and 8.8 μg/L respectively.[1]   The respective maternal plasma level was 42.9 μg/L.   The milk/plasma ratio for verapamil was 0.60.   No verapamil was detected in the infant's plasma.   Inoue reports that in one patient receiving 80 mg four times daily, the milk level peaked at 300 μg/L at approximately 14 hours.[2]   These levels are considerably higher than the aforementioned.   In another study of a mother receiving 240 mg daily, the concentrations in milk were never higher than 40 μg/L.[3] See bepridil, diltiazem, nifedipine as alternates.

Pregnancy Risk Category: C

Lactation Risk Category: L2

Theoretic Infant Dose: 45.0 μg/kg/day

Adult Concerns: Hypotension, bradycardia, peripheral edema.

Pediatric Concerns: None reported via milk.   Observe for hypotension, bradycardia, weakness.

Drug Interactions: Barbiturates may reduce bioavailability of calcium channel blockers (CCB). Calcium salts may reduce hypotensive effect. Dantrolene may increase risk of hyperkalemia and myocardial depression. H2 blockers may increase bioavailability of certain CCBs. Hydantoins may reduce plasma levels. Quinidine increases risk of hypotension, bradycardia, tachycardia. Rifampin may reduce effects of CCBs. Vitamin D may reduce efficacy of CCBs. CCBs may increase carbamazepine, cyclosporin, encainide, prazosin levels.

Alternatives: Bepridil, Nifedipine, Nimodipine

Adult Dosage: 80-100 mg TID

T½ = 3-7 hours	M/P = 0.94
PHL =	PB = 83-92%
PK = 1-2.2	Oral = 90%
MW = 455	pKa =
Vd = 2.5-6.5	

References:

1. Anderson, P. et. al. Verapamil and norverapamil in plasma and breast milk during breast feeding. Eur J. Clin Pharmacol. 31:625-7, 1987.
2. Inoue H, et.al. Level of verapamil in human milk. Eur. J. Clin. Pharmacol. 26:657,1984.
3. Andersen HJ. Excretion of verapamil in human milk, Eur. J. Clin. Pharm. 25:279, 1983.

VIGABATRIN

Trade: Sabril
Can/Aus/UK:
Uses: Anticonvulsant
AAP: Not reviewed

Vigabatrin is a newer anticonvulsant and a synthetic derivative of gamma-aminobutyric acid. It is an effective adjunctive anticonvulsant for the treatment of multi-drug resistant complex partial seizures. It has also shown efficacy in controlling seizures and spasm in infants 3 months and older. No data are available on its transfer into human milk. However, the plasma levels of this drug (dose=1.5 gm) are quite low, 93 μmol/L, which would suggest that the amount in milk would probably be low even if the drug had a milk/plasma ratio of 1 or greater, but this is not known for sure.[1] However, regardless of the kinetics of this drug, it irreversibly inactivates gamma-aminobutyric acid.[2] The effect of this property on neonatal brains is not known. Some caution is recommended in breastfeeding mothers.

Pregnancy Risk Category:

Lactation Risk Category: L3

Theoretic Infant Dose:

Adult Concerns: Changes in visual field defects have been noted. Drowsiness, fatigue, and acute psychosis (7%) have been described particularly in patients with a history of psychiatric disorders. Psychosis and an increased frequency of seizures have been reported upon abrupt withdrawal of vigabatrin therapy.

Pediatric Concerns: None reported via milk.

Drug Interactions: May decrease phenytoin levels by 30%. Few other interactions are noted which is a plus for this drug.

rnatives:

Dosage: 1-4 gm daily

T½ = 7 hours	**M/P** =
PHL =	**PB** = 0%
PK = 0.5-2 hours	**Oral** = 50%
MW = 129	**pKa** =
Vd = 0.8	

References:
1. Grant SM, and Heel RC: Vigabatrin: a review of its pharmacodynamic and pharmacokinetic properties, and therapeutic potential in epilepsy and disorders of motor control. Drugs 41:889-926, 1991.
2. Dichter MA, Brodie MJ. New Antiepileptic Drugs. NEJM 334:1583-1590, 1996.

VITAMIN A

Trade: Aquasol A, Del-vi-a, Vitamin A, Retinol
Can/Aus/UK: Aquasol A, Avoleum
Uses: Vitamin supplement
AAP: Not reviewed

Vitamin A (retinol) is a typical retinoid. It is a fat soluble vitamin that is secreted into human milk and primarily sequestered in high concentrations in the liver (90%).[1] Retinol is absorbed in the small intestine by a selective carrier-mediated uptake process. Levels in infants are generally unknown. The overdose of Vitamin A is extremely dangerous and adults should never exceed 5000 units/day. Use normal doses. DO NOT use maternal doses > 5000 units /day. Mature human milk is rich in retinol and contains 750 μg/Liter (2800 units). Infants do not generally require vitamin A supplementation.

Pregnancy Risk Category: A

Lactation Risk Category: L3

Theoretic Infant Dose:

Adult Concerns: Liver toxicity in overdose.

Pediatric Concerns: None reported via milk, but do not use vitamin A in excess of 5000 IU/day.

Drug Interactions:

Alternatives:

Adult Dosage: < 5000 IU daily

T½ =	**M/P** =
PHL =	**PB** =
PK =	**Oral** = Complete
MW = 286	**pKa** =
Vd =	

References:
1.   Lawrence RA. Breastfeeding, A guide for the medical profession. Mosby, St. Louis, 1994.

VITAMIN B-12

Trade: Cyanocobalamin
Can/Aus/UK: Anacobin, Cytacon, Rubramin
Uses: Vitamin supplement
AAP: Approved by the American Academy of Pediatrics for use in breastfeeding mothers

Vitamin B-12 is also called cyanocobalamin and is used for the treatment of pernicious anemia. It is an essential vitamin that is secreted in human milk at concentrations of 0.1 μg/100 ml. B-12 deficiency is very dangerous to an infant. Milk levels vary in proportion to maternal serum levels.[1]   Vegetarian mothers may have low levels unless supplemented.   Supplementation of nursing mothers is generally recommended.

Pregnancy Risk Category: A

Lactation Risk Category: L1

Theoretic Infant Dose:

Adult Concerns: Itching, skin rash, mild diarrhea, megaloblastic anemia in vegetarian mothers.

Pediatric Concerns: None reported with exception of B-12 deficiency states.

Drug Interactions:

Alternatives:

Adult Dosage: 25 ug daily

T½ =	M/P =
PHL=	PB =
PK = 2 hours.	Oral = Variable
MW = 1355	pKa =
Vd =	

References:
1.   Lawrence RA. Breastfeeding, A guide for the medical profession. Mosby, St. Louis, 1994.

VITAMIN D

Trade: Calciferol, Delta-D, Vitamin D
Can/Aus/UK: Calciferol, Calcijex, Drisdol, Hytakerol, Radiostol
Uses: Vitamin D supplement
AAP: Approved by the American Academy of Pediatrics for use in breastfeeding mothers

Vitamin D is secreted into milk in limited concentrations and is proportional to maternal serum levels.[1] Excessive doses can produce elevated calcium levels in the infant[2], therefore lower doses are suggested in undernourished mothers (RDA is 200-600 IU/day). There has been some concern that mothers deficient in vitamin D may not provide sufficient vitamin D to the infant, and hence impede bone mineralization in their infants. In a study by Greer[3], breastfed infants who received oral vitamin D supplementation had greater bone mineralization than those who were not supplemented. However, a more recent study of Korean women in winter who were not supplemented with vitamin D, and whose infants were either fed with human milk or artificial cow's formula (with vitamin D added), suggested that even though the breastfed groups plasma 25-hydroxyvitamin D concentration was lower, bone mineralization was equivalent in both breastfed and formula-fed infants.[4] The authors speculated that adequate bone mineralization occurs during the breastfeeding period from a predominantly vitamin D independent passive transport mechanism. Adequate intake of vitamin D is still recommended either from supplementation or via diet. RDA is 400 IU per day. Supplementation with therapeutic doses (> 5000 IU/day) may be hazardous leading to hypercalcemia in the infant. Plasma calcium levels in the infant should be monitored if therapeutic doses are used.

Pregnancy Risk Category: A

Lactation Risk Category: L3

Theoretic Infant Dose:

Adult Concerns: Elevated calcium levels in breastfed infants.

Pediatric Concerns: None reported via milk, but do not overdose. Significant renal toxicity can occur in infants.

Drug Interactions:

Alternatives:

Adult Dosage: 250 mcg to 1.5 mg QD

½ =		M/P =
HL=		PB =
K =		Oral = Variable
MW = 396		pKa =
Vd =		

References:
1. Rothberg AD, et. al. Maternal-infant vitamin D relationships during breast-feeding. J Pediatr 101;500-3, 1982.
2. Goldberg LD. Transmission of a vitamin-D metabolite in breast milk. Lancet 2:1258-9, 1972.
3. Greer FR, Searacy JE, Levin RS et.al. Bone mineral content and serum 25-hydroxyvitamin D concentration in breast-fed infants with and without supplemental vitamin D. J. Pediatr 98:696-701, 1981.
4. Park MJ, Namgung R, Kim DH, Tsang RC. Bone mineral content is not reduced despite low vitamin D status in breast milk-fed infants versus cow's milk based formula-fed infants. J. Pediatr 132:641-645,1998.

VITAMIN E

Trade: Alpha Tocopherol, Aquasol E
Can/Aus/UK: Aquasol E, Bio E
Uses: Vitamin E supplement
AAP: Not reviewed

Vitamin E (alpha tocopherol) is secreted in milk in higher concentrations than in the maternal serum. Following topical administration to nipples (400 IU/feeding), Vitamin E plasma levels in breastfeeding infants was 40% higher than controls in just 6 days.[1] Studies clearly indicate that high levels of Vitamin E are stored in the liver and tend to accumulate over time. In 1984, over 36 neonates receiving vitamin E in neonatal intensive care units died following the I.V. administration of just 25-50 IU/day for several weeks.[2] The maternal RDA during lactation is approximately 16 IU/day.[3] Do not overdose. Do not apply to nipples unless concentrations are low (< 50-100 IU), and then only infrequently. The application of pure vitamin E oil (1000 IU/gm) to nipples should be discouraged.

Pregnancy Risk Category: A

Lactation Risk Category: L2

Theoretic Infant Dose:

Adult Concerns:

Pediatric Concerns: None reported via milk, but caution is recommended. Do not use highly concentrated vitamin E oils directly on nipple.

Drug Interactions:

Alternatives:

Adult Dosage: 16-18 (1 mg d-A-tocopherol) daily

T½ = 282 hours(IV)	M/P =
PHL=	PB =
PK =	Oral = Variable
MW = 431	pKa =
Vd =	

References:
1. Marx CM, Izquierdo A, Discoll JW, et.al. Vitamin E concentrations in serum of newborn infants after topical use of vitamin E by nursing mothers. AM. J. Obstet. Gynecol. 152:668-70, 1985.
2. Hale TW, Rais-Bahrami R, et.al. Vitamin E toxicity in neonatal animals. Pediatric Res. 27(2):59A, 1990.
3. Lawrence RA. Breastfeeding, A guide for the medical profession. Mosby, St. Louis, 1994.

WARFARIN

Trade: Coumadin, Panwarfin
Can/Aus/UK: Coumadin, Marevan, Warfilone
Uses: Anticoagulant
AAP: Approved by the American Academy of Pediatrics for use in breastfeeding mothers

Warfarin is a potent anticoagulant. Warfarin is highly protein bound in the maternal circulation and therefore very little is secreted into human milk. Very small and insignificant amounts are secreted into milk but it depends to some degree on the dose administered. In one study of two patients who were anticoagulated with warfarin, no warfarin was detected in the infant's serum, nor were changes in coagulation detectable.[1]   In another study of 13 mothers, less than 0.08 μmol per liter (25 ng/ml) was detected in milk, and no warfarin was detected in the infants' plasma.[2]   According to these authors, maternal warfarin apparently poses little risk to a nursing infant and thus far has not produced bleeding anomalies in breastfed infants. Other anticoagulants, such as phenindione, should be avoided. Observe infant for bleeding, such as excessive bruising or reddish petechia (spots). While the risks in breastfeeding premature infants (which are more susceptible to cranial bleeding), is still low, oral supplementation with vitamin K1 will preclude any chance of hemorrhage. Even modest doses of Vitamin K1 counteract high doses of warfarin.

Pregnancy Risk Category: D

Lactation Risk Category: L2

Theoretic Infant Dose: 3.8 ng/kg/day

Adult Concerns: Bleeding, bruising.

Pediatric Concerns: None reported via milk, but observe for bleeding, bruising.

Drug Interactions: The drug interactions of warfarin are numerous. Agents that may increase the anticoagulant effect and the risk of bleeding include: acetaminophen, androgens, beta blockers, clofibrate, corticosteroids, disulfiram, erythromycin, fluconazole, hydantoins, ketaconazole, miconazole, sulfonamides, thyroid hormones, and numerous others. Agents that may decrease the anticoagulant effect of warfarin include: ascorbic acid, dicloxacillin, ethanol, griseofulvin, nafcillin, sucralfate, trazodone, amino glucethomide, barbiturates, carbamazepine, etretinate, rifampin. Due to numerous drug interactions, please consult additional references.

Alternatives:

Adult Dosage: 2-10 mg QD

T½ = 1-2.5 days	M/P =
PHL =	PB = 99%
PK = 0.5-3 days	Oral = Complete
MW = 308	pKa = 5.1
Vd = 0.1-0.2	

References:
1. McKenna Rk, Cole ER, Vasan U. Is warfarin contraindicated in the lactating mother? J Pediatrics 103:325-327, 1983.
2. L'E Orme M, et. al. May mothers given warfarin breast-feed their infants? Br Med J 1:1564-5, 1977.

WEST NILE FEVER

Trade:
Can/Aus/UK:
Uses: Viral febrile infection
AAP: Not reviewed

West Nile fever in humans usually is a febrile, influenza-like illness, characterized by an abrupt onset (incubation period is 3 to 6 days) of moderate to high fever (3 to 5 days, infrequently biphasic, sometimes with chills), headache (often frontal), sore throat, backache, myalgia, arthralgia, fatigue, conjunctivitis, retrobulbar pain, maculopapular or roseolar rash, lymphadenopathy, anorexia, nausea, abdominal pain, diarrhea, and respiratory symptoms. It is not known whether the virus transfers into human milk, nor if it is communicable if present in milk, although its transmission is believed unlikely. Thus far, there has been no documented occurrence of a mother passing the West Nile virus via maternal milk. Infected mosquitoes are the primary vector for West Nile virus although both hard and soft ticks have been found infected with West Nile virus in nature, but their role in the transmission and maintenance of the virus is uncertain. Mosquitoes, largely bird-feeding species, are the principal vectors of West Nile virus. The virus has been isolated from 43 mosquito species, predominantly of the genus Culex.[1-3]

For answers to questions about West Nile virus, please see the CDC web site http://www.cdc.gov/ncidod/dvbid/westnile/q&a.htm and the N Y C a d v i s o r y n o t i c e w e b s i t e http://www.ci.nyc.ny.us/html/doh/html/cd/encalert.html

Pregnancy Risk Category:

Lactation Risk Category:

Theoretic Infant Dose:

Adult Concerns: Febrile influenza-like illness, characterized by an abrupt onset of moderate to high fever, headache (often frontal), sore throat, backache, myalgia, arthralgia, fatigue, conjunctivitis, retrobulbar pain, maculopapular or roseolar rash, lymphadenopathy, anorexia, nausea, abdominal pain, diarrhea, and respiratory symptoms.

Pediatric Concerns: No transmission reported via milk but it has not been studied.

Drug Interactions:

Alternatives:

Adult Dosage:

References:
1. Hayes, Curtis. West Nile Fever. In: Monath TP (ed). The arboviruses: epidemiology and ecology, Vol 5. Boca Raton, Florida: CRCPress, 1989:59-88.
2. Shope, Robert E. Other Flavivirus Infections. In: Guerrant RL, Walker DH, and Weller PF (eds). Tropical Infectious Diseases:Principals, Pathogens, and Practice. Churchill Livingstone:Philadelphia, PA, 1275-1279.
3. Zdenek Hubalek Z. and Halouzka J. West Nile Fever: A Reemerging Mosquito-Borne Viral Disease in Europe. Journal of Emerging Infectious Diseases. 1999;5(5):643-650.

XENON-133

Trade: Xenon-133
Can/Aus/UK:
Uses: Evaluation of pulmonary obstruction.
AAP: Not reviewed

Xenon-133 (T1/2 = 5.3 days) and Xenon-127 (T1/2=36.4 days) are noble gases.[1] As such they are chemically inert and are used often for ventilation and for cerebral blood flow studies. The patient is asked to inhale a gas mixed with either of these isotopes, followed by a brief 5 min wash out period. Obstructions in the lung appear as hot spots.

Because these gases are inert, they would not be stored or any length of time in the human, and would be rapidly exhaled within minutes. This is a typical case were the biological half-life (time stored in body, minutes in this case) is incredibly short compared to the radioactive half-life (5.3 days).   Xenon-133 would not likely be hazardous to a breastfeeding infant as long as a brief wash out period of an hour or more is used.

Pregnancy Risk Category:

Lactation Risk Category: L3

Theoretic Infant Dose:

Adult Concerns: None.

Pediatric Concerns: None if brief wash out period is used.

Drug Interactions:

Alternatives:

Adult Dosage:

T½ = 5.3 days	M/P =
PHL =	PB =
PK =	Oral = None
MW =	pKa =
Vd =	

References:
1.   Fundamentals of Nuclear Pharmacy. Gopal B. Saha, 3rd edition, 1992, Springer-Verlag Publishers.

ZAFIRLUKAST

Trade: Accolate
Can/Aus/UK: Accolate
Uses: Leukotriene inhibitor for Asthma
AAP: Not reviewed

Zafirlukast is a new competitive receptor antagonist of leukotriene D4 and other components of slow-reacting substance of anaphylaxis which are mediators of bronchoconstriction in asthmatic patients. Zafirlukast is not a bronchodilator and should not be used for acute asthma attacks.

Zafirlukast is excreted into milk in low concentrations. Following repeated 40 mg doses twice daily (please note: average adult dose is 20 mg twice daily), the average steady-state concentration in breastmilk was 50 μg/L compared to 255 ng/mL in maternal plasma.[1] Zafirlukast is poorly absorbed when administered with food. It is likely the oral absorption via ingestion of breastmilk would be low. The manufacturer recommends against using in breastfeeding mothers.

Pregnancy Risk Category: B

Lactation Risk Category: L3

Theoretic Infant Dose: 7.5 μg/kg/day

Adult Concerns: Pharyngitis, aggravation reaction, headache, nausea, diarrhea have been reported.

Pediatric Concerns: None reported.

Drug Interactions: Erythromycin reduces oral bioavailability of zafirlukast by 40%. Aspirin increase zafirlukast plasma levels by 45%. Theophylline reduces zafirlukast plasma levels by 30%. Zafirlukast increase warfarin anticoagulation by 35%. Terfenadine reduces zafirlukast plasma levels by 54%.

Alternatives:

Adult Dosage: 20 mg BID

T½ = 10-13 hours	M/P = 0.15
PHL =	PB = >99%
PK = 3 hours	Oral = Poor
MW = 575	pKa =
Vd =	

References:
1. Pharmaceutical Manufacturers Package Insert, 1997.

ZALEPLON

Trade: Sonata
Can/Aus/UK: Sonata, Starnoc
Uses: Hypnotic agent used for insomnia.
AAP: Not reviewed

Zaleplon is a nonbenzodiazepine hypnotic sedative that interacts at the GABA receptor. In a study of 5 lactating mothers who received doses of 10 mg orally, the peak milk level occurred at 1.2 hours and averaged 14 μg/L.[1] Milk levels decreased rapidly following a peak at 1.2 hours to less than 3 μg/L four hours following administration. The authors estimate that the dose received by the infant would correspond to 0.0128% to 0.0166% of the maternal dose (10 mg). The authors suggest that these levels would be subclinical to the infant.

Pregnancy Risk Category: C

Lactation Risk Category: L2

Theoretic Infant Dose: 2.1 μg/kg/day

Adult Concerns: Headache, drowsiness, peripheral edema, dizziness have been reported. Avoid alcohol and other depressants.

Pediatric Concerns: None reported via milk. Milk levels were reported to be subclinical.

Drug Interactions: Zaleplon potentiates the CNS effects of alcohol, imipramine, thioridazine. Rifampin decreases the plasma levels of zaleplon. Cimetidine produces a significant increase in plasma levels of zaleplon.

Alternatives:

Adult Dosage: 10 mg nightly

T½ = 1.2 hours	M/P = 0.5
PHL =	PB =
PK = 1,2 hours	Oral = Complete
MW =	pKa =
Vd =	

References:
1. Darwish M, et.al. Rapid disappearance of zaleplon from breast milk after oral administration to lactating women. J. Clin. Pharmacol. 39:670-674, 1999.

ZANAMIVIR

Trade: Relenza
Can/Aus/UK: Relenza
Uses: Treatment of Influenza viral infections
AAP: Not reviewed

Zanamivir is a viral neuraminidase inhibitor, which blocks or prevents viral seeding or release from infected cells, and prevents viral aggregation. It is only moderately effective, and is believed to reduce symptoms by only 30% or several days, and only if treatment is instituted within 2 days of infection.

It is administered via inhalation using a Diskhaler device. Only 4-17% of the inhaled drug is systemically absorbed. Peak plasma concentrations are only 17-142 nanogram/mL within 2 hours of administration and then rapidly decline. The manufacturer reports that it is present in the milk of rodents, although no human data are available. Due to the poor oral or inhaled absorption, and the incredibly low plasma levels, it is unlikely to produce untoward effects in breastfed infants. However, due to its limited efficacy (reduces length of illness by 1 to 1.5 days), its use in breastfeeding mothers is probably not warranted, unless in high-risk patients with other severe medical conditions.

Pregnancy Risk Category: B

Lactation Risk Category: L4

Theoretic Infant Dose:

Adult Concerns: Bronchospasm may occur in patients with asthma or obstructive pulmonary disease.

Pediatric Concerns: None reported via milk but not studies exist.

Drug Interactions: None yet reported.

Alternatives:

Adult Dosage: 10 mg twice daily.

T½ = 2.5-5.1 hours	M/P =	
PHL =	PB = <10%	
PK = 1-2 hours	Oral = 4-17%	
MW = 332	pKa =	
Vd =		

References:
1.   Drug Facts and Comparisons. 1999 ed. Facts and Comparisons, St. Louis.
2.   Pharmaceutical Manufacturers Package Insert, 2000.

ZINC SALTS

Trade: Zinc
Can/Aus/UK:
Uses: Zinc supplements
AAP: Not reviewed

Zinc is an essential element that is required for enzymatic function within the cell. Zinc deficiencies have been documented in newborns and premature infants, with symptoms such as anorexia nervosa, arthritis, diarrheas, eczema, recurrent infections, and recalcitrant skin problems.

The Recommended Daily Allowance for adults is 12-15 mg/day. The average oral dose of supplements is 25-50 mg/day, higher doses may lead to gastritis. Doses used for treatment of cold symptoms averaged 13.3 mg (lozenges) every 2 hours while awake for the duration of cold symptoms. The acetate or gluconate salts are preferred due to reduced gastric irritation and higher absorption.   Zinc sulfate should not be used.   Excessive intake is detrimental. Eleven healthy males who ingested 150 mg twice daily for 6 weeks showed significant impairment of lymphocyte and polymorphonuclear leukocyte function and a significant reduction of HDL cholesterol.

Interestingly, absorption of dietary zinc is nearly twice as high during lactation as before conception. In 13 women studied, zinc absorption at preconception averaged 14%, and during lactation, 25%.[1] There was no difference in serum zinc values between women who took iron supplements and those who did not, although iron supplementation may reduce oral zinc absorption. Zinc absorption by the infant from human milk is high, averaging 41% which is significantly higher than from soy or cow formulas (14% and 31% respectively). Minimum daily requirements of zinc in full term infants varies from 0.3 to 0.5 mg/kg/day.[2] Daily ingestion of zinc from breastmilk has been estimated to be 0.35 mg/kg/day, and declines over the first 17 weeks of life, as older neonates require less zinc due to slower growth rate. Supplementation with 25-50 mg/day is probably safe, but excessive doses are strongly discouraged. Others have shown, that zinc levels in breastmilk are independent of maternal plasma zinc concentrations or dietary zinc intake.[3] Other body pools of zinc (ie, liver and bone) are perhaps the source of zinc in breastmilk. Therefore, higher levels of oral zinc intake probably have minimal effect on zinc concentrations in milk.

Pregnancy Risk Category:

Lactation Risk Category: L3

Theoretic Infant Dose: 0.35 μg/kg/day

Adult Concerns: Oral Zinc salts may cause gastritis, GI upset. Gluconate salts, and lower doses are preferred.

Pediatric Concerns: None reported via milk.

Drug Interactions: Zinc may reduce absorption of ciprofloxacin, tetracyclines, norfloxacin, ofloxacin. Iron salts may reduce absorption of zinc. Foods containing high concentrations of phosphorus, calcium (diary foods), or phytates (bran, brown bread) may reduce oral zinc absorption. Coffee reduces zinc absorption by 50%.

Alternatives:

Adult Dosage: 15 mg daily

T½ =	**M/P =**	
PHL =	**PB =**	
PK =	**Oral = 41%**	
MW =	**pKa =**	
Vd =		

References:
1. Fung EB, Ritchie LD, Woodhouse LR et al: Zinc absorption in women during pregnancy and lactation: a longitudinal study. Am J Clin Nutr 66:80-88, 1997.
2. Drug Facts and Comparisons. 1997. ed. Facts and Comparisons, St. Louis.
3. Krebs NF, et.al. Zinc supplementation during lactation: effects on maternal status and milk zinc concentrations. Am. J. Clin. Nutr. 61:1030-6, 1995.

ZOLMITRIPTAN

Trade: Zomig, Zomig-ZMT
Can/Aus/UK: Rapimelt, Zomig
Uses: Migraine analgesic
AAP: Not reviewed

Zolmitriptan is a selective serotonin-1D receptor antagonist that is specifically indicated for treating acute migraine headaches. Peak plasma levels of zolmitriptan during migraine attacks are generally 8-14 nanograms/mL and occur before 4 hours.[1,2]   Zolmitriptan is structurally similar to sumatriptan, but has better oral bioavailability, higher penetration into the CNS, and may have dual mechanisms of action. No data are available on its penetration into human milk. See sumatriptan as preferred alternate.

Pregnancy Risk Category: C

Lactation Risk Category: L3

Theoretic Infant Dose:

Adult Concerns: Asthenia, dizziness, paresthesias, drowsiness, nausea, throat tightness, tight chest. Tachycardia and palpitations have been reported.

Pediatric Concerns: None reported via milk. See sumatriptan as alternative.

Drug Interactions:

Alternatives: Sumatriptan

Adult Dosage: 2.5 mg q 2 hours PRN

T½ = 3 hours	M/P =
PHL=	PB =
PK = 2-4 hours	Oral = 48%
MW =	pKa =
Vd =	

References:
1. Seaber E. et.al. The absolute bioavailability and metabolic disposition of the novel antimigraine compound zolmitriptan. Br. J. Clin. Pharmacol. 43:570-587, 1997
2. Palmer KJ, Spencer CM. Zolmitriptan (Adis new drug profile). CNS Drugs Jun 7(6): 468-478, 1997.

ZOLPIDEM TARTRATE

Trade: Ambien
Can/Aus/UK:
Uses: Sedative, sleep aid
AAP: Approved by the American Academy of Pediatrics for use in breastfeeding mothers

Zolpidem, although not a benzodiazepine, interacts with the same GABA-BZ receptor site and shares some of the same pharmacologic effects of the benzodiazepine(Valium) family.[1] In a study of 5 lactating mothers receiving 20 mg daily, the maximum breastmilk concentration occurred between 1.75 and 3.75 hours and ranged from 90 to 364 μg/L.[2] The amount of zolpidem recovered in breastmilk 3 hours after administration ranged between 0.76 and 3.88 μg, or 0.004 to 0.019% of the total dose administered. Breastmilk clearance of zolpidem is very rapid and none was detectable (below 0.5 ng/ml) by 4-5 hours postdose.

One case of infant sedation and poor appetite related to zolpidem use has been reported following the nightly use of sertraline(100mg) and 10 mg Zolpidem.[3] Upon discontinuation of zolpidem, the infant regained appetite and became more alert.

Pregnancy Risk Category: B

Lactation Risk Category: L2

Theoretic Infant Dose: 54.6 μg/kg/day

Adult Concerns: Sedation, anxiety, fatigue, irritability.

Pediatric Concerns: None reported via milk in one study. One case of infant drowsiness and poor feeding.

Drug Interactions: Use with food may significantly decrease plasma levels by 25%.

Alternatives:

Adult Dosage: 5-10 mg QD

T½ = 2.5-5 hours	M/P = 0.13-0.18
PHL =	PB = 92.5%
PK = 1.6 hours	Oral = 70%
MW = 307	pKa =
Vd =	

References:

1. Pharmaceutical Manufacturers Package Insert, 1996.
2. Pons G. Francoual C. et.al. Zolpidem excretion in breast milk. Eur. J. Clin. Pharmacol. 37:245, 1989.
3. AK. Personnal communication, 1999.

ZONISAMIDE

Trade: Zonegran
Can/Aus/UK:
Uses: Anticonvulsant
AAP: Not reviewed

Zonisamide is a new anticonvulsant for the treatment of partial seizures. In a study of one patient for up to 30 days postpartum who received 300 mg/d zonisamide, maternal plasma levels were 10.16, 10.6, 9.52, and 10.24 mg/L at 3, 6, 14, and 30 days respectively (mean= 10.13 mg/L).[1] Corresponding milk levels were 8.25, 9.75, 9.12, and 10.5 mg/L at 3, 6, 14, and 30 days respectively (mean = 9.41 mg/L). Milk/plasma ratios ranged from 0.81 to 1.03. Using this data, an infant would consume approximately 28% of the maternal dose per day. No neonatal problems were reported although this dose is high.

Pregnancy Risk Category: C

Lactation Risk Category: L3

Theoretic Infant Dose: 1.4 mg/kg/day

Adult Concerns: Side effects include headache, abdominal pain, flu symptoms, anorexia, nausea, diarrhea, dyspepsia, dizziness, ataxia, somnolence, fatigue and confusion.

Pediatric Concerns: None via breastmilk but dose via milk is high.

Drug Interactions: Carbamazepine, phenytoin, phenobarbital, may increase the plasma clearance of zonisamide.

Alternatives:

Adult Dosage: 100-600 mg/day

T½ = 63 hours	M/P = 1.03
PHL=	PB = 40%
PK = 2-6 hours	Oral = 65%
MW = 212	pKa =
Vd = 1.45	

References:
1. Shimoyama R, Ohkubo T, Sugawara K. Monitoring of zonisamide in human breast milk and maternal plasma by solid-phase extraction HPLC method. Biomed Chromatogr. 13(5):370-2, 1999.

ZOPICLONE

Trade:
Can/Aus/UK: Apo-Zopiclone, Dom-Zopiclone, Imovane, PMS-Zopiclone, Rhovan, Zileze
Uses: Hypnotic sedative.
AAP: Not reviewed

Zopiclone is a sedative/hypnotic which, although structurally dissimilar to the benzodiazepines, shares their pharmacologic profile.[1] In a group of 12 women, who received 7.5 mg of zopiclone, the average peak milk concentration at 2.4 hours was 34 $\mu g/L$[2] but the average milk concentration was 10.92 $\mu g/L$. The milk half-life was 5.3 hours compared to the maternal plasma half-life of 4.9 hours. The milk/plasma AUC ratio was 0.51 and ranged from 0.4 to 0.7. The authors report that the average infant dose of zopiclone via milk would be 1.4% of the weight adjusted dose ingested by the mother.

Pregnancy Risk Category:

Lactation Risk Category: L2

Theoretic Infant Dose: 1.6 $\mu g/kg/day$

Adult Concerns: Sedation.

Pediatric Concerns: None reported via milk.

Drug Interactions:

Alternatives:

Adult Dosage: 7.5 mg orally

T½ = 4-5 hours	M/P = 0.51
PHL =	PB = 45%
PK = 1.6 hours	Oral = 75%
MW = 388	pKa =
Vd = 1.51	

References:
1. Gaillot J, Heusse D, et.al. Pharmacokinetics and Metabolism of zopiclone. Pharmacology 27(suppl 2): 76-91, 1983.
2. Matheson I, Sande HA, Gaillot J. The excretion of zopiclone into breast milk. Br. J. Clin. Pharmac. 30:267-271, 1990.

Appendix

Glossary

adipose	the fat tissue in the body
analgesic	drugs used to treat pain
androgen	drug that mimics the action of the male hormone testosterone
antiangina	drug used to treat the pain associated with reduced coronary flow in the heart
antidepressant	drugs that elevate or treat mental depression
antiemetic	compound used to treat nausea and vomiting.
antihypertensive	drug used to treat high blood pressure
antimetabolite	drug generally used to inhibit the immune response, such as in arthritis or cancer
antineoplastic	drug used to treat neoplasms, or cancers
antivertigo	compound used to treat dizziness bradycardia slow heart rate
anxiolytic	reduces anxiety. sedative drug
arthropathy	painful inflammation of joints
bronchodilator	drug that dilates the bronchi in the lungs
CCB	calcium channel blocker
candidiasis	fungal infection, candida, yeast, thrush
cholinergic	nerve transmitter, acetylcholine
diuretic	drug that induces excretion of water by kidneys
dL	deciliter, 100ml
DNA	deoxyribonucleic acid, chromosome, genetic components of human cells
estrogen	drugs that mimic the action of estrogens, or female hormones.
flora	bacteria normally residing within the intestine.
GI	gastrointestinal
half-life	the time required for the concentration of a drug to diminish by one-half in the specified compartment (blood).
hepatoxic	drug that produces liver damage
hyperglycemia	elevated blood sugar (dextrose)
hypoglycemia	low blood sugar (dextrose)
hypotension	low blood pressure
immune	antibody system which fights infection, foreign protein, etc.
immunosuppressive	drugs that diminish or reduce the immune (antibody) response.
L	liter, 1000 ml, 1000 cc, approximately 1 quart
lipid	fat
maternal	mother
mg	milligram, one thousandth of gram
mg/L	milligram per Liter

milk-plasma ratio	ratio of drug in milk to plasma. Higher ratios indicate more drug penetration into milk. A ratio of 1 means that the amount of drug in milk is identical to that in plasma.
ng	nanogram, 1×10^{-9} gm
NICU	Neonatal intensive care unit
NSAID	Nonsteroidal anti-inflammatory
perineal	area between the anus and scrotum.
progestational	drug that mimics the action of progesterone, a female hormone.
prolactin	hormone that promotes breast milk production.
pseudomembranous colitis	severe, sometimes bloody diarrhea caused by overgrowth of offending colonic bacteria.
RNA	ribonucleic acid, genetic component of human cell.
tachycardia	rapid heart rate
teratogenic	drugs or conditions that produce birth defects in pregnant women.
µg	microgram, one millionth of a gram
µg/L	microgram per liter

Normal Growth During Development

BOYS	Weight (lb).	Length (in.)	Head Circumference (in.)
Birth	7.5	19.9	13.9
3 months	12.6	23.8	16.1
6 months	16.7	26.1	17.3
9 months	20.0	28	18.1
12 months	22.2	29.6	18.6
15 months	23.7	30.9	18.9
18 months	25.2	32.2	19.2
24 months	27.7	34.4	19.6

Please note, these data were not derived from exclusively breastfed infants.

Normal Growth During Development

GIRLS	Weight (lb).	Length (in.)	Head Circumference (in.)
Birth	7.2	19.7	13.5
3 months	11.8	23.5	15.6
6 months	15.9	25.8	16.7
9 months	18.8	27.7	17.4
12 months	21.0	29.3	17.9
15 months	22.5	30.6	18.4
18 months	23.9	31.9	18.6
24 months	26.3	34.0	18.8

Please note, these data were not derived from exclusively breastfed infants.

Radiocontrast agents and their reported milk concentrations*

Drug	Dose	Milk (C_{max})	Clinical Significance	Bioavailability	References
Gadopentetate	6.5 g	3.09 μmol/L	Only 0.023% of maternal dose; total dose = 0.013 μmol/24h;safe	0.8%	See Monograph
Iohexol	0.75 g/kg	35 mg/L	Mean milk level was only 11.4 mg/L; virtually unabsorbed; safe	<0.1%	See Monograph
Iopanoic Acid	2.77 g	20.8 mg/19-29 h	Only 0.08% of maternal dose; virtually unabsorbed; safe	Nil	See Monograph
Metrizamide	5.06 g	32.9 mg/L	Only 0.02% maternal dose recovered over 44.3 h; poor oral absorption; safe	0.4%	See Monograph
Metrizoate	580 mg	14 mg/L	Mean milk level 11.4 mg/24h; only 0.3% of maternal dose; safe	Nil	See Monograph

* Adapted from Hale TW, Ilett KF. Drug Therapy and Breastfeeding: From Theory toClinical Practice, First Edition ed. London: Parthenon Publishing; 2002

Recommended Childhood Immunization Schedule --- United States, 2002

Age ► Vaccine ▼	Birth	1 mo	2 mos	4 mos	6 mos	12 mos	15 mos	18 mos	24 mo	4-6 yrs	11-12 yrs	14-16 yrs
Hepatitis B	HB1		HB2			HB3					HB*	
Diphtheria, Tetanus, Pertussis (DTP)			DtaP	DTaP	DTaP		DTaP			DTaP	Td	
H. influenzae			Hib	Hib	Hib	Hib						
Polio			IPV	IPV			IPV			Polio		
Measles, Mumps, Rubella						MMR				MMR	MMR*	
Varicella							Var				Var*	
Hepatitis A										Hep A		

* if previously missed or given earlier than recommended.

Table 3. Activities of Radiopharmaceuticals That Require Instructions and Records When Administered to Patients Who Are Breast-Feeding an Infant or Child. Regulatory Guide 8.39

Radiopharmaceutical	COLUMN 1 Activity Above Which Instructions Are Required		COLUMN 3 Examples of Recommended Duration of Interruption of Breast-Feeding*
	MBq	mCi	
I-131 NaI	0.01	0.0004	Complete cessation (for this infant or child)
I-123 NaI	20	0.5	
I-123 OIH	100	4	
I-123 mIBG	70	2	24 hr for 370 MBq (10mCi) 12 hr for 150 MBq (4 mCi)
I-125 OIH	3	0.08	
I-131 OIH	10	0.30	
Tc-99m DTPA	1,000	30	
Tc-99m MAA	50	1.3	12.6 hr for 150 Mbq (4mCi)
Tc-99m Pertechnetate	100	3	24 hr for 1,100 Mbq (30mCi) 12 hr for 440 Mbq (12 mCi)

urce: Nuclear Regulatory Commission. For a more complete
le see: http://neonatal.ama.ttuhsc.edu/lact/radioactive.html

Tc-99m DISIDA	1,000	30	
Tc-99m Glucoheptonate	1,000	30	
Tc-99m HAM	400	10	
Tc-99m MIBI	1,000	30	
Tc-99m MDP	1,000	30	
Tc-99m PYP	900	25	
Tc-99m Red Blood Cell In Vivo Labeling	400	10	6 hr for 740 Mbq (20 mCi)
Tc-99m Red Blood Cell In Vitro Labeling	1,000	30	
Tc-99m Sulphur Colloid	300	7	6 hr for 440 Mbq (12 mCi)
Tc-99m DTPA Aerosol	1,000	30	
Tc-99m MAG3	1,000	30	
Tc-99m White Blood Cells	100	4	24 hr for 1,100 Mbq (5 mCi) 12 hr for 440 Mbq (2 mCi)
Ga-67 Citrate	1	0.04	1 month for 150 Mbq (4 mCi) 2 weeks for 50 Mbq (1.3 mCi) 1 week for 7 Mbq (0.2 mCi)

Cr-51 EDTA	60	1.6	
In-111 White Blood Cells	10	0.2	1 week for 20 Mbq (0.5 mCi)
T1-201 Chloride	40	1	2 weeks for 110 Mbq (3 mCi)

* The duration of interruption of breast-feeding is selected to reduce the maximum dose to a newborn infant to less than 1 millisievert (0.1 rem), although the regulatory limit is 5 millisieverts (0.5 rem). The actual doses that would be received by most infants would be far below 1 millisievert (0.1 rem). Of course, the physician may use discretion in the recommendation, increasing or decreasing the duration of the interruption.

NOTES: Activities are rounded to one significant figure, except when it was considered appropriate to use two significant figures. Details of the calculations are shown in NUREG-1492, "Regulatory Analysis on Criteria for the Release of Patients Administered Radioactive Material" (Ref.2).

If there is no recommendation in Column 3 of this table, the maximum activity normally administered is below the activities that require instructions on interruption or discontinuation of breast-feeding.

Thyroid Function Tests

T$_4$(thyroxine)	1-7 days	10.1-20.9 μg/dL
	8-14 days	9.8-16.6 μg/dL
	1 month-1year	5.5-16 μg/dL
	>1 year	4-12 μg/dL
FTI	1-3 days	9.3-26.6
	1-4 weeks	7.6-20.8
	1-4 months	7.4-17.9
	4-12 months	5.1-14.5
	1-6 years	5.7-13.3
	>6 years	4.8-14
T$_3$ by RIA	Newborns	100-470 ng/dL
	1-5 years	100-260 ng/dL
	5-10 years	90-240 ng/dL
	10 years-adult	70-210 ng/dL
T$_3$ uptake		35-45%
TSH	Cord	3-22 μIU/mL
	1-3 days	<40 μIU/mL
	3-7 days	<25 μIU/mL
	>7 days	0-10 μIU/mL

Therapeutic Drug Levels

Reference (Normal) Values

Drug	Therapeutic Range	
Acetaminophen	10-20	μg/ml
Theophylline	10-20	μg/ml
Carbamazepine	4-10	μg/ml
Ethosuximide	40-100	μg/ml
Phenobarbital	15-40	μg/ml
Phenytoin		
Neonates	6-14	μg/ml
Children, adults	10-20	μg/ml
Primidone	5-15	μg/ml
Valproic Acid	5-15	μg/ml
Gentamicin		
Peak	5-12	μg/ml
Trough	< 2.0	μg/ml
Vancomycin		
Peak	20-40	μg/ml
Trough	5-10	μg/ml
Digoxin	0.9-2.2	μg/ml
Lithium	0.3-1.3	mmol/L
Salicylates	20-25	mg/dL

From Therapeutic Drug Monitoring Guide, WE Evan, Editor, Abbott Laboratories, 1988.

Pediatric Laboratory Values

Test	Age	Range	Units
pH	< 1 mo.	7.3-7.46	
pCO_2	2-5d	4.1-6.3	kPa(mmHg)
pCO_2	2-5d	5.6-7.7	kPa(mmHg)
Total CO_2	< 1 yr.	15-35	mmol/L
Albumin, Serum	< 1 yr.	3-4.9	gm/dL
Phenylalamine	Newborn	0.7-3.5	umol/L
Ammonia	< 1 yr.	68	umol/L
Total Bilirubin	< 2 w	< 11.7	mg/dL
	< 10 yr.	< 0.9	mg/dL
Calcium	< 1 yr.	7.8-11.2	mg/dL
Chloride	< 2 yr.	100-110	mmol/dL
Cholesteral Total	< 1 yr.	93-260	mg/dL
Copper, Serum	1-5 yr.	80-150	μg/dL
Copper, Wiring	< 6 yr.	8-17	μg/dL
Creatine Kinose	1-3 yr.	50-305	IU/L
Creatine, Serum	< 10 yr.	0.2-1.02	mg/dL
Ferritin	1-4 yr.	6-24	μg/L
Fructosamine	5-17 yr.	1.4-2.2	mmol/L
Glucose	1-6 yr.	74-127	mg/dL
Hemoglobin A_{1C}	2-12 yr.	5.1	$\%HbA_{1C}$
Cholesterol (HDL)	1-9 yr.	35-82	mg/dL
Iron	< 2 yr.	11-150	μg/dL
Magnesium	< 1 yr.	1.6-2.6	mg/dL
Osmolality	28d	274-305	mmol/dL
Phosphatose, alkaline	2-9 yr.	100-400	IU/L
Phosphorus, Serum	< 2 yr.	2.5-7.1	mg/dL
Potassium	< 2 mo.	3-7.0	mmol/dL
Prolactin	0-18 yr.	20 or less	ng/mL
Protein, Total	< 1 yr.	5-7.5	mg/dL
Protein, Urine	< 1 yr.	130-145	mmol/dL
Sodium, Urinary	1-6 mo.		
breast-fed		6.1	mmol/L
formula-fed		13.2	mmol/L

Typical Radioactive Half-Lives

Radioactive Element	Half-Life
Mo-99	2.75 Days
TI-201	3.05 Days
TI-201	73.1 Hours
Ga-67	3.26 Days
Ga-67	78.3 Hours
I-131	8.02 Days
Xe-133	5.24 Days
In-111	2.80 Days
Cr-51	27.7 Days
I-125	60.1 Days
Sr-89	50.5 Days
Tc-99m	6.02 Hours
I-123	13.2 Hours
Sm-153	47.0 Hours

Common Radiopaque Agents

Generic Name (Iodine Content)	Trade Name
Iocetamic Acid (62% Iodine)	Cholebrine
Iopanoic Acid (66.68% Iodine)	Telepaque
Ipodate Calcium (61.7% Iodine)	Oragrafin Calcium
Ipodate Sodium (61.4% Iodine)	Bilivist,Oragrafin Sodium
Tyropanoate Sodium (57.4% Iodine)	Bilopaque
Diatrizoate Sodium 41.66% (24.9% Iodine)	Hypaque Sodium
Diatrizoate Meglumine 66% and Diatrizoate Sodium 10% (37% Iodine)	Gastrografin, MD-Gastroview
Diatrizoate Meglumine 30% (14.1% Iodine)	Hypaque Meglumine 30%, Reno-M-Dip, Urovist Meglumine DIU/CT
Gadopentetate Dimeglumine 46.9%	Magnevist
Iodamide Meglumine 24% (11.1% Iodine)	Renovue-Dip
Iohexol (46.36% Iodine)	Omnipaque
Iopamidol 26% (12.8% Iodine)	Isovue-128
Iothalamate Meglumine 30% (14.1 % Iodine)	Conray 30
Ioversol 34% (16% Iodine)	Optiray 160
Metrizamide (48.25% Iodine)	Amipaque
Diatrizoate Meglumine 28.5% and Diatrizoate Sodium 29.1% (31% Iodine)	Renovist II
Diatrizoate Meglumine 50% and Diatrizoate Sodium 25% (38.5% Iodine)	Hypaque-M, 75%

Generic Name (Iodine Content)	Trade Name
Diatrizoate Meglumine 52% and Diatrizoate Sodium 8% (29.3% Iodine)	Angiovist 292, MD-60, Renografin-60
Diatrizoate Meglumine 60% and Diatrizoate Sodium 30% (46.2% Iodine)	Hypaque-M, 90%
Diatrizoate Meglumine 66% and Diatrizoate Sodium 10% (37% Iodine)	Angiovist 370, Hypaque-76, MD-76, Renografin-76
Iothalamate Meglumine 52% and Iothalamate Sodium 26% (40% Iodine)	Vascoray
Ioxaglate Meglumine 39.3% and Ioxaglate Sodium 19.6% (32% Iodine)	Hexabrix
Diatrizoate Meglumine 18% (8.5% Iodine)	Cystografin Dilute
Diatrizoate Meglumine 30% (14.1% Iodine)	Cystografin, Hypaque-Cysto, Reno-M-30, Urovist Cysto
Diatrizoate Sodium 20% (12% Iodine)	Hypaque Sodium 20%
Iothalamate Meglumine 17.2% (8.1% Iodine)	Cysto-Conray II

Oxytocin Intranasal Spray

Oxytocin intranasal spray is no longer available on the US market, but oxytocin powder is available through several vendors. Below is one.

Hawkins Chemical   800-328-5460

* Please note: milk level values are subject to change. Some authors report differing levels so check the individual monograph for complete other reported milk levels.

ANTIBIOTIC AGENTS

Drug	AHL	PB	M:P	Milk Level
Acyclovir	2.4hr	9-33%	0.6-4.1	4.16-5.81 mg/L
Amantadine	16hr	67%		
Amikacin	2.3hr	4%		
Aminosalicylic	1hr	50-73%		1.1 mg/L
Amoxicillin	1.7hr	18%	0.043	0.68-1.3 mg/L
Ampicillin	1.3hr	8-20%	0.2	1 mg/L
Azithromycin	68 hrs	7-51%		0.64-2.8 mg/L
Aztreonam	1.7hr	60%	0.005	0.18-0.22 mg/L
Bacampicillin	1.3hr	8-20%	0.2	
Carbenicillin	1hr	26-60%	0.02	0.26 mg/L
Cefaclor	0.5-1hr	25%		0.16-.21 mg/L
Cefadroxil	1.5hr	20%	0.019	0.10-1.24 mg/L
Cefazolin	1.2-2.2hr	89%	0.02	1.16-1.51 mg/L
Cefepime	2 hrs	19%	0.8	0.5 mg/L
Cefixime	7hr	70%		
Cefoperazone	2hrs.	82-93%		0.4-0.9 mg/L
Cefotaxime	<0.68hr	40%	0.17	0.26-0.32 mg/L
Cefotetan	3-4.6hr	76-91%		0.22-0.34 mg/L
Cefoxitin	0.7-1.1hr	85-99%		0.9 mg/L
Cefpodoxime	2.84 hrs	22-33%	0.16	
Cefprozil	78min	36%	0.05-5.67	0.7-3.4 mg/L
Ceftazidime	1.4-2 hrs	5-24%		5.2 mg/L

Drug	AHL	PB	M:P	Milk Level
Ceftibuten	2.4 hrs	65%		
Ceftriaxone	7.3hr	95%	0.03	0.6-7.89 mg/L
Cefuroxime	1.4 hrs	33-50%		
Cephalexin	50-80min	10%	0.008-0.14	0.20-0.50 mg/L
Cephalothin	30-50min	70%	0.06-0.51	0.27-0.47 mg/L
Cephapirin	24-36min	54%	0.068-0.48	0.26-0.43 mg/L
Cephradine	0.7-2hrs.	8-17%	0.2	0.6 mg/L
Chloramphenicol	4 hrs.	53%	0.5-0.6	1.7-6.1 mg/L
Chloroquine	72-120 hrs	61%	0.358	0.227 mg/L
Ciclopirox	1.7 hrs	98%		
Ciprofloxacin	4.1hr	40%	>1	2.26-3.79 mg/L
Clarithromycin	5-7hr	40-70%	>1	
Clindamycin	2.9hr	94%		1.0-1.7 mg/L
Clofazimine	70 days		1.7	0.9-1.33 mg/L
Cloxacillin	0.7-3 hrs	90-96%		0.2-0.4 mg/L
Cycloserine	12+hr		0.72	6-19 mg/L
Dicloxacillin	0.6-0.8hr	96%		0.1-0.3 mg/L
Dirithromycin	20-50 hrs	15-30%		
Doxycycline	15-25hr	90%	0.3-0.4	0.77 mg/L
Enoxacin	3-6 hrs	40%		
Erythromycin	1.5-2hr	84%		0.4-1.5 mg/L
Ethambutol	3.1hr	8-22%	1.0	1.4 mg/L
Famciclovir	2-3 hrs	20%	> 1	
Foscarnet	3 hrs	14-17%	3.0	
Fosfomycin	4-8 hrs	< 3%	0.1	
Fluconazole	30hr	90%	0.46-0.85	0.98-2.93 mg/L
Gentamicin	2-3hr	<10%	0.11-0.44	0.41-0.49 mg/L

Drug	AHL	PB	M:P	Milk Level
Grepafloxacin	15.7 hrs	50%		
Griseofulvin	9-24hr			
Hydroxychloro-quine	40 days	63%	5.5	1.1 mg/L
Imipenem-Cilistatin	1.3 hrs	20-35%		
Isoniazid	1.1-3.1hr	10-15%		6-16.6 mg/L
Itraconazole	64 hrs	99.8%		
Kanamycin	2.1hr	0%	<0.4	12-18.4 mg/L
Ketoconazole	2-8hr	99%		
Lincomycin	4.4-6.4hr	72%	0.9	0.5-2.4 mg/L
Lomefloxacin	8 hrs.	20.6%		
Loracarbef	1 hrs	25%		
Methacycline	7-15hr	75-90%		
Methicillin	1-2hr	40%		
Metronidazole	8.5hr	10%	0.4-1.8	15.5 mg /L
Miconazole	20-25hr	91-93%		
Minocycline	11-26hr	80%		
Nafcillin	0.5-1.5hr	70-90%		
Nalidixic	1-2.5hr	93%	0.08-0.13	5 mg/L
Netilmicin	2-2.5 hrs	< 10%		
Nitrofurantoin	20-58min	20-60%	0.27-0.31	0.3-0.5 mg/L
Norfloxacin	5hr	20%		undetectable
Ofloxacin	5-7hr	32%	0.98-1.66	0.05-2.4 mg/L
Penciclovir	2.3 hrs	< 20%		
Penicillin G	<1.5hr	60-80%	0.03-0.13	7-60 units/L
Piperacillin	0.6-1.3hr	30%		
Pyrimethamine	96hr	87%	0.2-0.43	3.3 mg/L
Quinacrine	> 5 days	High		

Drug	AHL	PB	M:P	Milk Level
Quinine	11hr	93%	0.11-0.53	0.4-1.6 mg/L
Rifampin	3.5hr	80%	0.16-0.23	3.4-4.9 mg/L
Rimantadine	25.4 hrs	40%	2.0	
Streptomycin	2.6hr	34%	0.12-1.0	0.3-0.6 mg/L
Sulfamethoxazole	10.1hr	62%	0.06	
Sulfasalazine	7.6 hr		0.09-0.17	
Sulfisoxazole	4.6-7.8 hr	91%	0.06	
Terbinafine	26 hrs	99%		0.65 mg/72 hrs
Terconazole	4-11.3hr			
Tetracycline	6-12hr	25%	0.6-0.8	0.43-2.58 mg/L
Ticarcillin	0.9-1.3hr	54%		
Tobramycin	2-3hr	<5%		0.5 µg/mL
Trimethoprim	8-10hr	44%	1.25	2.0 mg/L
Trovafloxacin	12.2 hrs	76%		1.2-5.5 mg/L
Valacyclovir	2.5-3 hrs	9-33%	0.6-4.1	
Vancomycin	5.6hr	10-30%		12.7 mg/L

ANTICONVULSANTS AND SEDATIVES

Drug	AHL	PB	M:P	Milk Level
Carbamazepine	18-54hr	74%	0.69	1.3-3.6 mg/L
Clonazepam	18-60hr	50-86%	0.33	11-13 µg/L
Ethosuximide	31-60hr	0%	1.0	55 mg/L
Ethotoin	3-9 hrs	< 41%		
Felbamate	20-23 hrs	25%		
Gabapentin	5-7 hrs	< 3%		
Lamotrigine	24 hrs	55%	0.56	6.51 mg/L
Magnesium	<3hr	0%	1.9	

Pentobarbital	15-50hr	35-45%		0.17 mg/L
Phenobarbital	53-140hr	51%	0.4-0.6	2.1 mg/L
Phenytoin	6-24hr	89%	<0.45	0.26-1.5 mg/L
Primidone	10-21 hr	<20%	0.72	2-13 mg/L
Topiramate	18-24 hrs	15%		
Valproic	14hr	94%	0.42	0.17-0.47 mg/L

ANTIDEPRESSANTS - MISCELLANEOUS

Drug	AHL	PB	M:P	Milk Level
Amitriptyline	31-46hr	94.8%	1.0	0.151 mg/L
Amoxapine	8 hr	15-25%	0.21	<20 µg/L
Bupropion	8-24 hr	75-88%	2.51-8.58	0.189 mg/L
Buspirone	2-11hr	95%		
Clomipramine	19-37 hrs	96%	1.62	211 ug/L
Desipramine	7-60 hr	82%	0.4-0.9	17-35 µg/L
Dothiepin	14-23.9hr		0.3	11 µg/L
Doxepin	8-24hr	80-85%	1.08-1.66	27-29 µg/L
Fluvoxamine	15.6 hrs	80%	0.29	0.09 mg/L
Imipramine	8-16hr	90%	0.5-1.5	12-29 ug/L
Nefazodone	1.5-18 hrs	> 99%		
Nortriptyline	16-90hr	92%	0.87-3.71	180 µg/L
Trazodone	4-9 hrs	85-95%	0.142	

ANTIDEPRESSANTS-SSRIs

Drug	AHL	PB	M:P	Milk Level
Citalopram	36 hours	50 5%	1.6-3	298 nMol
Fluoxetine	2-3 days	94.5%	0.286	28.8 ug/L
Nefazodone	1.5-18 hr	>99%		
Paroxetine	21 hrs	95%	0.09	7.6 ug/L
Sertraline	26-65 hr	98%		19-43 ug/L
Trazodone	4-9 hr	85-95%	0.142	
Venlafaxine	5hr	27%	4	4.3 mg/L

ANTIHISTAMINES
H-1 BLOCKERS

Drug	AHL	PB	M:P	Milk Level
Astemizole	20hr	96.7%		
Brompheniramine	24.9hr			
Cetirizine	8.3 hrs	93%		
Chlorpheniramine	12-43hr	70%		
Clemastine	10-12hr		0.25-0.5	5-10 µg/L
Doxylamine	10.1 hrs			
Diphenhydramine	4.3hr	78%		
Fexofenadine	14.4 hrs	70%		
Hydroxyzine	3-7 hrs			
Levocabastine	33-40hr			
Loratadine	8.4-28hr	97%	1.17	
Meclizine	6hr			
Promethazine	12.7hr	76-80%		
Terfenadine	11.7hr	97%	0.12-0.28	41.02 ng/ml
Trimeprazine	5hr			

Drug	AHL	PB	M:P	Milk Level
Tripelennamine	2-3hr			
Triprolidine	5hr		0.5-1.2	1.2-4.4 ug/L

ANTIHYPERTENSIVES
ACE INHIBITORS

Drug	AHL	PB	M:P	Milk Level
Benazepril	10-11 hr	96.7%		
Bepridil	42 hrs	> 99%	0.33	
Captopril	2.2 hr	30%	0.012	4.7 µg/L
Enalapril	35 hr	60%		5.9 ug/L
Fosinopril	11-35 hrs	95%		
Lisinopril	12 hrs	Low		
Losartan	4-9 hrs	99.8%		
Quinapril	2 hr	97%		
Ramipril	13-17 hr	56%		

ANTIHYPERTENSIVES
BETA BLOCKERS

Drug	AHL	PB	M:P	Milk Level
Acebutolol	3-4 hr	26%	7.1-12.2	
Atenolol	6.1 hr	5%	1.3-6.8	0.66-1.7 mg/L
Betaxolol	14-22 hr	50%	2.5-3.0	
Bisoprolol	9-12 hr	30%		
Carteolol	6 hr	23-30%		
Esmolol	9 min.	55%		
Labetalol	6-8 hr	50%	0.8-2.6	129-662 µg/L

Drug	AHL	PB	M:P	Milk Level
Levobunolol	6.1 hrs			
Metoprolol	3-7 hr	12%	3.0	0.38-2.58 umol/L
Nadolol	20-24hr	30%	4.6	146 µg/L
Propranolol	3-5hr	90%	0.5	35.4 ug/L
Sotalol	12hr	0%	5.4	4.8-20.2 mg/L
Timolol	4hr	10%	0.8	15.9 µg/L

ANTIHYPERTENSIVES
CALCIUM CHANNEL BLOCKERS

Drug	AHL	PB	M:P	Milk Level
Amlodipine	30-50hr	93%		
Bepridil	24hr	>99%	0.33	
Diltiazem	3.5-6hr	78%	1.0	200 µg/L
Felodipine	11-16hr	>99%		
Flunarizine	19 days	99%		
Isradipine	8hr	95%		
Mibefradil	17-25 hrs	99.5%	5	
Nicardipine	2-4 hrs	> 95%		
Nifedipine	1.8-7hr	92-98%	1.0	<46 ug/L
Nimodipine	9 hrs	95%	0.06-0.3	<3.5 ug/L
Nisoldipine	7-12 hrs	99%		
Nitrendipine	8-11hr	98%	0.5-1.4	4.3-6.5 µg/L
Verapamil	3-7hr	83-92%	0.94	25.8 µg/L

ANTINEOPLASTICS - ANTIMETABOLITES

Drug	AHL	PB	M:P	Milk Level
Allopurinol	1-3hr	0%	0.9-1.4	0.9-1.4 ug/ml
Azathioprine	0.6hr	30%		
Busulfan	2.6hr			
Chlorambucil	1.3hr	99%		
Cisplatin	0.53hr	90%	>1	0.9 mg/L
Cyclophosphamide	7.5hr	13%		
Cytarabine	1-3hr	13%		
Doxorubicin	30hr	85%	4.43	128 µg/L
Fluorouracil	11 min	8-12%		
Gallium	78.3hr			0.01-0.045uCi/mL
Mercaptopurine	0.9hr	19%		
Methotrexate	7.2hr	34-50%	>0.08	2.6 ug/L

ANTISECRETORY DRUGS

Drug	AHL	PB	M:P	Milk Level
Cimetidine	2 hr	19%	4.6-11.76	6 mg/L
Famotidine	2.5-3.5 hr	17%	0.41-1.78	72 µg/L
Lansoprazole	1.5 hrs	97%		
Nizatidine	1.5 hr	35%		nil
Omeprazole	1 hr	95%		
Ranitidine	2-3 hr	15%	1.9-6.7	0.72-2.6 mg/L

BRONCHODILATORS - B2 AGONISTS

Drug	AHL	PB	M:P	Milk Level
Albuterol	1.7-7.1hr			
Isoetharine	1-3hr			
Isoproterenol	1-2hr			
Pirbuterol	2-3hr			
Salmeterol	5.5hr	98%	1.0	
Terbutaline	14hr	20%	<2.9	3.2-3.8 ng/ml

Diuretics

Drug	AHL	PB	M:P	Milk Level
Acetazolamide	2.4-5.8 hrs	95%	0.25	2.1 mg/L
Bendroflumethiazide	3-3.9 hr	94%		
Bumetanide	1.5 hrs	95%		
Chlorothiazide	1.5 hr	95%	0.05	<1 mg/L
Chlorthalidone	54 hr	75%		
Dyphylline	3-12.8 hr	56%	2.08	
Ethacrynic	2-4 hr	90%		
Furosemide	92 min	95%		
Hydrochlorothiazide	5.6-14.8 hr	58%	0.25	
Indapamide	14 hrs	71%		
Spironolactone	10-35 hr	90%	0.72	47-104 ug/L
Torsemide	3.5 hr	99%		
Triamterene	1.5-2.5 hrs	55%		

GASTROINTESTINAL AGENTS

Drug	AHL	PB	M:P	Milk Level
Cisapride	7-10hr	98%	0.045	6.2 µg/L
Diphenoxylate	2.5hr			
Loperamide	10.8hr		0.37	0.27 µg/L
Metoclopramide	5-6hr	30%	0.5-4.06	20-125 ug/L
Prochlorperazine	10-20hr	90%		

NARCOTIC ANALGESICS

Drug	AHL	PB	M:P	Milk Level
Alfentanil	1-2 hrs	92%		0.21-1.56 ug/L
Buprenorphine	3 hrs	96%		3.28 ug/day
Butorphanol	3-4hr	80%		4 µg/L
Codeine	2.9hr	7%	1.3-2.5	140-455 ug/L
Fentanyl	2-4hr	80-86%		< 0.05 ug/L
Hydrocodone	3.8hr			
Meperidine	3.2hr	65-80%	0.84-1.59	0.13-0.275 mg/L
Methadone	13-55hr	89%	1.5	0.05-0.57 mg/L
Morphine	1.5-2hr	35%	1.1-3.6	< 0.5 mg/L
Nalbuphine	5 hrs		1.2	
Oxycodone	3-6hr		3.4	<5-226 µg/L
Pentazocine	2-3 hrs	60%		
Remifentanil	<20min.	70%		
Tramadol	7 hrs	20%		100 ug/16 hrs

ANALGESIC AND ANTI-INFLAMMATORY (NONNARCOTIC)

Drug	AHL	PB	M:P	Milk Level
Acetaminophen	2hr	25%	0.91-1.42	10-15 mg/L
Antipyrine		<1%	1.0	
Aspirin	0.25hr	49%	0.03-0.08	1.12-1.69 mg/L
Butorphanol	3-4hr	80%		4 µg/L
Diclofenac	1.1hr	99.7%		< 19 ug/L
Diflunisal	8-12hr	99%		
Etodolac	7.3hr	95-99%		
Fenoprofen	2.5hr	99%	0.017	
Flunisolide	1.8hr			
Flurbiprofen	3.8-5.7hr	99%	0.013	0.05-0.07 mg/L
Ibuprofen	1.8-2.5hr	>99%		< 0.5 mg/L
Indomethacin	4.5hr	>90%	0.37	
Ketoprofen	2-4hr	>99%		
Ketorolac	2.4-8.6hr	99%	0.015-0.037	5.2-7.3 ug/L
Nabumetone	22-30hr	99%		
Naproxen	12-15hr	99.7%	0.01	1.76-2.37 mg/L
Olsalazine	0.9hr	99%		
Oxaprozin	50 hrs	99%		
Piroxicam	30-86hr	99%	0.008-.013	0.22 mg/L
Propoxyphene	6-12hr	78%		
Tolmetin	1-1.5hr	99%	0.0055	0.18 mg/L

PSYCHOTROPIC DRUGS

Drug	AHL	PB	M:P	Milk Level
Alprazolam	12-15hr	71%		
Butabarbital	100 hrs			
Butalbitol	40 hrs	26%		
Buspirone	2-3 hrs	95%		
Caffeine	4.9hr	36%	0.52-0.76	
Chloral Hydrate	7-10hr	35-41%		3.2 mg/L
Chlordiazepoxide	5-30hr	90-98%		
Chlorpromazine	30hr	95%	<0.5	0.29 mg/L
Chlorprothixene			1.2-2.6	19 ug/L
Clomipramine	19-37hr	96%	0.84-1.6	<342.7 µg/L
Clonazepam	18-50 hrs	50-86%	0.33	11-13 ug/L
Clobazam	17-31 hrs	90%		
Clozapine	8-12hr	95%		
Dextroamphetamine	6-8hr	16-20%	2.8-7.5	55-138 µg/L
Diazepam	43hr	99%	0.2-2.7	51-78 ng/ml
Doxepin	8-24hr	80-85%	1.08-1.6	27-29 µg/L
Estazolam	10-24 hrs	93%		
Flunitrazepam	20-30 hrs	80%		
Fluphenazine	10-20hr	91-99%		
Flurazepam	47 hrs	97%		
Halazepam	14 hrs	High		
Haloperidol	12-38hr	92%	0.58-0.81	5 µg/L
Hydroxyzine	3-7hr			
Lithium	17-24hr	0%	0.24-0.66	0.3 mmol/L
Lorazepam	12hr	85%	0.15-0.26	8.5 µg/L
Meprobamate	6-17hr	15%	2-4	
Midazolam	1.9 hrs	97%	0.15	9 ug/L

Drug	AHL	PB	M:P	Milk Level
Nicotine	2hr	4.9%	2.9	
Nitrazepam	30hr	90%	0.27	10-15 µg/L
Oxazepam	12hr	97%	0.1-0.33	24-30 ug/L
Pentobarbial	15-50 hrs	35-40%		0.17 mg/L
Prazepam	30-100hr	>70%		
Quazepam	39 hrs	> 95%	4.19	
Risperidone	3-20 hrs	90%	0.42	130 ug/L
Secobarbital	15-40 hrs	30-45%		
Temazepam	9.5 hrs	60-96%		
Thiopental Sodium	3-8 hrs	60-96%	0.4	0.9 mg/L
Triazolam	5.5 hrs	89%		
Zolpidem	2.5-5 hrs	92.5%		90-364 ug/L

Drugs that are usually contraindicated in lactating women*

Drug	Nature of possible infant risk
Amiodarone	Relative infant dose 4-6% of maternal dose; may accumulate because of very long half-life; adverse cardiovascular and thyroid effects possible
Antineoplastic agents	Overtly toxic; avoid exposure; bone marrow suppression, damage to intestinal epithelial cells possible.
Chloramphenicol	Relative infant dose 2% of maternal dose. Blood dyscrasias, aplastic anemia, etc. possible
Ergotamine	Symptoms of ergotism (vomiting and diarrhea) reported; potential to inhibit prolactin secretion
Gold salts	Relative infant dose varies from 1-7%. Long half-life in adults suggests potential for accumulation. Possibility of diarrhea, dermatitis, nephrotoxicity and blood dyscrasias
Lithium	Not recommended as relative infant dose is around 18-23% of maternal dose, and severe rash also reported. Caution if use.
Phenindione	Relative infant dose calculated at around 18% of maternal dose and abnormal blood coagulation in an infant has been reported

Drugs that are usually contraindicated in lactating women

Drug	Nature of possible infant risk
Radiopharmaceuticals	Temporary discontinuation of breastfeeding may be necessary. See NRC table.
Retinoids	Secretion into milk is unknown, but is likely to be significant as these drugs are usually very lipid soluble (e.g. isotretinoin). Contraindicated because if the wide range of adverse effects in adults and mutagenic and carcinogenic actions in animals
Tetracyclines (Chronic)	While the acute use of tetracyclines for up to 3 weeks is ok, chronic use over many months may lead to staining of immature teeth, or changes in epiphyseal bone growth
Pseudoephedrine	Preliminary, unpublished results by the authors indicate that pseudoephedrine may inhibit prolactin and milk production significantly

* Adapted from Hale TW, Ilett KF. Drug Therapy and Breastfeeding: From Theory to Clinical Practice, First Edition ed. London: Parthenon Publishing; 2002

Drugs that are usually contraindicated in lactating women

Drug	Nature of possible infant risk

Index

Ordering Information

Pharmasoft Publishing
21 Tascocita Circle
Amarillo, Texas, USA 79124-7301
8:00 AM to 5:00 PM CST

Call....   **806-376-9900**
Sales....   **800-378-1317**
FAX....   **806-376-9901**

Online Web Orders...

http://www.iBreastfeeding.com

Single Copies   **$ 24.95 US**
Plus Shipping

(Texas Residents add 8.25% sales tax)